The Oil Price Revolution

Steven A. Schneider is a former research associate at the Third Century America Project at the Institute of International Studies in Berkeley, California, and author of numerous articles on energy policy. He has a Ph.D. degree from the University of California, Berkeley, and will soon receive his law degree from Harvard Law School.

THE OIL PRICE
REVOLUTION

Steven A. Schneider

THE JOHNS HOPKINS UNIVERSITY PRESS
Baltimore and London

The Johns Hopkins University Press, Baltimore, Maryland 21218
The Johns Hopkins Press Ltd., London

Library of Congress Cataloging in Publication Data

Schneider, Steven A.
  The oil price revolution.

  Includes bibliographical references and index.
  1. Petroleum products—Prices. 2. Petroleum
industry and trade. 3. Atomic energy industries.
4. International economic relations. 5. World
politics. I. Title.
HD9560.4.S26   1983   338.2'3   82–12639
ISBN 0–8018–2775–2

To my mother and my father

Contents

List of Tables

List of Figures

Preface

This book began as a short term paper for a seminar on the Nixon administration. As a newly arrived graduate student in sociology at the University of California at Berkeley, I thought I would satisfy a course requirement by writing something on the relationship between business and government. With the 1973–74 oil crisis only a few months behind us, Professor Franz Schurmann encouraged me to make that the focus of my research.

Like the oil crisis itself, that "term paper" never seemed to end. Yet, throughout the process, I sought to explain the oil crisis by examining the interrelationships between governments and companies. "Knowing" that the oil companies were the dominant force, I became increasingly impressed with the power of governments. And somewhere along the way I discovered that it was not just the great powers—the consuming-country governments—that mattered, but oil-exporting-country governments as well.

I also incurred a number of debts. The first of these was to the Danforth Foundation, which sponsored much of my graduate study. My work on energy policy was also encouraged by my participation in the Ford Foundation–funded Third Century America Project. The principal investigator on that project, Professor Franz Schurmann, became my dissertation adviser. He encouraged both my interest in contemporary issues and my respect for what many academics would disparage as "mere journalism." He also urged me to ask big questions. Indeed, with the current emphasis in academia on narrowly specialized issues, I hope that this work might come to stand as a counterexample.

Anyone who glances at the notes to this book will discover the extent to which it is dependent upon the work of the petroleum, business, and daily press. Were reporters not covering the news on a regular basis, a synthetic work of this character would not be possible. In particular, I wish to express my appreciation for the excellent reporting in the *New York Times, Business Week, Petroleum Intelligence Weekly,* and the *Petroleum Economist.* Like almost everyone who has written about international oil in recent years, I have benefited from the excellent investigatory work by the old Senate Subcommittee on Multinational Corporations (now the Subcommittee on International Economic Policy). And despite my differences with them, I have learned a great deal from the works of the three giants in the field—Edith Penrose, Morris Adelman, and Walter Levy.

My thinking about international oil has also been influenced by several discussions with Chris Rand. Others who have read part of the manuscript or discussed it with me include Fred Block, Michael Burawoy, Edwin M. Epstein, Peter B. Evans, J. M. Letiche, Roger Waldinger, and Harold L. Wilensky. I have also benefited from the process of anonymous peer review. In addition, I was generously granted access to the collections at both the Standard Oil of California and the American Petroleum Institute libraries. Peter Kubaska, Judy Smith, and Evelyn Rosenthal typed the manuscript. Dan McCarthy did a superb job in copyediting it, and Jane Warth guided it through the production process.

My parents have helped me in more ways than I can recount, having patiently accepted that "another month or so" to finish a dissertation can easily turn into a year and a half. The many days I spent working on the manuscript would have been far less enjoyable were I not regularly interrupted by my eight-year-old friend Celeste Agos.

Three people have been especially important in the completion of the work. John Case provided important encouragement at a time when I especially needed it, and he persuaded me to do what I really wanted to do; submit the whole enormous manuscript for publication. Anders Richter, my editor at The Johns Hopkins University Press, guided it through a long review process. Finally, I want to thank Ruth Milkman for the support and encouragement that she provided during the time that I worked on this project.

Note Regarding References

To reduce the total number of footnotes wherever feasible, all of the references for several consecutive statements have been combined into a single note, often at the end of the paragraph. In addition, the following abbreviations have been used in the notes:

BW   *Business Week*
MEES   *Middle East Economic Survey*
NYT   *New York Times*
PIW   *Petroleum Intelligence Weekly*
PE   *Petroleum Economist*

MNC Hearings.   United States Senate, Committee on Foreign Relations, Subcommittee on Multinational Corporations (now the Subcommittee on International Economic Policy), *Hearings on Multinational Corporations and United States Foreign Policy* (Washington: Government Printing Office, 1974–)

MNC Report.   United States Senate, Committee on Foreign Relations, Subcommittee on Multinational Corporations (now the Subcommittee on International Economic Policy), *Summary and Analysis of Hearings and Investigation Prepared by the Staff at the Request of the Chairman, Senator Frank Church* (Washington: Government Printing Office, 1975)

MNC Oil Embargo Report.   United States Senate, Committee on Foreign Relations, Subcommittee on Multinational Corporations, *U.S. Oil Companies and the Arab Oil Embargo: The International Allocation of Constricted Supplies* (Washington: Government Printing Office, 1975)

MNC Debt Report.   United States Senate, Committee on Foreign Relations, Subcommittee on Foreign Economic Policy, *International Debt, the Banks, and U.S. Foreign Policy* (Washington: Government Printing Office, 1977)

MNC Saudi Oil Report.   United States Senate, Committee on Foreign Relations, Subcommittee on International Economic Policy, *The Future of Saudi Arabian Oil Production* (Washington: Government Printing Office, 1979)

Introduction

With a new decade about to begin, in December 1979 world attention was riveted on Caracas, where the Organization of Petroleum Exporting Countries (OPEC) was set to fix a new world oil price. Would a barrel of the highly valued Arabian light crude, which costs about 50¢ to produce, sell for $24, as Saudi Arabia was insisting? Or would it go for $35, as the new revolutionary government in Iran wanted? Ten years earlier, such a scene would have been inconceivable. A decade before that, when OPEC was formed, hardly anyone had even noticed.

Yet during the 1970s the world had been shocked by two dramatic increases in the price of oil. The first came in 1973–74. In the aftermath of the fourth Arab-Israeli war, which had triggered both an oil embargo against the United States and a series of Arab oil-production cutbacks, the oil-exporting countries boosted the world oil price from about $2 a barrel on October 1, 1973, to more than $8 on January 1, 1974. By the end of the year the price was over $10. What was particularly startling about this was that since 1949 the world oil price had been relatively stable, fluctuating around $2.

After 1974 the price stabilized again, at about $12. High as this was, consumers could take some solace from knowing that, in real terms, prices had declined after 1974. Then, in 1979, following the shutdown of Iranian oil production during the Iranian revolution, the price took off again, reaching about $24 by year-end, and it was well on its way to more than $30 by the middle of 1980.

Together, these price increases constitute the largest nonviolent transfer of wealth in human history. They also represent the most fundamental reordering of power relationships since World War II.

The oil-exporting countries' triumph involved two victories. One was an assertion of the power of nation-states over multinational corporations. In the early 1970s the oil-exporting countries took the ownership of the oil reserves in their territories away from private multinational companies, establishing the claim that national sovereignty meant control over the resources of one's country, irrespective of signed contracts that ceded such control to the multinational oil companies. In this period, the oil-exporting countries also took control over oil pricing and production rates from the international oil companies, and they established their right to the bulk of the profits derived from the sale of crude oil.

1

The oil-exporting countries' second victory was won at the expense of the oil-consuming countries. It consisted of raising price levels, which forced the consuming countries to transfer an additional 2 percent of their national output to the exporting countries after the 1973–74 price increases and another 2 percent after the 1979 price increases. It was the working out of long-term economic forces that enabled prices to be raised, but it was political power that determined how the proceeds from these price increases would be divided.

Since World War II, the primary actors in the international oil trade have been the international oil companies, the consuming-country governments, and the oil-exporting countries. The international oil companies can be divided into two groups: the eight international majors that dominated the world oil trade in the decade following World War II (and that even today generally remain the largest and most powerful of the companies) and the newcomers, both independent private companies and consuming-country, state-backed companies that challenged the majors by beginning overseas operations in the 1950s and 1960s. In addition, there are several thousand oil companies whose activities are confined to the United States. Though not international actors per se, the opposition of these companies has often placed limits on the activities of the majors.

Of the consuming-country governments, the United States is by far the most important. Five of the eight major oil companies are United States based, as are many of the independents, and the United States constitutes the largest oil market. Most importantly, through its political and military power the United States has provided a "security blanket" for many of the exporting-country governments. However, unlike the other major oil-consuming countries, throughout the postwar period the United States has been a major oil producer. It also has the world's largest natural gas production and extensive coal reserves.

Western Europe provides the largest market for the oil-exporting countries. Historically, its indigenous energy production has consisted mainly of coal, but since the 1960s, natural gas from the Netherlands, North Sea oil, and nuclear power have become increasingly important European energy sources. Until 1973, when it was supplanted by the United States, Japan was the largest oil importer. Japan has almost no domestic fossil fuel reserves, and in terms of energy consumption it remains the country most dependent upon imported oil.

The history of international oil since World War II has been largely shaped by the conflicts among these consuming countries. As nation-states, each has sought to pursue its own interests, frequently at the expense of others. Moreover, their different interests have been accentuated by their uneven resource endowments and their unequal representation in the Middle East oil concessions. The dominance of U.S. companies in the international oil industry has been a severe impediment to consumer-country cooperation.

Of the thirteen oil-exporting countries that belong to OPEC, Saudi Arabia is the most important. It controls a quarter of the world's oil reserves, and since 1970 it has been the world's leading oil exporter; its exports more than double those of any other country. Of OPEC's four other founding members, two are

Arab states—Kuwait and Iraq—a third, Iran, is also a Middle East country, and only Venezuela is outside the strategic Middle East. In the 1960s, Libya became an important oil exporter and joined OPEC, as did four lesser exporters: Qatar, Abu Dhabi,[1] Algeria, and Indonesia. Nigeria began producing oil in 1958 and joined OPEC in 1971. Since then, Gabon and Ecuador have become members, although neither is a very important producer. In addition, there have always been non-OPEC oil exporters, and one of them, Mexico, has become an important exporter in the 1980s.

These actors have performed in a context that has been shaped by the evolution of the world market economy and shifts in the political balance of power. Yet the combination of a world market economy and a political system based on nation-states is highly unstable, particularly where a commodity such as oil is involved, for a market economy is highly dynamic. It tends to react sharply to new developments—the discovery of vast new reserves in the Middle East in the 1950s or temporary shortages during the Arab oil embargo of 1973 and again following the cessation of Iranian oil exports in 1979. On the national level, these reactions can be controlled, at least in principle, by the intervention of the state. Indeed, among the principal tasks the state performs are regulation of economic behavior and redistribution of the wealth that accrues to favored parties as a result of the functioning of the market. Yet, on the international level, there is no duly constituted authority that can perform these functions.

In an effort to provide stability for a system which is inherently unstable, attempts at cartelization have been common in the history of the world oil industry. In 1928 the leading oil powers of the day—British Petroleum, Royal Dutch/Shell, and Exxon[2]—met at the Achnacarry hunting estate and agreed on the principle that no company should seek to expand its share of the market. Other companies soon joined the agreement, but despite this it was continually plagued by the fact that both parties and non-parties sought to increase their share of the market above the cartel-stipulated levels. Subsequently, the major companies developed mechanisms to contain the working of market forces. These included understandings to limit production, joint-venture agreements, and long-term purchase agreements among the companies. Yet the protection against the working of market forces that these arrangements provided was only partial at best. Nor could the majors prevent new firms from entering the industry and eroding the price level, as they did in the 1950s and 1960s. In fact, the world oil price fell from a high of just over $2 in 1957 to a low of about $1.30 early in 1970.[3]

These developments seemed to confirm the teachings of economic theory, according to which cartels are inherently unstable structures. For the more a cartel raises prices over competitive levels, the greater the incentive for new firms to enter the industry and for members of the cartel to boost their production above cartel-specified limits. The effect of both these developments is to erode the price level. Indeed, this is what happened in the international oil industry in the 1950s and 1960s. New firms entered the industry and several of the majors sought to increase production above the levels desired by their partners in the joint-venture operations they maintained in the Middle East. In addition, as a cartel boosts the price of a commodity, incentives increase for the development of substitutes for the cartelized commodity—that is, new energy sources.

If these companies, with their years of experience and tightly interlocked structure, could not maintain a cartel, how could the exporting countries, whose relations were far less intermeshed? Until 1973, the organization that the exporting countries had created—OPEC—was little more than a forum for the discussion of pricing and production policies. Even today, OPEC lacks nearly all the bona fide characteristics of a cartel. It *does* fix a reference price for its members, but it *does not* set the prices that individual countries can charge for their crudes. And more often than not, its members are unable to agree on a reference price.

OPEC has never controlled its members' production, nor has it achieved an agreement on market shares. It has no mechanisms for detecting members who deviate from the reference price in the prices they charge for their crudes. Nor can it impose sanctions on members who fail to keep the price of their crudes in line with the prices of others.

Reviewing the literature on cartels, Paul Leo Eckbo found that cartels tended to be effective when the following conditions prevailed: the concentration of production was high; demand was inelastic (i.e., a large increase in price has only a small effect on demand); the cartel's market share was high; its membership had cost advantages over outsiders; and governments did not get involved in restraining the operations of the cartel.[4]

In the international oil industry, these conditions have long prevailed. The concentration of production, by exporting countries and by oil companies, has always been high. Demand for oil has always been price inelastic. Since its founding in 1960, OPEC's membership has accounted for about 90 percent of the oil in world trade; and the cost of producing oil in the Middle East exporting countries has always been much lower than anywhere else. Moreover, the possibility of governments' breaking the cartel was prevented by the fact that OPEC is a cartel of governments, which have sovereign rights and which operate in a world market that lacks a world government that could put restrictions on their behavior.

Eckbo also found that, typically, cartels break up as a result of production by those outside the cartel, development of substitutes for the products of the cartel, or rivalry among the cartel members.[5] This last factor—rivalry among members—was the bane of the exporting countries during the 1950s and 1960s. Throughout these years, each exporting country sought to boost its production as much as possible; as a result, the oil companies were able to play the countries against one another, foiling their efforts to increase the sums the companies paid them in return for their oil. Several times during this period, OPEC attempted to devise a system of prorationing among its members, but each time the system broke down as individual OPEC countries opted for production levels that exceeded their quotas.

Consequently, to raise prices to the levels attained in the 1970s, a way of restricting the production of each exporting country had to be found. Once this was done, the exporting countries have had to guard against erosion of the higher price levels, as a result of new oil resources beyond the exporting countries' control or new energy sources that could substitute for oil. Yet it was not OPEC that devised solutions to these problems. Solutions emerged as a result of the failure of consuming-country energy policies, the investment strategies pursued by the international oil companies, and political developments.

With international regulation lacking, the history of world oil since World War II has been shaped by three crises: a shortage of energy supplies at the close of World War II, the 1973–74 rise in oil prices, and the 1979 price increases. A crisis, which is a condition of instability that leads to decisive change, occurs as a result of contradictions that are embedded in a social system; however, it usually takes a precipitating event to transform these contradictions into a crisis. In the case of world oil, these events were World War II, the fourth Arab-Israeli war, and the Iranian revolution. But because they create changed circumstances and demand a response, crises also open new opportunities. As these opportunities are exploited, a new period of stability is ushered in; however, its durability depends upon the adequacy of the response to the crisis.

The first postwar energy crisis, which arose at the close of World War II, had economic and political/strategic aspects. As a result of the wartime destruction of their coal fields, economic recovery in Western Europe and Japan was jeopardized by their lack of energy resources. In this period, U.S. policy makers were afraid that Soviet expansion would lead to another war and that economic stagnation, due to a lack of outlets for domestic investment, would lead to another Great Depression.

These problems were resolved by two factors: the vast, largely untapped reserves of Middle East oil and the politically hegemonic position of the United States. Middle East oil could supply Western Europe and Japan with the energy they needed for recovery. Also, development of this oil and the building of refineries to process it would offer outlets for U.S. investment. And U.S. oil companies in the Middle East, funneling royalties to the Western-oriented governments in the region, would help to forestall Soviet expansion in the Middle East. In addition, by relying on oil company payments to pro-Western Arab governments, rather than direct foreign aid, the United States could maintain a dual foreign policy in the Middle East, supporting both Israel and the Arab states.

To take advantage of the opportunities presented by Middle East oil, a response had to be organized, which the hegemonic position of the U.S. government enabled. In advancing its own interests, the U.S. government gave shape to an international oil system, substituting its politically preponderant power for the absence of a world government.

In the decade following World War II, because control of Middle East oil was considered essential to the realization of U.S. foreign policy interests, the U.S. government strongly supported the efforts of U.S. companies to establish a dominant presence in Middle East oil, providing favorable tax treatment and direct political/military support. The government did this not because it was the "instrument" of the companies, as is commonly supposed, but because the companies served the foreign-policy interests of the United States.

The international oil system that the United States organized around Middle East oil resolved the first post–World War II energy crisis, and a period of stability ensued. Oil prices remained relatively stable and supplies were both abundant and secure. But because the system had been organized by the United States in accordance with *its* interests, the exporting countries and the other consuming countries regarded it as insufficiently favorable to *their* interests. Nor were international institutions that could regulate the system created. Consequently, as the predominance of the United States declined, conflicts among the consuming countries increased and, in this context, the exporting countries were able to make substantial gains. In short, the system that emerged after World War II was largely a product of U.S. power, and its breakup coincided with the decline of U.S. hegemony and the increased importance of new actors—Europe, Japan, and the Third World—in international politics.

The oil-price revolution of the 1970s stemmed from several contradictions that were inherent in the system established after World War II:
1. Growing reliance upon imported oil meant increased dependence upon a few states in the Middle East and North Africa.
2. The control that the major oil companies exercised brought them enormous profits, but this profitability attracted other companies to the industry, weakening the majors' control.
3. The availability of cheap oil facilitated the recovery of Western Europe and Japan, but it transformed them into rivals of the United States, weakening the prospects for consumer-country unity. Also, the consuming governments in Western Europe and Japan were hostile to the Anglo-American multinational oil companies. Consequently, as the governments of Western Europe and Japan grew in power, the unity that the consuming countries and the multinational corporations initially shared vis-à-vis the exporting countries tended to shatter.
4. The growth of dependence on imported oil contributed to the world's economic interdependence, but, at the same time, nationalism increased as a political force. In its attempt to establish its predominance in the Middle East, the United States opposed both Arab and Iranian nationalism; yet these movements persisted and led to disruptions of oil supplies in 1973 and 1979. Moreover, local and regional conflicts tended to interact with and gain force from global struggles between the superpowers. In these struggles the United States generally sought to maintain the status quo, while the Soviet Union sought to promote change.

Had any of these contradictions been absent, world oil prices would probably be considerably lower today. Indeed, it was their confluence that proved explosive.

By the 1970s, as a result of the industrial world's growing dependence upon imported oil, a small number of countries found themselves in control of a material that was vital to the advanced countries and for which there was no near- or medium-term alternative. In 1955, imported oil accounted for less than a fifth of Western Europe's energy needs, but by 1970 it accounted for more than half. Similarly in Japan, imported oil accounted for slightly less than a quarter of its energy consumption in 1955, but by 1970 it accounted for more than two-thirds. (See appendix tables A1, A2, and A3.) Moreover, about two-thirds of the world's oil imports came from a few states in the Middle East and North Africa.[6]

Although this growing dependence upon Middle East (and North African) oil is generally regarded as a fact of nature, it is the consequence of social choices. On the demand side, it reflects patterns of social organization—growing reliance upon air and motor transport and increased suburbanization—that were premised upon high levels of energy use and the availability of cheap oil. On the supply side, it reflects a failure to develop alternative energy sources. Prior to 1973, the only alternative energy source that received much attention was nuclear power, and its development lagged far behind expectations.

This dependence also stems from a lack of oil exploration and development outside the Middle East, North Africa, and the United States, for with the world oil market characterized by surplus until 1970 and with some of the major companies holding reserves twenty or forty times their level of sales, the majors were not very interested in developing new sources. And with prices falling, other companies were reluctant to make extensive capital investments in developing new areas because they doubted whether they would be able to compete with cheap Middle East oil. Consequently, until the 1970s, worldwide industry expenditures on exploration and development declined as a percentage of total capital expenditures and lagged far behind the growth of oil consumption.

Equally critical was the decline in the international position of the United States. It led to greater rivalry among the oil-consuming countries, which the oil-exporting countries were able to exploit, and it limited the ability of the consuming countries to respond to OPEC. Growing Soviet involvement in the Middle East, radical nationalist movements in the area, and the failure of U.S. policy in Vietnam limited the possibility of direct U.S. military intervention in the Middle East. Thus the United States became militarily and politically dependent upon regional powers—chiefly Saudi Arabia and Iran—which, in turn, increased the bargaining power of these oil-exporting countries.

Increasingly, with newcomers growing in importance, the exporting countries were able to play the companies against one another—a reversal of the previous situation. And at key points in the emergence of OPEC power, the more vulnerable newcomers capitulated to oil-exporting-country demands.

Rivalry between conservative and radical oil-exporting countries tended to spur OPEC on, encouraging a leapfrog process in which one group of countries would secure gains, only to be outdone by another group. As demand for oil increased, several underdeveloped, sparsely populated countries—Libya, Kuwait, Qatar, the United Arab Emirates, and Saudi Arabia—began to accumulate far more revenue than they could absorb domestically. That made these "rich" OPEC countries far less dependent upon additional oil revenues than the oil-consuming countries were upon continued crude supplies.

These broad historical developments combined with two specific factors to produce the price increases of 1973–74. One was a sharp rise in market prices for petroleum products, which resulted from an unprecedented convergence of economic growth in the consuming countries in 1972–73. The other was the Arab-Israeli war, which led the Arab oil-exporting countries to cut back on production. While the rise in market prices led to large increases in profit margins, the political power of the exporting countries enabled them to claim these profits for themselves, rather than continue to have them go to the oil companies, as they did initially (and as they undoubtedly would have ten years before). The production cutbacks brought on by the Arab-Israeli war aggravated an already tight market situation and led to further increases in prices, the profits from which the exporting countries successfully claimed for themselves.

The combination of these two factors was important, for had the market not already been tight, the Arab production cutbacks would not have had such impact. Similarly, had there been no politically motivated production cutbacks, the market would not have tightened as much as it did, and prices would not have risen as much.

The price increases brought on by these politically motivated production cutbacks constituted the second energy crisis of the post–World War II period. Like the first crisis, it had economic and political/strategic aspects. The rise in oil prices damaged economic growth prospects in the consuming countries and created the problem of "recycling" petrodollars—funds accumulated by the OPEC countries that they could not absorb domestically. More significantly, for the first time the flow of oil had been seriously disrupted by political events, and the West had to contend with the possibility of future politically motivated disruptions to badly needed energy supplies.

Once prices rose to the high levels attained in 1974, the "rich" OPEC countries found that they could meet their revenue needs at greatly reduced levels of production. They therefore had an interest in limiting their oil production. At the same time, the ability of the other OPEC countries to expand production was limited by their lack of proven reserves. As a result, it became possible to contain the internal rivalry, whereby one exporting country sought to boost production at the expense of another. Thus a solution had been found to the problem that had plagued the exporting countries throughout the 1950s and 1960s; but this was a highly contingent solution. If the "rich" OPEC countries had to cut production to the point where they were no longer able to meet their revenue needs, they would be tempted to cut prices in an effort to boost sales again, and this prospect would be intensified as these countries increased their revenue needs.

Indeed, the cartel had a great deal of strength, so long as demand for OPEC oil remained high enough to permit each of the "rich" exporting countries to meet all its revenue needs by selling as much oil as it could at the cartel-determined price. But if consumers could reduce demand for imported oil to the point where these OPEC countries would have difficulty meeting their revenue needs, the cartel would again be vulnerable to price cutting. This was the new opportunity opened up by the 1973–74 price increases. Moreover, with prices up, the incentives for conserving energy increased and the prospect for developing alternative energy sources and new supplies of oil and gas improved.

As important to OPEC's continued strength as a cartel, as important as the strength and cohesion of these exporting countries, were the weaknesses and divisions that continued to plague the consuming countries. After World War II, when it was politically hegemonic, the United States had organized a response to the first postwar energy crisis, but in the absence of either a hegemonic power or international mechanisms that could regulate the world oil system, the rivalries among the consuming countries prevented them from responding effectively to the second postwar energy crisis. The ability of the consuming countries to respond to the new situation was also limited by their failure to develop alternative energy sources in the 1950s and 1960s and by the oil companies' failure to develop significant reserves of oil and gas in non-OPEC countries. Indeed, these failures protected OPEC, at least for a time, from the forces that have plagued other cartels—competition from sources outside the cartel and development of substitutes for the cartel's product. Moreover, the OPEC countries were able to get the companies to do their bidding. The companies allocated production shares among the members of the cartel, thereby insulating the OPEC countries from this potentially divisive task, and because they made conditions lucrative for the companies, the exporting countries limited the companies' commitment to development of oil supplies in new areas.

Following the 1973–74 rise in oil prices, new political opportunities presented themselves as well. Egypt aligned itself with the West; the conservative Arab oil-exporting countries were strengthened by their new wealth; and the Arabs showed new interest in reaching a settlement with Israel. Initially, the rise in oil prices also strengthened the position of the United States in the Middle East.

After 1974, a period of relative stability followed; however, the opportunities that presented themselves in this period were not successfully exploited. The consuming countries remained divided, and failed to develop effective energy policies. The international oil companies made only modest efforts to develop new sources of oil and gas. And conditions in the Middle East remained highly volatile. These factors came to a head in 1979, when the Iranian people overthrew the Shah, halting Iranian oil production in the process. As in 1973, the consuming countries found themselves unable to compensate for what was, on a worldwide basis, only a small reduction in supplies. As a result, the third energy crisis of the postwar period emerged, only five years after the second.

1

THE CHEAP OIL ERA: WORLD WAR II THROUGH THE 1960s

1

The Making of the International Oil System

As World War II drew to a close, two groups sought to organize the world oil market: the major international oil companies and U.S. policy makers. The major international oil companies saw control of the prolific oil fields in the Middle East as the way to ensure their continued dominance of the world oil industry. U.S. policy makers saw control of petroleum resources as both a source of U.S. power in the postwar period and a way of facilitating recovery in Western Europe and Japan and integrating those areas into a world economy that was to be centered around the United States. Moreover, since they saw the companies' interests as complementing their own, U.S. policy makers strongly supported the major international oil companies in this period.

From the start, nonetheless, the efforts of these two parties to organize the world oil market met opposition from other consuming countries, independent companies, U.S. domestic interest groups, and Third World nationalism. As a result, the control that the majors and the U.S. government were able to achieve was limited. The structure that emerged was vulnerable to conflicts among the majors themselves and future assertions of power by those whose initial role in the system was highly circumscribed. What stability there was depended upon a continued coincidence of interest between the majors and the U.S. government.

In the midst of World War II a group of U.S. policy makers began to plan for a new world order. Two fears haunted them: depression and war; and each could be linked to a specific historical experience: the breakdown in world trade in the 1930s and the attempt to appease Hitler at Munich. Both were seen to have resulted, at least in part, from the failure of the United States to assume world leadership in the interwar period.

In the nineteenth century the predominance of Great Britain had ensured the maintenance of international order; the Bank of England coordinated international economic activities; and the British navy was a bulwark against military conflict. But after World War I Great Britain was too weak to continue playing this role and the United States was unwilling to do so. In the 1920s the United States refused to join the League of Nations, and in the 1930s it abandoned the gold standard, its principal link to the world economy.[1]

In the absence of international leadership, each nation pursued its own interests, engaging in such practices as competitive currency depreciation, quan-

13

titative trade restrictions, foreign-exchange controls, and exploitation of weaker countries through bilateral trade agreements. But the result was stalemate and continued stagnation. As Charles P. Kindleberger stated, "When every country turned to protect its national private interest, the world public interest went down the drain, and with it the private interests of all."[2]

A powerful group of U.S. policy makers was determined to see that these mistakes were not repeated in the post–World War II period. They would push the United States to take a strong leadership role in the postwar period, urging it to consolidate its power and to use that power to impose order on the world economy. By 1943 this internationalist current had become the dominant force in U.S. foreign-policy making. Centered in three powerful sectors of the federal government—the State Department, the Treasury Department, and the Board of Economic Warfare—it had the strong support of a group of corporate liberal business leaders who looked abroad for new markets for their products and profitable outlets for investment.[3]

The internationalists maintained that the division of the world into mutually exclusive trading blocs had aggravated the Great Depression and led to the war. They believed that by enmeshing all nations in a worldwide system of economic relations, a structure of peace could be created. Consequently, they sought a new world order in which private companies would be free to trade, invest, and profit—anywhere in the world—without discrimination. In practice, this would mean opposition to European restrictions against the sale of American goods, a worldwide reduction of trade barriers, elimination of rules against exchange of one currency for another, and abolition of colonial relationships that gave one country special privileges in another.

By seeking foreign markets, the United States could avoid the danger of economic stagnation due to inadequate domestic demand. But while the problem in the United States was thought to be inadequate demand (surplus), in the rest of the world it was inadequate supply (scarcity). Consequently, the internationalists held that by selling its products overseas, the United States would advance its own interests and those of its customers. But how were these customers to pay for the U.S. goods they imported? One possibility was for them to increase their exports to the United States. But because their war-torn economies lacked the capacity to compete with U.S. producers and because the substitution of foreign goods for U.S. goods would only worsen the U.S. surplus, that alternative had to be rejected.

The other possibility was for U.S. foreign investment to increase. By investing overseas, U.S. corporations would provide the host countries with the dollars they needed to pay for U.S. goods. Foreign investment would also provide the United States with control over the raw materials needed to ensure future prosperity. Hence at the close of World War II the internationalists sought to promote the flow of U.S. capital abroad to stimulate growth in world trade and demand for U.S. goods (in particular), promote the reconstruction of war-torn areas, aid in development of the Third World, provide an outlet for surplus U.S. capital, and ensure U.S. access to vital raw materials.[4]

The irony in the internationalists' commitment to a liberal economic order in which corporations would be free to trade and invest without government interference was that its realization in the postwar period would require widespread government intervention, for governments would have to create and maintain the institutions and "rules of the game" that a liberal economic order requires. Indeed, for international trade and investment to proceed, governments would have to establish an international monetary system; they would have to provide a world context in which companies would feel secure to do business in all parts of the globe; and they would have to maintain a legal system that would provide sanctions against the impairment of contracts.

Given the magnitude of the tasks to be accomplished and the likelihood of conflicts, the internationalists' vision would have little prospect of realization had it not been that, in the immediate postwar period, the preponderance of military, political, and economic power resided in the United States. With the active support of the United States, the internationalists might mobilize resources sufficient to realize their ends. The task would be difficult in any case, but without the support of the U.S. government there would be little chance of success. Recognizing this, the internationalists pushed for the U.S. government to play a strong interventionist role in world affairs.

The goals of the internationalists faced both domestic and foreign opposition. Domestic interests feared they would be unable to compete with foreign imports and with their internationally based compatriots, who would have access to cheap labor and cheap raw materials. In all the talk of internationalism, they "smelled" an alliance between big business and big government that would squeeze them out. At the same time, political conservatives feared that internationalism would mean big government and U.S. involvement in foreign conflicts. They preferred a return to more traditional U.S. policies of limited government and relative isolationism. Political and economic conservatives maintained that, because of its domestic resource base and geopolitical position, the United States did not have to become ensconced in world affairs.

Internationally, Great Britain and the Soviet Union were the principal opponents of creation of a liberal world economy, for they saw their future prosperity as dependent upon maintenance of their bloc systems. Great Britain looked to its traditional preferential trading system to help its exports and saw the preservation of a sterling bloc as essential to tying up its wartime debts.[5] The Soviet Union saw the East European bloc as a security belt that would buffer it from future attacks and as a trade bloc that would be insulated from the pressures of international capitalism. The Soviet Union was determined to maintain the distinctness of that bloc, keeping it out of the "one world" that the internationalists envisioned—which set Soviet objectives at direct odds with those of the internationalists.

Great Britain, the Soviet Union, and much of the rest of the world saw the open system that the United States was trying to establish as one which would favor the United States at their expense, for such a system tends to maximize the advantages of the nation with the highest level of technical development and the most enterprising and strongest firms. Countries that fail to compete successfully are left with idle resources—something the war-torn economies in Europe and Japan could hardly afford.

In this new system of multilateral trade, how were the crippled industries of Europe and Japan to compete with those of the United States? How were Europe and Japan to restore their own industrial capacity, if U.S. firms were free to buy up their industry? Was not the U.S. cry for anticolonialism simply a way of ensuring that the United States would have access to the raw materials in the underdeveloped world, at the expense of the former colonial powers? These concerns led Europe and Japan to insist on the need for continued economic controls to give them the opportunity to recover. Indeed, because they sought to maintain high levels of employment and to improve living standards, few nations were willing to subordinate their domestic policies to the needs of the international system, as they had under the operation of the gold standard in the late nineteenth century.

Still, the pleas of the Europeans and Japanese might have gone unheeded had it not been for the growing conflict between the United States and the Soviet Union, for it soon became apparent that Western Europe and Japan were too weak and too short of dollars to engage in a free market. In the context of an emerging cold war, U.S. policy makers came to fear that unless the European and Japanese economies were strengthened, these nations would be increasingly vulnerable to Soviet advances and leftist opposition. In response to this challenge, the United States decided to provide direct aid for the reconstruction of Western Europe and Japan.

The United States accepted restrictions on the liberal world order it sought in order to further the economic recovery of its allies, and this change in policy was signified by announcement of the Marshall Plan in June 1947. As Robert Gilpin stated, "The Marshall Plan signaled a profound shift in American policy, away from the pursuit of global multilateralism and American commercial interests to the promotion of European regionalism."[6] However, the acceptance of European regionalism was seen by U.S. policy makers as a temporary departure, made necessary by the Communist threat, but one that would ultimately contribute to realization of the long-term goal: a liberal world economy centered around the United States.

THE ROLE OF PETROLEUM IN THE ACHIEVEMENT OF U.S. POSTWAR OBJECTIVES

Control of petroleum had a crucial role to play in achieving the internationalists' objectives. It would aid in the consolidation of U.S. power, in maintaining national security, in resistance to Soviet advances and leftist opposition, in rebuilding Western Europe and Japan, and in construction of a liberal world economy.

There could be no clearer testimony to the importance of petroleum for consolidating a nation's power and maintaining its national security than World War II itself. As Charles Rayner, the State Department's petroleum adviser, told the Special Senate Committee Investigating Petroleum Resources in 1945, "World War II has been and is a war based on oil. The following examples show that the course of the present war has given ample evidence that military strategy and industrial output for continued military operations can be measured in terms of the availability of oil supplies." He pointed out that one of Germany's first acts was to force Rumania into the Reich in order to gain access to the oil fields and refineries of Ploesti, the German drive into the Caucasus was directed at capturing four-fifths of the Russian oil fields, and Germany's North African campaign was largely an attempt to gain control of Middle East oil fields. The failure of these campaigns was important in Germany's ultimate defeat. Similarly, according to Rayner, the main objective of the Japanese attack on Pearl Harbor was control of the "Netherlands East Indies, dictated by the imperative need of securing control of the oil resources of Borneo and Sumatra—more than sufficient to meet her annual requirements."[7]

In sharp contrast, the Allied forces that confronted Germany and Japan benefited enormously from U.S. petroleum supplies, which accounted for 80 percent of the Allies' wartime needs.[8] U.S. policy makers learned two lessons from this experience: the strategic value of maintaining control of as much of the world's oil as possible and the necessity of meeting U.S. oil needs from secure supplies. Indeed, U.S. power in the post–World War II period was to be based on three factors: nuclear superiority, control of international monetary reserves, and control of oil—the resource most essential to the world's economic recovery.[9]

At the close of World War II the United States was the world's only nuclear power and the dollar was unrivaled as an international currency. In contrast, the predominance of U.S. interests in the world oil industry was far less well established. Prior to World War II, the petroleum industry had been heavily concentrated in the Western Hemisphere; in 1938, more than three quarters of the world's oil was produced there and nearly 70 percent of all oil was consumed within the hemisphere. The United States accounted for about 60 percent of both the world's oil production and its consumption. After the United States, the largest producers were the U.S.S.R. and Venezuela, each accounting for about 10 percent of world production in 1938; and in Venezuela, U.S. companies controlled 60 percent of production, with Royal Dutch/Shell controlling the other 40 percent. In that year, the entire Middle East accounted for only 5½ percent of the world's oil production.[10]

In the postwar economic growth, the substitution of oil for coal and the expansion of ocean, air, and automotive transport were expected to increase worldwide demand for petroleum greatly. Most observers believed that the Western Hemisphere's reserves would not be capable of meeting this increase in demand. Indeed, in 1942–43 the fear was widespread that the United States was running out of oil, and in the postwar period the United States was expected to become a net importer of oil.[11] Hence to meet the growth in demand for oil in Europe and Asia and to supplement U.S. supplies, Eastern Hemisphere oil production would have to increase in the postwar period.

The Middle East was known to contain vast, untapped, and cheap oil reserves, whose development had been delayed by the war. In 1943 the U.S. government had sent a mission, headed by Everett Lee Degolyer, a well-known oil geologist, to investigate the potential of Middle East oil. In November it reported that "the center of gravity of the world of oil production is shifting from the Gulf-Caribbean areas [in which the U.S. fields were included] to the Middle East, to the Persian Gulf area, and is likely to continue to shift until it is firmly established in that area."[12]

In 1945, British/Dutch interests controlled 52 percent of the Middle East's petroleum reserves, the United States 42 percent.[13] The disparity in Middle East production just prior to and during World War II was even greater: the British accounted for roughly 80 percent, the United States for only about 15 percent.[14] In Iran, the oldest concession and leading Middle East producer in 1938, the British Petroleum Company ("Anglo-Iranian" at the time) was the sole concessionaire, whose exclusive rights extended to all of the country except the five northern provinces. In Iraq, the Iraq Petroleum Company (IPC)—a joint venture of British Petroleum (23.75%), Royal Dutch/Shell (23.75%), Compagnie Française des Pétroles (23.75%), Exxon (11.875%), Mobil (11.875%), and the Gulbenkian interests (5%)[15]—had exclusive rights to virtually the entire country, the only exception being a narrow strip on the eastern border that once was part of Iran. IPC also controlled the lesser concessions in Qatar, Abu Dhabi, and Oman. Only in the concessions south of Iraq did U.S. interests total as much as 50 percent, and prior to the end of World War II these areas were only marginal producers. In Kuwait, Gulf had become BP's 50 percent concession partner in 1934 as a result of State Department prodding. In 1938 they discovered oil, but the concession did not come onstream until after World War II.

The only major Middle East concession in which U.S. companies held a predominant position was in Saudi Arabia. The kingdom that Ibn Saud proclaimed in 1932 faced financial collapse because the world slump was undermining its main source of income, taxation of the *hajj* (Islamic pilgrimage) to Mecca. Consequently, in 1933 the king sold Standard Oil of California (SoCal) an exclusive sixty-year concession in Saudi Arabia. Needing both capital and market outlets, in 1939 SoCal took on Texaco as a partner in its new venture.[16] In that year, King Ibn Saud enlarged the concession to 440,000 square miles, giving the California-Arabian Standard Oil Company the exclusive right to all the oil in an area the size of Texas, Louisiana, Oklahoma, and New Mexico combined.[17] However, as in Kuwait, development of the concession was delayed by the onset of World War II.

The growing importance of Middle East oil was a direct challenge to the political position of the United States, for control of Middle East oil would play a major role in the determination of national power in the postwar period. Although U.S. companies were well represented in the international oil industry, they did not have a preponderant influence, and their position in the concessions in which they were represented was far from secure. At the same time, the prospect of vast amounts of cheap oil threatened to undermine the dominance of the world market that the three leading international oil companies—British Petroleum, Royal Dutch/Shell, and Exxon—had established. Both their market position and the mechanisms for control over supply (and hence price) that they had created over the previous two decades would be endangered by the growing importance of Middle East oil. Finally, if cheap Middle East oil was allowed to enter the United States, it could drive U.S. domestic producers out of business.

For the U.S. government and the major international oil companies, the immediate task was to establish control over Middle East oil, while, for domestic producers, the goal was to keep that oil out of the United States. If the companies and the U.S. government were to achieve their objectives, they would have to counter the efforts of the other advanced countries (principally Great Britain, France, and the Soviet Union) to maintain and extend their interests in Middle East oil, as well as the opposition that would emanate from domestic producers if their interests were threatened. Further complicating the aims of the U.S. government and the major U.S. companies was that, politically, Great Britain had long dominated the Middle East. At the close of World War II the British still maintained a strong military presence in the area: British troops occupied southern Iran; Kuwait was still a British protectorate; and the Iraqi king had been hand-picked and installed by the British. However, by insisting on an ''open door''—no special access for a colonial power—the United States hoped to increase the share of Middle East oil that was controlled by U.S. nationals. This would enable the United States to gain control of a resource that was vital to its military security, its political power, and its future prosperity.

By expanding the role of U.S. companies in the Middle East, the United States would secure its position in that strategic area, at the crossroads of Europe and Asia. The urgency of this endeavor became apparent in 1946, when the Soviet Union, in support of its demand for oil concessions similar to those obtained by Anglo-American companies, sent tanks toward the Iranian border. The tanks retreated in response to U.S. pressure, but the threat of future incursions remained.[18] Consequently, the United States embarked on a strategy of reinforcing British military power in the Middle East, at the same time that it sought to supplant Great Britain economically. The United States understood that if Great Britain was too weak in the region, Arab nationalism or Soviet influence could fill the vacuum. But if the British remained too powerful, they could deny the United States its ultimate goal in the region: control of oil.

U.S. corporate control of oil was to play a key role in establishing the liberal economic order that American policy makers sought to create, for cheap Middle East oil would facilitate the recovery of Western Europe and Japan. At the same time, it would incorporate them into an international system of trade, reducing the tendencies toward fractionalization and the formation of regional blocs that had characterized the interwar period. Therefore, the U.S. government encouraged foreign investment to alleviate the dollar shortage that was both limiting U.S. exports and hindering the recovery of U.S. allies, but most U.S. corporations were not anxious to go abroad. In the prevailing context of widespread political instability and economic weakness overseas, it was far more attractive for U.S. companies to take advantage of domestic investment opportunities. In fact, from 1946 to 1948 U.S. net exports of foreign capital were less than they had been from 1926 to 1928.[19]

In sharp contrast to this pattern was the situation of the petroleum industry, where it was understood that dominance of the world oil market would pass to whoever gained control of the vast reserves of Middle East oil. Newcomers to the international industry saw the availability of low-cost Middle East reserves as an opportunity to build their market shares. The established companies—Exxon, Royal Dutch/Shell, and British Petroleum—feared that if newcomers established a strong position in the Middle East, the well-protected price of international oil and their share of the market could be greatly reduced. As a result, newcomers and established firms had an interest in maximizing their control of Middle East reserves through foreign investment.

Yet, because Middle East reserves were so vast, they could be disposed of only in the expanding markets of Europe and Japan. Consequently, investments in Middle East reserves had to be complemented at the outset by investments in marketing and refining facilities in Western Europe and Japan. This led the petroleum industry to make large foreign investments abroad, which distinguished it from most other U.S. industries in the period. Of the $2,362 million in new capital outflow that U.S. firms sent abroad from the end of 1945 to the end of 1949, $1,762 million, or nearly three quarters, was accounted for by the petroleum industry.[20]

Like other U.S. companies, U.S. oil companies were concerned about the risks of foreign investments. Prior to World War II, U.S. oil companies had been ousted from Bolivia through confiscation and from Mexico through expropriation, and their activities had been curtailed by government action in Argentina, Chile, and Uruguay. In the emerging postwar world they would be especially vulnerable to anticolonial sentiments in the underdeveloped world and to anti-American sentiments in the Middle East in particular. This would be particularly true if radical governments, hostile to the United States, came to power. Hence in pursuing their overseas ventures the international oil companies sought the strong support of the U.S. government. They needed the U.S. government to establish their rights of entry vis-à-vis the old concessionary powers, primarily the British, and to secure their position with the oil-producing countries. But at the same time that they sought the support of the U.S. government, the companies were determined to resist government intrusions into regulation of the industry.[21]

As U.S. petroleum policy emerged, two principles became central: protection of Western Hemisphere reserves for U.S. needs and an "open door," ensuring the right of U.S. companies to invest in foreign petroleum resources. The first principle reflected U.S. concern with national security, the second the commitment to building a liberal economic order that was to be centered around U.S. power.

In April 1944 the Inter-Divisional Petroleum Committee of the State Department formulated the "Foreign Petroleum Policy of the United States," which declared: "General recognition should be achieved of the principle of equal opportunity for American enterprise in exploration for additional sources of supply of petroleum, and in the development of whatever reserves may be found in the future. A broad policy of conservation of Western Hemisphere petroleum reserves should be adopted in the interest of hemispheric security, in order to assure the adequacy for military and civilian requirements of strategically available reserves."

To achieve the conservation objective, three measures were recommended:

a. Curtailment, insofar as practicable, of the flow of petroleum and its products from Western Hemisphere sources to Eastern Hemisphere markets.
b. Facilitation, by international agreement and otherwise, of substantial and orderly expansion of production in Eastern Hemisphere sources of supply, principally in the Middle East, to meet increasing requirements of post-war markets.
c. Removal by international agreement and otherwise, of impediments to the exploitation of Middle Eastern concessions held by United States nationals.[22]

To assure prompt development of the Middle East reserves that were needed to meet the import needs of Europe, Africa, and parts of Asia, the policy established several "more specific policy objectives":

1. An agreement between the U.S. and Great Britain on a development program for the Middle East.
2. "Protection against alienation of American-held concessions into non-American hands."
3. The substitution of Middle East oil for Western Hemisphere oil in Eastern Hemisphere markets and
4. The establishment of an International Petroleum Council to resolve international petroleum disputes.[23]

SECURING THE U.S. POSITION IN THE MIDDLE EAST

During World War II the U.S. government took steps to ensure that either the U.S. government or U.S. nationals would have control of Middle East oil. In November 1943, Secretary of State Cordell Hull told Interior Secretary Harold

Ickes that "there should be a full realization of the fact that the oil of Saudi Arabia constitutes one of the world's greatest prizes."[24]

Yet SoCal and Texaco, the two U.S. companies that were operating in Saudi Arabia, were concerned that, with the war preventing both the resumption of pilgrimages to Mecca and the development of Saudi oil fields (Ibn Saud's only sources of income), the kingdom would be thrown into financial crisis. In such a context, it would be likely that King Ibn Saud would be overthrown and that the companies' concession would be lost in the process, for while the king's ascendancy in warfare had succeeded (at least temporarily) in uniting the many tribes in the Arabian peninsula, he still faced many rivals, who could take advantage of an economic slump. Consequently, the two American concessionaires urged President Roosevelt to provide aid to the Saudi regime; in return, they offered to set aside a petroleum reserve from which the U.S. government could be supplied at preferentially low prices.

At first the president rejected the companies' request, on the grounds that there was no legal basis for it, and that, in any case, it was a British responsibility, given that nation's extensive commitments in the area. But with growing U.S. involvement in the war, Roosevelt worked out an arrangement that would enable Great Britain to divert a portion of its U.S. Lend-Lease loan to the Saudis. Between 1941 and 1943 the British advanced $33.8 million to the Ibn Saud regime.[25] However, the concessionaires came to fear that this arrangement would increase British influence in the area and lead to loss of the concession. As Navy Undersecretary William Bullitt wrote:

The officials of both the Standard Oil of California and the Texas Company are much disturbed about the future security of their concession not only because of the normal insecurity in Arabia but also because they feel that the British may be able to lead either Ibn Saud or his successors to diddle them out of the concession and the British into it. American experts on Saudi Arabia are inclined to agree with this estimation of the situation. They point out that the Anglo-Iranian Oil Company had every opportunity to get this concession and, after examination, rejected it on the ground that there was no oil in Saudi Arabia—and have been regarding the concession with covetous eyes ever since the Americans struck oil.[26]

Consequently, on February 18, 1943, after three years of oil company lobbying, the president approved direct Lend-Lease aid to Saudi Arabia, declaring: "I hereby find that the defense of Saudi Arabia is vital to the defense of the United States."[27] Also during 1943, the Joint Chiefs decided to build an airbase at Dhahran in Saudi Arabia. By 1946, the United States had sent $17.5 million in aid to Saudi Arabia.[28]

With many government and industry experts afraid that an oil shortage would emerge in 1943, Harold Ickes, secretary of the interior and petroleum administrator for war, proposed that a federal oil corporation be created to develop foreign oil reserves. Ickes pointed out that such a corporation would aid in the conservation of U.S. oil, by exploiting Saudi Arabian oil, and would serve to counteract British influence in the area. On June 8, 1943, the Joint Chiefs of Staff endorsed

Ickes' proposal, recommending that the corporation begin by acquiring a controlling interest in Saudi Arabia's oil concessions. On June 26, 1943, acting on this recommendation, President Roosevelt authorized the Reconstruction Finance Corporation to establish the Petroleum Reserves Corporation (PRC).[29]

In the summer of 1943 the PRC began negotiations for purchase of the Saudi Arabian concession from its two American owners, Standard Oil of California and Texaco. Although the companies were anxious for the federal government to take direct diplomatic responsibility for the security of their enterprises in the Middle East, they wanted to keep all oil operations in private hands. Hence, while they had offered to set aside a petroleum reserve in exchange for Lend-Lease aid to Saudi Arabia, they refused to sell the U.S. government either the concession or a share in it. And though the companies got the United States to provide Lend-Lease assistance to Saudi Arabia, they never established the promised petroleum reserve, nor did the U.S. government secure a share in the Saudi concession.

Unable to purchase a share of the Saudi Arabian concession, in early 1944 the PRC attempted to gain a foothold position in Middle East petroleum by building a major pipeline from the Persian Gulf[30] to the eastern Mediterranean. Ickes reasoned that since full development of the Saudi Arabian concession was dependent upon rapid and cheap transportation to the major world markets, government control of the key pipeline would be almost as good as a government share in the concession. He proposed that the U.S. government build a thousand-mile pipeline to bring oil from Saudi Arabia to the Middle East and, in return, the companies that operated in the area would guarantee 20 percent of the oil fields as a naval reserve.

The three U.S. companies that were operating in the Persian Gulf area at the time—Gulf, SoCal, and Texaco—were glad to have the federal government assume responsibility for the local political issues and the enormous financing costs in building a pipeline. Consequently, an agreement was concluded in early February between the concessionaires and the U.S. government. Proponents of the pipeline argued that U.S. oil resources were being rapidly depleted, that the pipeline would provide protection against any attempt to take the Saudi concession from U.S. companies, and that the pipeline would increase the amount of oil available to Western Europe. Yet, because of the time it would take to complete the pipeline, it would not aid the Allied war effort so much as Europe's postwar recovery.

Because only three companies would benefit from the proposed pipeline, both their domestic and international competitors attacked it as providing an unfair competitive advantage. Furthermore, they reasoned that by giving the government a stake in Middle East oil, the pipeline would lead the federal government to favor Middle East oil at their expense. They denounced the plan as an unwarranted governmental intrusion into the free market, and domestic producers argued that, with proper incentives, U.S. oil needs could be fully supplied from U.S. sources. Liberal opinion saw the scheme as an imperialist endeavor, while conservatives objected to government interference in business. Traditional isolationist sentiment saw the pipeline as unnecessarily involving the United States in the politically turbulent Middle East.

The British government also attacked the pipeline proposal, fearing PRC's encroachment into traditional British preserves. Britain's resentment was especially great because it had just been denied the U.S. materials it needed to expand pipeline capacity in its Iraq concession, and now the United States was planning to build a pipeline more than twice as long as the one Britain proposed. And this U.S. pipeline would be used to expand the production of U.S. companies in Saudi Arabia at the expense of British companies in the Iraq Petroleum Company.

As a result of this varied opposition, in the spring of 1944 President Roosevelt shelved the PRC's pipeline plan and the PRC soon lapsed into nonexistence (the pipeline was eventually built by U.S. companies operating in the Middle East).[31] However, the PRC experience established an important constraint on U.S. policy, for it had shown that the U.S. government would not be able to secure its aims directly but would have to work through the oil companies. The companies had the political power to resist measures that went against their interests and encroached upon their traditional private enterprise rights. Consequently, rather than work independently of or contrary to the interests of the oil companies, the U.S. government would seek to make the companies an instrument of federal policy.

In an effort to guarantee U.S. companies access to Middle East petroleum and to safeguard the concessions they had already secured, the United States attempted to work out an international oil agreement—to reach an accord with Great Britain, the dominant power in Middle East oil at the time, and then invite other countries to endorse it. In this way, it was hoped, a system of rules for international oil operations would be created, just as a system of rules in international monetary operations would be established. However, when negotiations with Great Britain began in the spring of 1944, a major conflict between the two Allied powers became apparent, for Great Britain sought to preserve its concession rights but the United States wanted Great Britain to forgo colonial prerogatives that prevented U.S. companies from competing on an equal basis with British companies. The result was a vaguely worded agreement that called for "respect for valid concession contracts and lawfully acquired rights" and "the principle of equal opportunity in acquiring exploration and development rights." Probably the most significant feature of the treaty was that it called for establishment of an International Petroleum Commission that would aid in the resolution of disputes in the international petroleum industry.[32]

Fearing that the provisions of the treaty could lead to nationalization or extensive government involvement in the industry, the U.S. petroleum industry attacked the treaty. As a result, Roosevelt asked the Senate to return it for revision. While the federal government sought to establish a commission with powers of control over the international oil industry, the industry wanted a commission with advisory powers only.[33]

In November 1945 a revised treaty was resubmitted to the Senate. While hardly providing a comprehensive set of rules for regulation of the international oil industry, the treaty was an initial effort at establishment of a code of conduct. This code was to be approved by oil-importing and oil-exporting countries, and an international commission was to be created to aid in the resolution of disputes. Two principles of the code were particularly important to the United States. The first sought to protect the interests and thereby strengthen the governments of the oil-producing countries. The effect would be to bolster the ability of pro-Western governments to resist Soviet advances. The treaty also sought to protect U.S. and British companies against the threat of nationalization. As Secretary of State Dean Acheson stated, the treaty attempted ''to lay down the rule that once you have gotten a concession and it is a fair and honest one, you will not get expropriated without compensation.''[34]

Because of the protection against nationalization that it provided, the revised treaty won the support of the U.S. international companies; it was endorsed by the Petroleum Industry War Council and the American Petroleum Institute. Exxon President Eugene Holman told a Senate committee that ''in the absence of an oil agreement advocating—as the agreement before you does—the sanctity of contracts and the right of competitive business to compete, the present trend in various areas toward nationalization might be accelerated.''[35]

However, U.S. domestic producers continued to oppose the treaty, fearing it would lead to greater government regulation of the oil industry and increased oil imports. They were particularly alarmed by a radio broadcast by John Loftus, chief of the oil section of the State Department, in which Loftus stated that oil imports ''will continue to be a point of friction and conflict until the nations get together and work out some fair way of keeping disputes at a minimum, and in some orderly way of developing the world's oil resources.'' The ''Anglo-American agreement,'' he said, ''is only the first step toward the worldwide agreement that we need.'' Loftus also suggested that a world organization might have functions not assigned to the Anglo-American commission, that it might suggest revisions in oil concession agreements and function as an appeals board, and he said that a world organization might have more than advisory powers and that oil companies, like utilities, are a matter of public concern.[36]

Russell B. Brown, counsel for the Independent Petroleum Association of America, concluded that ''giving the State Department a degree of responsibility and power over the determination of international as well as national policy on oil would be harmful to our people.'' He added that, since any treaty would have this effect, the domestic oil producers would oppose any international agreement.[37] As a result of this opposition, the treaty was held up in the Senate Foreign Relations Committee by Texas Senator Tom Connally. Finally, on July 5, 1952, President Truman withdrew the treaty.[38]

Several things about the treaty episode are significant. Whereas the failure of the PRC showed that the government had to work through the oil companies, the failure of the Anglo-American agreement revealed that even the opposition of domestic producers could block federal initiatives. Any attempt to develop cooperation through the establishment of international institutions and rules, which the international oil companies seemed ready to accept, was ruled out by the likely opposition of more parochial domestic interests. As a result, operation of the international industry would be *more* anarchic, and the control that would be established would be mainly in private (oil company) hands. Instead of international agreements there would be private government.

Finally, the decision to seek a bilateral agreement—one that excluded both France and the Soviet Union, two important powers in international oil and, at the time the treaty was negotiated, two allies as well—set the stage for things to come. In the immediate postwar period control over international oil was to be mainly an Anglo-American affair, but the opposition to that control would come increasingly from those powers that had been excluded: France and the Soviet Union.

The Aramco Merger. When the war was over, everyone in the petroleum industry expected Saudi Arabian oil production to boom. Thus competition from cheap Saudi oil posed a threat to the market position of the established international majors: Exxon, Mobil, Royal Dutch/Shell, and British Petroleum. The only way the majors could nullify this threat would be to find some way of restraining Saudi production (simply sharing it would not be sufficient). Particularly vulnerable was Exxon, for the company's projections showed that it would need all its U.S. and Venezuelan production to meet the needs of its Western Hemisphere markets. It therefore needed to increase its Middle East holdings in order to supply Eastern Hemisphere markets.[39] Consequently, Exxon and Mobil attempted to purchase a share of the Saudi Arabian concession, now known as the Arabian-American Oil Company (Aramco).

The suitors had three things to offer: capital, market outlets, and the prospect that, through avoidance of competitive relations, all four companies would benefit. SoCal and Texaco believed that, in the long run, they would gain from the partnership and so they agreed to the merger.[40] The four partners then received antitrust clearance from the U.S. government;[41] however, a major barrier remained. In agreeing to the Red Line Agreement of 1928,[42] Exxon and Mobil had pledged that, as IPC partners, they would not acquire concessions within the boundaries of the old Ottoman Empire (which included Saudi Arabia) except through their joint ownership of IPC. In merging with Aramco, Exxon and Mobil were not only violating the terms of this agreement, but threatening the home markets of their European competitors with the prospect of cheap Saudi oil.

Exxon and Mobil insisted that the Red Line Agreement was no longer valid because two of the IPC partners, CFP and Gulbenkian, had become "enemies" as a consequence of being in France at the time of the German occupation.

Enlisting the support of the State Department, threatening to bring legal suit against the IPC partners (which would have exposed the secret agreement), and agreeing to purchase large volumes of oil from either Iran or Kuwait (at British Petroleum's option), Exxon and Mobil got the British to accept termination of the Red Line Agreement. Also, Exxon and Mobil agreed to allow CFP to lift more oil from Iraq than the IPC agreement provided for, but this failed to satisfy the French. Gulbenkian and the French continued to insist that the Red Line Agreement was still valid. As the Subcommittee on Multinational Corporations found, "It became increasingly clear that the French felt 'frozen out' of Saudi Arabia and that their national objective was not so much the negative one of blocking further American participation in Aramco as an aspiration to be included in the greatest oil deal in the history of the industry."[43]

To reduce the likelihood of an adverse court ruling, the two American companies considered the possibility that one of them sell its share in IPC to the other in exchange for a greater share in Aramco. If this had been done, it would have had major implications for the future of the international oil industry, for if Exxon and Mobil each had an interest in Iraq or Saudi Arabia, but not in both countries, each company would have had a much greater interest in expanding total production in its concession. Greater competition would have been the result.[44]

Paul Nitze, then serving as deputy director of the Office of International Trade Policy, saw two advantages in this "swap" alternative. It could help mollify the French, since their rights under the Red Line Agreement would not be violated, and it would help counter the objections that both Congress and the domestic oil industry were raising about the emergence of an increasingly interlocked group of American and British oil companies that, together, had a monopoly on the international oil industry. Nitze arranged a meeting with executives from Exxon and Mobil to discuss this alternative, but was told that the companies had already rejected the IPC/Aramco swap alternative and were going ahead with the merger.

Exxon and Mobil proceeded to acquire 30 percent and 10 percent of Aramco. Eventually they reached a settlement with their IPC partners, which included a provision that enabled them to increase their liftings in Iraq beyond the levels allowed by the IPC group agreement. The French never forgave the United States for keeping them out of Aramco, and they were hardly alone in thinking it was a strange kind of "open door" that allowed one nation to walk in, always and everywhere, but kept others forever out.

"Fifty/Fifty" and the Foreign Tax Credit. The assertion of U.S. "rights" vis-à-vis other advanced countries was only part of the process of establishing a predominant position for the United States in international oil. Equally important was the buttressing of pro-Western regimes in the oil-producing countries.

In October 1945, when a reformist coup brought the Acción Democrática to power in Venezuela, oil company executives feared that the new government might nationalize the industry or renounce the forty-year extension of concessions that the companies had secured in 1943. But because Venezuela was heavily dependent upon oil revenues, the measures the new government took against the foreign-controlled industry proved to be surprisingly restrained. Consequently, the companies went along with the government's 1948 decision to ensure itself 50 percent of the profits from the oil industry's operations in the country.[45]

In forcing the companies to pay higher taxes, Venezuela took advantage of the fact that the companies had already made substantial investments in the development of Venezuelan oil and would therefore be willing to pay more, rather than lose their assets. But Venezuela's apparent victory contained the seeds of defeat: even without the additional taxes, Venezuelan oil was more costly than Middle East oil, and by raising the companies' tax-paid cost,[46] Venezuela threatened to accelerate the industry's movement to the Middle East. To prevent this, Venezuela sent representatives to the other oil-exporting countries to urge them to adopt the "fifty/fifty" strategy, thereby boosting their own revenues and increasing the attractiveness of Venezuelan crude.[47]

Combined with another development, the Venezuelan action soon led to trouble for the companies in Saudi Arabia. After the Aramco merger, the American partners made a deal with Ibn Saud in which they relinquished their rights to the Neutral Zone in return for an offshore concession adjacent to their Dhahran field. The agreement enabled Aramco to keep its concessions centered around a single refinery and tanker port and to trade in a territory that belonged to both Kuwait and Saudi Arabia, but it opened a promising field to new competition. For the right to half the concession, Aminoil, a syndicate of American firms, offered Kuwait $7.5 million plus an annual royalty of at least $625,000 a year (figured at 35¢ a barrel). Inasmuch as in 1934 Gulf and BP had paid only $170,000 plus an annual royalty of $35,000 for the concession to Kuwait, this was an attractive offer. It indicated the extent to which independent companies would go to secure a foothold in the Middle East. For its half of the concession, J. Paul Getty offered Saudi Arabia $9.5 million down, an advance on royalties of $1 million (payable yearly), and royalty payments of 55¢ a barrel.[48]

Immediately, the deal raised questions for the Aramco partners. Why was Aramco paying a royalty of only 21¢ a barrel when Getty was ready to pay 55¢? And why was Venezuela receiving 50 percent of the profits on the companies' operations in that country when Saudi Arabia was getting only 20 percent?[49] Ibn Saud wanted an increase in payments from Aramco, but the Aramco partners were not anxious to give it to him.

By this time the United States' main concern was the threat of Soviet advancement into the Middle East. As a 1950 State Department memorandum stated,

The area is highly attractive to the USSR because of oil, its strategic location at the air, land and sea crossroads of Eurasia and its vulnerability to attack from without and within. Apart from the outer shell of resistance exhibited by Turkey and Iran, states historically familiar with the USSR, the ability of Middle East armed forces and the desire of local populations to resist Communist military forces appears almost non-existent. It is believed that Soviet striking forces could not be prevented by the West from fast overrunning Persian Gulf oil fields.

The vulnerability of the area and the oil to internal attack also appears high. Communism's alleged support for the underdog, in an area of underdogs, and its promise of quick relief have opportunity for expansion in the Middle East where masses of people live in circumstances of exceptional poverty and ignorance, where governments are often corrupt, inefficient and of, by and for the upper class and where increasing numbers of partially educated but frustrated younger generations are becoming available for explosive action. Communist propaganda tries to exploit this internal situation and to place responsibility on the West.

Unfortunately, Western powers are already unpopular, the European nations chiefly because of their lingering reputation for colonialism and imperialism, the U.S. chiefly because of its support for the Jewish state of Israel. There unfortunately also exists a history of friction and dissatisfaction over the oil operations of foreign interests in the area. ''Anglo-American oil imperialists'' receive their full share of attention not only from those preaching Communism but from the increasing numbers of xenophobes in the area who believe that both the West and the Soviets are interested in only the exploitation of the Middle East and that both should be rejected.[50]

The State Department recognized that to maintain the U.S. position in the Middle East, aid would have to be provided to improve the standing of U.S. oil companies with the host governments and to increase the durability of those governments. However, the State Department's ability to furnish that aid was impeded by political developments. Through a series of offenses, the Jews of Palestine (about 700,000 in number) had brought most of the land allocated to them in a U.N. partition plan under their control. On May 15, 1948, they proclaimed establishment of the state of Israel.

The oil companies, the U.S. armed forces, and the State Department all opposed establishment of a Jewish state because they feared it would worsen U.S. relations with the Arabs and provide an opening for the Soviets into the region. But Truman's political advisers pointed out that, with elections approaching, the president was dependent upon Jewish campaign contributions and Jewish votes, particularly in New York, the state with the greatest number of electoral votes. They also argued that if the Soviet Union were to recognize Israel first, it could drive the new state closer to the Soviet bloc. Consequently, against the advice of both the secretary of state and the secretary of defense, Truman recognized Israel a few minutes after the state was proclaimed.[51]

U.S. oil policy now had to contend with the fact that popular domestic support was pro-Israel and hostile to the Arabs, and the Israeli lobby emerged as one of the strongest forces in U.S. politics. Ironically, one of the few forces that could match it in terms of political muscle was the oil lobby itself. In response to all this, a dual foreign policy emerged, consisting of official, overt support for Israel and private, covertly government-backed support for the Arab states. Along with the failure of PRC, this further ensconced the oil companies as the instruments for achieving this secret or private foreign policy.

The State Department was anxious that something be done to appease Ibn Saud; however, domestic support for Israel made it unlikely that Congress would approve direct foreign aid to the Arab governments. Therefore the State Department recommended that the companies relinquish those parts of the Aramco concession that they had little intention of developing in the foreseeable future; the Saudi government could then auction them off and pocket the revenue. But the companies rejected this, fearing increased competition as other companies developed the relinquished territories. Another alternative was for the companies to increase their royalty payments and pass the increase on to customers in Western Europe. However, the U.S. government rejected this because higher oil prices would impede the recovery of Western Europe, which the United States, through the Marshall Plan, was doing so much to facilitate.

Finally, the State Department worked out an agreement with the Treasury Department to allow the companies to treat their payments to Saudi Arabia as income-tax payments.[52] Since U.S. law gives companies that operate abroad a dollar-for-dollar credit on their income-tax payments to foreign countries, the effect was to reduce the companies' U.S. tax obligations by the amount of "taxes" they paid to the oil-exporting countries. The decision was first implemented for Saudi Arabia, where Aramco had paid the United States $50 million in income taxes in 1950. In 1951, after the decision went into effect, the company paid only $6 million in U.S. income taxes. Payments to the Saudis increased from $66 million in 1950 to almost $110 million in 1951.

Since 1953 this credit has completely offset the companies' U.S. tax liability on their foreign earnings, the result being that the major oil companies have enjoyed an extraordinarily low effective tax rate. For example, in 1972 Exxon paid only 6.5 percent of its global income in U.S. taxes and Mobil only 1.3 percent.[53] Never approved by Congress, it has been a kind of privately arranged foreign aid, paid for out of funds that should have gone to the U.S. Treasury. Within a few years, the tax-credit scheme spread to the other oil-exporting states, and to maintain the competitive positions of their companies, other governments were forced to adopt comparable policies.

The American companies proceeded to make political profit out of the "fifty/ fifty" split that they had been forced to accede to in Venezuela. In April 1951, Exxon and Mobil explained the rationale to their IPC partners:

With its 50/50 slogan, it is attractive alike to governments and to the public. Its central idea can be easily understood by the man in the street and it makes an immediate appeal as something essentially reasonable and fair. For these reasons it is a strong formula from a public relations standpoint. Also, it provides a firm basis on which to stand and therefore may be considered as perhaps the most stable formula obtainable.[54]

In an effort to boost their share of production, in the 1950s and 1960s the oil-exporting countries granted "marketing allowances," discounts, and other rebates to the international oil companies. The effect was to keep the oil-exporting countries' share of the profits on Middle East oil below the stipulated 50 percent level until at least the mid-1950s.[55]

Since the foreign-tax credits could be used only to offset profits earned abroad, they provided a tremendous incentive for the oil companies to invest abroad rather than at home. While the favorable cost advantages of Middle East oil probably would have led the companies to invest in foreign production facilities in any case, the foreign-tax credit also gave the companies a strong incentive to build refineries and petrochemical plants outside the United States.

So long as the exporting countries had received a fixed per barrel royalty, the price at which the oil was sold and the companies' profits were of little direct concern to them. But now, with the oil-exporting countries officially entitled to 50 percent of the profits from the sale of a barrel of crude oil, they had a new interest in the price at which the oil sold. Yet most crude oil was *not* sold, but was transferred from a company's production affiliate to its refining affiliate. Consequently, to facilitate calculation of the revenue that host countries were entitled to, the companies announced "posted prices" for the various crudes they produced. These posted prices, established in 1950, were intended to correspond to the market price (or value) at the time, but in subsequent years the market price declined and the posted price became simply a tax-reference price or means of calculating the revenue the host country was entitled to. For example, with a posted price of $3, a market price of $1.80, and production costs of 20¢, one arrived at the producing-country government's per barrel entitlement, by ignoring the market price, subtracting the production cost from the posted price, and dividing the result in half: $3 − .20/2 = $1.40.

The Iranian Nationalization and the Consortium.   As soon as the tax-credit agreement vis-à-vis Saudi Arabia was reached, it intensified nationalist pressures for greater oil revenues in Iran, the one Middle East oil-producing country where U.S. companies still lacked a direct presence. The Iranians had long been dissatisfied with their arrangements with British Petroleum (Anglo-Iranian), which in 1950 brought the oil company's profits to nearly five times the amount it paid to Iran and resulted in BP's paying more in taxes to the British government than it paid to Iran. Moreover, in 1951 Bahrain was getting 35¢ per barrel for its oil, Saudi Arabia 56¢, and Iraq 60¢; but Iran was still receiving only 18¢.[56]

Spurred on by the fifty/fifty agreements in Venezuela and Saudi Arabia, the Iranians sought a change in their concession terms. But in contrast to its U.S. counterparts in the Middle East, BP lacked the advantages of a foreign-tax credit and, partly for this reason, was unwilling to boost Iran's per barrel revenues to the level of the other Middle East producers. As the dispute dragged on, public resentment against the company increased, and was given official expression by a small group of nationalists in the Iranian parliament. In 1951 the pressures for change were intensified when the anti-imperialist National Front, under the leadership of Premier Mohammed Mossadegh, came to power. Immediately, the new government nationalized BP's concession, creating the National Iranian Oil Company (NIOC) to take over its responsibilities. Both BP and the British government, which was heavily dependent upon the earnings of BP for foreign exchange, were determined to resist the nationalization. Consequently, later in 1951, at the height of the nationalization crisis, Britain sent gunboats to Iran to "show the flag."[57]

In contrast to Britain, the United States had a wider range of interests. On the one hand, the United States wanted to ensure that Iran remained firmly in the Western camp. That made the United States sympathetic to buttressing the Mossadegh regime, for it was Mossadegh who had led the opposition to the Soviet oil concession agreement in 1946–47. Also, the United States knew that both the British and BP were extremely unpopular in Iran. Consequently, with the Soviet Union threatening to counterattack and with the Communist Tudeh Party the main alternative to Mossadegh in Iran, the United States made it clear that it would not support military action by the British.[58]

On the other hand, the United States could not accept nationalization in Iran without adequate compensation, for fear it might spread to other oil-producing countries, jeopardizing U.S. interests in those areas and the sanctity-of-contracts principle that it sought to establish as one of the foundations of the liberal world economy it sought to create. Therefore, the United States went along with the boycott of Iranian oil that BP instituted. The boycott was remarkably effective, forcing Iranian oil production to drop from 640,000 barrels per day (b/d) in 1950 to 20,000 b/d in 1952.[59]

The boycott's success was due to the legal threat that BP held over the head of any purchaser of Iranian oil and, more importantly, to the fact that the oil companies had alternative sources of supply. BP was able to replace much of the oil it lost in Iran by boosting its liftings in Iraq, where it had a 23.75 percent share, and the U.S. majors profited enormously by boosting production in Iraq, Kuwait, and Saudi Arabia during this period. In addition, the U.S. majors had an interest in ensuring that nationalization schemes proved unsuccessful, for it would tend to secure their positions in the oil-exporting countries.

The companies and their consumers in the West emerged nearly unscathed by the boycott,[60] but the effect on Iran, where oil accounted for about a third of its total production, was nearly crippling.[61] Fearing a left-wing coup, the United States toyed with the idea of coming to the aid of the Mossadegh regime, but decided that the nationalization issue would have to be resolved first. Mossadegh lacked the financial resources to compensate BP for the loss of its physical assets in Iran and the value of the oil that still lay in the ground; however, the United States insisted that he either meet this demand or denationalize.

By this time, Mossadegh's political support was heavily dependent on his having nationalized Iranian oil—a move he could not renounce without renouncing his popular base; so he refused to accept either part of the U.S. proposal and declared that if the United States would not provide him with aid, he would turn to the Soviet Union. In retaliation, the CIA backed a coup, drawing on the opposition of the Iranian army, the police, and the landowning class.[62] In August 1953, Mossadegh was overthrown and the Shah assumed control of the government, appointing General Fazlollah Zahedi as prime minister.[63]

The U.S. government's next task was to stabilize this new pro-Western government, and the most effective way was to boost its oil revenues. But the new Iranian government was unwilling to return the Iranian oil concession to the British alone, fearing the impact this would have on its standing with the Iranian public. Besides, there was no assurance at this point that BP, acting alone, could absorb enough Iranian crude to provide the new Iranian government with all the revenue it required. Consequently, in a pattern that had become familiar, the U.S. government turned to the major U.S. oil companies, proposing that a consortium of oil companies be established to produce and market Iranian oil.

Theoretically, the United States could have turned to non-major American companies, but in practice, heavy reliance on these companies was not a good alternative: private companies would invest in Iranian crude only if they had market outlets for it, and most of the downstream marketing outlets were controlled by the majors. Other companies might absorb some Iranian crude, but not enough to provide Iran the revenues it required. With the Iranian government unstable and unable to safeguard the concessions it granted the companies, it was unlikely that independent companies would be willing to risk their capital on Iranian production and then compete to increase their share of world markets. And even if they did, this strategy would require that they lower prices, making them increasingly unable to pay large royalties to the Shah.[64]

Only the majors could substitute Iranian crude for Saudi or Kuwaiti crude without lowering prices, but they were reluctant to do so because they feared that if they cut back on production in the Arab world, they would antagonize the governments of these countries, jeopardizing their concessions in the process. Besides, why should they make costly investments in a high-risk area like Iran when they already had more low-cost oil than they needed in their concessions in Kuwait, Saudi Arabia, and Iraq?

As Howard Page, Exxon's Middle East coordinator at the time, told the Senate Subcommittee on Multinationals:

We knew when we went into the consortium that as a business deal, a straight business deal, it was for the birds. I mean, in other words, we had to spend money for capacity and reserves that we already had and had available and freely available so we lost money on every barrel. I mean once we were there, of course, then you didn't lose money on every barrel except of course you had to pay for the reserves, but the point was that we went in there as, to save the situation [sic], and it was in the interests of the United States and Britain at that time.[65]

Given Iran's recent history, the companies had little assurance that they would be able to maintain the concession once they established it. As Page said, "It was touch and go as to whether or not even after we did the consortium out there that the country would last. There was a very strong Tudeh Party there run by the Communists and they would whip up the excitement of people against foreigners."[66]

Like the State Department, the companies had an interest in opposing an extension of Soviet influence. As Page was later to state, "We recognized the dangers if Russia got in, we had a real interest in seeing to it that the problem was solved. We didn't balk at participation. Had the Russians gotten Iranian oil, and dumped it on world markets, that would have been serious."[67] Nor did the majors want to see Iranian oil pass into the hands of their competitors.

Moreover, in April 1953, after much debate within the federal government,[68] the Department of Justice had brought a civil antitrust suit against the five U.S. international majors. In January 1954, the companies indicated that they would go into the proposed Iranian Consortium only if they were promised antitrust immunity in the exploration, production, and refining of Iranian oil. The companies knew this would weaken the government's antitrust case since the Justice Department would be sanctioning a joint production/refining arrangement.[69] However, the Eisenhower administration agreed to this, on the grounds that the government's national security interests, which were dependent upon the cooperation of the major oil companies, took priority over prosecution of the antitrust case.

A plan for the Iranian Consortium was then worked out, giving BP a 40 percent share, each of the five U.S. majors an 8 percent share (totaling another 40%), Royal Dutch/Shell a 14 percent share, and CFP a 6 percent share. But once they learned of the planned Consortium, U.S. independent companies objected to this new cartel arrangement. In response to these protests, the State Department persuaded each of the U.S. majors to relinquish a 1 percent share of the Consortium. The resulting 5 percent was then divided among a group of U.S. independent companies—with the State Department specifying that they be U.S. companies.[70]

It was also agreed that BP would receive $510 million in compensation, most of it from the companies that bought into the concession, but a small portion from the Iranian government. Finally, the National Iranian Oil Company continued to exist, as the titular owner of the Iranian oil fields, but the Consortium was granted managerial rights for the next twenty-five years, with an additional fifteen-year option.

While the Iranian Consortium was considerably more inclusive than the Aramco concession, it was overwhelmingly an Anglo-American affair; and it excluded Italy, West Germany, and Japan, the three powers defeated during World War II, each of which was now firmly allied with the United States. Exclusion was particularly troublesome to Ente Nazionale Idrocarburi (ENI), the Italian national petroleum company, headed by Enrico Mattei. Prior to the Iranian nationalization, ENI had been supplied exclusively by BP from its Iranian concession. Though Mattei had the opportunity to buy oil from Mossadegh during the boycott, he had agreed not to do so. Later, when the Consortium was formed, he expected ENI to be given a share in it, and he greatly resented ENI's exclusion.[71]

At the request of the National Security Council, the five U.S. majors proceeded to bring Iranian oil production back into the world market in a manner that would preserve the world price, thereby enabling the companies to provide the Shah with the revenues he required. The U.S. majors persuaded the pro-Western rulers in Iraq, Saudi Arabia, and Kuwait that, by accepting limitations on their production and thereby making room for an increase in Iranian production, they would help keep Iran—and possibly the entire Persian Gulf region—out of the Soviet orbit.[72] Then, in February 1955, Iran joined Turkey, Iraq, Pakistan, and Britain in the U.S.-organized[73] Middle East Treaty Organization—the Baghdad Pact—a Middle East version of NATO. Secretary of State John Foster Dulles explained that the "basic purpose is to create a solid band of resistance against the Soviet Union."[74]

Along with these political developments, the Iranian nationalization dispute established an important precedent for the oil industry. A reformist government had acted in opposition to the interests of a major oil company, and the result was a crippling loss of revenue and eventual overthrow. This experience proved to be a powerful deterrent against similar actions by other exporting countries. As Geoffrey Chandler, an executive with Royal Dutch/Shell stated, "Throughout the 1960s the Mossadegh episode in Iran was remembered as indicating an ability on the part of the companies to frustrate the effective exercise of nationalization."[75] Indeed, not until twenty years after the Iranian nationalization would another major oil-producing asset be nationalized.

With the entrance of the U.S. companies into the Iranian Consortium, the basic structure of the international petroleum industry—which would endure for the next two decades—was firmly established. The United States had opened the door of the all-important Middle East concessions to U.S. nationals, which (as table 1–1 indicates) substantially increased their share of the area's production while blocking the entrance of newcomer nations to the principal producing concessions. And it secured the position of pro-Western regimes in the area.

The creation of the new system was clearly a joint venture of government and business, but a "division of labor" had to be respected. Rooted in the companies' hostility to direct government intervention in the industry, this division of labor reduced the likelihood that the tensions of Middle East politics would affect the flow of oil. The oil companies' task was to produce oil and deliver it to Europe, Japan, and (to a limited extent) the United States at affordable prices, all the while transferring enough revenue to the oil-producing countries to prevent their radicalization. The U.S. government, assisted by Great Britain, would maintain the security of the Middle East's political/military system, in which the oil companies operated. This meant maintaining preponderant military power and political influence, sufficient to deter Soviet encroachments and to contain the conflicts between Arabs and the new state of Israel.

Both partners had to be ever on guard against the oil-producing countries'

TABLE 1-1. OIL PRODUCTION CONTROLLED IN FOREIGN COUNTRIES (EXCLUDING U.S. AND U.S.S.R.), 1938–57*

	1938		1945		1953	
	Level	%	Level	%	Level	%
British-Dutch	810.0	52.5	813.0	41.1	1,818.4	32.6
U.S.	506.9	32.9	818.2	41.4	2,961.4	53.1
Others	225.3	14.6	346.0	17.5	797.6	14.3

Oil Production Controlled in Foreign Countries (Excluding North America and Communist Countries)*

	1950		1957	
	Level	%	Level	%
British-Dutch majors	1,336	40.0	2,215	31.9
U.S. majors	1,942	58.2	3,963	57.1
Others	60	1.8	764	11.0

Oil Production Controlled in Middle East*

	1939		1944		1953	
	Level	%	Level	%	Level	%
British-Dutch	247.5	78.3	353.4	87.2	760.2	31.4
U.S.	49.8	15.7	51.8	12.8	1,456.8	60.1
Others	19.0	6.0	—	—	207.3	8.5
Middle East as a % of total foreign	14.2		16.5		36.6	

*In thousands of barrels per day (tb/d).

Figures for 1938, 1939, 1944, 1945, and 1953 are from Fanning, *Foreign Oil and the Free World*, pp. 352 and 354; figures for 1950 and 1957 are from Adelman, *The World Petroleum Market*, pp. 80–81. The data from Adelman are not strictly comparable with the data from Fanning. British-Dutch majors include British Petroleum and Royal Dutch/Shell; U.S. majors include Exxon, Mobil, Standard Oil of California, Texaco, and Gulf.

unifying in opposition to the imposed system and renouncing the sanctity of contracts. The oil companies would do this by making the countries compete with each other for their respective market shares—the U.S. government by supporting its friends and punishing its foes.

The Suez Crisis. The conflict over the Iranian nationalization had shown that the advanced countries were largely unhindered by a cutoff in supplies from a single oil-exporting country. However, just two years after resolution of the Iranian nationalization, the forces that had led to this crisis—Third World nationalism and Western fears of Soviet advances—created a general crisis in the international oil industry. In 1952, Colonel Gamal Abdel Nasser overthrew King Farouk in Egypt, ushering in a new wave of Arab nationalism, and the new Egyptian regime embarked immediately on a program of economic and land reform, with one of its ultimate goals the nationalization of the Suez Canal. Pursuing their objectives, the Egyptians benefited from a change in Soviet policy toward the Third World.

Immediately following World War II, the Soviet Union had adopted a rigid bipolar position: countries were in either the "imperialist" or the "anti-imperialist" camp; there was no genuinely neutral position and, hence, no possibility of the Soviets' cooperating with any government that claimed to be neutral in the struggle between East and West. But following the death of Stalin, in the mid-1950s a new Soviet doctrine was formulated that held there are many paths to socialism and that a neutral government *could* play a progressive role. This made it possible for the Soviet Union to support national liberation struggles and nationalist regimes, which was to have immediate consequences for the Middle East and, ultimately, for the oil industry, for the new strategy made it possible for the Soviet Union to leap over the Northern Tier, Baghdad Pact countries and compete with the United States for influence with Nasser's new nationalist regime. And although the Soviet Union had originally adopted a position of neutrality on the Arab-Israeli conflict, in 1955 it adopted a pro-Arab position. In September 1955 the Soviet Union met Nasser's request for massive deliveries of arms by arranging for Egypt to buy arms from Czechoslovakia.

In December, in response, the United States and Great Britain offered to help finance the planned Aswan High Dam. But in the United States, the offer was opposed by fiscal conservatives, who objected to the dam's cost; by Southerners who feared competition from Egyptian cotton; and by the "China lobby," which objected to Egypt's recognition of Communist China. Consequently, the United States withdrew its Aswan Dam offer in July and the Soviet Union agreed to help finance the dam.

Still, Nasser decided to retaliate against the West by nationalizing the British-controlled Universal Suez Canal Company. Although Nasser did not plan to close the canal, the British and French viewed Egyptian control of the canal as a direct threat to the security of their oil supplies. They also believed that if Nasser was successful, he would press for nationalization of Middle East oil resources. In addition, Britain and France feared that as Nasser gained prestige and influence in the Arab world, their influence in the Middle East would decline. Britain feared that Nasser's success would lessen British hegemony in Jordan and Iraq, as well as its prestige and influence as a result of losing the canal. France was afraid that if Nasser was successful, it would have a destabilizing influence on its colony in Algeria.

In contrast, the United States did not view Nasser's move as a direct threat to its oil interests, and was far more concerned that if the West resisted Nasser's move, Egypt would be driven into the Soviet camp, eventually bringing much of the Arab world with it. The United States also feared that a hostile response to the Egyptian move would do further harm to the position of the United States vis-à-vis the Soviet Union in the new nations of Asia and Africa. Whereas Great Britain and France were concerned about their immediate interests in the area, the United States, as world leader, was far more concerned about the long-term, systemic consequences of opposing Nasser.

In opposing Nasser, Great Britain and France recognized that they had a common interest with Israel, which resented the continual border clashes with Egypt and Nasser's repeated intent "to drive Israel into the sea." Consequently, with the support of Great Britain and France, Israel invaded Egypt on October 29, 1956 and rapidly advanced toward the Suez Canal, and two days later, Britain and France entered the fighting. The Soviet Union declared it was ready to send "volunteers" to aid the Egyptian forces, if necessary, but proposed that peace be restored by a joint U.S.-S.U. force. The United States, determined to keep the Soviet Union out of the Middle East, rejected this offer and turned instead to the oil weapon.

With Egypt blocking the canal, Western Europe had to turn to the Western Hemisphere for oil.[76] Petroleum was available and an emergency plan (worked out during the summer) was ready, but the United States would not allow the oil to flow freely until Great Britain and France agreed to a cease-fire and withdrawal.[77] Their lifeblood threatened, France and Great Britain withdrew their troops and the canal was restored to Egyptian control by the end of the year, but the canal remained closed for another three months, during which time the loss in Middle East oil production was largely compensated by increases in U.S. and Venezuelan production.[78] During the crisis the United States boosted its shipments of petroleum and petroleum products to Western Europe from 50,000 to 475,000 b/d. Normally, oil supplies from the Western Hemisphere accounted for only 20 percent of Western Europe's supplies, but during the "oil lift" Western Hemisphere supplies accounted for roughly 60 percent of Western Europe's energy supplies.[79]

The Suez crisis had several important consequences. Like the Iranian nationalization, it seemed to demonstrate the ease with which the West could resist hostile actions by underdeveloped countries, for the oil companies had been able to minimize economic damage to the consuming countries by rearranging world oil flows. Insofar as there were problems, they stemmed more from the initial refusal of the United States to resupply Western Europe than from the closing of the canal. Nonetheless, the crisis greatly enhanced Nasser's prestige. It also demonstrated that, with the Soviet Union now an active competitor for influence in the Third World, underdeveloped countries could benefit by exploiting the rivalry between East and West. Only a few years before, in the conflict over Iranian nationalization, the United States appears to have been far more concerned about "just" compensation—and hostile to the aspirations of an underdeveloped nation—than it was in the Suez Canal crisis. Part of the reason was that rivalry with the Soviet Union and the consequent danger of appearing as a colonial power to the emerging nations of Asia and Africa made the principle of "just" compensation less important in the Egyptian nationalization.

Despite U.S. efforts, the Suez crisis also enhanced the prestige and influence of the "anti-imperialist" Soviet Union and marked a sharp decline in French and British influence in the Middle East. In the future, therefore, the United States would have to assume much greater responsibility for maintaining the stability of the area. Indeed, though the British continued to maintain a military presence "east of Suez," the United States had almost sole responsibility for maintaining security west of Suez.[80] In 1957, in recognition of these trends, the "Eisenhower Doctrine" gave the U.S. president authority to extend economic or military aid—and, if necessary, to send U.S. military forces—to the Middle East if any nation in the region requested help against Communist-instigated aggression.

Finally, the Suez Canal crisis greatly antagonized France and Great Britain, which found the oil weapon used against them not by an oil-exporting country but by the United States. Consequently, the nations of Western Europe, and France in particular, increased their efforts to free themselves from dependence upon oil supplies that were controlled by U.S. nationals.

THE STRUCTURE OF THE INTERNATIONAL OIL INDUSTRY

The international oil industry that emerged during the decade following World War II was dominated by eight interlocked firms: Exxon, Mobil, Standard Oil of California, Texaco, Gulf, British Petroleum, Royal Dutch/Shell, and Compagnie Française des Pétroles (CFP). The first five are U.S. companies (the first three having been part of Rockefeller's Standard Oil, with the Rockefeller family still owning a substantial share—1 or 2 percent—of each of them). As its name suggests, British Petroleum is British owned, with the British government owning 51 percent. Royal Dutch/Shell is 60 percent Dutch and 40 percent British. CFP is a French company, much smaller than the other seven.[81]

In 1950, virtually all the oil produced outside North America and the Communist countries was produced by these eight companies. The three best-established companies—Exxon, BP, and Shell—accounted for 70.5 percent of this production. In 1957 the eight majors still accounted for 92 percent of non–North American, non-Communist oil production and their refining totaled 68 percent.[82]

Not only was the market share of a few firms exceedingly high, but, as table 1–2 shows, these firms functioned in the crucial Middle East production concessions through joint ventures rather than independently; and each of the majors had holdings in at least two countries. In a period when the reserves in any country were more than adequate to supply a firm's production needs, this gave the companies tremendous advantage in dealing with the oil-exporting countries, for if any oil-exporting country made "excessive" demands upon a company, the company could reduce its production in that country and increase it elsewhere, thereby transferring revenue to the compliant country. This was clearly

TABLE 1–2. OWNERSHIP SHARES IN MAJOR MIDDLE EAST JOINT OIL PRODUCTION COMPANIES (PERCENT)

	Iranian Consortium	Iraq Petroleum Company	Aramco (Saudi Arabia)	Kuwait Oil Company
Exxon	7	11.875	30	
Texaco	7		30	
SoCal	7		30	
Mobil	7	11.875	10	
Gulf	7			50
British Petroleum	40	23.75		50
Royal Dutch/Shell	14	23.75		
CFP	6	23.75		
Iricon	5			
Gulbenkian		5		

Figures are from U.S. Senate, Committee on Foreign Relations, Subcommittee on Multinational Corporations, *Multinational Corporations and United States Foreign Policy* (1974) (*MNC Hearings*), part 5, p. 289.

demonstrated during the Iranian nationalization, when British Petroleum boosted production in Kuwait to make up for its losses in Iran.

Alternatively, if conditions became more favorable in a particular country, a company could boost its production there, without endangering the world price level, and cut back in another country. For example, after completion of a new pipeline from Iraq to the eastern Mediterranean in 1952, Iraqi production was increased from 192 tb/d (thousand barrels per day) to 514 tb/d. Exxon and Mobil, which had holdings in both Iraq and Saudi Arabia, accommodated the increased Iraqi production by cutting back on Aramco's production. BP did the same thing (to a lesser extent) by cutting back on production in Kuwait.[83] In short, because they had holdings in several countries, the majors had considerable power to determine the oil-exporting countries' production shares and therefore could play the countries against one another.

However, multiple holdings also imposed limitations on the companies' actions. Before a major oil company could agree to anything in one country, it had to consider its impact on the company's operations elsewhere. When accommodations to the demands of a particular country were called for, the majors would find that their room to maneuver was limited. In 1950, the advantages a company derived from having holdings in several countries clearly outweighed the disadvantages; but by 1970, as we will see, the disadvantages had grown.

The major oil companies were vertically integrated; that is, each operated in the production, transport, refining, and marketing sectors of the industry; and though not as great as their dominance over crude-oil production, the majors' control of these other sectors was quite substantial. Outside the United States and the Communist countries, in 1953 the eight majors controlled 95.8 percent of all reserves, 90.2 percent of all production, 75.6 percent of all refining capacity, and 74.3 percent of all product sales.[84] Moreover, control over production and control in these downstream sectors tended to reinforce one another, for would-be newcomers to the industry and oil-exporting countries alike knew that control over crude oil would do them little good unless they could find markets for the oil. And with the majors supplying themselves with crude and dominating product markets, that would not be easy. At the same time, independent refiners found it difficult to compete with the majors, who had access to low-cost, high-profit-margin crude oil.

Essentially, the oil companies sold crude oil to themselves; so development of a group of informed buyers who could bid the price down was prevented, and it was very difficult for the oil-exporting countries to determine the actual market value of their crude oil.

Vertical integration facilitated transmittal of changes in demand for petroleum products to the producing level without delay, thereby reducing the likelihood of crude surpluses that would lead to price reductions. A vertically integrated producer has an assured outlet for its crude and a refiner or marketer that is part of an integrated structure has an assured source of supply. In addition, vertical integration enabled a company to reduce its overall tax burden by setting transfer prices and notional profits among its affiliates in ways that would reduce its tax liability.[85] Vertical integration also meant that the majors were concerned not simply with maximizing profits on the production of oil, but on maximizing the profits of their entire integrated structure. If a company's profits on crude oil could be increased—say from an increase in production levels, but only at a cost to the company's profits in downstream markets—the company could be expected to oppose the production increase.

The majors have often been viewed as an all-powerful monolith, and certainly they have strong interests in common. All eight majors have sought to maintain a price level that is well above cost, to resist encroachments by others into the Middle East concessions, and to oppose the efforts of oil-exporting countries to alter concession terms in their favor. Yet there have also been important differences among the majors. Indeed, many changes that the industry has undergone since World War II have been due to these differences.

Companies that were partners in the producing concessions were competitors in downstream product markets, because each company had an interest in boosting its market share. The majors also differed in their positions in the various concessions, and they frequently had different interests in the level of production in a particular concession. If left to pursue its own competitive interest, each company would have been strongly tempted to use its access to low-cost crude to reduce prices in order to expand its market share. Recognizing this, the majors devised a series of mechanisms to restrict production and thereby maintain the price level; but these were imperfect, at best. Consequently, the behavior of the eight majors combined elements of independent, competitive, profit-seeking behavior, as well as policies designed to advance their common interests.

From the beginning, the cartel structure that the majors sought to establish was jeopardized by rivalry among the members of the cartel. As we have seen, in the immediate postwar period there was a particularly strong conflict between the best-established majors—Exxon, BP, and Shell—and the less-well-established majors, who sought to use their recently acquired low-cost crude oil to boost their shares in downstream markets. The established majors saw these efforts as threatening the price level and encroaching on their position in downstream product markets. Consequently, they used their position in the joint ventures to limit their partners' access to cheap crude oil.[86]

For example, in 1947 SoCal and Texaco (CalTex) sought to keep the price that Aramco charged its parent-company affiliates at $1.02 a barrel; but at that price, Arabian oil would reduce Exxon's sales of Venezuelan crude on the U.S. eastern seaboard and its sales in Western Europe. Therefore Exxon, with Mobil's backing, demanded that Aramco production be sold to the company affiliates at the world price of $1.48 a barrel. If CalTex, which owned only 60 percent of Aramco, still wanted to compete in downstream markets, it would be forced to share 40 percent of the profits with Exxon and Mobil, its Aramco partners. The dispute went on for a year and a half, but eventually Exxon, which threatened to sue its partners for breach of fiduciary responsibility, got the price raised to $1.43 a barrel.[87]

Similarly, in the Iraq Petroleum Company the established majors were afraid that if CFP had unrestricted access to cheap Iraqi oil, the French company would use it to cut prices in product markets. Consequently, they made rapid expansion difficult by requiring that production be planned for five-year periods, five years in advance, thereby making it difficult for a company to take advantage of immediate opportunities to boost its market share. And to discourage companies from taking more than their share in any one year, they decided that a partner would have to pay a price halfway between tax-paid cost and realized price on such excess liftings.[88]

In the Iranian Consortium, the threat of price cutting came from both CFP and the U.S. independents. To minimize this, it was decided that each member of the Consortium would submit a nomination for the Consortium's total liftings, called the "aggregate programmed quantity" or the APQ. The bids would be ranked in descending order, and one would read down the list—cumulating the shares in the Consortium represented by each of the companies,—until the 70 percent figure was reached. The nomination of the company that put the figure over 70 percent would be accepted as the APQ and each member of the Consortium would be able to take its equity share of that figure at tax-paid cost, or about two-thirds of the posted price. A company could have additional liftings, but only if it was willing to pay the full posted price.[89] By setting the APQ at the bid of the 70 percent partner, European and U.S. interests were able to counterbalance one another. With European interests totaling 60 percent and U.S. interests 40 percent, neither could set the APQ by acting as a bloc. Total liftings could not be more than the total sought by BP, the sole pre–World War II concessionaire, which retained a veto power with a 40 percent share in the Consortium.

Of the major Middle East concessions, only Kuwait had no restrictions on liftings; each of the two partners was allowed to take all the oil it wanted at cost. This liberality stemmed from an early agreement between the partners (apparently terminated in 1951) not to compete with one another in product markets.[90]

The output restrictions within the major concessions represented an attempt by the best established companies to inhibit the tendency of the smaller, less-established companies to reduce prices by using their control over cheap Middle East oil to expand their market shares. By enmeshing these recent arrivals in the network of concessions, the threat they posed to the established majors was reduced. But by maintaining artificial restraints on production, the system invited the antagonism of the host countries, each of which clamored for an increase in production. And with prices far above costs, other companies had a strong incentive to force their way in.

The combination of output restrictions within each major concession and interlocks between the concessions enabled the companies to keep the average annual rate of expansion in the oil-exporting countries as a group at a steady 9.55 percent between 1950 and 1972. In fact, as John Blair has pointed out, the "assumption that oil production would increase at an average annual rate of 9.55 percent explains all but one-tenth of one percent of the actual change." What makes this so remarkable is that the rates of production in the countries that made up this total varied enormously throughout this period.[91]

The precise manner in which this orchestration was achieved is not known, but it seems clear that the interconnections between the majors were essential, for when the majors met to formulate production plans in any joint venture, they learned of their partners' plans. Presumably, this knowledge was extended to the other international majors by way of the joint ventures. Every year, for example, the Aramco partners met to inform each other of the quantity of oil that each was planning to take in each of the next three years. From this exchange, each partner learned the production plans of three of its major "competitors," and presumably this information was passed on to the other companies when they met the Aramco partners in the other joint ventures.

Although this system provided no guarantee against a firm's raising its production level, to the detriment of prices, it provided a powerful deterrent for it gave all the other firms a good idea of each competitor's production plans. Consequently, the possibility that a firm would be able to increase its profits by expanding production, lowering prices, and securing a larger market share was significantly reduced by the fact that its competitors would be able to anticipate such action as a result of their substantial information about its production plans. In addition, the fact that the companies met as competitors in downstream markets increased their knowledge of each other's activities. Hence the would-be price cutter could expect that its competitors would be ready to protect their market shares by appropriate price reductions, if necessary. If, however, a company was unable to increase its market shares through lower prices, price reductions were not in its interest. As M. A. Adelman stated in 1972, each of the majors "can be assured that nothing is contemplated to threaten an excess of supply and a threat to the price. Each can hold back on output in the almost certain knowledge that all the others are doing the same."[92]

In addition, the companies were able to maintain a steady increase in oil supply by treating the Middle East as the "swing area" or "surge pot." If supply outside the Middle East exceeded the companies' needs, Middle East production was cut back. Alternatively, if the supply of oil outside the Middle East fell short of the companies' needs, Middle East production was increased. As the chief of Exxon's Middle East operations, George Piercy, testified: "As long as Middle East production was readily expansible, these variations could be accommodated."[93]

Within the Middle East, Kuwait played the role of swing supplier. Because of Kuwait's small population, it was easier for the companies to cut production in Kuwait, where oil revenues were less badly needed than in the far more populous nations, Iran and Iraq; and the simple "offtake" rules that the Kuwait Oil Company maintained facilitated this process. Moreover, because Shell received substantial volumes of Kuwait oil on long-term contract, three of the seven largest companies could use Kuwait as a balancing factor. The other four giants, the Aramco partners, were able to pursue a similar strategy in Saudi Arabia, where offtake rules were relatively flexible and the population relatively small.[94]

A persisting problem was that, even with concession output restrictions, some companies habitually had access to more crude oil than they had market outlets for. In such a situation the temptation to cut prices in product markets or, alternatively, to sell the oil at relatively low prices to third parties, enabling them to gain a foothold in the industry, was very great. Therefore, to reduce the probability of either development, the majors concluded long-term sales contracts among themselves, and their refusal to sell reserves provided a further protection against price cutting. This unwillingness continued, despite the fact that reserves were anywhere from 50 to 150 times sales and, at any reasonable discount rate, had a present value of zero.[95]

Largely as a result of the majors' control of the market, a barrel of Middle East oil, which cost about 15¢ to produce, sold for between $1.70 and $2 in the early 1950s—or more than ten times its cost.[96] Yet even at these inflated prices, Middle East oil was competitive with oil from other areas and with alternative energy sources. For example, in 1955, when a barrel of Middle East oil was estimated to cost about 12¢ to produce, a barrel of U.S. oil cost $1.88 to produce and sold for $2.78. Venezuelan oil was in between, at a cost of 41¢ a barrel, but it sold for $2.90.[97] Indeed, part of the reason why Middle East oil could be sold for so much more than its cost was because it competed in world markets with oil that was far more costly.

U.S. IMPORT CONTROLS AND THE MAINTENANCE OF WORLD OIL PRICES

Despite the substantial control the majors exercised, between 1947 and 1949 there was a strong tendency toward declining prices. During those years, the price of Middle East oil fell from $2.22 a barrel to $1.75, for basically two reasons. One was that the United States was anxious to promote European recovery, and the Economic Cooperation Administration (ECA), which administered the Marshall Plan in Europe, objected to the high prices the oil companies charged in Western Europe and pressured the companies to reduce them.[98] The other reason was that the international majors had an interest in reducing the price in order to expand their product markets.[99]

By late 1949 the price of Middle East oil had fallen enough to make its delivered price on the U.S. East Coast equal to the delivered price of Venezuelan or U.S. domestic crude—and the price reductions came to an abrupt halt. Shortly after that, the delivered price of Middle East oil exceeded the price of Venezuelan or U.S. crude on the U.S. East Coast. As Adelman has shown, neither the hypothesis of competition nor the hypothesis of collusion by the majors explains this result. Given the cost of Middle East oil, a genuinely competitive industry would have driven the price far lower; and it was in the interest of the majors to further lower the price to increase their share of the U.S. market. While it has frequently been contended that the majors did not want Middle East oil to compete with their U.S. production, Adelman explains the flaw in this reasoning. At the time, two of the majors—BP and CFP—had no U.S. interests at all and therefore no reason to restrict imports into the United States. The other six companies accounted for roughly 45 percent of U.S. refining and 30 percent of U.S. crude output; but, as Adelman explains,

Every one of them was in deficit on U.S. crude supply, even adding Esso and Shell Venezuela output. Had they done no more than substitute Persian Gulf crude for U.S. crude costing over twice as much, their profits would have been very great and the impact on U.S. domestic prices small, possibly negligible. For only very high-cost crude would have been backed out of the U.S. market.[100]

What stopped the majors from further reducing the price and expanding the production of their Middle East oil fields were the restrictions on imports that the U.S. domestic producers secured. In the 1930s, after discovery of the East Texas oil field drove the price down from $1.30 to 24¢ a barrel,[101] a system of production prorationing was devised to maintain the price of U.S. crude oil by limiting production. Officially based on the need to conserve oil, the system assigned each oil well a "total allowable," supposedly the amount that would maximize the amount of oil ultimately recoverable from the well. Then, each month, the state regulatory agencies—notably the Texas Railroad Commission—attempted to establish the amount of oil that was needed (at the existing price). Once a total need figure was arrived at, the expected output from wells exempt from prorationing restrictions was deducted and the remainder was prorated to the other wells, according to their "total allowable."[102] That is, to keep production (and consequently prices) at the desired level, wells were allowed to produce at only a given percentage of the "total allowable."

The effectiveness of this system was threatened by the prospect of cheap Middle East imports entering the United States. Consequently, U.S. domestic producers, landowners, and supplying industries that benefited from the prorationing system rallied to its defense by demanding restrictions on imports. They maintained that dependence on foreign oil was a threat to national security, and they were supported in this claim by U.S. defense officials.[103]

During 1949–50, three congressional investigations of the issue had the effect of serving notice on the companies that if they did not voluntarily keep imports down, legislative action would require them to do so.[104] During this period, moreover, though the majors sought to increase imports, their major objective was to preserve the prorationing system.[105] Consequently, the increase in imports began to lessen; but when the price of U.S. oil was raised in 1953 and again in 1957, it became more attractive to bring cheap Middle East crude into the United States, and imports increased. In 1954 President Eisenhower called for voluntary restraint by the importing companies, and in 1957 he established a "voluntary" import control program. The major international oil companies went along with the program, but several industry newcomers, who hoped to use cheap imports to boost their market shares, voiced dissatisfaction with the program and in some cases refused to cooperate with it.[106]

As noncompliance spread, the voluntary controls broke down, and between 1954 and 1958, imports increased from 10.3 to 14.2 percent of U.S. oil consumption.[107] In 1959, to halt this trend, Eisenhower established mandatory import quotas, which limited imports to 12 percent of the U.S. market. As a result, imports, which had been growing at 15 percent a year, would be able to grow only in accord with growth in U.S. oil consumption—about 3 percent a year.[108]

By imposing import quotas, the United States split the oil market in the non-Communist world; and for the next fourteen years the U.S. market would be separate from the market in the rest of the non-Communist world. This provided a tremendous boon to the U.S. domestic oil industry. It has been estimated that, without the import quotas, one-third to one-half of U.S. domestic oil production would have been closed down during the 1960s. The U.S. coal industry and the U.S. natural gas industry also benefited from the high price of U.S. oil; but the cost was borne by U.S. consumers, who paid from $1 to $1.50 a barrel more for oil as a result of the quotas. The quotas are estimated to have cost consumers between $3 billion and $4 billion a year.[109]

National security was the official rationale for the quotas, but at the time they were enacted there was little danger of a coordinated cutoff of foreign oil supplies, and most U.S. imports still came from highly secure areas: Venezuela and Canada. In any case, the import quotas were a very inefficient way of maintaining the security of U.S. petroleum supplies.

Outside the United States, the immediate effect of the imposition of U.S. import quotas was a surplus of oil on the world market, which put downward pressure on the world price. However, the long-term effect may have been just the opposite, for by limiting access to the U.S. market the federal government reduced the oil companies' incentive to cut prices in order to expand sales. With access to the world's largest market restricted, and demand in any one market relatively insensitive to changes in the price (i.e. demand was price inelastic), the major oil companies had little incentive to reduce prices, for by doing so they would simply be taking business from one another. Also, in the mid-1950s the restrictions on imports into the U.S. market were complemented by European concern for the protection of high-cost coal. This tended to further restrict the opportunities open to the majors for expanding markets by cutting price, and the protectionist policies in the consuming countries tended to support the international oil companies' high-price policies. As a result, the majors had strong incentives to maintain production controls.

When the state regulatory agencies permitted U.S. price increases, in 1953 and again in 1957, prices went up in the world market as well, despite the fact that prices were already several times cost and producible supply was far in excess of demand. The explanation for this strange result is that a concentrated world industry, whose prospects of expanding were limited by government policies, had little to gain by reducing prices. However, they could gain quite a bit by raising prices in response to the signal provided by the U.S. price increase and by using their interlocked structure and control of the market to avoid competitive price cutting among themselves. While the majors were well served by the restrictions on production that they maintained, their production controls were the only element of stability in what would otherwise have been an extremely erratic market. Indeed, the price stability that the majors provided, and the assurance of a steady supply of energy, were important elements in world economic recovery. Moreover, because Middle East oil was so cheap, prices could be kept high enough to ensure development of a foreign resource, but low enough to facilitate economic growth in the consuming countries.

Nor could Western Europe or the United States have easily endured the social disruption that would have resulted from a genuinely free market in Middle East oil. Even at the inflated prices that the majors maintained, Middle East oil created a "coal crisis" in Western Europe and an oil-import crisis in the United States. Nor was a lower price and a correspondingly higher level of consumption in the world's best social interest. Although oil company control was a very inefficient means of achieving such social goals as conservation, protection of domestic industries, and stability of price and supply, in the context of an unregulated world economy, in which there was strong opposition to direct government intervention, no other means was available. Nevertheless, the majors' restrictions on production worsened their relations with the oil-exporting countries, which were primarily interested in boosting sales in order to increase revenues. Indeed, during the 1960s the U.S. oil-import quotas reduced the sales of the major oil-exporting countries by about 25 percent and cost them about a billion dollars a year.[110]

However, in preserving a strong domestic oil industry in the United States and the prorationing system, the import quotas also maintained "spare" productive capacity in the United States. When U.S. producers were allowed to produce only a fraction of their capacity, extra capacity resulted, which served as a powerful deterrent to the exporting countries. So long as production losses could be made up in the United States, any effort by the exporting countries to pressure the companies or the consuming countries by withholding supplies was not likely to be successful. In short, the power of the majors vis-à-vis the exporting countries and the high price levels were buttressed by the policies of the consuming countries. Had those policies been altered, the world price would not have been as high. Nor would the power of the majors have appeared so awesome.

The mid-1950s marked the high point of Anglo-American control over the world oil system. Whereas the Anglo-American majors controlled the bulk of the world's oil and were tightly interlocked, the exporting countries were disunited, and in response to pressure from any exporting country, the majors could shift production elsewhere. Equally significant was the fact that the United States and Great Britain exercised political hegemony over the all-important Middle East. All of the major oil-exporting countries in this area were closely linked with the West, and the regimes in these countries were directly dependent upon either the United States or Great Britain for their political security. The United States was the dominant power in the Mediterranean and Great Britain maintained preponderant military power in the Persian Gulf, and the governments in both Great Britain and the United States were strongly supportive of the major oil companies.

In addition, the United States was not dependent upon Middle East oil imports; spare capacity in the United States was both a safety device against a breakdown in the flow of oil from the exporting countries to the consuming countries and, as the Suez crisis demonstrated, a source of political leverage for the United States vis-à-vis its allies in Western Europe and Japan.

Yet the dominance of the international majors, on the one hand, and Great Britain and the United States on the other did not last long. Their power was challenged by those emerging forces that had been excluded from control of the system: the oil-exporting countries, which demanded greater revenues and national control, and the other consuming countries and a growing number of newcomers to the international oil industry, both of which demanded a greater role in the system. Yet the ability of the majors to respond to the demands of any of these forces was limited by the demands of the others. In addition, worldwide dependence upon Middle East oil would increase and eventually the United States would come to rely on oil imports from that area, having lost its spare capacity in the process. It is to this development that we now turn.

2

The Development of Dependence upon Middle East and North African Oil

Middle East oil provided the solution to the first postwar energy crisis, but dependence upon Middle East and North African oil is at the root of the current energy crisis. In the decade following World War II, the economic recovery of Western Europe and Japan was threatened by energy shortages. During the winters of 1945–46 and 1946–47, complete stoppage of industrial activity (except for continuous-process industries) was ordered for two to three weeks in France and Denmark, and in other countries, production stoppages occurred in particular industries.[1] Middle East oil enabled Western Europe to overcome these problems, but the solution to the first postwar energy crisis planted the seeds for future crises.

It was not dependence upon Middle East oil per se that was the problem, but the fact that this dependence became excessive. Several factors contributed to this: a pattern of economic growth that was premised on high levels of energy consumption and the continued availability of petroleum, the failure of the consuming countries to develop alternative energy sources, and a lack of exploration and development outside the Middle East and North Africa.

During the two decades following World War II, as a result of the availability of cheap Middle East oil, oil replaced coal as the dominant energy source in the capitalist world. Prior to World War II, this transformation was much further along in North America than in Western Europe or Japan,[2] but in North America natural gas also became an important source of fuel—something that did not occur in Western Europe or Japan, where gas reserves are far less extensive. Consequently, in the postwar period the dependence on oil as an energy source occurred more rapidly and reached higher levels in Western Europe and Japan than in North America[3] (see figures 2–1, 2–2, 2–3, and appendix tables A1, A2, and A3).

In the Communist countries, in contrast to the capitalist world, the shift to oil was far less pronounced, due in part to a scarcity of oil resources. Of the Communist countries at the end of World War II, only the Soviet Union and Rumania were known to have significant oil resources, and these did not compare in magnitude with the prodigious reserves of Middle East oil. And because the Communist nations stressed self-reliance, particularly in energy policy, they were reluctant to become dependent upon Western-controlled Middle East oil.

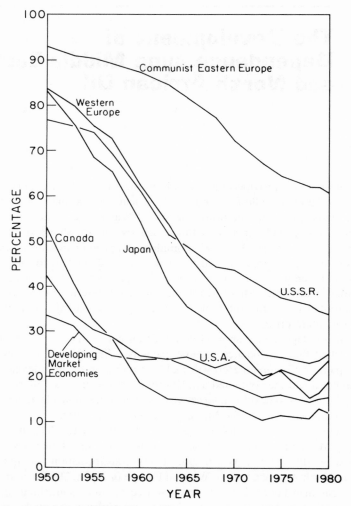

Figure 2–1.   Percentage of Energy Consumption in Solid Fuels, 1950–80. The figures on the percentage of energy consumption in solid fuels, liquid fuels, and natural gas are derived from data in Darmstadter, *Energy in the World Economy*, table 11 (through 1965), U.N., *World Energy Supplies, 1961–70*, table 2 (1968), and U.N., *Yearbook of World Energy Statistics, 1979 and 1980*, tables 1 and 6. "Communist Eastern Europe" does not include the U.S.S.R. There are minor discrepancies between the data in the U.N. series and the data in Darmstadter. See Darmstadter, *Energy in the World Economy*, pp. 826–27, for a discussion of why this may be the case.

Moreover, because of their isolation from the capitalist world economy, the Communist countries lacked the hard currency the Western oil companies would demand in payment for Middle East oil. Just as the United States attempted to integrate Western Europe and Japan into the "free world" by encouraging their dependence upon Anglo-American-controlled Middle East oil, the Soviet Union

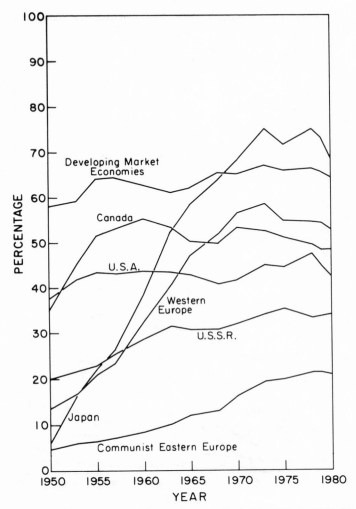

Figure 2–2.   Percentage of Energy Consumption in Liquid Fuels, 1950–80.

used its control of Eastern Europe's oil supplies to further the dependence of those countries upon the Soviet Union.[4] Finally, the stress on heavy industry and the relative neglect of the consumer sector in general and the private automobile in particular has tended to curtail demand for oil in the Communist world.

THE SHIFT FROM COAL TO OIL IN WESTERN EUROPE AND JAPAN

Prior to World War II in Western Europe and Japan, regionally produced coal had been the dominant energy source, accounting for about 80 percent of energy

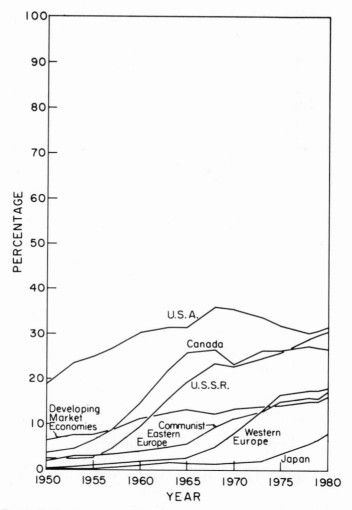

Figure 2–3.   Percentage of Energy Consumption in Natural Gas, 1950–80.

consumption in Japan and more than 90 percent in Western Europe. Oil, a
secondary fuel, had been used primarily for road, water, and air transport and
accounted for about 10 percent of all energy consumption.[5] However, as a result
of the war, coal production in Western Europe and Japan was severely damaged,
because many coal fields had been destroyed; others suffered from a lack of
maintenance and capital investment; and the industry faced a shortage of skilled
and experienced workers.

In this context, foreign oil was greatly desired by the nations of Western
Europe and Japan. However, the United States, which was expecting petroleum

shortages of its own, did not have enough oil to supply Western Europe directly, nor did the Europeans have the dollars needed to purchase oil from the United States.[6] This forced the Europeans to look to the Middle East, where oil was readily available. However, insofar as this oil was controlled by U.S. companies, which demanded payment in dollars, the European dollar shortage remained an obstacle. Several developments helped alleviate this problem—and facilitate the shift from coal to oil. One was a European emphasis on purchasing nondollar oil from BP, Shell, and CFP;[7] another was economic aid from the United States. From April 1948 to December 1951, 56 percent of the sales by U.S. oil companies in European Marshall Plan countries were financed by the ECA. Altogether, 20 percent of the Marshall Plan funding was used for the purchase of petroleum and petroleum products or for development of facilities in Europe for processing crude oil.[8]

Increasingly, Europe's oil came from the Middle East. Prior to World War II, about 20 percent of Western Europe's oil had come from the Middle East, but in 1947, before the Marshall Plan, Europe was already receiving 43 percent of its crude oil from the Middle East; and by 1950 the percentage had increased to 85.[9]

Another factor that helped remedy the developed countries' oil-financing problems was that the international companies began to build their refineries primarily in the oil-consuming countries. In 1939, roughly 70 percent of all refining capacity outside North America and the Communist nations was near the oil fields; by 1951 this had fallen to about 50 percent, and by 1965 to about 16 percent.[10] There were several reasons for this trend. The growth of demand for a variety of oil products made it possible to build technically efficient refineries in the consuming countries; the development of large tankers made it much cheaper to transport crude oil than equivalent amounts of petroleum products; and refineries in the oil-consuming countries were thought to be less vulnerable to nationalization.

Yet, in the immediate postwar period, probably the most compelling reason for locating refineries in the consuming countries was that it reduced the foreign-exchange cost of oil consumption, since only the crude oil had to be imported. But this meant that the consuming country, not the exporting country, gained the economic benefits: jobs, tax revenues, stimulus to supply industries, etc. And the oil companies were more willing to accept payment in local currencies, since they needed this currency to pay for part of the construction of refineries.

In Japan, where opposition to foreign investment has always been strong, the U.S. military authorities pressured the international oil companies, which preferred to go it alone, to join forces with local refining companies. Each party put up half the capital, with the international companies providing all the foreign exchange. In return, the international oil companies gained the right to supply all the crude ever needed by the refineries.[11]

Still short of foreign exchange, the Japanese government developed a complex scheme for allocating it, forcing the oil companies to compete with other industries for their share. Since the total amount of foreign exchange was limited by the Japanese government, the oil companies could expand their share of the energy market only by keeping the price of crude oil down. Consequently, Japan paid lower prices for crude oil than any other country. Moreover, Japan embarrassed the majors by publicizing the prices it paid. Then, in 1962, the International Monetary Fund pressured Japan into eliminating the foreign-exchange control system. As a result, by 1966–67 oil prices in Japan were higher than in Western Europe.[12]

Between 1950 and 1955 the consumption of oil practically doubled in Western Europe, and in Japan it quintupled (see appendix tables A2 and A3). Yet the demands of economic recovery meant that the countries in these areas needed all the energy they could get. Foreign-exchange pressures still limited their access to oil; consequently, until the mid-1950s, they continued to maximize the production of indigenous coal, which was still the dominant fuel. In this period, demand for oil supplemented rather than replaced demand for coal.

With the 1957–58 recession, the demand for energy in Western Europe leveled off.[13] Instead of coal *and* oil, it became a question of coal *or* oil, and oil had several advantages. It was easier to transport and use; for example, oil-fired boilers could operate automatically, while labor was required for coal handling and ash disposal.[14] Oil was environmentally cleaner and its quality as a fuel was more consistent. To be competitive with oil, coal had to have a substantial price advantage to offset oil's considerable nonprice advantages. On the basis of energy supplied (BTUs), the price of fuel oil was about equal to the price of coal before 1958, and after 1958 it fell below the price of coal.[15]

This decline in the price of fuel oil was largely due to a decline in the price of crude oil, which began after 1957. Several factors contributed to this: the reopening of the Suez Canal in 1957, growing sales of Soviet oil in the world market, rising competition to the majors, and the imposition of U.S. import controls, which left many independents without market outlets for their oil. And supplies of this low-cost fuel were reliably available.

In addition, the international oil companies priced heavy fuel oil at a low level in order to gain market penetration and displace coal. At the same time, prices for gasoline—a product that had no substitutes—were kept high, enabling the companies to exploit the inelasticities of demand for gasoline. Rather than challenge the companies' pricing policies, the consuming countries reinforced them by taxing gasoline heavily, while minimizing taxes on fuel in order to encourage industrial growth.[16]

Then, largely as a result of U.S. military aid and defense spending abroad, in Western Europe and Japan, the dollar shortage of the early 1950s became the dollar glut by the end of the decade. In 1958, all the major West European currencies were made convertible[17]—a key objective of the internationalists. This development was as significant as fuel prices in bringing the subsequent boom in European oil consumption, because it meant there was no longer a currency barrier to the purchase of imported oil.

In facilitating the economic recovery of Western Europe, oil had helped make the European economies strong enough to erect this milestone in the internationalists' schema. Moreover, during the decade following World War II, when dollars were scarce and most U.S. companies were reluctant to invest abroad, the oil companies poured more than $1.5 billion into Western Europe; and in 1955 they accounted for 54.6 percent of all U.S. direct investments in Western Europe.[18] In short, oil was both a cause and a beneficiary of European convertibility and the economic strength that lay behind it. Also, in 1958 Japan abolished controls on the importation of crude oil, paving the way for enormous growth in its dependence upon foreign oil.

By facilitating recovery and by establishing a direct link between Japanese and European energy supplies and the Anglo-American companies that provided them, the international oil industry tended to encourage development of a more interdependent world. Indeed, during the postwar period the value of world trade in petroleum far exceeded the trade in any other commodity. In 1970, for example, the value of petroleum imports accounted for 8.3 percent of the value of all imports by the world market economies.[19] Moreover, the importance of petroleum gave the United States considerable leverage in the world economy, for U.S. nationals dominated the oil industry and, more importantly, through a system of political alliances, the U.S. government maintained the security of the international oil system.

With oil readily available for less than the price of coal and with the dollars to pay for it flowing freely, there was no way that coal could maintain its dominance as a fuel. In 1963 oil became the chief source of energy in Japan, and in 1966 in Western Europe. By 1970 oil was the leading energy source in every West European country except Great Britain.[20]

Proportionally, more oil was consumed in sectors where oil and coal were competitors than in sectors where oil was the only feasible alternative. In 1960, 43 percent of the oil consumed in Western Europe and 34 percent of the oil consumed in Japan were used for purposes for which coal was not a feasible substitute—either in transportation or in the production of nonenergy products, mainly petrochemicals. But by 1970 these percentages had fallen to 35 and 28 percent respectively. This was not true in the United States, where, in 1960, 57 percent of the oil consumed was used for transportation and nonenergy products—and 58 percent in 1970.[21]

With oil assuming a dominant role, coal production in Western Europe peaked at 543 million metric tons in 1957 and fell to 340 million metric tons in 1970, despite the fact that Europe has extensive coal reserves. Indeed, it is likely that the energy content of European coal reserves is equal to that of the world's oil reserves.[22] Similarly, coal production peaked in Japan in 1961 at 55 million metric tons and fell to 40 million metric tons in 1970.[23]

The immediate effect of the decline in coal production was the European "coal crisis" of the late 1950s. An industry that had been urged to boost production as rapidly as possible was suddenly confronted by declining demand.

Mine owners and workers protested, decrying the "predatory" tactics of the oil companies. In response, the governments of the European coal-producing countries—West Germany, Belgium, the United Kingdom, the Netherlands, and France—embarked on a dual policy of protectionism and rationalization. They sought to maintain their coal industries by reserving a share of the energy market for them, by taxing oil products heavily, and by direct subsidization. As these measures proved uneconomical, they attempted to boost coal productivity by closing uneconomic pits and introducing higher levels of mechanization. In Great Britain and France, concern for the coal industry was intensified by the fact that, as major powers, both countries sought to be self-sufficient in meeting their energy needs. According to Adelman, the total cost of supporting the European coal industry was $3.5 billion in 1964.[24] Yet, despite these efforts, coal production continued to decline.

In Japan, the situation was similar, but considerably aggravated by geological conditions in the mines.[25] To prevent excessive contraction of the coal industry, in 1955 the Japanese government placed restrictions on the conversion of coal-fired boilers to oil. In 1958 a five-year coal-rationalization program was introduced to equate the price of coal with that of oil. But in 1967, when the government introduced new coal-support measures, the real cost of domestic coal was still one-third higher than its subsidized selling price. In 1969 and again in 1972, further government subsidies were instituted, but production continued to fall.[26]

CONSUMER-GOVERNMENT ENERGY POLICIES

One effect of consuming-government attempts to maintain their coal industries was to buttress the price of oil, for the more oil companies cut prices, the more likely they were to be accused of acting ruthlessly and "unfairly" taking business away from coal. This tendency, to suspect the companies of competing unfairly, was reinforced by the fact that, in making their plans for the future, the Europeans habitually overestimated the cost of imported oil.[27] And as consuming governments became committed to the support of high-cost coal (and, later, high-cost nuclear energy) programs, high oil prices served to reduce the level of subsidy required, to improve the likelihood of success for these programs, or to make an expensive policy appear not so costly.

By seeking to ensure a share of the market for coal (and, later, nuclear power), consuming governments tended to limit the ability of the international oil companies to expand production in the oil-exporting countries—even reducing prices to increase their share of the market. In short, the efforts of governments in Western Europe and Japan to support their coal industries were quite similar in effect to the efforts of the U.S. government to support its domestic oil producers.

Although the growing dependence on Middle East oil tended to reduce the level of energy self-sufficiency throughout Western Europe and Japan, the effects varied considerably, depending upon each country's domestic resource base and attitude toward imports (see table 2–1). These substantial differences in national energy self-sufficiency undermined consumer-country cooperation and precluded consumer unity which might have brought oil prices down. Countries that were more energy self-sufficient had far less interest in reducing oil prices than countries that were more dependent upon imports. Indeed, countries with substantial domestic coal industries often seemed more concerned about protecting those industries than about the level of oil prices.

Other conflicts of interest persisted as well. Because of its interests in British Petroleum and Royal Dutch/Shell, Great Britain tended to identify (as an oil-producing country) with high oil prices. Indeed, the profits these companies repatriated to Great Britain substantially reduced the balance-of-payments cost of Great Britain's oil, and this identification increased as interest in North Sea oil picked up in the 1960s. But at the same time that Great Britain supported high oil prices, it opposed Continental protectionism as a barrier to British coal exports.

Like Britain, France was a major power and French nationals were among the international majors, but the French company, CFP, had always been the "poor sister," much smaller than the others, excluded from the Aramco concession, etc. Partly for this reason, the French were hostile to the international oil companies, but the key to France's energy policy was de Gaulle's foreign policy. De Gaulle believed that a great power must be self-sufficient in key raw materials; but given the French resource base, this was no easy task. France has no major oil or gas reserves, and its coal fields are hard to mine and difficult to mechanize.[28] Consequently, the focus of French energy policy was to have French

TABLE 2–1. RATIO OF ENERGY PRODUCTION TO CONSUMPTION, 1938, '55, '70

	1938	1955	1970
U.S.	1.084	1.002	.901
Japan	.838	.751	.165
Western Europe	.958	.767	.412
Belgium-Luxembourg	.959	.835	.194
France	.621	.626	.307
Federal Republic of Germany	1.114*	1.021	.550
Italy	.174	.277	.183
Netherlands	.887	.518	.740
Austria	.353	.792	.420
Denmark	.024	.040	.002
Finland	.129	.166	.006
Norway	.327	.402	.408
Portugal	.201	.242	.150
Sweden	.113	.154	.103
Switzerland	.191	.272	.186
U.K.	1.176	.869	.547

*Includes what is now the German Democratic Republic.

Figures for 1938 and 1955 are from Darmstadter, *Energy in the World Economy*, table 10; figures for 1970 are computed from data in U.N., *World Energy Supplies, 1961–1970*, pp. 48–53.

companies control as much oil worldwide as France consumed domestically and to limit the share of foreign companies in the French market to less than one-half.

Legislation enacted between 1926 and 1929 gave the French government control over oil imports into French territory, and the government used this authority to reserve 25 percent of the market for CFP. Then, in 1963, the French government decreed that 50 percent of domestic oil consumption be of French-owned oil—that is oil produced in the franc zone (mainly Algeria) and by the French state-owned corporation, ERAP, in Iran. However, this franc-zone oil tended to be high-cost oil, and could only be sold if prices were kept high.[29] As a result, French oil policy came to be characterized by contradictions. In its hostility to the international majors, France supported high oil prices—exactly what those companies wanted—and by limiting the companies' activities and reserving a share of the market for French companies, it kept profit margins high. As Adelman has pointed out, "High profit margins are precisely what draw the detested foreigners into the French market like bees to the jam pot."[30]

Like Great Britain, the Netherlands also identified itself as a producing nation because of its interest in Royal Dutch/Shell, and in the 1950s it hoped to become a major coal producer. Again, just as the discovery of North Sea oil reinforced the commitment to oil-industry welfare in Great Britain, the discovery in the Netherlands of the Groningen natural gas fields in 1959 had a similar effect, for it was understood that the value of these fields would increase with the price of oil. In addition, the Netherlands benefited as a major center of oil shipping and refining in Europe. Thus the Netherlands opposed restrictions on the international majors and precipitate oil price declines.[31]

In contrast to France, Great Britain, and the Netherlands, the main energy concern of West Germany during the 1950s and 1960s was to slow the replacement of coal by oil, but the effect on world prices of a "coal champion" was quite similar to the effect of an "oil champion," for both groups saw their policy interests advanced by high oil prices. Indeed, it was mainly those countries that had neither a substantial domestic coal industry nor major international oil interests that had a strong interest in lower world oil prices. But their interests were more than counterbalanced by the interests of the other oil-consuming countries.

As a result of the substantial differences of interest among the oil-consuming countries, formulation of a common energy policy eluded them. Efforts to develop such a policy in the European Economic Community and the Organization for Economic Cooperation and Development (OECD; earlier, the Organization for European Economic Cooperation) repeatedly faltered, the basic conflict being between countries with domestic coal industries, which desired protection for them, and those without such industries, which sought greater reliance upon oil imports, hopefully at lower prices.[32]

In addition, efforts to arrive at a European energy policy were hindered by the structure of the European bureaucracy. From the start of the European Community's organization, coal and oil were treated as separate commodities. Coal policy was assigned to the European Coal and Steel Community, established in 1951.

Nuclear policy became the province of the individual states and of Euratom, established in 1956. And in 1959, oil, natural gas, and electricity became the responsibility of the European Economic Community (EEC). In 1967 the secretariats of these three agencies merged, but prior to the 1970s little effort was made to formulate a common energy policy. The fragmentation of energy policy was also a problem in the United States, where sixty-one federal agencies were involved in the formulation of energy policy.[33]

In the absence of common consumer-country policies, each nation was free to pursue its own interest as competitively as it deemed advisable. Yet no country developed a comprehensive energy policy that resolved questions of fuel shares, types of demand growth, environmental standards, and economic efficiency, and this lack of public policy increased the international oil companies' freedom to maneuver and the consuming countries' dependence upon them.[34]

ENERGY CONSUMPTION PATTERNS

Prior to World War II, the United States relied much more on oil than did either Western Europe or Japan. Then, following the war, the United States, which had pioneered the use of oil, became the first nation to make substantial use of natural gas, boosting its share of energy consumption from 12.9 percent in 1938 to 30.4 percent in 1960; and between 1950 and 1970, natural gas accounted for more than half the growth in U.S. energy consumption.[35] In Western Europe and Japan, oil replaced coal; in the United States, natural gas made up for the decline in coal's share. Consequently, in the United States, oil's share of energy consumption increased only slightly during the postwar period (see figure 2–2 and appendix table A1).

Because the United States maintained quotas on the importation of foreign oil, its domestic fuel industries were shielded from the disruptive impact of Middle East oil. Coal's share of U.S. energy consumption declined, and though the coal industry showed many signs of being a depressed industry, the decline was far more moderate in the United States than in Western Europe or Japan (see figure 2–1 and appendix tables A1, A2, and A3). And after declining in the 1950s, U.S. coal production increased throughout the 1960s.[36]

In the United States, a "three fuel" pattern emerged; but in Western Europe and Japan, natural gas did not become a major energy source—it accounted for less than 10 percent of total energy consumption throughout the 1950s and 1960s (see figure 2–3). The main reason was that, for much of this period, Western Europe and Japan lacked extensive proven reserves of natural gas.[37] It became possible to transport natural gas by ship (after liquefying it) only in 1964–65, and this is an expensive and dangerous undertaking.

In 1959 a major discovery of natural gas was made in the Netherlands, but to conserve the benefits of this resource, the Dutch government kept the price high, and until the 1973 oil-price increases, this made it difficult for the gas to compete against fuel oil in other West European countries. During the 1960s, substantial quantities of natural gas were also discovered in the North Sea, but this gas did not enter production in significant quantities until after the 1973 oil-price increases.[38]

The United States used energy far more intensively than did either Western Europe or Japan (see table 2–2). This was only partly due to the higher standard of living in the United States: per dollar of GNP, the United States used roughly twice as much energy as most of the nations of Western Europe and Japan (see table 2–3). Indeed, the U.S. became committed to a pattern of economic growth that was dependent upon high levels of energy consumption in general and petroleum and natural gas in particular.

No interest was more important in promoting this pattern of development than the "highway lobby," an alliance of roadbuilders, truckers, automobile manufacturers, tire companies, and the petroleum industry. In 1932, under the leadership of GM President Alfred P. Sloan Jr., these interests joined together to promote a continuing program of highway construction and to ensure that highway taxes were used solely for highway purposes. Their greatest victory was the 42,500-mile Interstate Highway system; conceived in 1944 and approved in 1956, it was the largest public works project ever undertaken. Between 1956 and 1970, as part of this project, the federal government spent roughly $70 billion on highways (in contrast, the federal government provided only $795 million for rail transit during this period). The highway lobby also got forty-four of the fifty states to require that gasoline taxes be used solely for highway construction. As a result, from 1945 to 1970 states and localities spent $156 billion constructing roads.[39]

This burst of roadbuilding encouraged dependence upon automobiles and trucks. Between 1945 and 1973, U.S. automobile registrations climbed from 25 million to over 100 million; and the bigger the car, the more profitable it was. Consequently, Detroit kept making them bigger—the result being that fuel economy decreased by more than 10 percent between 1950 and 1973.[40] Similarly, between 1945 and 1972 truck registrations increased from 5 million to roughly 21 million,[41] and trucks increased their share of intercity freight traffic from 15.8

TABLE 2–2. PER CAPITA ENERGY CONSUMPTION (IN KILOGRAMS), 1938–73

	1938	1950	1960	1970	1973
U.S.	5,150	7,886	8,578	11,128	11,742
Western Europe	2,035	1,931	2,602	3,791	4,285
Japan	885	553	1,191	3,215	3,936
	Ratio of U.S. per Capita Energy Consumption to:				
Western Europe	2.53	4.08	3.30	2.94	2.74
Japan	5.82	14.26	7.20	3.46	2.98

Figures for 1938, 1950, and 1960 are from Darmstadter, *Energy in the World Economy*, p. 57; for 1970, from U.N., *World Energy Supplies, 1961–70*, pp. 25, 41, and 49; for 1973, from U.N., *World Energy Supplies, 1971–75*, pp. 19 and 27. Ratios computed by author.

TABLE 2–3. RATIO OF TOTAL PRIMARY ENERGY CONSUMPTION TO REAL GNP, 1960 and 1970

	1960	1970
U.S.	1.81	1.86
Japan	.80	.91
France	.67	.71
U.K.	1.47	1.41
W. Germany	.85	.85
Italy	.63	.97
Netherlands	.74	.95
Canada	1.38	1.54
U.S.S.R.	1.44	1.47

Computed from data in CIA, *Handbook of Economic Statistics, 1976,* pp. 76 and 31. Energy consumption is in million metric tons of coal, GNP in billions of 1975 U.S. dollars.

percent in 1950 to 21.3 percent in 1970. During this period the railroads' share of freight traffic declined from 57.4 to 39.8 percent, despite the railroads' greater energy efficiency.[42]

As table 2–4 shows, there was a shift in this period from energy-efficient modes of intercity traffic, and throughout this period cars were used for roughly 90 percent of intracity passenger travel.[43] Altogether, the transportation sector accounted for roughly a fifth of the U.S. gross national product, a quarter of its total energy use, and more than half of its petroleum consumption.[44]

More important than the transportation sector was the pattern of economic development it facilitated. Between 1950 and 1970, suburbs accounted for 75 percent of the increase in the population of Standard Metropolitan Statistical Areas, and to accommodate this growth, housing, retail stores, and factories were built in the suburbs. Between 1950 and 1970, two-thirds of all new housing units were built in suburbia. In 1948 there were only eight planned shopping

TABLE 2–4. ENERGY EFFICIENCY IN TRANSPORTATION, 1970
Energy Efficiencies of Major Intercity Transportation Modes (in BTUs per passenger mile)

Passenger Modes	Actual Load	100% Load
Bus	1,600	740
Railroad	2,900	1,100
Automobile	3,400	1,600
Airplane	8,400	4,100

Passenger Modes	Percentage Distribution of Intercity Traffic		
	1950	1960	1970
Bus	5.2	2.5	2.1
Railroad	6.4	2.8	0.9
Automobile	86.2	90.1	86.6
Airplane	2.0	4.3	10.0

Compiled from tables in Dumas, *The Conservation Response,* pp. 110–11. See Dumas for original sources.

centers in the United States; by 1960 there were an estimated 3,800. And though manufacturing and trade employment in the central cities of the twenty-five largest metropolitan communities declined between 1948 and 1963, manufacturing employment outside the central city grew by 61 percent and trade employment by 122 percent.[45]

Real estate interests thrived on this development, but the effect of these decentralized development patterns was to greatly increase the demand for energy. To move passengers and freight, rails require about a quarter as much energy as cars and trucks,[46] but because patterns of settlement are so dispersed in the United States, the demand for transportation is huge, and the concentration of people, required to make rails a viable form of transport, is rarely present. Similarly, dispersed single-unit housing (often poorly insulated) requires more energy than compact housing, and though compact housing makes such conservation measures as "district heating" possible, dispersed housing increases the waste of electrical energy through transmission losses.[47] However, since energy prices were kept low, there was little concern for energy efficiency in construction and, consequently, energy consumption in buildings increased steadily as a result of increased lighting, air conditioning, window area, etc. For example, buildings in New York City, constructed in the late 1960s, require about twice as much energy per square foot as buildings constructed in the early 1950s.[48]

The rapid growth in natural gas pipelines after World War II also encouraged increases in energy consumption. Between 1945 and 1953, nine of the thirteen major interstate pipelines that serve the United States today were built. These pipelines were financed mainly by insurance companies, which increased their investments in pipeline bonds from $5 billion to $14 billion between 1945 and 1955. To ensure their investments, the insurance companies insisted that the pipelines operate at full capacity for a twenty-year period, which led the pipeline transmission companies to push for rapid increases in the consumption of natural gas—the nation's scarcest and most valuable energy source.[49]

Another fossil fuel-based industry that took off after World War II was the petrochemical industry. Few things proved more profitable than the replacement of natural materials with artificial ones, derived from petroleum- and natural gas-based inputs. Petrochemicals have therefore come to dominate textiles, furniture, home furnishings, paints, and building materials. Consequently, production of synthetic organic chemicals increased from about 300 million pounds in 1946 to 39 billion pounds in 1974. By the early 1970s, the chemical industry had become the largest industrial energy consumer, accounting for 28 percent of the energy used in industry or about 9 percent of the U.S. total.[50]

Finally, the United States also became highly dependent upon electricity—indeed, the electric motor played a key role in boosting productivity in manufacturing. Electricity is a high-quality form of energy, but it is also very wasteful. For every BTU of electricity used, roughly two BTUs are lost in the process of generation and transmission. Nonetheless, with real electrical prices falling until the 1970s,[51] electricity was increasingly used for air conditioning, home heating, etc.,[52] and since government regulation assured utilities a fixed return on their total investment, utility shareholders' profits grew with the growth in demand for electricity. Because fuel costs could be passed on to customers, and there were no profits in energy conservation, the utilities did everything they could to promote demand for electricity. From 1960 to 1972, consequently, electricity went from 15 percent to 25 percent of U.S. energy consumption.[53]

During the decade following World War II, energy-short Europe and Japan could hardly afford to adopt the energy-intensive U.S. model, but as a result of the availability of cheap Middle East oil, in the 1960s they came to imitate it. As table 2–2 shows, during the 1950s and 1960s per capita energy consumption increased more rapidly in Western Europe and Japan than in the United States,[54] and after the mid-1950s, heavy energy- and oil-consuming industries, such as steel, nonferrous metals, petrochemicals, and synthetic fibers, played a leading role in Japan's economic growth.[55]

As a result of the availability of oil, a revolution in the means of transport occurred in Western Europe and Japan. As the first country to be heavily dependent upon oil, the United States was also the first nation to make the automobile a mass consumer item. By the 1920s there was a motor vehicle for every ten people in the United States, a figure that West European countries did not reach until the late 1950s; and as late as 1960 Japan had only one automobile for every forty-four people.[56] But as table 2–5 shows, automobiles proliferated in Western Europe and Japan in the 1960s. In the late 1960s, there was also a trend toward the production of large-engine cars in Western Europe.[57]

Along with greater reliance upon the automobile, there was a huge increase in airplane travel in the 1960s. Between 1960 and 1970, passenger air mileage increased by 239.2 percent in the United States, by 161.5 percent in France, by 160.2 percent in the United Kingdom, and by 1,263.6 percent in Japan.[58] Western Europe and Japan also increased their use of electricity in this period. Indeed, between 1945 and 1973 in most countries, electricity consumption grew at twice the rate of energy consumption as a whole.[59]

The United States was also the first country to develop a strong petrochemical industry, initiating the production of plastics and synthetic fibers in the immedi-

TABLE 2–5. POPULATION PER CAR, 1960–75

	1960	1968	1975
U.S.	2.4	2.2	2.0
Japan	43.8	7.9	6.4
U.K.	7.2	4.4	4.0
France	7.2	3.8	3.4
W. Germany	10.2	4.6	3.4
Italy	20.4	5.8	3.7

Figures for 1960 and 1968 are from "Motorization in Postwar Japan," *Wheel Extended* (Spring 1972), p. 34; figures for 1975 are from Motor Vehicle Manufacturers' Assn., *Motor Vehicle Facts and Figures, 1975*, pp. 28–31.

ate postwar years. Between 1945 and 1960, the industry grew at more than 15 percent a year. Other countries began to develop petrochemical industries on a significant scale only in the 1950s, but with cheap imported oil available, as a feedstock, their industries soon boomed.[60]

The case of Japan was particularly striking—whose first petrochemical venture was launched in 1955. In the 1960s, the Japanese petrochemical industry grew at an average annual rate of 25 percent, and by 1970 Japan trailed only the United States as a producer of petrochemicals. In Western Europe between 1960 and 1970, demand for oil products for nonenergy purposes, mainly petrochemicals, grew at an annual rate of about 16 percent, or one and a third times the rate for oil.[61]

Worldwide, the key to the development of the petrochemical industry was the availability of low-cost feedstocks, chiefly imported oil in Western Europe and Japan and price-controlled natural gas in the United States. Until 1973, this enabled the industry to penetrate markets for natural products by reducing the selling price of its major products. The result was shirts made from synthetic fibers, rather than cotton; chairs made from plastic, rather than wood; intensified use of artificial fertilizers; etc. The effect was to further increase dependence upon low-cost oil and natural gas.

NUCLEAR POWER AND ALTERNATIVE ENERGY SOURCES

During the 1950s, the growth in real gross national product was greater than the growth in energy consumption in the United States, Western Europe, and Japan. In the 1960s, however, the growth in energy consumption exceeded the growth in real gross national product in Japan and Western Europe, and from 1967 to 1970 this was also true in the United States[62], (see appendix table A4). But despite the increasing energy intensity of the developed capitalist economies, very little was done to ensure that the energy needed in the future would be available. The operating assumption was that Middle East oil would long be available to close the gap between supply and demand, and governments and industry neglected development of alternative energy sources. With oil relatively cheap, private firms deemed it unlikely that they could develop a competitive alternative, and few cared to take the risk. With oil supplies abundant, the need for government action did not seem urgent; besides, governments had a long-term solution to the problem: nuclear power—or so they thought.

In the 1950s, promising coal liquefaction and gasification efforts were abandoned in the United States, West Germany, and Great Britain.[63] Little effort was made to develop heavy crudes, tar sands, or shale oil,[64] and Japan did little to exploit its extensive geothermal prospects. The utilization and development of solar energy was neglected everywhere, and no country had a major conservation research and development program. Indeed, with energy prices falling, countries had little incentive to develop more efficient ways of using energy.[65] The bulk of research and development in the international oil industry was concerned with refining processes and products and with a range of products only indirectly related to energy applications, that is, petrochemicals, plastics, and pesticides.[66]

Only in the area of nuclear power was a significant effort made to develop a new energy source. For example, in 1973 the United States, the United Kingdom, West Germany, France, and the Netherlands devoted between 60 and 80 percent of their energy research and development budgets to nuclear fission technology. Within the nuclear programs, funding in all five countries was heavily concentrated on the development of the liquid metal fast breeder reactor (LMFBR).[67] Although U.S. expenditures on alternative energy sources—coal gasification and liquefaction, geothermal, and solar—dwarfed those of Japan and the European countries, public funding for nuclear energy in the United States in 1973 was 8.6 times as great as for all alternative energy sources combined.[68]

There were several reasons for nuclear's predominance. As a result of the wartime development of the atomic bomb, there was considerable knowledge about nuclear reactors, as well as a "nuclear establishment" in the United States that enjoyed great public prestige. After World War II, consequently, U.S. nuclear interests were able to gain public funding, despite the fact that nuclear power was far from economical and the need for it was perceived as many years off.

In the mid-1950s, Great Britain and France developed similar nuclear constituencies as a result of their decisions to become nuclear weapons powers. The political power of these interests, the connection between civilian nuclear and military technology, and the fact that nuclear power promised greater energy self-sufficiency encouraged its development in these countries. Indeed, in 1956 the United Kingdom launched a civilian nuclear R&D program against a background of growing concern about the security of Middle East oil supplies (due to the Iranian and Suez crises) and the military need for plutonium. Similarly, in 1957 France became the first EEC country to use nuclear power; its development of civilian nuclear technology was closely connected with its 1956 decision to build an atom bomb and its desire for greater self-sufficiency in energy supplies. Moreover, the desire for greater energy security and recognition that coal production would probably continue to decline led several West European nations to form Euratom in 1957. In the 1960s, the United States also came to see nuclear power as the long-term solution to the problem of supply security.

In contrast to the Europeans and the Americans, the Japanese were slow to embark on a nuclear power program. The availability of cheap hydroelectric power in the 1950s and cheap oil in the 1960s left Japan with little incentive to establish a major nuclear power program; and because Japan did not have a nuclear weapons program, it did not have a nuclear constituency to lobby for development of nuclear power. However, in 1966 the Japanese adopted a target of building 30,000–40,000 megawatts of nuclear plant by 1985. They purchased the necessary design and know-how licenses from the U.S. nuclear industry and imported their first reactors from the United States. In 1971 the 1985 target was increased to 60,000 megawatts. At that level, nuclear power was expected to account for 25 percent of Japan's generating capacity.[69]

Yet, by the early 1970s all efforts to develop nuclear power had met with little success. Since its founding, Euratom has been plagued by commercial rivalries among its members, so that the ideal of a joint European nuclear program has never been approximated. In the late 1960s, as a result of performance and pricing problems, France and the United Kingdom were forced to substantially abandon their commercial reactors and adopt U.S. technology. Like Japan, most European countries had become dependent upon U.S. firms for construction of their reactors or for the licensing of the requisite technology. As late as 1973, nuclear power accounted for less than 2 percent of all the energy consumed in Western Europe, Japan, and the United States.[70]

OIL COMPANY INVESTMENT STRATEGY AND DEPENDENCE ON MIDDLE EAST OIL

Even without alternative energy sources, dependence upon Middle East and North African oil and vulnerability to supply disruptions could have been avoided. Since the mid-1950s, more than 60 percent of the world's proven oil reserves have been in the Middle East and North Africa; more than half the world total has been in the Arab states, and more than 20 percent in Saudi Arabia alone.[71] Nonetheless, the reserves outside this area were substantial and had the potential to reduce significantly dependence upon Middle East and North African crude.

For example, in 1973 world oil consumption totaled 20.7 billion barrels, and at the end of that year the *Oil and Gas Journal* estimated proven reserves outside the Middle East and North Africa at 224.6 billion barrels. If one assumes a reserves/production ratio of 10:1, it would have been possible to supply world demand for oil without reliance upon the Middle East or North Africa,[72] and the undiscovered potential in these other areas was far greater.[73] According to a highly respected study by J. D. Moody, a petroleum consultant and former vice-president of Mobil, in 1974 there were 742 billion barrels of oil waiting to be discovered outside the Middle East and North Africa (see table 2–6).

At any reasonable reserves/production ratio, it would have been possible to satisfy world demand for oil for many years from any of a number of areas or from various combinations of several areas. High dependence upon the Middle East and North Africa was not inevitable. Indeed, while this area contains more than 60 percent of the world's proven reserves, only about a third of the world's ultimately recoverable reserves are estimated to be in this region, (see table 2–7). Similarly, the world's reserves of natural gas are vast, and outside the United States, very little of it has been developed (see tables 2–8 and 2–9). Indeed, outside North America there has been very little exploration for natural gas; most of it has been found "accidentally" in the search for oil.[74]

Consequently, while by 1974 the United States had consumed about two-fifths of its 1.267 trillion cubic feet (tcf) of natural gas, the rest of the world was below the 10 percent level. Moody estimated that the Middle East had 1,492 tcf of natural gas and Africa 540 tcf, but only about 3 percent of this had been produced. Latin America, with 398 tcf, had produced about 13 percent of its potential, while Asia had produced less than 1 percent of its 786 tcf.

To convert these potentials into usable productive capacity, substantial exploration and development would be required, and until the 1970s the industry's efforts to do this were quite limited. Indeed, between 1956 and 1970 non-Communist world expenditures on exploration and production declined by 18 percent in constant dollars, despite a 158.5 percent increase in oil consumption (see appendix table A5), and the effort made was concentrated in the United States, the area of the world with the greatest percentage of its total recoverable reserves already produced. Though the United States' share declined throughout this period, in 1970 the U.S. still accounted for nearly 60 percent of total industry expenditures on exploration and production, despite the fact that the United States is not a specially favored geological region.[75]

Though expenditures outside the United States increased, their rate of increase was far below the rate of increase in both worldwide oil consumption and other industry capital investments outside the U.S. Particularly striking was the limited effort in Africa, Latin America, and the Far East. In 1973, exploration expenditures in the United States were nearly twice as large as in these three areas combined and production expenditures were more than three times as large. Yet, according to Moody's estimates, both the proven and the undiscovered reserves in these underdeveloped areas were roughly three times as large as the reserves in the United States.

Similarly, in 1976 a U.N. conference concluded that, regardless of the measure used, "discounting the Middle East, less than five percent of the exploratory effort has been in the developing countries."[76] Bernardo F. Grossling, a senior scientist at the U.S. Geological Survey, found that while the developing countries account for half the world's prospective petroleum producing area, only about 4.3 percent of all exploratory drilling has taken place in these countries. And this was true despite the fact that the amount of oil found per well drilled was much higher in Latin America and Africa than in the United States or Western Europe.[77]

Between 1970 and 1973, there were substantial increases in exploration and production expenditures, but, given the lead times involved, it would be several years before these expenditures would have much impact. Even at these higher levels, it is doubtful that these exploration and development efforts were sufficient to meet future world needs. Also, while it lessened slightly, the preponderant role of the United States in the worldwide total persisted. As a result, by the 1970s there were twice as many oil wells in Kansas as in all of South America, and three times as many in Arkansas as in all of Africa. The continental slopes, most of China, and large parts of the rest of the world have never been systematically explored for oil or natural gas.[78]

There were several reasons for this lack of exploration and development. In

TABLE 2–6. PROVEN AND ULTIMATELY RECOVERABLE RESERVES OF CRUDE OIL
(BILLION BARRELS)

	Fields Discovered		
	(1) Cumulative Production (through 1974)	(2) Proven Reserves	(3) Total (1 + 2)
U.S.	106	51	157
Canada	7	9	16
Total North America	113	60	173
Western Europe	3	24	27
Middle East	78	435	513
North Africa	14	40	54
Other Africa	5	30	35
Total Africa	19	70	89
Latin America	45	39	84
Asia	11	30	41
Antarctica	—	—	—
Total Non-North America, Non-Communist	156	598	754
Total Non-Communist World	269	658	927
Total Communist World	50	128	178
Total Worldwide	319	786	1,105

Columns 1 through 6 are from a paper presented by J. D. Moody to the World Petroleum Congress in
on 1973 oil consumption (col. 7) are from BP, *Statistical Review of the World Oil Industry, 1973.*
reflects the later date of Moody's estimates and his differing assessments. ''North America'' includes

general, companies would not develop an oil field unless they had refining and
marketing outlets for its production. Consequently, companies whose crude
sources exceeded their market outlets were not particularly interested in developing additional oil resources. Throughout the 1960s their principal problem was a
surplus of crude and pressure from host governments for an increase in liftings.
Additional crude sources would only aggravate these problems by forcing additional crude onto the market or causing the companies to ''backout'' on their
production in existing concessions, further aggravating relations with the host
governments.[79]

Of course, if a new area opened up, all companies were likely to seek an
interest in it, if only to protect their market position. But in general, ''crude
long'' companies were probably better off if additional reserves were left undiscovered and undeveloped. Exxon's Howard Page expressed the ethos well
when he told a Senate subcommittee that

	Undiscovered			
(4) Expected Value	(5) Range		(6) Ultimate (1 + 2 + 4)	(7) 1973 Consumption
85	(50–150)		242	6.2
70	(40–110)		86	.6
155	(100–250)		328	6.8
57	(27–97)		84	5.5
150	(75–280)		663	.5
33	(15–60)		87	
38	(18–65)		73	
71	(33–125)		160	.4
82	(41–145)		166	1.3
90	(38–170)		131	3.0
20	(5–50)		20	—
470	(270–700)		1,224	10.7
625	(450–900)		1,552	17.5
300	(70–700)		478	3.2
925	(600–1,400)		2,030	20.7

Tokyo in May 1975; the figures were provided to the author by the U.S. Geological Survey. Figures
Note that Moody's estimates of proven reserves differ from those in the *Oil and Gas Journal;* this
Canada and the U.S. only; Mexico is included in "Latin America."

I had recommended to the executive committee that although we had the opportunity to go into Oman that we shouldn't do it because we were unable to provide adequate outlet for our Aramco concession, and I didn't see, I thought it would endanger our Aramco concession if we went into a new concession in the same area, and backed up on Aramco and if it did produce oil would have to back up further on Aramco and, therefore, on Saudi Arabia.

Just at this time, the producing department brought in their geologist who had just come back from Oman, and he stated, "I am sure there is a 10 billion oil field there," and I said, "Well, then, I am absolutely sure we don't want to go into it, and that settles it[.]" I might put some money in if I was sure we weren't going to get some oil, but not if we are going to get oil because we are liable to lose the Aramco concession, anyway, if we were going to back up any further on it by going into new areas.[80]

While the ready availability of cheap Middle East oil led to huge increases in consumption throughout the world, it discouraged the development of petroleum reserves outside the Middle East, for oil discovered in new areas was unlikely to cost as little to produce as oil in the Persian Gulf. Moreover, in August 1971 the *Petroleum Press Service* expressed the widely held industry view that the accumulations of oil remaining to be found were smaller and more hidden than those already found. While it cost about 10¢ to produce a barrel of oil in the Gulf in the 1960s, costs in North Africa ranged from 15¢ to 30¢, Venezuela averaged as high as 46¢, production costs in the United States were estimated at $1.22,[81] and drilling in a new area that lacked a developed infrastructure was likely to be more expensive than drilling in an established area. Consequently, with prices falling and all countries likely to seek per barrel payments comparable to those the Middle East countries received, companies without access to Middle East reserves were generally unwilling to make the substantial investments required to develop a new area. The tendency has been strong for the industry to go for the "easy" oil.

Rather than channel the bulk of their production through their own marketing outlets, in the 1960s the majors began selling large quantities of crude oil on the

TABLE 2–7. PERCENTAGE OF PROVEN OIL RESERVES, UNDISCOVERED POTENTIAL, AND 1973 PRODUCTION BY AREA

	Proven Reserves	
	World	Non-Communist World
U.S.	6.5	7.8
Canada	1.1	1.4
Total North America	7.6	9.2
Western Europe	3.1	3.6
Middle East	55.3	66.1
North Africa	5.1	6.1
Other Africa	3.8	4.6
Total Africa	8.9	10.7
Latin America	5.0	5.9
Asia	3.8	4.6
Antarctica	—	—
Total Non-North American, Non-Communist	76.1	90.9
Total Non-Communist World	83.7	100.0
Total Communist World	16.3	—
Total Worldwide	100.0	

The percentages on proven reserves and undiscovered potential are computed from the figures in table 2–6, cols. 2 and 4; those on 1973 production are computed from figures in BP, *Statistical Review of the World Oil Industry, 1973.*

open market. This made it possible for crude-short companies to acquire oil at relatively low prices, and it reduced their interest in developing their own sources for crude.

The main factors that worked against these tendencies were the companies' interests in diversifying their supplies to ensure against political risks and to save on transportation costs to major markets. Yet even where these interests might have proved dominant, they tended to run into political obstacles. The development of reserves in Southeast Asia for export to Japan was deterred by the Korean and Vietnam wars and by conflicting offshore territorial claims.[82] Latin American reserves could have been developed for sale in the U.S. market had import quotas not substantially cut this market off. Moreover, in response to company practices, most Latin American countries prevented or greatly restricted the access of foreign companies to exploration and development in their territories.

Since the early 1960s, the Soviet Union has encouraged Japanese participation in Siberian oil and gas projects, and since 1966 Japan has expressed interest in

Undiscovered Potential		1973 Production	
World	Non-Communist World	World	Non-Communist World
9.2	13.6	18.3	22.7
7.6	11.2	3.6	4.4
16.8	24.8	21.9	27.1
6.2	9.1	.7	.9
16.2	24.0	36.8	43.8
3.6	5.3	6.2	7.6
4.1	6.1	4.1	5.0
7.7	11.4	10.3	12.6
8.9	13.1	9.6	11.1
9.8	14.4	3.9	4.6
2.2	3.2	—	—
50.8	75.2	61.3	72.9
67.6	100.0	83.2	100.0
32.4	—	16.8	—
100.0		100.0	

TABLE 2–8. PROVEN AND ULTIMATELY RECOVERABLE RESERVES OF NATURAL GAS (TRILLION CUBIC FEET)

	Fields Discovered		
	(1) Cumulative Production (through 1974)	(2) Proven Reserves	(3) Total (1 + 2)
U.S.	482	300	782
Canada	23	83	106
Total North America	505	383	888
Western Europe	34	176	210
Middle East	43	643	686
North Africa	14	236	250
Other Africa	4	71	75
Total Africa	18	307	325
Latin America	52	94	146
Asia	6	131	137
Antarctica	—	—	—
Total Non-North American, Non-Communist	153	1,351	1,504
Total Non-Communist World	658	1,734	2,392
Total Communist World	101	630	731
Total Worldwide	759	2,364	3,123

Sources: Same as table 2–6.

developing the Tyumen oil fields in west Siberia; however, both the United States and China have objected. The United States, concerned about the strategic implications of Siberian development, continually put pressure on Japan to avoid making major agreements with the Soviet Union, and the Chinese objected to any move that would aid the Soviet economy, improve Japanese-Soviet relations, or increase the Soviet Union's ability to invade China.[83]

Where Third World countries have sought to develop their oil and gas resources, they have been constrained by a shortage of skilled personnel and capital,[84] and the policies pursued by the advanced countries and the various international agencies have not alleviated these problems. During the 1960s, neither the United States nor Great Britain would provide aid for oil exploration in the Third World. And the World Bank, the various regional development banks, and the United Nations Special Fund maintained policies, formulated with U.S. support, against the granting of loans for oil development except in the case of proven reserves.[85]

The high levels of exploration and development in the United States reflect the other side of many of the factors already discussed. The United States had a long

| | Undiscovered | | | |
(4) Expected Value	(5) Range		(6) Ultimate (1 + 2 + 4)	(7) 1973 Consumption
485	(320–700)		1,267	23.6
410	(220–650)		516	1.7
895	(600–1,300)		1,783	25.3
280	(115–500)		490	5.4
806	(400–1,500)		1,492	1.0
117	(50–240)		367	
98	(33–225)		173	
215	(83–465)		540	.1
252	(110–510)		398	1.5
649	(220–1,550)		786	.9
80	(20–200)		80	—
2,282	(1,500–3,500)		3,786	8.9
3,177	(2,200–4,800)		5,569	34.2
2,000	(700–3,500)		2,731	10.4
5,177	(3,500–7,000)		8,300	44.6

history of petroleum activity, so that supplies and personnel were readily available. Consequently, it was generally cheaper to drill in the United States, and import quotas protected U.S. oil against competition from cheap Middle East oil. Finally, U.S. tax benefits, including the oil depletion allowance and the "expensing" of intangible drilling costs,[86] provided substantial incentives for domestic drilling. Indeed, the benefits from these provisions were so great that it became common within the industry to speak of "drilling up the taxes."

Despite these incentives, industry expenditures on exploration and development in the United States declined from 71.9 percent of the non-Communist world total in 1956 to 58.3 percent in 1970.[87] This was mainly because the geological prospects for developing new fields were much greater in areas of the world that had been much less intensively explored than the United States. Also, in the 1960s foreign markets were growing more rapidly than the U.S. market. Along with the foreign-tax credit, these factors ensured that rates of return were much higher overseas than in the United States.

In the United States, in addition, the Northern Slope of Alaska and the offshore areas held the greatest remaining potential. However, the leasing of federal

TABLE 2–9. PERCENTAGE OF PROVEN NATURAL GAS RESERVES, UNDISCOVERED
POTENTIAL, AND 1973 PRODUCTION BY AREA

	Proven Reserves	
	World	Non-Communist World
United States	12.7	17.3
Canada	3.5	4.8
Total North America	16.2	22.1
Western Europe	7.4	10.1
Middle East	27.2	37.1
North Africa	10.0	13.6
Other Africa	3.0	4.1
Total Africa	13.0	17.7
Latin American	4.0	5.4
Asia	5.5	7.6
Antarctica	—	—
Total Non-North America, Non-Communist	57.1	77.9
Total Non-Communist World	73.4	100.0
Total Communist World	26.6	—
Total Worldwide	100.0	

The percentages on proven reserves and undiscovered potential are computed from the figures in
Data Book, sec. 13, table 4 (originally from various issues of U.S. Bureau of Mines, *Minerals*

offshore acreage declined from 3.5 million acres in 1960–64 to 1.6 million acres
in 1965–69,[88] and the development of Alaska was delayed by the controversy
over the Alaska pipeline. Finally, public debate about maintenance of the oil
import quotas, and their gradual easing, reduced the incentives for domestic
development.

All told, the abundance of North African and Middle East oil fields was a boon
to both the international oil companies and the oil-consuming countries, for it
enabled them to meet ever increasing levels of energy consumption with minimal
expenditures on the development of new energy sources. Not surprisingly, the
Department of Commerce estimated the annual return to the petroleum industry
in the Middle East in 1970 at 79.2 percent.[89] And the companies used their
profits on Middle East oil to help finance the building of refineries and other
investments in the developed countries.

More importantly, the low cost of imported oil became a key component in the
economic growth of Western Europe and Japan. Between 1960 and 1973,

Undiscovered Potential		1973 Production	
World	Non-Communist World	World	Non-Communist World
9.4	15.3	49.1	64.4
7.9	12.9	6.8	8.9
17.3	28.2	55.9	73.3
5.4	8.8	11.2	14.6
15.6	25.4	2.8	3.6
2.3	3.7		
1.9	3.1		
4.2	6.8	1.3	1.7
4.9	7.9	3.5	4.6
12.5	20.4	1.7	2.2
1.5	2.5	—	—
44.1	71.8	20.3	26.7
61.4	100.0	76.2	100.0
38.6	—	23.8	—
100.0		100.0	

table 2–8, cols. 2 and 4; those on 1973 production are computed from figures in *Basic Petroleum Yearbook* and *World Natural Gas*).

Japan's gross domestic product grew at 10.3 percent a year and Western Europe's at 4.7 percent—rates more than twice as high as those attained during the five years following the 1973–74 oil price increases.[90] It would be facile to attribute this change solely to the increase in the price of oil, but it would be wrong to discount the role that the rise in oil prices has played in bringing it about. As a result of the bounty the oil-consuming countries enjoyed until the 1970s, dependence upon Middle East and North African oil increased enormously. In the 1970s, the bill would come due.

3

International Oil in the 1950s and 1960s

The mid-1950s marked the zenith of the Anglo-American majors' control of the world oil industry—yet during the next decade the parties that had been excluded from that system would undermine it. The Soviet Union, excluded from the Anglo-American oil pact in 1944 and shut out of Iran after World War II, reentered the world oil market. Italy, which had been denied admittance to the Iranian Consortium, pioneered new arrangements with the oil-exporting countries, and France, which had been excluded from Aramco and then had its victory in the 1956 war snatched away as a result of its dependence upon U.S.-controlled oil supplies, developed a new oil-producing area in Algeria and plotted with the governments of Iran and Iraq in its efforts to become a major international oil power.

Private companies of varying nationality (the independents) and national oil companies, organized by many of the oil-consuming countries, also sought to gain a role in the international oil industry. These newcomers were attracted by the rapid growth in world oil consumption and by the huge profits the majors secured on their international operations.[1] The national oil companies were also interested in the prestige, political influence, and supply security that they believed control of foreign oil would bring them. To establish their presence in the international oil industry, the newcomers appealed to the exporting countries' interest in national control and greater revenue through increased oil liftings, and in return for the right to explore for oil, they were willing to offer the oil-exporting countries much higher bonus payments and seemingly better terms than those provided by the international majors, most of whom already had far more oil than they required for their market outlets. Moreover, while the majors always had to consider the effect that agreeing to new terms in a particular area would have on their concessions, the newcomers were not constrained by this factor.

With the majors holding the exploration rights to nearly all the promising territory in the oil-exporting countries, the chief obstacle confronting the newcomers continued to be access to crude-oil supplies. Hence when Venezuela offered concessions in 1956–57, many newcomers, most of them American, bid handsomely and secured concessions. However, the majors still controlled the bulk of Venezuela's oil, and in 1960 the new administration in Venezuela announced that no further concessions would be granted. Similarly, Indonesian oil

was controlled by the majors, and from 1951 until 1961 the Indonesian government maintained a freeze on granting new concessions.

To obtain oil, the newcomers were left with the choice of developing a new
oil-producing area or securing a stake in the Middle East. However, prior to
formation of the Iranian Consortium in 1954, only two independents, Getty and
Aminoil, had obtained significant concessions in the Middle East. Then, with
formation of the Consortium, nine U.S. independents gained a foothold in the
Middle East as a result of U.S. government pressure. But beyond that, the
Middle East seemed sealed.

THE NEWCOMERS AND NORTH AFRICA

After World War II the French government began subsidizing companies
whose mission was to find oil in franc-zone areas. France's goal was for French-
owned companies to produce as much oil worldwide as France consumed domestically. In 1947, CFP produced only a little over a million tons a year, while
France consumed 5 million tons a year.[2] To realize the government's objective,
French companies began investing heavily in exploration and development
throughout the franc zone, including such areas as Gabon and the Middle Congo,
but most important was the French effort to find oil in Algeria. Between 1947,
when the Algerian effort began, and 1962, when Algeria gained its independence, French government-sponsored oil enterprises put roughly $1.2 billion into
exploration and development in the Sahara. In contrast, the Anglo-American
majors, which had more oil that they knew what to do with, had little interest in
Algerian oil. By their standards, it was too costly, and they were deterred by the
political instability in the country.[3]

France discovered oil in Algeria in the mid-1950s, and exports began in 1959.
At that point the French government required that refiners who operated in
France purchase certain quantities of this oil.[4] In 1959, as part of this effort to
guarantee a market for Algerian crude, the French government purchased much
of France's domestic refining and marketing capacity.

While in 1950 France received 21 percent of its crude-oil imports (14 million
tons) from CFP's operations in Iraq and imported the rest from sources under the
control of non-French companies, in 1961 32 percent of France's imports (35
million tons) came from Algeria and 20 percent from Iraq. French companies
were producing 94 percent as much oil worldwide as France was consuming
domestically.[5]

In bringing Algerian production onstream, France established the first important oil-producing area outside the control of the major international oil companies. In using that production to supply the French market, France also contributed to erosion of the majors' control of downstream operations. However, in
resisting Algeria's demand for independence, France incurred enormous ill will
in the Arab world, which set back its efforts to secure a greater role in world oil.

The big breakthrough for the independents came in Libya, another new producing area, just east of Algeria. The Italians had found oil in Libya prior to World War II, and after the war the French had discovered oil there as well. Consequently, the area was seen as promising when the government proclaimed its Petroleum Law of 1955, which was designed to maximize the speed with which production would begin in desperately poor Libya. Rather than offer most of its territory as a single concession to a company or group of companies, as the Middle East oil-exporting countries had done, Libya invited the companies to bid for a series of concessions, each of them quite small by Middle East standards. By offering the companies many concessions, Libya increased the probability that some of them would go to the newcomers. This, in turn, increased the likelihood that production would be developed quickly, since, unlike the majors, the newcomers would not have to choose between Libyan oil and oil in established Middle East concessions. In short, the development of Libya represented an alliance between a new producing area and industry newcomers, all of whom were determined to force their way into a system dominated by the international majors and the established oil-producing countries.

The Petroleum Law contained several other provisions which were intended to encourage rapid production by providing special benefits to the companies. One provision allowed companies to deduct all their exploration expenses in the year they were incurred, after they had begun exporting oil. Another offered the companies a generous 20 percent depreciation allowance on their physical assets

TABLE 3–1. SHARES OF PRODUCTION, MAJORS VS. NEWCOMERS, 1966

| | (Percent) | | | (Thousand Barrels Daily) |
	Anglo-American Majors	CFP	Others	Total Production
Iran	83.5	5.6	10.9	2,110
Iraq	71.3	23.7	5.0	1,390
Qatar	79.3	15.7	5.0	280
Abu Dhabi	69.6	26.2	4.2	355
Kuwait	100.0	—	—	2,275
Saudi Arabia	100.0	—	—	2,395
Persian Gulf	85.3	6.3	8.4	9,250
Libya	44.1	—	55.9	1,500
Algeria	11.8	18.5	69.7	715
Nigeria	94.5	—	5.5	420
Indonesia	82.9	—	17.1	550
Venezuela	85.2	—	14.8	3,370
Non-North America, Non-Communist Total	78.2	4.5	17.3	15,805

Computed from data in Adelman, *The World Petroleum Market*, p. 80.

before production and an equally generous 25 percent depletion allowance on their gross income.

Yet the greatest inducement that Libya offered the companies was that it taxed them not on the basis of the posted price, as the Middle East oil-exporting countries did, but on the basis of the much lower realized prices. This provision cost Libya millions of dollars, since, after 1960, posted prices remained rigid while market prices declined. But as a result, companies that operated in Libya did not face the same price floor as companies that paid taxes on the basis of posted prices. This left them free to cut prices—an important inducement to newcomers anxious to break into established markets[6]—and it led to rapid expansion in Libyan production. In addition, Libya retained the right to repossess areas that were not developed.

Libya's strategy made it a major oil-exporting country. In the first round of bidding, seventeen companies received eighty-four concessions areas. By 1961, at least ten good fields had been discovered, and Libya was exporting oil. By 1965 it was the world's sixth largest exporter, accounting for 10 percent of the world's crude-oil exports.[7]

While the majors accounted for well over 80 percent of all production in the other exporting countries, newcomers in Libya accounted for 56 percent of production and, in Algeria, 70 percent (see table 3–1).

COMPANY-COUNTRY JOINT VENTURES

While France pioneered development of the Sahara, Italy's national oil corporation, Ente Nazionale Idrocarburi (ENI), initiated a new kind of arrangement between an oil company and an oil-exporting country. ENI's chairman Signor Enrico Mattei maintained that both the oil-consuming and the oil-exporting countries could get a better deal by bypassing the majors and concluding agreements with one another. In the mid-1950s he proposed such an arrangement to Iran and Egypt. Despite the coup in Iran and the formation of the Iranian Consortium, the new Iranian government was anxious to secure greater national control over Iran's oil resources; indeed, it had retained the National Iranian Oil Company partly for this reason. Yet the Consortium had secured the exclusive rights to most of Iran, the main exception being the Iranian offshore territory.[8]

In 1957 NIOC and ENI reached a partnership agreement, giving ENI the right to explore for oil in Iranian offshore territory. ENI would provide all the initial capital, but in the event that oil was found, NIOC would become a full partner in the operation, paying half the cost of development and receiving half the profits from the venture, and the joint venture would continue to pay a 50 percent tax to the Iranian government (as was now customary).

This arrangement provided the basis for the government's heralded claim that it had secured a 75/25 profit split, breaking the standard 50/50 division. As a government taxing the joint venture, it would receive half the profits and then, as a partner in the operation, it would receive half the remaining profits ($.50 + .50(.50)) = .75$). Financially, however, it was far from clear that this was a better deal for Iran than a more traditional concession-type arrangement would have been, for ENI failed to pay an initial—and customary—cash bonus. Once it started producing oil, it would pay only the usual 50 percent tax on its share of production, and the additional profits that Iran received would be the result of investments it made itself.

The real significance of the Iranian deal was not its financial advantages, but that it made an oil-exporting country an actual partner in the production operations. In so doing, it opened the possibility of new kinds of arrangements between the international oil companies and the oil-exporting countries. It also demonstrated new ways in which the oil-exporting countries and the newcomers could aid each other in their respective efforts to improve their position vis-à-vis the international majors, for by providing the technological expertise to find oil and assuming the initial risk, ENI made it easier for Iran to gain some control over its oil resources. Yet by agreeing to help finance development of the fields once oil was found, Iran was helping the newcomers, who had less capital to dispense than the majors, to meet their capital requirements.

At the same time, it was difficult for the majors to enter into joint-venture agreements in these new areas because, as joint-venture partners, they would be continually torn between development of a new area and their interests in established concessions. The majors were also afraid that if they took the oil-exporting countries as partners in new ventures, they would soon be pressured into taking them on as partners in their established concessions, which they sought to avoid because of the effect it would have on profits and because they did not want to share control. (In 1957 ENI also made a joint-venture agreement with Egypt, similar to the one it had made with Iran. Yet, despite the precedent-setting character of its agreements, ENI never found significant quantities of oil.)

Three months after the ENI deal, Iran announced that another offshore area was being offered on a joint-venture basis. None of the Consortium members bothered to apply, but fifty-seven other companies expressed interest and a deal was soon concluded with Standard Oil of Indiana. The terms were similar to the ENI deal, except that the American independent agreed to an immediate bonus payment of $25 million.

Shortly after that, in 1958, the Japanese company, Arabian Oil, secured offshore concessions in the Neutral Zone from both Saudi Arabia and Kuwait. Japan agreed to provide the Arabian and Kuwaiti governments with the right to 10 percent of the oil found, bringing the governments' profit shares to 56 percent and 57 percent respectively. In addition, these agreements contained provisions for relinquishing part of the concession area. By 1964 the Japanese were producing 240,000 b/d in the Neutral Zone.[9] Like France, Japan insisted that all the refineries in Japan take proportions of the unattractive Neutral Zone crude oil; however, the foreign companies that controlled the Japanese refineries were willing to take only a limited amount. Consequently, in desperation, Arabian Oil attempted to sell the oil outside Japan, despite the fact that the field had been developed to supply Japanese markets with Japanese-produced oil.

As the exporting countries witnessed the offers the newcomers made for new areas, they insisted that new concessions contain relinquishment provisions and that the majors relinquish parts of their concessions, which they had failed to develop. By the end of the 1950s, provisions for relinquishment of unexploited areas became a standard part of new concession agreements. By 1963, Aramco had relinquished approximately three quarters of its original concession area and Kuwait Oil Company had given up about half of its concession area.[10] This further weakened the majors' control over the industry and, correspondingly, increased the opportunities available to the newcomers. However, the majors were careful to relinquish only the least promising oil territory.

The growing importance of the independents posed a serious challenge to the predominance of the majors, but the effects were mitigated by the rapid growth in oil consumption. An expanding market made it possible for the majors to maintain high rates of growth, despite the rise in competition. Also, as countries developed national oil companies with access to high-cost oil, their willingness to accept higher world oil prices increased, for, as we saw in the case of France's development of Algerian oil, high prices were often needed to permit "national champions" to remain solvent.

THE SOVIET OIL OFFENSIVE

The most disruptive force in the late 1950s was the reentry of the Soviet Union into the world oil market.[11] Prior to World War II the Soviet Union had been an important oil exporter, supplying roughly 19 percent of the West's oil imports between 1930 and 1933. However, as a result of the wartime destruction of its oil facilities, it remained a net oil importer until 1954.[12] Then, in the mid-1950s, the Soviet Union launched a major oil-export offensive. Between 1955 and 1960 Soviet oil exports increased by a factor of four. One reason for this was that, with recovery of the Soviet oil industry, the Soviet Union was able to produce more oil than it could consume, and under Khrushchev the Soviet Union embarked on a policy of economic modernization through trade collaboration with the West. By exporting oil, the Soviet Union planned to earn much of the hard currency it needed to purchase sophisticated technology from the West. Indeed, in 1960 fuels and lubricants accounted for 26 percent of the Soviet Union's trade with the industrial West. Finally, the Soviet Union sought to use oil exports as a way of gaining political influence, particularly in the Third World.[13]

To penetrate Western markets, the Soviet Union generally sold oil at 10–20 percent less than world prices. The oil companies objected vigorously to the Soviet price-cutting tactics, urging the consuming countries to refuse to purchase the Soviet oil on the grounds that dependence upon Communist oil was politically risky. Appealing to Cold War anxieties, the companies argued that the Soviet motives were "political" and that competition from the Soviet Union was "unfair," since a state-owned company did not have to take account of ordinary economic costs in setting prices. As evidence that Soviet prices were based on noneconomic considerations, the oil companies pointed out that from 1955 to 1960 the Soviet Union charged Communist countries 50 percent more on average than they charged non-Communist countries.[14]

The oil companies limited the export of Soviet oil by refusing to purchase it for their refineries and by boycotting firms that distributed it. In addition, the U.S. government was concerned that Soviet imports would be cut off at a time of crisis, and therefore, it pressured countries into limiting their imports of Soviet oil. The United States also banned the export of pipe to the Soviet Union and refused to lease oil tankers to the U.S.S.R.

As a result of U.S. pressure, the EEC countries informally agreed to limit Soviet oil to no more than 10 percent of each country's imports. However, Sweden, which was not a member of NATO or the EEC, was among the first to take large quantities of Soviet oil, allowing it to reach 15 percent of its total imports. With both NATO and the EEC attempting to put a halt to Soviet oil sales, Italy's ENI made sizable long-term contracts with the Soviets and used the relatively cheap Soviet oil to expand into downstream markets at the expense of the international majors.[15]

The Japanese government also pressured its importers to take supplies from the Soviet Union, and independent refiners took advantage of the availability of cheap Soviet oil to help increase their market shares. As a result, by 1960 Soviet oil sales became an important counterweight to the dominance of the majors in Italy, West Germany, and Japan—the three largest non-Communist importers of Soviet oil.[16]

While Soviet oil sales were opposed on security grounds, the real threat they posed was to the international price level, for in 1960 only about 4 percent of Western oil imports came from the Soviet Union.[17] The threat that these supplies would be cut off was hardly a major security risk, but a small amount of oil, particularly if it was targeted on a particular market, could exert real downward pressure on the price level. In many large Western markets, the Soviet Union *did* lead prices down, and in markets where the majors were entrenched, with virtually no competition, the Soviets introduced an element of real competition. Still, private oil companies in this period—many of them newcomers—repeatedly sold oil at prices as low or lower than those for which the Soviet Union was accused of "dumping."[18]

In pursuing its oil policy, the Soviet Union *did* have political interests. Surely, officials in the Kremlin were delighted to learn that their price-cutting tactics caused problems for those pillars of modern capitalism—the international oil companies—and they looked on with glee as the NATO countries fought bitterly over whether it was all right for countries to buy cheap Communist oil. But these were not the primary motivations for Soviet oil sales.

Insofar as political motives were primary in Soviet oil sales, it was in reference to dealings with the Third World, not developed countries. To fan distrust of the "imperial West" and win friends in the Third World, the Soviet Union sometimes sold oil cheap—a policy that had its greatest success in Cuba.[19] The Soviet Union also gained considerable influence in India, partly as a result of providing low-price Soviet oil, and it attempted to use oil policy to gain influence in the Middle East. In the late 1950s the Soviet Union sent technicians and oil-drilling equipment to Algeria, Egypt, and Syria. In 1959 the Soviet Union offered to explore for oil in northern Iran and give the Iranian government 15 percent of the oil it found, in exchange for a promise from Teheran not to permit any foreign (U.S.) military bases on its territory—an offer that was politely refused.

OPEC

In 1957, as indicated, in response to a U.S. price increase, the world petroleum price was raised to its highest level since 1948, despite the fact that costs were not increasing and there was no oil scarcity or higher pressure of demand on supply.[20] Indeed, the price rise was a reflection of the powerful control exercised by the international majors at the time and of the way in which U.S. energy policy buttressed high international oil prices.

From 1957 to 1960, however, the world oil price fell, from $1.97 a barrel to $1.84.[21] There were several reasons for this decline. First, between 1955 and 1960 the newcomers' share of non-U.S., non-Communist oil production increased from 8 percent to 16 percent.[22] This and the growth in Soviet oil sales exerted downward pressure on the price level. In addition, U.S. import quotas were enacted in 1957 on a "voluntary" basis, and in 1959 they were made mandatory. The immediate effect was that many American independents, who were planning to import oil into the United States, had no outlets for their crude. Consequently, to dispose of their crude they were forced to discount heavily.[23]

As a result of competition from the newcomers and the Soviet Union and the prospect of growing world oil markets (due to the shift from coal to oil in Western Europe and Japan), the differences among the majors became intensified. To boost or simply maintain their positions in downstream markets, the majors were forced to cut their profit margins. And companies that still had more crude than they had market outlets for began selling it to third parties, the result being that, for the first time, substantial amounts of crude oil were sold on an open market at significant discounts, rather than through the majors' integrated channels.[24]

As competition within the international oil industry intensified, the companies attempted to shift part of the pressure onto the oil-exporting countries. With prices falling, the majors decided to reduce their payments to the producing countries. To do this, they cut the posted price first by 10 percent in February 1959 and then by 7.5 percent in August 1960, but, did not consult the countries about either move.[25]

Following the first price reduction, in April 1959 the First Arab Oil Congress met. Venezuela's minister of mines and hydrocarbons, Perez Alfonzo, was invited to attend the congress as an observer, and at his urging the congress established an oil consultation commission. However, Iran objected to participation in a group that included several radical Arab regimes (notably the United Arab Republic and Iraq), and Iraq disliked the presence of the U.A.R. Consequently, the group was short lived.

Then in May 1960, Alfonzo, along with Saudi Arabia's director general of petroleum affairs, Abdullah Tariki, proposed formation of another group of oil-exporting countries (this time the U.A.R. was excluded). Angered by the oil companies' unilateral decision to cut the posted price, the Shah was willing to collaborate with Arab regimes, and particularly with the revolutionary, anti-monarchical regime in neighboring Iraq. In September 1960, as a result, Iraq, Iran, Kuwait, Saudi Arabia, and Venezuela joined together to form the Organization of Petroleum Exporting Countries (OPEC). The founding members accounted for 67 percent of the world's petroleum reserves, 38 percent of its production, and 90 percent of the oil in international trade.[26]

OPEC provided the oil-exporting countries a clearinghouse for the exchange of information and a forum for discussion of mutual problems and common strategies, yet OPEC met with only limited success during the first decade of its existence. Its first demand—restoration of the posted price to its previous level—was rejected by the oil companies. Consequently, while from 1957 to 1959 production in Middle East countries had risen by 30 percent and payments to the governments of these countries by 26.5 percent, from 1959 to 1961 production rose by 22 percent but payments rose only 13.7 percent.[27] However, the oil companies agreed that they would not reduce the posted price further—a considerable concession in a period of falling market prices.

Stymied in their efforts to get the posted price restored, the OPEC members attempted to increase their per barrel revenues through another route. After the fifty/fifty tax agreements were reached, the companies continued to pay royalties of 12.5 percent, but counted these payments as a credit against the total taxes owed. The countries argued that royalty payments should be treated as an expense and that taxes should be paid on the total profits, after the deduction of royalty payments.[28]

In 1964 an agreement was reached in which the companies agreed to expense royalties, on the condition that the OPEC countries allow discounts off posted prices in the calculation of taxable profits. In agreeing to this, for the first time the exporting countries implicitly accepted that tax prices might be influenced by market prices. The companies were anxious to have this principle acknowledged by the exporting countries, but it had little immediate effect since the agreement also called for the gradual elimination of discounting. At the same time, the companies accepted the principle that OPEC per barrel revenues could increase in a period of declining prices.[29]

In addition, in exchange for the expensing of royalties, OPEC abandoned its demand for restoration of posted prices to their 1959 level. The exporting countries did this, knowing that their increased revenue from the expensing of royalties would be about equal to what they had lost as a result of the 1959–60 reduction in posted prices.[30] As a result of the royalty-expensing agreement and the maintenance of posted prices, between 1960 and 1969 the oil-exporting countries' per barrel revenues increased from 71¢ to 84¢ in the Eastern Hemisphere, while those of the companies declined from 56¢ to 36¢,[31] an indication of the shifting balance of power in the international oil industry.

The OPEC countries also agreed to a "most favored company" clause, which stipulated that no company could be given favored treatment in an OPEC country. This was sought by the majors as a way of putting pressure on the independents, who relied on favorable terms in order to reduce prices and expand their market share. The majors recognized that if they could get the oil-exporting countries to impose a uniform tax, it would serve as a floor to prices and prevent disruptive outbreaks of competition.

This had immediate implications in Libya, where companies discounted heavily, relying on Libya's practice of taxing them on the basis of realized rather than posted prices. Although independents and majors discounted on their sales to third parties from Libya, it was much more important to the independents to be able to do this, for the independents were seeking to establish significant positions in new markets while most of the majors' oil moved through their own established, integrated channels. The majors recognized that the market gains the independents made were at their expense and that the competitive price cutting that resulted was injurious to the profitability of their worldwide operations. Similarly, the oil-exporting countries saw the growth in Libya's market share cutting into their production. Consequently, as soon as the OPEC agreement was adopted, the majors and the other OPEC countries urged Libya, which had joined OPEC in 1962, to adopt its provisions.

By the mid-1960s Libya had established itself as a major oil exporter, and consequently, from the Libyan government's perspective, the incentives that had been offered the companies in 1955 to draw them in were no longer desirable. In 1965, with Exxon's assistance,[32] Libya enacted a law requiring the companies to pay per barrel taxes comparable to those paid in the other OPEC countries; this meant both the expensing of royalties and the elimination of discounting. The majors were quick to accept the new terms, but the independents strongly objected to them. The independents argued that, unlike the majors, they had not participated in the 1964 negotiations with OPEC, and that they had come into Libya with the understanding that taxes would be paid on the basis of realized, not posted, prices. They argued that, in order to sell Libyan oil, they had to be able to discount it. Finally, they told the Libyan government that if they were forced out of Libya, the majors would substitute Arabian for Libyan oil, greatly reducing Libya's revenue.[33]

But the Libyan government refused to capitulate. Because the majors were ready to go along with the new terms and OPEC had reached an agreement that no company could receive preferential terms in a single country, there was little that the independents could do. By January 1966, they agreed to pay taxes on the basis of posted prices and to expense royalties, as was done in the other OPEC countries.[34]

OIL POWER IN THE 1960s

By the 1960s the international majors' and the U.S. government's control over international oil had been considerably eroded. As table 3–2 shows, the new-comers had established a substantial presence in the world oil industry, and France and the Soviet Union had assumed an active role in the world oil market.

Competition in oil production and competition in downstream operations tended to reinforce one another. In the early 1950s the great bulk of the world's oil had moved through the majors' integrated networks, but by 1968 open-market sales accounted for 28 percent of the world market,[35] which made it much easier for independent refiners and other third parties to secure crude supplies. Independent refiners could now purchase oil from the newcomers at prices comparable to those the majors paid their producing affiliates. At the same time, by providing new outlets for production, independent refiners tended to encourage greater production by the newcomers, and differences in the size and rates of growth of the majors tended to reduce the commonality of their interests and make them behave more competitively. The growth in competition at both the upstream and downstream levels made it increasingly difficult for the majors to control the growth in supply, for now the independent producers could boost supply on their own and the prospect of increasing their market share made it likely they would do so. On the other hand, majors with access to more oil than they had market outlets for would be strongly tempted to boost production and sell to independent refiners. As a result, between 1957 and the spring of 1970 the world price of crude oil declined steadily, from about $2 a barrel to about $1.30.[36]

This increase in industry competition had several consequences for the oil-exporting countries. The willingness of newcomers to pay substantial bonuses for the right to explore for oil showed the exporting countries the enormous value of their resources. The growing heterogeneity in the industry made it increasingly difficult for the industry to respond to the oil-exporting countries in a coordinated and unified way, and the growth of competition in downstream

TABLE 3–2. EIGHT MAJORS' SHARE OF NON-COMMUNIST, NON-U.S. OIL INDUSTRY OPERATIONS, 1955–65

	Production	Refining	Product Sales
1955	92%	81%	n.a.
1960	84	74	70%
1965	76	58	66

Mikdashi, *The Community of Oil Exporting Countries*, p. 49. Reprinted by permission of the publisher, George Allen & Unwin Ltd.

operations tended to greatly weaken the majors' "power of disposal." Now, if the majors refused to purchase a country's oil, as they had in Iran from 1951 to 1953 (see chapter 1), it was likely that independent refiners could be persuaded to take it.

The growth in industry competition also eliminated the majors' near monopoly on industry expertise. This expertise was now held by many heterogeneous, large firms. This, in turn, made it possible for the oil-exporting countries to appeal to alternative sources for technological and financial assistance. Combined with the political motivations of France and the Soviet Union, this factor took on considerable importance in shaping the development of relations between oil companies and the oil-exporting countries.

At the same time, the oil-exporting countries began to develop greater domestic expertise regarding the industry's operations. Indeed, in the early 1960s, Iraq, Kuwait, Saudi Arabia, and Venezuela established national oil companies (Iran, as indicated, already had one).

While these factors tended to improve the bargaining position of the oil-exporting countries, during the 1960s the countries were plagued by the majors' continuing ability to play the countries against one another. Despite the huge increase in oil consumption, the supply of oil greatly exceeded the demand for it throughout the 1960s. In this context, most oil-exporting countries sought to maximize their revenues by appealing to the companies to produce as much oil as possible, which left it to the companies to decide how much oil they took in each country in which they held concessions, and the companies used this power to reward countries that provided favorable terms and to punish those that attempted to stiffen their terms. To a considerable extent, this meant taking the cheapest oil available, but, to strengthen their bargaining position, in particular disputes the companies appear to have cut back more on production than their immediate commercial interests would have dictated. (Of course, this may have been fully consistent with their long-term commercial interests.)

The exporting countries recognized that to limit the power of the companies, they would have to control their members' production. Yet, because no country was willing to accept limitations on its production, OPEC's efforts to establish output quotas (production prorationing) repeatedly failed in the 1960s. Predictably, when the subject arose, countries argued for prorationing on the basis of criteria that would work to their advantage. Iran, the most populous of the Middle East oil-exporting countries, argued for prorationing on the basis of population. Kuwait and Saudi Arabia, which had the largest oil resources, insisted that oil reserves be the criteria. Venezuela, the largest producer until 1970, pushed for prorationing on the basis of historic shares. Consequently, despite repeated efforts, OPEC was unable to develop a workable prorationing scheme in the 1960s.

Cooperation was also inhibited by conflicts between the best-established oil-exporting countries and countries that were attempting to increase their market share. On one level, this was a conflict between Venezuela and the Middle East, for as Middle East production increased, Venezuela saw its role as an exporter decline. On another level, it was a conflict between Libya and the other oil-exporting countries, for in its efforts to become a major oil-exporting country, Libya offered the oil companies oil on far more favorable terms than the other oil-exporting countries, threatening the price level in the process.

In the absence of exporting-country unity, individual countries were able to secure gains by exploiting the competition among the newcomers and the majors and the political rivalries among the great powers in the Middle East; but there was little improvement for the exporting countries as a group. Moreover—from the perspective of the oil-exporting countries—many new arrangements that they had worked out with the newcomers turned out to have inherent weaknesses.

The companies benefited from knowing their actual profit margins in each country while the exporting countries did not. As a result, the exporting countries never knew at what point their oil would become uneconomical, and in bargaining, the companies continually exploited this uncertainty. For example, if a government threatened to stiffen its terms, the companies would declare that that would make their oil noncompetitive, and the government never knew whether the companies were bluffing. Even if a government persisted, the companies could reduce their liftings to lend credibility to their claims.

The companies' ability to play the countries against one another was also enhanced by the companies' insistence on dealing with the countries individually, rather than as a group. As a result, individual countries frequently made concessions to the companies in order to boost their market share, thus weakening OPEC's ability to secure a fixed per barrel payment from the companies. On the other hand, countries which stiffened their terms were forced to pay the penalty of reduced oil production.

Iraq. Since the end of World War II, development of Iraq's oil resources lagged behind the other major Middle East oil-producing countries, as the IPC parents preferred to take their oil in Saudi Arabia and Iran.[37] Iraq had been disadvantaged by the entrance of Mobil and Exxon into Aramco and by the highly restrictive procedures that governed the expansion of output in the IPC. Of the five IPC partners, only CFP and (to a lesser extent) Shell had an interest in rapid expansion of Iraqi output; the other companies had ample supplies of cheap crude elsewhere. As a result, IPC consistently understated the nation's oil reserves, failed to follow promising geological leads, and left the middle third of Iraq completely undeveloped, while refusing to relinquish it.[38]

In 1958 the autocratic regime of King Faisal was deposed by an army general, Abdel Karim Kassem. Under the monarchy, Iraq had been closely allied with the United States and Great Britain; it belonged to the Baghdad Pact, was hostile to international communism, and welcomed foreign capital. Consequently, when the coup occurred, the United States and Britain sent troops to Lebanon and Jordan to guard against the possibility of nationalist upheavals in those countries and to prepare for a possible invasion of Iraq. However, it soon became clear that there was little internal opposition to the new regime, and the Kassem government declared that oil interests would not be touched. So the United States and Great Britain decided against military action.[39]

In sharp contrast to the monarchy it replaced, the Kassem government was based on nationalism, domestic reconciliation, nonalignment in foreign affairs, and hostility toward Western capitalism. Kassem reached a rapprochement with the secessionist Kurdish minority, brought Communists into the government, concluded a technical-aid agreement with the Soviet Union, and in 1959 renounced the Baghdad Pact, of which Iraq had been a founding member.

Initially, Kassem had been reluctant to confront the oil companies, though he entered into negotiations with them. With a surplus of oil on the world market and with most of the IPC members able to obtain all the oil they could sell from their other concessions, Iraq's bargaining position was not strong. Besides, the new government needed the revenues the oil companies provided—and the memory of what had happened to Mossadegh was still vivid. However, relations between the Kassem regime and the oil companies worsened as a result of two developments in 1959–60. In 1960 the Iraqi government raised port dues substantially, to the level charged in the other Gulf ports. The companies argued that this made Iraqi oil noncompetitive with other oil from the Gulf and announced that, as a result, Iraqi production would be reduced to 8 million tons a year—a reduction of over 4 million tons. Following threats from Kassem to take "measures," the companies agreed to negotiate the issue and raise production in the interim, but not before Iraqi resentment intensified. The Iraqis were also angered by the reductions in the posted price in 1959 and 1960.[40]

It was in this context that Iraq and the companies resumed negotiations on a series of demands, the most important being that (1) a large portion of the unexploited concession territory be relinquished, with the government having the right to choose the areas to be given back; (2) Iraq be given a 20 percent share in the ownership of IPC;[41] and (3) the fifty/fifty profit split be altered in the government's favor. In making these demands, Iraq was attempting to take advantage of precedents established in previous Middle East agreements. The Iraqi goverment pointed out that other Middle East governments had won relinquishment provisions and had broken the fifty/fifty principle in arrangements with the newcomers.

However, it was one thing for the newcomers to breach the fifty/fifty principle in a new venture and something quite different for the majors to do so in an old, established concession. The majors that made up the IPC were unwilling to agree to fundamental changes in concession arrangements, partly because they feared they would have to grant these terms to the other countries in which they held concessions; consequently, they refused to compromise on the participation demand. Although they were willing to relinquish territory, as they had done in other concessions, they were not willing to allow Iraq to choose the areas to be given up. Therefore, negotiations broke down, and in December 1961 Iraq enacted Law 80, which expropriated, without compensation, the IPC's rights to

99.5 percent of its original concession area. However, the companies were left all the territory in which they had active, producing wells. The expropriated area included the North Rumailia field, which was known to have great potential, but which had not yet been brought into production.

To leave room for future accomodation with the companies, Law 80 stipulated that IPC might regain an area equal to what had been left it under the new law. In 1961, though the government had taken control of most of its territory, it had no plan for developing it.

In leaving the companies with all of their producing territory, Iraq hoped to continue to obtain revenue from petroleum, which it badly needed. At the same time, the Iraqi move left the companies in a dilemma. They were anxious to punish Iraq for its action and demonstrate that an oil-exporting country could not "get away" with a unilateral, uncompensated expropriation, but the companies were also anxious to recover the North Rumailia field, if only to keep it out of the hands of their competitors.

The companies' immediate response was to hold Iraqi production even, despite the fact that an expansion program, initiated in 1959 and aimed at doubling Iraqi production, had been largely completed. Iraq's production for 1962 increased by only .5 percent, while production in Kuwait, Iran, and Saudi Arabia increased by 11.5, 12, and 9.2 percent respectively.[42] Then, in February 1963, Kassem was assassinated and his government replaced by a more moderate regime. By June an agreement had been reached on the port dues at Basra, and the companies agreed to raise their output. In 1964, with the other issues unresolved, the government created the Iraq National Oil Company (INOC). The state-owned company was to develop the country's oil reserves, and since it lacked the capacity to do this, it was authorized to make agreements with foreign companies.

In response, the IPC partners pursued a twofold strategy. To prevent other companies from going into Iraq, they threatened lawsuits and enlisted the cooperation of the U.S. State Department, which pressured the American independents to stay out of Iraq.[43] At the same time, the IPC partners sought to reach an agreement with Iraq,[44] and to pressure the radical oil-exporting country, the companies withheld the benefits of the OPEC royalty-expensing agreement from Iraq until the Law 80 dispute was resolved.

In June 1965 a draft settlement was reached, restoring North Rumailia and other proven areas to the IPC and creating a joint venture, including INOC and four of the IPC members (Exxon refused to participate), that would develop oil resources in the expropriated territory. When it was learned that the agreement would allow the IPC partners back into the expropriated areas, public opposition mounted and ratification of the agreement was delayed. With the outbreak of the Arab-Israeli War in 1967, hostility toward Western oil companies intensified, and the agreement was abandoned.[45]

By 1967, Iraq's situation had changed in two other ways as well. First, Iraqi and French relations had improved dramatically. During the 1950s and early

1960s, considerable Iraqi hostility toward France had resulted from France's role in the Algerian war and its support for Israel, particularly its role in the 1956 Suez crisis, but by 1967 the Algerian war had been settled, de Gaulle was parading as a champion of the Third World, and France had moved away from its pro-Israeli position.

De Gaulle saw concessions on oil as a way that France could forge an alliance with the Third World and become a "third force" in world politics. In 1966 ERAP, a state-owned French company, had introduced the service contract agreement into the Middle East in a deal with Iran. Under this arrangement, ERAP agreed to work as a contractor to the National Iranian Oil Company, receiving a share of the oil for its services but leaving NIOC with entire ownership of the concession. Such an arrangement was of particular interest to Iraq, since it would provide the country technical assistance while allowing it to retain its nationalized property. And once it became clear that IPC would not be allowed back into the expropriated territory, France's interest in supporting the majors was considerably reduced. Consequently, both ERAP and CFP, acting independently of its IPC partners, expressed interest in aiding INOC with development of the expropriated territory.

The other important change, from Iraq's perspective, was that, following the ouster of Khrushchev, the rate of growth in Soviet exports began to slow in the mid-1960s, and in 1966 the Soviet Union and East European countries began contracting (on a barter basis) for the import of crude oil from the Middle East. There were several reasons for this change in policy. Soviet oil production was declining and consumption was increasing, so that the Soviet Union was no longer able to meet East Europe's growing oil needs and its own need for the hard currency that exports of oil to the West provided. Besides, it was cheaper to import oil from the Middle East than to develop the oil resources in Siberia.[46]

There were also political motivations for the change in policy, for the Soviet Union recognized that by contributing to the lowering of world oil prices, its exports were benefiting the advanced capitalist countries but weakening the price levels that the oil-exporting countries depended upon. Moreover, the Soviet Union had become a competitor of the Middle East countries, whose good will it was attempting to win. Thus the Soviet Union had much to gain by becoming a purchaser of Middle East oil, as it did in the late 1960s.

The effect on Iraq was to open a new potential market for the sale of oil from its nationalized territory. Following discussions with the Soviet Union and with the French and Italian state oil companies, in August 1967 Iraq enacted legislation that gave INOC exclusive rights to develop the expropriated territories. New oil concessions were prohibited, but INOC, which still lacked the technological expertise to go it alone, was permitted to associate with others in development of the territory.

This time the State Department attempted to prevent foreign national oil companies from coming to Iraq's aid, to no avail. In November, an agreement was reached between ERAP and Iraq for exploration of some of the expropriated areas. ERAP agreed that, five years after the beginning of exports, INOC would become a partner with joint-management responsibility, and ERAP agreed to strict relinquishment provisions. While many criticized the agreement as less advantageous than what the IPC partners had offered in 1965, the fact that a Western oil company agreed to operate in an area in dispute with the majors was looked on in Iraq as an important political step. The Iraqi government also maintained that the deal was a "reward" for France's support of the Arabs in the struggle with Israel.[47]

ERAP was anxious to participate in development of the North Rumailia oil field, but Iraq rejected its offer and decided to have INOC develop the field with the assistance of the Communist countries. In December 1967 the Soviet Union had agreed to provide INOC with equipment and technicians and to aid in the drilling, transport, exploration, and marketing of Iraq's oil—in return for crude oil. The Soviet Union did not go ahead with these oil projects until June 1969, but numerous other Iraqi/Soviet oil agreements have been reached since then.

As a result of the aid it secured from France and the Soviet Union, Iraq was able to gain control of most of the territory that had originally been granted to the IPC. Unlike Mossadegh, the Iraqis did not have to back down from their nationalization. Indeed, the Iraqi success was to become an important precedent in establishing the nationalization alternative of the 1970s, but Iraq paid a heavy price for its "victory." Between 1961 and 1969, Iraqi production increased by only 26.9 million tons. In contrast, the figures for Iran, Kuwait, and Saudi Arabia were 109.1, 48.5, and 80.6 million tons respectively.[48] And though the Soviet Union was able to provide outlets for Iraqi oil, it was unable to rival the majors' marketing outlets or to pay hard currency for the oil. Equally significant: from 1961 until 1968, Iraq's proven oil reserves declined, from 27 billion to 23.5 billion barrels. In contrast, with the exception of Venezuela (see next section), all the other major oil-exporting countries saw their proven reserves increase during this period (Saudi Arabia from 50 billion to 74.7 billion barrels, Kuwait from 62 billion to 70 billion barrels, Iran from 35 billion to 43.8 billion barrels).[49]

Aside from CFP, the majors were aided by the restrictions on Iraqi production, for with Libyan production surging and continual demands for increased production in Iran (see chapter 5), the majors were confronted with a surplus of oil that threatened the price level. By holding Iraqi production down, they were able to achieve a high degree of protection against this downward price pressure.

Venezuela. Aside from Iraq, in the 1960s the only other oil-exporting country that was willing to accept a slower rate of development in order to secure better financial terms from the majors was Venezuela. The impetus for change in both countries came from the ouster of dictatorships. In Iraq, a radical nationalist government came to power; in Venezuela, it was a reform-oriented, popularly elected government. Also—in comparison with Iraq—Venezuela exploited international rivalries to a much lesser extent.

The military dictatorship that ruled Venezuela from 1948 to 1957 posed few challenges to the international oil companies. During this period the government's profit share declined gradually while Venezuelan production doubled.[50] Then, in 1958, the Jimenez dictatorship was ousted and a period of popularly elected government was initiated in Venezuela—the only oil-exporting country to be so governed. Subsequently, the oil companies were confronted by a series of competitive nationalist moves by political forces that sought to boost revenues and gain popular support through tough dealings with the oil companies.

In 1958 the provisional government boosted the government's share of the proceeds from petroleum from 52 to 65 percent, breaking the fifty/fifty split that officially prevailed in the Middle East.[51] Then, in 1960, the Betancourt administration announced that it would grant no additional concession areas to the oil companies (a policy that was continued throughout the 1960s), and it established a state petroleum company.[52]

Fearing that Venezuela's high taxation and bothersome controls would spread to other countries, the companies began to disinvest in Venezuela. Between 1960 and 1968 the companies decapitalized their Venezuelan operations by nearly $1.2 billion.[53] In doing this, the companies were not simply responding to market forces, but attempting to shape them by a strategy that would prevent other countries from adopting Venezuelan-type policies and, they hoped, get Venezuela to reverse its policies. Despite the companies' efforts, competitive nationalism led the government to impose stricter terms on the companies. In 1966 Venezuela proposed a selective tax on oil industry profits in excess of 15 percent. As the debate proceeded, the industry slowed production to its lowest rate in nearly a decade. Finally, a compromise agreement was reached on retroactive tax claims, prices, production levels, future taxation, and Venezuela's participation in the industry.[54]

In 1969, in an attempt to increase oil production, the recently elected Caldera government (which the oil companies had secretly supported) proposed to offer the companies additional concession areas on a new contract system. However, the opposition party, Acción Democrática, controlled the congress and voted to stiffen the terms on which the contracts would be offered. Twenty-five companies expressed interest initially, but only three—Occidental, Shell, and Mobil—were willing to sign up on the revised terms. The contracts were not signed until the summer of 1971—two and a half years after Caldera had begun to promote them—and by the beginning of 1975 only small quantities of commercially exploitable oil had been found.[55]

With Venezuelan oil more costly to produce than Middle East oil,[56] the oil companies maintained that the country's high taxation policies were making it uneconomical. On the U.S. East Coast, however, Venezuelan oil had about a 40¢ per barrel freight advantage over oil from the Persian Gulf. And though the average cost of Venezuelan oil was greater than the cost of Middle East oil, a substantial portion of Venezuelan oil cost considerably less than the average, and could have been developed and produced had the oil companies chosen to do so.

Adelman estimates that Venezuelan oil could have undersold Middle East oil on the U.S. East Coast, and a substantial portion would have been competitive in Europe.[57]

By restricting the entry of imported oil, U.S. import controls cut Venezuela off from what would otherwise have been the market for its oil. And while, throughout the 1960s, Venezuela sought the same kind of preferential access to the U.S. market that Canada received, its requests were repeatedly denied—a U.S. government policy that the major oil companies supported.[58] Consequently, throughout the 1960s Venezuela's position as an oil exporter declined. In 1960 Venezuela had accounted for 27.4 percent of all crude-oil exports, but by 1970 for only 10.9 percent. Indeed in 1970, for the first time, both Iran and Saudi Arabia surpassed Venezuela as oil exporters.[59]

Between 1958 and 1970, as part of the companies' program of disinvestment, the number of exploratory wells drilled in Venezuela fell by 83 percent (from 598 to 102).[60] Consequently, between 1960 and 1970 Venezuela's proven reserves fell from 18 billion barrels to 14.75 billion. During this period, in contrast, Saudi Arabia's proven reserves increased (in billion barrels) from 50 to 140, Iran's from 35 to 55, Kuwait's from 62 to 68, and Iraq's from 25 to 27.5.[61] As a result of this stalemate between a popularly based government and an international industry, Venezuela's role as an oil exporter declined and its reserve base was increasingly inadequate as an alternative to Middle Eastern supplies, a factor which redounded ultimately to the detriment of the advanced capitalist countries.

Minor Exporters and the Supply of Oil. Indonesia (formerly the Dutch East Indies) was an important oil-exporting country prior to World War II; however, the Indonesian oil fields were badly damaged during World War II. Production was restored after the war, but, as a result of disputes between the oil companies and the nationalist government (headed by Sukarno), Indonesia was only a minor oil producer throughout the 1950s and 1960s.

After gaining independence in 1951, the Indonesian parliament passed a law urging a freeze on the granting of concessions, while the government attempted to formulate an oil policy. The freeze lasted ten years, during which the three major oil companies in Indonesia—Shell, Stanvac (a joint venture of Exxon and Mobil), and CalTex (a joint venture of SoCal and Texaco)—controlled virtually all the country's oil production. However, because of the freeze on new concessions, no exploration in new areas took place during this time, and Indonesia's oil industry "lived" off its proven reserves.[62]

In 1961 the government passed Law 44, mandating that, from then on, the companies would be contractors rather than concessionaires. Several U.S. and Japanese independents signed exploration agreements under these terms, but the majors refused to accept the provisions of Law 44. They were concerned about the impact that acceptance of the Indonesian terms would have on their Middle East concessions.

Negotiations dragged on, and in 1963 the Indonesian government declared that if an agreement were not reached soon, the companies would be nationalized. Since the Hickenlooper Amendment (passed in 1962) mandated that an uncompensated nationalization of a U.S. company would lead to an automatic cutoff of foreign aid, and since that would increase the probability of a Communist revolution in Indonesia, the U.S. government sought to resolve the dispute. In June 1963 a special team of U.S. negotiators secured an agreement between the companies and the Indonesians under which the companies would continue operating under "contracts of work." The companies became "contractors," but retained management control. Under the terms of the new arrangement, the Indonesian government would receive 60 percent of the profits from the companies' Indonesian operations.[63]

From Indonesia's perspective, the major advantage of the agreement was that it gave the government formal ownership, while still requiring the companies to provide the funds for capital investment. In so doing, it reduced the foreign-exchange burden that Indonesia would otherwise have had to assume as "owner." Yet, as a result of its freeze on concessions and its nationalization dispute, the increase in production in Indonesia lagged behind the rate in the Middle East,[64] and despite the 1963 agreement, between 1963 and 1965 the oil industry came under increasing attack in Indonesia. During this period Sukarno moved more and more to the left, and the influence of the Indonesian Communist Party increased. On March 19, 1965, a series of strikes, demonstrations, and takeovers by Communist-dominated unions culminated in a decree that placed the oil companies under government supervision. However, the companies were not nationalized and Western managements remained in place.

Then, following an unsuccessful Communist-backed effort to gain control of the government in September 1965, the right, led by General Suharto, gained increasing power in Indonesia. In March 1966 Sukarno transferred power to Suharto. In sharp contrast to the Sukarno government, the Suharto government welcomed foreign investment, and worked out a new arrangement with the oil industry, the "production sharing contract." Under this agreement, oil production is shared between the exploring oil company and the Indonesian national oil company, Pertamina. When it was first proposed, the major oil companies, with U.S. government support, opposed the production-sharing contract because it would reduce their managerial control and deprive them of the opportunity to market the government's production share. However, a number of Japanese companies and U.S. independents entered into such contracts and the majors soon acceded to the new arrangements.[65]

Under the production-sharing contract, the contractor is responsible for financing the entire operation and can retain up to 40 percent of the annual production to cover amortization of capital costs and operating expenses. The rest of the production is split between Pertamina and the contractor—in some cases in a fixed proportion of 65/35, in others rising to 70/30 above certain levels of production. As a result of these arrangements, the Indonesian government was supposed to get 65 percent of the total profits from the country's oil industry operations. Also in January 1967, Suharto withdrew the 1965 decree that placed foreign companies under government supervision.[66]

Between 1963 and 1965—the years of left ascendancy in Indonesia—Indonesian oil production leveled off. In 1965, in response to the developments in those years, Shell, whose operations in Indonesia went back to 1885, sold out to Pertamina, an Indonesian state company. However, Shell agreed to be paid mainly in oil and its employees remained in Indonesia under a service-contract agreement.[67]

As the right increased in strength and the production-sharing contract was adopted, Indonesian production began to pick up, growing at a healthy annual rate of 11.8 percent between 1965 and 1970. During this period, Middle East production grew at 10.8 percent.[68] Indonesia's offshore areas were opened to foreign companies in 1967, but offshore production did not begin until September 1971.[69]

Indonesia joined OPEC in 1962, but the unique character of its arrangements with the oil companies tended to work against Indonesian cooperation with the other oil-exporting countries. Indeed, the other oil-exporting countries continually sought an increase in posted prices, but, as a result of its profit- and production-sharing schemes, Indonesia did not even have posted prices. Nonetheless, by the late 1960s the prospects for continued rapid growth in Indonesian production looked good, for the country's oil was low in sulfur and tended to be near ground level. Also, Indonesian oil was ideally suited for the booming Japanese market, and under Suharto, economic and political conditions had stabilized.

Like Indonesia, Nigeria remained a minor oil-exporting country throughout the 1960s. Though exploration had been undertaken as early as 1938, until the late 1950s Nigeria's oil potential was neglected, for Nigeria's original concessionaires, Shell and BP, were principally concerned with development in the Middle East. Only after the explorations of several independents proved successful were Shell and BP roused to greater activity in Nigeria, and exports from Nigeria began in 1962. Encouraged by a favorable petroleum law, which limited the government's share of the profits to only 35 percent, Nigerian production grew rapidly. However, between 1967 and 1970 the growth of Nigerian production was interrupted by the Nigerian civil war.[70]

As a result of its favorable location (west of Suez), its noninvolvement in the Arab-Israeli dispute, and the low-sulfur quality of its oil, once the war ended—in 1970—Nigeria's growth as an oil exporter was assured. By 1972 it was exporting almost 2 million barrels per day (compared with 300,000 b/d in 1967), and by 1973 it had become the world's sixth largest exporter of oil. Nigeria joined OPEC in 1971.[71]

Despite the Nigerian civil war, the limited development of Indonesia's oil resources, and the oil industry's disinvestment program in Venezuela and its punitive slow-growth policies in Iraq, more than enough oil was available to meet a booming world demand throughout the 1960s. In the Arabian Peninsula,

TABLE 3–3. OIL PRODUCTION IN OPEC COUNTRIES, 1955–70

	Production (Thousands of Barrels Daily)			Percentage Increase	
	1955	1960	1970	1955–70	1960–70
Iran	328.9	1,067.7	3,829.0	1,064.2	258.6
Kuwait	1,103.6	1,691.8	2,989.6	170.9	76.7
Saudi Arabia	976.6	1,313.5	3,799.3	289.0	189.3
Qatar	115.0	174.6	362.4	215.1	107.6
United Arab Emirates	—	—	779.6	—	—
Iraq	697.0	972.2	1,548.6*	122.2	59.3
Algeria	—	181.1	1,029.1	—	468.2
Libya	—	—	3,318.0	—	—
Venezuela	2,157.2	2,846.1	3,708.0	71.9	30.3
Ecuador	9.9	7.5	4.0	−60.0	−40.0
Indonesia	235.5	409.6	853.6	262.5	108.4
Nigeria	—	17.4	1,083.1	—	6,124.7
Gabon	—	15.4	108.8	—	606.5
6 Middle East members	3,221.1	5,219.8	13,308.5	313.2	155.0
Total OPEC Members	5,623.7	8,696.9	23,413.1	316.3	169.2

*Excludes government's production.

OPEC, *Annual Statistical Bulletin, 1973*, pp. 12–25. Since countries joined OPEC at different times, not all of the countries listed were OPEC members during the years listed.

Iran, and North Africa, oil was cheap and readily available, and the oil industry faced generally favorable terms. As a result, the oil-exporting countries in this area experienced rapid rates of growth throughout the 1960s (see table 3–3), and the industry had little problem meeting consumer demand.

THE THREAT OF FALLING PRICES

By exploiting the competition between the majors and the newcomers and the rivalry among the great powers, the oil-exporting countries gained significant control over their oil resources. However, by the late 1960s there was growing awareness of the weaknesses inherent in many of the agreements the oil-export-ing countries had reached with the newcomers. By this time, all of the major oil-exporting countries had established national oil companies.[72] In addition to serving as suppliers in their local markets, most of these companies had estab-lished joint-venture agreements with foreign companies, and though the amount of oil produced through these arrangements was relatively small,[73] the fact that the national oil companies had the responsibility for exploration and develop-ment in the vast relinquished territory meant that, by acting in concert with foreign partners, they had the potential to become a major force in the interna-tional oil industry.

However, as this development emerged, concern was expressed about the likelihood that, to establish themselves in international markets, the national oil companies would engage in competitive behavior that would weaken the price structure. One of the pillars of the price structure was that the majors had to pay taxes on the basis of a fixed posted price, which maintained a price floor of about $1. This consisted of the cost of the oil (roughly 10¢) plus the tax that the oil-exporting countries levied on each barrel (90¢ = .50(1.80)).

But unlike the majors, the national oil companies, which were agents of their governments, did not have to pay taxes on the basis of posted prices, nor did many of the newcomers operating in joint-venture arrangements. Indeed, as Thomas R. Stauffer found, "In general the tax-paid cost to the foreign partner for his share of any crude produced under these newer agreements is less than would be the tax-paid cost to an 'OPEC' concessionaire under otherwise identical conditions."[74]

As a result, the national oil companies and the newcomers, operating in joint ventures with them, had the advantage of a price floor that included only the cost elements and not the tax element. Theoretically, they could sell a barrel of oil, which the majors had to sell for at least $1 for just over 10¢ and still make a profit on it. In practice, this difference was mitigated by the higher cost of the oil that these joint-venture operations had access to and by the fact that they had to pay a per barrel tax to their host governments. But according to Stauffer's calculations, their average tax-paid cost was 22¢ per barrel less than the price of an OPEC concessionaire,[75] and the joint-venture partners could use this cost advantage to discount their oil and expand their market shares.

As early as 1964 the National Iranian Oil Company began offering heavy price discounts on the oil produced in its joint venture with Standard Oil of Indiana.[76] In addition, with the growth of world demand for oil expected to slow in the 1970s and with production expected to increase in Nigeria and Indonesia, the growth in Middle East and North African production was expected to decline, which would increase the likelihood of price competition. The international majors recognized that the potential for price cutting by newcomers and national oil companies was a threat to both their profits and their dominance of world markets, and by the middle of the 1960s the oil-exporting countries saw that while the agreements with the newcomers had provided individual exporting countries with many immediate advantages, their long-term effect was to weaken the price level that the oil-exporting countries as a group depended upon for their revenues.[77] Consequently, countries began openly to discuss whether new concessions should be withheld from the newcomers, for they were the most aggressive price cutters.[78]

Along with this, the exporting countries expressed interest in cementing an alliance with the international majors, but on a new basis. In the spring of 1969 in a major address, "Participation versus Nationalization: A Better Means to Survive," Saudi Arabia's oil minister, Sheik Zaki Yamani, called for the participation of the oil-exporting countries in both the production and the refining and marketing operations of the international oil companies.[79] Yamani explained that the majors' dominant position in world markets gave them the ability to preserve the price level, and their vertically integrated structure gave them an interest in maintaining it. The majors, he declared, "are now really the only bulwark of stability in the world market." Consequently, he dismissed national-ization of the majors, on the grounds that

nationalization of their upstream producing properties would inevitably deprive the majors of any further interest in maintaining crude oil price levels. . . . They would put their full weight behind efforts to drive down crude oil prices, and in this they would undoubtedly succeed. . . . We in the producing countries—having become the operators and sellers of our oil—would find ourselves in a competitive production race. . . . It is even extremely doubtful that we would be able to sell at the level—say $1.05 or $1.10—which would enable us to maintain our present unit income of 90 cents per barrel. The market forces ranged against us—the consumers and the majors—would be too strong in the present oversupply conditions. . . . Financial instability would inevitably lead to political instability.

After noting the difficulties that the oil-exporting countries would have if they attempted to form a cartel of their own, Yamani declared that "we like the majors because they provide the buffer element between us and the consumers which is indispensable for the maintenance of world prices."[80]

However, Yamani recognized that, as a result of the rise of the newcomers, the majors' control of the market had been declining. Consequently, participa-tion was intended to strengthen the worldwide structure that the majors had created over decades to maintain the price level and, at the same time, allow the producing countries' national oil companies to become part of that structure. As Yamani said, participation "would be like a long-term two-way compromise between the majors and the producing countries, with the former assuring their position upstream by taking on the latter as partners downstream."[81]

In June 1968 the principle of participation was endorsed by all nine OPEC members. The oil-exporting countries saw participation as a way of gaining genuine control of the international oil industry and still maintaining the high per barrel revenues that stemmed from the majors' worldwide structure. But for the majors, participation meant sharing control in both the oil-exporting and the consuming countries, and it threatened to reduce both their assets and their future profitability, since, under participation, these would have to be shared with the oil-exporting countries. Consequently, throughout the 1960s the majors resisted the proposal.

Participation was only one of the possible responses to the problem of price erosion as a result of increased competition from the national oil companies. In the late 1960s Ashraf Lutfi, a Kuwaiti official and former OPEC secretary general, proposed a program of production prorationing.[82] But OPEC's previous efforts to work out such a system had failed, and there was little reason to believe that renewed efforts would prove more successful. Even if such a scheme were established, the temptations of individual countries to violate it and sell more oil than their allocated quotas would remain strong. In fact, the incentives to "cheat" would increase with the success of the cartel. Moreover, without the companies' vertically integrated structure it would be difficult to detect violations, since secret deals could be made between buyers and sellers of crude. It was for these reasons that Yamani rejected production prorationing.[83]

More important, however, was the radical nationalist alternative to Yamani's participation proposal. Drawing on the experience of Iraq, a small group of radicals urged the exporting countries to nationalize their oil operations. A leading spokesman for this view was Yamani's predecessor as Saudi Arabia's oil minister, Sheikh 'Abd Allah al-Tariki, who in 1968 declared that "the only sound way to fulfill the objectives of the principle of participation . . . would be to nationalize the existing old-style concessions and form new companies to operate these concessions and undertake the exploration of areas where no oil had been found."[84]

In the 1970s, nationalization and participation would contend for support. Rather than genuine alternatives, the threat of nationalization would make participation more likely, as the two strategies tended to converge. Advocates of participation would demand increasingly more, while those who favored nationalization would see the advantages of continued collaboration with the major international oil companies. The result, an alliance that would shake the world, materialized in the 1970s.

2

THE OIL PRICE REVOLUTION

4

The Basis of Oil-Exporting Country Power in the Early 1970s

In the midst of the fourth Arab-Israeli war, the oil-producing countries took control of crude-oil pricing. On October 16, 1973, the Middle East oil-producing countries boosted the price of the oil they exported by a whopping 70 percent. A day later, in retaliation for Western support of Israel, the Arab oil-exporting states, with only Iraq dissenting, decided to cut back production. Within a few days each of the Arab states also imposed an oil embargo against the United States and the Netherlands. In December, though the war had ended, the oil-exporting countries announced a second and far larger price increase. As a result of these actions, the world oil price went from about $2 a barrel on October 1, 1973, to more than $8 on January 1, 1974. Subsequently, the oil-exporting countries not only maintained this high price level but raised it further.

These developments stunned the world. The oil-exporting countries had secured the greatest nonviolent transfer of wealth in human history. After years of quiescence, they had become a powerful force in world politics.

From its inception in the late 1940s and until 1973, the Arab ''oil weapon'' had been ineffectual. Throughout the 1950s the world oil price had been relatively stable; it went from about $1.80 a barrel in 1949 to a high of just over $2 in 1957. Then, from 1957 until 1970, the price declined, reaching a low of about $1.30.[1] In the late 1960s, most of the experts on international oil expected the price to continue to decline (contracts signed at the time demonstrate the expectation of further price declines).[2] Moreover, in the first decade of its existence OPEC had gained a raise of only a few cents a barrel, and in September 1967 the *London Times* had reported that OPEC was deeply divided and might split up.[3]

In the 1970s, in sharp contrast to these expectations, world oil prices began to rise and OPEC established itself as the most successful cartel in history. The annual *Strategic Survey,* published by London's prestigious International Institute for Strategic Studies, said in its review of 1973: ''The successful use of the oil weapon by the Arab states in connection with the Middle East war of October produced the greatest shock, the most potent sense of a new era, of any event of recent years.''[4]

Several broad historical trends combined to make this change possible. As a result of the energy policies of the oil-consuming countries and the investment strategies of the international oil companies, by the 1970s a small number of countries found themselves in control of a resource that was essential for the economies of the advanced countries and for which there was no near- or medium-term alternative. As demand for oil increased, several underdeveloped, sparsely populated countries—Libya, Kuwait, the United Arab Emirates, Qatar, and Saudi Arabia—began to accumulate far more oil revenue than they could absorb domestically, which made them far less dependent upon additional revenues than the oil-consuming countries were on continued supplies. At the same time, the predominance of the United States in world affairs declined. This meant that there was no politically hegemonic power that could shape the international oil system, as the United States had done after World War II.

In this context, rivalries among the oil-consuming countries became rampant, greatly weakening their ability to respond to OPEC gains. Indeed, the exporting countries found that they could exploit the divisions among the consuming countries. In addition, the possibility of direct U.S. military intervention in the Middle East was limited by a growing Soviet presence in the region, by indigenous, radical nationalist movements in the area, and by the failure of U.S. policy in Vietnam. As a result, the United States became militarily and politically dependent upon regional powers, chiefly Saudi Arabia and Iran, and the effect was to increase the bargaining power of these oil-exporting countries.

As U.S. political hegemony declined, so did the control formerly exercised by the major international oil companies, which found themselves increasingly challenged by newcomers. That too increased the bargaining power of the exporting countries, for as the newcomers grew in importance, the exporting countries were able to play the companies off against one another—a reversal of the previous situation. Moreover, in many of the initial confrontations between oil companies and exporting countries, the more vulnerable newcomers were the first to capitulate.

These historical trends were ignited by two political developments: the Libyan revolution in September 1969 and the Arab-Israeli war, four years later. With Qaddafi's coming to power, Libya became the first "rich" radical Arab oil-exporting country. Strategically positioned, Libya was able to take risks that the other radical Arab oil-exporting countries—Iraq and Algeria—could not afford and that the other "rich" Arab exporters—Kuwait, Qatar, the United Arab Emirates, and Saudi Arabia—were disinclined to take because of their alignment with the West. But with Libya leading, others followed. Indeed, the rivalry between conservative and radical oil-exporting countries tended to spur OPEC on, encouraging a leapfrog process in which one group of countries would secure gains, only to be outdone by another group. Finally, the Arab-Israeli war led the conservative Arab oil-exporting countries to cut back production, which led to skyrocketing prices—something the conservative Arab exporting countries never directly sought.

THE NATURE OF THE ENERGY CRISIS: DEPENDENCE ON MIDDLE EAST AND NORTH AFRICAN OIL

Its causes are complex, but the energy crisis of the 1970s was not due to any physical shortage of oil. As the OECD's oil committee concluded in 1972, "World proved reserves of crude oil are more than ample to satisfy projected needs for the foreseeable future."[5]

Since 1970, the proven (discovered) reserves of oil have been more than thirty times consumption levels, and half the world's recoverable reserves has yet to be found. Nor are increases in the cost of producing oil at the root of the problem. According to Adelman's calculations, when oil was selling for more than $10 a barrel, existing fields could have greatly expanded production at a cost of 10–20¢ a barrel in the Persian Gulf, 50¢ in Venezuela, and $1.60 in the North Sea.[6]

The crisis stems from the fact that, in the 1970s, a system of interdependencies that had favored the importers shifted to favor the oil exporters. Throughout the postwar period the advanced capitalist countries had become increasingly dependent upon imported oil for a growing proportion of their energy supplies (see appendix tables A1, A2, and A3); however, until the mid-1960s their vulnerability to a supply cutoff was considerably reduced by substantial spare productive capacity throughout the world, much of it in the United States. At the same time, the economies of the oil-exporting countries were extremely dependent upon their oil revenues, and for the production of their oil they required the technical know-how of the international oil companies. Moreover, the governing regimes in most of these countries depended upon the United States and Great Britain for their stability. Yet, by the early 1970s, each of these dependencies had been altered in fundamental ways.

As tables 4–1, 4–2, and 4–3 show, between 1955 and 1973 Japan's dependence upon oil—virtually all of it imported—increased from 22.9 to 80.4 percent of its total energy consumption. In Western Europe during this period, oil imports increased from 24.4 to 64.5 percent of total energy consumption, and in the United States they increased from 7 to 18.1 percent. Increasingly, this oil came from Iran and a few Arab states in the Middle East and North Africa. Between 1963 and 1973, Western Europe's dependence upon oil imports from this area increased from 32 to 54 percent of its total energy consumption; in Japan, it increased from 44 to 65 percent. Until the 1970s, the United States had relied on this area for only a marginal portion of its energy supplies, but in a clear departure from policy, formulated at the close of World War II (of relying on Western Hemisphere sources for its oil), in the early 1970s the United States also became dependent upon imports from the Middle East and North Africa. Their shares increased from 1.7 percent of United States oil consumption in 1970 to 7 percent in 1973, and seemed destined to shoot way up in the future.

Nor was there any near- or medium-term alternative to this dependence. De-

TABLE 4–1. OIL CONSUMPTION AND OIL IMPORTS AS A SHARE OF U.S. ENERGY CONSUMPTION (PERCENTAGE)

	1955	1960	1965	1970	1973	1975	1978	1979	1980	1981
Oil Consumption	45.5	46.0	44.1	44.6	47.2	43.9	46.7	45.5	42.9	41.1
Oil Imports from										
Western Hemisphere		7.1	8.1	9.0	11.7	8.8	7.2	7.8	6.7	6.5
Western Europe				.7	.8	.1	1.0	.9	1.0	1.4
Middle East		1.7	1.4	.6	2.4	3.3	6.0	5.5	4.2	3.4
North Africa			.2	.2	1.0	1.4	3.3	3.4	2.8	1.8
Other Africa			.1	.2	1.5	2.4	2.6	3.1	2.5	2.0
S.E. Asia & Australasia			.4	.2	.7	1.1	1.4	1.4	1.1	1.1
Communist nations				<.1	.1	<.1	<.1	<.1	—	<.1
Total World	7.0	9.1	10.1	10.9	18.1	17.3	21.5	22.1	18.3	16.3
Imports as % of oil consumption	15.4	19.9	23.0	24.4	38.4	39.3	46.1	48.6	42.6	39.5
From the Middle East as a % of oil imports		18.7	13.9	5.5	13.3	19.1	27.8	24.9	22.9	20.9
From the Middle East & North Africa as a % of oil imports			15.8	7.3	18.8	27.2	43.1	40.4	38.0	32.0

Figures on total energy consumption for 1955, 1960, and 1965 are from Darmstadter, *Energy in the World Economy*, table 11. All other figures are from BP, *Statistical Review of the World Oil Industry* (various issues). Conversions into comparable units and percentages were made by the author. Reexports and changes in stocks make it possible for total imports to exceed total consumption.

TABLE 4–2. OIL CONSUMPTION AND OIL IMPORTS AS A SHARE OF WEST EUROPEAN ENERGY CONSUMPTION (PERCENTAGE)

	1955	1960	1965	1970	1973	1975	1978	1979	1980	1981
Oil Consumption	23.4	36.1	51.3	61.2	63.9	56.0	57.7	54.8	53.2	50.7
Oil Imports from										
Western Hemisphere		5.8	6.2	2.9	1.9	1.9	1.8	1.5	3.2	4.2
Middle East		23.9	27.9	30.1	43.9	36.8	34.6	32.5	28.2	23.3
North Africa			11.2	21.5	10.3	6.4	6.8	6.7	5.5	5.4
Other Africa		2.0*	2.1	4.3	4.3	3.5	3.1	3.8	3.8	2.6
S.E. Asia & Australasia		.4	.2	<.1	<.1	<.1	<.1	<.1	.1	.2
Communist nations		3.1	3.9	3.8	4.2	4.1	5.8	4.2	5.0	5.6
Total World	24.4	35.0	51.5	62.7	64.5	52.7	52.3	48.8	45.9	41.4
Imports as % of oil consumption	104.3	97.0	100.5	102.5	101.1	94.2	90.7	89.1	86.3	81.6
From the Middle East as a % of oil imports		68.3	54.2	48.0	68.1	69.8	66.2	66.5	61.5	46.0
From the Middle East & North Africa as a % of oil imports		74.0	75.9	82.3	84.0	81.9	79.3	80.3	73.6	56.7

*Includes all Africa.

Ibid. (table 4–1).

TABLE 4–3. OIL CONSUMPTION AND OIL IMPORTS AS A SHARE OF JAPANESE ENERGY CONSUMPTION (PERCENTAGE)

	1955	1960	1963	1965	1970	1973	1975	1978	1979	1980	1981
Oil Consumption	22.9	42.6	59.4	71.9	74.1	80.4	70.3	72.2	69.7	66.5	63.4
Oil Imports from											
Western Hemi-sphere			5.4	3.0	1.8	.7	.7	.6	.6	1.2	2.8
Middle East			44.3	58.6	64.1	65.0	53.5	54.5	53.9	48.6	41.9
North Africa					.7	.3	1.0	.1	.2	.7	1.0
Other Africa					.2	1.6	1.0	—	—	.2	.3
S.E. Asia & Australasia			6.3	5.3	11.1	16.5	13.4	14.8	15.6	14.6	13.5
Communist nations			3.2	3.4	.3	.8	2.3	2.1	2.1	2.5	2.7
Total World			59.4	70.7	78.2	85.4	71.9	72.2	72.4	67.9	62.2
Imports as % of oil consumption			99.6	98.3	105.5	106.2	102.3	100.0	103.8	102.0	98.1
From the Middle East as a % of oil imports			74.6	82.9	82.0	76.1	74.4	75.4	74.5	71.6	66.1
From the Middle East & North Africa as a % of oil imports			74.6	82.9	82.9	76.5	75.8	75.6	74.7	72.7	67.6

Ibid. (table 4–1).

veloping oil and natural gas resources in new areas, building additional nuclear capacity, restoring a moribund coal industry, pushing ahead with development of new energy sources, or substantially boosting the efficiency with which the economy uses energy, would each take several years.[7] Moreover, the cost of most of these measures was likely to be considerably higher than the 1970 cost of imported oil, and the cost of alternatives that could substitute directly for oil (i.e. synthetic fuels) was greater than either the pre- or post-1973 cost of imported oil.[8] Consequently, as James E. Akins, head of the State Department's Office of Fuels and Energy, told the American Petroleum Institute in April 1973: "In the short run—that is, in the next ten to twenty years—it is unlikely that any alternative source of energy will be available in sufficient quantities to preclude substantial increases in hydrocarbon prices." He indicated that the upper limit would be set by the consumer's willingness to pay.[9]

It was clear that, as a result of this dependence, consumers would be willing to pay considerably more for petroleum than the oil-exporting countries received. Indeed, because of consumer-country taxes, in the 1960s the price that consumers paid for imported oil was already based (to a considerable extent) on the price of higher-cost alternatives, and OPEC had long objected that the greatest part of the consumer's expenditure (47.5% in 1969) consisted of taxes levied by the consuming-country governments. In contrast, the revenue of the producing countries accounted for only 7.9 percent of the final selling price of a barrel of petroleum products.[10] Consequently, the producing government's take could almost double if prices to the consumer went up only 15 percent. Nor would this have much impact on demand, for a 100 percent increase in price would reduce demand by no more than 50 percent, and probably by a lot less.[11] While the demand for oil was not very sensitive to changes in price, the demand for energy was very responsive to economic growth in the consuming countries. Estimates were that in the developed countries a 10 percent increase in GNP would typically be accompanied by a 9 percent increase in energy requirements.[12]

The growing dependence upon imported oil, the lack of immediately available alternatives,[13] the inelasticity of demand for oil, and the strong relationship between economic growth and demand for energy helped lay the groundwork for a rise in oil prices. Yet each of these factors had prevailed during a decade in which oil prices actually fell and the oil-exporting countries were able to increase their take by only a few cents per barrel. The reason for this was that the oil-exporting countries were as dependent upon their oil revenues as the importing countries were upon their crude supplies. With the exception of Kuwait, the major exporting countries were characterized by low levels of per capita income and limited foreign currency reserves. Consequently, most of them sought to maximize revenues by maximizing oil production.

As we have seen, the only exporters that were not "production maximizers" were Venezuela, which raised per barrel taxes and accepted the consequent decline in its production levels, and Iraq, whose production growth was limited as a result of its expropriation of the area left undeveloped by the IPC. But the amount of oil taken off the world market as a result of these actions did not eliminate the surplus that characterized the world market until the 1970s. Consequently, the international oil companies were able to resist demands from the oil-exporting countries by playing them off against one another.

Substantial levels of spare productive capacity tended to strengthen the consumers' bargaining position. Estimates are that in 1960 the productive capacity of the non-Communist world exceeded its consumption by 40–50 percent.[14] In this context, if any oil-exporting country sought to pressure the companies by cutting back on production, consumers could turn to alternative sources for supplies. Of course, if several major oil-exporting countries got together and restricted supplies, they had the potential to create major problems for the consuming countries, but the oil-exporting countries had been unable to do this because most of them lacked the ability to forgo immediate revenues. And despite the existence of OPEC, they had little cohesion. Their efforts to allocate production shares—in 1965, 1966, and 1968—had all broken down.

The exporting countries' problems were compounded by the fact that, until the mid-1960s, most of the world's spare capacity was in the United States. In 1956, the year of the Suez Canal crisis, the United States had enough spare capacity to replace two-thirds of the oil exported from the Middle East. Until 1966, only Venezuela could shut off more production than the United States could replace.

In the unlikely event that several producers could agree on a concerted plan of action, they would have to be willing to accept substantial reductions in their export levels to pressure the West (see table 4–4).

From the mid-1950s until the mid-1960s, dependence upon Middle East and North African oil increased, but the level of U.S. spare capacity remained essentially constant, increasing the West's vulnerability to a production cutback. In 1966, for the first time, there were Middle East countries—Kuwait and Saudi Arabia—whose exports exceeded the level of U.S. spare capacity.[15] Then, in the mid-1960s, as dependence upon Middle East and North African oil continued to increase, the level of U.S. spare capacity began to decline sharply. In 1968 the State Department informed foreign governments that U.S. oil production would soon reach its limits.

The failure to expand spare capacity as imports grew is not difficult to fathom. No profit-maximizing company would make substantial investments in new productive capacity with the intent of holding it idle against the contingency of a major production cutback. Nor would any oil-producing country permit the bulk of its productive capacity to go unused. The U.S. government might have maintained spare capacity, but the opposition to direct government involvement in the

TABLE 4–4. U.S. SPARE CAPACITY IN RELATION TO OIL-EXPORTING COUNTRIES' EXPORTS, 1956–73 (TB/D)

	1956	1960	1967	1970	1973
U.S. Spare Capacity	2,080	2,709	2,122	1,331	—
U.S. Spare Capacity as a % of					
Middle East Oil Exports	66.0	57.8	23.2	10.5	—
Middle East & North African oil exports		55.0*	18.3	7.7	—
Arab oil exports			21.7	9.1	
Oil Exports from					
Iran			2,356	3,581	5,425
Iraq			1,163	1,493	1,934
Kuwait			2,256	2,728	2,813
Saudi Arabia			2,461	3,400	7,093
Libya			1,718	3,307	2,173
Venezuela			3,361	3,470	3,198
Arab countries			9,781	14,549	18,224
Middle East	3,152	4,690	9.145	12.715	19,970
North Africa		237*	2,460	4,665	3,420
Middle East & North Africa		4,927	11,605	17,380	23,390

*Includes all Africa.

The figures on spare capacity were furnished to the author by the Independent Petroleum Assn. of America; the figures on Middle East and North African exports are from BP, *Statistical Review of the World Oil Industry* (various issues). Figures on exports by country and on Arab oil exports are from U.S. Bureau of Mines, *International Petroleum Annual* (various issues), but include reexports and are not strictly comparable with the figures from BP. Percentages were computed by the author.

The figures on spare capacity are rough approximations and probably overstate the aid the U.S. could provide in periods of crisis, because well owners had a tendency to exaggerate the aid they could provide and because of problems likely to arise in transporting oil over new routes.

industry tended to work against this. Indeed, at the close of World War II Secretary Ickes had proposed that the Petroleum Reserves Corporation hold a security reserve, but his plans were shot down as a result of oil industry opposition. In 1957 a cabinet-level committee on oil imports considered an increased government role "in exploring for oil reserves which, when discovered, would not be put into production," but the committee rejected it because "such a course would be costly to an already overburdened government and would be contrary to the principles of free enterprise which characterize American industry."[16]

What was peculiar was that spare capacity had been maintained at such high levels in the United States. Rather than a deliberate policy, this was an unintended consequence of the means of protecting domestic oil interests—the prorationing system. As explained earlier, under the prorationing system various state regulatory agencies limited production, in order to maintain the domestic price of oil, thereby forcing private producers to do what they would never do on their own: systematically maintain high levels of expensive, secure, spare productive capacity. However, in the mid-1960s several contradictions inherent in U.S. energy policy began to manifest themselves. As a result of price controls, which kept the price of natural gas almost constant throughout the 1960s, its supply failed to keep pace with demand.[17] The growth of nuclear power lagged behind expectations, and a burgeoning environmental movement challenged the unrestrained use of coal, forcing utilities to convert from coal to oil.[18]

The net effect of these developments was to increase demand for oil, but after 1967, U.S. productive capacity began to decline, for the prospects of expanding capacity in the continental United States were very limited. The environmental movement had delayed both the Alaskan pipeline project and the leasing of federal offshore areas, and following the Union Oil spill in 1969, a ban was placed on drilling in the Santa Barbara Channel, one of the few growth areas left in the United States. In a desperate effort to meet demand, the "allowable" production levels were raised on U.S. capacity and spare capacity began to fall precipitously. By 1970 the oil exports from each of five countries—Iran, Kuwait, Libya, Venezuela, and Saudi Arabia—were more than twice the level of spare capacity in the United States. At a confidential briefing of the OECD's Energy Committee in January 1970, the U.S. delegate warned the Europeans that if serious supply difficulties developed, they could no longer count on U.S. help.

In March 1971, Texas allowables reached the 100 percent level for the first time since 1948. In response, Byron Tunnel, chairman of the Texas Railroad Commission, declared that "we feel this to be an historic occasion. Damned historic, and a sad one. Texas oil fields have been like a reliable old warrior that could rise to the task when needed. That old warrior can't rise anymore."[19] By 1973 the United States had no spare capacity.

Elsewhere in the Western Hemisphere the situation was similar. During the short-lived Arab oil embargo of 1967, both Canada and Venezuela had increased their oil exports. At that time, Alberta, which supplies most of Canada's oil, was estimated to have roughly 1.5 mb/d in spare capacity, and Venezuela had another 500,000 b/d. However, largely as a result of the oil companies' strategy of disinvestment, by 1970 spare capacity in Venezuela was virtually exhausted, and as a result of U.S. price controls and uncertainty over U.S. import policy, exploration in Alberta had been inhibited. Consequently, by December 1972 Alberta had no spare capacity either.[20] These developments greatly increased the West's vulnerability to production cutbacks, for, by the early 1970s, even a partial cutback in a single oil-exporting country could cause serious problems.

In retrospect, the significance of the decline in spare capacity may seem apparent, but during the 1960s few people expressed concern about it. For domestic producers, it was far cheaper to meet increasing demand from existing capacity than to develop additional capacity. And U.S. policy makers were misled by their own dissimulation, for while the official explanation for the oil import quotas was "national security," everyone knew that, in reality, the program was to protect domestic producers. Thus, the real security problem—the maintenance of spare capacity to counter possible production cutbacks in the oil-exporting countries—was neglected.

Similarly, because of their perceptions of their security problem, the countries of Western Europe and Japan had failed to protect themselves against a major supply disruption. Rather than a concerted shutdown by the oil-exporting countries, the concern in the principal consuming countries was loss of a single country's exports and the possibility that, in times of crisis, the major oil companies would favor their home countries at the expense of others. Diversified supply sources and the creation of national oil companies were seen as the appropriate response to these problems.

In practice, this strategy failed to protect the security of these countries' oil supplies. The development of North Africa in the 1960s enabled Western Europe to reduce its oil imports from the Middle East (see table 4–2), but the political ties between the countries in North Africa and those in the Middle East greatly reduced the practical significance of this diversification. And because they lacked the majors' range of oil sources, the national oil companies, like the U.S. independents, proved to be much more vulnerable to producer-government pressure. Nor were they able to give special aid to their home countries during the Arab oil embargo. When U.S. spare capacity disappeared, Western Europe and Japan lost their only security against loss of supplies from a single oil-exporting country.

Despite the rise in allowables, in 1970 U.S. oil production began to decline. Consequently imports, which between 1960 and 1970 had increased from 20 to 24 percent of U.S. oil consumption, shot to 38 percent in 1973. In absolute terms, between 1970 and 1973 U.S. oil imports increased from 3.4 to 6.2 mb/d, equivalent to 32 percent of the increase in world oil imports during this period. In 1970 the United States imported only 250,000 b/d from North Africa and the Middle East; by 1973 it received 1.18 mb/d from those areas.[21]

This increase in U.S. imports was far greater than had been expected. In

February 1970, President Nixon's Task Force on Oil Imports, relying on information from the oil industry and the federal government, predicted that as late as 1980 the U.S. would import only 5 mb/d. The main reasons for this underestimation were the task force's acceptance of oil industry estimates of domestic producing capacity and its failure to take adequate account of the impact the decline in natural gas supplies would have on oil consumption. The task force split, but its majority report recommended that the oil import quotas be abolished and replaced with a high but gradually declining tariff that would favor Western Hemisphere oil. It also urged that dependence upon Eastern Hemisphere oil be limited to 10 percent of U.S. oil consumption—a level that was exceeded by 1972.[22]

Both domestic and multinational oil companies objected to abolition of the oil import quotas,[23] which they feared would reduce domestic prices and force many high-cost U.S. wells to shut down. Concern was also expressed about the foreign-policy implications of a differential tariff, for countries subject to higher tariffs were bound to protest. And with the political situation in the Middle East deteriorating, many questioned the wisdom of increased reliance on oil from that area.

Several months after the report was submitted,it became clear that it had underestimated both future U.S. oil consumption and U.S. oil import needs. Then, by the summer of 1970, the rise in transport costs had pushed the landed price of Middle East oil on the U.S. East Coast above the price of U.S. oil from the Gulf of Mexico—a reversal of the traditional situation in which Middle East oil sold for $1.40 to $1.50 less than domestically produced oil. Consequently, Nixon rejected the proposed tariff scheme and appointed another committee to study the matter, but in the absence of an alternative energy policy, the government simply raised oil import quotas to meet the pressure of growing demand, and finally abolished them in April 1973.

Despite growing imports, the United States might have avoided increased dependence upon Middle East and North African oil, for Venezuela was anxious to supply the U.S. market and the cabinet task force had recommended that it receive preferential treatment under the proposed tariff system. Yet the multinational oil companies, which had a stake in the Middle East and were involved in conflicts with the Venezuelan government, opposed any Venezuelan preference; and many U.S. foreign-policy officials feared that a Venezuelan preference would worsen U.S. relations with the Middle East oil-exporting countries. Consequently, after the Venezuelans increased oil company taxes in December 1970, U.S. officials informed them that, as a result, their hopes of gaining special preference for their oil were "fruitless." In 1971, after Venezuela passed a hydrocarbon reversion law, giving the government control of all its oil fields as soon as concessions expired (in the 1980s), the United States let it be known that it would look to Canada, rather than Venezuela, to meet its petroleum needs. With its access to the U.S. market still restricted, Venezuela's oil production declined from 3,760 tb/d in 1970 to 3,460 tb/d in 1973.[24]

Similarly, development of Canada's oil and natural gas resources was inhibited by U.S. price controls and the uncertainty surrounding U.S. import policy. Consequently, by the early 1970s Canada's export capability was considerably reduced, and growing resentment, toward the U.S. companies that dominate the Canadian oil industry and the United States in general, led Canada to assume a more nationalistic stance in the 1970s. In the early 1970s, Canada decided to conserve its petroleum supplies for Canadian needs, and in 1973 the Canadian government told the United States not to assume the availability of Canadian petroleum in the future. To meet its growing demand for oil, the United States was forced to turn increasingly to the Eastern Hemisphere, a development that U.S. policy toward Canada and Venezuela had encouraged.

The problems created by the widespread failure among forecasters to anticipate the full growth in U.S. imports were compounded by the almost unprecedented concurrence of high growth rates in all the advanced countries between 1971 and 1973. Demand for energy exceeded the levels that both industry and nonindustry sources had predicted,[25] and because other energy sources failed to expand as rapidly as expected, the gap between the projections and the demand for oil was greater than it was for total energy consumption.[26] This combination of largely unexpected factors brought demand in the world oil market closer to the limits of immediately available supply than it had ever been.

By the end of 1972, only the countries in the Middle East—particularly Saudi Arabia—had the ability to substantially expand production in the immediate future. Therefore, with demand increasing, concern began to grow about an oil shortage in the 1980s, resulting from either lack of productive capacity or refusal by Middle East countries to produce enough. As a result, the bargaining leverage of the oil-exporting countries increased. In the early 1970s it was not simply the control of the majors that kept prices up, but the tightness in the world oil market.

CONSUMING-COUNTRY DISUNITY AND COMPETITION IN THE INTERNATIONAL OIL INDUSTRY

In the 1970s, the oil-exporting countries continued to exploit the rivalries among the consuming countries and the international oil companies. Indeed, these rivalries tended to increase as a more multipolar world produced a more heterogeneous oil industry.

Historically, the power of the major oil companies vis-à-vis the oil-exporting countries stemmed from several factors. In response to pressure from any oil-exporting country or group of countries, the majors would increase production elsewhere. Their control of capital, markets, and technology added to their bargaining power, and they benefited from the political and legal support they received from their home governments. However, by the 1970s the power the majors derived from each of these factors was considerably eroded. We have seen how the ability to shift production was limited as a result of growing dependence upon Middle East and North African oil and the decline in spare capacity, and the rise of the newcomers meant that other companies were anxious to provide the oil-exporting countries with capital, market outlets, and technology. As table 4–5 shows, since 1953 the share of the seven largest companies declined in every phase of the world oil industry.

France and Italy had long been suitors of the oil-exporting countries, and in the late 1960s this role was also assumed by two economic giants, West Germany and Japan. Apart from its development of the Neutral Zone (where oil was discovered in 1959), Japan had taken little interest in foreign oil ventures, apparently content to rely on the majors for its imports, but in 1967 this policy was altered when a report to the minister of International Trade and Industry (MITI) declared that Japan should seek to obtain 30 percent of its oil from Japanese firms or firms with a major Japanese interest. Thus in October 1967 the Petroleum Development Public Corporation was created to provide financial assistance to Japanese companies engaged in overseas exploration and production. Largely as a result of this, between 1967 and 1973 Japanese expenditures on overseas exploration and development increased by more than a factor of ten. Despite these efforts, the Japanese had only limited success, but they made their desire to secure foreign oil evident to the oil-exporting countries.[27]

Similarly, until the late 1960s West Germany had relied on the international majors for its oil supplies, showing little interest in either a national oil company or the problems of supply security. But in 1969 the West German government began providing subsidies to Deminex, a joint oil exploration and development enterprise (begun by eight German-owned oil companies) for overseas operations. The government supplied three quarters of Deminex's first five-year fund (1969–74). In the winter of 1969–70, Germany sought a 5 percent participation share for Deminex in the Iranian Consortium, but its bid was rejected by the international oil companies, which feared the precedent that this would establish. Nonetheless, Deminex's move made it clear that, like Japan, West Germany was attempting to secure a substantial foreign crude base under the control of German

TABLE 4–5. CHANGES IN WORLD OIL INDUSTRY CONCENTRATION BY SECTOR (FIGURES EXCLUDE U.S. AND COMMUNIST COUNTRIES)

	1953		1962		1972	
	7 Largest	Others	7 Largest	Others	7 Largest	Others
Concession areas	64%	36%	33%	67%	24%	76%
Proven reserves	92	8	79	21	67	33
Production	87	13	74	26	71	29
Refining capacity	73	27	59	41	49	51
Tanker capacity	29	71	23	77	19	81
Product marketing	72	28	59	41	54	46

Figures for 1953 and 1972 are from Jacoby, *Multinational Oil*, p. 211; figures for 1962 are from *MNC Hearings*, part 7, p. 353.

nationals. In 1970, the German cabinet urged Deminex to establish bonds with the Arab oil-producing governments, presumably on a Deminex-to-government basis.

With other companies anxious to increase their shares of the lucrative Middle East and North African oil fields, which the world had grown dependent upon for its energy supplies, the principal concern of the companies with well-established concessions was to maintain their privileged access to the oil-exporting countries' reserves. To do this, companies were willing to give the exporting countries better terms. Indeed, higher tax-paid costs, which could be passed on to consumers, were of much less concern to the established companies than either the threat that they would be displaced by other companies or that their competitors in other concessions would gain a significant market advantage as a result of access to crude on more favorable terms than they themselves received. Yet the majors retained substantial bargaining power. They still controlled a preponderant share of every phase of the industry. Their control of enormous amounts of capital would continue to play a major role in determining where resource development would occur. And because of the worldwide scope of their operations, they could take risks in various countries that other companies could not afford.

The majors also had an assemblage of technological skills that could not easily be replaced and that the oil-exporting countries depended upon for the exploration and development of their reserves. The majors also had the most reliable data on costs, reserves, and opportunities in the industry—the information needed for decisions about investments. Finally, because of their interlocked network, logistical skills, and vertically integrated structure, the majors were able to coordinate production and market sales, reducing the likelihood that crude surpluses would materialize and threaten the price level. As Yamani clearly recognized, without the majors the control of supply would be severely impaired, and would threaten the price level, to the detriment of the oil-exporting countries.

In comparison with the majors, the newcomers were far more vulnerable to producing-government pressure. While the tightness of the world market made it increasingly difficult for the majors to shift production from one exporting country to another, the majors could still do this to some extent, and they could still choose among countries in their allocation of investment funds and production growth. The newcomers, with holdings in only one country, were unable to do this. Since they lacked the multiple-country concessions of the majors, they were less concerned about how developments in a single country would affect developments elsewhere. Indeed, they had much less interest in preserving the concession system. Consequently, it is hardly surprising that between 1970 and 1973 the independents were usually the first to be singled out and the first to capitulate to producer-government demands.

Like the oil companies, the consuming countries were deeply divided; each country was more concerned about maintaining its supply of oil than about the price it paid for it. In the past, the United States provided leadership for these countries, but Europe and Japan were now increasingly hesitant to be associated with the United States. This was the result of an economic independence that came with increasing economic strength and reluctance to work with the United States for fear of being identified with U.S. support for Israel.

With their nationals still in control of the seven largest international oil companies, the United States, Great Britain, and the Netherlands tended to be much more supportive of the majors than were Japan or the other European countries. In fact, the latter saw little reason to risk their oil supplies by supporting companies in which their nationals had no stake; and France went one step further. Still resentful about its exclusion from Aramco, France attempted to turn Arab resentment of the United States, for its support of Israel, to its advantage. Following the 1967 Arab-Israeli war, France, which had been a leading supporter of Israel, sought a rapprochement with the Arab world. It pushed for direct arrangements between the oil-exporting countries and the European countries, hoping to reduce the role of the Anglo-American majors.

For its part, the United States, or certain factions within it, saw the maintenance of low world oil prices as contrary to their interests. Low oil prices strengthened European and Japanese exports in international markets and impeded U.S. efforts to regain self-sufficiency in energy supplies. Moreover, the suspicion—widespread in Europe and Japan—that the United States was secretly in favor of high oil prices tended to work against efforts at international cooperation.

In the absence of unity, the oil companies and the consuming countries were vulnerable to two dangers: being picked off one by one and bidding against one another in periods of scarcity. And because the countries were widely distrusted and consumers were primarily interested in the supply of crude oil, not its price, the companies could expect little support if they attempted to resist oil-exporting-country demands for a price increase and, therefore, a supply shortage resulted.

The position of the oil-consuming countries was also weakened by their neglect of energy issues. Largely because oil was readily available at low prices, energy policy was not a high priority in any consuming country until the early 1970s. Aside from France, none of the governments of the major oil-consuming countries had systematically considered energy options. No country had formulated a comprehensive energy plan that resolved such issues as the proper energy mix, environmental issues, energy pricing, etc. As a political issue of secondary importance, oil policy did not receive much scrutiny from either top policy makers or the public. It was often subordinated to issues of more pressing concern.

THE SHIFTING CHARACTER OF OIL-EXPORTING COUNTRY DEPENDENCE

The disunity of the consuming countries, their dependence upon imported oil, and their lack of emergency preparedness left them extremely vulnerable to a cutback in oil supplies from the exporting countries. Moreover, cutting off the flow of petroleum is relatively simple: companies can be ordered to halt production; pipelines can be severed; the channels that the supertankers pass through can be mined or blocked—the entrance to the Gulf, the Strait of Hormuz, is only 26 miles wide; and oil fields can be sabotaged. The ease with which these things can be done gave the exporting countries considerable protection against military intervention by the consuming countries ''to protect their interests.''

In response to military intervention, an oil-exporting country would be likely to destroy its oil fields. After several months, production might be restored, but in an already tight market, the intervening period might prove catastrophic to the consuming countries. Moreover, to remain in control, an invading power would have to commit itself to permanent occupation—a blatant violation of national security that would poison relations with other Third World countries. After the U.S. experience in Vietnam, it would probably result in substantial domestic opposition as well; and it would risk a Soviet response. Even if these obstacles could be overcome, success would not be ensured: the dangers of guerrilla activity and sabotage would persist.

Consequently, the consuming countries had to maintain regimes in the exporting countries that were friendly to the West, that had an interest in ever higher levels of oil production, and that could prevent their opponents from interfering with the flow of petroleum. Fortunately for the West, until the 1970s the exporting countries were as dependent upon their oil revenues as the consuming countries were upon their crude supplies. Although the exporting countries espoused common goals, in practice they remained divided and were unable to restrict production, their principal bargaining weapon. In 1965, in an effort to support the world price, OPEC adopted a plan for restricting production, allocating production shares among its member governments. However, Saudi Arabia, Libya, and Iran exceeded their allotments, bringing OPEC's first effort at production programming to an abrupt halt. Similar efforts failed in 1966 and 1968.

The basic problem was that effective production programming required production quotas for member countries and mechanisms to enforce decisions and impose sanctions for noncompliance. Yet, with each OPEC country seeking to maximize its oil reveneus, few countries were willing to accept limitations on their production, and OPEC, as an organization, lacked the means of operating a cartel and the authority to compel member nations to adhere to group decisions. The lack of cohesion among the oil-exporting countries was demonstrated by their failure to aid Iraq in its dispute with IPC during the 1960s. Rather than aid a member country, Iraq's neighbors preferred to see their own revenues increase as the companies shifted production away from Iraq. Similarly, when the Arab exporting countries embargoed oil during the Arab-Israeli war of June 1967, Iran, Venezuela, and Indonesia increased their exports. Saudi Arabia, unwilling to accept a continuing loss of revenue, took the lead in arguing for quick termination of the embargo. Indeed, the conservative exporting states—Libya, Kuwait, and Saudi Arabia—had shut down less out of solidarity with the states that were fighting Israel than out of fear of reprisals by indigenous radicals and labor unions.

The Arab radicals—Iraq, Syria, Algeria—proposed a total, three-month ban on oil shipments, to be followed by selective exports to friendly countries, but about a week after the embargo began, individual countries resumed production without consulting one another. By the end of June, Arab oil operations were 50 percent of normal. The last countries to resume production were Iraq and Libya, where a strike by oil workers had prevented the government from resuming oil operations.[28]

The Arabs maintained an embargo against shipments to the United States, Great Britain, and West Germany, but this had little effect. The United States was not very dependent upon Arab oil at the time, and spare capacity made it possible to increase domestic production by about a million barrels per day between May and August. Great Britain and West Germany made up their losses by turning to alternative sources (including the U.S.). Inasmuch as the Arabs did not impose overall cutbacks on production, it is likely that Arab oil either found its way into Great Britain and West Germany or enabled the oil companies to shift non-Arab oil to these countries, replacing it with Arab oil in its usual markets.

Following the war, the radical Arab oil-exporting countries, Algeria and Iraq, and the radical "confrontation states," Egypt and Syria, continued to urge that strong measures be taken against the oil-consuming countries. In opposition, Saudi Arabia argued that the Arabs themselves had been the main victims of the embargo. Yamani declared that the embargo "hurt the Arabs themselves more than anyone else and the only ones to gain any benefit from it were the non-Arab [oil] producers." He proposed that oil production be resumed, with some of the revenue used to aid the Arab cause.[29] In this conflict between radicals and conservatives, the Saudi view prevailed, for, as a result of the June defeat, the confrontation states had grown dependent upon financial backing from the conservative oil-exporting countries. Consequently, at the Khartoum Arab summit in August–September 1967, a rapprochement was reached between Egypt and Saudi Arabia. The two countries agreed to end their intervention in the Yemen civil war, removing the major conflict between them, and Egypt went along with a Saudi demand for the formal lifting of the Arab oil embargo. The conference stipulated that "nothing should be done to impair the financial capability of the Arab oil-producing states to back the unified Arab effort; and that the responsibility for deciding on appropriate measures should be left to the producing countries themselves." As part of these agreements, Saudi Arabia, Kuwait, and Libya agreed to provide a $378 million annual subsidy, two-thirds of which would go to Egypt and the remainder to Jordan.[30]

Following the June war, there was considerable discussion of starting an organization to coordinate the use of oil as a weapon in Arab strategy. This alarmed the conservative oil-exporting countries, which became concerned that they would be pressured into cutting back oil supplies. To preempt this, Saudi Arabia, Kuwait, and Libya formed the Organization of Arab Petroleum Exporting Countries (OAPEC) in January 1968. The requirements for membership excluded Egypt and Algeria, as well as all Arab countries that were not oil producers (or only minor exporters), and while Iraq was invited to join OAPEC, it declined because of the conservative character of the organization. As oil historian Benjamin Shwadran explained, at the time of its founding OAPEC "had all the earmarks of an effort on the one hand to protect its members from non-producing Arab countries, and on the other hand guarantee the western companies not only the uninterrupted flow of the oil but also the protection of the necessary investments for the development of the industry."[31] In response to the creation of OAPEC, on February 1, 1968, the radical Arab oil-exporting countries, Iraq and Algeria, signed an agreement pledging to promote cooperation against the major international oil companies and to coordinate the policies of their national oil companies.

There were two basic reasons for the reluctance of the conservative exporting countries to cut back oil production. One was their dependence upon oil revenues, the other was that the regimes in these countries were dependent upon the United States and Great Britain for their political and military security. Yet, by the 1970s, both of these factors had changed. Because of the rapid increase in world oil demand and the targeting of this demand on a few countries, Kuwait, Libya, Qatar, the United Arab Emirates, and Saudi Arabia accumulated international currency reserves that were quite high in relation to their imports (see table 4–6). This would enable them to hold back oil production for a fairly long

TABLE 4–6. FOREIGN-EXCHANGE RESERVES, RATIO OF RESERVES TO IMPORTS, AND OIL AS A PERCENTAGE OF EXPORTS FOR OPEC COUNTRIES, 1966–73

	Foreign-Exchange Reserves (Millions of U.S. Dollars)			Ratio of Reserves to Imports			Oil as a % of Exports
	Dec. 1966	Dec. 1970	Sept. 1973	Dec. 1966	Dec. 1970	Sept. 1973	1970
Iran	268	208	984	.29	.13	.29	88.6
Iraq	325	462	1,230	.66	.91	1.37	93.7
Kuwait	932	1,173	3,210*	2.01	1.88	3.08*	95.5
Saudi Arabia	748	662	4,080	1.26	.96	2.05	96.8
Libya	339	1,590	2,435	.79	2.87	1.41	99.7
Algeria		339	527		.27	.23	66.0
Venezuela	777	1,021	1,660	.53	.51	.59	90.3
Ecuador	61	83	181	.35	.30	.34	20.3[†]
Indonesia		160	917[‡]		.16	.39[‡]	38.5
Nigeria	226	224	446	.36	.21	.24	57.5

*First quarter 1973; [†]1972; [‡]third quarter 1973.

Figures on foreign-exchange reserves and imports are from International Monetary Fund, *International Financial Statistics, December 1973*, p. 19, and *December 1974*, p. 39. All figures refer to the end of the period (i.e. Dec. 31, 1966). Figures on government reserves for Kuwait are from the country table and include all government reserve assets, not just those held by the central bank. Figures on Indonesian and Algerian reserves are from the Dec. 1975 issue, as are figures on 1973 Saudi imports. Figures on oil as a percentage of total exports are from OPEC, *Annual Statistical Bulletin, 1973*, table 4, pp. 3–5. Ratios were computed by the author. Figures on the reserve holdings of Abu Dhabi, Qatar, and Gabon were not available. Imports are annual.

period.[32] And as we have seen, because of the growing tightness in the world oil market, by the 1970s Kuwait, Libya, and Saudi Arabia each had the ability to cause a serious supply disruption.

These countries were able to accumulate large currency reserves because they had very small populations and extremely underdeveloped economies, whose abilities to absorb revenue were quite limited. Indeed, in the topsy-turvy world of international oil, backwardness became a source of bargaining strength. In a developed economy, an increase in revenue in the oil sector stimulates growth in the other sectors, but in these Arab kingdoms the oil sector had been isolated from the rest of the economy. It provided enough revenue to meet the needs of the ruling groups, but they were not under pressure to develop the domestic economy. In Saudi Arabia in the 1960s, half the population was still engaged in agriculture and pasturing.

The international oil industry had taken far more capital out of these countries (through repatriation of profits) than it had put in in new investments. Very little industrialization had taken place in any of these societies; the bulk of the populations was unskilled; and the distribution of income was highly unequal. As a result, the internal market remained quite limited and was oriented toward luxury rather than consumer goods. Consequently, there were few domestic outlets for absorption of capital, and a substantial portion of the dominant groups in these societies opposed industrialization and the accumulation of additional wealth because they saw this as disruptive of the traditional social patterns they sought to preserve.

Moreover, foreign investment was discouraged by the Arabs' lack of entrepreneurial skills, the hostility they faced in the West, and the high rates of inflation worldwide, which devalued foreign assets. Just as the international monetary system (created at Bretton Woods) facilitated the growth of the international oil system, its breakdown undermined the stability of the world oil system. Monetary instability in the developed world and the consequent devaluation of major international currencies discouraged the Arab exporters from expanding oil production simply to accumulate additional currency reserves. Indeed, as holders of foreign exchange, many rich OPEC countries were badly hurt by devaluation of the dollar.

Economists in the advanced countries frequently dispute it, but in the exporting countries the view became prevalent that "oil in the ground is worth more than money in the bank." As Akins stated:

From an economic standpoint an increase in present income should be vastly more useful than the discounted value of income deferred for 10–20 years—and that with other energy sources in prospect oil may not even command high prices in such future periods. To Arab countries, such arguments are simply not persuasive. In the personal experience of their leaders, past income has been wasted and even current income is not invested profitably. Moreover, just about every top official in OPEC, starting with Perez Alfonso in Venezuela 20 years ago and including Zaki Yamani of Saudi Arabia today, is convinced that his country can sell its oil profitably in ten or 100 years as a raw material (primarily for petrochemicals) if not as a fuel.[33]

Finally, because oil is not labor intensive, it was possible to cut back production without displacing many workers. For example, in Saudi Arabia oil provided over 50 percent of the GNP but accounted for only 1 percent of the labor force.[34] The effect of these factors was to leave the oil-consuming countries far more dependent upon increasing oil supplies than these "rich," underdeveloped, oil-exporting countries were on increasing oil revenues.

At least as important to the governments of the oil-exporting countries as utilization of their oil wealth was their concern with political security. Since World War II, they had depended upon the United States and Great Britain for that security. We have seen the role the United States played in consolidation of the Saudi regime and restoration of the Shah in 1953. The United States also aided in building up the Saudi armed forces, and in 1963 a U.S. combat force was assigned to Saudi Arabia during the Yemen civil war. In Iran, the United States helped establish the State Organization for Intelligence and Security (SAVAK) and provided nearly $1.5 billion of military assistance between 1946 and 1967.[35] Following Iraq's defection from the Baghdad Pact, in 1959 the United States concluded mutual security agreements with Iran, Turkey, and Pakistan—the "Northern Tier" countries. And the United States was the dominant naval power in the Mediterranean.

Aside from the special relationship it cultivated with Saudi Arabia, the United States did not play a major or direct role in the Arab world. That role fell to Great Britain, because of its long history in the area and because of the U.S. interest in good relations with Israel.

The most direct threat to a pro-Western oil-exporting country that Britain guarded against was Iraq's claim to Kuwait, which Iraq maintained had once been part of its territory. Consequently in 1961, when Kuwait—till then a British colony—was granted independence, Iraq invaded Kuwait and Britain, with several Arab states, countered the Iraqi move. However, Iraq did not abandon its claim; so Kuwait found its sovereignty protected by an Anglo-Kuwaiti defense agreement, concluded in 1961, and by British forces on the neighboring island of Bahrain. Similarly, Britain pledged to protect Bahrain against external attack. It also maintained the security and conducted the external affairs of the Trucial states—tiny sheikdoms on the southeast corner of the Arabian Peninsula—whose relations were characterized by border disputes, many of them involving areas believed to contain oil. Any ruler who abandoned a territorial claim faced a loss of legitimacy and possible overthrow; however, the British presence tended to freeze the status quo, preventing the sheikdoms from resorting to war without requiring their rulers to renounce their territorial claims. Britain mediated other disputes among the states and helped to preserve their internal security.

To perform these roles, Britain maintained naval facilities on the island of Bahrain and in the port of Aden, but more significant than the actual British presence, which had been quite modest for much of the postwar period, was that it signified a commitment of British power to the maintenance of the regimes. As a result of these commitments, a symbiotic relationship developed between the

United States and Great Britain, on the one hand, and the conservative pro-Western regimes in the oil-exporting countries on the other, for while the United States and Great Britain worked to preserve the internal and external security of these regimes, they responded by maintaining the flow of oil to the West. By 1970, however, the system was threatened by the growth of Arab radicalism and Arab nationalism, an increased Soviet presence in the region, and the relative incapacity of the United States and Great Britain to respond to these forces. Consequently, the West faced a series of dangers to the security of the international oil system.

Since World War II, the British position north of the Indian Ocean had eroded under the pressure of Third World nationalism and Britain's deteriorating economic status. In 1947 Great Britain withdrew from India. In 1956 Nasser nationalized the British-owned Suez Canal Company. In 1958 in Iraq, the British-installed Hashemite dynasty was overthrown, establishing the first radical regime in an oil-exporting country and virtually dismantling the Baghdad Pact only a few years after its creation. Moreover, the Iraqi revolution had demonstrated that the Baghdad Pact was incapable of ensuring the survival of a member state. Then, in 1967, following five years of struggle, the liberation movement in South Yemen forced Great Britain to abandon its colony in the port of Aden, which the British had occupied for 128 years.

Following a sharp devaluation of the pound, in 1968 Britain announced that by 1971 its military forces would be withdrawn from the Gulf area and its protection treaties with the Gulf states would be canceled. From the British perspective, the loss of empire meant that the benefits it derived from maintaining its position in the Gulf no longer justified the costs it might incur in the event of a major upheaval in the area. For the oil-consuming countries, the 1968 announcement signified that Britain was no longer willing to commit itself to maintaining the security of pro-Western regimes in the Persian Gulf area. Nor was the United States in a position to assume this role, for it had only a token force in the Gulf: a naval facility on Bahrain, consisting of three small ships and about 400 men; and its involvement in Vietnam, the domestic opposition it generated, and its balance-of-payments problems all worked against assumption of this additional responsibility.[36]

In the absence of external power, it was likely that dynastic rivalries, border disputes, and tribal differences would lead to conflicts that would almost certainly affect the minor oil exporters (Abu Dhabi, Sharjah), and that might spill over into the major exporting countries as well, disrupting oil operations and possibly transferring power to governments less hospitable to the West. Indeed, Abu Dhabi and Saudi Arabia had long disputed both their frontiers and their claims to the Buraimi Oasis. Iraq and Iran had conflicting claims over navigation rights in the Shatt-al-Arab waterway at the mouth of the Tigris-Euphrates. Iraq disputed Iranian sovereignty in Khuzistan province, where most of Iran's oil fields were located, and Kuwait, far more vulnerable than Iran, might be forced to join the radical Arab states, if Iraq pressed its claim to the sheikdom.

THE THREAT OF ARAB RADICALISM

As the 1960s drew to a close, hostility to the West and radicalism were on the ascendancy in the Arab world. In June 1967, the Arabs suffered a stunning defeat at the hands of Israel, which occupied the Sinai Peninsula, the West Bank, the Golan Heights, and the Old City of Jerusalem. These developments had several consequences. They provided a basis for greater Arab unity, for, as we have seen, defeat had forced Egypt, the leading Arab radical, to turn to the conservative oil-exporting states for financial aid, blunting Egyptian radicalism in the process. At the same time, the religious Saudis, who had long stood apart from the Arab-Israeli conflict, were deeply offended by Israel's capture of Jerusalem, Islam's third Holy City. And as Israel's presence in the occupied territories became firmly established, concern intensified throughout the Arab world about the dangers of Israeli expansionism. Whatever their differences, all Arab nations supported recovery of the occupied territories and restoration of Palestinian rights.

The June war also led to the worsening of U.S.-Arab relations, for the war seemed to mark a reversal of U.S. opposition to preventive wars by Israel. Following the war, the United States accepted Israel's concept of security through enlarged boundaries and helped to maintain Israeli military superiority by supplying sophisticated weaponry.

In addition, many of the Palestinians displaced by the war found themselves "guest workers" in the oil-exporting countries, engendering both genuine support and fear of trouble in the event the "host" countries failed to do their part in the struggle against Israel. Consequently, in the 1970s the conservative Arab states reconsidered the possibility of cutting back oil production to get the West to pressure Israel into making concessions. This was encouraged by the growing vulnerability of the United States, Israel's principal supporter, to an embargo or production cutback as a result of its growing dependence upon Arab oil.

The June defeat also encouraged Arab radicalism. Humiliated by defeat, the Arabs were determined to right the wrong that had been done to them, and to many this meant that Arab society had to be transformed. Prior to 1967, most Palestinians were aligned with one or another of the Arab states; following the war, many Palestinians, disenchanted with the Arab heads of state, appealed directly to the Arab masses. The effect was to radicalize public sentiment throughout the Arab world.

In November 1967, when the People's Republic of South Yemen was created, the new government proclaimed its intention to expel Britain from the Arabian Peninsula, and it became a base for revolutionary movements throughout the Gulf. In international politics, the new regime aligned itself with the Communist world; indeed, Soviet warships entered Aden's deep-water harbor several days after the British withdrew. Diplomatic relations with the United States were broken in October 1969, and a month later Saudi and Yemeni troops clashed openly. Then, on the new regime's third anniversary in 1970, the name of the country was changed from the People's Republic of South Yemen to the People's Democratic Republic of Yemen—the omission of "South" reflecting the new state's claim to be the legitimate government of the whole of Yemen, north and south.

In 1965, following the conflict in Yemen, guerrilla war had broken out in Dhofar, a southern province of Oman. The expulsion of the British from Aden and the establishment of the People's Democratic Republic of Yemen paved the way for intensification of the struggle in Dhofar, and by 1969 the guerrillas controlled most of the province. In 1968 the Dhofar Liberation Front decided to extend its revolutionary struggle to the rest of Oman, the lower Gulf, Bahrain, and Qatar. With this change in emphasis, the name of the organization was changed to the Popular Front for the Liberation of the Occupied Arab Gulf (PFLOAG). The organization saw its main enemies as "imperialism," Arab "reaction," and Iran, and in December 1971 it merged with a guerrilla organization operating elsewhere in Oman. It received support from China, the Soviet Union, and the PDRY. By the early 1970s it maintained cadres throughout the lower Gulf area. For the first time there was a revolutionary organization of significance targeted on the oil-exporting countries of this region.[37]

If these revolutionary currents were not contained, Saudi Arabia and Kuwait could find themselves squeezed between radical forces: Iraq in the north and the PFLOAG in the south. At that point, their vulnerability to radical demands for changes in concession arrangements and for production cutbacks would increase and their security would be in immediate jeopardy. Given the ease with which the flow of oil could be halted, Saudi Arabia and Kuwait could be continually subject to terrorist attacks by those with little interest in the continued flow of oil, and without Western backing, these conservative regimes would be more vulnerable to internal opposition.[38]

The most immediate transformation of an oil-exporting country occurred in Libya, where, on September 1, 1969, a group of young Nasserite army officials, the Revolutionary Command Council (RCC), seized power in a bloodless coup, deposing King Idris. Akins described the Idris regime as "one of the most corrupt in the area and probably one of the most corrupt in the world. Concessions were given, contracts were given on the basis of payments to members of the royal family. This was widely known throughout Libya, widely known through the Arab world."[39] Within Libya, there was widespread support for the new government, and almost no attempt was made to defend the king. The U.S. ambassador to Tripoli, noting the anti-Communist orientation of the RCC, predicted that it would serve U.S. interests well.[40] This prediction seemed borne out by the new government's initial caution in dealing with the international oil companies.

Great Britain and the United States had maintained military bases in Libya, and the new, nationalistic government asked that these be closed. Not wishing to antagonize the RCC, the United States agreed and withdrew its military personnel from Wheelus Air Force Base (its only military base in an Arab country) by the end of the year. Britain did likewise. Moreover, when the United States learned of a planned coup against the RCC in 1970, it informed the Libyan government. Yet the anti-imperialist, pan-Arabist orientation of the new Libyan government was to lead to important changes. Unlike the other "rich" oil exporters, the government in Libya was not dependent upon the United States and Great Britain for its political security. Consequently, it put the bargaining advantages that came from its high currency reserves, small population, and underdevelopment to work in the service of Arab revolution.

In May 1970 the three radical oil-exporting countries—Iraq, Libya, and Algeria—agreed to form a united front to work together in OPEC and in dealing with the international oil companies. These three countries also shared a commitment to government control of all oil operations and were ready to take joint positions in negotiating with the companies. When they created a fund to strengthen their position vis-à-vis the companies, their communique said they favored "legislative or regulatory measures" to reach their goals, rather than "lengthy and fruitless" negotiations with the companies.[41]

This radical oil-exporting bloc placed the rivalry between radical-nationalist and conservative Arab states, which had been central to inter-Arab politics since the Egyptian revolution in 1952, at the center of international oil politics. By 1970 the radical-nationalist camp included the military or single-party republics of Egypt, Syria, Iraq, Southern Yemen, Libya, Sudan, and Algeria, as well as the Ba'ath Party, the Palestinian resistance movements, and several other revolutionary organizations. The conservative camp, led by Saudi Arabia, included the monarchies in Morocco, Jordan, Kuwait, Bahrain, Qatar, Oman, and the seven tiny sheikdoms in the lower Gulf. Neither camp was highly unified, but the member nations had common characteristics. The radical-nationalists, which stressed their socialist and anti-imperialist character, shared an ideological hostility to "Western imperialism," by which they meant primarily the United States, and to "Arab reaction," by which they meant those Arab states, including most of the monarchies, whose political systems they regarded as "undemocratic," "feudal-capitalist," and as "puppets of Western imperialism." They were also hostile to the multinational oil companies, and in international politics they tended to align with the Soviet Union. In contrast, the conservative regimes were traditional and paternalistic, and viewed communism and the threat of revolution as their principal enemies. Accordingly, they remained solidly aligned with the West and heavily dependent upon the oil companies.

Both camps shared a long-term commitment to a unified Arab nation—on their own terms, of course—and deep hostility to Israel. However, the radicals were far more inclined to urge the use of oil to advance Arab political goals.

For the oil-exporting countries, this rivalry between radicals and conservatives was a source of strength. In dealing with the international oil companies, the radicals did not seek simply to gain a few cents more on the barrel; rather, they sought to end imperialism by throwing the hated international oil companies out, and they were determined to demonstrate their superiority to the conservative states by showing that they could secure better terms. As Libya's prime minister stated in 1973, "We warned the obstinate U.S. companies that they must understand that they were facing a revolution here, unlike the situation in the Gulf or Saudi Arabia or Iran. To compare us with these countries would lead them to an erroneous assumption and falsify all their calculations."[42]

To advance their objectives, the radicals were willing to take risks and endure setbacks, but as the radicals' initiatives met with success, the conservatives demanded comparable terms, because they wanted them and because to have accepted less would have discredited them in the Arab world. In the early 1970s, consequently, the pattern emerged of a radical state making a bold move and the conservative regimes responding with comparable demands. Disunity within the oil industry and among the consuming countries was exploited, and the exporting countries gained. Moreover, with each small victory the bargaining position of the exporting countries vis-à-vis the companies improved, for with their per barrel revenues and the demand for their oil increasing, their currency reserves mounted. This made them increasingly able to afford production cutbacks—at the very time the consuming countries' appetite for imported oil made them more vulnerable to a reduction in supplies. And with the positions of Great Britain and the United States deteriorating in the Middle East, the conservative Arab oil-exporting countries were better able to advance their economic interests and more responsive to the anti-Western sentiments of the radical forces in the Arab world.

THE ROLE OF THE SOVIET UNION

Complementing the growth in Arab radicalism, the expansion of Soviet power, regionally and globally, further weakened the predominance of the United States and Great Britain in the Middle East. Following the Cuban missile crisis in 1962, the Soviet leadership decided to seek parity with the United States in nuclear weapons and to expand its naval forces so that it could exert power at particular points around the globe, as the need arose. By the late 1960s, both objectives had been attained.

While Khrushchev's successors reduced Soviet involvement in many parts of the Third World, they deepened Soviet involvement in the Middle East, for the Soviet Union had several interests in the area. The most important was the historic Russian concern with securing access to the warm waters of the Mediterranean and maintaining the security of its southern borders. In addition, in the mid-1960s the Soviets began bartering for Middle East oil. This enabled them to rely on Middle East oil for part of their domestic consumption while maintaining oil exports to Eastern and Western Europe. Consequently, they could continue to earn hard currency from the West while maintaining the political influence derived from oil sales to Eastern Europe. As a world power, the Soviet Union also sought to extend its influence in the Middle East, and Soviet leaders saw the ability to deny Middle East oil to Western Europe and Japan as a potential trump card in the struggle between East and West.

Following the death of Stalin, in the mid-1950s the Soviet Union adopted a new policy toward the Third World, based on support for "progressive" regimes rather than revolutionary movements. As a result of this policy, the Soviet Union gained considerable influence in Iraq, Syria, and most significantly Egypt. Stalin's successors also abandoned the Soviet Union's longstanding territorial claims in the Northern Tier countries and attempted to pursue a policy of detente in that area. In 1956 the Soviet Union concluded a trade pact with Iran, but political relations between the two countries remained cool. Then, in 1958, the Iraqi revolution brought a shift in the Shah's attitude toward the Soviet Union, for the revolution demonstrated the inadequacy of the Baghdad Pact to ensure the survival of a member state and established the first regime in the Persian Gulf region that was interested in and capable of supporting radical movements and overt aggression in the Gulf states. Moreover, the threat from that regime would increase as it received Soviet backing.

In this context, the Shah began to envision an Iranian/Soviet detente as a way of blunting Soviet support for Iraq and enabling the Shah to shift the focus of his troops from the Soviet Union to the increasingly volatile Gulf area. In 1958 the Shah gave serious consideration to concluding a treaty of friendship and nonaggression with the Soviet Union. However, agreement could not be reached, and the Shah signed a security treaty with the United States instead.

In the mid-1960s the Shah became increasingly concerned about the threat of radicalism in the Persian Gulf and the readiness of the United States and Great Britain to maintain the security of his regime. Consequently, he moved toward an accommodation with the Soviet Union so that he could give greater attention to the security problems that stemmed from the south. In March 1965 the Shah declared that, in the future, Iran's military preparations would be focused on the Persian Gulf. He feared that the antimonarchical position of Iraq and the revolutionary movements in the Gulf could lead to direct attacks on Iran or to interference with the oil lanes in the Gulf that Iran depended upon.

The first major improvement in Soviet-Iranian relations came in 1962, when the Shah announced that no foreign (U.S.) missiles would be permitted on Iranian soil. Then, in 1964, a trade agreement was concluded between Iran and the Soviet Union. But the big breakthrough came in 1965, after the United States failed to come to the aid of Pakistan in the second Kashmir War. Since Pakistan, like Iran, had a security agreement with the United States, this increased the Shah's doubts about whether the United States could be relied upon to aid Iran in the event it was attacked by a neighboring power. At that point, the Shah decided to embrace a policy of detente with the Soviet Union, and in 1966 Iran concluded a major agreement with the Soviet Union. It agreed to provide the Soviet Union with natural gas in exchange for a Soviet steel mill, a machine-tool factory, and other industrial plants (gas deliveries to the Soviet Union began in 1970). In 1966 agreement was also reached on Soviet-Iranian exploration and development in the promising Iranian Caspian area.

In 1967 Iran reached agreement with Moscow for the purchase of $110 million of Soviet military equipment. This was the first time that any country tied to a

Western alliance acquired arms from a Communist state; moreover, the Shah had long objected to U.S. reluctance to grant Iran more sophisticated military equipment. In 1970 Iran and the Soviet Union concluded a treaty that was expected to double trade between them, and in April of that year there were discussions about building a pipeline for the transport of Arab oil from Iran to the Soviet Union.

Despite these gains, the Six-Day War had been a setback for the Soviet Union in the Arab world. After encouraging Nasser's early moves, which brought about the crisis, the Soviet Union failed to support the Arabs during the war, then backed efforts to achieve a cease-fire while Israeli troops still occupied Arab territory. To restore its influence in the Middle East, following the war, the Soviet Union undertook massive rearmament of the defeated Arab radicals, Egypt, Syria, and Iraq, and for the first time the Soviet Union provided arms to the new radical regimes in the Sudan,[43] Libya, and South Yemen. In 1970, following Israeli raids into Egypt, the Soviet Union rescued Nasser by sending pilots and missile crews into Egypt, along with new deliveries of Soviet equipment.

By providing armaments and military support, the Soviet Union cemented its ties with the radical Arab states and implied a commitment to protect these states against Western intervention. Also, by championing the Arab states against Israel, the Soviet Union hoped to solidify anti-Western sentiments and increase its power in the area. As a result of these efforts, by 1970 Soviet influence in the Arab world had reached new heights.

To advance its Middle East interests, in the mid-1960s the Soviet Union had begun to maintain a significant naval presence in the Mediterranean, formerly regarded as an "American lake." Following the Six-Day War, the Soviet fleet was rapidly expanded, reaching a peak of more than sixty ships in 1969. In 1968, Soviet vessels had made occasional visits to the Indian Ocean, the Red Sea, and the Persian Gulf; and it was likely that, following the British withdrawal, the Soviet Union would become the dominant power in the Indian Ocean. In the 1960s the Soviet Union also acquired air and naval bases in Egypt and port rights in Syria, the Sudan, Yemen, South Yemen, and Iraq. As a 1969 report by the Center for Strategic and International Studies concluded, "Moscow will use sea power much as it has been used by Britain in the past—and indeed, still is in the Gulf—to bring political pressure to bear by displays, albeit limited, of on-the-spot military power."[44]

The Soviet Union's attainment of nuclear parity and its growing presence in the Middle East deterred Western military intervention in the area. Prior to the mid-1960s, the West could take military action with little fear of a Soviet military response, so that, following the Iraqi revolution in 1958, U.S. troops were landed in Lebanon, and in response to the Yemen conflict in 1963, the U.S. Air Force was sent into Saudi Arabia. However, before taking such actions in the future, the West would have to weigh the possibility of a Soviet response. Thus the effect of this growing Soviet presence was to provide a protective cover for a wide range of anti-Western regimes and movements and to put the West in the position of having to rely less on military force and more on political and economic accommodations with friendly regimes in the region. Perhaps most significantly, the growing inability of the West to protect them made the conservative regimes in the oil-exporting countries more vulnerable to internal threats and regional pressures and less responsive to Western interests.

In its efforts to increase its influence in the Middle East and weaken the West, the Soviet Union encouraged Arab radicalism and assertions of Arab nationalism. It supported the radical Arab states, the Palestinians, and the Dhofari guerrilla movements. Indeed, the greatest long-term danger to the West was that an alliance between the Soviet Union and Arab radicalism would gain control of the oil fields. In pursuit of that objective, the Soviet Union encouraged the oil-exporting countries to nationalize their concessions; moreover, it offered to buy the nationalized oil ("hot oil") and to provide technical assistance, as it had done in Iraq. Finally, in the 1970s, the Soviet Union began urging the oil-exporting countries to use the "oil weapon" against the West.

Despite the problems that the Soviet role in the Middle East posed for the West, several major obstacles continued to limit Soviet influence. The Soviet Union could not replace the West in meeting the needs of the exporting countries for tanker capacity, technically trained personnel, or market outlets, though in particular situations it could make a contribution to each of these. And the oil-exporting countries clearly preferred payment in hard currency to the barter terms that the Soviet bloc offered. In addition, the Soviet Union's ability to project its naval power into the Persian Gulf was seriously impeded by the closure of the Suez Canal (from 1967 to 1975).

Also, the Soviet Union fell victim to the rivalries that characterized the Middle East. By gaining influence with the radical Arab nations, the Soviet Union further alienated itself from the conservative regimes. It frequently found that it had to choose between support for existing regimes and support for radical movements. In the mid-1950s, Khrushchev adopted a policy of support for "progressive" regimes. This strategy gained the Soviet Union considerable influence in the Arab world, particularly in Egypt, but these regimes were basically hostile to communism, and their suppression of Communist parties, which the Soviets accepted, left the Soviet Union without a strong system of ideologically based parties that would serve its interests in these countries. If the Soviet Union championed revolutionary movements in the Arab world, it would alienate not only the conservative Arab regimes but many "progressive" regimes as well.

Unable to avoid these conflicts, the Soviet Union found itself aiding both South Yemen and the Dhofari guerrilla movement while recognizing the states these guerrillas were fighting and whose legitimacy the PDRY challenged. Similarly, the Soviet Union was reluctant to support the Palestinian guerrilla movement, and did not provide it substantial backing until after the death of Nasser and the Jordanian civil war in 1970. And although the Soviet interest in the

Northern Tier had led to a policy of detente with Iran in the 1960s, Soviet backing for Iraq, Iran's principal antagonist, and Soviet support for the Dhofaris tended to worsen Soviet-Iranian relations. The official Soviet commitment to atheism also impeded its influence in the Arab world, where the influence of religion is strong.

The Soviet Union's lack of influence with Israel meant that it could not provide the Arabs what they most wanted: recovery of the occupied territory. While the Soviet Union supplied Egypt with advisers and armaments to fight Israel, it was also, by permitting Jewish emigration to Israel, supplying the Arabs' enemy with skilled personnel, who could work in both civilian and military sectors. Finally, the Soviet Union was still reluctant to risk a direct confrontation with the United States.

It was likely that, where it could, the Soviet Union would seek to extend its influence, make alliances with friendly regimes and radical movements, and take advantage of developments adverse to the West. These factors would be of considerable significance, but equally significant was what the Soviet Union would not or could not do: take over the oil fields, risk direct confrontation with the United States, or become an overt champion of revolutionary movements in the Middle East.

U.S. STRATEGY

U.S. policy sought to respond to the security problems posed by the British withdrawal, the growing presence of the Soviet Union, and the rise of Arab radicalism and Arab nationalism. Both domestic and foreign-policy considerations led the United States to seek to keep the Arab-Israeli conflict separate from the "oil politics" of the Persian Gulf—maintaining the dual policy that went back to the foreign-tax credit decision in 1950—for so long as the two issues were kept separate, the Arab-Israeli conflict and the anti-American feelings it engendered in the Arab world would not lead to disruption in the flow of oil to the West. It would be possible for the United States to continue to support both Israel and the conservative oil-exporting countries. That, in turn, would prevent the oil lobby and Israel's supporters from clashing in U.S. domestic politics.

The second tenet of U.S. policy was to prevent local conflicts by promoting cooperation among the pro-Western governments in the area. From the perspective of the United States, a regional approach to security offered several advantages over a U.S. presence. It would enable the United States to avoid another costly world commitment; it would minimize the risks of an anti-American backlash in the Arab world; and, perhaps most importantly, the Soviet Union would be less likely to expand its role in the Persian Gulf if the U.S. military stayed out of the area.

The first step in this effort to promote regional security involved a British proposal for a federation of Bahrain, Qatar, and the seven Trucial "tribalities." However, Bahrain and Qatar resisted the proposed union, each declaring its independence in 1971. Consequently, in December 1971 a federation of only the seven Trucial sheikdoms resulted: the United Arab Emirates. Yet even this truncated grouping was highly unstable, being an amalgam of oil-rich and oil-poor tribalities that had long been at odds with one another. More promising than this hurriedly patched together federation was the effort to get Saudi Arabia and Iran to assume cooperative responsibility for maintaining regional security. As Joseph Sisco, assistant secretary of state for Near Eastern and South Asian affairs told Congress:

One of the principal U.S. policies in the Gulf since the British announced in 1968 their intention to end their protective treaty relationships there, has been to encourage friendly states in the area to assume increasing responsibility for collective security in the region. In the Gulf, this has been shared primarily by Iran and Saudi Arabia. Elsewhere in the peninsula Saudi Arabia now bears the primary responsibility.[45]

As a result of the Yemen civil war, in the mid-1960s the United States had begun building Saudi Arabia into a military force capable of crushing internal threats and intervening in neighboring states. However, because of its small population and lack of skilled personnel, Saudi Arabia's potential as a military power was quite limited, and it was incapable of countering Iraq. Consequently, in 1965 the Johnson administration began selling Iran sophisticated air and naval weaponry, and in 1966 the decision was made to sell Iran several squadrons of F-4 Phantom fighter-bombers, the most sophisticated aircraft to be deployed in the Middle East to that time. Then, when the Suez Canal was closed, following the Six-Day War, it became increasingly important to protect the sea lanes of the Persian Gulf. Consequently, once the British withdrawal from the Gulf was announced, the efforts to strengthen Saudi Arabia and Iran were stepped up. In 1968 the United States agreed to supply Iran with $600 million of modern arms over the next five years.[46] Also, in October 1968 Iran and Saudi Arabia agreed on a Gulf median line, ending a major dispute between them, and in 1970 Iran abandoned its century-old claim to Bahrain, removing a point of conflict between itself and the Arab world.

Nonetheless, there were problems from the beginning with this reliance on local powers to maintain Western security interests, for Saudi Arabia's opposition to Israel, its solidarity with other Arab nations, and its vulnerability to local pressures tended to make it an unreliable guardian of U.S. interests. For his part, the Shah of Iran was every bit as threatened by the radical forces in the Persian Gulf as the United States and, consequently, so long as the Shah remained in power Iran could be relied upon to oppose the spread of Arab radicalism. However, not being an Arab state, and maintaining relatively close ties with Israel, Iran was resented in the Arab world. Consequently, any action it took to maintain security in the Gulf was likely to intensify Arab nationalism, and as Iran built up its military capability, it caused concern in the Arab world, triggering a regional arms race. Moreover, Saudi Arabia and Iran could extract a price for the security role they were asked to assume. Indeed, in the 1960s the Shah had already begun to exploit East-West rivalries in order to advance his interests.

To contain Soviet advances and Arab radicalism, the United States also sought to maintain a strong Israel. Prior to the 1967 war, overt U.S. support for Israel had been quite limited; to avoid antagonizing the Arabs, the United States had attempted to minimize its support for Israel. During the first Arab-Israeli war (in 1948–49), the United States had denied Israel's requests for military assistance. In the Suez conflict, the United States opposed Great Britain, France, and Israel; and in 1957 the United States pressured Israel into withdrawing from the captured Sinai territory.

As early as 1954, however, the United States was covertly subsidizing the transfer of French weapons to Israel, but did not directly supply major weapons to Israel until 1962. Following the June war, France—as part of its effort to improve its standing in the Arab world—refused to release fifty Mirage supersonic fighters that Israel had purchased prior to the war, and the United States, fearing that a Soviet-backed Egypt might gain the upper hand, replaced France as Israel's principal arms supplier. In 1968 the United States agreed to provide Israel with fifty supersonic F-4 Phantoms. The sale signified a dramatic increase in U.S. support for Israel and worsened U.S. relations with the Arab world; it also brought a Soviet response. To defend against the Phantoms, the Soviet Union agreed to provide Egypt with a missile defense system and Soviet personnel and pilots to ensure that the system operated effectively. By March 1970, large quantities of Soviet arms and advisers were arriving in Egypt.

Initially, the Nixon administration sought to follow an "even-handed" policy in the Middle East, long advocated by the State Department. This meant restraint on arms sales to Israel and support for a negotiated settlement, based on the principles spelled out in U.N. Resolution 242, which called for "withdrawal of Israeli armed forces from the territories occupied in the recent conflict" in exchange for "termination of all claims of belligerency and respect for and acknowledgement of the sovereignty, territorial integrity and political independence of every state in the area." In short, the resolution envisioned an exchange of territory for peace, without calling on Israel to abandon all the territory it had captured or requiring the Arabs to make "full peace" with Israel.[47] However, the administration's attempt to arrange a comprehensive settlement along these lines—the Rogers Plan—was rejected by both Israel and the Arab states.[48]

Then, in the summer of 1970, a U.S.-arranged cease-fire between Egypt, Jordan, and Israel broke down almost as soon as it had been agreed to. In September, heavy fighting broke out between the Palestinian fedayeen, based in Jordan, and the Jordanian army. Relations between the Palestinians and the Hussein regime, long uneasy, had been brought to a head when Egypt and Jordan (but not Syria or Iraq) had accepted the U.S. cease-fire proposal, for the Palestinians feared that their interests would receive short shrift in any settlement. Consequently, they disrupted the cease-fire through intensified guerrilla activity and the hijacking of European commercial airliners. Hussein responded by attacking the guerrillas, and it seemed clear that, in the ensuing conflict, either the

Palestinians would lose their base of operations in Jordan or Hussein would be overthrown.

The United States considered survival of the Hussein regime vital, for Hussein was a close ally, a nonradical Arab, and possibly a means to an Arab-Israeli settlement. If he were overthrown, Israel would take preemptive measures against a radical Jordan and another Arab-Israeli war would result; but this time the Soviet Union might be drawn in. As President Nixon later stated, "Since the U.S. could not stand idly by and watch Israel being driven into the sea, the possibility of a direct U.S.-Soviet confrontation was uncomfortably high. It was like a ghastly war of dominoes, with a nuclear war waiting at the end."[49]

Consequently, when Syrian tanks (destined to aid the Palestinians) crossed the Jordanian border, the United States put 20,000 troops on alert and moved additional naval forces into the Mediterranean. If Syria or Iraq were to enter the battle, the United States was prepared to intervene militarily; however, its ability to do so was highly circumscribed. As the chairman of the Joint Chiefs pointed out, without bases east of Suez, the United States lacked the capability for ground intervention. The air support that it could provide would not compare with the Israelis'. And again, U.S. intervention would increase the risk of Soviet retaliation.

On September 21 the Israelis decided to intervene if the Syrian tanks continued to advance, and they began to move forces toward Jordan. The United States agreed in principle to Israeli air and land strikes. However, General Assad, who controlled the Syrian air force at the time, refused to fly covering missions for the Syrian tanks; so the Syrian tanks withdrew and a cease-fire was soon announced.

Several factors played a role in the withdrawal: the Soviets had urged the Syrians to back off, and in refusing to provide air cover, General Assad sought to embarrass his political rival, Prime Minister Jedid. Nonetheless, what most impressed U.S. policy makers was that Israel had been prepared to protect Hussein on terms favorable to the United States. Consequently, following the Jordanian crisis, the Nixon administration became committed to ensuring Israel's military superiority, for its efforts at securing a comprehensive agreement (or even a workable cease-fire) had met with little success and Soviet influence in the area seemed to have increased. If a Soviet-backed Egypt were to recover the Sinai, or a Soviet-backed Syria the Golan Heights, both Soviet influence in the Middle East and Arab radicalism would increase enormously; and if prospects of success seemed reasonable, the radical forces in the Arab world would take up arms to advance their objectives.

In this context, a strong Israel was seen as a way of containing radical forces throughout the region and preventing another Arab-Israeli war. As a result, U.S.-Israeli relations flourished from the fall of 1970 until the October war in 1973. The supply of Phantoms continued with only a brief interruption between the summer of 1971 and March 1972. During fiscal years 1968 to 1970, U.S. military credits to Israel averaged $47 million, but during fiscal years 1971–73 they averaged \$384 million.[50] By ensuring Israeli military superiority, the United States removed the pressure on Israel to negotiate a settlement and prompted a flow of arms from the Soviet Union to the Arab states; but Washington did not attempt to pressure Israel to return portions of the occupied territories. Yet if Israel would not make concessions, neither would the Arabs; so each side grew more intransigent.

The final U.S. response to the growing security problems in the Middle East occurred at the level of global politics. Plagued by economic problems, the Soviet Union was anxious to conclude arms-limitation agreements with the United States and to receive credits for the purchase of U.S. technology. President Nixon responded to these Soviet concerns by attempting to extract foreign-policy concessions from the Soviet Union. At his first presidential news conference, on January 27, 1969 he declared:

What I want to do is to see to it that we have strategic arms talks in a way and at a time that will promote, if possible, progress on outstanding political problems at the same time— for example, on the problem of the Middle East and on other outstanding problems in which the United States and the Soviet Union, acting together, can serve the cause of peace.[51]

The president hoped to get the Soviet Union to back off in the Middle East in exchange for an arms-limitation agreement and U.S. technical assistance, yet U.S. efforts to maintain political stability in the Middle East were to have only limited success. Between the Libyan revolution in 1969 and the Iranian revolution in 1979, the oil-exporting-country governments aligned with the West remained in power. But increasingly, these pro-Western regimes demanded, and were able to secure, greater oil revenues. Because the United States was increasingly dependent upon these governments for maintaining security in the area, it was not in a position to support the companies in resisting these demands. And without the support of their home government, the companies were forced to capitulate.

Nor did the U.S. strategy prevent the outbreak of a fourth Arab-Israeli war, during which the Arab oil-exporting countries cut back production, which "shocked" the world economy and led to skyrocketing oil prices. That a production cutback could have such devastating effects was due to the extent to which the world had become dependent upon Middle East and North African oil and to the failure of the consuming countries and the oil companies to coordinate their strategy in anticipation of a cutback. Their mounting currency reserves enabled the Arab oil-exporting countries to "afford" the production cutbacks, and the growing political challenges they faced in the Arab world pressured them into it.

The Libyan Breakthrough and the Teheran/Tripoli Agreements

As the 1960s drew to a close, the international oil companies still controlled the pricing of crude oil and the actual production levels in the OPEC countries. The process by which the exporting countries increased their power and boosted their revenues began gradually.

In June 1968 OPEC adopted a "Declaratory Statement of Petroleum Policy in Member Countries."[1] As sovereign powers, the countries invoked the legal doctrine of "changing circumstances"[2] and asserted their right to equity participation or an ownership share in the companies' concessions. They also maintained that the governments of the exporting countries had the right to unilaterally determine the price the oil companies paid them and that their per barrel payments should keep pace with the prices of the industrial products they imported. They declared that the oil companies did not have the right to "excessively high net earnings after tax"; accordingly, excess profits, as determined by the government, "shall be paid by the operator to the Government."[3]

At the time it was issued, the international oil companies did not pay much attention to the statement, for they did not believe that OPEC had the power to achieve its objectives. Yet, as a result of the actions of individual exporting countries, by the mid-1970s the OPEC countries had secured the objectives in the 1968 statement.

At the close of the 1960s, both Iran and Libya sought higher revenues. While Iran's efforts were largely rebuffed, Libya, because it was strategically situated, made substantial gains. Libya's victory led to demands for comparable gains in the other exporting countries, which produced a direct conflict between the international oil companies and the oil-exporting countries; and surprisingly, the exporting countries won. In retrospect, it seems a small victory, but it was OPEC's first victory, and in many respects it laid the basis for those that followed.

In the 1960s the surge in Libyan production had forced the majors to adjust the growth rate in their Middle East production programs downward. This was particularly resented in Iran, where the Shah was dependent upon oil revenues to realize his goal of making the country a major industrial power.[4] The Shah objected to the fact that Saudi Arabia, which had a much smaller population than Iran, had a larger production base and therefore received larger annual produc-

135

tion increments. In his efforts to get the Consortium to boost Iran's share of the market, the Shah appealed to the U.S. State Department, but prior to the late 1960s, the department was reluctant to tell the oil companies how to allocate their production.[5] The companies, for their part, refused to make any commitment to Iran for fear that, if they did, the other exporting countries would demand similar commitments.

In 1966, following extended negotiations involving Iran, the Consortium members, and the U.S. State Department, the Consortium agreed to increase Iranian production by 11 percent per year in 1967 and 1968, to relinquish about a quarter of its concession, and to allow the National Iranian Oil Company to buy oil at a price midway between the company's tax-paid cost and the posted price. Rather than attempt to compete with the Consortium members in downstream markets, Iran would take advantage of its growing detente with the Soviet Union and barter this oil to the East European countries in exchange for goods.

The agreement was not much of a concession on the companies' part. A commitment to expand production by 11 percent per year was not much of a breakthrough, considering that, since 1958, the Consortium's annual production increase had fallen below 11 percent only once, and in 1966 the Shah had demanded a 17 percent increase. Also, by this time relinquishment agreements were common, and the price at which Iran received the oil and the stipulation that it be sold to Eastern Europe protected the Consortium from competition from Iran's national oil company. Consequently, it is not surprising that the agreement failed to satisfy the Shah.[6]

By the late 1960s, oil revenues accounted for roughly half of Iran's national budget, yet Iran's expenditures were approaching the limits that its oil revenues, supplemented by foreign borrowings, could sustain.[7] In 1968 the Shah had announced a five-year, $11 billion industrial program. The Shah's dream of making Iran a major military power and its new role as "guardian" of the Persian Gulf meant that costly military expenditures lay ahead. Finally, since the Shah lacked a popular base of support, he maintained his power by relying on a costly national secret police, SAVAK, that was estimated to have roughly 70,000 agents.[8]

These budgetary pressures, coupled with a lack of alternative sources of funding, led Iran to seek an increase in oil revenues. In February 1968 the Shah demanded that the Consortium guarantee him production increases over the next five years sufficient to meet the revenue needs for his Fourth Development Plan. From 1963 to 1967 the Consortium's production increases had averaged 13.8 percent, but the Shah's new demand would mean a 20 percent increase per year over the next five years.[9] The companies, which were planning to increase production in Iran by only 8 percent, objected to the Shah's demand. It would be difficult for them to make commitments five years in advance. And if they agreed to the Shah's demands, other producers would demand similar production increases, which would make it difficult for the companies to maintain the price level by limiting production.

The State Department's concern with consolidating Iranian support led it to put increasing pressure on the oil companies. At a meeting with U.S. oil company executives in March 1968, Under Secretary of State Eugene Rostow explained that while the State Department would not normally interfere in commercial matters, the Consortium's current problem with Iran had serious national security implications. He expressed concern about the growth of Soviet influence in the area, following the departure of the British military, and indicated that the State Department expected the Soviet Union to encourage the Arabs in their efforts to gain control of the oil that Europe had become dependent upon. He said that since Iran was the strongest state in the area, it was very important to the United States in maintaining influence in the region. He also expressed concern about the possibility of another Arab-Israeli war, and he indicated that while Iran was not anxious to embargo oil, it might be pressured into doing so, particularly if the companies continued to resist its demands for increased production and revenue. Finally, he said that, based on the State Department's discussions with Iran, he believed the Iranians would accept a two-year schedule if production were increased. [10]

The representatives from the major companies replied that, were they to meet the Iranian demands, similar demands would be made in the other oil-exporting countries. They argued that rather than an improvement in the overall situation, this would lead to a deterioration in relations with the other exporting countries. [11]

The meeting also brought out a basic split within the Consortium. On one side were the crude-short companies—Mobil, Shell, the U.S. independents in the Consortium, and CFP. Since they needed the crude for their downstream operations, they were far more anxious to meet the Shah's demands for increased production. On the other side were the crude-long majors—BP, Texaco, Exxon, and Gulf. They did not want to give their price-cutting competitors additional crude, and they feared that any concessions to Iran would trigger increased demands elsewhere in the Middle East.

In fact, the crude-long majors suspected that their crude-short partners leaked information about the overlifting rules in the Consortium to the Shah. For example, in 1967 CFP aggravated relations between the companies and Iran by informing the Shah that the penalty for lifting ''extra'' crude oil in Aramco was less severe than in the Consortium. Similarly, at the meeting with Rostow, the representatives of the independents in the Consortium (Iricon) pointed out that the overlifting penalty had been modified as a result of pressure from the Shah, following the CFP disclosure. But in the judgment of the independents, it was still too high, their proposal having been rejected by the majors-dominated Consortium. [12]

The meeting broke up with the State Department officials agreeing to tell the Shah that they had consulted the oil companies, that the companies were trying to solve the problem, and that the actual ''offtakes'' were likely to be closer to what the Shah was demanding than it currently appeared. It was hoped that this would prevent the Shah from taking action on April 20, when he was scheduled to meet with the oil companies. The undersecretary concluded the meeting by asking the companies to do whatever was possible to avoid an open confrontation with the Shah.[13]

At the April 20 meeting, the Shah told the companies that if his demands were not met, he would seize a Consortium oil field, put his own company on the Consortium's board, or take additional oil at a discounted price to sell in Eastern Europe. The Consoritum attempted to stall for time—going from the Gregorian to the Persian calendar to do so—and agreed to make an advance payment of $75 million to Iran. Then, in October, the Shah demanded that the Consortium install 5 million b/d of additional capacity, arguing that this would enable Iran to meet a supply emergency arising from another Arab oil embargo. The Consortium refused, believing that if the capacity were added, the Shah would either coerce them to utilize it or seize it himself.[14]

Finally, in 1969, the Shah secured a boost in revenues by making a series of threats. In March he stated that he planned to expand the Iranian armed forces, and that if the United States would not provide credits for this, he was prepared to turn to the Soviet Union. Less than a month later, the Shah threatened to nationalize half of Iran's oil reserves, unless the companies agreed to expand production. He argued that Iran, with a population of 27 million, should be entitled to considerably more oil revenue than Kuwait, a nation of 500,000; yet in 1968 Iranian production averaged 2.84 mb/d while Kuwaiti production averaged 2.64 mb/d. In addition, the Shah mounted an international campaign in which he suggested that if the Consortium could not increase Iran's production, it should allow outsiders to come in. Furthermore, the *New York Times* reported that "beyond the argument of national need for royalties and tax income, Iran contends that she should be rewarded by the American and European oil companies for her contribution to political stability in the Middle East."[15]

In response to these pressures, the Consortium sought an accommodation with the Shah. It increased production by about 10 percent, substituted a more expensive for a less expensive crude (enabling it to increase payments to Iran), and agreed to make another advance payment to the Shah.[16] However, the Consortium had not agreed to boost Iranian production to the levels that would provide the Shah the billion dollars in oil revenue that he demanded, for that would have required them to cut back production elsewhere, and both the Kuwaiti prime minister and the Iraqi oil minister had warned the companies against doing that. Consequently, the Consortium's principal concession was its agreement to provide the Shah an advance on future petroleum revenues, to bridge the gap between Iran's current revenues and the Shah's billion-dollar demand.[17]

Nonetheless, on May 15, 1969, the Shah announced that the oil companies had met his demand for a billion dollars in revenue payments in 1969, upping their earlier "best endeavor" offer of $900 million. But he expressed only "qualified satisfaction" with this, for he had not altered his basic concession terms, and he still lacked the long-term financial assurances that his military and economic plans required. Five days later, he declared that he was prepared to turn to the Soviet Union for combat equipment. Clearly, the Shah was not satisfied: he wanted more money than he was getting.[18]

While the Shah had pressured the companies into raising production, and had registered his discontent with the arrangements between Iran and the Consortium, he had not won any basic alteration in concession terms. Despite his repeated threats, the main weakness in his bargaining position was that, because of Iran's great dependence on oil revenues and its limited currency reserves (see table 4–6), the Shah could not afford to pressure the companies by withholding substantial amounts of production. Moreover, even if the Shah reduced Iranian production, the companies, because the world market was still characterized by surpluses, would not have had much difficulty replacing the crude the Shah took off the market. Nor were the other oil-exporting countries likely to support the Shah's bid for greater Iranian production, since that would be at their expense.

THE LIBYAN BREAKTHROUGH

Despite the Shah's repeated efforts, the real breakthrough came in Libya, which had several advantages in confronting the international oil companies. Libya and Algeria were the only oil-exporting countries in which independents controlled most of the production (see table 3–1). In 1970, although independents controlled only 15 percent of the output in all OPEC countries, they controlled 55 percent of Libya's production;[19] and unlike the majors, each of which had extensive holdings in several countries, many independents were entirely dependent upon Libya for their foreign production. The majors could respond to a threat in any country by increasing their production elsewhere, but the independents could not do this. The capitulation of the independents during the royalty-expensing negotiations of 1965–66 had indicated their vulnerability to pressure from even a single exporting country.

The closing of the Suez Canal following the 1967 war increased the benefits of Libya's Mediterranean location. Oil from the Persian Gulf had to be transported to Europe by tanker around Africa or through pipelines to the Mediterranean, but Libyan oil could be shipped directly across the Mediterranean. Indeed, a barrel of oil from the Gulf required four times as much tanker capacity as a barrel of oil from the Mediterranean,[20] and with the closing of the canal, tanker capacity was scarce. This locational advantage had not been very significant in the early 1960s, when most tankers passed through the canal, but in the future Libya could expect to retain an important edge, since closure of the canal was accelerating a trend to supertankers that were too large to pass through the canal.

Because of the Mediterranean freight advantage, the oil companies shifted production from the Gulf to Libya, and though other producers with outlets west of Suez might have been expected to gain as well, political factors intervened. Iraq, which sent much of its production by pipeline to the Mediterranean, was still in controversy with the IPC; Algeria was in a dispute with France; and in

1967–68, Nigerian oil production was halted as a result of the Biafra civil war (though it picked up substantially in 1969). As a result, Middle East oil exports increased by 30.5 percent between 1967 and 1969, but Libyan exports increased by 78.7 percent (see table 5–1). By the end of 1969, Libya accounted for more than a quarter of Western Europe's oil imports,[21] which meant it would be extremely difficult for Western Europe to replace Libyan oil, particularly since demand was pushing against the limits of tanker capacity. Thus rapid increases in Libyan production enabled the sparsely populated country[22] to accumulate huge currency reserves. According to Akins, these were sufficient to keep the Libyan government "at current expenditure and import levels for four years."[23]

Finally, at a time when pollution concerns were growing more important, Libya was able to take advantage of the low-sulfur content of its oil, something that prior to the 1970s it had not received any premium for. Yet even if pollution concerns are left aside—and in Europe, where most Libyan oil was burned, they were not given much consideration—high-sulfur crudes are more costly to process. They also lead to corrosion and other hazards in refining operations. Consequently, as George Henry Mayer Schuler (at the time an executive with Bunker Hunt Oil Company) explained, many small independent companies had built refineries in Europe that could only "run a particular kind of Libyan crude oil, and to cut off that oil was to cut off their life blood."[24]

Because of these advantages, Libya received the highest per barrel payments of any Arab government, but most observers still considered Libyan oil underpriced. In recognition of this, the prerevolutionary government of King Idris had given the companies that were operating in Libya an ultimatum, requiring them to raise posted prices to government-stipulated levels or face unilateral legislation. Negotiations with the companies were to begin September 1, 1969, but on that day the Idris regime was swept away and replaced by a government headed by twenty-six-year-old Colonel Muammar Qaddafi. Upon seizing power, the new government notified the United States, Great Britain, and France that it would respect all agreements in force. However, a month after the regime came to power it announced that the battle for higher posted prices would be resumed.

According to Schuler, the new government's oil policy had several objectives.

TABLE 5–1. INCREASES IN OIL EXPORTS, 1967–69 (IN TB/D)

	Exports		Increase in Exports 1967–69
	1967	1969	
Iraq	1,169.5	1,445.4	23.6%
Total Middle East	9,639.9	12,582.7	30.5
Libya	1,717.3	3,069.5	78.7
Algeria	773.2	892.5	15.4
Nigeria	546.8	544.7	−.3
Venezuela	3,283.8	3,386.5	3.1

OPEC, *Annual Statistical Bulletin, 1970*, table 62, p. 80.

It sought a large increase in its per barrel take, so that it could both increase government revenue and discredit the Idris regime; it hoped to gain control of the companies' producing operations, so that it could "manipulate oil supplies for political and commercial purposes"; and it wanted the success it envisioned for these policies "to demonstrate to people governed by more moderate regimes that revolution and 'Arab socialism' are the wave of the future." Finally, the Libyan government planned to utilize oil and the revenues derived therefrom in "the battle to liberate Palestine."[25]

Libya, whose expertise on oil matters was quite limited, was advised by Algeria and Venezuela. It coordinated its pricing strategy with Algeria, which was engaged in a conflict with the French companies operating within its borders. (Like Libya, Algeria had the advantages of a Mediterranean location and an industry structure in which independents controlled the majority of its production.) While in August the conservative regime of King Idris had sought a 10¢ increase in the posted price, the radical Qaddafi regime began by demanding a 44¢ increase. The RCC based its demand on the alleged underposting of Libya's first crude exports in 1961, on its freight advantage since the closing of the Suez Canal, and on the quality of its low-sulfur crude. Libya's demand was equivalent to what Algeria was asking of France.[26]

The Libyan demands posed a major challenge to the international oil companies, for the advantages of Libyan crude—its location and low-sulfur quality— could not be duplicated elsewhere and consequently, they resulted in pure windfalls. For example (aside from sulfur content), a barrel of Libyan and a barrel of Saudi Arabian crude were worth about $2.50 in Europe, but since it cost 40¢ less to ship the Libyan oil to Europe, that 40¢ was windfall profit. (In economic terms, it was a "true rent.") The issue was who got the 40¢, and that was a question of political power.

Since 1967 the Libyan windfalls had gone mainly to the international oil companies, and now the RCC was demanding that the bulk of the windfall be transferred to Libya. On the face of it, that may have seemed only fair; indeed, Akins later testified that he considered the Libyan demands "quite reasonable."[27] But if the companies acceded to the Libyan demand, they would lose the windfall profits they had become accustomed to. More significantly, the other exporting countries would perceive it as a per barrel revenue increase for Libya and demand comparable increases; and if the companies acceded, Libya would ask that this second increase be added to its freight differential or low-sulfur premium, which would set the process of price increases in motion again.[28] In short, the Libyan demands posed the threat that they would initiate an unending process of leapfrogging, in which gains would be granted to Libya, and extended to the Gulf producing countries, only to have Libya come back and ask for more. To avoid this, the companies hoped to settle for an increase of about 5¢ per barrel.[29]

After an initial meeting in late January with all the companies operating in Libya, the RCC adopted a new bargaining strategy. Instead of dealing with the companies as a group, it would attempt to exploit their disunity by negotiating with them one at a time. After calling each company in for individual negotiations, Libya decided to focus on Exxon and Occidental; Exxon was the largest producer in Libya and Occidental had the largest reserves.[30] As discussion proceeded, Qaddafi warned that because of U.S. support for Israel, U.S. interests in the Middle East were "balanced on a razor's edge." In April, he told the Libyan people to prepare for the "coming fight with the oil companies," which he linked with "world Zionism and local forces of reaction." He also said that Libya's ultimate goal was to operate the industry as a "sole and exclusive government enterprise."[31]

Libya sought to exploit the differences among the companies by exploring the possibility of selling its oil to companies not currently operating in the country. Following a three-day visit to Moscow in March, Libyan Oil Minister al-Mabruk said that Libya sought to cooperate with the U.S.S.R. in the exploration and development of Libyan oil, and wanted to open East European markets to Libyan crude. A Beirut press report said the threat of Libyan cooperation with the Soviet Union was Libya's trump card in its negotiations with the Western oil companies. Libya also pursued discussions with Japanese, German, French, and Hungarian companies.[32] The companies, for their part, resorted to the classic weapon of cutting back on exploration and development. As many as fifty-two exploration rigs had operated in Libya in 1969, but by early 1970 the number had fallen to twenty-six.[33]

In May, to pressure the companies, Libya began ordering a series of production cutbacks. Occidental's production, which had been scheduled to expand, was cut from 800,000 to 425,000 b/d in a matter of months. Exxon was denied export rights from its new $350 million liquefied natural gas plant. The cutbacks imposed on other companies' operations in Libya ranged from 15 to 31 percent. By September 1970 Libyan production had been reduced from 3.6 mb/d to 2.8 mb/d.[34] Exxon's vice president, George Piercy, explained the significance of the Libyan cutbacks:

This was the first time since the Iranian nationalization in the early 1950s that a major Middle Eastern producing country was willing to sacrifice current revenues to achieve changes in concession arrangements. Libya was in a unique position to do this. Its population was small, its monetary reserves high, and its oil increasingly valuable because of the transportation shortage. The new revolutionary government was determined to pursue its nationalistic aims which included ever increasing control over its oil.[35]

Also in May, shortly after Libya's first production cutbacks, a bulldozer ruptured the Trans-Arabian pipeline (Tapline), which pumped a half million b/d of Arabian oil to the eastern Mediterranean, and the Syrians, who were seeking an increase in toll charges, refused to allow its repair—a decision that clearly aided the Libyans. Oil was available in the Persian Gulf, and rather than support Libya, several Gulf producers were willing—even anxious—to expand production.[36] But with the Suez Canal closed, the demand for tankers boomed and their single-journey rate skyrocketed.

Algeria was the first to take advantage of this situation, in mid-July unilaterally raising the posted price for the French companies operating in Algeria from $2.08 to $2.855 a barrel. In doing this, Algeria increased its take from 78.6¢ to $1.21 a barrel.[37] More significantly, for the first time an oil-exporting country had unilaterally raised prices. Still, though the Algerian move encouraged the Libyans, it was less significant than a Libyan breakthrough would be. Since Algeria had already nationalized the minor holdings of non-French companies, its change in the posted price would not affect the Anglo-American majors and would therefore be less likely to affect arrangements elsewhere in the Middle East.

In 1965 Algeria had granted the French companies a preferentially low posted price in exchange for a promise to develop Algerian oil resources. The 1970 price increase was in part an attempt to alter—in Algeria's judgment, rectify— the 1965 agreement. Moreover, rather than being based on commercial considerations, oil was a factor in the Franco-Algerian state-to-state relationship; and since most Algerian oil still went to the protected French market, it was less likely to be a standard for pricing crudes in other parts of the world.

Yet the oil companies continued to resist an agreement with Libya. They knew that any concession to Libya would have to be extended to the other oil-producing states. As the report of the Senate Subcommittee on Multinational Corporations stated:

Saudi Arabia, Iran, Kuwait and Iraq politically could not afford to leave the impression that the new Libyan regime could negotiate better terms with the international oil companies than they; hence a major Libyan posted price increase could "leap frog" into the Persian Gulf countries. There was also the additional risk that Libya would then seek to "leap" ahead of more politically conservative Persian Gulf producing nations as a further demonstration of its revolutionary vitality. The Libyan negotiations thus were of critical importance to the entire structure of international oil pricing.[38]

Exxon attempted to resolve the impasse by offering Libya a 10¢ increase in the posted price and an 11¢ "freight premium," reasoning that it would then have to extend only the 10¢ increase to the other oil-producing countries. Libya refused the offer and broke off negotiations with Exxon, which shifted the burden of negotiations onto Occidental, probably the most vulnerable of the newcomers. In early 1970 Occidental received most of its profits, roughly half its crude supply, and virtually all of its foreign production from Libya.[39] In addition, there were widespread rumors that Occidental was damaging its Libyan fields by overproducing.[40] Consequently, Libya could keep Occidental shut back on the grounds of "good conservation practices."

The only way Occidental could resist Libya's demands would be if it secured oil elsewhere (i.e. from another country). Yet in July, when Occidental had asked Exxon, its negotiating partner, to guarantee an emergency supply of oil at little more than cost, Exxon "rejected the request, offering Occidental only back-up oil at third party market price."[41] Tanzer reports that "according to the testimony of an oil company insider, the critical turning point in the early Libyan negotiations was the refusal of the major international oil companies, particularly Exxon, to help Occidental Petroleum resist Libya's demands.''[42]

Several factors influenced Exxon's decision. The majors still resented the intrusion of the independents and their price-cutting tactics, and as a maverick, Occidental was especially scorned. In 1968 Occidental had requested an import quota to enable it to bring large volumes of cheap Libyan oil into the United States, but since Occidental's proposal threatened to disrupt the oil-import quota system and, with it, the balance between domestic and foreign production, it was vigorously opposed by both the majors and the U.S. domestic producers. Then, in 1969, Occidental offered to operate an oil field that the Peruvian government had expropriated from an Exxon subsidiary.

The most significant factor in Exxon's refusal to supply Occidental with "cost oil" was that it would be contrary to its immediate economic interest. Given Libya's enormous currency reserves, it could keep Occidental's production shut back for a long time, and Exxon, during this time, would not gain any economic benefits by supplying Occidental with cost oil, particularly since Occidental would use it to compete with Exxon in downstream markets. Moreover, if Occidental and the other independents were successful, and were allowed to expand production of underpriced Libyan oil, they could continue to increase their market shares. In contrast, if Occidental remained shut back and lacked cost oil, it would be possible for Exxon to increase its own market share without cutting prices.

Since Exxon's offer left Occidental without access to cheap crude, the latter was forced to reach an agreement with Libya. On September 2, 1970, Occidental agreed to a 30¢ increase in the posted price and an increase in its income tax rate from 50 percent to 58 percent. As the report of the Subcommittee on Multinational Corporations noted, the agreement "represented the most radical increase in revenues that any oil-producing country had won since the 1950 Aramco tax agreement." In return, Occidental was allowed to increase production from 450,000 to 700,000 b/d.[43]

After the Occidental settlement, Libya went after the Oasis group, a consortium of Continental, Marathon, Amerada-Hess, and Royal Dutch/Shell. Again, Libya had made a strategic choice. Like Occidental, the three U.S. Oasis independents were heavily dependent upon Libyan crude supplies, and Shell was a crude-short major. Moreover, Shell's agreement to Libyan terms would set a precedent that the other majors would find difficult to resist. Each of the three independents secured more than half their output from Libya, but Shell received only 3 percent of its worldwide production from Libya.[44]

The principal concern of the Oasis independents was protection of their crude supplies; however, they were afraid that if they accepted higher Libyan terms, their crude might be priced out of many markets. To assuage this concern, the Libyans told the Oasis independents that they would treat all companies alike and that the price increases would eventually spread to the other producing countries. Libya agreed not to impose the new terms on the Oasis independents until similar agreements were concluded with the other companies operating in Libya—a concession not granted to Occidental.[45] As a result, on September 21, 1970, the Oasis independents agreed to terms comparable to the Occidental package. But Shell resisted Libya's demands, maintaining that it had worldwide commitments to consider. Negotiations between Libya and Shell broke down, and Shell was forced to stop exporting from Libya.[46]

Libya's bargaining position was strengthened by the precedent established in the settlements with the independents, and Libya could now shut down the remaining operating companies in the country and live reasonably well on the 1.6 mb/d produced by Occidental and the Oasis independents. Consequently, Libya gave the majors and the remaining independents until September 27 to accept terms comparable to the Occidental/Oasis package;[47] so the majors confronted a dilemma. If they acceded to Libya's demands, they would undoubtedly face similar demands from the other exporting countries; if they resisted, they faced the prospect of losing their Libyan concessions. Consequently, they turned to their home governments for support.

James Akins, then in charge of petroleum matters at the State Department, later testified that he considered the Libyan demands reasonable and the companies' position unwarranted. "It was also to our interest I thought that the companies have a reasonable working relationship with the Libyans and with the other producers. If the Libyans concluded they were being cheated, this I thought guaranteed a breakdown in relations with the companies and all sorts of subsequent problems."[48] Akins feared that if the companies resisted Libya's demands, the RCC would nationalize their holdings and that countermoves by the companies would prove unsuccessful because the Europeans would be unwilling to boycott Libyan oil.

If Libya moves in and takes over the companies, Europe one way or another is going to get Libyan oil, and if the companies then try to block the sale of Libyan oil, as they said they would, through controlling their tankers or people that bought the Libyan oil, in this case, they would find themselves nationalized in Europe as well.[49]

Nonetheless, at a meeting of oil company executives and State Department officials on September 25, Sir David Barran, then serving as Shell's chief executive officer, argued that

the dangers of permanent damage to our own and the consumers' interests lay much more in yielding than in resisting the demands then being made on us. . . . Our conclusion was that sooner or later we, both oil company and consumer, would have to face an avalanche of escalating demands from the Producer Governments and that we should at least try to stem the avalanche.[50]

Shell's position was supported by BP and Mobil. They argued that the industry could do without Libyan oil and still supply Europe with 85 to 90 percent of its petroleum needs for at least six months.[51] However, SoCal and Texaco, which would have a hard time replacing Libya's low-sulfur crude, were reluctant to put their Libyan concession at risk in a confrontation with the RCC. The European governments were not prepared to risk cutting off Europe's oil supplies, and the U.S. State Department officials who were present were not convinced by Barran's line of reasoning.[52]

According to John J. McCloy, who participated in the September 25 meeting as counsel to a number of the companies, Under Secretary Johnson told the companies that they could not expect much assistance from the U.S. government. The United States had little influence with the radical Libyan government, and U.S. intervention would be "ineffective at best."[53]

If one examines the choices confronting the State Department at the time, a decision to support the companies hardly made sense, for higher international oil prices would be paid largely by Western Europe and Japan, which would further improve the competitive position of U.S. export industries, particularly those like the petrochemicals, in which energy costs are a large proportion of total costs. As the world oil price rose, the heated domestic conflict between U.S. oil producers and those who advocated cheap Middle East imports would be eliminated. A decline in tanker rates following resolution of the Libyan crisis was expected to reduce the landed cost of Middle East oil, but a high world price would reduce the attractiveness of imports, and if it were high enough, it would pull U.S. prices up, benefiting U.S. producers.

In contrast, if the United States were to support the companies and a confrontation resulted, U.S. firms were likely to be displaced by firms from Western Europe and Japan. U.S. relations with both its alliance partners and the Middle East countries would deteriorate. Given the limited U.S. dependence on oil imports and the magnitude of the price increases that were being discussed, it was not in the United States' interest for the federal government to support the oil companies.

Lacking unity among themselves and strong government support, it would be doubly difficult for the companies to hold out against Libya, for if Libyan exports were cut off, it would be essential that the companies have their home governments attribute any resulting shortages to Libyan intransigence rather than corporate unreasonableness. To Libya, the lack of response by consuming-country governments to the Libyan threats seemed to imply that the risks of retaliation were not great. And for the companies to mount an effective boycott of Libya, they would have to have the support of most of the companies operating in Libya and be able to keep other companies from moving in. Moreover, by this time Libya had the support of the other OPEC countries, so that the companies could not be certain that replacement oil would be available elsewhere if negotiations with Libya broke down.[54] Not surprisingly, SoCal and Texaco were the first of the majors to agree to Libya's demands, and rather than stand alone, the other majors soon followed. By the end of September, virtually all the companies operating in Libya had agreed to RCC's demands. However, aside from Occidental, none of the companies got their production cutbacks restored.[55]

As a result of these settlements, the companies' per barrel tax-paid cost in Libya increased from $1.40 to $1.70. The agreement also contained provisions for five automatic increases in tax-paid costs. Since market prices had declined from 1957 through the spring of 1970, the majors found this provision particularly difficult, and Libya got the companies to increase the tax rate to 55 percent, destroying the fifty/fifty principle that had been inaugurated in 1950.[56] Moreover, while the companies never accepted the logic or evidence behind Libya's claim that its oil had been underpriced since 1965, they signed a letter ascribing the increase in the tax rate to this alleged underpricing.[57]

Libya took the position that its gains simply redressed past injustices and did not represent a significant advance. *Petroleum Intelligence Weekly* (*PIW*) reported that, despite the agreement, Libyan crude "will still be a bargain."[58] Consequently, Libya determined to continue pressing for higher posted prices, a larger freight differential, and a low-sulfur premium.

As the majors had warned, the Libyan agreement had an immediate impact on the other oil-exporting countries. Following the agreement, Iran, Iraq, Kuwait, and Algeria made new demands on the companies. In an effort to stem the tide, in the fall of 1970 the majors agreed to extend the 55 percent tax rate to Nigeria and the Gulf producing states[59] and make some adjustments in posted prices. However, the demand for a general increase in posted prices was postponed until after a forthcoming OPEC meeting. Then, in December, Venezuela increased its effective tax rate from 52 percent to 58 percent and declared that from then on the government would unilaterally set posted prices, as Algeria had done in July. Since the tax increase was retroactive to the beginning of January, it cost the oil industry a third of its 1970 Venezuelan profits.[60]

Following these developments, prices rose in Western Europe and the United States. While significant, the increases stemming from Libya's breakthrough were not disruptive, yet the 1970 developments in Libya had consequences that went well beyond their immediate financial impact, for in pressing its advantages Libya had been testing the waters. That it resorted to negotiation, argument, and economic pressure rather than unilateral government action suggests its initial uncertainty.[61]

The success of Libya's efforts encouraged the oil-exporting countries, for the developments in Libya revealed a lack of resistance by consumers and considerable disunity among the oil companies. In the face of this, Libya's tactics had proved highly effective. Singling out the companies, one by one, enabled Libya to take advantage of corporate disunity. The companies and the consuming countries alike appeared vulnerable to Libya's production cutbacks. Libya had forced the companies to negotiate posted prices with an exporting country, whereas the companies had previously set prices unilaterally. Also, it had demonstrated that sovereign states could abrogate agreements with the world's most powerful multinational corporations. Moreover, the assistance that Libya received from Algeria and Venezuela encouraged further cooperation among the exporting countries. To the oil companies, it must have become evident that the support they could expect from their home governments was limited.

Recognizing the key role of Libya's breakthrough in the emergence of OPEC's power, Adelman has argued that the U.S. government could have contained Libya and nipped OPEC in the bud.

When the first Libyan cutbacks were decreed, in May 1970, the United States could have easily convened the oil companies to work out an insurance scheme whereby any single company forced to shut down would have crude oil supplied by the others at tax-plus-cost from another source. . . . Had that been done, all companies might have been shut down, and the Libyan government would have lost all production income. . . . The OPEC nations were unprepared for conflict. Their unity would have been severely tested and probably destroyed. The revenue losses of Libya would have been gains to all other producing nations, and all would have realized the danger of trying to pressure the consuming countries.[62]

Yet, even if it could have been agreed upon, it is far from clear that Adelman's proposal would have been successful, for, with enormous currency reserves, Libya might have been able to outlast the West, which would be plagued by shortages stemming from both the lack of spare production capacity and the tanker shortage. But the real problem with Adelman's proposal is that it would have required a unity among consuming countries and oil companies that did not exist. The United States could easily have endured the loss of Libyan production, but Europe could not. Nor were the Europeans likely to pass up an opportunity to strengthen their position in international oil by displacing Americans from their Libyan concessions. As Akins stated:

The loss of oil from Libya alone would have meant the drawing down of more than half of the European oil reserves within a year. It seemed unlikely, indeed inconceivable, that France, Germany, Spain or Italy would have allowed that to happen; especially as the goal would apparently have been only to protect the Anglo-Saxon oil monopoly, which they had long sought to break. To have tried to explain to them that they would themselves suffer in the long run, would have been less than futile. We in the State Department had no doubt whatever at that time, and for those particular reasons, that the Europeans would have made their own deals with the Libyans; that they would have paid the higher taxes Libya demanded and that the Anglo-Saxon oil companies' sojourn in Libya would have ended.[63]

Similarly, the majors, with holdings in several countries, could have accepted and even benefited from a Libyan shutdown, but without their Libyan production, the independents would have been in serious trouble. And it was probably fanciful to expect the majors to keep their rivals—the independents—in business by providing them substantial quantities of oil at cost over a sustained period of time. The oil-exporting countries' first victory, like those that followed, was made possible by the disunity of the West.

THE TEHERAN AGREEMENT

Encouraged by the success in Libya, in December 1970 OPEC demanded extension of the 55 percent tax rate to all exporting countries, elimination of disparities in payment among countries, and an increase in posted prices. This was the first time the exporting countries formally sought a worldwide price increase. OPEC also supported Libya's efforts to secure premiums for its ordinarily favorable location (the short-haul premium) and the additional value of its locational advantage that was due to closure of the Suez Canal (the Suez premium). If its demands were not met, OPEC threatened to achieve them "through a concerted and simultaneous action by all Member countries."[64]

OPEC also summoned the oil companies to begin negotiations in Teheran by January 12, 1971, with only the Persian Gulf countries. OPEC had several reasons for wanting the Mediterranean and Gulf producers to negotiate separately. The conservative exporting countries were concerned that Libyan and Algerian insistence on raising "political issues," notably U.S. support for Israel, would prove disruptive to both OPEC unity and the continued flow of oil, and Libya insisted that it did not want to be seen in the same room as the "reactionaries" and "feudalists" of the Gulf, though it consulted with them. Moreover, certain issues were unique to the Mediterranean producers: the freight advantage and Libya's demand for compulsory reinvestment.[65]

In the demand for split negotiations, the companies saw an unending process in which they would reach a settlement with one group of producers, only to find another group asking for more. This corporate fear was confirmed when, on January 2, before negotiations had even begun on the OPEC demands, Libya sought further increases in the posted price, beyond those obtained the previous fall; a further tax increase; a larger freight premium; and a provision that, for every barrel of Libyan oil a company produced, it would have to reinvest 25¢ in Libya. The *Petroleum Press Service* estimated that acceptance of these demands would raise the tax-paid cost of Libyan oil from $1.70 to $2.60 a barrel.[66]

The Libyans threatened to stop production if their demands were not met. The RCC stated that they were intended in part to "hurt" the oil companies until they prevailed upon the United States to change its Mideast policy.[67] In announcing these demands, Libya had upstaged the Gulf negotiations, taking the lead again, but its demand for an increase in per barrel revenues, beyond what the Gulf countries got, was hardly surprising. In September, its tax rate had been increased to 55 percent in compensation for the alleged underpricing of its crude since 1965. Then, in November, the companies agreed to raise the tax rate to 55 percent in the Gulf exporting countries. However, once the industry standard became 55 percent, Libya was without compensation for the formally admitted underpricing.

The Libyan demands placed the companies in a real dilemma, for the other oil-exporting countries were demanding elimination of disparities between countries in the posted price. As a result, no matter how the companies met Libya's demand for compensation for back payments, the other exporting countries were likely to insist on a similar increase, just as they had insisted on the 55 percent tax. But if the companies met the other exporting countries' demands for equivalent terms, Libya would be back, insisting on compensation for the previous underpricing of its crude. McCloy explained the industry reaction to the new Libyan demands:

The companies were thus faced with the threat of repeated "leapfrogging" on pain of seizure of oil-producing properties or serious stoppages with consequent disruption of the supply of oil to the consuming countries. In the circumstances, it was clear that the only hope of achieving stability of supply was for the companies to join together and negotiate with all the members of OPEC as a group. Unified action by the governments required unified action by the companies.[68]

The companies knew they would have to pay more for OPEC oil, but they were determined to restabilize their relations with the exporting countries. That meant they had to stop the ever spiraling demands, accompanied by continual threats of shutdown. And the companies were convinced that the way to do this was to conclude a long-term agreement with all the exporting countries. However, as *PIW* stated, OPEC's insistence on limiting talks to oil from Persian Gulf terminals "made it clear that what they have in mind is an 'open-end' agreement that would be up for revision the moment new Mediterranean prices were set in Libya."[69]

In January, to strengthen their bargaining position, fifteen international oil companies, a group that included all the majors and most of the leading independents, formed a united bargaining front, known as the London Policy Group. They sent a "Message to OPEC" that stated:

We have concluded that we cannot further negotiate the development of claims by member countries of OPEC on any other basis than one which reaches a settlement simultaneously with all producing governments concerned. It is therefore our proposal that an all-embracing negotiation should be commenced between representatives of ourselves . . . on the one hand, and OPEC as representing all its Member Countries on the other hand, under which an overall and durable settlement could be achieved.[70]

The companies' approach signified the change in bargaining power, for prior to the 1970s they had always sought to deal with the exporting countries individually. When OPEC was founded, in 1960, it had sought to negotiate as an organization with the companies, but the companies resisted, refusing to "recognize" OPEC for bargaining purposes. Then it was the companies that sought to "divide and rule"; now OPEC seemed to be exploiting the disunity among the companies.

The fifteen signatories of the "Message to OPEC" were soon joined by German, Spanish, and Belgian companies, but there were two important absences. Italy's ENI, a large purchaser of Libyan and Algerian crude, refused to join the companies' group, and though France's CFP joined, Elf, which had large Algerian holdings, stayed out. This equivocal stance did little to dispel the view, widely shared among both the oil companies and the exporting countries, that France was the weak link in the companies' united front, likely to break ranks and reach a settlement on its own.[71]

While the impetus behind the companies' approach to OPEC came principally from the majors, each independent was afraid it might be singled out and forced to capitulate, as had happened to Occidental in the fall. Consequently, the independents sought an agreement in which any company that was forced to cut back on production would have its supplies replaced at cost by the other companies. This resulted in the Libyan Producers' "Safety Net" Agreement, in which the signatories pledged not to make an agreement with the Libyan government without the assent of the other companies. Also, the agreement provided that if any company's production were cut back by the Libyan government, it would receive assistance from the other operating companies in Libya.[72]

However, other provisions of the agreement reduced its effectiveness. The cutback company's production would not be replaced in its entirety, since each company would have to bear its prorated share of the cutback. Consequently, if several companies were cut back, a company could suffer considerable losses. Moreover, this would be particularly hard on the independents, which got most of their oil in Libya, and instead of providing crude oil, companies had the right to make monetary payments: 10¢ for every barrel of Persian Gulf oil lost and 25¢ for every Libyan barrel. This was a poor substitute, because the payments were low, relative to the market value of a barrel of crude oil, and because nickels and dimes would not enable the companies to keep their refineries going and maintain their market shares. The independents fought vigorously, but unsuccessfully, against insertion of this clause into the agreement.[73]

In addition, enforcement of the agreement was by no means sure, and several countries later reneged on their commitments. The "insurance" provided by the agreement was worth considerably less to a company than the value of its concession; it was therefore doubtful that any company would stay with the group if it feared that, by doing so, it would lose its Libyan concession. Consequently, as Schuler testified, the Safety Net Agreement "wasn't worth a hell of a lot."[74] It represented an advance in corporate cooperation over the companies' failure to aid Occidental the previous summer, but it fell far short of what was required to prevent each independent from being singled out and pressured by the oil-exporting countries.

The companies were concerned that either their negotiating stance vis-à-vis OPEC or the Libyan Safety Net Agreement might prompt antitrust proceedings against them. To prevent this, McCloy got both the State and the Justice departments to agree to support the companies' global negotiating strategy and their sharing agreement.[75] In January, Assistant Attorney General for Antitrust Richard McLaren issued "Business Review" letters, in which he indicated that the Department of Justice did not intend to institute proceedings against the companies for any actions they took pursuant to either the proposed "Message to

OPEC'' or the Libyan Producers' Agreement. This action made the London Policy Group the first governmentally approved intercompany bargaining body. The LPG and the Libyan sharing agreement were seen as arrangements that would be disbanded after the negotiations were completed, but this turned out not to be the case, and the Justice Department continued to sanction the companies' joint bargaining stance with "Business Review" letters. The United States also consulted other consuming countries. As Under Secretary of State John Irwin stated: "Out of these talks emerged a consensus among the consuming countries and the oil companies that, although another increase in revenues of the producing countries could be expected, an effort should be made to prevent a spiral of increasing demands by the producers—a process in which a Libyan settlement would be followed by further rounds of escalating demands in all producing areas."[76]

The joint approach was first challenged in Libya. Going back to the tactics it had used so successfully the year before, in January 1971 Libya attempted to single out the most vulnerable firms and get them to accede to its demands. A number of threats to independent companies were made, which culminated in an ultimatum to Bunker Hunt and Occidental to dissociate themselves from the companies' united front by January 24 or suffer "appropriate action." Although Hunt and Occidental expected Libya to cut their production back, they refused to abandon the united front or to accept higher per barrel taxes. Libya, which had learned that a production-sharing agreement existed, though it did not know its terms, took no action.

Apparently, the oil companies' oil-sharing agreement strengthened the independents' resolve to hold out and reduced Libya's readiness to resort to production cutbacks. According to Schuler, this "proved the soundness of the joint approach agreed [to] in New York. It should have demonstrated also that much of the Libyan bravado was still bluff at that point in time."[77] Also, the companies hoped that the U.S. government could get the exporting countries to moderate their demands, and after several meetings between company executives and the State Department, President Nixon authorized a mission by Under Secretary of State John Irwin II to the moderate oil-exporting countries, Iran, Saudi Arabia, and Kuwait. Irwin later explained:

The general objectives of my mission were:
A. To prevent an imminent impasse in discussions between the oil-producing countries and the oil companies from resulting in an interruption of oil supplies;
B. To explain the reasons why the U.S. Government had taken steps to make it possible under our antitrust laws for the oil companies to negotiate jointly; and
C. To seek assurances from the Gulf producers to continue to supply oil at reasonable prices to the free world.[78]

However, subsequent testimony revealed that the oil companies and Irwin had different ideas about the purpose of his mission. Irwin saw it as meeting a need to impress the leaders of the conservative oil-exporting countries with the United States' concern with maintaining the flow of oil; the oil companies thought

Irwin's task was to convince these leaders that the U.S. government supported the industry's call for joint negotiations with the producing countries.[79]

On January 18, Irwin and Douglas MacArthur II, the U.S. ambassador to Iran, met with Iran's finance minister, Amouzegar, and with the Shah. The Iranians claimed that, at the OPEC conference in December, they had taken the lead in demanding split negotiations while some OPEC countries had sought an overall settlement. They maintained they now had a proxy to negotiate for Kuwait and Saudi Arabia, and they felt there would be no disagreement from Abu Dhabi or the other sheikdoms to any settlement they agreed to. But both the Shah and Dr. Amouzegar insisted that a worldwide approach would be a "most monumental error," for, as the companies knew, the Gulf producers could not impose their will on Venezuela or the other Arab states. Consequently, if the companies insisted on a worldwide agreement, they would likely have to meet the most radical demands, rather than the more moderate demands of the Gulf producers.[80] The likely result would be a breakdown in negotiations and, eventually, a cutoff in oil production, which Dr. Amouzegar indicated the Gulf producers would go along with.

If, on the other hand, the Iranians maintained, the negotiations were split, the Gulf producers were prepared to conclude a five-year agreement with the companies and stick to it, even if producers in other areas obtained better terms. However, the Iranians indicated that they hoped the companies would not give the radicals a great deal more, since that would put considerable pressure on Iran.[81] Iraq would be part of a Gulf settlement, but there was no reason to believe that Iran could say what Iraq would do in the event Libya secured better terms.

Though the industry negotiators were to arrive in Teheran the next day, Irwin did not wait to consult with them. Following his discussions with the Iranians, he recommended to Washington that the negotiations be split. He later testified that his recommendation was based on the concern expressed to him by the conservative exporting countries about the consequences of a unified negotiation and their assurances that they would honor a Gulf-only agreement, regardless of what happened elsewhere.[82] Akins and MacArthur supported Irwin's recommendation, which was immediately endorsed by Secretary of State Rogers, who recommended to McCloy that the companies open negotiations with the Gulf countries and conduct parallel negotiations with Libya. On January 19 MacArthur urged the company negotiators to agree to split negotiations.

Thus the State Department abandoned the strategy of seeking a global settlement with all the oil-exporting countries at the same time, despite the fact that the "Message to OPEC," the Libyan Producers' Safety Net Agreement, the "Business Review" letters, and the extensive consultations between the industry and the Departments of State and Justice had been premised on this strategy.[83] Yet neither McCloy nor the company representatives in Teheran were convinced by the State Department's recommendation. As McCloy telegraphed his associate:

I would imagine the companies would repose little faith in assurances by Iran and others that they would stand still even if more favorable terms were granted the Libyans. Substantially unrelated but parallel negotiations might, I fear, impair the basis not only on which the Justice Department based its concurrence respecting the statement to OPEC, but also the rationale of the objectives of the entire operation from the industry's point of view.[84]

But the companies' bargaining position was considerably eroded by the lack of support that they could now expect from their home governments. Indeed, since it involved direct confrontation between the companies and the exporting countries, the question of joint versus split negotiations implicitly raised the question of who would make the crucial decisions in international oil: the companies or the exporting countries. Despite the State Department recommendation, the companies attempted to salvage their global strategy, but their bargaining position was weak. Recognizing that the U.S. government now supported the split negotiating strategy, on January 19 the Gulf producers gave the companies forty-eight hours to agree to "Gulf-only" negotiations. If the companies refused, the producers threatened to convene an OPEC meeting on January 25 and legislate new terms, as Venezuela had done the previous December and Algeria the previous July. The companies responded by proposing that negotiations be conducted in both Libya and the Gulf, but that no settlement be concluded with the Gulf countries prior to conclusion of a settlement with Libya and Algeria. With this "separate but necessarily connected" formula, the companies hoped to meet the demand for separate negotiations and still prevent leapfrogging.

When the formula was rejected, the companies sought to get the Gulf countries to agree that the Teheran negotiations would set posted prices for the eastern Mediterranean terminals of the Gulf exporting countries.[85] In this way, they hoped to ensure that the Gulf countries would not demand higher prices for their eastern Mediterranean exports once a settlement was concluded with Libya, and they hoped to "hinge" Libya to the Gulf settlement by tying it to the posted prices established for the eastern Mediterranean. But the Gulf countries rejected this proposal as well—a clear indication that they planned to take advantage of any improved terms Libya secured. Finally, on January 30, with only two independents (Bunker Hunt and Gelsenberg) dissenting, the companies abandoned their efforts to secure a global agreement and recognized the total separation of the Gulf and Libyan negotiations.[86]

The companies' negotiating team was split into two groups, one to negotiate with the Gulf countries and one to negotiate with Libya. Libya, however, refused to proceed with substantive discussions until after the Teheran negotiations were concluded, making it clear it would wait to see the terms for Gulf terminal oil, then seek to outdo them.

Like the Occidental-Libyan settlement the previous fall, the companies' agreement to split negotiations between the Gulf producers and Libya was a major breakthrough for the oil-exporting countries, for in direct confrontation with the exporting countries, the companies were forced to back down, opening themselves to the prospect of leapfrogging. Moreover, the momentum changed. The companies' attempt to work out a joint strategy had been foiled, and all the old animosities reemerged. As Schuler stated, at the beginning of the 1970 Teheran negotiations "there was a certain air of confidence on the part of the companies that, for the first time, all companies were ready and willing to work together towards a reasonable settlement. By January 31st these roles were reversed: the OPEC countries were confident of their ability to face-down the oil companies, home governments of those companies and consumers [sic] governments; and the companies had reverted to an attitude of narrow self-interest."[87]

The OPEC country that insisted most strongly on split negotiations was Iran. By January 1971 it was heavily in debt, but anxious to assume costly new responsibilities, which meant that it was badly in need of increased revenues and extremely vulnerable to the loss of revenue that would accompany a production shutdown. By splitting the negotiations, Iran solved both problems, for without the radical Libyans present, making "crazy demands," Iran could conclude a settlement without resorting to production cutbacks, and as leapfrogging continued, it could increase its revenues step by step.

Because Iran was financially vulnerable, it might have been forced to yield had the companies held fast; however, in assessing the reasons for the companies' capitulation to OPEC's demand for split negotiations, the lack of support they received from the U.S. government stands out. As in the Libyan negotiations the previous fall, if the companies had confronted the exporting countries and a loss of supplies resulted, the companies would need the support of the U.S. government. Yet, with the United States courting the Shah and asking Iran to assume a new security role in the Gulf, the United States could not oppose the Iranian demand for a split in the negotiations. This was in marked contrast to the support the companies received from the U.S. government in the decade following World War II, and it suggests that a state's support for its multinational corporations is contingent on its foreign-policy interests and the relationship of the companies to those interests.

Moreover, while the State Department's primary concerns were the diplomatic situation in the Middle East and the threat of an oil embargo, these were important, but secondary concerns for the oil companies. The industry's primary goal was halting OPEC's leapfrogging demands so that its relations with the exporting countries could be restabilized. Consequently, the industry was much more committed to the strategy of one global negotiation than the State Department. In short, the primary concern of the State Department, to avoid an oil embargo, was most jeopardized by a single, overall negotiation, while the primary concern of the international oil companies, to halt OPEC's leapfrogging demands, which threatened continued instability, was most jeopardized by split negotiations.

It is also likely that, at this point, U.S. policy makers supported an increase in world oil prices, for at a time of growing U.S. balance-of-payments problems, higher world oil prices would enhance the competitiveness of U.S. industries. In the face of growing Arab radicalism, higher prices would strengthen the conservative regimes that the U.S. was allied with in the exporting countries, and with the United States attempting to get Western Europe and Japan to assume a greater portion of the West's defense burden, the increases would be absorbed mainly by consumers in Western Europe and Japan. In addition, higher world oil prices would encourage U.S. efforts at regaining energy self-sufficiency, and as world oil prices rose, the conflict between U.S. oil producers and U.S. oil consumers would lessen.

For the major oil companies, leapfrogging also offered certain benefits. If the tax-paid cost of Libyan oil rose, it would weaken the independents in the world oil industry, and since a breakdown in negotiations could threaten their concessions, the majors were much better off with leapfrogging than with impasse. Higher prices could be passed on to consumers, but loss of a Middle East concession could not be made up. Moreover, consumers would be far more angered by loss of supply than by the price increases that would result from OPEC's demands.

The independents also prefered accommodation to confrontation; however, they had far more to lose from split negotiations than the majors. If the price of Libyan crude rose above the price of Gulf crude, their market position would be in jeopardy. It is no accident, therefore, that the two companies that protested the split to the very end were independents, or that the only ''industry'' critique of the companies' performance came from the representative of an independent, George Henry Mayer Schuler. But on their own, the independents were powerless to resist.

In Teheran, after the negotiations were split, the companies sought assurances from the Gulf states that they would not cut back production in support of increased demands by Libya. However, OPEC announced on February 7 that if an agreement were not reached with the companies by February 15, the exporting countries would legislate new terms, as Algeria had done the previous July and Venezuela the previous December. If any company refused to accept these new terms by February 22, the exporting countries threatened to ''take appropriate measures including total embargo on the shipments of crude oil and petroleum products by such company.'' This was the first time the OPEC countries, as a group, threatened to withhold supplies. However, supplies were to be withheld from noncomplying companies, not from consumers; consequently, if a company resisted, it ran the risk of another company's taking the oil on OPEC's terms.[88]

The companies now had to choose between reaching an agreement or risking a confrontation with the exporting countries. Once again, their rivalry and their lack of support in the consuming countries tended to resolve the issue in favor of settlement, for while OPEC might have backed down before a united industry front, buttressed by the consuming-country governments, that was not what it faced. On January 20 the United States had convened a meeting of the OECD countries in Paris but little support for the oil companies emerged, for the consuming countries were too divided to take action. As one of the company negotiators later wrote:

The French were too anti-American, the British too bemused by their debt to Pompidou, the Italians too much governed by Mattei's legacy of dislike for the Seven Sisters, and the Japanese too scared of the OPEC reaction for any discussion to get started toward what was needed.

All these governments had no conception of the scale of the disaster to which their lack of initiative and solidarity was exposing them. In this climate, the companies had no sound alternatives; they saw themselves as damned if they did, and damned if they didn't.[89]

Also, the United States assured the countries that if they went along with a settlement, they could count on five years' supply at stable or only slightly increasing prices. While the consuming countries were reported to be more concerned about a loss of supplies than a price increase, an OECD spokesperson said the meeting did not discuss "contingency arrangements for coping with an oil shortage."[90] Then, on February 3, the Shah told a press conference:

The major governments happily, after my warning two weeks ago—when I said that if the major governments stand behind the oil companies and intend to support them this would be the ugliest sign of economic imperialism and new colonialism—have shown not the slightest sign of any interference or support of the companies.[91]

By threatening to embargo oil to noncomplying companies, rather than consumers, the exporting countries encouraged disunity between the companies and the consuming governments and among the companies themselves. The threat was not that supplies would be cut off to consumers, but that particular companies would lose their concessions. In the face of this threat, the Italians, French, and Japanese planned separate initiatives vis-à-vis OPEC.[92] In response to these challenges, the primary concern of the existing concessionaires became the preservation of their concessions, not the maintenance of low prices.

Given the hostility to the companies that existed in the consuming countries, it is not likely that they would have received much public support if they had resisted the OPEC demands and shortages resulted. Indeed, the exporting countries told the companies that if their demands were not met, production would be halted and the companies would have to face the wrath of the consuming countries. Moreover, by embargoing the companies, not the consuming countries, the exporting countries hoped to shift the blame for shortages to the companies. In contrast, higher prices could be passed on to consumers, and the consuming-country governments had made it clear that they would intervene only if the talks broke down. Thus the industry's interest in keeping government out of its operations became another reason for preferring even a high-price settlement to confrontation. Finally, once the exporting countries began setting prices unilaterally, it was doubtful that they would stop, so that the power to determine prices would pass from the companies to the exporting countries. The companies seemed to believe they would be better off negotiating prices than allowing that to happen.[93]

On February 14, one day before the OPEC deadline, the companies accepted the demands that the Gulf exporting countries had made on February 2. The government take was increased about 30¢ per barrel, bringing it to $1.26. (The OPEC countries had initially sought a 45¢ increase, and the companies' initial offer was 9.1¢.) In addition, the companies agreed to make the 55 percent tax uniform. They also agreed to eliminate all marketing and other OPEC allowances (i.e., discounts granted by the OPEC countries from the official prices) and to adjust the posted price of particular crudes upward. These actions removed several items that had caused tension between the companies and the OPEC countries in the past. The agreement was to last five years. It included provisions for an annual upward adjustment of 2.5 percent for worldwide inflation and a further annual 5¢ per barrel increase.

As a result of the Teheran Agreement, the revenues of the Gulf producing countries were expected to increase by $1.4 billion in 1971, and by $11.7 billion if the agreement ran the full five years.[94] The industry characterized the financial cost as "extremely high." Indeed, at the time the agreement was concluded it was the most costly settlement in the history of international oil. The industry justified the cost on the grounds that the agreement would provide both supply security and price stability for a five-year period. It contained an "antileapfrogging" clause, which provided that no Gulf country would seek the more advantageous financial terms that might be negotiated by other states. The Shah also pledged that there would be no leapfrogging, and the Gulf exporting countries agreed not to take any action "in the Gulf" to support the demands of other OPEC members for terms better than those agreed to at Teheran.[95]

However, even at the time it was concluded, there were reasons to doubt that the Teheran Agreement would last five years. The exporting countries refused to make a commitment on oil prices in the Mediterranean. Rather, they secured a provision that stipulated that if Libya secured a freight premium that was justified by the high tanker rates, and if tanker rates then fell (as they were expected to, with the reopening of the Suez Canal and the building of more and larger tankers), the companies would have to reduce the Libyan advantage or extend it to the other exporting countries.[96] This gave the Gulf countries an interest in Libya's violation of whatever agreement it might reach with the companies (it became known as the "reverse hinge"). In addition, though the Gulf countries agreed not to take action "in the Gulf" in support of increased demands by other countries, nothing was said about action in the Mediterranean. Nor did they agree to increase production to make up for a Libyan cutback.

The recent history of the exporting countries and the oil companies gave little reason for confidence in the durability of their agreements. As *PIW* asked in January, "Why put so much emphasis on getting assurances and agreements from the Persian Gulf governments when if such agreements were worth anything the present crisis wouldn't exist?"[97] Indeed, toward the end of the Teheran negotiations Yamani is reported to have told Piercy that the agreement was not likely to be long lived.[98]

THE TRIPOLI AGREEMENT

In Tripoli on February 23, ministers from the Mediterranean exporting countries—Algeria, Libya, Iraq, and Saudi Arabia—agreed to let Libya represent
them in negotiating a Mediterranean price. But the ministers pledged that if terms
were not quickly agreed to, they would meet again to discuss retaliatory measures, including an oil stoppage. The companies sought to tie the Libyan settlement to the Teheran Agreement and to rectify some of the "excesses" that Libya
had won in September. In particular, they hoped to reduce the Libyan freight
differential from 63¢ to no more than 40¢ to 45¢, thereby reducing their vulnerability to the "reverse hinge" that the Gulf countries had won.[99] Yet Libya
soon made it clear that it had no intention of settling for the Teheran terms plus a
"reasonable" freight differential. Indeed, according to the *Middle East Economic Survey,* Libya and Algeria considered the Teheran Agreement "something of a sell-out,"[100] and on February 23 Libya presented the companies with a
list of increased demands, including a short-haul premium, retroactive to June
1967, and a 25¢ per barrel obligatory reinvestment provision. According to the
Petroleum Press Service, the demands would cost the companies 65¢ a barrel
more than the equivalent of the Gulf terms; moreover, the Libyans would not
sign a five-year agreement. The Libyans' demands made it clear that they were
attempting to establish a separate Mediterranean pricing zone, so that when
tanker rates eased, the pressure would be on Gulf prices to move up rather than
for Mediterranean prices to go down.[101] The day after Libya presented its demands, Algeria announced it was taking a 51 percent controlling interest in the
French oil companies within its borders, which accelerated the pace of change.

However, Libya's bargaining strength was somewhat weaker than it had been
the previous fall, for on January 29, 1971, Tapline had reopened. That, along
with additional tanker capacity, meant that tanker rates, which had peaked in
November, were falling; therefore Libya's locational advantage and its ability to
create a supply shortage were reduced. *PIW* estimated that if Libya cut off its 3
mb/d, half of this could be made up: a sixth from the Gulf by tanker, a sixth from
Tapline, and a sixth from increased supplies in West Africa and the Western
Hemisphere. That would still leave Europe with a shortfall, but its stockpiles
could fill the gap for well over a year.[102] Moreover, in the fall the Gulf countries
had looked to a Libyan breakthrough as a way of improving their terms, but by
the spring of 1971 they had concluded a new pact with the companies in which
they pledged not to embargo their oil in support of demands for better terms
elsewhere. Libya, therefore, repeatedly backed away from the militant action it
threatened.

In early March, the Libyans threatened to embargo their oil on March 9 if
agreement had not been reached by then. On March 9, the deadline was extended
to March 13, which also passed with no indication that the "drastic action" that
Libya had warned of was imminent. Instead, Libya sent delegates to the other
oil-producing states, not to ask them to join an embargo, but to find out if they

planned to increase production in the event of a Libyan embargo; and Yamani seems to have persuaded Libya to refrain from drastic action and to continue negotiating.[103] At the same time, Libya sought technical assistance from Algeria, the Soviet Union, and U.S. independents, and announced, during the negotiations, that it was studying a project to sell oil directly to foreign state companies.

Yet the basic dispute persisted. As Ian Seymour explained: ''In a nutshell, the companies' objective is to defend the albeit already attenuated bastions of the Teheran price framework at all costs. That of the Libyan side—for a wide variety of compelling reasons, at once economic, political and psychological—is to break it apart beyond defense or repair. Obviously, the two sides cannot both succeed in their endeavor, which is why agreement is proving so difficult.''[104]

On March 11, Syria pledged support for joing action against the companies—possibly a hint to nationalize the IPC and Aramco pipelines. Then, on March 15, the four countries that exported from the Mediterranean threatened to shut-in production if their demands for higher Mediterranean prices were not met. While Iraq and Saudi Arabia were not against Libya's winning better terms, they made it clear that they would not participate in an embargo to back up Libya's demands for an increase beyond the Teheran terms.[105] After Libya made several threats to nationalize the companies, as Algeria had done, the company executives met on March 17 to consider the situation. As Schuler relates:

They listed on the blackboard the pros and cons of making a settlement as follows:
1. Pro settlement:
   a) Defers nationalization and makes it less tempestuous.
   b) Helps to maintain the industry as the middleman.
   c) Keeps the oil flowing.
2. Con settlement:
   a) Puts strains on Teheran.
   b) Makes Libyan oil uncompetitive.
   c) Whets appetite in Libya and elsewhere.
   d) Possibly difficult to convince Europe of its necessity.
   e) Strengthens appeal of Libyan-type approach.
   f) Could keep Canal closed because Libya will finance.[106]

Once again, the companies' interest in retaining their concessions proved dominant and they dropped their Persian Gulf–plus approach and negotiated the Teheran terms on top of the ''inflated'' Libyan price structure. As the *Middle East Economic Survey* said, the result was ''a thumping victory for the Libyans''; they retained all their September gains and secured all the benefits of the Teheran Agreement as well. They won new ground in building the low-sulfur premium into the posted price for the first time and in gaining a compulsory reinvestment provision. Whereas the companies had sought to reduce the Libyan freight differential, the final settlement increased it.[107]

The Teheran Agreement had provided about a 30¢ increase in per barrel take, but the Tripoli Agreement provided Libya an additional increase of about 65¢ a barrel. In six months the companies' tax-paid cost in Libya had gone from $1.40 to $2.30 a barrel. Like the Teheran Agreement, the Tripoli Agreement was supposed to last five years, but shortly after it was agreed to, Libya Vice Premier Jalloud said that if the cost of Libya's imports continued to increase sharply, the Tripoli Agreement might not last the full five years. As Schuler stated, "We knew we were *not* getting a *real commitment* for five years no matter how much we were prepared to give."[108]

The companies could take solace in the fact that Libya settled for substantially less than its earlier "nonnegotiable" demands, and it agreed to cease making claims for back payments during the duration of the agreement. The companies also weakened Libya's proposal for a 25¢-a-barrel company reinvestment program, agreeing only that the six largest companies in Libya would each keep at least one rig busy on exploration and development drilling—an important victory, since compulsory reinvestment was the only Teheran/Tripoli demand to infringe directly on the companies' control of industry operations and investment decisions. The companies also kept the tax-paid cost of Libyan oil low enough to remain competitive in Europe, though that was likely to change (and did) as tanker rates declined and the Suez Canal reopened. Still, as a result of the changes brought about by the Qaddafi regime, the companies' per barrel profits were estimated to have declined from between 45¢ and 48¢ a barrel in 1969 to between 18¢ and 20¢ a barrel in 1972.[109]

Following the Tripoli Agreement, Venezuela, Algeria, and Indonesia adjusted their prices upward to correspond with the Libyan terms, and the companies reached agreements with Nigeria and Saudi Arabia (for its Mediterranean exports) that were patterned after the Libyan Agreement. Also, the companies offered Iraq the Libyan terms (minus the low-sulfur premium, since Iraq did not have low-sulfur oil), but Iraq wanted the same increase that Libya got, arguing that if a premium were paid for one special characteristic (low sulfur), it should be paid for all special characteristics. The Iraqis recounted the special characteristics of their oil: high lube oil yield, low pour point, low H_2S, etc., but the companies knew that if they gave Iraq the same increase, the Libyans would be back, asking for a new sulfur premium.

Thus, the companies were in the same sort of dilemma they'd encountered the previous fall. If they acceded to an exporting country's demand for special treatment, other countries would demand comparable treatment and leapfrogging would ensue. Historically, to avoid such dilemmas, the companies had sought to avoid paying premiums for quality characteristics; however, the companies no longer had the power to resist such demands. But in this case they wriggled out by agreeing to a number of the Iraqi government's longstanding demands on minor matters.[110] However, the general problem—the companies' vulnerability to leapfrogging—had not been resolved by the Teheran/Tripoli agreements, and was likely to persist.

In its settlement with the companies, Iraq received all the Teheran/Tripoli terms. The government and the companies saw the agreement as the prelude to a comprehensive settlement of the issues that had divided them since the Law 80 expropriation in 1961.[111] With world supplies tightening and Iraq no longer the lone radical, or even the leading OPEC militant, its oil was held in higher regard. Finally, when the Shah learned of the "generosity" of the Libyan settlement, he demanded concessions on several longstanding Iranian issues: cheaper barter oil, maximization of exports from the Abadan refinery, and special port dues.[112] These demands indicated that, despite the Teheran assurances, the leapfrogging would continue.

In several respects, the Libyan breakthrough in the spring of 1971 was the most enigmatic of OPEC's victories. The opening of Tapline and the general improvement in transport had weakened Libya's bargaining advantage. At the same time, the Gulf producing states had agreed not to embargo oil in support of Libyan demands that went beyond the terms of the Teheran Agreement, and it seemed likely that they would abide by this pledge. In short, the companies seemed to have gone a long way toward isolating Libya—still, they caved in.

This is explicable only in terms of the deep suspicions that characterized relations among the companies. The independents, who feared loss of their concessions, were willing to pay higher prices in order to protect them. The majors were concerned about the effect of a Libyan breakthrough on the stability of the Teheran Agreement, but they were not aggrieved by the prospect of their competitors' paying higher prices for their Libyan crude. During the companies' strategy meetings, consequently, the majors were willing to agree to higher per barrel payments than the independents.[113]

By this time, moreover, the momentum was on Libya's side. The companies had yielded to pressure the previous fall, and again in January and in February. It was doubtful that, at this late point, they would confront the exporting countries.

THE IMPACT OF THE 1970–71 AGREEMENTS

Any assessment of the developments of 1970–71 must be cognizant of the magnitude of the increases. From the perspective of the oil-exporting countries, the Teheran/Tripoli agreements were an enormous victory. By mid-1971 their per barrel income was roughly 50 percent higher than it had been in 1969. In 1971 alone, the total increase in government revenues was expected to be $4.3 billion.[114]

In the decade after the 1959–60 cut in posted prices, the exporting countries had gained an increase of about 13¢ a barrel. At that point, their per barrel revenue was about equal to what it had been in 1957.[115] Now, in less than one year, per barrel revenues in the oil-exporting countries had gone up by 40¢ or more.[116]

From the perspective of consumers in the West, the price increases that resulted from the Teheran/Tripoli agreements were of minor significance. For every dollar the consumer spent on petroleum products in 1970, 7.9¢ went to the producing countries; following the Teheran/Tripoli agreements, this would increase to about 10¢—hardly cause for alarm. In fact, following the settlements with the exporting countries, the retail price of petroleum products in Europe rose only 3 to 5 percent. And with tanker rates down, the landed price of imported oil was again less than the price of U.S. crude.[117]

As table 5–2 shows, the real cost of crude oil in Europe and Japan was generally less in January 1972 than in 1957. Partly, this was due to the fact that, since 1957, greater tanker efficiencies had reduced the cost of shipping oil from the Persian Gulf by about two-thirds, but mainly it was a consequence of the growing strength of the currencies of other countries relative to the U.S. dollar, as oil was generally priced on a dollar basis.[118] Nonetheless, there was widespread opposition to the companies' efforts to pass the increased costs from the Teheran/Tripoli agreements onto the consuming public. As the *Petroleum Press Service* said, "At a time of rampant worldwide inflation, and of recurrent currency troubles, governments are understandably displeased that the long tradition of low prices for imported mineral oils can no longer be fully maintained."[119] However, little was done to thwart the companies' plans.

The OPEC countries had frequently complained about the high prices the companies charged for petroleum products, but the Teheran/Tripoli agreements placed no restrictions on the companies' pricing in downstream markets. Consequently, in the spring of 1971 *PIW* found that the price increases the oil companies announced in the consuming countries more than covered their OPEC cost increases. Moreover, for most of the previous decade the seven largest companies had after-tax returns on their net assets in the Eastern Hemisphere of about 11 percent, and in 1971 this went up to 12.3 percent. And while earnings per barrel in the Eastern Hemisphere had fallen steadily, from 54.3¢ in 1961 to 33¢ in 1970, in 1971 they increased by .5¢ to 33.5¢.[120]

These developments strengthened the oil companies' preference for a strategy of accommodation, rather than confrontation, with the exporting countries. So long as price increases could be passed on, the financial position of the oil companies would not be jeopardized. Indeed, the OPEC increases provided a

TABLE 5–2. INDEX OF LANDED CRUDE PRICES, 1957–72 (IRANIAN LIGHT: APR. 1970 = 100)

	1957	11/14/70	1/20/72
Germany, Hamburg	174.2	117.9	120.4
Netherlands, Rotterdam	166.5	115.1	120.2
Sweden, Gothenburg	157.8	116.0	125.8
U.K., London	115.3	128.1	123.1
France, Lavera	85.9	128.9	123.1
Italy, Genoa	134.6	116.8	127.7
Japan, Yokohama	183.7	112.9	120.8

Petroleum Intelligence Weekly, Mar. 27, 1972, p. 5.

signal that all the companies could respond to by raising their prices without colluding. In contrast, confrontation would threaten companies with loss of their concessions, and might lead consuming-country governments to act on their threats to bypass the companies and make direct government-to-government deals with the exporting countries. This strategy of accommodation avoided the immediate dangers of confrontation, but it meant continued instability in relations between the companies and the exporting countries, for it invited the countries to make further demands in the future.

At the same time, their success in the Teheran/Tripoli negotiations greatly strengthened the bargaining power of the OPEC countries, for in confronting the international oil companies, the exporting countries had won. As a result, they had a new sense of their power, which would encourage them to seek further victories.

The limited resistance that the exporting countries met from both the consuming countries and the international oil companies made it likely that they would press for more, exploiting the disunity of the West in the process. The ease with which the companies passed price increases on to consumers and the maintenance of high taxes on oil products in the consuming countries indicated that the exporting countries could raise the price of crude substantially without significantly reducing sales. And the success of the exporting countries in threatening unilateral action, nationalization, and production cutbacks virtually assured that such threats would be made in the future.

OPEC's financial success also made it likely that its members would resort to pressure tactics, for with higher prices, several OPEC countries accumulated significant currency reserves, increasing their ability to withhold supplies (see table 4–6). This raised the level that consuming countries would have to stockpile to be adequately protected; but higher prices increased the cost of stockpiling. Consequently, rather than promising five years of stability, as the companies claimed, the Teheran/Tripoli agreements made oil supplies less secure than before.

Another effect of higher per barrel revenues was that exporting countries gave more consideration to conserving their oil resources,[121] and Kuwait, the OPEC country with the highest ratio of currency reserves to imports, was the first to act on this concern. In April 1972, when production in Kuwait reached 3.86 mb/d, the Kuwaiti government announced that, from then on, production would be limited to an average of 3 mb/d. As a result, Kuwait denied the industry access to between 800,000 and 1.2 mb/d of producing capacity, which further tightened the world oil market.[122]

In taking this action Kuwait, like Libya before it, was asserting greater control over its production level, traditionally a prerogative of the companies. Similarly, in 1970 Algeria and Venezuela had begun setting the prices of their crude oil, and by negotiating the Teheran and Tripoli agreements the other exporting countries were asserting greater control over oil-pricing policy. Still, at the end of

1971 the power to set pricing and production policy was primarily in the hands of the international oil companies.

Finally, the Teheran/Tripoli agreements can be viewed as an extension of the dual policy the U.S. government inaugurated with the foreign-tax credit in 1950. Once again, increased oil revenues, rather than direct foreign aid, were used to buttress regimes that were friendly to the United States—except that the larger revenues, rather than being transferred from the U.S. Treasury, would come mainly from consumers in Western Europe and Japan, a development appropriate to the world's growing multipolarity.

Immediately following the Teheran/Tripoli agreements there was an enormous arms buildup in the Middle East. In 1971 the United States agreed to assist Saudi Arabia in expanding its navy, a program that would last until 1983. In the summer of that year the United States agreed to sell F-5 aircraft to Saudi Arabia, and in September the Saudis requested assistance in the modernization of their national guard, which the United States formally agreed to in April 1973. A month later, the United States agreed in principle to sell Saudi Arabia a limited number of Phantom jets. Similarly, in 1972 a U.S. mission made a defense survey of Kuwait, and a year later the Kuwaitis announced plans to purchase $500 million worth of arms from the United States.[123]

The biggest military buildup came in Iran. In May 1972 President Nixon and his national security adviser, Henry Kissinger, agreed to sell Iran virtually any conventional weapons it wanted. In the spring of 1973 Iran concluded what was then the largest military sales agreement ever arranged by the U.S. Defense Department, a $2 billion order that included helicopter gunships, supersonic interceptors, Phantom jet bombers, C-130 cargo planes, and other military equipment. It accounted for more than half of all U.S. foreign military cash sales in 1973. Iran also concluded a Treaty of Friendship and expanded economic ties with the Soviet Union in 1972, enabling the Shah to move the bulk of his armed forces from the northern frontier and toward the Gulf.[124]

As table 5–3 shows, in 1971 and 1972 there was an enormous increase in U.S. military aid and arms sales to both Saudi Arabia and Iran. Moreover, in 1972

TABLE 5–3. U.S. MILITARY AID AND ARMS SALES TO IRAN AND SAUDI ARABIA, 1970–72 (MILLIONS OF DOLLARS)

	Arms Purchases from U.S.			Total Military Aid and Arms Purchases from U.S.		
	1970	1971	1972	1970	1971	1972
Iran	91.2	445.9	499.2	93.8	568.0	612.8
Saudi Arabia	2.6	73.1	306.8	3.2	73.8	307.3

Adapted from table in *MERIP Reports*, no. 30 (Aug. 1974), pp. 12–13.

both Saudi Arabia and Iran launched regional policing operations. In September of that year, the Saudis organized exiles in North Yemen to attack the South (which came to a halt after about two weeks of war). More significant and more effective were the efforts by Saudi Arabia and Iran to suppress the rebellion in Dhofar. In 1971 the Sultan of Oman appealed to Iran and Saudi Arabia for aid in his struggle against the Dhofaris; in 1972 Iran sent a small helicopter squadron and military equipment and Saudi Arabia agreed to provide financial assistance, which financed a mercenary army. On December 20, 1973, Iran's involvement escalated when the Shah sent 10,000 troops to crush the Dhofari rebellion. The Iranian intervention was a heavy blow, which confined the PFLOAG to Oman's southern province.[125]

From the perspective of U.S. foreign–policy makers, the Iranian intervention was a boon, for it contained a radical threat to an essential U.S. interest while avoiding the problems that would accompany direct U.S. intervention. Moreover, it underscored the Shah's willingness to use military force to protect the conservative regimes in the Gulf area. Insofar as the Shah's increased oil revenues made this possible, the U.S. State Department must have viewed it as money well spent.

6

Forging the Grand Alliance: Nationalization and Participation

Less than six months after the Tripoli Agreement, in September 1971 OPEC demanded that the exporting countries be granted "effective participation"[1] in the companies' oil-producing concessions and that they be compensated for the adverse effect of the August devaluation of the dollar on the purchasing power of their oil revenues.[2] In what had become a familiar pattern, the exporting countries threatened "concerted action" if their demands were not met.[3]

The oil companies contended that the demands for participation and currency-related revisions were violations of the Teheran/Tripoli agreements. They cited the provision in the Teheran Agreement that stated: "The existing arrangements between each of the Gulf states and each of the companies to which this Agreement is an overall amendment, will continue to be valid in accordance with their terms." The Tripoli Agreement contained a similar clause.[4] In rebuttal, the exporting countries argued that the Teheran/Tripoli agreements had not dealt explicitly with participation and had been negotiated under the assumption of a dollar with a fixed price against gold.[5] While technically the companies' contention may have been correct, the pressing of narrow legal points would do them little good. Whatever illusions they nourished about five years' stability were shattered by the new demands.

The demand for price adjustments due to changing currency values was dealt with first, and once again Libya initiated action. In September, the RCC revalued the Libyan currency, forcing the companies to increase their dollar payments by 3.6 percent.[6] Yet, with the value of the world's major currencies continuing to fluctuate, resolution of the issue proved difficult. Indeed, the impact of the dollar devaluation and subsequent currency realignments varied for each exporting country, depending upon the currencies it was paid in and the mix of countries that met its import needs.

However, the prospects for a settlement improved in December, when the Smithsonian Agreement provided for a formal devaluation of the dollar against gold and a revaluation of leading currencies against the dollar. This provided both the companies and the exporting countries a framework within which they could negotiate. When OPEC and the companies met in Geneva on January 20, the companies accepted OPEC's demand that they be compensated for the effect that the devaluation of the dollar had on the purchasing power of their oil revenues. This led immediately to an increase in posted prices of 8.49 percent and to creation of an index that would link future payments to changes in the value of a basket of eleven currencies, rather than to the dollar itself.[7]

When Libya refused to go along with the agreement, the companies agreed that if Libya secured better terms, as it threatened to do, they would be extended to the other countries as well. But Libya's bargaining strength was weakened by the decline in tanker rates. As a result, in May it settled for what were essentially the Geneva terms.[8]

While the demand for price adjustments as a result of changes in currency values became largely a technical issue, the demand for participation[9] raised far more fundamental questions about the future relationship of the exporting countries to the international oil companies. On one hand, it reflected the interest of the exporting countries in gaining both national control and increased benefits from oil industry operations. But the countries also recognized their continued dependence upon the international oil companies.

The countries relied on the companies to market their oil. While, in a tight market, countries could probably find buyers for their crude without much trouble, once the market loosened up again, it would be up to the companies to decide where they purchased their crude. And undoubtedly most companies would go first to the countries where they had concessions that offered them "cost crude."

The exporting countries also wanted to preserve the advantages of the industry's vertically integrated structure. Historically, this had enabled the industry to transmit changes in market demand to the production level without delay, thereby reducing the likelihood that crude surpluses would materialize and threaten the price level. Since most of the companies' refineries were in the consuming countries, they were protected from nationalization by the exporting countries.[10] Moreover, the cost of acquiring or building substantial refining capacity was beyond the means of most exporting countries. However, while the participation demands were formally limited to the companies' production operations, Yamani indicated that the OPEC countries would use their surplus funds to invest in refining and marketing operations in the consuming countries.[11]

In addition, nearly all the countries still required technical assistance from the companies in exploration and production. Indeed, at the time the participation demand was raised, no host-government oil company had ever made a major oil find or drilled in 3,000 feet of water.[12] Most countries also needed the companies to supply a high proportion of the capital required for continued exploration and production. As Yamani explained:

Nationalization does not guarantee the state concerned the means to market its crude, particularly if the quantities involved are substantial. . . . But this is not the real problem in my opinion. The real problem is how can any state, Arab or otherwise, continue to search for new oil resources once it embarks on nationalization. If I nationalize the oil resources of my country, the oil companies will withhold investments for oil exploration and there will be difficulties.[13]

And the exporting countries still needed the companies' assistance in the production of their oil.

Moreover, it was in the interest of both the exporting countries and the majors to preserve the concentrated structure of the international oil industry, for that would help to maintain a price level that was already roughly ten times cost. That price level would be jeopardized if the exporting countries were forced to sell their crude to companies that lacked established markets, for in order for such companies to market the oil, they would have to discount it. Nor would it be in the exporting countries' interests to strengthen the competitive position of either their own or the consuming countries' national oil companies vis-à-vis the majors, for that too would threaten the price level that both the exporting countries and the majors benefited from. As Yamani stated, "If we do business with the consumers, and some of them have already approached us, for this, I think there will be very severe competition between them—the international and the national oil companies."[14]

Most countries valued their concessionaire's expertise and sought to preserve the working relationships and stability that the majors' dominance brought to the industry. Consequently, the specialists whom OPEC consulted on its participation demands recommended overwhelmingly that the governments' prospective share of the oil be marketed through existing company channels. Indeed, the OPEC countries wanted their participation share to be treated as part of the companies' overall production and export programs, rather than as incremental output, for a 20 percent increment in production could have devastating consequences on the price level.[15]

By assuring that the major international oil companies had a continuing interest in the profitability of Middle East crude production, the exporting countries would be assured of their continued support. That would mean that these companies, which as refiners were the principal "purchasers" of crude oil, would be less likely to act as aggressive purchasers of crude supplies, seeking at every opportunity to reduce the price. It would also reduce the incentive of the organizations most skilled at finding and developing new oil supplies to develop alternatives to Middle East oil. And the international oil companies were potentially powerful political allies, able to moderate opposition to the exporting countries in the consuming countries. Furthermore, regardless of the final arrangement, it was in the interest of each exporting country for the companies to agree to it. If the companies challenged the settlement, the threat of continued legal action could make it extremely difficult for an exporting country to sell its crude oil or to develop arrangements with other companies. Indeed, uncompensated nationalization would make it hard for an exporting country to attract capital.

At the same time, the concessionaires could benefit from OPEC's participation program, for by the 1970s the predominance of the concessionaires in the international oil industry was threatened by potential opposition within the exporting countries and by the emergent competition from other Western oil companies. Despite its still considerable bargaining strength, each concessionaire was vulnerable to pressure because it might lose its privileged access to a country's crude oil to another company or group of companies. So to protect their privileged positions, the concessionaires were willing to modify their arrangements with the exporting countries. Many oil industry executives recognized that the concession system was no longer viable and that, to secure their interests, a new relationship with the exporting countries would have to be developed.

Given this, the participation program that the exporting countries were to propose had several advantages for the concessionaires. The most important was that it would enable them to maintain control over the bulk of the world's oil supply. In addition, if OPEC established a firm buy-back price that all companies would have to pay for the oil they bought from the countries, it would provide the industry with a worldwide price floor, thereby reducing the likelihood that either the companies or the exporting countries would reduce prices.

Consequently, the broad outlines of an agreement could have been guessed at the outset. The companies would cede the countries an ownership share in the concessions in return for continued preferential access to the countries' crude oil. To be sure, the companies would bargain long and hard over the size of the exporting countries' equity share, the price they would pay for it, the terms under which the companies would buy the "participation" oil back from the exporting countries, etc., but the concessionaires' bottom-line concern was that, in the end, the crude oil would remain in their refining/marketing networks. So long as that was the case, the companies could continue to make profits from it. Yet it was also in the interest of the exporting countries that the concessionaires continue to produce and market the bulk of the crude. The terms of the partnership still had to be spelled out, but it would be a partnership.

NATIONALIZATION

The demand for national control of the oil fields had a long history. As we have seen, in 1951 the Mossadegh regime nationalized the Iranian oil fields, only to give them back three years later, and in 1961 Iraq nationalized the unexploited acreage in the IPC concession. Yet it was Algeria that became the first major exporting country to gain national control of its oil industry. The combination of emphasis on national development and exploitation of the advantages that non-major companies were willing to provide enabled Algeria to achieve this success.

In July 1965 Algeria had concluded an agreement with France for cooperation between the French companies operating in Algeria and Sonatrach, the Algerian national oil company, established in 1963. France provided Algeria with grants, loans, credit facilities, and special access to the French market while Algeria granted the French companies additional concession areas. With France agreeing to pay a tax of 53 percent in 1965–67, 54 percent in 1968, and 55 percent thereafter, the agreement broke the hallowed fifty/fifty principle that officially prevailed in the major Middle East concessions. The agreement served the interests of both countries. For France, it became the symbol of the new relationship to the developing countries that de Gaulle was trying to foster. France also gained oil produced by French companies and paid for in francs. At the same time, Algeria needed the protected French market to sell its high-cost oil. Algeria also used the relationship between Sonatrach and the French companies to develop its own skilled labor and management and professional expertise, so that Sonatrach became the most developed of the producing-country state oil companies.

In January 1967 Algeria nationalized BP's Algerian retail network. The 1967 Arab-Israeli war provided Algeria a pretext for nationalizing all the other oil industry retail networks in the country and for taking control of the small U.S. producing assets, a move that was planned before the war. In response to the Algerian move, the U.S. government was unwilling to make strong representations on behalf of the U.S. companies, because of the U.S. desire to reopen diplomatic relations with Algeria and the growing U.S. interest in importing Algerian natural gas.[16]

Then, in October 1968, Getty Oil agreed to grant Sonatrach 51 percent of its Algerian interests. In return, Getty received the lifting of government controls, recovery of 49 percent of its assets, an exploration permit in a promising area, and easy financial obligations. The agreement marked the first time that a producing country acquired a majority participation in an existing production facility. It also went beyond the fifty/fifty profit-sharing principle, with Getty agreeing to be taxed at 55 percent. In addition, while Getty agreed to provide needed capital, Sonatrach acted as the operating company, and Algeria was to receive 88 percent of the profits from the jointly owned company.[17]

Algeria sought to get the other non-French operating companies within its borders to agree to similar terms, but they resisted. Consequently, in April 1969 Algeria rescinded Sinclair's concession, and in June 1970, four non-French companies were nationalized: Royal Dutch/Shell, Phillips, Italy's AMIF, and Germany's Elwerath-Sofrapel. As a result, the only crude oil not under Algerian control was held by French companies, but these companies accounted for about three quarters of the country's production.[18]

Algeria grew dissatisfied with its relationship with the French companies. It objected to the French companies' rate of investment in the country and the slow rise in its discovered reserves, and its dissatisfaction with the French companies increased as a result of the more favorable agreement concluded with Getty. Consequently, when the 1965 agreement came up for renegotiation in 1969, Algeria sought substantial changes in the relationship. It wanted higher per barrel receipts and greater investment on the part of the French companies. Its bargaining position was strengthened by an agreement on technical cooperation with the Soviet Union; and even before the formal agreement was concluded, Soviet technicians were advising and working with Sonatrach in all aspects of exploration and production.

Negotiations with France broke off in June 1970 and, as we have seen, the following month Algeria unilaterally raised posted prices. France then proposed the opening of overall cultural, economic, and social talks, provided Algeria would temporarily suspend the price increases. Algeria agreed to this, and on October 5 negotiations opened. However, by this time Libya had won major price increases from the companies, and Algeria upped its demands. France was now willing to meet the Libyan terms, but Algeria wanted a further increase. In addition to its price demands, Algeria wanted a 51 percent participation share. Fearing the continual escalation of Algeria's demands, on February 5 France postponed talks until after the Teheran negotiations concluded. Once the Teheran Agreement was announced, France proposed that no final agreement be reached until after the Tripoli Agreement was concluded. Algeria had waited long enough. On February 24, President Boumedienne announced that Algeria was taking a 51 percent controlling interest in French oil companies and nationalizing oil and natural gas pipelines.[19]

France did not contest the nationalization per se, but objected vigorously to the $100 million that Algeria proposed to pay in compensation—a sum that France estimated to be about one-seventh the true value of its Algerian interests. And worse, Algerian claims for back taxes would more than offset the proposed compensation. In retaliation, France in mid-April broke off negotiations with Algeria and instituted a series of reprisals. Technical personnel were withdrawn; France stopped purchasing Algerian oil; and both CFP and Elf-Erap warned prospective buyers that they would take legal action to stop the sale of "hot" oil or gas from nationalized fields. These moves reduced Algerian production to a third of its former level. France also threatened to get the World Bank and the Export-Import Bank to deny credits to Algeria. It attempted to halt the twenty-five-year liquefied natural gas deal which El Paso and Sonatrach had agreed to in the spring of 1970, but this effort met with only limited success. In response to French diplomatic pressure, the White House further delayed approval of the LNG project by voicing concern to the Federal Power Commission, and an Algerian application for a World Bank loan was rejected with U.S. support.[20]

Yet the long-term effectiveness of France's moves was dubious. The Soviet Union sent technicians to replace the ones that France had withdrawn. Major international banks continued to furnish Algeria with loans and credits. Beginning in May, U.S. companies interested in purchasing Algeria's low-sulfur crude began negotiations with Algiers. El Paso denied that France had any valid legal claim, and negotiated for an additional 5 billion cubic meters a year of gas, to be added to the 15 billion already contracted for shipment to the U.S. East Coast. The United States, badly in need of natural gas, was unlikely to deny Algeria access to its markets on any long-term basis, especially since it would mean siding with France and against the only U.S. company involved in the situation. In addition, the State Department, encouraged by the recent improvement in U.S.-Algerian relations, was unlikely to support measures that would reverse this.[21]

Consequently, on June 30 CFP, which had a hard time replacing Algeria's low-sulfur crude, reached an agreement with Algeria, pretty much on the exporting country's terms. CFP agreed to withdraw its boycott and Algeria agreed to increase its compensation offer and reduce its demand for per barrel remittances. However, Algeria's compensation payments were more than offset by its claims for back taxes. Shortly after this agreement was reached, the U.S. State Department informed the Federal Power Commission that it had no objections to long-term imports of Algerian LNG. Elf-Erap, which could draw on its low-sulfur Libyan production, held out longer, but in October it agreed to similar terms. While Algeria's immediate achievement was not overwhelming—the 1965 agreement had given the government a 20 percent interest in most producing fields and as much as 49 percent in some—Algeria became the first major oil-exporting country to establish majority ownership in its oil-producing properties.[22]

Following the conclusion of these agreements, Sonatrach controlled three quarters of Algeria's oil production, all of its natural gas production, and all of its refining, marketing, and transport operations. The only foreign companies still operating in Algeria's oil industry were Getty and the French companies, and, contrary to the expectations of many, Sonatrach was successful in selling its oil. Historically, the major oil companies had refused to deal with state-owned companies, but majors and independents bought oil from Sonatrach,[23] which was able to secure the financing it needed to expand its operations. The state oil company relied on both Western companies and the socialist countries for technical assistance. Algeria was well represented in Washington, with John Connally representing its legal interests until the time he became Treasury secretary, at which point former Secretary of Defense Clark Clifford took over.[24]

Probably the most significant aspect of the Algerian nationalizations were the effect they had on the other exporting countries. With Algeria having taken control of its oil industry, other countries came under political pressure to do the same. As Yamani stated on July 1, 1971, participation in the ownership of concession-holding companies "has become a national demand, especially after the Algerian action nationalizing 51 percent of the assets of the French companies operating in Algeria."[25] And Algeria's success in selling its crude oil indicated that an exporting country could market significant quantities of oil without a direct link to the international oil companies.

In several respects, Algeria's situation was different from that of the other exporting countries. It had a far more developed indigenous technical capability. Exporting far less oil than Venezuela, Libya, Kuwait, Iraq, or Saudi Arabia, it faced fewer problems in marketing its oil. It used the back taxes it was owed by the companies to pay for its 51 percent ownership shares, but few of the other exporting countries could claim such credits. To secure national control of their oil industries, the other exporting countries had to devise methods of paying for their ownership shares.

Venezuela was the first to resolve the issue. On July 30, 1971, a Hydrocarbon

Reversion Law was enacted, giving the Venezuelan government control of the concessions as soon as they expired (in the early 1980s). The law also stipulated that concession areas that were not exploited within three years would revert to the state, and to ensure that their facilities remained in good working order, companies were required to post bonds.[26]

In September, with the Algerian and Venezuelan precedents established, OPEC announced the demand of the oil-exporting countries for effective participation in ownership of the companies' producing assets. OPEC did not stipulate the equity share that the countries envisioned, but it was understood that the six Gulf exporting countries sought an initial 20 percent. But Libya maintained that this was inadequate and rejected collective OPEC bargaining on participation. Reports indicated that the Qaddafi regime would insist on the 51 percent share that Algeria had obtained.[27]

Political developments encouraged Libya to assert its militance. On December 1, 1971, the British were scheduled to complete their withdrawal from the Gulf area, and the day before, Iran, with tacit British support, seized three uninhabited islands in the Gulf. While the islands were not vital strategically, the Shah was apparently concerned that they might be taken over by another power or used by guerrillas as a base of operations.[28] Iran's move was strongly opposed throughout the Arab world, but the strongest response came from Libya. On December 7 the RCC announced the nationalization of British Petroleum's 50 percent share of the Libyan concession it held with Bunker Hunt; Qaddafi declared that this was in retaliation for British support for Iran's action. He also warned U.S. companies, producing in Libya, that if the United States did not change its policy toward Israel, they faced a similar fate.[29]

The BP nationalization was precipitated by political factors, but Libya's interest in securing a 50 percent participation share also played a role. At the time that Libya issued its nationalization decree, the other exporting countries were holding a meeting on participation, and the BP nationalization put pressure on the Gulf countries to increase their demands and to secure a "respectable" participation share. Moreover, like Libya's demands a year before, for terms that exceeded those that the Gulf countries were demanding, the BP nationalization was a warning to the companies that, regardless of what they settled for with the Gulf countries, Libya would ask for more.

Still, the immediate impact on BP was limited. BP needed all the low-sulfur crude it could get, but Libyan oil was only about 5 percent of its worldwide production. And though they were not legally required to do so, the other operating companies in Libya extended the Safety Net Agreement to provide BP with alternative supplies in the event they were needed. However, to prevent BP from making up its losses, Libya placed a freeze on the other companies' production levels.[30]

The BP nationalization demonstrated the pitfalls an exporting country would face in unilaterally altering concession terms. Desperately short of technicians, Libya got Bunker Hunt, Britain's Overseas Technical Services Corporation, and the Soviet Union to provide skilled personnel to operate the field. Yet the major obstacle to resuming production from the nationalized field was that, with replacement oil available in the Middle East, BP was able to mount an effective boycott. The British government, with U.S. support, asked the consuming countries not to buy oil from the nationalized field—which France and Germany quickly accepted. In addition, Bunker Hunt refused a series of requests by the Libyan government to market the nationalized oil, despite the fact that Hunt was selling its crude from the concession, and BP's threat to take legal action against any purchaser of the nationalized Libyan crude prevented sales of this oil to Western markets during 1972.[31] However, on June 1, 1972, the Eastern bloc countries agreed to purchase roughly half the nationalized crude on barter terms. According to Schuler, "This willingness of the U.S.S.R. and other Eastern countries to 'fish in troubled waters' and the West's inability or unwillingness to discourage these contracts emboldened the Libyans and permitted a resumption of momentum which had flagged during the first half of 1972."[32]

Soon after the BP nationalization, another test of the market for "disputed" oil occurred, with similar results. In April 1972 the North Rumailia field, which Iraq had nationalized in 1961, finally came onstream. The IPC immediately contested sale of this oil, threatening prospective buyers with legal action; however, Iraq's exports from the field came to about half of North Rumailia's 1972 planned productive capacity. The bulk of this oil went to the Communist countries that helped develop the field. In addition, companies in Brazil, Ceylon, India, and Italy purchased North Rumailia oil, despite the threat of legal suits.[33]

The quantities of oil involved in the BP nationalization and the sale of North Rumailia crude were small, about 230,000 b/d in the case of Libya and much less in the case of Iraq. In principle, it should have been easy to find markets for such small quantities, but it was easy for the West, and BP and IPC in particular, to do without this oil. Hence, on the basis of these experiences, one cannot say what would have happened had Saudi Arabia (for example) unilaterally nationalized the Aramco concession, with its 5.6 mb/d. Nor did Saudi Arabia seem anxious to find out.

PARTICIPATION

In January 1972 negotiations between the international oil companies and the six Gulf exporting countries began on the participation issue. Saudi Arabia's oil minister, Sheikh Zaki Yamani, the leading advocate of participation, represented the Gulf countries in the negotiations. They demanded an immediate 20 percent government participation,[34] rising gradually to 51 percent, and offered to pay the companies on the basis of net book value; that is, for 20 percent participation they would reimburse the companies for 20 percent of what they had invested in the concessions (minus depreciation). The companies objected, arguing that the market value of the concessions, with their extensive reserves, was far greater than what the companies had invested in them. The differences are illustrated by the fact that, on net book value, a 20 percent share in Kuwait Oil Company would have come to approximately $50 million, but, on a market basis, its value was estimated at from $600 million to $800 million.[35] In addition, the companies argued that net book value failed to take account of interim inflation. In this argument the companies were supported by the U.S. State Department, which indicated that it would consider compensation based on net book value as confiscation and, hence, in violation of international law.[36]

The second major issue between the companies and the exporting countries concerned prices. With 20 percent participation, 20 percent of the oil produced in a concession would belong to the host country. However, the companies and the countries agreed that the bulk of this oil would be sold back to the companies, which would be responsible for marketing it. The question was: What price would the companies have to pay for this oil? The exporting countries proposed a buy-back price midway between the companies' tax-paid cost and the posted price. However, since posted prices were far above market prices, the companies argued that they would lose money on oil purchased at this price.[37]

Other issues included the ownership share that exporting countries would receive and the rate at which this would increase; the amount of oil the countries would market themselves; when and how the countries would pay for their equity shares (In oil or dollars? Right away or over the next twenty years?); and how the future capital needs of the concession would be met (Would the countries, as equity owners, help finance investment projects, or would this continue to be an exclusively company role?).

What made resolution of these issues particularly difficult was the divergent interests of the exporting countries. For example, a capital-rich country like Saudi Arabia might be glad to contribute to the financing of capital projects while a revenue-short country like Iran would probably find this burdensome. Similarly, a small exporter like Abu Dhabi might want to market all of its participation crude, but a giant exporter like Saudi Arabia would be hesitant to take on such a task. Consequently, Yamani proposed a two-phase procedure in which general principles would be agreed to for all the Gulf states, then negotiations with individual countries would follow. Even so, agreement proved difficult.

With both Algeria and Libya having nationalized oil companies, the political pressure on the Gulf states to achieve a breakthrough was strong. Consequently, toward the end of January, Yamani declared that if agreement was not reached by the end of the year, the exporting countries would take unilateral action. In response, Aramco offered Saudi Arabia a 50 percent share in several established but undeveloped areas, but Saudi Arabia rejected this, partly because several other Gulf exporting countries objected on the grounds that they lacked such areas and, therefore, were not able to make similar arrangements.[38] In February, King Faisal told the Aramco partners that participation was imperative, yet the companies were still reluctant to agree to terms.

To coordinate their strategy, the exporting countries called an "extraordinary" OPEC conference for March 11. Yamani indicated that the conference would single out one or two companies at a time and take action to force them to accept the terms that the OPEC countries dictated. However, the conference would not call for nationalization.[39] In addition, Saudi Arabia threatened the companies with unilateral legislation if they refused to accept participation terms within a month. On March 1 Yamani reported to Aramco on his trip to the other OPEC states.

Who are the so-called moderates? There is only Saudi Arabia, Kuwait, and a handful of small Gulf states. There is a worldwide trend toward nationalization and Saudis cannot stand against it alone. The industry should realize this and come to terms so that they can save as much as possible under the circumstances.[40]

Then, on the eve of the OPEC conference, Yamani revealed that Aramco accepted the principle of immediate 20 percent government participation; and the implication was that the other major oil companies would accept it as well. However, the agreement was largely formal; all major issues, including the buy-back price and the basis on which the companies would be compensated, were still to be resolved. It is likely, however, that if the companies had not reached agreement in principle, Libya and Iraq would have taken 51 percent ownership immediately, and the other exporting countries would have supported their action. Had that occurred, "in the escalating situation thus created it would have been extremely difficult if not impossible for the more moderate Gulf producers to have remained restricted to their initial target of an initial twenty percent participation," the *Middle East Economic Survey* explained.[41]

As it was, at the OPEC conference the exporting countries agreed to a majority takeover of the companies if the participation talks failed. In addition, the OPEC members pledged concerted retaliation against firms that refused to accept OPEC participation demands. The possibility of establishing a common defense fund of perhaps $150 million to $200 million was also discussed. According to *PIW*, OPEC's new sanction policy was aimed at preventing the oil companies from agreeing to participation in some countries but not others. Shortly after the OPEC conference, the other companies operating in the Gulf formally accepted the 20 percent participation principle for Abu Dhabi, Qatar, Kuwait, and Iraq.[42]

Along with the Gulf participation talks, in January 1972 Iraq and the IPC began negotiations to resolve the dispute over the territory that Iraq had nationalized in 1961 (the Law 80 dispute). However, by the time negotiations got under way, Iraq had become incensed by a fall off in IPC's exports from its Mediterranean ports. Then, after negotiations broke down in February, Iraqi exports from the Mediterranean fell by nearly 44 percent, to about half of total capacity, in March and April. The companies claimed that the fall in tanker rates and the high taxes on Mediterranean exports (stemming from the 1971 price agreements) made the oil uncompetitive. But the Iraqis viewed the cutback as a form of pressure by the companies. They pointed out that there had been no comparable reduction in Aramco's Mediterranean output via Tapline and that Nigeria's production had increased despite the decline in tanker rates.[43]

In May the companies offered to increase Mediterranean exports if Iraq would reduce its taxes. This outraged the Iraqis, who, with the other OPEC members, saw it as an attack on the 1971 agreements. In addition, the companies sought compensation for the territory that Iraq had expropriated in 1961. If Iraq agreed to this, it would undermine the position that the moderate Gulf exporting countries were taking in the participation talks. They insisted that there could be no compensation for the value of reserves still in the ground. On the other hand, if the companies failed to secure compensation from Iraq, *their* position in the participation negotiations would be weakened. As Geoffrey Stockwell, managing director of IPC at the time, stated:

We could have done a deal, but only by complete capitulation. We would have sold the pass on the current industry talks on participation. Equally if the Iraqis had met our terms they would have sold the pass on the OPEC side. The question of participation and compensation in Law 80 were obviously intermingled. Both sides had their hands tied by the attitudes of OPEC and the oil industry.[44]

Negotiations broke down, and on June 1, 1972, Iraq announced that it was nationalizing the IPC's Kirkuk fields in northern Iraq, leaving the IPC parents with only their holdings in the Basrah Petroleum Company in southern Iraq.[45] Having nationalized its oil, Iraq confronted the problem of selling it. In April, Iraq had signed a fifteen-year Treaty of Friendship and Cooperation with the Soviet Union. The Soviets had encouraged Iraq to nationalize the IPC, and in April a $224 million Soviet loan helped strengthen Iraq's bargaining position. Following the nationalization, the Soviet Union began to purchase Kirkuk oil, aided in transporting it, and agreed to build a refinery in nearby Mosul. However, the Soviet Union could absorb only a small fraction of the output of the Kirkuk fields, and it was unable to pay for this in the hard currency that Iraq badly needed.[46]

Consequently, immediately after nationalizing the Kirkuk fields, the Iraqis sought an accommodation with the IPC, which was also anxious to reach a settlement. Indeed, both parties had an interest in maintaining market outlets for the Kirkuk crude. Accordingly, the IPC quickly agreed to the two conditions that OPEC had stipulated for negotiations: that they be conducted within the framework of Iraq's nationalization law and that the companies take no legal action to hamper the sale of oil from Iraq's northern fields so long as the negotiations were in progress.[47]

While the companies refrained from legal action, Iraq had a hard time selling its nationalized oil, nor was this unexpected. In July, Iraq's vice president, Saddam Hussein, said that in nationalizing the IPC, Iraq anticipated that the worst eventuality would be two years "of being a non-oil country." And though they had pledged not to "unduly" increase production, other OPEC countries boosted their exports in order to replace the Kirkuk oil. Consequently, in early October Iraqi exports from its Mediterranean pipeline were only a third of capacity, and its per barrel income was less than it was under the concession agreement.[48]

In contrast to Libya, Iraq did not have extensive currency reserves. Consequently, there was considerable danger that, in order to sell its oil, Iraq would sharply discount it, breaking the OPEC price in the process. In an effort to prevent this, Kuwait and Libya provided loans to Iraq.[49] However, aside from this "transitional" financial aid and an offer by Algeria to provide technical assistance, Iraq received little support from the other OPEC countries.

As part of its efforts to resolve the dispute, Iraq sought to cultivate a special relationship with CFP, citing "the just policy pursued by France towards our Arab causes and more specifically towards the Palestinian cause."[50] On June 18, a ten-year agreement was concluded, giving CFP the right to buy 23.75 percent of the production of the former IPC fields (its percentage shareholding in the IPC) at the prenationalization price (tax-paid cost) plus any increases OPEC might secure in the future. However, the French made it clear that implementation of the agreement would be contingent upon a satisfactory conclusion of compensation arrangements with the IPC shareholders. In the meantime, CFP attempted to mediate the dispute between IPC and Iraq. While Iraq and its IPC partners were glad to have CFP mediate their dispute, the IPC partners were concerned that CFP might gain an advantage at their expense and that the principle of bilateral intergovernmental deals might gain currency as a result of the Iraqi-French relationship. The French also agreed to provide technical and financial assistance for the development of Iraqi oil and other Iraqi industrial projects.[51]

While both Iraq and the IPC were anxious to reach a settlement, no agreement was likely until the participation talks were concluded. Yet the Iraqi nationalization tended to put additional pressure on the other Gulf countries and the companies to come to terms. As Yamani stated in September: "The nationalization of IPC was a shock to the oil companies. Some of them were not aware of the facts of life, and now realize that they have to face either nationalization or participation. And this is why, in my opinion, they are moving closer to our side."[52]

The next shock came less than a month after the Iraqi nationalization. On June 28 Iran announced that it had reached agreement on the outlines of a separate deal with the Iranian Consortium and was therefore dropping out of the Gulf participation negotiations. The agreement reflected Iran's concern with maximizing its oil revenues, but was quite compatible with the interests of the Consortium. Capital-short Iran agreed to forgo participation in ownership and management. However, it did not have to pay compensation for assets acquired or help finance future Consortium investment projects. In addition, the Consortium agreed to expand Iranian production from its present 4.3 mb/d to 8 mb/d by 1976 and to provide a small quantity of oil to the National Iranian Oil Company for marketing downstream. The main advantage of the agreement for the Consortium was that Iran reaffirmed its right to remain in the country as the principal producer/marketer of Iranian oil for an additional fifteen years after expiration of the existing agreement in 1979. Legally, the Consortium had this right anyway, but Iran and the Consortium recognized that the pace of change in the international oil industry would make it impossible for the Consortium to enforce this option, if Iran did not want it to stay in the country.[53]

The Iranian/Consortium agreement angered the moderate Arab states, which resented the companies' efforts to exploit differences between Iran and the other Gulf exporting countries. Yet the final terms of the Iranian agreement would not be determined until the conclusion of the Gulf participation agreements. In the meantime, the companies had left themselves open to the danger of continual leapfrogging, for the Gulf participation talks, the Iraq nationalization of IPC, and the Iranian/Consortium agreement involved offtake/price agreements and compensation terms. Whatever was agreed to in one set of negotiations would affect the other negotiations, with the probability that each exporting country would try to do a little better than its neighbor. And in the unlikely event that the companies got all three parties to accept "reasonable" terms, Libya was prepared to up the ante again.

The majors' efforts to reach a settlement were also complicated by the challenge they faced from the state-backed or state-owned oil companies in Italy, Germany, Spain, Austria, and Japan. In 1971, oil economist Paul Frankel had arranged to bring these companies together. During 1972, while the participation negotiations proceeded, they met informally to exchange ideas on how they might secure a stake in upstream oil producing operations. Their goal was to buy into the existing concessions. In addition, the state-owned companies in Italy (ENI) and France (Elf-Erap) were discussing the possibility of direct government-to-government deals with the oil-exporting countries.[54] In the event that the participation negotiations broke down, each of these companies would have been happy to provide the exporting countries with industrial equipment, capital, technological expertise, and downstream marketing opportunities.

In addition to facing rivalries from industry newcomers, the majors were divided among themselves. One split was between the four Aramco partners and Gulf, the only U.S. major not part of the Saudi Arabian concession, whose principal concession was in Kuwait. But the reserves of the Kuwaiti concession were not nearly as extensive as those that Aramco had. And while Saudi Arabia planned to greatly expand production, the Kuwaiti government maintained strict limitations on production. Hence Gulf cared less about tying up the crude than the Aramco partners. Moreover, Gulf maintained that the Aramco partners' concern with retaining control over the participation crude weakened their bargaining position on the price they would pay for this oil. At several points, Gulf proposed that the only way to secure a reasonable buy-back price was to let the exporting countries try to market the crude. However, Gulf's position was consistently rejected by the Aramco partners.[55]

The other major split among the majors was between Mobil and the other three

Aramco partners. Each of the other three partners had a 30 percent share of the Aramco concession, but Mobil had only a 10 percent share. Consequently, the other three partners feared that, to increase its share of Saudi Arabia's oil, Mobil might seek a separate deal with the Saudi government. Indeed, on September 12, 1973, Mobil formally notified its partners that it reserved the right to make its own deal with the Saudi Arabian government if the group efforts failed. Yamani was aware of this split between the companies and used it to extract concessions.[56]

In the participation negotiations themselves, the main issues that still divided the concessionaires and the exporting countries were the compensation terms and the amount of oil that would be sold back to the companies. The companies wanted the right to buy back all but 4 percent of the total product whereas the governments wanted no restrictions on the amount of participation oil that they could market directly. The companies still insisted on compensation for the value of future profits from the concession shares the OPEC countries would take over, but the governments wanted to pay only net book value.[57]

After repeated threats by the exporting countries that they would take unilateral action, on October 5, 1972, a Gulf participation agreement was reached between the international majors and the five countries still represented by Yamani. It provided for an immediate 25 percent participation share, rising gradually to 51 percent in 1983. Compensation to the companies would be based on "updated book value," that is, net book value plus an adjustment for inflation.[58]

The governments' share of the oil was to be divided into three categories: oil sold directly by the national oil companies, oil sold back to the companies, and a "balancing factor," that is, oil that the governments would have the option of marketing themselves or selling back to the companies. Agreement on this "balancing factor" was intended to enable the governments to rechannel the crude they could not market back to the companies, and it paved the way for the increase in the government's participation share, from the 20 percent initially sought to the 25 percent actually agreed upon. The companies agreed to pay somewhat more, somewhat less and about the equivalent of the halfway price between tax-paid cost and actual market price for the three categories of oil. Thus the companies would lose about half of the profits they would have made on this buy-back oil if it had remained theirs. The resulting increases in government revenues were expected to be large enough to enable the exporting countries to cover their cash-compensation obligations to the companies.[59]

The agreement did not require the companies to make investments in the exporting countries or provide for participation in the companies' worldwide refining and marketing operations. However, Yamani said that Saudi Arabia would not give long-term supply commitments to anyone who was not prepared to build, or participate in building, new refinery capacity in Saudi Arabia. He also indicated that Saudi investments in downstream operations in other countries would come later.[60] Exxon's Chairman, Kenneth Jamieson, described the participation agreement as a way of building "more stable future relationships." He said that, through the participation agreement, "we have maintained the essential intermediary role of the private international oil companies as the most effective agents for the production, transportation and distribution of oil products."[61]

At the OPEC meeting on October 26–27, Saudi Arabia, Kuwait, Abu Dhabi, and Qatar declared that they intended to become part of the general participation agreement that Yamani had negotiated. However, each country still had to work out the details of its arrangements with the companies, including the exact buy-back prices. Several OPEC countries were unhappy with the agreement. Though it had been represented by Yamani in the negotiations, Iraq refused to endorse the agreement.[62] It objected to the updated book-value compensation formula, which would be disproportionately costly to Iraq as a result of the IPC's lack of new investment in recent years and which would also set a precedent for the compensation to be paid for the nationalization of the Kirkuk fields. They were not directly affected by the pact, but Algeria and Venezuela indicated that they were not pleased with it.[63]

The agreement was also criticized at a Baghdad conference, "Oil as a Weapon in the Struggle against Imperialism and Israeli Aggression and as a Means of Independent Economic Development." The conference was attended by delegates and private observers from the United States, France, Italy, Latin America, Iran, the U.S.S.R. and other Communist countries, Egypt, Syria, Lebanon, Kuwait, and Iraq—but not Saudi Arabia or Libya. The conference issued a statement, declaring that

the international oil cartel is putting forward participation between the imperialist oil companies and the oil producing countries as an alternative to nationalization after the Iraqi nationalization of IPC, and this is aimed at maintaining the domination of the imperialist oil monopolies in the Middle East. Such participation, and the goals it embodies, aims to continue a monopolistic exploitation which runs counter to the issue of liberating national oil resources.[64]

The opposition to the participation agreement that had the greatest impact came from Libya. Libya's oil minister, Mabruk, said that Libya wanted to attempt to market all of its participation crude itself, without automatically having to sell any of it back to the concessionaires. Libya also sought an immediate 50 percent participation share, with compensation based on net book value, and further increases in its equity in the next few years.[65] To achieve this objective, Libya refused to allow ENI to begin exports from a newly developed Libyan field that ENI had spent tens of millions of dollars to bring into production. In addition, ENI was not a party to the Libyan Producers' Sharing Agreement and could expect no help from the other companies operating in Libya. Consequently, shortly after the Gulf agreement was announced, ENI agreed to grant the Libyan government a 50 percent share in the ENI concession. For its 50 percent share, Libya agreed to pay ENI cash compensation on the basis of updated book value. The agreement also left ENI as the permanent operator of the concession, with all management decisions in its hands, and for the first five years it left it up to ENI to market Libya's entire share of the concession's production. Despite these terms, Libya was able to cite the ENI agreement as a case of 50 percent participation at a time when the Gulf states were only getting 25 percent. In an effort to end support for the Gulf participation terms, Libya sent a copy of its ENI agreement to Kuwait, a country that had already expressed reservations regarding the participation pact.[66]

Then, a week after the ENI deal, Libya demanded 50 percent of the profits that Hunt had earned on its sales from the unnationalized portion of the Sarir field, since the nationalization of British Petroleum from the other half of the field. Citing the ENI precedent, Libya demanded a 50 percent participation in Hunt's share of the concession and sought an option that would require Hunt to purchase Libya's share of the oil, produced at a price calculated to drive up (rather than reflect) market prices, as the Gulf arrangements did. Schuler, who worked for Hunt at the time, stated: "It was clear to all concerned that industry acceptance of the Libyan demands would force some or all of the Gulf states to abandon the Yamani agreement and seek equivalent terms to Libya's."[67] With the backing of the majors,[68] Hunt resisted Libya's demands. If Libya cut off its production, Hunt, under the terms of the Libyan Producers' Sharing Agreement, was entitled to receive backup crude from the other companies operating in Libya. However, Libya refrained from taking immediate action.

In addition to the Libyan leapfrog, the other factor that put pressure on the October participation terms was the rapid increase in market prices; as a result of this, the four countries that had accepted the agreement outlined in October sought to win higher buy-back prices from the companies before ratifying the participation agreement. Consequently, although the October agreement was intended to go into effect on January 1, 1973, only Saudi Arabia and Abu Dhabi signed agreements by that date, and to get them to sign, the companies had to agree to several sweeteners over the October terms. Buy-back prices were raised and a timetable for increasing the government's share was speeded up in order to reach the 51 percent mark in 1982 rather than 1983.

Instead of stipulating a minimum percentage of oil for direct sale that the governments would have to take, the final agreement divided the participation crude into only two categories: "bridging" crude, what the governments would be required to sell to the companies, and "phase-in" crude, which the governments could either market themselves or sell to the companies. During the first four years of the agreement, the companies would have to buy whatever portion of the phase-in crude the governments wished to sell them. Phase-in crude would be 15 percent of the participation oil in the first year, 30 percent the second, and 50 percent the third. And rather than get the bridging crude at tax-paid cost, the companies would have to pay market prices for it. Phase-in crude would be purchased at slightly less than market prices.[69]

As table 6–1 indicates, the participation agreement would raise the com-

TABLE 6–1. THEORETICAL FORMULA FOR 100 BARRELS OF ARABIAN LIGHT AS A RESULT OF PARTICIPATION

75 barrels at tax-paid cost of $1.621	$121.575
18.75 barrels at bridging price of $2.05	38.438
3.75 barrels at phase-in price of $1.97	7.388
2.50 barrels at market price to replace oil sold directly by oil-exporting countries	5.375
Total cost for 100 barrels	$172.776
Minus preparticipation cost of 100 barrels	162.100
Additional cost of 100 barrels due to participation	$ 10.676

PIW, Jan. 8, 1973, p. 2.

panies' costs by roughly 10¢ per barrel, or about 6 percent. For crude-short companies, the increase would be slightly greater, since these companies would have to pay market prices to replace the oil they had been overlifting (producing in excess of entitlements as a shareholder). Yet, with market demand strong and with clauses in their long-term contracts that enabled them to increase prices as a result of increased costs stemming from changes in fiscal arrangements with the producing countries, the companies did not have much trouble passing these increased costs on to consumers. Moreover, with the participation agreements, the concessionaires retained a substantial advantage over other oil companies, which would still have to purchase all their oil at market prices.[70]

In mid-January, Qatar and Kuwait, but not Iraq, concluded similar agreements with the companies. However, Kuwait's National Assembly refused to approve the agreement, reopening the negotiations between Kuwait and the companies.[71]

As expected, acceptance of the participation agreements by Saudi Arabia and Abu Dhabi set off fireworks in the Middle East. Citing the increase in the government's participation share from 20 percent to 25 percent and the last-minute increases in the buy-back prices, the Shah demanded that the Consortium renegotiate the agreement reached with Iran the previous June. He insisted on financial terms equivalent to those in the Gulf. In addition, the Shah offered the Consortium a choice between (1) continuing the current relationship until the existing agreement expired in 1979, and then being treated as any other buyer, or (2) agreeing to a complete and immediate takeover in return for guaranteed supplies at a special discounted price for the next twenty to twenty-five years.[72]

The companies might have tried to resist the Shah's demands, but they feared competition from new parties in the event they failed to cement their relationship with Iran. In fact, shortly after the Shah made his new demands, the West German cabinet reaffirmed its support for the government-subsidized petroleum company, Deminex, which expressed interest in combining joint exploration-production ventures in the OPEC countries with long-term crude-supply contracts. In early February *PIW* reported that Deminex planned to sound out Iran on the possibility of such a venture.[73]

Anxious to tie up the Iranian crude at a preferential price, on March 5, 1973, the Consortium accepted the Shah's guaranteed-supply option. According to the agreement, for the next twenty years the Consortium would remain as a service contractor, operating the concession for the Iranian government. The Consortium would have the exclusive right to export 96 percent of Iran's oil in 1973 (which would decline gradually to 81 percent in 1981); however, Iran became the legal owner-operator, with official responsibility for financing and investment decisions, including the layout of funds and the choice of capacity to develop and of oil to be made available for sale. The agreement also gave Iran control of the Abadan refinery. And the Shah indicated that, eventually, Iran planned to sell all of its export oil through its own downstream facilities.[74]

The settlement provided that the companies would purchase the oil at cost plus a fee, a formula that guaranteed Iran the financial equivalent of the Gulf participation terms. The Consortium also reaffirmed its commitment to expanding Iran's export capacity to 8 mb/d by 1976. Finally, as a prepayment for crude oil, the Consortium agreed to provide 40 percent of the funds Iran would require for its annual budgeted capital expenditures between 1973 and 1980.[75]

The Gulf participation agreements also paved the way for a settlement of the Iraqi nationalization dispute. On February 28, 1973, IPC and Iraq reached an agreement, resolving all major issues that had divided them since 1961. The agreement was a masterpiece of issue linkage and face-saving accommodation. The companies implicitly recognized Iraq's nationalization. Though the word "compensation" was never officially mentioned, Iraq agreed to provide the companies with 15 million tons of Kirkuk oil free of all cost. In settlement for back claims against the IPC, the companies agreed to pay Iraq $345 million.

For the companies, it was a relatively good deal. They had never doubted that they would eventually have to pay Iraq for the royalty expensing that they had denied the radical oil exporter since 1964, and compensation for other claims had been expected as well. Consequently, they had the free oil in compensation for the Iraqi nationalization. For Iraq, it was not a bad bargain either. The value of the oil was about equal to the amount it would receive from the companies in payments on back claims, so that Iraq was able to resolve its nationalization dispute successfully, without reducing its hard currency resources. The settlement also removed all legal impediments on the sale of North Rumailia crude. In addition, IPC retained its ownership of the Basrah Petroleum Company in southern Iraq and agreed to expand output there from 35 million tons in 1973 to 80 million tons in 1976. And in accordance with the agreement reached the previous June, CFP secured the right to purchase 23.75 percent of the oil produced from the nationalized fields at a preferential price.

Ironically, the first nationalization of a major Middle East oil producing field in twenty years had actually led to a major improvement in relations between Iraq (historically the most radical OPEC member) and the major international oil companies. The settlement also enabled Iraq to reduce its dependence upon the Communist countries for capital goods, technology, skilled personnel, and markets. Indeed, as soon as the settlement was concluded, Iraq announced that all future sales would be for cash not barter (the "currency" the Communist countries paid in).[76] As a result, there was some movement toward, and considerable potential for, a shift in Iraq's political orientation—from East to West.

Yet Iraq was not a wholly reformed state. Less than a month after the IPC agreement, Iraqi and Kuwaiti troops clashed. Kuwait charged that Iraq occupied its territory without provocation. Iraq, which had never given up its claim to Kuwait, was reported to be interested in gaining an outlet through Kuwait for its North Rumailia crude. Indeed, Iraq later demanded that Kuwait hand over two Gulf islands, one for use as an export terminal and one for use as a military base.

Aside from concern about its sovereignty, Kuwait was alarmed by the Soviet involvement in the North Rumailia project. However, following the mediation efforts of several Arab states, the Iraqis withdrew and the dispute subsided. In the meantime the Shah had made clear that, if necessary, he would intervene to protect Kuwait.[77]

Unlike Iraq and Iran, Libya did not seek simply to benefit from the general participation agreement, but to tear it apart. Using the tactics of divide and conquer that it had employed so effectively in 1970, Libya, in January 1973, summoned the three independents in the Oasis group for participation talks. Conspicuously absent from the Libyan summons was the fourth Oasis partner, Shell, one of the international majors.[78] In February, Libya proposed a 50 percent participation deal, which would be twice as costly as the Gulf terms. Then in May, Libya demanded 100 percent participation in the Oasis, Occidental, and Chevron-Texaco Amoseas concessions. Libya proposed compensation at net book value and sales to the companies at market prices. Yet Libya did not regard these demands as tantamount to nationalization, for the concessionaires would remain as service contractors with a preferred right to buy the oil.[79]

Largely as a result of its lack of success in selling nationalized oil,[80] the RCC was reluctant to take unilateral action. As Qaddafi explained, Libya "won't unilaterally nationalize its oil resources and industry" because from a takeover by Libya alone, "other wealthy Arab states would profit to boost their own production and help imperialist powers to declare an economic blockade against Libya."[81] Instead, Libya explored the possibility of bringing in the consuming-country national oil companies, which would buy out the concessionaires in Libya and establish joint-venture arrangements with the Libyan national oil company.[82] In the end, realization of Libya's objectives had to await a further tightening in the world oil market, which was not long in coming.

The participation agreements and accompanying nationalizations were significant in several respects. First, they kept the momentum building toward acquisition of greater and greater oil-exporting-country power. The demands for participation also put an end to any illusions the oil companies might have harbored about the Teheran/Tripoli agreements' resulting in five years of stability. As in the earlier agreements regarding oil pricing, in the participation negotiations the oil-exporting countries again showed that they could threaten unilateral action and production cutbacks and that they could exploit the disunity among the international oil companies.

By gaining an equity interest in the companies' producing operations, the oil-exporting countries further increased their control over industry operations. Most significantly, by resisting the companies' demand that compensation be paid for the value of the oil reserves that the companies returned to the exporting countries, the countries established the claim that national sovereignty meant control over the resources in one's country, irrespective of the fact that contracts signed in an earlier period had ceded such control to the companies. Nonetheless, despite these gains, through the participation agreements the exporting countries acknowledged their continued dependence upon the international oil companies for technological assistance and aid in the marketing of their oil.

7

Market Forces and Political Forces: Prelude to the Oil Crisis

The oil-price increases between October 1973 and January 1974 were cataclysmic, but the forces that produced those increases had been germinating for several years. The oil-consuming countries failed to develop an effective, coordinated strategy for responding to the rise in the exporting countries' power, nor did the individual consuming countries develop effective energy policies. With the world economy booming and U.S. oil production declining, demand for OPEC oil increased sharply during 1972–73, which further strengthened the exporting countries' bargaining position and led them to make new demands. At the same time, the United States failed to respond to Egypt's efforts to enlist its aid in bringing about a resolution of the Arab-Israeli conflict. By the end of 1973, Egypt had little recourse but war, and the Arab oil-exporting countries were under increasing pressure to use the "oil weapon" to advance the Arab position in the struggle against Israel.

By the early 1970s it was evident that major changes were occurring in the international oil industry. To protect their interests, the oil-consuming countries would have had to reduce their dependence upon Middle East and North African oil by diversifying their supply sources, developing alternative energy sources, and cutting their growth in energy consumption. To cope with a short-term loss of supplies, oil stockpiles had to be built up and spare productive capacity (which could be drawn upon in times of emergency) created. To minimize the danger that, in periods of tight supply, consumers would bid up prices, the consuming countries had to limit the amount they would pay for oil and to share equitably whatever supplies were available. Finally, to maintain both price stability and supply security, the consuming countries could have attempted to work out cooperative arrangements with the exporting countries. Yet prior to the Arab oil embargo, very little progress was made in any of these areas.

The United States took the lead in pushing for consuming-country cooperation and pointed out the dangers of a supply cutoff. The United States also warned against consuming countries' bidding up prices and urged the other advanced countries to refrain from concluding bilateral deals with the exporting countries. The United States proposed formation of an international authority to prevent competitive bidding for available energy in periods of shortage, and it suggested cooperation to find new sources of oil and natural gas and to develop alternative energy sources, but the Europeans and Japanese were reluctant to follow the U.S. lead.

In the fall of 1969, at a meeting of the OECD Oil Committee, the Department of State first raised the possibility of a common consumer-country approach to energy problems. The following May, the United States urged that energy problems be dealt with in a multilateral context; the issue was raised again in the fall of 1971 and in the spring of 1972. On all these occasions the U.S. proposals received little positive response. The United Kingdom, the Netherlands, and a few other countries supported the U.S. initiative, but most countries did not. In an official statement at an OECD meeting in 1972, the United States declared that

it is imperative for the world's major consumers of oil and other forms of energy to take joint and coordinated action—starting now—to increase the availability of all types of energy resources; to lessen, to the degree possible, an overdependence on oil from the Middle East, to coordinate the response of consuming countries to restrictions on the supply of Middle East petroleum, and to develop jointly and cooperatively a responsible program of action to meet the possibility of critical energy shortages by the end of this decade.[1]

The United States demanded that the Europeans and Japanese indicate whether they preferred a cooperative or autarkic approach to energy issues. The European Community said it favored the cooperative approach, and while the Japanese response was ambiguous, it seemed inclined toward cooperation. Yet even after this formal declaration, the United States was the only country that favored establishment of an oil consumers' front; and very little positive action resulted.[2] There were several reasons for this. There was little recognition of the nature of the impending problem, and for most policy makers the need for dealing with it did not seem urgent; the price increases that stemmed from the Teheran/Tripoli agreements seemed manageable; and in the winter of 1970–71 the United States had assured its allies that the agreements would safeguard the stability of supply for the next five years. Nor were the Europeans or Japanese concerned about the participation agreements, which were viewed as an issue between the Anglo-American oil companies and the exporting countries.[3]

More significant than their lack of awareness were the differences of interest among the consuming countries. It was not simply that they were unconcerned by the demand for participation, but that many people in Western Europe and Japan believed they could benefit from the changing relationship between the oil-exporting countries and the Anglo-American companies. In addition, the nations of Western Europe and Japan avoided alignment with the United States because of their fear of being identified with U.S. support for Israel.

The OPEC nations had indicated that they were opposed to formation of an ''importers' OPEC'' and, consequently, many consuming countries feared they had more to lose by offending OPEC than they had to gain from collective action. The Japanese were hesitant to cooperate with the United States because they suspected that part of the reason for the U.S. capitulation to OPEC demands in 1970–71 was U.S. interest in boosting oil prices in order to retard the growth of Japanese exports,[4] but France pursued the most independent policy. The French were still deeply hostile to the Anglo-American oil companies. As a result of the recent nationalization of the French companies in Algeria, France had lost its principal foreign crude base and once more was unable to meet its longstanding goal of having French companies control as much crude worldwide as France consumed domestically. But despite the setback in Algeria, France's post-1967 policy of seeking better relations with the Arab world appeared to be paying off. In 1972 Iraq had signed a special agreement with the French, and it seemed that, rather than cooperate with the consuming countries, France would be better off going it alone. Certainly the vague promises about the benefits of consumer cooperation would not persuade the French to pass up an opportunity to gain a piece of the long-coveted Arabian Peninsula. France also saw energy as another issue on which the United States was attempting to subordinate Europe's interests to its own. Thus energy issues became part of France's wider campaign against Kissinger's "Atlantic charter."[5]

While France and Italy identified themselves as consumers (both countries were heavily dependent upon imported oil), as a result of the North Sea discoveries Great Britain and Norway increasingly identified their interests with those of the oil-producing countries. High prices were fine if one were about to become an oil exporter. Moreover, the balance-of-payments benefits the United Kingdom derived from the profit remittances of its major oil companies were proportionately greater than those the United States received from its oil companies.[6] Consequently, while the United States became increasingly concerned about the growing cost of imported oil, Great Britain was much more inclined to see a rise in oil prices as in its interests.

Yet the U.S. emphasis on consumer cooperation was paradoxical. The United States was far less dependent upon imported oil and had far better prospects of becoming self-sufficient in energy than most of the nations of Western Europe and Japan. Also, the United States had several advantages in developing a special relationship with the oil-exporting countries. It offered the largest market, and because of the historic dependence on declining domestic sources, it offered the greatest growth potential. The United States had sophisticated technology, particularly oil industry technology, to offer the oil-exporting countries, and the United States could provide more outlets for the exporting countries' capital investments than any other country. Finally, its military and political power made it a much sought ally. In short, if any country could go it alone, it was the United States. But because of this, many consuming countries regarded the U.S. initiative on cooperation with suspicion, fearing that the United States was attempting to subordinate them politically.

Leadership on the energy issue, nevertheless, had to come from the United States, for the capital it could pour into research and development on alternative sources and the extensive domestic resources that it could exploit were essential to the success of any consumer-country program. But in the context of growing international economic competition, the United States was unwilling to subordinate its national interests to those of responsible international leadership. While the United States assumed leadership on the issue, it acted ambivalently, which reconfirmed the suspicions of many consuming countries and further impeded the prospects for cooperation. This wariness was intensified in the fall of 1972, when Yamani proposed that Saudi Arabia be given a "special place" in the U.S. market. Saudi oil imports would be exempted from restrictions and duties and Saudi investments in U.S. marketing and refining would be encouraged. The United States would also aid in the development of Saudi Arabia. In return, the United States would have a preferential claim on Saudi oil.[7]

The prospects of a special relationship between the world's leading oil exporter and its leading consumer sent chills up the spines of European and Japanese officials, who feared that such an arrangement would preempt oil supplies and force them to pay higher prices for what was left. Moreover, Iran had proposed a similar arrangement to the United States four years before, and was still believed to be interested;[8] and Venezuela had long sought a special relationship with the United States. If the United States accepted the Saudi offer, who knew what sort of "polygamy" would follow? The mere prospect of a U.S.-Saudi deal led several consuming countries to scurry about, seeking to lock up enough crude to meet their needs. According to Akins, between the time the Saudi offer was made and the summer of 1973, at least three governments made overtures to Saudi Arabia with offers of attractive long-term contracts.[9]

While the Saudi offer was contrary to the multilateral principles the United States asked others to subscribe to, the United States was reluctant to reject it. Finally, in June 1973, the United States said it would accept no bilateral arrangements. Several factors influenced the U.S. decision: the proposed U.S.-Saudi arrangements ran against the principle of most-favored-nation dealings in energy with Venezuela and Canada; an agreement with Saudi Arabia would have angered Iran and other exporting countries; and a special relationship would involve the sale of sophisticated military equipment to Saudi Arabia, which supporters of Israel would oppose. However, the United States agreed informally to provisions enabling Saudi Arabia to invest in U.S. oil refining and marketing; and in September 1973 *Platt's Oilgram News Service* reported that, with Kissinger's ascension to secretary of state, the United States had secretly decided to pursue the "special relationship" with Saudi Arabia.[10]

The equivocation (and partial capitulation) of the United States would further arouse the suspicions of the other consuming countries, yet this was one of several instances in which the United States put its national interest ahead of its commitment to the principles of a liberal world economic order. Another was the insistence of the United States on including only oil that traveled by water in an emergency sharing plan, which meant that, in a worldwide shortage, oil consumption would be cut back proportionally less in the United States than in countries that imported the bulk of their oil. For example, with the United States importing only a third of its oil supply and getting about a sixth of this by pipelines from Canada, a 10 percent cutback in seaborne imports would reduce U.S. consumption by less than 3 percent. In Japan, in contrast, where nearly all oil was imported by tanker, a 10 percent cutback in imports would mean a 10 percent cutback in consumption.

Not surprisingly, the Japanese maintained that all consumers should be cut back in proportion to their total energy requirements, and the French supported a plan based on each nation's "vital needs." However, while the United States advocated an oil sharing agreement, Congress refused to permit the sharing of domestic production. Consequently, the United States refused to accept either the Japanese or the French approaches, and the Europeans and Japanese regarded the U.S. position as unreasonable. If a cutoff in Middle East supplies occurred, it was likely to stem from U.S. support of Israel. Why, then, should the Europeans and Japanese have their oil supplies cut back more than the Americans?

The European OECD countries had a sharing plan since 1960, but disagreements between the United States and the other consuming countries prevented inclusion of Japan or the United States. Yet as Geoffrey Chandler, head of government relations at Royal Dutch/Shell, warned in the summer of 1973, an oil sharing agreement was urgently needed to prevent competitive price bidding in the event of a supply crisis, and the absence of an international sharing plan made an embargo more likely.[11]

The failure of the United States to champion consumer cooperation successfully stemmed in part from its declining predominance in the international oil industry. The decline in U.S. spare capacity limited the ability of the United States to supply Japan and Western Europe in emergencies, and because the ability of the United States to intervene in the Middle East was limited, the United States was no longer able to guarantee the flow of oil to Western Europe and Japan. In addition, the ability of the United States to support Western Europe and Japan was limited by its growing dependence upon Arab oil, its interest in maintaining good relations with the Arab world, and its commitment to Israel.

Like the other consuming countries, the United States did not want to appear to confront OPEC by creating a common front of consuming countries, and in May 1973 a State Department official ruled out the use of force in the event of an oil embargo, a policy which was confirmed by the National Security Council that summer. And though the United States had repeatedly warned against the dangers of competitive bidding, in the summer of 1973 it refused to support a proposal to put a ceiling price on oil. At that time, the price of oil was being bid up by a wide range of companies, including U.S. independents and consumer-country national oil companies. However, with domestic supplies running short, the United States badly needed the oil. That summer, a proposal for cooperation on the development of alternative energy sources was also rejected.[12]

CONSUMER-COUNTRY RESPONSES

In the absence of consumer-country unity, the EEC, Japan, and the United States each attempted to develop its own energy policies; however, several problems were inherent in this multicenter approach. It did not facilitate either the coordination of strategy or the pooling of resources for developing new energy sources, and the options of Western Europe and Japan were limited by their lack of domestic energy resources. Moreover, in practice, the determination and implementation of policy proved difficult.

In Japan, the emphasis continued to be on securing foreign oil under the control of Japanese nationals. The Japanese still feared that, in a supply crunch, the U.S. and European governments would direct the international oil companies to give their home countries preferential treatment. During the first quarter of 1973, four new Japanese oil groups were formed (making a total of nine), with the stricture that they get into the international oil industry in a hurry. Yet, rather than additional energy supplies, the immediate effect of this policy was to put additional upward pressure on world oil prices. Moreover, the idea that, in a supply crunch, it would help countries to have foreign oil controlled by its nationals was questionable, for in such a situation, particularly if it were politically motivated, the exporting countries—not the companies or their home governments—were likely to control the allocation of supplies. In addition, in May 1971 Japan raised its 1985 planning target for nuclear power from 30,000–40,000 megawatts to 60,000 megawatts. At that level, nuclear power would account for a quarter of Japan's electric generating capacity. However, by the end of 1972 Japan had only 1,823 megawatts of nuclear capacity in operation. [13]

In May 1973, when the European Council of Ministers held its first meeting on energy policy in more than three years, a dispute immediately broke out between France and the other members. France maintained that, before considering its relations with either the exporting or the other consuming countries, the Community had to work out a common internal energy policy. What France had in mind was adoption of common regulations on oil prices and imports, similar to those that France herself had long employed. Most of the EEC members were opposed to enacting such controls over the internal market. They wanted to defer the issue and, instead, formulate a common external policy. But France maintained that the Community had no authority to define a common position vis-à-vis the outside world and insisted on the right of each country to formulate its own policy with respect to the exporting countries. In taking this position, France maintained the freedom to make its own deals with the exporting countries and prevented the Common Market from entering into agreements with the United States. [14]

As a result of the disagreements between France and the other EEC members, the Community was unable to adopt a resolution on energy policy, but the council agreed to a directive requiring that, by June 30, 1974, member states provide themselves with "instruments" to mitigate the effects of a sudden oil shortage. These included stockpiling, rationing, emergency price controls, mutual consultation, and free exchange of information. In addition, the council allocated $25 million for Community energy projects in 1974.[15]

However, the unresolved issues included relations between the oil-importing and -exporting countries, organization of the Community oil market, promotion of nuclear energy, the future role of coal, the use of natural gas, the implications of energy policy for the environment, ways of making more efficient use of energy, and development of new energy sources. The Community also failed to agree on restraints to prevent the bidding up of prices by its members, and received no mandate to propose such a system to the United States or Japan. Finally, as part of their effort to deal with the insecurity of Middle East oil supplies, the nations of Western Europe, like Japan and the United States, gave renewed emphasis to development of nuclear power.[16]

In comparison with Europe and Japan, the United States had far greater energy options. Nonetheless, on June 4, 1971, when President Nixon delivered the first presidential energy message in U.S. history, he warned Congress and the American public that the United States could no longer take energy self-sufficiency for granted. (Indeed, several urban areas had experienced "brownouts" the previous summer.) The president proposed a comprehensive energy research and development program, whose principal objective would be demonstration of a nuclear breeder reactor by 1980. The president also called for increased efforts to develop technology for the gasification of coal, control of sulfur oxide emissions, and production of shale oil, and he cited the need for long-range efforts in geothermal, solar, and nuclear fusion. However, $77 million of the roughly $100 million in new funding that the president proposed was for the breeder and $16 million more was to improve the supply of enriched uranium.

A month later, Nixon asked for $2 billion in federal funding over the next decade for breeder reactors. His proposed program was designed to shift the U.S. energy mix away from oil and toward greater use of nuclear power and coal. The president also proposed that all federal energy resource development programs (some fifteen of them) be put under one agency. He called for more rapid sale of oil and gas leases on the Outer Continental Shelf and he removed all restrictions on oil imports from Canada. But the president failed to say anything about policy on the Alaska pipeline, oil imports, or tax and price incentives for U.S. oil production.[17]

In the fall of 1972 the United States entered negotiations with Venezuela on development of that country's heavy oil deposits (almost tar). The Faja Bituminosa, in eastern Venezuela, was estimated to contain 700 billion barrels of petroleum. The oil companies had known about these deposits for years, but, doubting their commerical viability, had shown little interest in developing the area.[18] However, with the world oil situation worsening, the U.S. government proposed a bilateral deal under which it would guarantee Venezuela access to the

U.S. market and have private U.S. companies make investments in developing the area. In return, Venezuela would guarantee that the U.S. companies that made these investments would have long-term rights to remain in Venezuela and earn profits from their investments.

When word of the negotiations leaked out, it caused a furor in Venezuela. The opposition party in Venezuela accused the government of negotiating behind the country's back and compromising Venezuelan sovereignty—charges that struck a responsive chord among the Venezuelan electorate. Consequently, with Venezuelan elections scheduled for 1973, the government announced that it would not turn the Faja over to foreign companies.[19] Having been denied free access to the U.S. market for thirteen years, Venezuela would deny the United States access to its resources.

Aside from the initiative on the Faja, the United States concentrated on development of domestic resources. Between 1971 and 1973 the U.S. energy research and development budget increased by nearly 50 percent; yet, despite the budget's emphasis on nuclear power, the nuclear program fell behind schedule.[20] Between 1970 and 1973, U.S. production of oil and coal declined. Growing environmental concern played a role in these declines. In 1970, the Clean Air Act placed restrictions on the burning of coal, and the Alaska pipeline, with its 2 mb/d capacity, was delayed by an injunction that prevented the Interior Department from issuing a construction permit until it evaluated the pipeline's adverse environmental impacts. The injunction had been secured as a result of legal action by a coalition of environmental groups. Scheduled to begin operation in 1972, the pipeline's delay slowed the pace of exploration and production in Alaska.[21] Also, after the Union Oil spill in the Santa Barbara Channel, the United States imposed a moratorium on drilling in the area and subsequent offshore leasing was delayed. In the early 1970s, U.S. natural gas production began to level off as well (see table 7–1).

Yet U.S. energy consumption continued to increase, so that there was a growing gap between supply and demand. Indeed, in the winter of 1972–73 many consumers in the Midwest had to shift from natural gas to heating oil, and several Northeastern cities experienced a shortage of fuel oil. In the short term, the only way of closing the gap was to import more oil. Consequently, industry and government officials began to predict huge increases in U.S. oil imports. In 1972 a National Petroleum Council study found that by 1975 the United States

TABLE 7–1. U.S. ENERGY PRODUCTION, 1970–73

	1970	1973	1970–73
Oil (billion barrels)	4.12	4.00	−3.0%
Natural gas (billion cubic feet)	1,135	1,152	1.5%
Coal (million short tons)	612.7	598.6	−2.1%

Adapted from U.S. Dept. of Interior, *Energy Perspectives*, pp. 86, 148, and 134. Percentages computed by author.

would be importing 9.7 mb/d, or 51 percent of its total supply—nearly three times the 3.4 mb/d the United States imported in 1970. Despite this prediction, the National Petroleum Council urged retention of the oil import quota system to protect the nation against "unrestrained imports." At an OECD meeting in the winter of 1972–73, Under Secretary of State John Irwin warned the other consuming countries that by 1980 the United States would have to import half of its crude oil needs—12 mb/d, or nearly twice as much as any country was exporting in 1972.[22]

These projected increases in U.S. oil imports were expected to put enormous pressure on world oil supplies, and by the beginning of 1973 the impact had begun to be felt. In 1972 U.S. oil imports had increased by 20 percent; then, in January 1973, the United States increased its oil import quotas by nearly a million barrels a day, potentially doubling the amount of oil from the Eastern Hemisphere that could enter the United States in 1973, compared with 1972. For the first time, Eastern Hemisphere imports would account for more than half of all U.S. imports. As PIW reported, "Further upward pressure on already soaring crude prices and tanker charter rates is likely to result from the sharp rise in U.S. import quotas, industry sources generally agree."[23]

By spring the landed price of imported oil was generally higher than the price of domestically produced oil. Nonetheless, at the end of March the president empowered the Oil Import Appeals Board to grant additional quotas, without limit, whenever refiners, distributors, etc., could prove "exceptional hardship." In March, further compounding the problem, Canada announced that to meet its own domestic needs, it was freezing its level of oil exports to the United States.[24]

In April, with oil prices rising rapidly, Akins told the American Petroleum Institute that the main short-run task of consumers was to work out mutually satisfying arrangements with the oil producers to prevent a skyrocketing of prices. He proposed a "multilateral consumer-producer commodity agreement," aimed at avoiding ruinous price competition. He warned that if an international oil shortage resulted and countries bid against each other, a "postulated" price of $10 a barrel by the end of the decade would not seem "unrealistic" but would be "almost intolerable." The $10 price would be unavoidable, he said, in the absence of a national-international production price formula.[25] Yet the international cooperation that would make such an agreement feasible did not exist; so the proposal drew little response.

With imported oil selling for more than domestic oil in the United States, oil industry opposition to elimination of the import quotas waned.[26] For the first time it became possible for increases in the price of OPEC oil to pull the price of U.S. oil up. Indeed, only the maintenance of domestic price controls prevented this, and it was in this context that Nixon delivered his second energy message, on April 18, 1973. The president abolished the fourteen-year-old oil import quota system, but in so doing he sought to restore the differential between the prices of domestic and foreign oil that the import quotas had preserved until recently. According to the president's proposal, imports up to 1973 levels would be permitted free of charge for seven years. However, imports above those levels would be subject to an import fee that was designed to reduce U.S. import dependence by pushing up the price of oil in order to reduce demand and boost supply (especially since, at the proposed prices, domestic oil would be far more profitable to the companies than foreign oil).

The president also sought to boost coal consumption by delaying the toughest part of air quality standards, sulfur emission limitations, for up to two years; and he called for tripling the federal leasing program for offshore oil and gas exploration in 1974 and for deregulating the price of newly discovered natural gas by an amendment to the Natural Gas Act. Yet the president did not say anything about U.S. relations with the oil-exporting countries.[27] Shortly after his energy message, Nixon established a White House Energy Policy Office and named John Love to head it. He also urged Congress to establish a Department of Energy and Natural Resources and an Energy Research and Development Administration.

The president's energy program was designed to reduce long-term dependence upon imported oil, but the immediate effect was to boost demand for imported oil, for the program placed no restraints on 1973 imports. As a result, in the first nine months of 1973 U.S. oil imports were 33.6 percent higher than during the same period in 1972.[28] Even this increase did not prevent spot shortages of gasoline in the summer of 1973; but it put tremendous pressure on world oil supplies, forcing prices up.

THE RISE IN MARKET PRICES AND THE PARTICIPATION AGREEMENTS

During 1972–73, several factors combined to push the price of petroleum products up. The most important were an almost unprecedented convergence of boom conditions in the advanced capitalist countries and the growth of U.S. demand for oil imports. In 1971, as a result of a worldwide economic slowdown, demand for oil fell below its historic pace. Between 1965 and 1970, world oil demand had increased at an average annual rate of about 8 percent, but in 1971 the growth in demand fell to a modest 5.4 percent.[29]

By 1972, most of the major capitalist economies were in roughly the same phase of the business cycle—expanding together.[30] As a result, between 1972 and 1973 the world's real gross domestic product grew by 7.3 percent, its highest annual increase since at least the 1950s.[31] The effect was to boost demand for oil. However, by the standards of the previous decade, the annual rate of increase in oil consumption (7.3 percent in 1973) was not especially high (see table 7–2). What was high in comparison with previous years (though not inordinately) was the increase in world oil imports, and the main reason for this was the growth in U.S. demand for oil imports. While outside the United States, throughout the 1970s the increase in oil imports was less than the average between 1965 and 1970, in the United States in the 1970s the growth in imports greatly exceeded its

TABLE 7–2. AVERAGE RATES OF INCREASE IN GDP, ENERGY CONSUMPTION, OIL CONSUMPTION, AND OIL IMPORTS, 1965–73

	1965–70	1970–71	1971–72	1972–73
Developed Market Economies				
GDP	4.6%	3.7%	5.5%	6.0%
Energy consumption	5.6	3.7	5.8	5.5
Oil consumption	7.9	4.4	7.5	6.8
Oil imports	11.2	6.6	6.8	14.9
Non-Communist World				
GDP	4.8%	4.0%	5.4%	6.3%
Energy consumption	5.8	3.1	5.3	4.9
Oil consumption	8.0	4.9	7.7	6.8
Oil imports	10.9	7.3	9.4	13.3
World				
GDP	5.3%	4.6%	5.6%	7.3%
Energy consumption	5.5	4.0	5.2	5.1
Oil consumption	8.1	5.4	8.0	7.3
Oil imports	11.1	7.3	10.6	13.1
Oil imports, developed market economies, excluding U.S.	12.2%	4.7%	3.6%	11.4%
U.S. oil imports	6.3	16.9	22.0	29.2

Figures on GDP (gross domestic product) are from U.N., *Yearbook of National Accounts, 1976*, vol. 2, table 4A. Figures for oil and energy consumption for the developed market economies from 1970–73 are from BP, *Statistical Review of the World Oil Industry* (various issues). Figures on energy consumption for 1965–70 and for the non-Communist world and the world from 1970–73 are from U.N., *World Energy Supplies, 1971–75*, table 1, p. 3. These figures are not strictly comparable with those from BP, but the differences should be slight. Figures on oil imports are also from BP. All rates of increase, except for GDP, were computed by the author.

historic rate (see table 7–2). Between 1965 and 1970 the United States accounted for only 8.7 percent of the increase in world oil imports, but between 1970 and 1973 it accounted for roughly a third of the increase.[32]

Unlike previous increases in the demand for imported oil, the increases in the early 1970s began to push against the limits of productive capacity. Partly, this was because the increase in U.S. imports, delay in bringing nuclear reactors into operation, and pressures on demand that stemmed from growing environmental concern were largely unforeseen. In addition, Kuwait and Libya placed restrictions on production, depriving the industry of badly needed productive capacity.

The combination of a tight oil market and an economic boom in the consuming countries drove the price of petroleum products up. Yet, as a result of the participation agreements, the major international oil companies became reluctant to make sales to third parties. With the market tight, the majors wanted to keep all their crude for their own refineries, and because the participation agreements were unstable, the amount of oil that the exporting countries would market themselves was still uncertain. Moreover, the exporting countries were demanding revisions in the buy-back prices the companies would have to pay. Consequently, the majors were unwilling to enter into long-term contracts for the sale of oil to third parties at fixed prices. As Dillard Spriggs, executive vice president of Baker Weeks Company, explained, "They could not know whether they would be able to honor any commitments they might make. The name of the game in international oil became 'hold on to supply.' "[33]

Because the majors were unwilling to sell to them, the independents scrambled desperately to secure oil supplies, and their ranks were increased after President Nixon removed import controls in April 1973. In removing all restrictions on U.S. imports, the president placed no restrictions on the freedom of U.S. companies to bid against each other in an already tight world market. As Edith Penrose stated, "Although United States import demand was instrumental in creating a continuing crisis, the United States did nothing either to control it or to manage the way it hit the market."[34] Furthermore, discussion of an energy crisis and anticipation of winter shortages led many buyers to build their inventories during the summer. In this context, independent oil companies eagerly bought the participation crude that Abu Dhabi had to sell, paying undisclosed but very high prices for it.[35]

In May, the Saudi government was able to sell participation oil directly for $2.55 a barrel—93 percent of the posted price. Twenty-three independents, but not a single major, were willing to purchase the oil at that price.[36] At the time the sale was made, Aramco was paying Saudi Arabia only $1.61 for every barrel of equity oil it produced and $2.39 for the participation oil (bridging price) that the Saudis sold back to Aramco. However, the Saudi sale represented only 2.5 percent of Aramco's production.[37] A month after the Saudi sale, Iran sold participation crude for 5¢ more than Saudi Arabia. By the end of July the Iranian government had sold all the crude it was entitled to under the new agreement with the Consortium, and all its joint-venture crude. This was the first time the National Iranian Oil Company had been able to sell the bulk of its joint-venture crude by itself. In June, it was reported that Qatar had sold all its participation oil for 1973–75 above posted prices.[38]

The rise in market prices led the exporting countries to demand revisions in the participation agreements. As early as April 1973, Kuwait, Saudi Arabia, and Abu Dhabi had demanded that the buy-back prices agreed to the previous December be renegotiated. Why should they sell their participation oil back to the concessionaires for less than others were willing to pay for it? When the participation agreements were negotiated, the exporting countries had been concerned about their ability to market the crude. But as *PIW* explained:

Since then, however, soaring demand, entry of the United States as a major oil importer, and near-panic buying by U.S. and European independents as well as the Japanese, have all set oil prices skyrocketing. Far from needing to sell oil back to the major companies, the producing countries have been swamped with buyers for every barrel available at prices well above the buy-back levels fixed in the participation agreements.[39]

By the summer of 1973 Aramco was paying 50¢ a barrel less than the market price for bridging crude and 63¢ less for phase-in crude;[40] Libya therefore became convinced that it could sell significant quantities of nationalized oil. Indeed, during the first four months of 1973 Hunt was lifting 118,000 b/d from the Sarir field and Libya was lifting 115,000 b/d. On May 24, to pressure the companies on participation, Bunker Hunt was denied the right to produce in Libya, and on June 11 the company was nationalized. Qaddafi declared the nationalization a "slap in the face" for U.S. support of Israel, and Sadat described it as the "start of the battle against American interests in the Middle East."[41]

Immediately after the Libyan move, the State Department reiterated the U.S. position on nationalization: states have the right to nationalize properties in their territories, but adequate compensation must be paid. However, the United States objected strongly to the political motivation behind Libya's action. The United States was also concerned that if Libya secured better participation terms than the Gulf countries, the political position of Arab radicals would be strengthened at the expense of the moderates. Washington branded the Bunker Hunt nationalization "invalid and not entitled to recognition by other states"; a sharp note of protest was sent to Libya on July 8; and the United States made its position known to other countries, particularly those that might import the nationalized oil. However, Washington did not directly prohibit the purchase of "hot" oil by U.S. companies. Hence, despite official U.S. protestations, Libya was able to sell between 210,000 and 245,000 b/d of the nationalized oil—roughly half the capacity of the field. Additional sales were limited not by an unwillingness of buyers to purchase the oil but by a shortage of technicians who could produce it.[42]

Much of this hot oil was sold to U.S. independents, who, in a tight market, desperately sought crude supplies. These companies took the position that they would be delighted not to purchase hot oil—if someone could show them where they could get other crude. Among the purchasers of oil from the Libyan government was Sohio, which had recently been acquired by BP, the company that Libya had nationalized originally. In addition, sales of the nationalized oil were made to the Communist countries; to Petrobras, the Brazilian state oil company; to Italy's ENI; and to several European independents.[43]

Under the terms of the Libyan Producers' Sharing Agreement, Bunker Hunt was entitled to up to 150,000 b/d in crude supplies from the companies still operating in Libya. However, while Texaco, SoCal, Exxon, and BP provided Hunt with back-up oil, the crude-short companies, Mobil and Shell, failed to live up to their commitments, and Gulf, which was subject to production limitations in Kuwait, was unable to provide Hunt with back-up crude. Moreover, most independents, though unaffected by the Persian Gulf participation agreements, failed to honor their commitments under the sharing agreement. Consequently, Hunt did not get the backing it sought, but it did receive enough back-up oil to remain in business.[44]

Following the nationalization of Bunker Hunt, Libya went after Occidental. In

July it ordered Occidental's production cut back from 549,000 b/d to 320,000 b/d, and in August, encouraged by its success in selling hot oil, Libya demanded that Occidental and the Oasis independents agree to 51 percent participation by the anniversary of the Libyan revolution, September 1. With worldwide demand for crude skyrocketing, the main concern of the companies operating in Libya was tying up the crude; so on August 11 Occidental acquiesced to Libya's demands and concluded a settlement that went far beyond the terms of the Gulf participation agreement. Instead of being compensated on the basis of updated book value, Occidental was paid only the net book value of the assets it gave up, and rather than get a discount on the participation crude it bought back from Libya, Occidental agreed to pay a buy-back price that was 40 percent above the going market price.[45]

In the context of booming prices, the deal was attractive for Occidental because it secured the right to buy back all of Libya's participation crude for the next thirty years. Consequently Occidental's chairman, Armand Hammer, declared that his company would make as much from its 49 percent share as it had from its former 100 percent share. Indeed, as soon as the deal was concluded, Occidental raised its prices by 97¢ a barrel, at that time the largest price increase in the history of the oil industry. In September, Hammer pointed out that as a result of the rise in market prices, the $4.90 that Occidental had to pay Libya for its buy-back crude was already "a low price today—and only a month has gone by." Moreover, after the deal was concluded, Libya ordered Occidental to increase its production from 335,000 b/d to 475,000 b/d, which Hammer described as "unsolicited and welcome."

Soon after the Occidental settlement, the other independents in Libya settled on terms similar to those that Occidental had agreed to and announced comparable price increases. Libya's Prime Minister Jalloud stated that, as a result of its nationalizations, Libya's per barrel income had increased from $2.30 to $4.70. Immediately after the Libyan/Occidental deal, Nigeria concluded a 35 percent participation agreement with Shell and BP, giving the concessionaires the right to buy its participation crude at market prices.[46]

In August, Sohio also agreed to pay Libya more than the posted price for 40,000 b/d of crude. The delivered cost would be between $6.25 and $7 a barrel, but *PIW* estimated that because of the rise in petroleum product prices, Sohio would realize $8.50 a barrel from the sale of products from Libya's sweet crude. Since Sohio was a crude-short company, it could use the Libyan crude to keep its refineries operating at capacity, and since most refining costs were fixed, *PIW* estimated that Sohio would make a healthy profit on its incremental Libyan supplies. Nonetheless, many industry executives feared that the high price Sohio was paying would be the "kiss of death" for the majors in their negotiations with the exporting countries on buy-back prices. However, others pointed out that Sohio had little choice; it had been unable to secure adequate supplies of low-sulfur crude from the majors.[47]

Following the participation agreements with the independents, Libya went after the majors. In August, Libya ordered Texaco and Chevron, the first majors to capitulate to Libyan demands in 1970, to cut back production from their Amoseas joint venture by more than 50 percent. Then Libya gave all the majors until August 25 to accede to its demands for 51 percent participation shares, but the majors refused to give in. They objected to both the 51 percent participation level and the demand for compensation at net book value, for were they to agree to these terms, they would undermine the participation agreements concluded for the Gulf. Indeed, Yamani had warned the Aramco partners in May that if Libya secured better terms, the Gulf participation agreement would have to be renegotiated.[48]

On September 1, the anniversary of the Libyan revolution, the RCC decreed a 51 percent nationalization of the majors' Libyan concessions; yet Libya was still reluctant to market nationalized oil in the face of opposition from the majors. Consequently, the September 1 decree gave the companies thirty days to think the situation over and come to terms. In the meantime, the majors were permitted to continue exporting from both the nationalized and the retained shares of the concessions, provided they did not take legal action to prevent the sale of the nationalized crude; however, they would be charged $4.95 for the nationalized oil. Concerned about the effect that even tacit acquiescence to the Libyan terms would have on the Gulf agreement, the majors rejected Libya's offer and notified prospective buyers that legal action would be taken against anyone who purchased the nationalized oil.[49]

The State Department supported the companies, urging the majors' customers to refuse to buy oil from the Libyan government, and at a press conference on September 5, President Nixon warned that "oil without a market, as Mr. Mossadegh learned many, many years ago, does not do a country much good."[50] Yet in the fall of 1973 the international oil market was far different than at the time of the Iranian nationalization. In 1951 it had been relatively easy to make up the loss of Iranian production by increasing production elsewhere, but in the fall of 1973 this was far more difficult. Demand was pushing against the limits of spare capacity, and many refineries were dependent upon Libya's low-sulfur crude. In addition, many prospective purchasers were not concerned about how resolution of the Libyan nationalization dispute would affect the worldwide position of the major oil companies. Hence, despite protests by the United States and Great Britain and a ruling by a World Court–appointed arbitrator, Libya had little trouble selling the nationalized crude. Soon after the nationalization, the New England Petroleum Company, the largest third-party purchaser of Libyan oil, had begun purchasing from the Libyan government rather than from its previous supplier, Standard Oil Company of California,[51] and other companies, in the United States and in Eastern and Western Europe, made purchases from the Libyan government, regardless of the legal consequences. However, Libya had to sell disputed oil for 20 percent less than its undisputed oil.[52]

Libya also sought to make deals directly with the consuming countries for the nationalized oil, and by early October a deal was concluded with India. In

October, Libyan Prime Minister Jalloud went to France to discuss a plan under which sales to Europe would be made directly between governments, without the companies serving as middlemen, and Italy's ENI was also reported to be interested in purchasing Libya's nationalized oil.[53]

Libya's success in marketing its nationalized oil demonstrated the extent of the West's dependence upon Arab oil and, as expected, its success in securing 51 percent participation and improved buy-back terms led to further demands for revision of the Gulf participation agreements. Indeed, in the summer of 1973 the exporting countries began canceling their buy-back pricing agreements and demanding new participation shares. As W. Jones McQuinn, an Aramco vice president, explained, "Yamani was under great political pressure from his critics as were the Saudis generally in the sense of having made an arrangement whereby he was selling oil to the companies at a price demonstrably lower than what was otherwise obtainable in the marketplace."[54]

At a meeting on September 13, Yamani told the companies that Kuwait, which had yet to ratify an agreement, would no longer accept even a 51 percent participation. Yamani also stated that, because of the agreement with the Consortium, the Shah could now claim to have full control of his nation's oil industry and, in response, Saudi Arabia would have to act forcefully. He explained that Saudi Arabia faced political problems that the companies did not understand. The participation agreement was being attacked as a sham, in which ownership was given with one hand and taken back with the other. Finally, he reiterated the Gulf countries' demand for an immediate increase in buy-back prices and he threatened to withhold crude supplies from Aramco if the companies did not comply.[55]

The Aramco partners felt they had no choice but to accede to Yamani's demands for higher buy-back prices, and so in September 1973 Aramco agreed to pay market prices—93 percent of the posted price—for the participation oil it bought back from Saudi Arabia. However, Saudi Arabia then demanded the right to directly market more of its participation oil. Similarly, in the wake of the Libyan moves, Abu Dhabi wanted to accelerate the rate at which it secured its 51 percent share.[56] As a result, when the October War broke out, the participation issue was still unsettled. On one hand, the concessionaires had the outlines of a partnership that could be extremely lucrative for them, despite their reduced role and the stiffer conditions the exporting countries were exacting, for they had the prospect of preferential access to a commodity of rapidly increasing value. On the other hand, the fragility of the agreement threatened the concessionaires with the possibility of losing everything.

THE DEMAND FOR REVISION OF THE TEHERAN/TRIPOLI AGREEMENTS

The participation agreements were only one of the casualties of a tight market, for aside from buying up participation oil at what seemed exorbitant prices, the independents also went into the highly visible spot market[57] and bid up prices there, as table 7–3 shows. By the summer of 1973, for the first time in years, crude oil was sold on the spot market above its posted price. In August, demand from U.S. refineries for low-sulfur fuel was pushing prices in the Mediterranean, Latin America, and Nigeria over $5 a barrel.[58] At the same time, the majors took advantage of the tight market by raising prices way above the level required to cover their increased payments to the oil-exporting countries. As Edith Penrose concluded, "Between the spring of 1970 and the summer of 1973, market prices for crude oil more than doubled measured in dollars, and nearly doubled in terms of other currencies, but the fiscal income of the host governments accounted for less than half of the increase."[59] As a result, major oil company profits increased from 30¢ a barrel in 1971 to 90¢ a barrel in the spring of 1973.[60]

The gap between the increase in petroleum product prices and oil-exporting-country revenues was even greater. According to OPEC's Secretary General Dr. Abderrahman Khene, between 1970 and the summer fo 1973 petroleum product prices increased from $29 per metric ton to $52 while the oil-exporting countries' revenue increased from $7 per metric ton to $13.[61] Hence almost three quarters of the increase was taken by the oil companies and the consuming governments. As a result of the equity oil that they still received at tax-paid cost, the majors reaped an enormous windfall in this period of rising prices. In August 1973 *PIW* estimated that if a major oil company met all its refinery needs from its own sources, its average crude cost would be 93¢ a barrel less than that of an independent company that had to purchase all its oil at market prices; and because they had tankers on long-term contract, the majors were estimated to have an additional transport cost advantage of 30 to 62¢ a barrel.[62]

In this transformed market situation, the three OPEC radicals took the lead in demanding revisions of the 1971 Teheran/Tripoli agreements. As early as August 1971, Iraq, Algeria, and Libya had demanded a revision in the agreements because they failed to protect the exporting countries against losses due to the devaluation of the dollar, and as we have seen, in January 1972 a formula was agreed to, compensating the OPEC countries for the devaluation of the dollar. However, this formula did not compensate the OPEC countries for their indirect losses from the revaluation of major world currencies. Consequently, when a

TABLE 7–3. AVERAGE ROTTERDAM SPOT CARGO PRICES, 1971–73

	Apr. 1971	Apr. 1972	Apr. 1973
Gasoline–premium	$35.00	$32.11	$70.08
Gasoline–regular	26.00	24.40	60.58
Gas oil	34.00	24.35	40.69
Heavy Fuel Oils			
Maximum 1% sulfur	22.50	16.72	23.86
Bunker C	22.50	14.59	16.06

From *Petroleum Intelligence Weekly*, Apr. 16, 1973, p. 6.

second official dollar devaluation occurred in February 1973, the three OPEC radicals demanded revisions in the compensation formula. On June 1 a new dollar parity pact, designed to be more sensitive to changes in currency values, was agreed to, and the immediate effect of the new agreement boosted posted prices by 11.9 percent.[63]

Having secured revision in the Teheran/Tripoli agreements because of monetary instability in the West, the Arab radicals also took the lead in demanding that the agreements be revised because, in the face of worldwide inflation, they failed to protect the exporting countries' purchasing power. Indeed, the cost of the OPEC countries' imports were increasing from 6 percent to 8 percent a year, but the Teheran Agreement provided for only a 2.5 percent annual inflation adjustment.[64] As a result, the OPEC radicals maintained that the 1971 agreements should be abrogated.

At an OPEC meeting in March, Algeria called for scrapping the 1971 agreements but received little support from the moderate OPEC states. Saudi Arabia vetoed the Algerian proposal, maintaining that the Teheran/Tripoli agreements had to be respected. Then, at an OPEC meeting in June, Iraq called for a change in the 1971 agreements, and by this time there was widespread support among the OPEC delegates for an improved inflation-adjustment factor. However, Iran's Oil Minister Amouzegar opposed Iraq's proposal for the scrapping of the Teheran Agreement and the unilateral determination of posted prices by the exporting countries. Saudi Arabia's Yamani did not attend the meeting, but as market prices escalated in the summer of 1973, pressure on the moderate OPEC governments to seek a revision in the 1971 agreements mounted. In July, Libya's oil minister declared that the Tripoli Agreement was obsolete, and during the summer Iraq sent delegations to Saudi Arabia and Kuwait to urge those countries to push for changes in the Teheran Agreement.[65]

What led the moderate Gulf countries to seek a change in the Teheran Agreement was that, in the face of rapidly increasing market prices, the 1971 agreement failed to protect the countries' profit share. The agreement provided for only a fixed 5¢ a barrel annual increase in posted prices; therefore, since autumn of 1972 the prices the companies realized from their sale of crude oil had increased more rapidly than the posted prices that the exporting countries' revenues were based upon. Consequently, according to OPEC estimates, when the Teheran Agreement was signed in the winter of 1971, the exporting countries received 80 percent of the per barrel profits. However, even though their absolute per barrel revenues had increased, as a result of the rise in market prices, by September 1973 their profit share had declined to 64 percent.[66]

In September, after market prices had risen above posted prices, Yamani declared that "the Teheran Agreement is either dead or dying and is in need of extensive revision." At the time the Teheran Agreement was signed, both the companies and the exporting countries had expected posted prices to remain above market prices, as they had since 1950. Moreover, during the Teheran negotiations the Shah had asked the companies to agree not to raise petroleum product prices. The issue was dropped, but it was raised again when product prices began rising faster than crude prices. At an OPEC meeting to discuss revisions in the Teheran Agreement, called for September 15, Yamani made it clear that Saudi Arabia now favored a "sizable lump sum increase in posted prices," a mechanism that would keep posted prices permanently above market prices, and a more realistic inflation-adjustment factor. "If we fail to obtain the cooperation of the oil companies in amending the Teheran price agreement," he stated, "we would have to exercise our rights on our own."[67]

Following the September OPEC meeting, the exporting countries announced that they would seek a large increase in posted prices; however, they maintained that this increase would be aimed at transferring the "excessive profits" the companies were earning (as a result of the increase in market prices) from the companies to the exporting countries. The exporting countries argued that there was no reason for the companies to pass the increased costs on to consumers. In support of its demand for higher postings, OPEC cited its 1968 "Statement of Petroleum Policy," which declared that "the financial provisions of contracts which actually result in such excessively high net earnings shall be open to renegotiation."[68] In 1968, no one had paid much attention to the OPEC statement, but as a result of the Teheran/Tripoli agreements, the participation settlements, and the transformed market situation, the oil-exporting countries had become powers to be reckoned with in 1973. Moreover, their earlier successes strengthened their solidarity and confidence.

Also, throughout the 1960s the companies had argued that changes in market forces should be taken into account in determining payments to the exporting countries. Of course, at that time, with market prices declining, this was an argument for lower per barrel payments to the exporting countries.[69] Now, with the tide turning, the companies were not quick to endorse the principle, though in the 1960s OPEC had not accepted it either. Finally, the Gulf exporting countries summoned the companies to begin negotiations on revising the posted price (and hence the Teheran Agreement) on October 8, but Algeria did not wait to see what would happen in the Gulf; in September it raised the posted price on its oil, from $3.50 a barrel to $5.[70]

By the fall of 1973 the 1971 price agreements and the participation agreements were in disarray. This may have been a threat to the major international oil companies, but it was not necessarily a threat to the consuming countries. In addition, there were reasons for the West to expect the international oil situation to become more favorable. Western economies were expected to slow, easing the pressure on world oil supplies. The consuming countries, while still divided, were beginning to reduce their dependence on Middle East and North African oil, and radical Iraq seemed finally to have made its peace with the international oil companies and was moving toward improved relations with the West. If these developments had run their course, OPEC might well have remained an obscure acronym and the "energy crisis" might be only a subject for scholarly debate.

What transformed a changing situation into a crisis, hastening developments that the West was unable to deal with, was the Arab-Israeli conflict.

THE EMERGENCE OF SAUDI POWER

In the 1970s the rapid increase in the world's demand for oil imports led to an enormous increase in Saudi production—far greater than that of any other major oil-exporting country (see table 7–4). As a result, between 1970 and 1973 Saudi Arabia's share of world oil exports increased from 12.8 percent to 21.4 percent.[71] Increasingly, Saudi Arabia was called upon to meet the rise in world oil demand. Between the beginning of 1973 and the end of 1975, Saudi Arabia was to account for nearly half the increase in productive capacity that was planned outside North America and the Communist countries (see table 7–5), and this was expected to just cover the increase in world demand.[72] In 1973 alone, Saudi export capacity was increased by 2.5 mb/d, the equivalent of another Libya. As *PIW* pointed out, Saudi Arabia was rapidly achieving the same dominance in the international oil industry that Texas had had in the U.S. industry in the 1930s.[73]

There were several reasons for this emphasis on Saudi production. Its reserves were much greater than those of any other country—yet this had long been true, without resulting in the concentration on Saudi production that occurred in the 1970s. Consequently, it is necessary to consider the ways in which political and economic factors encouraged the growing dependence upon Saudi production.

The oil-exporting country with the second largest reserves was Kuwait. In 1971 its production increased about 7 percent, to 2.9 mb/d.[74] Then, in the spring of 1972, Kuwait placed a ceiling on 3 mb/d on its production—the only Gulf state to institute such controls. Kuwait explained its decision by citing the need for conservation, but at the time the ceiling was imposed Kuwait's proven reserves were sufficient to produce at the existing level for another sixty years.[75] Regardless of the Kuwaiti government's motivation, Kuwait could not afford to conserve its reserves were it not that its population was small (about 800,000 in 1972) and its economy was receiving more in oil revenues than it could absorb. In addition, as a result of devaluation of the dollar and monetary instability in the West, Kuwait was reluctant to accumulate additional foreign-currency reserves, preferring oil in the ground.

Like Kuwait, Libya maintained a 3 mb/d ceiling on production. A small population, limited revenue needs, reluctance to accumulate additional foreign-currency reserves, and conservation were factors in the Libyan policy. However, Libya's motivation was somewhat different from what prompted Kuwait's production ceiling. The limitations on Libyan production were originally imposed in 1970 as part of Libya's efforts to secure better terms from the companies. In addition, Libya's population and revenue needs were somewhat greater than Kuwait's, but its proven reserves were less than half as large, making conservation a more pressing concern.

TABLE 7–4. WORLD OIL PRODUCTION BY COUNTRY AND AREA, 1965, 1970, 1973

	Production (TB/D)		
	1965	1970	1973
Iran	1,905	3,830	5,895
Iraq	1,315	1,565	2,020
Kuwait	2,170	2,735	2,755
Saudi Arabia	2,025	3,550	7,345
Abu Dhabi		695	1,305
Total Middle East	8.340	13,825	21,110
Algeria	560	1,040	1,095
Libya	1,220	3.320	2,180
Nigeria	275	1,085	2,055
Total Africa	2,215	6,215	6,015
Indonesia	480	855	1,335
Total Eastern Hemisphere	17,050	29,675	39,455
Venezuela	3,505	3,760	3,460
United States	9,015	11,295	10,950
Canada	925	1,475	2,115
Total Western Hemisphere	14,635	18,065	18,390
Non-Communist world	26,290	39,930	48,200
Total World	31,685	47,740	57,845

BP, *Statistical Review of the World Oil Industry* (various issues). Some computations by author; others taken directly from BP.

Yet the investment policies of the international oil industry were at least as responsible for the emphasis on Saudi production as the production ceilings imposed by the exporting countries, for the oil industry shifted production, exploration, and development expenditures from the militant exporting countries while boosting them in the compliant countries (principally Saudi Arabia and Abu Dhabi) above their historic rates. From 1970 to 1973 the average rate of production increased by 27.4 percent in Saudi Arabia and 23.4 percent in Abu Dhabi.

Yet in radical Libya during this period, the production rate declined at an average of 13.1 percent. Due to its militance on pricing and participation, Libya found its production cut below the maximum levels stipulated by the RCC, and exploration in Libya declined as well. As a result of the better terms that Libya secured through the Tripoli Agreement, Libya's crude became more costly than crude from the Gulf when tanker rates declined in 1971–72, and the companies shifted their liftings accordingly. Between April 1970 and the winter of

Share of World Total (%)			Annual Increase (%)	
1965	1970	1973	1965–70	1970–73
6.0	8.0	10.3	15.0	15.5
4.2	3.3	3.4	3.5	8.9
6.8	5.7	4.9	4.8	.2
6.4	7.4	12.9	12.0	27.4
	1.5	2.3		23.4
26.3	29.0	36.8	10.8	15.2
1.8	2.2	1.9	12.3	1.7
3.9	7.0	3.8	22.0	−13.1
.9	2.3	3.6	31.3	23.7
7.0	13.0	10.3	22.5	−1.1
1.5	1.8	2.3	11.8	16.0
53.8	62.2	68.5	29.8	10.0
11.1	7.8	6.3	1.3	−2.7
28.5	23.6	18.3	4.8	−1.0
2.9	3.1	3.6	8.8	12.8
46.2	37.8	31.5	4.5	.6
83.0	83.6	83.3	8.8	6.5
100.0	100.0	100.0	8.5	6.6

1971–72, Libyan production fell from a high of 3.7 mb/d to 2.5 mb/d, far below the government ceiling of 3 mb/d, and the militant policies of the RCC discouraged corporate exploration and development in Libya. In January 1972 the *Petroleum Press Service* stated that "few operators show much enthusiasm for developing new discoveries."[76]

Libya would have been glad to offer new exploration contracts, but in November 1972 the *Middle East Economic Survey* reported that the companies were sticking to the absolute minimum (as established by the Tripoli Agreement) on Libyan exploration.[77] As a result, in 1973 Libyan production was far below projections. For example, Exxon's George Piercy testified that "in 1969, we believed that, based on our view of the geological potential, Libyan production would reach an average level of 4,100,000 barrels per day in 1973. Actual production was about 1,900,000 barrels per day less."[78]

Algeria's nationalization of the French companies and the high prices it established for its oil had a similar effect. After the French companies were na-

TABLE 7–5. PLANNED CRUDE-OIL CAPACITY OUTSIDE NORTH AMERICA AND THE COMMUNIST COUNTRIES, 1973–75 (MB/D)

	Jan. 1, 1973	Jan. 1, 1974	Nov. 1, 1975	Dec. 31, 1975
Aramco	6.550	9.085	10.485	11.640
Iranian Consortium	4.993	5.186	5.873	6.493
Abu Dhabi	1.390	1.840	2.270	2.270
Iraq (Basrah)	.671	.800	1.200	1.650
Kuwait Oil Co.	3.000	3.000	3.000	3.000
Persian Gulf Total	16.604	19.911	22.828	25.053

	1973	1974	1975
Venezuela	3.6	3.5	3.4
Libya	2.3	2.3	2.4
Algeria	1.1	1.1	1.1
Nigeria	1.9	2.1	2.4
Indonesia	1.5	1.7	1.9
Iraq (Kirkuk)	1.2	1.2	1.2
Europe	.4	.6	1.3
Other	1.4	1.5	1.6
Total outside Persian Gulf	13.4	14.0	15.3

From *Petroleum Intelligence Weekly*, May 14, 1973, p. 7; see also *MEES*, June 15, 1973 (supplement).

tionalized (in 1971), France began to purchase less oil from Algeria and more from the Gulf countries. In 1970 only a third of France's oil imports came from the Gulf, but by 1972 France received more than half its imports from that area. As a result, Algerian production, which increased at an average rate of 12.3 percent between 1965 and 1970, increased by only 1.7 percent a year between 1970 and 1973.[79] As in Libya, prospects for expanding production in Algeria were severely circumscribed by the lack of exploration and development. Indeed, Algeria was plagued by a lack of capital for exploration and development.[80]

Because of its decision to terminate concessions in the 1980s and the stringent price and profit terms it imposed on the companies, Venezuela's production declined in the early 1970s. Moreover, faced by the prospect of imminent nationalization,[81] by 1973 the international oil companies were attempting to minimize their new investments in Venezuela.[82]

In addition, development of Iraq's oil resources had been delayed more than a decade, until the February 1973 settlement between Iraq and the IPC. While production in Iraq declined by 14.3 percent in 1972, it increased by 34.7 percent in 1973.[83] Moreover, as the *Petroleum Economist* stated in the summer of 1975, "Unlike most other Middle Eastern countries, whose oil potential is known with reasonable accuracy, Iraq still has areas which have not yet been thoroughly explored and the possibility, according to Iraqi officials, of at least doubling its reserves, to place them perhaps second only to Saudi Arabia.''[84] Yet, neglected for a decade and a half, it would be many years before Iraq's production would approach its potential.

In the early 1970s Nigeria, Indonesia, and Abu Dhabi experienced rapid increases in production. However, none of these countries was a major producer and their reserves made it unlikely that they would ever join the ranks of OPEC's big exporters—which left only Iran and Saudi Arabia. The Aramco partners, well represented in the Consortium, had always preferred to expand in Saudi Arabia rather than Iran, for in Saudi Arabia they controlled the entire output while, in Iran, production had to be shared among the seventeen companies that comprised the Consortium. In addition, the Consortium had far more restrictive offlifting rules than Aramco, and Iran's oil fields were subject to conservative British development practices.[85] Besides, Saudi reserves were at least twice as large.

Despite the Aramco partners' preference for Saudi output, throughout the 1960s the Shah's protests kept Iran's expansion above the rate in Saudi Arabia; but in the 1970s, with the growth rates in Kuwait and North Africa held back, it became possible to boost Saudi production way up and keep Iran's expanding fast enough to appease the Shah. While the Shah was anxious to reach a level of 8 mb/d, he indicated that he was not much interested in going above that figure.[86] In any case, many industry officials maintained that because of the limitations of Iran's reserve base, its production would eventually peak at 8 mb/d. In contrast, Saudi reserves were then estimated to be capable of sustaining a level of 20 mb/d,[87] and with political constraints removed, the Aramco partners were prepared to surge ahead with Saudi production. Indeed, once again the U.S. majors chose to produce the "easy" oil rather than develop new sources.

The immediate consequence was that by fall of 1973, Aramco's production program was running into problems. Because of forecasts that turned out to be too low and construction delays, demand was approaching the limits of Saudi capacity, and technical problems arose because of the rapid pace at which Aramco attempted to expand production from existing fields. As Christopher Rand states: "The engineering reports show quite clearly that in 1972 and 1973—and by implication during most if not all of 1971—Aramco so increased production from Ghawar and Berri, and then Abqaiq, that its water injection facilities became outdated and inadequate, pressure in the fields dropped markedly, and production of sand and salt increased—all at alarming speed."[88] Consequently, as W. W. Messick, SoCal's top engineer for Aramco matters, stated: If there had not been an embargo, Aramco would have confronted the dilemma of cutting back production, at a time when consumers were clamoring for more oil, or risking permanent damage to the Saudi fields.[89]

More significant than these short-term production problems was the growth of Saudi production and the role envisioned for it, which gave the country tremendous economic and political power. Though Saudi Arabia's population was considerably larger than Kuwait's or Libya's, the Saudis' oil revenues began to exceed their economic needs and they began to accumulate extensive currency reserves (see table 4–6). In the summer of 1973, with Saudi Arabia producing more than 8 mb/d, Aramco estimated that the Saudis could comfortably meet all their revenue needs at a production level of only 5.5 mb/d.[90]

Consequently, like Kuwait and Libya, Saudi Arabia was in a position to cut back, or even cut off, its oil production; and while the loss of Kuwaiti or Libyan production would cause major problems for the West, the loss of Saudi production, because it was so much greater, could be catastrophic. Indeed, even a 10 or 20 percent production cutback by the Saudis, or refusal to expand production in the future, could have major repercussions for the West.

THE ARAB OIL WEAPON AND MIDDLE EAST POLITICS

Fortunately for the consuming countries, until 1973 the Saudis had always been eager to expand production, and they had opposed restricting oil exports in order to advance Arab political interests. Indeed, since 1964 the Saudis had opposed all OPEC efforts to limit production. In 1967, as we have seen, the Saudis lobbied to end the Arab oil embargo. Historically, the two basic motivations for Saudi policy, maximum oil revenues and reluctance to alienate the United States, helped to maintain the security of the Saudi regime against the threat of revolutionary forces in the Arab world.[91] In the early 1970s, however, as a result of the West's dependence upon Arab oil, there was much discussion in the Arab world of using the oil weapon to force concessions from the consuming countries in the Arab-Israeli conflict.[92] Arab radicals, who had long supported use of the oil weapon, now argued for a policy of production cutbacks and nationalization.

There was also a body of "moderate" Arab sentiment, which maintained that if the United States refused to alter its pro-Israeli policy, the Arab countries should refuse to expand production. As Dr. Nadim Pachachi, a former OPEC secretary general and leading proponent of this position, explained, by simply refusing to expand production the Arabs could "cause a worldwide supply crisis in a fairly short period of time." However, by maintaining production at constant levels, the Arab exporting countries could continue to meet their financial needs. Consequently, Pachachi recommended that the production level be frozen until Israel withdrew from the occupied territories.[93]

In response to these arguments, the conservative Arab exporting countries, led by Saudi Arabia, reiterated several longstanding positions. In opposition to the nationalization proposal, they maintained that a distinction had to be made between the oil companies and their home governments, implying that the companies should not be punished for the actions of their governments. As late as 1972, Kuwait and Saudi Arabia insisted that, rather than restrict production, the best way of using oil to promote the Arab cause was by continuing to increase production and using the revenues to promote Arab interests.[94]

Early in 1973, however, there was a distinct shift in Saudi Arabia's position, for several reasons. With the Saudis producing at a level that provided more revenue than they could absorb domestically, they could easily afford to limit or even reduce production. (Prior to the 1970s and the great expansion of Saudi production, this had not been the case.) In addition, the Saudis did not have much economic incentive for expanding production and accumulating surplus revenues. As a result of the February devaluation of the dollar, the OPEC countries that had significant currency reserves—Kuwait, Libya, and Saudi Arabia—were estimated to have lost nearly $300 million, and while Saudi Arabia had expressed interest in making investments in the United States, it was discouraged by the failure of the United States to endorse its proposal for a special U.S.-Saudi relationship. Indeed, when he proposed that Saudi Arabia be given a "special place" in the U.S. market, Yamani had warned that if consumers did not encourage investments by the exporting countries, the exporting nations might find it more profitable to leave their oil in the ground.[95] Now, with the removal of U.S. import controls and its growing dependence on Arab oil, the United States for the first time was vulnerable to a cutback in Arab supplies; hence the Saudi argument that an Arab cutback would not hurt the United States was no longer valid.

Probably more important than any of these factors was Saudi Arabia's foreign-policy interests, and the three concerns that shaped Saudi policy: radicalism, both internationally and in the Arab world; Israeli expansion, with King Faisal's strong interest in recovery of Jerusalem; and the security of the Saudi regime.

Each of these concerns had its own roots. The Faisal regime had long been anti-Communist; indeed, in 1973 Saudi Arabia was the only member of the Arab League that did not recognize any Communist country. King Faisal opposed even trade with Communist countries, and Saudi Arabia had used its oil wealth and its troops to oppose the South Yemenis and the PFLOAG. Furthermore, on numerous occasions the deeply religious King Faisal had stated that, before he died, he intended to pray in a Jerusalem freed from Israeli occupation. Thus, solidarity with the Palestinians and fear of further Israeli expansion were also factors in Saudi opposition to Israel. Finally, having been deposed in one coup and returned to power in another, King Faisal understood the difficulties of maintaining his regime. Consequently, he put thousands of his political opponents in Saudi jails and permitted no legal opposition to his regime, no trade unions, no constitution, and no elections.

Yet from the Saudi perspective, its foreign-policy concerns were intimately linked. As the Saudis saw it, Israeli expansionism was leading to radicalization of the Arab world, and that, in turn, was the principal threat to the Saudi regime. King Faisal went so far as to maintain that Zionists were behind the Palestinian terrorists.[96] Historically, Saudi Arabia had looked to the United States to guarantee its security and was therefore reluctant to alienate the United States by using the oil weapon against the West; however, U.S. support for Israel and the hostility this engendered in the Arab world made it increasingly difficult for Saudi Arabia to ally itself with the United States. In fact, Faisal maintained that the U.S. Middle East policy was driving the Arabs into the Communist camp. Consequently—as an Aramco briefing paper summed up the situation—"King Faisal's foreign policy is based on his feeling that his interests and those of the United States are—with the single and very critical exception of Israel—virtually identical. . . . He also realizes that he cannot long maintain his pro-American position unless the U.S. mitigates its pro-Israeli policies."[97]

Radicalism was a growing force among the Arab masses, but toward the end of 1971 several developments opened new opportunities for Arab conservatives. As we have seen, in September 1971 the Palestinian guerrillas were forced to abandon their bases in Jordan and, as a result, the Western-oriented King Hussein was strengthened. In November General Hafez Assad seized power, deposing the left wing of the Syrian Ba'ath Party and replacing it with a more moderate and more Western-oriented government. But the most significant development was the death of Nasser (Sept. 29, 1970) and his replacement by Anwar el-Sadat. Nasser and King Faisal had been bitter enemies, for Nasser was the pro-Soviet leader of the Arab radical camp, who wanted to overthrow Arab reaction and unite the Arab world, while Faisal was the anti-Communist champion of Islamic conservatism. For five years Egypt and Saudi Arabia had fought each other directly in the Yemen civil war, in which Egypt's real target was Saudi Arabia.[98] But after the 1967 Arab-Israeli war, Egypt became dependent upon the financial support of the conservative exporting countries. Thus it was no longer a military threat to Saudi Arabia, and the hostility between the two countries was muted, but the differences between Nasser and Faisal persisted.

In sharp contrast to the pan-Arabist Nasser, Sadat was an Egyptian nationalist whose main interest was Egypt's economic development. Nasser believed that Israel was an insuperable barrier to his goal of uniting the Arab nation, and as a result, its existence was intolerable. But Sadat could "live with" Israel, and upon assuming office, he proceeded to take Egypt in new directions. Early in 1971 he told U.N. Ambassador Gunnar Jarring that Egypt was prepared to sign a "peace agreement" with Israel, recognizing its right to exist, provided Israel committed itself to total withdrawal in accordance with U.N. Resolution 242. In addition, Sadat expressed interest in reaching an interim or partial agreement with Israel.[99]

In May, in an effort to consolidate his power, Sadat purged the pro-Soviet Ali Sabry faction from the Egyptian government. That same month, Secretary of State Rogers visited Cairo, the first U.S. secretary of state to do so since John Foster Dulles in 1953. In June, King Faisal visited Egypt, a week-long trip that marked the beginning of a new entente between Egypt and Saudi Arabia. Relations between Egypt and Iran also improved. Whereas Nasser had discouraged foreign investment, Sadat was anxious to lure foreign capital into Egypt. He signed a fifteen-year Treaty of Friendship and Cooperation with the Soviet Union in May, but despite this, under his leadership in the early 1970s, Egypt seemed to be moving toward a rapprochement with both the conservative Arab camp and the West.

Egyptian-Soviet relations deteriorated in the summer of 1971, when, in the struggle between Sudanese President Nimeri and the Sudanese Communists, Sadat backed Nimeri and the Soviet Union backed the Communists. When Nimeri emerged victorious, the Sudan became another radical Arab state that had moved decidedly to the right.[100]

While Egypt seemed to be moving away from both domestic radicalism and the Soviet Union, it seemed to be heading into an alliance with another Saudi rival, Libya. On April 17, 1971, Egypt, Libya, and Syria had formed the Federation of Arab Republics and Sadat and Qaddafi were discussing a plan to merge their two countries. As a pan-Arab Nasserite, Qaddafi[101] was anxious to merge with the most populous of the Arab countries, and Sadat was eager to use Libya's oil wealth to help develop his country. However, Qaddafi was both anticapitalist and anti-Communist; he sought to forge an Islamic "third force" that would be allied with neither Moscow nor the West. Consequently, he insisted that there could be no merger so long as Soviet military advisers remained in Egypt.[102]

At the same time, there was growing opposition to the Soviet presence in Egypt, particularly among Egyptian military officers, who resented Soviet interference in their affairs. Sadat, long distrustful of the Soviets, grew impatient with their reluctance to provide the arms he sought; in April 1972 he had gone to the Soviet Union, seeking advanced weapons and Soviet support for renewed hostilities. However, at the time of Sadat's trip the U.S.-Soviet summit was only a month away, and Moscow was eagerly pursuing detente with the West. Consequently, the Soviet Union refused Sadat's requests.[103] Then, at the summit, the Soviets failed to promote the Arab cause, promising the United States that they would limit their support for the Arabs and thereby seeming to accept continued stalemate in the Middle East.[104] In fact, stalemate may have been the preferred Soviet policy, for while a Soviet-backed offensive would signify the end of U.S.-Soviet detente, stalemate would perpetuate Egyptian dependence on the Soviet Union.

Stalemate, however, was unacceptable to Sadat. It would mean that the Egyptian economy would continue to suffer from costly military expenditures but would achieve little militarily. (In 1972 Egypt had the dubious distinction of devoting a higher percentage [20.2%] of its GNP to military expenditures than any other country).[105] And it seemed clear that while the Soviet Union was unable to get Israel to withdraw from the occupied territories by diplomatic means, it was unwilling to expel Israel by force. In contrast, the United States was capable of exerting diplomatic leverage on Israel. In June, however, Sadat learned from Saudi Arabia that the United States would not press Israel for concessions until the Soviet presence in Egypt was eliminated.[106] Consequently, Sadat decided upon a major reorientation of Egyptian foreign policy. On July 18,

1972, he expelled the Soviet military advisers (estimated at 20,000 in all) from Egypt. The official explanation was dissatisfaction with the weapons the Soviets provided and lack of progress at the Nixon-Brezhnev summit.[107]

Less than a month after the expulsion, Egypt and Libya announced plans to merge, which they said would take place on September 1, 1973. In the intervening year, however, serious differences emerged. Sadat sought a peaceful settlement with Israel, which would restore the territories lost in 1967, while Qaddafi called for a "war of liberation" against Israel. Sadat was dismantling the public sector (introduced by Nasser) and seeking private foreign investment by Western companies while Qaddafi sought decreased economic dependence on the West. Furthermore, because Libya had alienated so many Arab states, Sadat recognized that a union with Libya would be a barrier to the coalition of Arab states that would be necessary to confront Israel successfully.[108]

Thus by 1973 there was a very real prospect of pulling Egypt, historically the leader of the radical Arab camp, into the conservative camp. In expelling the Soviets, Sadat was inviting a U.S. Middle East peace initiative; but to the great annoyance of the Egyptians and the Saudis, no U.S. initiative was forthcoming. Initially, part of the reason was that, with the U.S. presidential election approaching, President Nixon adopted a strongly pro-Israel position and was not about to pressure Israel into doing anything; nevertheless, U.S. intransigence persuaded Sadat that his only option was war. On November 14, 1972, he informed the "higher council" of Egypt's only legal political party, the Arab Socialist Union, that he intended to launch a war against Israel, perhaps within six months, certainly within a year; and in the winter of 1972–73 the Soviets began a large new shipment of military equipment to Egypt.[109]

In February 1973 Sadat sent his special national security adviser, Hafez Ismail, to Washington to find out if there would be a shift in U.S. policy. Ismail got little encouragement from Washington, but he learned that, in response to the Soviet shipments to Egypt, the United States was planning a new shipment of Phantom jets to Israel. The news strengthened Sadat's determination to go to war. On May 2, 1973, Aramco Vice President J. J. Johnston reported to Aramco headquarters in New York on a conversation with a Saudi official, Kamal Adham, who had told Johnston that the Saudi Arabian government

as well as other Arab countries were amazed that Sadat's moving out of the Russians failed to produce results in the Israeli situation. He said that all felt sure that this would give USG [U.S. Government] opportunity to push Israel into meaningful negotiations. He stated that only USG could cause such negotiations since Israelis absolutely had no reason to want to do anything themselves. He stated that he therefore was quite sure that Sadat would embark on some sort of hostilities even though the Egyptians themselves considered it hopeless. By so doing Sadat, who Adham characterized as being most courageous and farsighted, might marshal opinion in the U.S. for moving ahead with settlement initiative.[110]

At this point, Sadat had little choice but to go to war. He had offered to sign either a peace treaty or an interim agreement with Israel, but nothing was in the offing. He had appealed in vain to the Soviet Union for advanced weaponry, and had sent the Soviet advisers away and turned to the United States, only to learn that the United States was sending more arms to Israel. In addition, by this time Sadat was under strong domestic attack. His government was almost bankrupt and heavily in debt to Libya. Early in 1973, militant students and workers had clashed with Egyptian security forces over foreign and domestic policy, and Egypt's position in the Arab world was threatened by the rising influence of the oil-exporting countries. Indeed, Libya had gained considerable stature in the Arab world as a result of its militance in the oil negotiations and its use of oil revenues to finance Palestinian "freedom fighters" and other radical Arab groups. So a successful military operation promised to restore both Sadat's prestige as a leader and Egypt's dominance in the Arab world.[111]

In this context, the Arab oil weapon could serve several of Saudi Arabia's political objectives. Instead of the proposed Libyan-Egyptian merger, it could create a Saudi-Egyptian alliance—the axis of a powerful conservative camp in the Arab world, uniting the most populous and the wealthiest Arab states. It could force the United States to pressure Israel into making the concessions that were required for the peace agreement that Egypt was now prepared to make. It would enhance Saudi power and prestige in the Arab world and reduce the threats to the security of the Saudi regime. And it might lead to the recovery of Jerusalem.

Despite these potential advantages, the Saudis were still reluctant to alienate the United States. However, the growth of anti-U.S. sentiment in the Arab world and U.S. obstinacy on the Israeli question were forcing Saudi Arabia to deploy the oil weapon, and the first indication came in April 1973. Yamani was sent to Washington, where he warned government officials that if the United States did not make greater efforts to force Israel's compliance with U.N. Resolution 242, Saudi Arabia would find it difficult to raise, or even maintain, its present output. Saudi officials explained that as a result of their pro-U.S. attitudes and enormous oil resources, they were coming under tremendous political pressure from the rest of the Arab world.[112]

On January 6, 1973, the Kuwait National Assembly had adopted a resolution for a "freeze" on oil production in the event of another Middle East war and suggesting that, even before the start of such a war, Kuwait should use its oil resources in the struggle against Israel.[113] Then, in a symbolic protest on May 15—the twenty-fifth anniversary of the creation of the state of Israel—Iraq, Algeria, and Kuwait suspended their oil exports for an hour, and Libyan exports were halted for twenty-four hours.[114]

Though Saudi Arabia did not join the May 15 action, it was becoming increasingly difficult for the Saudis to resist the Arab world's support for use of the oil weapon. In fact, many Saudis believed that if Saudi Arabia failed to take action, Palestinian commandos might blow up key installations, cutting production for months. On June 2, to appease popular sentiment, Saudi Arabia's foreign minister, Omar al-Saqqaf, publicly declared that "the Arabs are ready to freeze the level of deliveries of crude oil to countries which support Israel."[115] An even more significant development occurred May 3, when several Aramco executives paid a courtesy call on King Faisal. The king told them that U.S. interests in the Middle East were threatened by both Zionism and Communism, and that it was the urgent responsibility of U.S. companies with interests in the area to do something to change the position of the U.S. government.[116]

Another meeting between Aramco executives and King Faisal occurred May 23. According to a report on the meeting by Aramco Vice President J. J. Johnston, the king stated that "the unequivocal support of Israel by the U.S. is allowing the Communist/radical elements in the Arab world to take over and sway the opinion of the Arab populace against the U.S." The king warned that "if these circumstances remain unchanged then all American interests in the Arab world will suffer. If there is no significant change in the Arab/Israeli problem, then the Saudis will find themselves becoming more isolated in the Arab world and they cannot permit this to happen and therefore American interests in the area must be removed. Action must be taken urgently; otherwise, everything will be lost."[117]

Faisal told the Aramco partners that they had to inform the American public, which was being misled by the news media, of its true interests in the area; and they had to inform government leaders. The king added that time was running out and that the companies might lose everything.[118] In delivering this warning, Faisal threatened to end the separation between U.S. policy toward Israel and its policy toward the Arab oil-exporting countries in the Gulf area. Faced with loss of the valuable Aramco concession, the Aramco partners proceeded to lobby U.S. government officials and the American public.

On May 30, executives from the four parent companies and an Aramco vice president, J. J. Johnston, conveyed the king's message to officials in the White House, the State Department (including Assistant Secretary Joseph Sisco), and the Defense Department (including Acting Secretary William Clements). However, although these officials acknowledged that a problem existed, they doubted that drastic action was imminent and did not believe that measures other than those already under way were called for. Several officials indicated that, in their judgment, the political pressures from Nasser that Saudi Arabia had faced in the past were much greater than those it currently faced. Having weathered those earlier pressures, these officials saw no reason why Saudi Arabia could not resist the pressures in the current situation. As Johnston reported, "The impression was given that some believe H.M. [His Majesty King Faisal] is calling wolf when no wolf exists except in his imagination. Also, there is little or nothing the U.S. Government can do or will do on an urgent basis to affect the Arab/Israeli issue."[119] Indeed, with President Nixon under attack as a result of Watergate, it was not a propitious moment for the United States to exert pressure on popular Israel.[120]

Because Washington discounted the likelihood of an embargo, it failed to take measures to protect against it. Less dependence on Arab oil, greater consumer-country cooperation, or a change in U.S. Middle East policy would have reduced the danger of an embargo, but because government officials failed to assess the probability of an embargo accurately, none of these objectives had much urgency for them. Throughout the summer of 1973, nevertheless, the Aramco partners continued to lobby Washington. The companies maintained that if the United States shifted its Middle East position, Saudi Arabia could argue that its pro-American policy had paid off and the Saudis could strengthen their ties to the United States.[121]

The companies also attempted to lobby the American public. In June, Mobil placed advertisements in U.S. newspapers, calling attention ''to the U.S. stake in the Middle East'' and warning against deterioration in U.S. relations with the Arab world.[122] In July, SoCal's chairman, Otto Miller, sent a letter to stockholders that stated: ''It is highly important at this time that the United States should work more closely with the Arab governments to build up and enhance our relations with the Arab people. . . . There must be understanding on our part of the aspirations of the Arab people, and more positive support of their efforts toward peace in the Middle East.''[123]

While these moves had little impact on U.S. Middle East policy, they caused quite a stir in the United States and the Arab world. SoCal's annual meeting was picketed by supporters of Israel and a consumer boycott put a quick halt to its public campaign for a change in U.S. Middle East policy. These developments also threatened to bring the oil lobby and the Israeli lobby into direct conflict.[124] Nonetheless, Miller's letter received excellent coverage in the Middle East. Several Saudi newspapers described it as the result of King Faisal's pressures on the Aramco partners and cited the strong Israeli and Jewish-American reaction as an indication of its effectiveness. Later in the year, the Saudis indicated that they were pleased with the Aramco parents for responding to King Faisal's directives and being more ''pro Arab'' than they had been in the past.[125]

Still, King Faisal told a *Washington Post* reporter in July that if U.S. support for Israel continued at its current level, Saudi Arabia would find it ''difficult'' to maintain close cooperation with the United States. Faisal also indicated that the debate in the Saudi government was between those who wanted to limit production increases and those who wanted to freeze production at current levels. *PIW* reported that Yamani was the only member of Saudi Arabia's Supreme Petroleum Council who was still pushing for production increases.[126] In July the PLO endorsed the freezing of production at current levels. Saddam Hussein, vice president of Iraq's RCC, said Iraq was prepared to be the first to use the oil weapon in an Arab-Israeli confrontation, provided a coordinated plan among (at least) a few Arab states could be worked out; Iran threatened embargoes and nationalizations; and Qaddafi warned, for the second time in two months, that oil might be used as a weapon. By this time, relations between Egypt and Libya had deteriorated to the point where Qaddafi marched 40,000 Libyans across the Egyptian border.[127]

On August 23 Sadat made a secret visit to Riyadh. What was discussed during Sadat's meeting with Faisal is not known, but it is likely that Sadat informed Faisal of the coming war with Israel (though probably not the date it would start) and asked him to use the oil weapon against the United States in the event of such a war. It also seems likely that Faisal agreed to provide Egypt with financial backing, and he may have made commitments on use of the oil weapon in the event of war.[128] In any case, immediately following Sadat's visit King Faisal announced that if U.S. policy in the Middle East did not change, he would restrict increases in Saudi production to 10 percent a year, far short of world requirements. Then, on August 30, Faisal proclaimed on American television:

We do not wish to place any restrictions on our oil exports to the United States, but America's complete support of Zionism against the Arabs makes it extremely difficult for us to continue to supply the U.S. petroleum needs and to even maintain our friendship with the United States.

If the U.S. does not change its policy in the Middle East and continues to side with Zionism, then I am afraid, such course of action will place us in an untenable position in the Arab world and vis-à-vis the countries which Zionism seeks to destroy.

Faisal also made increases in Saudi production conditional on aid in the industrialization of Saudi Arabia.[129]

Faisal's announcement may have convinced Egypt and Syria that Saudi Arabia would deploy the oil weapon in the event of another Arab-Israeli war, and Abu Dhabi, at the end of August, indicated that it would join a coordinated move to use oil as a weapon.[130] In any case, in response to the Saudi move, President Nixon declared at a press conference on September 5 that so long as Congress refused to pass his energy proposals, "it means that we will be at the mercy of the producers of oil in the Mid-East." He termed the Arab threats to cut off oil "an area of major concern," and with respect to the Arab-Israeli conflict, the president said that "both sides are at fault. Both sides need to start negotiations. That is our position."[131]

In blaming both the Israelis and the Arabs for the impasse, President Nixon did something that U.S. presidents had been reluctant to do in the past. Previously, Washington had also avoided linking Middle East diplomacy with oil supplies.[132] Yet there was little real change in U.S. Middle East policy, and though Faisal threatened to cut production, at this point the Saudis' preference seemed to be to use the Arab oil weapon gradually, progressively restricting production growth. Also, they did not want to do damage to Western Europe and Japan.[133] However, with the outbreak of war, the Saudis were forced into taking stronger action.

The October War, the Embargo, and the Price Explosion

For twenty-five years the United States had succeeded in keeping the Arab-Israeli conflict separated from international oil politics, but during that time it refused to recognize the claims of Arab nationalism to the occupied territories and to a homeland for the Palestinians. In 1973 the Arab people asserted those claims, launching the fourth Arab-Israeli war, which "unleashed" the Arab oil weapon, and the politically motivated production cutbacks that resulted created the most serious energy crisis of the postwar period.

Yet these production cutbacks would not have had the impact they did had dependence upon Middle East and North African oil not reached high levels. Moreover, substantial as the Arab oil-production cutbacks were, their effects were intensified because of competitive rivalries among the consuming countries and the international oil companies. Also, the consuming countries were victimized by their failure to develop alternative energy sources and their lack of emergency preparedness.

On October 6, the Jewish Day of Atonement, Sadat launched the fourth Arab-Israeli war. On September 22 he had informed the Soviet Union of his decision to go to war and, in the weeks before the war began, Moscow had sent large quantities of ammunition to both Syria and Egypt.[1]

The war caught both the United States and the Israelis by surprise. Officials in both countries had thought that so long as Israel retained military superiority, the Arabs would not resort to war. In addition, Kissinger had arranged for talks between the Egyptians and the Israelis to begin in November, after the Israeli elections. Foreign-policy specialists believed that the Arabs would not go to war so long as a political alternative for recovering the occupied territories remained open. Finally, because of detente, U.S. policy makers expected the Soviet Union to restrain Egypt.[2]

The Israelis learned of the impending attack in time to launch a preemptive strike; however, the United States had strongly warned them against striking first. Consequently, Prime Minister Golda Meir decided to "accept" the first attack, refusing even to put the country on full alert.[3] As a result, the Arabs were able to make impressive military advances. Syria nearly recaptured all of the Golan Heights; Egypt broke through the heralded Bar-Lev Line and consolidated its position on the east back of the Suez Canal. In the initial fighting, Israel suffered heavy losses of troops and equipment and quickly turned to the United States to replace its supplies.[4]

Initially, the United States was reluctant to resupply Israel; with oil growing in importance, the United States did not want to further antagonize the Arab world. U.S. policy makers also believed that a stalemate in the fighting might finally lead Israel to make the concessions necessary for conclusion of a peace agreement and give Sadat the "victory" he needed before he could sign a peace treaty with Israel. But on October 9 the United States agreed to resupply Israel. Initially, the resupply was kept at a minimal level and deliberately delayed in order to minimize U.S. involvement and to pressure Israel to agree to a cease-fire. However, by October 12 Egypt had rejected the U.S. call for a cease-fire-in-place, and the Soviet Union had begun to resupply the Arab side.

If Egypt secured a victory with the aid of Soviet arms, the Soviet-Egyptian alliance would be refurbished, but if the Arabs were shown that they could not win a victory with Soviet arms, they would be forced to seek the kind of diplomatic aid that only the United States could provide. And if the United States failed to supply Israel with arms, its influence in the Middle East and its credibility as a global power would be undermined. In addition, with President Nixon under increasing attack as a result of the Watergate scandal, Israel threatened to "unleash" its U.S. supporters if it did not get the arms it requested. Consequently, on October 13 President Nixon ordered a full-scale airlift of U.S. military supplies to Israel.[5]

With the outbreak of war, the Palestine Liberation Organization and the radical nationalists in the Kuwait national assembly called for use of the oil weapon, and the Iraqi Ba'ath Party stressed the importance of using oil in the current battle. In addition, the *Oil and Gas Journal* noted the gravity of "a threat from the Kuwaiti oil workers' union to stop production unless oil shipments to the United States were cut by at least 50 percent. Such an action could well spread to workers in other Arab states, even in those where unions are illegal."[6]

During the first ten days, the war had little impact on the international oil industry. As soon as the war began, Algeria declared an embargo on exports to the United States, but it had never sent much oil to the United States anyway. A day later, Iraq nationalized the holdings of the U.S. companies (Exxon and Mobil) in its Basrah Petroleum Company in retaliation for U.S. support for Israel. While symbolically important, this measure was of limited significance. The Iraqis had already nationalized the IPC's major production facilities in northern Iraq, and they agreed to pay compensation for their latest acquisition. Also, the Iraqis gave Exxon and Mobil continued access to the nationalized oil, the only penalty being that they had to pay market rather than preferential prices for it. And since neither Exxon nor Mobil had been the operator of the Basrah Petroleum Company (that role fell to their partners in the joint venture), Iraq's nationalization had no effect on day-to-day operations.[7]

Despite the outbreak of war, on October 8 the oil industry and the Gulf exporting countries met, as scheduled, to discuss the countries' demand for a revision in the 1971 Teheran price agreement. The countries claimed that the companies' profits were excessive and that the improvement in downstream product prices should accrue to the exporting countries. They sought to restore the eighty/twenty profit ratio that had prevailed at the time the Teheran Agreement was signed and to gain protection against reduction in their real income as a result of inflation. In essence, the countries' demand raised the issue of how the benefits from the improved market situation should be divided between the companies and the exporting countries.

The following day, the companies submitted an offer for a 15 percent increase in posted prices and a revised inflation-adjustment index. They also offered to pay a premium for low-sulfur crude. The exporting countries replied that they would accept an immediate 100 percent increase in the posted price, a mechanism that would permanently keep the posted price 40 percent above the actual market price (as it had been at the time of the Teheran Agreement), and an improved inflation adjustment factor.[8] With the two sides obviously far apart, the companies' negotiating team requested permission to consult with the governments of the consuming countries. They explained that the increases the Gulf countries were seeking "had exceptionally serious implications not only for the companies, but for the economy of the world at large."[9] With inflation a mounting worldwide concern, the companies were worried about the reaction of the consuming countries and feared that they might not be permitted to pass higher prices on to consumers, and their fears were intensified because they had already been criticized for the "ease" with which they had agreed to previous OPEC price increases. Consequently, between October 9 and 11 industry representatives consulted with officials from the United Kingdom, the Netherlands, Germany, Italy, Belgium, France, Spain, Japan, the United States, and the EEC and the OECD. These officials were almost unanimous in recommending that the companies not improve their offer to the point where it had a reasonable chance of being accepted by the exporting countries.[10]

On October 12, the chairmen of the four Aramco parent companies sent a memorandum to President Nixon, noting that there was "essentially no spare capacity" in the non-Communist world and that market forces had "pushed crude prices up substantially."

A significant increase in posted prices and in the revenues of the producing countries appear justified under these circumstances; but the magnitude of the increase demanded by OPEC, which is in the order of a 100 percent increase, is unacceptable. Any increase should be one which allows the parties an opportunity to adjust to the situation in an orderly fashion. Accordingly, the companies are resisting the OPEC demands and they are seeking an adjustment of them which can be fair to all the parties concerned.

The memo then discussed the political situation in the Middle East:

We have been told that the Saudis will impose some cutback in crude oil production as a result of the United States' position taken thus far. A further and much more substantial move will be taken by Saudi Arabia and Kuwait in the event of further evidence of increased support of the Israeli position.

We are convinced of the seriousness of the intentions of the Saudis and Kuwaitis and that any actions of the U.S. government at this time in terms of increased military aid to Israel will have a critical and adverse effect on our relations with the moderate Arab producing countries.

In the present highly charged climate in the Middle East, there is a high probability that a single action taken by one producer government against the United States would have a snowballing effect that would produce a major petroleum supply crisis.

The bulk of the oil produced in the Persian Gulf goes to Japan and Western Europe. These countries cannot face a serious shut-in. Regardless of what happens to United States' interests in the Middle East, we believe they will of necessity continue to seek Middle East oil and that they may be forced to expand their Middle East supply positions at our expense.

Much more than our commercial interests in the area is now at hazard. The whole position of the United States in the Middle East is on the way to being seriously impaired, with Japanese, European, and perhaps Russian interests largely supplanting United States presence in the area, to the detriment of both our economy and our security.[11]

When negotiations with the exporting countries resumed on October 12, the companies immediately requested an additional two weeks to consult with the consuming-country governments. The exporting countries granted them a week, and warned that they might not be willing to wait two weeks before taking unilateral action. Negotiations broke off, without a date for resumption, and on October 13 the companies' representatives left Vienna, where the negotiations had been held.[12] Three days later, as they had warned, the Gulf exporting countries unilaterally raised the posted price by 70 percent to $5.11 a barrel—the first of a series of dramatic changes that were to occur within the next two and a half months. Algeria and Venezuela had been unilaterally setting their oil prices since 1970, but this was the first time the Gulf countries had done this, and they indicated that, from that point on, they would set crude-oil prices themselves. Until 1970 this had been a power reserved exclusively for the companies; then, as a result of Libya's actions and the Teheran/Tripoli agreements, it became subject to joint determination by the companies and the exporting countries. Now, in the midst of the fourth Arab-Israeli war, the power passed entirely to the exporting countries.[13]

The exporting countries explained that their intention was "to re-establish the same relationship between posted and realized prices as existed in 1971 before the Teheran agreement, and by extension, a roughly similar profit-sharing ratio as well." They indicated that in the future they would seek to keep the posted price 40 percent above the market price,[14] which meant that, in practice, the market price would determine the posted price and that, for the first time since they were introduced in 1950, posted prices would vary on a commercial basis rather than remain fixed for long periods of time—historically, a major source of stability in the industry.

In arriving at the new posted price of $5.11 for a barrel of Arabian light, the Gulf exporting countries had taken $3.65 as the market price and added 40 percent to it. The countries claimed that a market price of $3.65 was only 17 percent above the actual price, $3.12, of the same crude in a recent sale. However, many crude-oil marketers disputed this, maintaining that $3 was about the highest price obtained for a barrel of Arabian light and that, in general, the market price was still between $2.80 and $2.85 on a spot basis. They said that a price of $3.12 might have been paid, but only if the crude were available on a long-term basis. The companies also disputed the exporting countries' claim that at the time of the Teheran Agreement the posted price had been 40 percent above the market price.[15]

Iran's oil minister maintained that once transport and crude-oil quality differences were taken into account, the cost to the consumer of Gulf oil at the new prices would be no higher than they were already paying for North African crude. Indeed, because of the tightness in the world market in recent weeks, Libya and Algeria had been able to sell oil for as much as $5.30 a barrel.[16]

The immediate effect of the Gulf exporting countries' action was to raise their per barrel income from about $1.80 to about $3.[17] Sizable as that was, it was less than what an OPEC study had recommended. That study had found that between January 1971 and August 1973 the price the companies realized from petroleum product sales in seven European countries had increased by at least $2.20 a barrel. However, during this period the exporting countries' take had increased by only $0.537, bringing it to $1.804. The study recommended that the companies be left the same profit margin they had at the time the Teheran Agreement was signed, which would mean increasing the government's per barrel take by $1.903 a barrel, bringing it to $3.707, and to do that a posted price of $6.205 would be required.[18]

It was also estimated that the OPEC move would leave the companies with a handsome profit margin of about 50¢ a barrel (realized price of $3.65, tax-paid cost of $3.15). Moreover, the Gulf countries defended the price hike by maintaining that crude oil must be underpriced so long as the consuming-country governments received 66 percent of the retail price while producing-country governments received only 9 percent.[19]

In announcing their decision, the oil-exporting countries said that if the companies refused to lift the oil at the newly established prices, they would make it directly available to others who were interested in purchasing it. Yet, with the market still tight and buyers more concerned with availability of supplies than with price, the exporting countries were not expected to have trouble making the new prices stick. And so long as the price increases could be passed on to customers, the companies were not about to give up access to their crude supplies.[20]

The company representatives had left Vienna, despite the exporting countries' threat of unilateral action, because they did not want to be associated with the kind of price increases the exporting countries were seeking. Had they negotiated such a settlement, they would have been strongly criticized in the consuming countries and the threat of consumer-government controls on petroleum product prices and oil company profits would have greatly increased. In contrast, a price increase that the companies were not held responsible for might well serve their interests, for unlike the situation in 1970–71, by the fall of 1973 the landed price of oil imported into the United States was above the price of oil produced in the United States. Consequently, an increase in the world oil price would put upward pressure on prices in the United States, where nearly all of the international oil companies had extensive production interests and where price controls on newly discovered oil had recently been removed.[21]

Shortly after the Gulf countries' action, Venezuela boosted its prices to the new Gulf level. While the Gulf countries had raised their posted prices by 70 percent, Libya and Nigeria boosted their posted prices by 94 percent, which threatened a new round of leapfrogging on price.[22]

While the October 16 price increase had been imposed during the October War, it stemmed from developments in the world oil market during the previous two years. The outbreak of the war affected the climate in which the exporting countries acted, but, had there been no war, it is likely that a price increase, comparable to the one enacted on October 16, would have occurred anyway. However, the war directly affected what followed.

THE PRODUCTION CUTBACKS AND THE EMBARGO

On October 9 Kuwaiti Oil Minister Atiqi had responded to pressure from Kuwait's national assembly by calling an emergency meeting of Arab oil ministers, and he stated: "Now the atmosphere is more propitious than in 1967 and we can accept a reduction in production at the same time denying supplies totally to any country which supports Israel materially and practically."[23] Then, on October 15, Aramco President Frank Jungers cabled from Saudi Arabia that the Saudis were upset by the pro-Israeli role the United States was playing. The cable warned that unless there was a change in the tone of remarks by top U.S. officials, the United States could expect imposition of an embargo. Also, the cable said, Yamani had indicated that the pressure for curtailing supplies came mainly from the Libyans and the Iraqis, but it was strongly supported by the Kuwaitis[24] and would therefore be very difficult to reverse.[25]

By this time the airlift of supplies to Israel that Nixon had authorized on October 13 had been widely reported, and on October 16 Israeli armored units had driven a wedge through Egyptian lines on the east bank and hundreds of Israeli troops had broken through, turning the battle tide on the Suez front. The move had been considered for some time but had been delayed because of a shortage of ammunition and equipment. However, upon receiving word of the U.S. supply airlift, the Israelis had acted.[26] On October 17, with Israeli troops rapidly advancing toward Cairo, the oil ministers from ten Arab states met at the

OAPEC headquarters in Kuwait.[27] Yamani later stated that he had been sent to the meeting by King Faisal with instructions to resist the radicals; so when Iraq proposed nationalizing all U.S. companies on Arab soil, the withdrawal of funds from U.S. banks, and a total embargo of the United States, Yamani refused to go along.

The Saudis opposed the Iraqi proposals because they wanted to maintain their relationship with Aramco and because they viewed the nationalization strategy as not well suited to increasing pressure gradually, the approach they favored. Yet, during the October War, Aramco's President Frank Jungers feared that if the cutbacks did not produce results, nationalization was a real possibility.[28] After their proposals were rejected, the Iraqis walked out of the OAPEC meeting, and subsequently they absented themselves from all meetings of the Arab oil ministers during the embargo. In the end, the plan adopted by OAPEC was in all essential respects the one proposed by Saudi Arabia, with strong and close support from Egypt. It called for each Arab state to cut its oil production by at least 5 percent from September levels. In addition, the OAPEC members declared that

the same percentage will be applied in each month compared with the previous one, until the Israeli withdrawal is completed from the whole Arab territories occupied in June 1967 and the legal rights of the Palestinian people restored. The conferees are aware that this reduction should not harm any friendly state which assisted or will assist the Arabs actively and materially. Such countries would receive their shares as before the reduction.[29]

Syria and Libya had argued for more stringent cutbacks and nationalization of U.S. companies in the Arab world. However, while Saudi Arabia, Qatar, Algeria, and Kuwait reduced their production by 10 percent, Libya (and Bahrain) cut its production by only the minimum 5 percent, and Iraq did not cut production at all.[30]

The day before the Arab oil ministers met, President Sadat had called for an immediate ban on Arab oil exports to the United States, a move that the majority of delegates at the Kuwaiti conference supported. Yet Saudi Arabia wanted to give the United States more time to change its policy of active support for Israel. Consequently, the adopted formula left it up to each country to decide whether it would embargo exports to the United States. The next day Abu Dhabi declared an embargo against the United States and, the day after, Libya did likewise.[31] However, other countries refrained from declaring embargoes, though Saudi Arabia indicated that it would cut off exports to the United States if its efforts to get the United States to change its Middle East policy did not soon produce tangible results. Saudi Arabia had expected the United States to replace Israel's losses, but it warned President Nixon that a large bequest to Israel would make it impossible for the Saudis to resist the pressure of Arab opinion. Despite this warning, on October 19 President Nixon asked Congress for $2.2 billion for military assistance to Israel, and in contrast to recent U.S. policy toward Israel, this was to be a gift, not a sale.[32]

Saudi Arabia responded the following day by declaring a total embargo against the United States, and within a few days all of the remaining Arab states declared embargoes against the United States. The Arab countries also embargoed the Netherlands because of its strong support for Israel.[33] In addition, the Arab states distinguished a "most favored" group of "friendly" countries that would continue to receive 100 percent of their September 1973 oil supplies and a "neutral" group of countries that would receive what was left.

Kuwait and Saudi Arabia added the volume of oil that normally went to the embargoed countries to their production cutbacks, which brought the total cutback to almost 20 percent by early November, or 12 percent of the oil in world trade.[34] Yet, even as it took this action, Saudi Arabia was concerned about endangering its relationship with the United States. As Yamani told a visiting delegation of U.S. congressmen at the end of October, "King Faisal has done his best in the last two weeks to represent American interests. . . . We did not want the embargo. We hope that we can do something, but there must be something that we can show as change."[35]

Once Israel had gained the offensive, the Soviet Union pressed for a cease-fire in order to save Egypt. The United States was also anxious to restabilize the situation, but in a way that would maximize prospects of achieving a peace agreement.[36] Consequently, in response to Moscow's call for a cease-fire, Kissinger sought Egyptian agreement to direct negotiations with Israel, something Egypt had always refused. With Kissinger taking the lead in the negotiations, the United States got Israel to agree to a cease-fire, and the Soviet Union got Egypt to agree to direct talks with Israel. The two superpowers then sponsored a U.N. resolution for a cease-fire-in-place, which the Security Council unanimously adopted on October 22 and called for it to go into effect within twelve hours. However, shortly after the cease-fire was adopted, Israel charged Egypt with violating it and resumed its offensive.

The Security Council issued a second call for a cease-fire, but before it went into effect the Israelis announced that their forces had reached the outskirts of Suez and had effectively surrounded the Egyptian Third Army Corps. Israel was now in position to block access to Suez City and destroy the highly touted Egyptian Third Army, possibly toppling Sadat in the process. The Egyptian leader appealed to Brezhnev for a joint U.S.-Soviet peacekeeping force in the Middle East. On October 24 Brezhnev sent a note to President Nixon urging that the United States and the Soviet Union send military contingents to the Middle East and indicating that, if the United States did not agree, the Soviets would consider acting unilaterally. The United States strongly opposed both introduction of U.S. and Soviet troops into the area and unilateral Soviet action. To enunciate the depth of U.S. opposition, on the night of October 24–25 President Nixon put U.S. forces on a worldwide military alert. The United States also warned Israel against further advances. As a result, on October 25 a cease-fire took hold, though not at the October 22 lines, and the fourth Arab-Israeli war came to a halt.[37]

As the cease-fire went into effect, Kissinger was preparing for a new diplomatic effort in which the United States would take an active role in trying to bring about an Arab-Israeli peace agreement. The cease-fire and the U.S. efforts, already under way—to bring about an agreement between the Arabs and the Israelis—were expected to reduce the pressures for maintenance of the Arab oil embargo and the policy of monthly production cutbacks. As Johnston cabled Aramco headquarters in New York on October 25, "There is now little doubt in my mind that the Kissinger initiatives and cease-fire [have] brought time to the extent that no radical move or push on their [the Saudis'] part will occur as long as forward momentum continues and as long as they are able to tell themselves and others that initiative must be given a chance."[38]

Yet when the oil ministers from the Arab countries met in Kuwait on November 4, they immediately increased the cutback level to 25 percent (20 percent plus the promised 5 percent monthly increment). However, they decided to include the volume that normally went to the embargoed countries in the 25 percent.[39] At the conference, the Arab countries also clarified the point that the consuming countries had been divided into three categories: (1) preferred countries, receiving 100 percent of September levels, (2) neutral countries, receiving a reduced percentage of September levels, and (3) embargoed countries, receiving no crude oil or refined products.[40] Consumer countries were warned that, to be in the "preferred" category, they would have to adopt a more positive attitude toward the Arab cause. It was also decided that Saudi Arabia's Yamani and Algeria's Oil Minister Abdelsalam Belaid would tour the major consumer countries to explain the embargo/cutback program.[41]

After the November 4 meeting, Algeria and Libya boosted their cutback level to 25 percent but Iraq continued to export as much as it could, actually increasing its production by 7 percent between September and December 1973.[42] Officially, Iraq maintained that since the production cutbacks did not distinguish between friend and foe, they would lead countries that had moderated their Middle East positions to conclude that it had done them no good. Consequently, Iraq advocated that the exporting countries nationalize the oil companies, banks, and other assets in their countries owned by nationals from the United States and other unfriendly countries.[43] Iraq also recommended that the exporting countries shift their foreign-exchange holdings from the currencies of unfriendly countries.

Behind Iraq's official position lay two major concerns. First, Iraq correctly saw the production cutback policy as part of a moderate Arab strategy designed to reach eventual accommodation with Israel. As the Iraqi leadership stated in an official Ba'ath Party radio broadcast, the objective of the October War was "to contain the sweeping revolutionary current by seeking to bring about a cease-fire and to return to bargaining with the Zionist enemy and United States imperialism."[44] Yet, as a radical Arab state that rejected any settlement with Israel, Iraq had little sympathy for this campaign. Second, since the Law 80 dispute in 1961 Iraq's production had lagged behind the other major Middle East oil-exporting countries'. Consequently—unlike Saudi Arabia, Kuwait, Abu Dhabi, Qatar, and

Libya—Iraq had only modest foreign-exchange reserves, and it could not afford to cut back production, especially since it was in the midst of a major economic development program. By expanding production while others cut back, Iraq hoped to increase its immediate production share and to encourage companies to increase their future liftings in the country. Yet, despite its refusal to go along with the production cutbacks, Iraq maintained an embargo against the United States and the Netherlands (and later Portugal, South Africa, and Rhodesia).[45]

The country closest to the Iraqi position was Libya. However, unlike Iraq, Libya had substantial foreign-currency reserves and therefore could much more easily endure a production cutback. In Iraq, the nationalization of U.S. companies left the operators in place, but if Libya were to confiscate U.S. assets it would have to find other companies to operate the fields. During the embargo, therefore, Libya's policy conformed much more closely to the embargo/production cutback strategy pursued by the other Arab oil-exporting countries than to Iraq's.[46]

As table 8–1 shows, November 1973 was the peak of the Arab cutbacks. In that month the Arab states produced 5 mb/d, or 24 percent less than the previous September. Of this total, Saudi Arabia accounted for 2.3 mb/d, or nearly half of the reduction.[47]

Had the Arab exporting countries reduced their production by 24 percent in 1967, the United States would have been able to replace nearly the entire deficit in a few months, and Canada and Venezuela could have provided the rest. However, in 1967 Arab oil production totaled 9.95 mb/d, or 26.9 percent of the world total, while by September 1973 Arab production had more than doubled, to 20.8 mb/d or 35.1 percent of the world total, and U.S. spare capacity had declined from 2.1 mb/d to virtually nothing.[48] In addition, while the oil companies had planned that by 1972 Alaska would be producing 2 mb/d, as a result of the delays created by the Alaska pipeline controversy there was no oil from Alaska at the time of the Arab oil embargo.

Nor was there much spare capacity outside the United States. In June 1967 Venezuela had had 500,000 b/d in spare productive capacity, and in response to the Arab cutbacks it had increased production. Yet largely as a result of the

TABLE 8–1. ARAB AND NON-ARAB OIL PRODUCTION PRIOR TO AND DURING THE EMBARGO (MB/D)

	1973				1974		
	Sept.	Oct.	Nov.	Dec.	Jan.	Feb.	Mar.
Arab	20.8	19.8	15.8	16.1	17.6	17.9	18.5
Non-Arab	38.4	38.9	39.0	39.3	39.6	39.5	39.5
Total	59.2	58.7	54.8	55.4	57.2	57.4	58.0

MNC Embargo Report, p. 7 (figures originally from *Oil and Gas Journal*).

strategy of disinvestment that the companies adopted in response to Venezuela's reversion law and high tax policies, in the fall of 1973 Venezuela had no more than 200,000 b/d in spare capacity. In any case, the country's opposition party argued that Venezuela should not boost production but should raise prices.[49]

In Iran, the Shah had long clamored for the companies to add to their productive capacity, and early in 1973 the Consortium had agreed to boost Iranian capacity to 8 mb/d by 1979. But at the time of the embargo, Iran had only 6.5 mb/d in productive capacity and nearly all of it was already in use.[50] Yet, as Christopher Rand has pointed out, at the end of 1973 the Consortium had seventeen undeveloped fields in Iran that "in the aggregate . . . could produce at least one and perhaps two million barrels a day."[51]

The failure to exploit these and other opportunities meant that while the loss of Arab supplies, 5 mb/d, represented only 8.4 percent of September's world oil production, after five months non-Arab oil production could be boosted by only 1 mb/d; and in the absence of the Arab cutbacks, world demand would have increased above its September level. In fact, world oil consumption had been growing at an annual rate of about 7.5 percent and world demand for oil imports had been increasing by about 11 percent a year. In November, consequently, the estimated gap between supply and demand (the "shortfall") was between 4 mb/d and 5 mb/d, or about 7.5 percent of world demand. As a percentage of the world's demand for imports, the net loss came to roughly 15 percent.[52]

Still, it was generally thought that most industrial countries could reduce their oil consumption by 10 to 15 percent without serious economic impacts.[53] The real threat was not the actual shortfall but that, if the Arabs continued to reduce production by 5 percent per month, as they promised, things would get worse. However, the consuming countries were victimized by their lack of readiness for the crisis. No country had a coherent plan for dealing with a loss of oil supplies, nor did the consuming countries as a group have a strategy for responding to the oil-exporting countries.

When the embargo was announced, most European countries had stocks equivalent to only sixty to ninety days' consumption, with another thirty days' supplies in transit, and unlike the Europeans, neither the United States nor Japan had official emergency stockpiling programs. However, Japan had enough oil on hand to last fifty-five days, with another twenty days' supplies in transit, and the United States had its normal commercial inventories, equal to about fifty days' consumption or 128 days' imports.[54]

As soon as the embargo cutbacks were announced, the consuming countries attempted to get the Arab states to remove them. On November 8 Kissinger met with King Faisal and told him that because it served to generate anti-Arab sentiment in the United States, continuation of the embargo policy made it difficult for the United States to pursue a more "evenhanded" or pro-Arab policy in the Middle East.[55] Consequently, the embargo was a barrier to his efforts to induce an Israeli withdrawal from the occupied Arab lands.[56] Faisal replied that while he would like to remove the embargo,

I, too, am in a difficult position. It would be easier if the United States would announce that Israel must withdraw and permit the Palestinians to return to their homes. . . . The Communists are accusing some Arabs of bowing to American pressure. To those who accuse you of bowing to Arab pressure, you can reply that the only reason the Arabs are doing this is because you support the enemy of the Arabs.[57]

The king made it clear that the cease-fire was not sufficient for lifting the embargo and that the embargo would continue until Israel withdrew from the occupied territories. However, the king's ministers indicated that there might be some easing in the production cutbacks once there was progress on an Israeli withdrawal. Yet, as a result of the embargo, Saudi prestige—in the Arab world and internationally—had increased enormously and the king enjoyed his new power. Faisal was reported to be the Arab leader who was most firm in continuing the oil cutbacks until progress was made on issues stemming from the 1967 war.[58]

When the carrot failed, Kissinger tried the stick. On November 21 he warned that the United States would consider countermeasures if the embargo continued "unreasonably and indefinitely." Yamani replied that if the United States took military measures to counter the Arab oil policy, Saudi Arabian oil installations would be blown up, which would deny oil to Europe and Japan for several years and lead to their economic destruction.[59] Still, it is extremely unlikely that the United States was seriously considering military intervention at this time, for it would be most difficult to invade an Arab country, install a new, compliant regime, and withdraw. In the wake of Vietnam, U.S. public opinion was unlikely to countenance a sustained military occupation, nor were U.S. forces well prepared for desert warfare.[60] Nor did the situation in November warrant such action. The effects of the embargo were still minimal, and the price increases, while substantial by historic standards, were not high enough to be a major threat to the world economy.[61]

European efforts to get the embargo/cutback eased met with somewhat greater success than those of the U.S. On November 6, two days after the OAPEC Kuwaiti conference, the nine foreign ministers of the EEC passed a resolution urging both parties in the Arab-Israeli war to withdraw to the positions occupied on October 22, the initial U.N.-sponsored cease-fire line. The resolution also called for a peace settlement based on U.N. Resolution 242. While the Arab countries recognized this as a friendly gesture, they wanted the EEC countries to insist on Israeli withdrawal from all the territories occupied in 1967. Nonetheless, in appreciation of the EEC move, on November 18 the Arab states suspended their decision to cut back supplies to the EEC countries by another 5 percent in December.[62]

Japan, which received 45 percent of its crude oil from the Arab Gulf states, also sought to appease the Arabs. As the country most dependent upon oil imports, Japan was particularly alarmed when, in October, OAPEC classified it as an "unfriendly" country. The *Middle East Economic Survey* reported that the Arabs would be looking for Japan to make a dramatic gesture (e.g., breaking ties with Israel) in exchange for being placed in the "friendly" category.[63] Then, on November 12, Yamani confirmed that to ensure complete restoration of oil supplies, Japan would have to sever economic and diplomatic relations with Israel. He spelled out Arab policy: "If you are hostile to us you get no oil. If you are neutral you get oil but not as much as before. If you are friendly you get the same as before."[64]

Kissinger urged Japan not to capitulate to OAPEC pressure, which seemed to confirm suspicions already prevalent in Japanese business and political circles of a Kissinger-Israeli conspiracy. That, along with the suspicion that U.S. oil companies were diverting oil to the United States at Japan's expense, convinced the Japanese that they should endorse the OAPEC position. Consequently, on November 22, only four days before the Arab summit meeting, Japan made a strongly pro-Arab statement on the territorial issue and promised to reexamine its policy toward Israel in the light of future developments. According to Professor Yoshi Tsurumi, "This was the first open break with American foreign policy in post-war diplomatic history that Japan had dared to make."[65] In recognition of the Japanese move, at their summit conference on November 28 the Arab governments exempted Japan from the December cutbacks. Yet Japan managed to resist breaking diplomatic and economic relations with Israel, as the Arabs had demanded.[66]

At the Algiers summit the Arab states also decided to impose an embargo against South Africa, Rhodesia, and Portugal, which had allowed the United States to use its bases in the Azores to resupply Israel, and a secret resolution stipulated that the monthly cutbacks would continue until an exporting country's oil revenues fell 25 percent below its 1972 level. Since prices had already increased by 70 percent, that meant the Arab producers could decrease their output to roughly 45 percent of its 1972 level before calling a halt to the successive monthly cutbacks.[67] (Iraq and Libya boycotted this meeting because they opposed both a negotiated settlement of the Arab-Israeli conflict and the October cease-fire.)

Despite the militant stance taken at the Algiers summit, early in December there were signs that the Arabs might relax their conditions for restoring production. The oil ministers of Saudi Arabia and Algeria toured the major European capitals, emphasizing Arab demands for Israeli withdrawals but offering to restore production progressively in response to a staged Israeli pullback, and with Washington playing a mediating role in an effort to bring about an Arab-Israeli settlement, Kissinger and Yamani met in Washington on December 5. The Saudi oil minister indicated that once Israel agreed to withdraw from the occupied territories, a timetable for greater Arab oil production could be matched with a timetable for withdrawing Israeli troops. Saudi conditions for boosting production to the level of world demand were unclear, but Yamani told Der Spiegel: "Industrialize Saudi Arabia. Then we will give you as much oil as you need."[68]

At a meeting of Arab oil ministers on December 8–9, a Saudi proposal for linking production increases to a timetable for Israeli withdrawal was formally adopted—a substantial retreat from the decision taken in October, in which the Arab exporting countries had stipulated that the production cutbacks would continue "until the Israeli withdrawal is completed from the whole Arab territories occupied in June 1967 and the legal rights of the Palestinian people restored." At this meeting the Saudis announced that they were postponing their December cutback until January but would not boost production above September levels even if Israel withdrew immediately.[69]

Shortly after the meeting of Arab ministers, Yamani stated that, rather than waiting until Israel began to withdraw from the occupied territories, production increases could begin as soon as Israel accepted the principle of withdrawal and the United States guaranteed Israeli compliance. Output would be restored in stages as Israel withdrew. Moreover, he stated, "I think all the Arab leaders surrounding Israel are talking about recognizing this state, living in peace with Israel. So this is not an issue at all." Yamani reiterated that, eventually, Saudi production might go to 20 mb/d, and he indicated that Saudi Arabia was still interested in making downstream investments in the United States. He explained that Saudi Arabia had been producing more oil than its economic interests required and would rather produce less; however, he stated, if it were necessary for the West, Saudi Arabia would produce more. "We hate to use oil as a weapon," he said, "and I don't think we'll ever use it again."[70]

THE SECOND PRICE INCREASE AND THE PARTICIPATION AGREEMENTS

While these developments were proceeding on the diplomatic front, the politically motivated embargo drove prices up by limiting production—something the oil-exporting countries had previously attempted but had never been able to do. In 1965, 1966, and 1968 OPEC had attempted to limit production by allocating production shares among its member countries, but all of these plans had failed because the countries were unwilling to limit their production. As recently as March 1973, OPEC had tabled still another proposal for production prorationing because prospects of agreement were dubious.[71]

Historically, the main reason for OPEC's inability to allocate production among its members was the unwillingness of the conservative exporting states to limit their production. When Libya imposed production cutbacks in 1970, Saudi Arabia boosted its production; and after the Iraqi and the Libyan nationalizations, the conservative Arab oil-exporting countries increased their exports.[72] But the political motives behind the Arab oil embargo got Saudi Arabia and the other conservative Arab exporting countries to reduce their production and the embargo brought the Arab-Israeli conflict and international oil politics together, marking the end of the dual policy that had been a cornerstone of U.S. Middle East policy since 1950, and this linking of what had been two separate issues is what accelerated and intensified the world energy crisis.

The resulting supply shortage was especially threatening to oil companies that lacked foreign concessions. While the concessionaires were still guaranteed preferential access to Middle East and North African oil, they were not about to sell any (as they normally did) until their own needs were met. In addition, the concessionaires had to pay the recently increased prices for participation and equity oil, but in the context of an increasingly tight market, these prices were considerably less than the market prices that other companies had to pay for their oil. Nonetheless, to stay in business, companies had to have crude oil, and since (generally) they could still pass crude-price increases on to consumers, they would be better off paying high prices for oil than if they were left crude short. The result, a mad scramble for crude supplies, put enormous upward pressure on prices.

What made this particularly threatening to the oil-consuming countries was that, when the Gulf exporting countries announced their price increase on October 16, they stipulated that in the future the posted price would remain 40 percent above the market price.[73] In doing this, they practically invited consumers to bid up the price they paid the oil-exporting countries. As Iran's Finance Minister Jamshid Amouzegar explained at the time: "Now it is not we as producers that will determine the price but you as consumers; we will wait and see what the market prices are and then calculate posted prices on this basis[,] keeping the same ratio between the two sets of prices that existed in 1971."[74] Consequently, if the oil companies bid up the market price, it would pull up the price that consumers paid to the exporting countries. And since the companies could not pass the full OPEC increase to consumers without triggering the 40 percent rule, the formula opened the door to continual price spiraling. For example, prior to October 16 both the posted price and the market price of a barrel of Arabian light had been $3. The cost was roughly 10¢, the government's take $1.86, and the companies' profit $1.04.[75] After October 16, the posted price was $5.11 and the government's take was about $3, or $1.14 more than it had been. If the companies passed this increase on to customers, it would boost the market price to $4.14. However, at that market price the posted price would have to go to $5.80 to remain 40 percent above the market price. If that happened, it would mean a further increase in a government's take. The companies might then try to pass that increase on, triggering still another application of the 40 percent rule, and so on.

In October, to avoid this, Exxon and Shell, the world's two largest oil companies, agreed to keep their crude market prices below the level that would trigger application of the 40 percent rule. In doing this, they reduced their profit margins by more than 50 percent a barrel—a strong indication that these companies were not trying to encourage further price increases by the exporting countries. Indeed, on October 29 the *Petroleum Intelligence Weekly* reported that the majors were concerned about their ability to raise prices as crude costs rise.[76]

The international oil companies were also anxious to restore price stability. At a meeting in November with the exporting countries, representatives from the companies were reported to have urged government restraint on follow-up action. They said that if further price increases occurred, they should be "gradual, predictable," and not marked by "constant volatility and uncertainty." And both the Gulf countries and the companies agreed on the need for a new oil pricing system that would cover all OPEC members and avoid the threat of continual leapfrogging.[77] However, the industry newsweekly *Petroleum Intelligence Weekly* indicated that there were "some crude producers—without heavy downstream investments—who would like to see higher prices"; and many crude-short companies, which did not favor higher prices, were willing to pay higher prices in order to get the crude they needed.[78] Consequently, in the absence of consumer-country controls to limit price bidding, these companies engaged in the upward price bidding that Akins had warned against the previous spring. To prevent this, several major companies asked Britian's minister for trade and industry to refuse foreign currency for bids over $6 a barrel, and a Shell executive tried to get Japan's Prime Minister Tanaka to restrain bids by Japanese companies. Yet these efforts met with little success.[79]

In November, Tunisia announced plans to auction 40,000 b/d of oil, and Nigeria put 300,000 b/d up for sale. Despite concern about the impact that sale of this oil would have on the market price, *PIW* found that "virtually every non-major oil firm" it canvassed planned to bid in both sales. Consequently, while a barrel of oil had sold for about $3 prior to the October price increases and production cutbacks, the Tunisian oil sold for $12.64 and the low-sulfur Nigerian crude for more than $16. Meanwhile, Algeria had established a price of $16 for its oil.[80]

In December, Iran set out to test the market, offering substantial quantities of oil on a long-term (six-month) basis. The successful bids ranged from $9 to $17.34 a barrel, and most of the bidding was by U.S. independents, who secured 48 percent of the Iranian oil. European companies received 35 percent and the Japanese took the remaining 17 percent.[81] As *PIW* said at the time, this sale demonstrated that some crude-short companies would pay almost anything to get nonembargoed oil in a supply crunch. Yet many oil companies feared that OPEC would take this sale as the basis for calculating the market price.[82]

While this upward price bidding did nothing to increase the availability of oil, it encouraged the oil-exporting countries to boost prices; and the only country that attempted to restrain its oil companies from unlimited bidding was Japan. The Japanese government advised its oil firms to exercise restraint, and they agreed among themselves not to go beyond $13 a barrel—a rather high limit.[83] Yet the failure of consumer-country governments to restrain their oil companies was related to their failure to work out an emergency sharing agreement, for in the absence of an agreement on sharing supplies, any country that put restraints on its oil companies was likely to suffer a disproportionate share of the short-fall.[84] As Exxon's Piercy later testified:

There was one basic thing that could have been done in the October crisis and that would have been something that the OCED has been working on for years, which is in times of a crisis a shortage of supply like that to have an agreement among the consuming nations as to how and how much each of them would get of their oil demand. Had we had such a thing and had we not had many countries out trying to project their own sources of supply by scrambling around in the market trying to get oil[,] I think we would have had a much more stable situation.[85]

In any case, immediately after the Iranian auction Libya raised its price by an additional $2, and Venezuela boosted its price by 56 percent.[86] Then, on December 22–23, less than two weeks after the Iranian auction, OPEC met in Teheran to determine the future world oil price. Iran took the lead in pushing for higher prices, calling for an increase in the per barrel price from its current level of $3.15 to between $12 and $14. The Shah argued that the price of oil should be just under the price of the nearest available substitute, which OPEC estimated to be the equivalent of $17 for a barrel of oil. As evidence of the exporting countries' ability to obtain such prices, Iran cited the prices it had just been paid for the oil it had auctioned. Iraq and Kuwait were inclined to support the Iranian position, and Venezuela favored even higher prices.[87]

However, Saudi Arabia, with only the support of several tiny sheikdoms, argued for a price of about $5. It was unreasonable, the Saudis argued, to take the prices at the Iranian auction as the true market prices, for they were paid in the midst of a politically motivated oil embargo/production cutback program for oil that had no restrictions on its destination, that is, oil that could be sent to the embargoed countries. In addition, Yamani argued that the increases the Iranians were demanding would ruin the economies of both the developed and the underdeveloped countries. After considerable debate, the two sides compromised on a price for equity oil of $7.11, a 126 percent increase over the price established on October 16 and 280 percent over the price that prevailed on October 1. Yet the Shah called the increase a "minimum," Amouzegar warned that the future world oil price would depend on world inflation and oil company profits, and the Shah declared that "the industrial world will have to realize that the era of terrific progress and even more terrific income and wealth based on cheap oil is finished."[88]

The other OPEC countries soon raised their prices as well. However, while in October the Mediterranean countries had pushed their prices above the level that prevailed in the Gulf, they were now brought into balance with the Gulf prices. Also, at the December meeting the link between posted prices and realized prices, established in October, was abandoned, with OPEC fixing the government take, then deriving the corresponding posted prices.[89] Had there been no October War and no production cutbacks, it is likely that the smaller October 16 price increase would have occurred anyway, but the December increase was largely a consequence of the production cutbacks and the panic-stricken response of the consuming countries.

Immediately following the OPEC meeting, OAPEC met and decided to cancel the 5 percent monthly production cutback scheduled for January and to reduce the total production cutback from 25 percent to 15 percent. In addition, the consumer countries were divided into four categories: most-favored countries, entitled to receive as much oil as their requirements dictated; friendly countries, entitled to receive supplies at their September level; neutral countries, to which general export cutbacks applied; and hostile countries, to which the full embargo applied. Britain, France, and Third World countries that had broken relations with Israel were placed in the most-favored category; Belgium and Japan were put in the friendly category; and the United States, the Netherlands, Portugal, Rhodesia, and South Africa were placed in the hostile category.[90]

There were several reasons for easing the production cutback policy. On December 21, Egypt, Jordan, Israel, the United States, and the Soviet Union had met in Geneva to begin the long process of peacemaking, and Egypt and Israel were about to begin their talks on disengagement of forces. In this context, the easing of the oil weapon was in keeping with its character as a flexible instrument that could be tightened when it was necessary to apply pressure and loosened as a reward for conciliatory behavior.[91] Also, the Arab oil ministers who visited consuming countries during November and December were reported to be impressed by the opposition to the production cutbacks. Saudi Arabia, in particular, did not want to cause extensive damage to the Western economies or provoke military reprisals. By easing the cutbacks, the Arab exporting countries would soften the impact of the price increase, for though the price was going up, consuming countries could console themselves with the knowledge that they would be getting slightly more oil. It was hardly much of a bargain, but the actions of the consuming countries and the international oil companies had helped prompt the increases.

The split between Saudi Arabia and the other major oil-exporting countries— especially Iran—over the size of the price increase reflected several basic differences in interest. As a substantial holder of foreign currency and close ally of the United States, Saudi Arabia was concerned about the impact a huge price rise would have on the world economy. In contrast, Iran was still badly in need of additional oil revenue, and because the prestige of the Saudi regime had been enhanced by the embargo and the production cutbacks, the Shah sought to boost his own prestige through a large increase in the world oil price. The Shah also maintained that the increase in the price of oil made only a small contribution to the increase in worldwide inflation.[92]

In contrast to most of the exporting countries, Saudi Arabia's oil reserves were so extensive that its leaders may have believed it could maximize its long-term revenues at a lower price and a higher production level. Insofar as they believed that a high price would speed development of alternative energy sources, this would be particularly true. While the Saudis maintained that they preferred to produce at a lower level, and that they could sell oil as a petrochemical feedstock long after its value as an energy source was exhausted, this explanation of Saudi behavior cannot be ruled out. In contrast, Iran and most of the other OPEC countries had much higher ratios of production to reserves than Saudi Arabia and, accordingly, were not so concerned about the impact higher prices would have on the development of alternatives to imported oil.

Saudi Arabia also feared that a drastic increase in prices would tilt the balance of power in the Gulf in favor of its rivals, Iran and Iraq, for while the revenues of all three countries would increase, Iran and Iraq, as "revenue-short" countries with large populations, would be strengthened more than Saudi Arabia, which already had more revenue than it could absorb; and many members of the Saudi ruling family were known to be concerned about the dangers that unspendable wealth would pose for maintenance of their traditional society.[93]

Furthermore, a steep price increase could undercut the effectiveness of the embargo/cutback policy, for the Saudis maintained that one of the strengths of the embargo/cutback was that it enabled the Arab countries to distinguish between "friendly," "unfriendly," and "neutral" countries and to reward countries for conciliatory moves while punishing others for hostile actions.[94] The price rise was not conducive to this flexible sort of reward and punishment since it treated friend and foe alike. In fact, since the "friendly" countries were more dependent upon oil imports than the "unfriendly" United States, higher prices would hurt them more. But this concern was of no interest to the non-Arab oil-exporting countries, and of less interest to the other Arab states than to Saudi Arabia, the principal architect of the embargo/cutback program.

Finally, the Saudis were aware of hints and discussions in the United States about seizing the Arab oil fields, and fearing this eventuality, they did not want to further antagonize the United States.[95] Other exporting countries were concerned about this, but their interest in higher revenues took precedence. And in contrast to the Arab radicals, Saudi Arabia sought to preserve a much closer long-term relationship with the United States, despite their differences over the Arab-Israeli conflict.

The October War and the embargo also marked the death of the participation agreement that Aramco had concluded with Saudi Arabia a year before—not that Saudi Arabia wanted to throw the U.S. companies out; far from it. But with the rise in anti-U.S. sentiment in the Arab world that accompanied the October War, Saudi Arabia could not agree to terms with U.S. companies that appeared to be less favorable than those Iran and Iraq had secured in the past year or that Libya had extracted in the fall. As a result of the embargo, the production cutbacks, and the price increases, the oil-exporting countries had a new awareness of their power. Consequently, on October 25 Johnston sent a cable to Aramco headquarters in New York in which he stated "I am now certain that Saudis will not sign any 25 percent implementation deal in any form and most probably will not sign it if percentage raised beyond fifty percent."[96]

However, it was not the participation share that mattered to the Aramco parents, but their preferential access to the oil and their financial arrangements with the Saudi government. The Saudis themselves were anxious to reach an agreement that would stabilize their arrangement with Aramco and end the leapfrogging on the participation issue;[97] hence Johnston recommended that the Aramco parents

look for a unique deal with some of the following characteristics:

(1) Something no one else has. This is why he [Yamani] pooh-poohed remarks in San Francisco which suggested something like Indonesian deal. They must have unique deal that cannot be copied by other countries.

(2) Something that utilizes the ARAMCO image and structure in Saudi Arabia which is in itself unique and exists only in Saudi Arabia.

(3) Current ARAMCO management control will remain (in fact believe we could improve control under some relaxed deal. Yamani and others characterize ARAMCO as "National Asset" and will continue to give us leeway.)

(4) Revised deal need not contain any lost financial position for current four owners. Saudis quite aware they can control this through postings and tax. (Incidentally got long playback of why unilateral action was taken on posted prices.)

(5) Am convinced could tie up crude if deal was right. Saudis not really interested in big increased crude volumes especially if we could fuzz up deal somehow.

(6) Yamani will make no more demands as such but will merely let nature take its course such as was case in posted prices, thus cannot expect him come up with demand or push such as was done in participation. Initiative must come from other four shareholders.

(7) General atmosphere created by negotiations, etc. on one hand versus attitude of OPEC countries on the other have precluded any possibility of going in with some bargaining position. I doubt that some horse trading approach would even be heard. On the other hand if we were to come in with some deal that had elements outlined above[,] believe crude volumes and financial effects could be preserved.

(8) One of unique elements might be ARAMCO's growth potential.

In summary if we could be ingenious enough[,] believe present shareholders can preserve present deal both in volume and financially but participation deal won't stand. We must develop something new that will remain unique.[98]

On November 13, 1973, Saudi Arabia formally notified Aramco that 25 percent participation was no longer acceptable. Yamani called for "immediate control" and stated that even a 51 percent share would be "insufficient and unsatisfactory." Abu Dhabi and Qatar were reported to be taking the same position. Then, in December, Abu Dhabi said it had to get a 51 percent share "long before 1982," and on December 19 Jungers told the Aramco parents that Yamani had told him the "key to making lasting agreement was for the State to have 100 percent control."[99] Yet the companies' main concern continued to be preferential access to the crude.

On January 29, 1974, Kuwait concluded an agreement with BP and Gulf that provided Kuwait with 60 percent participation at net book value. The Kuwaiti government said it might sell its participation crude back to BP and Gulf, but it reserved the right to sell it in international auctions, if possible. *PIW* reported that Gulf and BP would probably continue to buy back 75 percent of the government's participation share. Under the agreement, buy-back prices would not be fixed, but negotiated from time to time.[100]

Following the Kuwait deal, the companies offered Qatar and Abu Dhabi comparable terms, but while Qatar concluded a 60 percent agreement, Abu Dhabi held out for more. By January, Saudi Arabia was also renegotiating its participation agreement, and the Shah had notified the companies that if the Arab Gulf countries secured better participation terms, he would reopen the agreement that Iran had concluded in July with the Consortium.[101] In February, Libya totally nationalized the Libyan operations of Texaco, SoCal, and ARCO, which Tripoli Radio described as "a severe blow to American interests in the Arab world" and as a reply to the Washington Energy Conference, a meeting of major oil-consuming countries organized by the United States.[102]

Revision of the Gulf participation terms also paved the way for the peaceable resolution of two other Libyan nationalization disputes, for with the Gulf countries moving past 51 percent participation, the majors no longer had to fear that by agreeing to 51 percent participation in Libya they would set a precedent that would undermine the Gulf agreements. In April, consequently, Exxon and Mobil accepted Libya's 51 percent nationalization at "net book value." At the same time, these two U.S. majors agreed to new exploration and production-sharing agreements with the Libyan government.[103] Shell, which had been part of the Oasis concession, was fully nationalized, and in July agreed to compensation on the basis of net book value. In February, Libya also concluded a production-sharing agreement with Occidental that gave Libya the right to 81 percent of the oil while requiring Occidental to put up the bulk of the exploration costs.[104]

As these developments unfolded in Libya, the Kuwait national assembly decided not to ratify the Kuwait participation agreement—opening it up again and leading to the assumption of 100 percent participation by Kuwait in 1975. Similarly, in June 1974 Saudi Arabia concluded a 60 percent participation agreement, but it proved short lived. By December 1974, Aramco had agreed in principle to 100 percent participation by the Saudi government; but despite this, the four Aramco partners continued to have the right to buy back a substantial amount of Saudi Arabia's oil at a price somewhat lower than the market price. They had "fuzzed up" the deal by keeping it secret and learning to live with it.[105]

The old concession system had come to an end but the old concessionaires were still strong. They would continue to make handsome profits by servicing the oil-exporting countries and by marketing the crude that they retained preferential access to.

Moreover, during the transition the participation agreements provided the concessionaires an incredible advantage over their competitors, for by January 1974 most companies had to pay more than $10, the full market price, for their oil; and though the concessionaires paid this price for their participation oil, they paid only about $7 for their equity oil, reaping windfall profits on its resale.

Indeed, the desire of the exporting countries to capture this windfall accelerated the movement toward 100 percent participation. However, since the exporting countries earned more on participation oil than on equity oil, the increase in their participation shares meant further increases in their per barrel revenues, a further OPEC price increase that was not generally recognized.[106]

LIFTING THE EMBARGO

In November, Kissinger got Israel to withdraw to the original October 22 cease-fire line, relieving the pressure on the Egyptian Third Army. Sadat felt that this was the first time since 1957 that the United States had forced the Israelis to make a military move that Israel had opposed. In December, therefore, Sadat told Kissinger that he would get the embargo lifted during the first half of January; however, on December 28 Nixon sent a note to Sadat declaring "it is essential that the oil embargo and oil restrictions against the United States be ended at once."[107] On January 6, Secretary of Defense Schlesinger warned that the Arabs ran the risk of violence if they used their control over oil supplies to "cripple the large mass of the industrial world," and a day later the secretary added that the embargo would create domestic pressure favoring a U.S. show of force.[108] Kuwait's minister of foreign affairs, al-Sabah, replied that in the event of U.S. military intervention, Kuwait would blow up its oil fields, and Yamani reiterated that Saudi Arabia would do likewise.[109]

In January, Kissinger arranged a disengagement agreement under which Israel would withdraw from the east and west banks of the Suez Canal, pulling its forces about twenty miles back into the Sinai. This strip would then be divided into three zones, with the Egyptians maintaining up to 7,000 troops in the zone nearest the canal, the United Nations maintaining a buffer force in the middle zone, and Israel maintaining up to 7,000 troops in the third zone.

In return for the disengagement agreement, Sadat had promised to work for elimination of the embargo; consequently, following the agreement, Kissinger stated that "failure to end the embargo in a reasonable time would be highly inappropriate and would raise serious questions of confidence in our minds with respect to the Arab nations with whom we have dealt on this issue." The *Middle East Economic Survey* reported that U.S. diplomatic pressure on Saudi Arabia and Egypt was "very intense." Sadat publicly indicated that he felt the U.S. position had changed sufficiently to warrent reconsideration of the embargo, and privately he argued strongly for its lifting. At the end of January he told Nixon that King Faisal and the other Arab leaders had agreed to lift the embargo and would announce this at a February meeting.[110] However, noting that the conditions for lifting the embargo, stipulated in December, had not been met, on February 3 King Faisal told President Nixon that the embargo would not be lifted until a disengagement agreement had been reached on the Syrian-Israeli front as well. Nixon replied that unless the embargo was lifted, U.S. diplomatic efforts would come to a halt. Then, on February 13, Syrian President Assad, Algerian

President Boumedienne, Sadat, and King Faisal met in Algiers, where Sadat argued strongly for lifting the embargo; however, the three other leaders voted not to lift the embargo until further progress on a Syrian-Israeli agreement had been made.[111]

U.S. pressure for lifting the embargo continued. At a press conference on March 6, President Nixon noted that a meeting of Arab oil-exporting countries was scheduled in Tripoli on March 13, and he warned that if the embargo was not lifted at this meeting, the U.S. diplomatic effort would be undermined. U.S. officials contended that the embargo was provoking a backlash in the United States against Arabs and making it extremely difficult to shift toward a more "evenhanded" or pro-Arab policy.[112]

At the Tripoli conference, agreement in principle was reached on easing or removing the embargo/cutbacks; however, final action was delayed for a meeting of Arab oil ministers on March 16–18, at which the Arab exporting countries agreed to provisionally end the embargo on the United States until June 1. However, the announcement on lifting the embargo stated that since U.S. policy was not "compatible with the principle of what is right and just toward the Arab-occupied territories and the legitimate rights of the Palestinian people," production would not be fully restored to pre-embargo levels and a review of the situation would be made. Privately, King Faisal stressed the importance of obtaining a Syrian-Israeli disengagement agreement within two months to avoid reimposition of the embargo.[113] Libya, which had opposed the October cease-fire, and Syria opposed the lifting of the embargo; Iraq, which also opposed the cease-fire, was absent from the meeting. The only remaining radical Arab oil-exporting country, Algeria, supported the decision, but on a provisional basis.[114]

Following further "shuttle diplomacy" by Kissinger, a Syrian-Israeli disengagement agreement was signed May 31. As a result, on June 3 the Arab oil ministers tentatively agreed to remove all export restrictions, except the embargo on the Netherlands. Then, on July 11, the embargo/cutback policy was permanently and completely ended. However, in both their June and July statements the Arab oil ministers warned that embargos could be reinstated if a new war broke out.[115]

The Arab oil embargo was intended to pressure the United States into greater support for the Arab cause, and it was lifted in response to the pressure the United States placed on Israel, but in retrospect it is doubtful that the embargo had much immediate impact on U.S. Middle East policy, for the United States had long sought to promote stability in the Middle East.

Following the outbreak of the October War, U.S. policy shifted: from trying to achieve stability, through the maintenance of Israeli military superiority, to pressuring Israel into making the concessions required for conclusion of a peace agreement. Along with this, the United States assumed a much more active role in Middle East diplomacy. However, these shifts had much more to do with the changes created by the war itself than with the Arab oil embargo, for the war, not the embargo, had demonstrated the inadequacy of the earlier U.S. policy. The war had also given Egypt the "psychological victory" it needed before reaching a settlement with Israel, and this increased the likelihood that a U.S. initiative would prove successful. The military situation created by the war also provided the context for active U.S. intervention and cultivation of an Egyptian-U.S. alliance.

While the embargo underscored the need for stabilizing the Middle East, it is doubtful that it did much more than that. Indeed, throughout the negotiations Kissinger sought to avoid the appearance that the United States was reacting to the Arab oil embargo. Early in December, when the Israeli defense minister told Kissinger that a disengagement agreement need not await the outcome of the Israeli elections (scheduled for Dec. 31), Kissinger cautioned the Israelis against moving too quickly in the negotiations. And during the negotiations with Syria, Kissinger sought to convince Assad and the U.S. public that U.S. action in the Middle East was not primarily a function of its oil interests.[116]

Although the production cutbacks prompted the EEC and the Japanese to make symbolic shifts toward the Arabs, neither the EEC countries nor Japan could exert much influence on the outcome of the Arab-Israeli conflict. Nor is there any evidence that the Europeans or the Japanese sought to sway U.S. policy toward Israel during the embargo.[117]

Finally, while the embargo had been designed to punish the United States, ironically, following the embargo, U.S. influence in the Middle East was probably stronger than at any time since the mid-1950s. Egypt was moving further and further away from the Soviet Union and toward the United States, a move that was symbolized by President Nixon's visit to Cairo in June 1974. Following the disengagement of troops in the Golan Heights, relations between the United States and Syria improved; and Saudi Arabia, the United States' longstanding ally in the Arab world, had gained new power and prestige as a result of its deployment of the Arab oil weapon and the huge increase in oil prices.

ALLOCATING THE SHORTFALL: THE IMPACT OF THE EMBARGO ON SUPPLY

By the time the embargo ended its effects were hardly noticeable. The combination of a mild winter in both the United States and Western Europe, an impending recession, higher prices, and conservation measures[118] served to reduce demand and blunt the impact of the Arabs' supply restrictions. Nor was the United States or the Netherlands particularly hurt by the Arab oil embargo.

During the 1967 embargo the U.S. government had taken an active role in redirecting world supplies; during the 1973 embargo the international oil companies took responsibility for international oil allocations, while Washington concentrated on domestic allocation. In doing this, the companies reversed their traditional role of allocating production among the exporting countries, and allocated supplies among the consuming countries. Rather than allow the United

States and the Netherlands to bear the brunt of the shortfall, as the Arab countries intended, the international oil companies sought to even it out, so that all countries faced the same reduction in their consumption.[119] A directive of a U.S. major explained this policy as serving three goals: minimizing the risks of litigation and reprisals by consuming countries, maintaining political neutrality and preserving the company's role as a buffer, and providing flexibility of supply from many sources.

In addition, the fear was widespread within the industry that if the companies failed to redistribute supplies equitably, it would lead to greater governmental interference in their operations. At the same time, the companies did not want to jeopardize their standing with the exporting countries. Indeed, Yamani had threatened the companies with nationalization if they failed to comply with the rules laid down by the Saudi government.[120]

To meet their objectives with respect to both the consuming and the exporting countries, the companies shifted supplies of non-Arab oil to the United States and the Netherlands and redirected the Arab oil that normally went to these countries to nonembargoed markets. Had they not done this, the majors would have had to reduce their crude imports into the United States by 29 percent. Yet by increasing their deliveries from non-Arab countries into the United States, the majors were able to keep the reduction in their crude imports into the United States down to 16.4 percent. In this way the major oil companies were able to meet the rules of the embargo while frustrating its stated intent: punishment of the United States and the Netherlands and more favorable treatment of the other nations of Western Europe and Japan. Despite this, there is no evidence that the Arab exporting countries ever tried to stop the oil companies from shifting supplies in this way.[121]

During the embargo, therefore, comparatively little Arab oil entered the United States. Before the Arab oil embargo, the United States imported 6.6 mb/d, of which roughly 20 percent came from the Arab countries,[122] but during the first quarter of 1974, U.S. imports averaged only 5.3 mb/d, with only about 1 percent from Arab countries.[123] However, this decline in imports was only a 10 percent reduction in U.S. oil consumption. Similarly, in the Netherlands the availability of petroleum declined by 16 percent over its year-earlier level;[124] and as table 8–2 shows, while Japan fared better than the United States, Western Europe— supposedly a ''friendly'' area—fared worse. As a report by the U.S. Federal Energy Administration's Office of International Affairs concluded, ''It is difficult to imagine that any allocation plan would have achieved a more equitable allocation of reduced supplies.''[125]

Historically and at the onset of the crisis, the belief was widespread that during a supply shortage the oil companies would favor their home countries, but this turned out not to be the case. As a percentage of projected current demand, during the period January to April 1974 the five U.S. majors reduced supplies to the United States by 17 percent, to Europe by 18.6 percent, and to Japan by 16 percent. The independents allocated their supplies somewhat less evenly, but

TABLE 8–2. ESTIMATED INLAND CONSUMPTION OF PETROLEUM BY AREA: FIRST
QUARTER 1974 COMPARED WITH FIRST QUARTER 1973 AND FORECAST FOR FIRST
QUARTER 1974

	Consumption (MB/D)	
	1st Quarter 1973	1st Quarter 1974
Japan	4.78	5.26
U.S.	18.24	16.88
Western Europe	14.09	12.39
U.K.	2.31	2.13
France	2.68	2.39
Netherlands	.58	.48
W. Germany	2.90	2.31
Rest of world	19.94	22.90

From Stobaugh, "Oil Companies in the Crisis," in Vernon, ed., *The Oil Crisis,* p. 202. (This table is
a slightly revised version of the original, reprinted by permission of *Daedalus,* Journal of the
American Academy of Arts and Sciences, Fall 1975, p. 202, Boston, MA.) In the U.K., the coal
miners' strike reduced the consumption of coal and brought total energy consumption 13% below the
forecast, instead of 6%. The forecast for the Netherlands' petroleum consumption in the first quarter
of 1974 is actually a forecast for Benelux. Also, the figures for the U.S., Western Europe, and Japan
exclude bunkers (fuel for ships, equal to about 6% of inland consumption in Western Europe and
Japan), but the figures for "Rest of World" include bunkers. (See Stobaugh for the sources on which
this table is based.)
    There are several others problems with these comparisons. Rather than actual forecasts, the
forecasts are "assumed to be the same as compounded growth rate for consumption of all petroleum
between 1968 and 1973 as reported in BP, *Statistical Review of the World Oil Industry.*" Another is
that the U.S. devotes a higher proportion of its oil consumption to nonessential uses (pleasure
driving, excessive heating, display lighting, etc.) than Japan. Consequently, it should be easier for
the U.S. to cut demand and, accordingly, a sharp reduction in supplies might be a lesser hardship in
the U.S. Western Europe falls between the U.S. and Japan on this factor. *OECD Observer* (Dec.
1973), pp. 20–21.

since they operated in fewer national markets, they had more limited supply
options; and their supply allocations favored Japan, if anyone—not the United
States.[126]

    Moreover, consuming countries that attempted to secure favored treatment
from the companies met with little success. Shortly after the production cutbacks
were announced, the British government told the companies that serviced the
British market, including British Petroleum (51% state owned) and Royal Dutch/
Shell, that because Great Britain was on the list of "friendly" countries, it did
not expect to see its supplies reduced. The companies replied that Britain would
be treated like any other country, and if Britain wanted it otherwise, the government should enact legislation to that effect. Since this would hurt Britain's
relations with its allies, the government accepted the companies' dictates. In the
end, Britain fared slightly worse than the United States, but better than the
European average; however, this relatively favorable treatment was a response

Differences between 1st Quarter 1973 and 1st Quarter 1974 as a % of 1st Quarter 1973		Differences between "Actual" and "Forecast" during 1st Quarter 1974 as % of Forecast	Effect of Changes in Petroleum Supply on Total Energy
			Differences between "Actual and "Forecast" during 1st Quarter 1974 as % of Forecast
Actual	Forecast		
10%	13%	− 3%	− 2%
− 7	5	−11	− 5
−12	8	−19	−12
− 8	5	−12	− 6
−11	12	−21	−15
−17	7	−22	−12
−20	8	−26	−15
15	8	6	2

by the oil companies to the emergency created by the British coal strike rather than an attempt to comply with the government's directive.[127]

The French government also sought to secure favored treatment, directing the companies not to reduce their scheduled deliveries from non-Arab nations and to give France the consideration it was entitled to as a "friendly" nation. In addition, Algeria directed CFP and Elf-Erap to send their entire Algerian output to France, and it ordered non-French companies to maintain their shipments of Algerian oil to France. Despite these directives, and France's post-1967 policy of seeking improved relations with the Arab world, France suffered a large reduction in its oil imports (see table 8–2). Indeed, despite its national oil companies, France fared no better than many countries that relied entirely upon the major international oil companies—and CFP followed the same allocation policies as the majors.[128] Italy also told the companies it expected to receive crude oil at normal levels, but this did not stop the majors from announcing a 10 percent reduction in supplies for December. In contrast to Great Britain, Italy, and France, there is no evidence that the United States tried to secure special treatment from the oil companies or that the U.S. government ever objected to the companies' carrying out the embargo directives issued by the Arab governments.[129]

In general, the companies appear to have been more responsive to the long-term political implications of their allocations than to their short-term commercial interests. For example, while prices were higher in West Germany than France, the companies supplied France more generously than West Germany.[130]

Despite the modest level of the crude-oil supply shortfall and the great extent to which the companies evened it out, consumers had to bear unnecessary hardships, the consequence of several misguided consumer-government policies. In

Europe, Belgium, the Netherlands, Italy, Spain, and Great Britain imposed export controls on refined products, which distorted trade patterns and cut countries off from their traditional sources of supply. For example, West Germany could not obtain adequate supplies of certain petroleum products because refiners in other countries were not permitted to export them.[131]

Yet, as Prodi and Clo conclude, "there was at no time a real shortage of petroleum on the European market." Between October 1973 and April 1974, they point out, the reserves of oil products in the EEC countries never fell below 80 days' consumption. They conclude that, in Europe, "the difficulties of the crisis were mainly the result of disturbances in the internal distribution of oil products, which were triggered by the resistance of governments to the price increases imposed by the oil companies, and which led to delays in deliveries, discrimination against independent companies, and the speculative hoarding of stocks."[132]

Similarly, in the United States the newly created Federal Energy Office (FEO; later the Federal Energy Administration, or FEA) consistently overestimated the shortfall. To build up supplies of home heating oil and other distillate products, on December 5, 1973, the Cost of Living Council, which had the power to set petroleum product prices, increased the price of distillate products by 2¢ a gallon (15.4%) while setting back the wholesale price of gasoline by 1¢ a gallon (between 6% and 7%). This led to a surplus of home heating oil, but a serious shortage of gasoline. In fact, on February 1, 1974, gasoline stocks were 1.7 percent below their levels of a year before while distillate fuel-oil stocks were 38.4 percent above their year-earlier levels. During the embargo U.S. stocks of every major petroleum product, except gasoline, increased, over their year-earlier levels.[133]

To protect small refiners from being denied the crude they needed to stay in business and to provide for a geographically even sharing of the shortfall, Congress required the FEA to work out a plan for the sharing of crude oil supplies; however, during January and February 1974 the plan actually discouraged importation of crude oil. As a result of price controls, there were three categories of crude oil in the United States:

1. "Old oil," from wells in production prior to January 1, 1973, which sold at the controlled price of $5.25 a barrel.
2. "New oil," from wells not in production prior to January 1, 1973, plus any production from a preexisting well that exceeded its 1972 level. To encourage additional U.S. production, price controls on this oil had been removed in August 1973, and as a result of the OPEC price increases in January and February, it sold for roughly $10 a barrel. In addition, oil from small "stripper" wells was free of price controls, and as a special incentive for domestic production, companies were allowed to remove a quantity of "old oil," equivalent to their supply of "new oil," from controls. This oil was referred to as "released oil." As a result of these provisions, roughly 60 percent of all domestically produced oil was free of price controls by January 1974.

3. Imported oil, which sold for about $10 a barrel in the United States (the world price plus transportation).[134]

As a result of this two-tier price system, companies with access to price-controlled oil had a strong advantage over their competitors. Moreover, this advantage would be especially great if companies that had more oil than their refineries required were allowed to keep all their price-controlled oil for their own use and sell their imported and nonprice-controlled oil to other refiners. To prevent this, the FEO ruled that companies had to sell their crude oil at its weighted average price, which reduced the incentive of companies to import oil.

There was oil on the international market, but what profit-maximizing oil company would pay $10 or more to bring it into the United States, where it would be required to sell it to a crude-short refiner at a price of, say, $7.50? Similarly, why should any crude-short refiner seek additional crude on the international market, at $10 or more, when it could purchase crude oil from a "surplus" crude holder at $7.50? It is not surprising, therefore, that in January and February—the months when this "buy-sell" program was in effect—crude imports fell by about 25 percent but product imports, which were unaffected by the buy-sell program, fell by less than 5 percent.[135]

As a result, more crude oil went to Western Europe and Japan, and for the first time their refineries operated at higher rates than U.S. refineries. In fact, industry sources estimated that this buy-sell program cost the United States as much as 1 mb/d in oil imports, which approached the FEA's inflated 1.2 mb/d estimate of the gasoline shortfall. While this disincentive to import had the unintended consequence of reducing pressure on world markets, by January it was a bit late for this. On February 28 the FEA, which had opposed the buy-sell program from its inception, issued an amendment allowing refiners to exempt whatever additional imports they could procure from the buy-sell scheme. Not surprisingly, shortly after this ruling was announced, gasoline lines vanished.[136]

The FEA was also unable to work out a satisfactory plan for the sharing of gasoline supplies. As Deputy FEA Administrator John Sawhill testified on February 24, 1974, "We have these very long lines in some parts of the country, and we have adequate supplies—I hate to use the word 'surplus'—in other parts of the country."[137] In general, the eastern seaboard—the area of the country most dependent upon imports—faced the most severe shortages; yet certain other areas were hard hit as well.[138]

Part of the reason for these regional inequities was that Congress had mandated that supplies be allocated on the basis of 1972 consumption patterns. That meant that as a percentage of current demand, areas that had experienced rapid growth in 1972 (e.g., southern Florida and southern Arizona) had to bear a disproportionate share of the cutbacks. Yet Congress had chosen 1972 as the base because independent gasoline marketers had complained of a loss of market share in 1973. In addition, the FEA shifted crude oil from one refinery to another, without adequate consideration of regional demands for the products that particular refineries could make,[139] and when regional imbalances resulted,

FEA was unable to correct them. This was partly because the nation's petroleum and storage facilities were set up to handle the normal, pre-embargo traffic, not to make rapid shifts from one region to another in response to shortages—but it was also due to the poor quality of FEA's data. As FEA chief William Simon stated, "Our numbers are so bad we could have 50,000 people running around this country with a stick trying to gauge the inventories."[140]

The buy-sell program also shifted crude from more efficient to less efficient refiners, and this contributed to both a shortage of specialized petroleum products (kero-based jet fuel, aromatics, olefins, etc.) and to the gasoline shortage. In the end, many of FEA's problems stemmed from the agency's youth and the inexperience of its personnel. As a report by the Federal Trade Commission concluded, "The current [FEA] staff, still mainly detailees from other agencies, have neither adequate background, nor a long-term commitment to the program." This was a serious problem, but it was greatly compounded by FEA's involvement in detailed, day-to-day industry decisions. The agency attempted to do too much with too little experience and too small a staff. As the FTC said, it was an "overburdened and undermanned program."[141]

Yet, given the conditions under which FEA was created, it is hard to see how it could have been different, for the petroleum industry involves highly complex institutional arrangements. The experience, expertise, and skills to make it work on a day-to-day basis are lodged in the industry itself, and so long as this remains the case, no one else can manage it—certainly not a group of civil servants with little commitment to their jobs. Consequently, during the crisis created by the Arab oil embargo, the United States confronted the dilemma of choosing between inexperienced people to staff its oil allocation program or falling back upon people whose primary commitment was to the industry, not the public.[142] It was a not unfamiliar problem, which has recurred many times since in the determination of U.S. energy policy, but in 1973–74 it had highly damaging effects.

In retrospect, it seems that with better planning in Western Europe and the United States and among the oil-consuming countries as a whole, most of the negative impacts of the 1973–74 Arab oil embargo could have been avoided. As it was, the immediate hardships were not great, and nothing like what might have occurred had the Arab cutbacks increased, as was originally stipulated. But as a result of the hindrances that consumers experienced and the bidding up of prices, consumers had a new sense of vulnerability, and the oil-exporting countries a new sense of their power. Equally significant, the consuming countries had to confront high oil prices, a problem they had been relatively unconcerned with during the supply crisis created by the Arab cutbacks.

3

THE WORLD OF HIGH OIL PRICES

The Consequences of the Oil Price Revolution

The 1973–74 rise in oil prices posed a greater challenge to the world economy than any event since the Great Depression. Consuming countries feared that higher oil prices would mean slower rates of economic growth, increased inflation, and unmanageable balance-of-payments deficits. The poorer countries worried that they would be unable to secure funds to pay their higher oil bills, the richer ones that the system of international finance and world trade would collapse as countries resorted to import controls, restrictions on exchange of foreign currency, and debt repudiation—in a vain effort to pay for badly needed oil.

The exporting countries, unable to absorb their increased revenues domestically and fearful about the security of their investments in the developed world, might decide to cut back production rather than accumulate more surplus funds. Prices might then rise to astronomical levels, or energy resources might be unavailable at any price. In either case, economic growth would come to an abrupt halt. Nor could one discount the possibility that renewed instability in the Middle East would lead to another loss of supplies. Even in the unlikely event that all these pitfalls were avoided, energy experts warned that sometime between 1980 and 1990 the world's demand for oil would outrun the supply.[1]

Responding to the oil crisis was particularly difficult because actions that would alleviate part of the problem were likely to aggravate other parts. The fundamental issues were availability of adequate energy supplies and the price that had to be paid for it. The higher energy prices went, the greater the impact on inflation, the greater revenue that had to be transferred to the oil-exporting countries, the greater the balance-of-payments deficits of the consuming countries and the slower their economic growth. On the other hand, by encouraging conservation and development of new energy sources, higher prices promoted the availability of adequate energy supplies, and by strengthening the position of the conservative oil-exporting countries, higher prices contributed to the stability of the Middle East.

As a result of the increase in prices, the consuming countries paid $88.8 billion to the OPEC countries for oil imports in 1974 as opposed to $22.8 billion in 1973.[2] The increase in costs represented about 2 percent of the output of the oil-importing countries—between half and two-thirds of a normal year's growth.[3] This transfer of wealth to the oil-exporting countries posed several immediate problems for the consuming countries. Because a worldwide recession was expected even before the price rise, the transfer of wealth to the exporting countries reduced aggregate demand in the consuming countries. The Keynesian prescription for such a development would ordinarily be to boost demand through monetary and fiscal policies, but the mounting inflation and balance-of-payments problems that many oil-importing countries were experiencing, and the impetus that higher oil prices would give to both these trends, made consuming countries reluctant to adopt reflationary policies.

Early in 1974, as attention shifted from the problem of supplies to the problem of higher oil prices, much of the concern centered on the consequences that mounting OPEC surpluses would have on international payments and trade. The OECD estimated that by 1980 OPEC's cumulative surplus would rise to $650 billion.[4] Indeed, because of their underdeveloped economies and the rapidity with which their revenues increased, it would be some time before the "rich" OPEC countries (Saudi Arabia, Kuwait, Libya, the United Arab Emirates, and Qatar) could spend all the revenue they would accumulate. The image of a few rich oil countries, unable to spend their wealth, while others staggered about, grasping desperately for dollars to meet their oil bills, became widespread.

The fear was not that financing would fall short of the demand, for even in the early days of high oil prices policy makers recognized that the OPEC countries would have little choice but to return the bulk of their surplus funds to the consuming countries. There was no alternative to Western financial markets for investments as large as those the OPEC "surplus countries" would make. Rather, concern centered on channeling these OPEC funds to countries that needed them, for the OPEC countries were likely to place the bulk of their surplus funds where they would be safest—in the largest multinational banks, in the consuming countries with the strongest economies and the most prominent international financial organizations. But that meant that the countries with the greatest need for these funds, to cover their balance-of-payments deficits, would have access to them only through the mediation of the commercial banks and international lending agencies, which were being asked to lend funds of unprecedented magnitude to the deficit countries. How were these deficit countries, already plagued by serious financial problems, to maintain their creditworthiness in the face of new burdens? Would they not be crushed by the choice that confronted them: greater indebtedness at high interest rates, on one hand, or a lack of requisite energy supplies on the other?

This was only one of many dangers in "recycling" petrodollars from the exporting to the consuming countries. To maintain their creditworthiness, the consuming countries would have to make difficult adjustments: restraining aggregate demand, even as unemployment grew, and reducing oil imports. For many of the financially weak countries, that would mean serious recession, with political crises likely to follow. Rather than accept such policies, countries might default on loans, which could lead to an international financial crisis.

On the other hand, if easy money was available, countries could delay adjusting to the transformed energy situation, allowing their oil imports to continue to rise and putting further upward pressure on the world oil price level. Investment banker Felix G. Rohatyn gave voice to this concern when he said that "recycling means lending larger and larger sums to people who are less and less creditworthy, for the purpose of keeping up the fiction that nothing has changed."[5] Since private banks and international organizations would be dictating terms to sovereign governments, the potential for political conflict was great. As Federal Reserve banker Paul A. Volcker stated, the process threatened to "leave in its wake a trail of failing institutions, disturbed markets and political crises."[6]

The OPEC countries, at least initially, complicated the problems of the lending institutions because they placed their funds in short-term assets, enabling them to withdraw them on little notice. But the lending institutions would be asked to make long-term loans to the consuming countries, which left them with the problem of matching short-term funds with demands for long-term loans. Bad enough in itself, many feared that this problem would be aggravated as the OPEC countries began to shift their funds around to advance their political interests, upsetting international financial markets by making huge withdrawals on short notice.

Still, if oil prices could be stabilized, these problems of aggregate demand and the financing of trade deficits would decline over time. As the OPEC countries developed, their imports would increase, boosting aggregate demand in the consuming countries and reducing the OPEC surpluses. However, as these problems lessened, the transfer of real resources to the OPEC countries would increase, for so long as the OPEC countries were willing to run balance-of-payments surpluses, transferring oil for dollars, the consuming countries could defer the real transfer of wealth to the OPEC countries. But as OPEC surpluses declined, at a fixed oil price the consuming countries would have to transfer more goods and services to the oil exporters to secure the same quantity of oil.

To secure adequate supplies and help pay for their oil imports, the consuming countries were negotiating bilateral deals with the OPEC countries. France concluded a government-to-government deal with Saudi Arabia in December 1973 for 27 million tons of oil over three years at 93 percent of the posted price. (France had approached the Saudi government after trying for more than a year to get Aramco to guarantee regularly increasing long-term supplies.) By the end of January, France had also concluded provisional negotiations to buy 800 million tons of Saudi oil over a twenty-year period—enough to cover a quarter of France's consumption. In February, France's state-owned company, Elf-Erap, signed a long-term agreement to purchase oil from Libya at $16 a barrel (which Finance Minister Giscard d'Estaing later forbade the company to pay). France was also negotiating with Iran and Libya.[7]

In the latter part of 1973, Japan had proposed a series of bilateral economic and technical projects to the Middle East states, and in January 1974 Japan agreed to lend Iraq a billion dollars and to carry out refining, petrochemical, and other industrial projects in exchange for 160 million tons of crude oil and petroleum products over ten years. Japan made a similar proposal to Iran. Britain concluded a bilateral deal with Iran, exchanging industrial goods for 5 million tons of oil, and was negotiating with Saudi Arabia and several other oil-exporting countries. West Germany agreed to build a petrochemical complex in Iran in exchange for oil supplies and natural gas, and was discussing two major deals in exchange for Iranian oil and gas. Italy agreed to provide Libya economic and technical aid and equipment in exchange for 7 million tons of oil per year. Belgium, Spain, Greece, and Austria were reported to be anxious to secure supplies through direct deals with the oil-exporting countries, and the Nordic countries set up a joint commission to explore the possibilities for government-to-government deals.[8]

The problem with these bilateral agreements was that, while they were usually intended to secure supplies, they did not necessarily do this, since the exporting countries might renege on their agreements, particularly in the event of political conflict. Yet with consuming countries clamoring for supplies, prices were likely to be bid up, or at least stabilized at their already high levels. Insofar as particular consuming countries tied up supplies, they made it more difficult for the other consuming countries to secure supplies. Similarly, by assuring export markets for one's goods or establishing special relationships with exporting countries, particular consuming countries made it more difficult for other consuming countries to increase their exports to the OPEC countries. Consequently, if these bilateral agreements became widespread, they would trigger enormous conflict among the consuming countries, scrambling for scarce supplies and for export markets. Moreover, the agreements threatened to disrupt the multilateral trade pattern that had prevailed since World War II, potentially dividing the world into trade blocs.

Despite their substantial drawbacks, the bilateral deals gained impetus from the fact that, in the absence of a general agreement among consuming countries, each consuming country feared that if it hesitated to act, its neighbor would make a deal first, locking up supplies. In addition, the more oil that was transferred directly between consuming and producing governments, the more the oil companies would be bypassed. As a result, the international oil companies saw the bilateral deals as a direct threat to their position in the world oil industry.

THE CONSUMING-COUNTRIES' RESPONSE

The stance that the consuming countries took toward one another would deeply affect the effectiveness of their response to OPEC and the constellation of international power in the years ahead, for the benefits of any country taking unilateral actions to restrict oil imports would be much less than the benefits of concerted action. And if each country adopted an independent approach and advanced its own interests, the outcome was likely to be a profusion of bilateral deals, skyrocketing prices, and atomization. Alternatively, trading blocs might form as particular consuming countries developed alliances with particular OPEC countries. For example, a European bloc might exploit the ''French connection'' by strengthening ties with Algeria and Iran, or a trend toward regionalization might develop, with the United States joining Canada and Mexico in a North American energy market, Japan linking up with China and Southeast Asia, and Western Europe forming a bloc with North Africa and the Middle East. Another possibility would be for the consuming countries to line up *against* OPEC, taking either a confrontational or a conciliatory approach. Further complicating these possibilities were the non-OPEC, less developed countries (LDCs). They would be courted by the consuming countries, which would stress their common interest in lower oil prices, and by the OPEC countries, which would emphasize Third World solidarity and their common interest in higher commodity prices.

As in the pre-embargo period, the United States again took the leadership, urging a collective, multilateral consumer-country response to OPEC. The United States discouraged other consuming countries from concluding bilateral agreements with the oil-exporting countries and sought to unite the consuming countries in a group and thereby bring down the world oil price. On December 12, 1973—the evening of a Common Market summit meeting in Copenhagen—Secretary of State Henry Kissinger called for the nations of Western Europe to join the United States in an Energy Action Group that would collaborate on conserving energy, developing new sources of oil, giving oil-producing countries incentives to increase supply, and common research efforts. He said that while the United States could solve the energy problem alone, albeit ''with great difficulty,'' it was a problem ''Europe can't solve in isolation at all.''[9] Later, Kissinger warned that unless immediate steps were taken to overcome the crisis, the world would be threatened ''with a vicious cycle of competition, autarchy, rivalry and depression such as led to the collapse of the world order in the thirties.''[10]

Fearing repetition of the competitive devaluations of the 1930s, the finance ministers of the International Monetary Fund's Committee of Twenty met in Rome in January 1974 and pledged to avoid policies that would only shift payment problems among members of the group and be detrimental to world trade and economic activity. They noted the importance of avoiding competitive currency depreciations and escalating restrictions on trade and payments. Ten days after the meeting, the United States, which was expected to receive a disproportionate share of the OPEC funds, agreed to abolish controls over capital outflows. This made it easier for countries that failed to attract adequate OPEC funds to counter their balance-of-payments deficits by borrowing from the United States.

However, the countries of Western Europe and Japan were reluctant to follow the U.S. lead. They did not want to antagonize the OPEC countries, which had proclaimed their opposition to a ''countercartel.'' Nor did they want to be associated with U.S. support for Israel. In addition, the October War tended to divide the consuming countries. Of all its allies, only Portugal had allowed the United States to use its air bases to resupply Israel, which had infuriated Kissinger, who was also displeased by the November 1973 Copenhagen resolution, endorsing Palestinian rights, and by Japan's later statement along the same lines. For their part, the Europeans were angered by the failure of the United States to consult them on the decision to resupply Israel and the October military alert. Similarly, the embargo and the Arabs' categories "friendly," "unfriendly," etc., tended to divide the consuming countries.

The other consuming countries also questioned U.S. motives. They feared that by emphasizing development of consuming-country resources, the United States was attempting to get them to help underwrite the cost of developing the extensive but high-price shale and coal resources in the United States. Besides, a cooperative approach that emphasized the sharing of supplies in crises would reduce the risks to the United States as the primary target of a future Arab embargo.

While other consuming countries might improve their position through bilateral deals, the United States, by opposing such deals, was seen as protecting the predominant position of its nationals in the world oil industry. Many consuming countries feared that while the United States asked them to refrain from concluding bilateral deals, it would not do so itself, and this suspicion increased when the United States made overtures to Saudi Arabia in December 1973. Indeed, of all the consuming countries, the United States had the best prospects of concluding bilateral deals, and both Iran and Saudi Arabia had proposed such relationships to the United States in recent years. Other consuming countries feared that emphasis on a cooperative approach was also a means whereby the United States could reassert its leadership over the non-Communist world.

In addition, the consuming countries had different interests with respect to world oil prices. Those without significant domestic energy resources, like Italy, France, and Japan, clearly had an interest in lower prices; but with North Sea oil putting them on the verge of becoming oil exporters, Norway and Great Britain had an interest in higher prices. Indeed, North Sea oil would not have been profitable had world oil prices not risen substantially. The interests of other consuming countries, on the other hand, were less clear. As net importers of oil, Canada, West Germany, and the United States had an interest in lower prices, but the fact that they had extensive domestic energy resources made them more ambivalent about high oil prices than the resource-poor countries. Italy, France, West Germany, and Japan were heavy oil importers, but West Germany and Japan, because of their strong balance-of-payments position, would have a much easier time paying high prices than Italy or France.

While the United States was the country most vulnerable to a selective embargo, most consuming countries feared the consequences of another loss of Middle East oil supplies. But because of North Sea oil, Great Britain and Norway were much less vulnerable,[11] as were Canada and the Netherlands, because of their high levels of energy self-sufficiency. Not surprisingly, France took the lead in opposing the U.S. call for a united bloc of consuming countries, advocating establishment of a special relationship between Europe and the Arab world. The

French urged the consuming countries to bypass the multinational oil companies and conclude deals directly with the exporting countries. Even before Kissinger's call for a meeting of the consuming countries, France had urged a European-Arab "dialogue."

France's opposition to the U.S. position was based in part on a different view of the world oil situation. While the United States believed that prices could be brought down, France accepted the irreversibility of what had happened and sought to secure guaranteed supplies at existing prices, rather than at the higher prices that would prevail later. France also sought to use the oil crisis to regain a foreign crude base through special relations with the oil-exporting countries, to strengthen its relations with the Third World, and to establish itself as the key intermediary between the commodity-producing countries and the developed world. And with his government under attack from the left, French President Pompidou hoped to use his anti-U.S. stance to bolster his domestic popularity. Finally, France feared that the United States would use the policy of cooperation on energy to extract concessions from Europe on such other Atlantic issues as defense, trade, and finance.

Initially, Kissinger's proposal for a meeting of consuming countries received a lukewarm response in Western Europe. In contrast, France's proposal for a Euro-Arab dialogue was endorsed at the December 1973 summit of the EEC heads of government. In response to this move, the United States threatened to withdraw its troops from Western Europe;[12] but despite this threat, in early January the EEC agreed to convene the Euro-Arab dialogue before the end of 1974. Later in January, President Nixon invited the EEC countries and Norway, Japan, and Canada to a Washington energy conference to be convened February 11. After Kissinger's December call for such a meeting, Iran had expressed interest in attending, but the United States insisted that before they consulted the exporting countries, the consuming countries had to establish solidarity among themselves, for before they had done so, they could hardly present a counterweight to OPEC. Moreover, when such a dialogue did get under way, Kissinger insisted that "the main subject must inevitably be price."[13] The U.S. plan was for the leading consuming countries to meet first, then with the other consuming countries, and only after they had agreed upon a common strategy would they meet with the exporting countries. Saudi Arabia and Algeria responded to Nixon's call for an energy conference by warning the consuming countries not to "gang up" on the exporting countries, and as an alternative to the U.S. plan, France proposed a meeting of consuming, exporting, and Third World countries under U.N. auspices; not limited to oil, it would discuss the whole range of issues involving the developed and underdeveloped countries.

A week before the Washington Energy Conference, the foreign ministers of EEC adopted a joint position for presentation at the conference. It was very close to the French line, holding that the Washington conference was not to be used as a confrontation against the exporting countries, that no new organization was to be created as a result of the conference, that Europe must retain its freedom to establish direct relationships with the exporting countries, and that a dialogue with the exporting countries and non-OPEC less developed countries be entered into by April.[14] At the conference, however, a split emerged between France and the other eight EEC countries. West Germany assumed a leading role and "the Eight" were persuaded to adopt a "comprehensive action program" along the lines advocated by the United States. This shift was due partly to awareness by the EEC countries of the need for consumer-country cooperation that extended beyond Western Europe[15] and partly to concessions by the United States. The United States urged the consuming countries to adopt an emergency sharing plan and indicated, for the first time, that it would be willing to include its domestic oil in such a plan. Also, the United States agreed to drop not only its proposed "code of conduct" but all references to direct deals between consuming and exporting countries from the final communique.

Probably the most significant factor in the shift was the pressure exerted by the United States. U.S. spokesmen warned that if an agreement were not reached, neither access to U.S. markets nor the U.S. security commitment to Western Europe could be taken for granted. Indeed, President Nixon told the conference that "security and economic considerations are inevitably linked and energy cannot be separated from either,"[16] and Kissinger told German Foreign Minister Walter Scheel that Washington would reconsider the presence of U.S. troops in Germany unless the Europeans rejected the French position and supported establishment of the Energy Action Group.[17] As a result (with only France dissenting), the conference agreed to

I. Joint action in 1) conserving energy 2) allocating oil supplies in times of emergency 3) accelerating research efforts and 4) developing alternative energy supplies
II. Financial and monetary measures to avoid competitive depreciation and to establish long-term machinery to strengthen credit facilities
III. Establishment of a coordinating group to implement the agreement
IV. Plans for conferences of consumers and producers "at the earliest possible opportunity"

The conference also called for a moratorium on trade restrictions.[18]

France continued to oppose any joint action by consuming countries that the exporting countries might construe as aggressive. It was influenced by the fact that Kuwait and Saudi Arabia had indicated that in return for agreement on specific bilateral deals, they expected France to cooperate in blocking establishment of an oil consumers' group.[19] In refusing to go along with its EEC partners at the conference, France's actions led to a low point in post–World War II efforts toward European unity, for the Washington Energy Conference and the Energy Coordinating Group that it established led directly to creation of the sixteen-nation International Energy Agency in November 1974 (membership has since increased to twenty-one). France was not part of the ECG, and refused to join the IEA. It did not want to give the impression that the consuming countries were forming a countercartel, and it wanted to preserve its freedom in dealing with the oil-exporting countries. France made no attempt within the OECD or the

EEC to prevent formation of the IEA;[20] nonetheless, its refusal to join IEA clouded the prospects for consumer-country unity. In an effort to gain French cooperation, the new organization was officially made part of the OECD, to which France belonged, and was based in Paris; but OPEC countries continued to view both the ECG and the IEA as a U.S.-dominated countercartel.[21]

The United States saw the Washington Energy Conference as a clear triumph for its broad-based consumer unity strategy and one that would put France's Euro-Arab strategy to rest. But two and a half weeks after the conference, the EEC Council of Ministers adopted a plan for long-term economic, technical, and cultural cooperation between the EEC and a group of twenty Arab states. This indicated that while the European countries were prepared to cooperate with the United States and pursue the multilateral approach, they were not willing to submit to U.S. domination or to abandon the bilateral approach. They would pursue both options, hoping to derive benefits from each. By straddling, they hoped to avoid an open break with the United States, which the West Germans and British would have found intolerable, and retain the possibility of a common European energy policy, for which they needed the French.[22]

Kissinger was outraged by the European initiative, and much of U.S. diplomacy in 1974 was devoted to thwarting the Euro-Arab dialogue. In March, Britain vetoed a proposal for EEC negotiations with the Arabs, a decision undoubtedly influenced by the fact that, that same month, the United States lent Britain $2.5 billion from its Eurodollar reserves.[23]

In the end, the Euro-Arab dialogue yielded little. Plans for convening the meeting were delayed by Arab demands that the PLO be represented and then by Arab objections to an EEC trade agreement with Israel. A preliminary meeting was held in June 1975, but it consisted mainly of political posturing. Then, in May 1976, an inaugural meeting of the Euro-Arab dialogue took place, but so far little has been achieved.[24]

In contrast to the Europeans, the Japanese were much more inclined to follow U.S. leadership. At the close of 1973 the fear of oil shortages had led the Japanese to defy U.S. wishes, making a conciliatory statement on the Palestinian question and pursuing a series of bilateral deals in the Middle East. But once the fear of shortages eased, the Japanese aligned themselves with the United States, readily attending the Washington Energy Conference and joining the Energy Coordinating Group. They also quickly lost interest in bilateral deals.

In adopting this policy, the Japanese recognized that their export economy was dependent upon maintenance of an open, multilateral system of world trade and finance and that the United States was the key to this. In addition, Japan was dependent upon the United States to protect its oil supply line from the Persian Gulf. The Japanese also feared the consequences of a no-holds-barred competition for oil supplies with the United States. Still, they did not want to be too close to the United States for fear of being associated with U.S. policy toward Israel, nor did they want to abandon their freedom to deal independently with the exporting countries.[25]

By the spring of 1974, interest in bilateral deals had waned, due more to a change in market forces than to U.S. opposition to such deals. With oil supplies readily available and prices stabilizing, fear of shortages and skyrocketing prices had subsided, and consuming countries were afraid of locking themselves into long-term deals that might prove disadvantageous. In fact, most of the oil supplied through bilateral deals turned out to be more costly than oil supplied by the multinational companies.[26]

In March, President Pompidou announced that France would not sign any agreements stipulating higher prices than those charged by the international oil companies, yet there still was interest in bilateral deals as a way of assuring markets for exports and reducing balance-of-payments deficits. In June, France signed an elaborate ten-year agreement with Iran for some $4 billion worth of contracts and industrial plants, including five nuclear reactors, development of natural gas, electrification of railroads, subway construction, petrochemicals, and the training of scientists and technicians. However, oil was not directly involved. By the end of 1974, France had increased the value of the deal to $7 billion and had concluded similar deals with Iraq ($3 billion), Algeria ($3 billion), and Saudi Arabia ($800 million). By December, however, France was unhappy with the three-year pact it had signed with Saudi Arabia in January and was attempting to reduce a second oil agreement with the Saudis from twenty years to ten years and from 800 million tons to 200 million.[27]

In June, the United States concluded a cooperative agreement with Saudi Arabia that called for establishment of two U.S.-Saudi commissions to oversee economic and military programs in Saudi Arabia. It included a U.S. commitment to reequip and train the Saudi national guard, the group responsible for the security of the royal family and the Saudi oil fields. It also provided for expansion of Aramco's export capacity by about 2 mb/d, to 11.2 mb/d by the end of 1975. The State Department insisted that this was not the kind of bilateral deal the United States had objected to other consuming countries' making, because it did not give the United States a preferred position regarding access to Saudi oil supplies and because an increase in Saudi production would be in the interest of all consuming countries. However, the other consuming countries believed that secret agreements regarding access to oil were involved and that the United States was trying to outflank the Europeans and the Japanese. The United States also concluded a five-year, $15 billion trade pact with Iran in March 1975, and in mid-1976 was investigating the possibility of an arms-for-oil barter with Iran.[28]

In the summer of 1974 Iran and Italy concluded a $3 billion deal, and in November Saudi Arabia agreed to provide West Germany's Veba with 12 million tons of oil over three years in exchange for Veba's participation in Saudi Arabia's petrochemical industry. Nonetheless, by 1975 the danger of a widespread trend toward bilateralism had vanished. In fact, in June 1976, when Iran proposed to barter crude oil for goods and services, the French discouraged them.[29]

In 1974 the consuming countries also found themselves divided over methods of financing their oil deficits. Traditionally, the IMF was the major source of balance-of-payments financing, but its funds were not enough to meet the needs of countries with increased deficits due to the rise in oil prices. Western Europe and Japan therefore argued that the IMF's funds be increased, so that it and its sister organization, the World Bank, could play a large role in petrodollar recycling. But the United States argued that the private-capital markets could manage the recycling of OPEC petrodollars and that creation of a special oil facility that would provide OPEC with a ready outlet for its surplus dollars and ease countries' balance-of-payments problems would make it easier for OPEC to continue its high-price policy. The United States also feared that, as the largest guarantor of IMF transactions, it would have the greatest burden in the event that any nation defaulted on a loan from the oil facility.[30]

By June a compromise was reached. The consuming countries established an IMF "oil facility" that would borrow funds directly from the oil exporters and lend them to oil importers suffering balance-of-payments problems. However, with the 1974 OPEC surplus estimated at $65 billion, the fund would have a capitalization of only $3.4 billion, thus assuring that it would play only a limited role in recycling. During the first year of its existence, 87 percent of the facility's funds came from the OPEC countries and 57 percent of its loans went to the developed countries.[31] In addition, the World Bank borrowed $565 million from the OPEC countries in fiscal 1974, and almost $2 billion in fiscal 1975, and re-lent it to the non-OPEC LDCs.[32] And in 1974 the U.N. created an emergency fund to aid those LDCs that were worst hit by the oil-price rise.

Despite these efforts, in the summer of 1974 a crisis arose in Italy. Even before the oil-price increases, Italy had been plagued by inflation and serious balance-of-payments deficits. Then, during the first half of 1974, Italy ran a balance-of-payments deficit of $1 billion per month. If these deficits continued, the Italian government would be unable to finance them and Italy would be forced to default on its loan repayments, a development which would reverberate throughout the international monetary system. With the Italian Communist Party growing in strength, Italy's financial problems also threatened to bring about the collapse of the Christian Democratic government.

Italy was rescued by its own central bank, its European trading partners, and the efforts of international bankers. With the Italian cabinet paralyzed, the Italian central bank took the lead in imposing special restrictions on imports, tight monetary and fiscal policies, and vigorous export efforts aimed at fostering Italian recovery. These measures held Italy's balance-of-payments deficit at $7.5 billion in 1974, and Italy financed this debt by a special $2 billion loan from West Germany, another $1.88 billion in special financial assistance from the EEC, $1 billion from the IMF special oil facility, and $3 billion from private markets. As a result, a financial crisis that might have marked the end of the Italian government was avoided, and by 1975 its austerity measures had nearly eliminated the deficit.[33]

The Italian crisis demonstrated that West Germany was prepared to use its monetary reserves to hold Europe together by coming to the aid of the weaker European nations. Indeed, with German prosperity heavily based on exports, the country could hardly afford to see its trading partners collapse, and with the Italian Communist Party growing in strength, the Germans were particularly anxious to restore Italian financial stability.

After the Italian crisis, the major consuming countries agreed that the various central banks would serve as lenders of last resort for commercial banks that ran into difficulty and that each central bank would take responsibility for both its domestic banks and the foreign branches of those banks. However, while the central banks agreed to take more responsibility for mishaps, they did not increase their control over the day-to-day operations of the international financial markets.[34] Like Italy, Great Britain and France faced serious balance-of-payments problems in 1974; however, their financial crises were considerably reduced when Iran lent each of them over $1 billion.[35]

While the consuming countries argued about how to respond to the 1973–74 oil-price increases, the OPEC countries debated whether prices should be reduced or raised further. After the large price hike had been instituted, in January 1974 the OPEC countries convened in Geneva and agreed to freeze prices for three months. Later that month, Saudi Arabia publicly called for a price reduction. However, when the OPEC countries met again in March, the OPEC Economic Commission recommended an increase of $1 to $2.50 in the posted price, stating that the market would support a price rise of this magnitude. Algeria, Indonesia, Nigeria, and Iran argued that the posted price should be raised from $11.65 to $14, with Iran maintaining that the price of oil should keep pace with worldwide inflation. In opposition to this view, the Saudis held that the price should be reduced by at least $2. As a compromise, the conferees agreed to freeze prices for another three months.[36]

But in June the dispute reemerged. To compensate for worldwide inflation and to curb the excess profits that the companies were realizing on the sale of equity oil, the OPEC Economic Commission recommended raising the companies' tax-paid cost by over $3 a barrel. The Commission also recommended that, in view of the slack that had developed in the world oil market, OPEC should consider instituting a system of production prorationing. While most OPEC members were inclined to go along with the Commission's recommendations, Saudi Arabia called for a $2.65 reduction in the posted price. The Saudis indicated that they would refuse to go along with any restrictions on production until the price was brought down to a level they considered acceptable. In response, Algeria, Venezuela, Libya, and Iraq threatened to cut their production by amounts equal to any increases by the Saudis.[37]

The conference compromised. Another three-month freeze was maintained on the posted price, but all the exporting countries, with the exception of Saudi Arabia, raised their royalty rate from 12.5 percent to 14.5 percent. The effect was to raise the price of equity oil by about 11¢ a barrel, raising the companies' average tax-paid cost by 5 to 6¢ a barrel. The other significant development at the conference was the agreement of all the members, except Saudi Arabia, to freeze their production levels until the next conference, in September.[38]

While the Saudis succeeded in keeping the price of equity oil frozen during the first six months of 1974, this did not keep the companies' and, ultimately, the consumers' cost from rising during this period. The price of equity oil remained fixed, but the percentage of oil that was classified "equity crude" declined. Correspondingly, the percentage of the more costly "participation crude" increased as a result of changes in the participation agreements during the period. As we have seen, following the Kuwait Agreement in January 1974 the new norm in the Middle East became 60 percent rather than 25 percent participation. Moreover, regardless of when they were concluded, most 60 percent participation agreements were backdated to January 1, 1974. The effect of this was to raise the average price that officially applied on January 1 from $8.04 to $9.34, or about 16 percent.[39]

In an effort to reduce the price, in July 1974 U.S. Treasury Secretary William Simon got Prince Khaled, the heir apparent in Saudi Arabia, to promise that by September the Saudis would hold an auction to determine the true market price of oil. The amount to be auctioned was not stipulated, but discussion ranged from 500,000 b/d to 2 mb/d. With the market weakening, there was every expectation that an offering in this range would break the OPEC price.

As a result, the Saudis came under enormous pressure from the other OPEC members. These countries maintained that if, in an attempt to bring down prices, Saudi Arabia increased its production, then they would reduce their production in order to maintain prices. The *Petroleum Economist* reported that "there is reason to believe that the 'hawks,' notably Iran, Kuwait and Algeria, have actually agreed on a level of production cutbacks in such an eventuality."[40] Also, following Simon's visit, the Saudis failed to receive much encouragement from the United States for holding the auction. In August, consequently, Saudi Arabia canceled its plans to hold the auction.[41]

During the first half of 1974 the U.S. government relied on the combination of market forces and Saudi pressure to bring oil prices down. U.S. officials believed that as surpluses mounted, OPEC would have to lower prices.[42] In addition, U.S. policy makers did not want to upset the Middle East negotiations by directly pressuring the Arab oil-exporting countries. As we have seen, in this period the United States also advocated reliance upon the existing international financial institutions and private banks to recycle OPEC's surplus funds.

However, by September 1974 there was a distinct shift in U.S. policy. The United States decided to take a much tougher line with OPEC and became much more concerned about the adequacy of existing institutions to handle the OPEC surpluses. This shift was due to recognition that despite Saudi efforts and the growing pressure of market forces, oil prices had not come down but had risen, as countries cut production rather than prices. Moreover, the prospects for bringing prices down dimmed with cancellation of the Saudi auction, and the Italian financial crisis led to growing concern about the risks of default.

Addressing the United Nations on September 18, President Ford stated that "exorbitant prices can only distort the world economy, run the risk of a worldwide depression and threaten the breakdown of world order and safety." The president warned that "throughout history nations have gone to war over natural advantages such as water or food." Ford also raised the possibility that the United States would link its exports of food to the price of oil.[43] During the next six months, articles advocating use of military force to bring down the world oil price appeared in popular magazines, and *Business Week* reported that private bankers in Western Europe believed there was no alternative to military action in the Middle East, but that they wanted the United States to take this action.[44]

Despite this bravado, the risks of resorting to military force were as great as ever. It risked a Soviet response. It would decrease prospects for an Arab-Israeli settlement and unleash radical forces in the Middle East. It threatened relations with the Third World. It might well be opposed by countries in Western Europe, particularly France, and there was a high probability that, in response to such a move, the oil-exporting countries would blow up their oil fields. Nor were U.S. soldiers well trained in desert warfare, and their ability to sustain an operation in the Middle East was questionable in view of the Vietnam debacle and the transition to an all-volunteer army.[45]

Given these limitations and the risks involved, it was unlikely that any rational leader would resort to force in a dispute over price. Military action was credible only when issues of supply (as well as price) were involved. In his much heralded *Business Week* interview, Secretary of State Kissinger acknowledged as much, stating: "I am not saying that there's no circumstance where we would use force. But it is one thing to use it in the case of a dispute over price, it's another when there's some actual strangulation of the industrialized world."[46]

As for Ford's suggestion that the United States might curtail the export of food to pressure the OPEC countries, the reality was that the food needs of the OPEC countries were quite modest in relation to world supplies and could be satisfied from a wide range of sources. On the other hand, the United States needed to export food to help pay its oil-import bill. Consequently, it was not surprising that after the tough speeches by Ford and Kissinger, when asked what plans the United States had for getting the price down, FEA chief John Sawhill replied that there were none.[47] Similarly, Treasury Secretary Simon conceded at a press conference that the only United States leverage on oil prices was to conserve energy and develop alternative sources.[48]

In November, Kissinger proposed a bold plan for consuming-country cooperation on energy. Basically, there were two parts to the plan. One part was designed to reduce the consuming countries' sense of vulnerability by offering them protection against the twin dangers of financial collapse and a loss of oil supplies. The emergency sharing plan that the Energy Coordinating Group had worked out was designed to reduce the danger of a loss of supplies, but in addition, in a sharp reversal of U.S. policy, the secretary called for creation of an international facility to recycle petrodollars. The fund was to have an initial capitalization of $25 billion, rising to $50 billion in 1976. Kissinger also said that the IMF should establish a special fund to lend to the non-OPEC LDCs at low rates. The fund would be financed by IMF gold sales and funds from the industrialized and oil-exporting countries. Kissinger believed that by increasing the consuming countries' sense of security, these measures would make them less inclined to negotiate on the producers' terms.

The other part of the Kissinger plan was designed to alter the fundamentals of energy supply and demand by reducing consumption through conservation measures and increasing production of non-OPEC energy resources. With the industrialized countries relying on imported oil for roughly a third of their energy supplies, the secretary called on them to reduce it to 20 percent. He asked for conservation measures that would achieve a 10 percent reduction in oil imports by the end of 1975, and said that over the next decade the United States would reduce its imports from 7mb/d to 1mb/d. Kissinger also recommended ''a full-scale program of research and development of alternative energy sources on a scale dwarfing the atomic bomb project.''[49]

Kissinger later indicated that, as a result of these measures, the United States believed a situation could be created in two or three years ''in which it will be increasingly difficult for the cartel to operate.''[50] Finally, Kissinger indicated that once the consuming countries had taken steps to deal with their energy problems, the United States would be ready to participate in a meeting between the consuming and the exporting countries. But he warned that it would be futile to meet with the OPEC countries before the conditions for a price cutback had been created.[51]

Despite Kissinger's warnings, a month later at his meeting in Martinique with French President Giscard d'Estaing, President Ford modified the U.S. policy slightly. With the EEC countries consulting one another before taking positions in the IEA, the United States was concerned about the possibility that France would block formulation of IEA policies through its power over EEC decisions. To resolve this problem, President Ford agreed that the United States would attend a preparatory meeting of producing, consuming, and non-OPEC LDCs (proposed by France) in exchange for an agreement by President Giscard to refrain from blocking IEA actions, to maintain liaison with the IEA, and to cooperate with the IEA on research and development. Giscard also agreed that the consuming countries should attempt to coordinate their positions before meeting with the exporting countries.

This compromise between the United States and France reduced the conflicts that had divided them for most of the year and it paved the way for greater consuming-country cooperation. Though France never joined IEA, it cooperated with that organization through its membership in EEC and OECD. The agreement between Giscard and Ford also led to the Paris Preparatory Conference in

April 1975, a meeting of four oil-exporting countries (Saudi Arabia, Iran, Algeria, and Venezuela), three oil importers (the U.S., Japan, and the EEC), and three non-OPEC LDCs (India, Brazil, and Zaire) that was to plan the agenda for a world energy conference.

THE NORTH/SOUTH TALKS

Since the 1973–74 oil price rise, the OPEC countries and the non-OPEC LDCs have had an ambivalent relationship. The non-OPEC LDCs are probably the countries most badly hurt by the rise in oil prices, but as commodity producers they support what OPEC has achieved: sovereignty over natural resources, the right to unilaterally determine the price of the commodities they export, a shift in the terms of trade between the industrialized and the exporting countries and, with this, a transfer of power from the industrialized world to a portion of the nonindustrialized world. The OPEC example has had a powerful psychological impact on the non-OPEC LDCs, despite the fact that differences in their situations have made it impossible for other commodity producers to duplicate the OPEC success.[52] In addition, these countries have looked to the OPEC countries to provide them with financial and political support.

For their part, the OPEC countries as a group have sought good relations with the non-OPEC LDCs, primarily because of the legitimacy it gives them. Aligning themselves with other commodity producers has helped them resist demands from the industrialized countries for a decline in oil prices and enabled them to deflect these demands onto the more general issues of the relationship between the industrialized countries and the Third World. Nor have they had to sacrifice much to do this. In addition, both Algeria and Venezuela have sought to play a leading role among the Third World countries and have used the preeminence and revenues derived from their control of oil to advance this objective; and the Arab oil-exporting countries have seen good relations with the other Middle East countries as essential to their stability.

One consequence has been the role of OPEC nations in the North/South dialogue. Even before the 1973–74 oil-price rise, Algeria played a leading role in the movement of Third World countries for a new international economic order. In September 1973, at the Algiers summit meeting of nonaligned nations, the goals of this movement crystallized around demands for higher prices for raw materials and greater access for Third World commodity producers to the markets of the developed countries. In fact, the dramatic rise in oil prices, which began only a month later, can be seen as the first (and only) victory of this movement.

Then, early in 1974, Algeria endorsed the French proposal for an energy conference consisting of consuming, exporting, and non-OPEC less developed countries, but said that the conference should deal with *all* raw materials. Since many OPEC countries were not anxious to enter into dialogue with the consuming countries about oil prices, the call for a conference to discuss all raw materials seemed an effective way of avoiding a head-on issue. In April 1974 the principles for a "New International Economic Order" were set out at a U.N. Special Session on Raw Materials. Moreover, the non-OPEC LDCs saw the power of the OPEC countries as a vehicle for realization of these principles. In February 1975 the nonaligned nations endorsed the idea of using OPEC revenues to finance buffer stocks of other primary commodities.

When the Paris Preparatory Conference convened in April 1975, Algeria took the lead in insisting that the proposed world energy conference be broadened to include other issues of concern to the Third World, such as nonenergy raw materials and commodity prices, aid, technology transfer, and international monetary reform. Algeria's position won the support of the other OPEC and non-OPEC countries attending the preparatory conference; however, the conference broke up, without reaching any agreement, when the industrialized countries backed the United States in insisting that the conference be limited to energy. The apparent unity of the OPEC and non-OPEC countries concealed a basic difference. While Algeria, only a modest oil exporter, and the non-OPEC LDCs were willing to link the price of oil to other raw materials in an overall settlement of North/South issues, Saudi Arabia, Iran, and Venezuela were not willing to make this direct linkage.[53]

Following the failure of the preparatory conference, the United States adopted a more conciliatory tone toward the Third World, for several reasons. With Europe trying to build its links to the Third World through the Lomé Convention,[54] several European countries warned the United States that its stance vis-à-vis the Third World was too obstructionist. Nor had the United States' hard line weakened OPEC. Consequently, the United States became interested in drawing OPEC into a dialogue on oil supplies and prices, and saw the North/South dialogue as a means of doing this. In addition, the United States hoped to use the North/South dialogue to divide the oil-exporting countries from the non-OPEC LDCs and to get the OPEC countries to provide the non-OPEC LDCs with greater financial aid.[55]

The first indication of the shift in the U.S. position came in May 1975, when Kissinger announced that he was ready to broaden the dialogue between producers and consumers "to include the general issue of the relationship between developing and developed countries" and to discuss "all issues of concern to developing countries."[56] The secretary proposed that three separate commissions be set up — on energy, nonenergy raw materials, and economic development aid. After this proved unsatisfactory to the OPEC countries, on September 1, in a major U.N. address, Kissinger indicated that the United States was ready to participate in a full-fledged North/South dialogue. The secretary also put forth a series of proposals aimed at propping up Third World economies; these included financial aid, tariff commissions, technical assistance funds, commodity agreements, a new special $10 billion IMF lending facility to stabilize the export earnings of poor countries, and an international investment trust to be administered by the World Bank. Kissinger called for these schemes to be financed by both the industrialized and the OPEC countries.

With the United States ready to participate, the North/South dialogue got under way. In October, France reconvened another preparatory conference of the same ten nations that had met in April. Then, in December, twenty-seven countries met in Paris for the first plenary session of the Conference on International Economic Cooperation (CIEC), which became an encounter between the nineteen developing countries (which included seven OPEC members) and the eight industrialized nations (there were no Communist countries present). The "Group of 19" wanted a new international economic order that would include a commodity program and a common fund that would be used to stabilize raw materials prices, generalized debt relief, a new approach to development aid and technology transfer, and protection of the purchasing power of the export earnings and financial reserves of the developing countries through indexation and other means. The OPEC countries also hoped that by dealing with other issues of concern to the Third World, the conference would deflect the resentment of the oil-exporting countries that was growing among the non-OPEC LDCs. Nonetheless, at the opening session Kissinger criticized the oil producers for adding to the problems of developing countries and for contributing to unemployment and inflation in the industrialized countries. The meeting adjourned with a decision to set up four commissions: energy, other raw materials, economic development of poor countries, and international finance.

For the next year and a half, CIEC continued its work in committee and plenary sessions, but achieved virtually nothing. The United States opposed all schemes for supporting commodity prices at high levels as a means of transferring wealth to the suppliers, and the industrialized world was generally uninterested in negotiating anything but energy. The oil-consuming countries sought restraint on oil pricing and assurances of steady supplies, but were unwilling to agree to the exporting countries' demand for indexation of the price of oil to the price of the goods the OPEC countries imported. The consuming countries also refused to provide guarantees for the investments OPEC countries made in the industrialized countries, with the United States arguing that this would encourage high oil prices, and proposals for a moratorium on the debts of the Third World countries foundered on the opposition of the industrialized countries and the fear of the richer non-OPEC LDCs that such a measure would cut off their access to international capital markets.

In June 1977 the majority of the participating developing countries voted to disband CIEC and pass the issues it had been discussing to the U.N. Conference on Trade and Development. The industrial countries proposed creation of a new international body where oil exporters and consumers could continue to consult. While Saudi Arabia indicated willingness to go along with this, it was rejected by the developing countries.[57]

The closest CIEC came to a substantive achievement was a tentative agreement to establish a common fund to stabilize the price of primary commodities. However, final agreement on establishment of the fund was delayed until 1979 because of disagreements over its financing and the purposes it could be used for. Even then, the fund was much smaller than the fund the Third World had asked for.

The failure of CIEC was largely due to the industrialized countries' disinterest in talking seriously about anything but energy, and while the industrialized countries might have made concessions on nonenergy issues in exchange for concessions on energy issues, the OPEC countries refused to make such concessions. They refused to discuss energy prices in the CIEC framework on the grounds that determination of oil prices was the sovereign right of OPEC and its member governments. As a result, oil pricing was discussed in CIEC only insofar as it was one of the factors in long-term supply. In addition, the OPEC countries' leverage was reduced by the surplus that characterized the world oil market during the period that CIEC met. Moreover, rather than pressure the exporting countries to use what leverage they had in the CIEC talks, the non-OPEC LDCs tended to settle for promises of aid from the OPEC countries. In the end, the non-OPEC LDCs gained little from the CIEC dialogue, but that was also true of the industrialized countries, which failed to gain concessions on oil pricing or to divide the OPEC countries from the non-OPEC LDCs.

RECYCLING PETRODOLLARS

Kissinger's call for a $25 billion "safety net" fund to meet the oil-related balance-of-payments problems of the consuming countries was in response to the growing recognition that, since oil prices probably would not come down in the near future, there was a need to exert greater official control over petrodollar recycling. With multinational banks making loans of unprecedented magnitude to deficit countries, fear was growing that, rather than repay their loans, the weakest countries might default on them, provoking an international financial crisis.

In contrast to the IMF oil facility, the Kissinger safety-net plan was to be financed primarily by contributions from the United States and West Germany, without any contribution from the OPEC countries. And unlike the IMF oil facility, it would provide financing only for the industrialized countries. It was designed to provide emergency funding to countries that were unable to pay their oil bills and to force borrowers to adjust by taking painful measures to bring their external payments into balance in return for help. Countries that received aid from the fund would also have to eschew restrictive trade measures and cooperate with the consuming countries' overall effort to conserve energy and develop alternative supplies.

The Europeans objected to the safety-net plan because it was likely to be dominated by the United States and West Germany and because it did not provide for adequate participation by the exporting countries. In September 1974

Britain's Chancellor Healey had proposed a plan whereby the oil-exporting countries would provide funds for expansion of the IMF, and in return they would gain a greater share in IMF voting. In November the EEC had set up a $3 billion community loan program, financed with funds to be borrowed from the oil-exporting countries. After intense prodding by the United States, in April 1975 fifteen industrial countries, including France, reached agreement on a $25 billion compromise plan. It was agreed that risks on loans would be shared among all OECD members, according to a formula that gave equal weight to each member's GNP and foreign trade. Decisions would be made by a governing board composed of representatives of member states. Also, it was agreed that the IMF's oil facility would be extended and its capitalization increased to $6 billion. Of this sum, 70 percent came from the OPEC countries.[58]

However, the U.S. Congress refused to approve the safety-net plan. Congressmen objected to it as both unnecessary and costly, and many feared that it would be used simply to bail out banks that had overextended themselves. Since German participation in the plan was contingent upon U.S. participation, the failure of Congress to ratify it killed the scheme.

With the role of official organizations limited, a few private, multinational banks became the primary financial intermediaries between the oil-exporting and -importing countries. In fact, official sources provided only about 20 percent of the total deficit financing between 1974 and 1976. During these years the OPEC countries lent $9.75 billion to international organizations, but placed $49 billion with private commercial banks, mostly in New York and London.[59] Anxious to find secure outlets for their money, Kuwait and Saudi Arabia, the countries with the bulk of the OPEC surplus, deposited most of their funds with the largest and most prestigious multinational banks. These banks then lent this money to nations with balance-of-payments deficits.

It was a role the banks eagerly assumed, for in 1974–75 they faced a liquidity squeeze as a result of losses on their domestic portfolios, particularly on real estate investment trusts (REITs) and tanker leasing operations, and with the oncoming recession, loan demand from their traditional customers (the multinational corporations) slumped. But with OPEC funds pouring in and loan demand from the oil-importing countries rising, both problems were considerably lessened. Moreover, as a result of the involvement of banks in the recycling of petrodollars, governments replaced private corporations as the largest users of the private international capital market.[60]

The needs of the oil-importing countries for balance-of-payments financing varied tremendously. By exporting, West Germany was able to run a surplus on current account, while Japan substantially reduced its deficit. By contracting its economy, the United States was able to maintain a surplus on current account. The United States benefited from its ability to attract a disproportionate share of the OPEC surplus as well. However, the deficits of the other oil-importing countries increased from $3 billion in 1973 to $60 billion in 1974, and roughly $55 billion in both 1975 and 1976.[61] Consequently, many of the poorer industrial countries and the non-OPEC LDCs experienced serious balance-of-payments problems in 1974–75 (see table 9–1).

The balance-of-payments problems of the non-OPEC LDCs were due to the combined effects of higher oil prices and inflation and recession in the advanced countries. Between 1973 and 1974 the oil-import bill of the non-OPEC LDCs increased by $17.3 billion.[62] In addition, inflation in the developed countries increased the cost of LDC imports and recession reduced the demand for their exports, and these problems were intensified by the fact that the developed countries tended to respond to their economic problems by putting additional restrictions on imports from the LDCs. Nor were the non-OPEC LDCs able to earn much by exporting to OPEC. In fact, between 1974 and 1976 the OPEC countries spent over $100 billion on imports from the industrial countries, or 40 percent of what they had earned on exports to these countries, but they spent only $20 billion, or 33 percent of what they had earned, on exports to the non-OPEC LDCs.[63]

Between 1973 and 1974 the combined current account deficit of the non-OPEC LDCs increased by $25 billion.[64] To finance these deficits, these countries were forced to turn to the banks for aid.[65] According to a survey by Morgan Guaranty, between 1971 and 1973 the non-OPEC LDCs increased their borrowings by $45 billion, with the commercial banks supplying 20 percent of the total, but between 1974 and 1976 these nations borrowed an additional $109 billion, with the banks supplying 42 percent of the total.[66] Similarly, Walter Levy found that between 1973 and early 1978 the total foreign debt of the non-OPEC LDCs had increased from $95 billion to $210 billion. While in 1973 $30 billion was owed to the commercial banks, the figure in 1978 was $90 billion.[67]

This borrowing was heavily concentrated among the most creditworthy non-OPEC LDCs. By the end of 1978, eleven countries accounted for three quarters

TABLE 9–1. PAYMENTS BALANCES ON CURRENT ACCOUNT, 1973–81 (BILLIONS OF U.S. DOLLARS)

	1973	1974	1975	1976	1977	1978	1979	1980	1981
Industrial countries	17.7	−13.9	17.8	−2.2	−4.9	30.5	−10.2	−43.7	−3.7
Non-oil developing countries	−11.6	−37.0	−46.5	−32.0	−28.3	−39.2	−58.9	−86.2	−99.0
Oil-exporting countries	6.7	68.3	35.4	40.3	30.8	2.9	69.8	116.4	68.6
U.S.	2.5	1.4	22.3	9.0	−10.0	−11.6	3.1	6.2	9.0
Japan	0.1	−4.5	−0.4	3.9	11.1	18.0	−8.0	−9.5	6.2
W. Germany	6.7	12.3	7.1	7.3	7.9	13.4	0.1	−8.8	−1.0
U.K.	−1.2	−7.8	−3.4	−0.6	1.6	5.1	2.4	11.6	17.7
France	−0.1	−4.8	1.2	−4.9	−1.6	5.2	3.0	−6.3	−6.6
Italy	−1.2	−6.6	.7	−1.6	3.1	7.9	6.4	−9.5	−7.5

Figures for individual countries for 1973 & '74, 1975 & '76, and 1977 are from IMF, *Annual Report* (Washington, D.C.: IMF, *1977, 1979,* and *1981*), pp. 16, 21, and 22. All other figures are from IMF, *Annual Report, 1982,* pp. 18 and 21.

of all private bank debt to non-OPEC LDCs, with Brazil and Mexico accounting for 45 percent of the total.[68] Similarly, only a few banks accounted for the bulk of the loans. In fact, a survey by the Subcommittee on Multinational Corporations found that two-thirds of all U.S. private bank lending to twenty-five developing countries was by just six banks. Two-thirds of all non-OPEC LDC private bank debt was owed to U.S. banks.[69]

A symbiotic relationship developed between the large multinational banks and the most creditworthy non-OPEC LDCs, similar to the one between the oil-exporting countries and the multinational oil companies. The loans provided by the banks enabled the non-OPEC LDCs to weather the recession without drastic cutbacks in spending. The LDC borrowers also found that the loans from private banks tended to carry fewer political strings or other types of conditionality than loans from official lending institutions, such as the IMF; and of course the banks profited nicely from the interest.

However, it was far from clear that the relationship was in the long-term interest of either party. In effect, the OPEC surplus represented an increase in world savings that could be used to expand the capital available for long-term investment, but very little of this money was used to expand productive capacity. The loans to foreign governments were mainly used to maintain domestic consumption, which did little to enhance the earning power of the borrowing countries. Consequently, as table 9–2 shows, these countries found themselves saddled with ever higher levels of debt as a percentage of their GDP, and increasingly they had to devote more of their export earnings to repayment of debt, rather than to productive purposes. While their immediate problems eased with the 1976 recovery, this mounting level of debt meant that either another downturn in the world economy, which would reduce their exports, or another sharp rise in oil prices, which would boost their import costs, could prove catastrophic.

By the end of 1978 the position of the poorest LDCs, such as India, Bangladesh, and Pakistan, had become severely strained, for these countries lacked access to the international financial markets and to the flow of direct investment that had contributed substantially to financing the current account deficits of the non-OPEC LDCs as a group.[70] Nor has the inflow of foreign aid kept pace with the needs of these countries.[71]

TABLE 9–2. DEBT AMONG TOP 11 BORROWERS IN NON–OPEC LDCS

	1973	1974	1975	1976	1977	1978	1979
Current account deficit as % of GDP	1.2	4.8	5.9	3.5	2.2	2.2	3.1
Net debt as % of GDP	5.0	6.5	9.9	10.6	12.3	13.6	13.6
Debt service as % of exports	14.5	11.5	13.7	13.4	16.9	20.5	21.0

Citibank, *Monthly Economic Letter* (Mar. 1980), p. 10.

The banks, whose net claims on the LDCs increased from $3 billion in 1974 to $44 billion in 1978,[72] became increasingly fearful of a Third World country or group of countries' either defaulting or declaring a moratorium on the repayment of debt—a course of action advocated by left-wing forces in many LDCs. Were either development to occur, it could trigger a liquidity crisis in the international financial system. Once one bank called in a doubtful loan, other banks, fearing they might not be paid back, would be likely to follow. This could produce a mad scramble, with bankers bidding against one another and the financial position of the Third World countries completely undermined. And in 1978 the bankers' fears intensified when workers went on a general strike in Peru and a revolt broke out in Zaire's Shaba province, the center of its copper industry.

Yet with the banks dependent upon the profits from Third World loans and fearful about a Third World country's defaulting, the non-OPEC LDCs gained important leverage over their creditors. For example, in the summer of 1976 Peru needed $300 million to meet the interest and principal payments on its foreign debt of $3.7 billion. Had Peru gone to the IMF for funds, it would have been forced to submit to tough credit standards and to comply with strict monetary and fiscal targets. So, instead, the Peruvian government turned to the private banks for yet another loan. If the banks refused the request, they risked seeing their existing loans go sour; consequently, they agreed to lend Peru another $390 million. The banks demanded that Peru put its financial house in order, but their conditions were less strict than those the IMF would have mandated.[73]

Nor were the banks happy to assume the role of financial disciplinarian— something they would have preferred to see the IMF do. Nonetheless, in addition to Peru, banks rescheduled the debts of Argentina, Chile, Brazil, Uruguay, South Korea, the Philippines, and Zaire. Moreover, between 1974 and the end of 1978 the number of countries in arrears on current payments or conducting or seeking multilateral debt renegotiation increased from three to eighteen.[74]

By 1977 many bankers were looking to either the consuming-country governments or the OPEC states to assume the risks of additional loans to the LDCs. Similarly, Saudi Arabia was increasingly concerned about the security of the funds it had deposited with the private banks. Both the Saudis and the private banks wanted a reinvigorated IMF to impose strict disciplinary measures on deficit countries. They recognized that if the IMF's lending capabilities were not expanded, it would lack the funds needed to get countries to accept the disciplinary conditions it sought to impose.[75]

Yet, for all these problems, the banks, which had become dependent upon profits from loans to the Third World, could not stop lending. The same banks that worried about countries defaulting in 1976–77 complained when several countries prepaid loans in 1978, reducing the banks' earnings. Nor was any central bank in the home country likely to place effective controls on the private banks of its nationals so long as it saw them as competing for a bigger share of the world market. And with countries able to turn to the private banks for loans, the clout of the IMF, despite its increased resources, was considerably reduced.[76]

Recognition of these dangers led U.S. officials and private bankers to call for the IMF and other international organizations to assume a greater role in the recycling process. In response to this concern, the Carter administration backed a plan for a new $14 billion IMF oil facility, as proposed by the Fund's managing director, H. Johannes Witteveen. Witteveen maintained that for the Fund to force countries to correct their balance-of-payments problems, the Fund's resources had to be increased. However, negotiations on creation of the new fund stalled on two issues: the reluctance of the industrialized countries to grant the OPEC countries power in the new facility commensurate with their financial contribution to it,[77] and the OPEC countries' demand that the developing countries be given loans at preferentially low interest rates.

In August 1977 agreement was finally reached on creation of a $10 billion facility designed to enable the IMF to increase its share of the financing of balance-of-payments deficits from 7 percent to 11 percent. OPEC countries agreed to provide nearly half the funding, with Saudi Arabia providing $2.58 billion—the largest contribution. The IMF promised to give "special consideration" to developing countries when it reviewed loan requests; however, with Congress reluctant to ratify the $1.7 billion U.S. share, the fund did not begin operations until 1979.[78]

Despite the consuming countries' failure to develop a multilateral recycling mechanism prior to 1979, petrodollar recycling proved manageable. The main reason was that the OPEC surplus turned out to be far smaller than originally imagined. Initial estimates had failed to take adequate account of either the effect of the rise in oil prices on the level of oil imports in the consuming countries or the effect of inflation on the cost of OPEC imports—and OPEC's imports turned out to be far larger than anyone had thought possible. In fact, between 1974 and 1978 OPEC's imports grew at an average annual rate of nearly 38 percent.[79] Largely as a result of this, the OPEC current account shifted from a surplus of $72 billion in 1974 to a deficit of $1 billion in 1978 (see table 9–3).

As these trends became apparent, estimates of the cumulative 1980 OPEC surplus began to decline. For example, by mid-1974 the OECD had cut its earlier estimate of the cumulative 1980 surplus by more than half—to $250–$300 billion. At this level the OPEC surplus would equal about 5 percent of the value of all stocks and bonds in the major OECD countries in 1980, or 2 percent of their fixed assets.[80] Other estimates of the surplus showed a similar downward trend.[81] In addition, in 1974, when the annual OPEC surplus was at its peak, the importing countries were able to draw upon their accumulated foreign-exchange reserves to help finance their balance-of-payments deficits. Also, the private banks, which received the bulk of the OPEC funds, proved extremely skilled at matching short-term deposits with long-term demand for loans and at transferring funds to the deficit countries.

Another important factor in assessing the "OPEC" surplus was the extent to which it was concentrated in just a few countries. The cumulative 1974–78 OPEC current account surplus reveals that four OPEC countries—Algeria, Indonesia, Gabon, and Ecuador—remained in deficit during this period. Of the total surplus accumulated by the other OPEC countries, Saudi Arabia accounted for nearly 40 percent, Kuwait for 18.1 percent, Iran for 16.2 percent, and the United Arab Emirates for 12.2 percent; the other OPEC countries had only marginal shares. (see appendix table A6). Consequently, the investment decisions of these four, solidly pro-Western governments were crucial to recycling. Moreover, by 1978, when OPEC's combined current account surplus had disappeared, the U.S. Treasury estimated that six OPEC countries—Iraq, Libya, Saudi Arabia, Kuwait, Qatar, and the United Arab Emirates—still had a combined surplus of $19 billion whereas the other six major oil exporters had a combined current account deficit of $13.6 billion.[82]

Fortunately for the consuming countries, the OPEC "surplus countries" showed little inclination to shift their funds around precipitously—to promote their political interests or for any other reason. As holders of vast wealth, they had an interest in the continued stability of the Western economic system; nor did they want to provoke the West, fearing this might lead to seizure of their assets. Moreover, if the OPEC countries had shifted their funds from, say, U.S. to European banks en masse, this would have lowered the interest rates they received. Nor could they have stopped the European banks from transferring funds to U.S. banks. In addition, most OPEC bank deposits were subject to withdrawal limitations or penalties.

As time passed and the OPEC countries gained increasing confidence in their ability to make investments, a larger proportion of their surplus funds was invested in long-term assets. Bank deposits and short-term government securities were estimated to account for two-thirds of the OPEC surplus in 1974, but by 1976 this had fallen to a little more than one quarter.[83] Between 1974 and 1978 the largest share of the OPEC surplus, 29.9 percent, went into the Euro-banking market. The United States received the largest share of any single country, 20.4 percent of the total.[84] Nor was this surprising, for the international money markets, based primarily in New York and London, and the market in U.S. government securities were the only outlets for funds as large as those the OPEC nations had accumulated. Only 19.1 percent of OPEC's surplus funds went directly to developing countries and only 4.9 percent went to international organizations.

In addition, while the United States and the United Kingdom sought to attract OPEC funds, Germany, Switzerland, and Japan—the strong-currency countries—tried to limit the inflow of OPEC funds because they feared that an inflow of OPEC funds would boost their exchange rates and make their exports uncompetitive. These countries have also been afraid that, as their currencies become reserve currencies, they will have to subordinate their domestic monetary policy to the needs of the international financial markets.[85]

While the OPEC "surplus countries" did not move their funds around pre-

TABLE 9–3. OPEC INVESTIBLE SURPLUS AND ITS DISPOSITION, 1974–81
(BILLION DOLLARS)

	1974	1975	1976
Invested in			
U.S.	11.5	7.9	11.1
Euro-banking market	22.5	8.0	11.0
U.K.	7.5	.25	−1.0
Other developed countries	6.0	7.75	8.0
Non-market countries	.5	2.0	1.25
Less developed countries	6.0	7.25	7.5
International financial institutions	3.75	4.25	1.25
Total Allocated	57.75	37.4	39.1
Estimated Current Account Surplus	72.25	36.75	39
Lag in receipt of oil revenues	−11.25	−.25	−7.5
Net borrowings	.5	3.75	7.75
Investible Cash Surplus	61.5	40.25	39.25
Discrepancy in Estimates			
(Investible Cash Surplus less Total			
Allocated)	3.75	2.85	.15
U.S.	19.9	21.1	28.4
Euro-banking market	39.0	21.4	28.1
U.K.	13.0	.7	−2.6
Other developed countries	10.4	20.7	20.5
Non-market countries	.9	5.3	3.2
Less developed countries	10.4	19.4	19.2
International financial institutions	6.5	11.4	3.2
	100.1	100.0	100.0

From U.S. Dept. of the Treasury. After 1977, figures for Other Developed Countries and Non-Market Countries are available only in aggregate. Cumulative totals and Percent Distribution were calculated by author. Because the sources vary, the figures in this table are not strictly comparable with those in table 9–1.

cipitously, as rational investors they reacted to unfavorable developments, and this tended to accentuate the balance-of-payments and currency problems that both the United States and Great Britain experienced. As indicated, with its large financial markets and historic links with many of the oil-exporting countries, Great Britain initially attracted a substantial share of the OPEC surplus, enabling it to finance its balance-of-payments deficits. Indeed, in 1974 Britain ran a balance-of-payments deficit of $7.8 billion, but received $7.5 billion in capital inflows from the OPEC countries. However, as Britain's economic situation continued to deteriorate, the OPEC countries, which accounted for half of all foreign-government holdings of pounds, began to shift their funds elsewhere, and withdrew more than $6 billion in 1975 and 1976, when the pound was sinking fast. They also reduced the percentage of sterling that they would accept

1977	1978	Cumulative 1974–78	1979	1980	1981	Cumulative 1974–81
7.4	.4	38.3	7.1	14.0	16.4	75.8
12.0	2.5	56.0	29.0	32.0	2.75	119.75
.75	.25	7.75	2.5	3.5	1.0	14.75
8.0 1.25	5.75	40.5	8.25	25.75	20.0	94.5
8.5	6.5	35.75	8.5	10.25	12.75	67.25
.5	−.5	9.25	−.5	4.5	4.25	17.5
38.4	14.9	187.55	54.85	90.0	57.15	389.55
31.5	−1	178.5	63.0	119.0	67.0	427.5
2.5	1.25	−15.25	−6.25	1	4.25	−16.25
9.75	18.75	40.5	8.25	4.25	4.0	57.0
43.75	19.0	203.75	65.0	124.25	75.25	468.25
5.35	4.1	16.2	10.15	34.25	18.10	78.7
Percent Distribution of Allocated Surplus						
19.3	2.7	20.4	12.9	15.6	28.7	19.5
31.3	16.8	29.9	52.9	35.6	4.8	30.7
2.0	1.7	4.1	4.6	3.9	1.7	3.8
20.8 3.3	38.6	21.6	15.0	28.6	35.0	24.3
22.1	43.6	19.1	15.5	11.4	22.3	17.3
1.3	−3.4	4.9	−.9	5.0	7.4	4.5
100.1	100.0	100.0	100.0	100.1	99.9	100.1

in payment for their oil, from 20.3 percent in 1974 to 5.7 percent in the first quarter of 1976.[86]

The withdrawal of OPEC funds and the diminished willingness of OPEC countries to accept payment in sterling were significant factors in the sharp fall of the pound during 1976 (from $2.05 in March to $1.55 in December). By raising the price of imports, the pound's decline wrecked the government's plan to reduce inflation. In an effort to ward off disaster, in June 1976 the U.S. joined with other industrialized countries in setting up a $5.3 billion line of short-term credit for Britain to use in bolstering the pound. The United States provided $2 billion of the total.[87]

Despite this aid, Britain's financial situation continued to deteriorate. In the fall of 1976 Britain requested nearly $4 billion from the IMF, but the IMF lacked the funds to meet this request and still continue lending to the other oil-importing countries that were making demands upon it. However, the other oil-importing countries again came to Britain's rescue. Nine countries agreed to provide the IMF just under $3 billion in additional funds, enabling it to make a $3.9 billion loan to Great Britain in January 1977—the largest loan in the Fund's thirty-year history.[88]

Britain also negotiated a $3 billion line of credit with the Bank for International Settlements in Basel, the central bankers' central bank, to finance reductions in the official sterling balances below their year-end 1976 level. With these two credit accords, Britain was able to secure a $1.5 billion loan from a group of private banks. As a result of the credits that Britain secured, the value of the pound began to increase, and with the IMF demanding that Britain reduce the expansion of its monetary supply as a condition for receiving the IMF loan, the British economic situation began to stabilize. By 1977 Britain was able to retire a significant portion of the sterling balances, reducing its vulnerability to currency attacks. Then, as North Sea oil came onstream, Britain was able to attract foreign funds, and by the end of 1977 was running a substantial balance-of-payments surplus.[89]

When Britain ran into financial problems, it called in a $486 million loan it had extended to Italy as its part of the EEC package put together in 1974. That provoked another financial crisis in Italy; however, the other EEC countries agreed to replace the British loan, and the major industrial nations agreed to extend another $500 million to Italy through the IMF. In return for this, Italy had to adopt an austerity program and reduce its balance-of-payments deficit. Despite cutbacks, Italy failed to keep its federal budget deficit below the levels agreed to with IMF. Nevertheless, Italy kept afloat by restricting the growth of its money supply and mounting a huge export drive.[90]

When the OPEC countries shifted out of sterling, they put more of their money into the United States and dollar-denominated assets. But less than a year later, when the dollar came under attack, as the U.S. balance-of-payments deficit mounted in 1977–78, the OPEC countries reduced the share of surplus funds that they invested in the United States, which further aggravated the U.S. balance-of-payments problems. And in January 1978 a report that Saudi Arabia was going to abandon the dollar as the standard for oil pricing weakened the dollar in international markets.[91] This development points to another consequence of the OPEC surplus. Since it is so large and concentrated, rumors about a shift in the way it will be allocated can have a significant impact on financial markets, encouraging speculation.

When the OPEC surpluses mounted, there was considerable concern in the Western press about the "danger" of the OPEC countries' buying up a considerable portion of consuming countries' real assets. These fears were encouraged by several well-publicized OPEC investments. In July 1974 Iran bought 25 percent of the stock of Krupp Huttenwerke of Essen, Germany. Later, Iran negotiated to purchase large shares of Ashland Oil and Pan American World Airways, but neither deal materialized, and in 1976 Iran expressed interest in buying an equity stake in both BP and Occidental. Kuwait bought a seventh of Germany's Daimler-Benz; Libya purchased a 10 percent share in Fiat; and Middle Easterners bought real estate in the Champs Elysées, in the London financial district, and along choice South Carolina beaches.[92]

Yet, despite these highly publicized acquisitions, the OPEC countries acquired a very small slice of the world's capital stock. Even at its 1974 peak, the OPEC surplus was equal to only about 13 percent of the net increase in the rest of the world's capital stock. At the end of 1978, OPEC countries accounted for only 12 percent of foreign investment in the United States and for less than 1 percent of all investments in the United States.[93] In addition, the OPEC countries have shown very little interest in direct investment; in the United States, less than 1 percent of the OPEC countries' investment has been direct investment.[94] This is partly because direct investment requires special competence by the purchaser in conducting some line of business, which investors from OPEC countries generally lack because of the underdeveloped character of the OPEC nations' economies. Also, OPEC investors preferred portfolio investments, because they feared xenophobic reactions in the developed countries and therefore sought to keep their investments "low profile."[95] This was part of the reason why a high percentage of the OPEC surplus went into the Eurodollar market. Moreover, Iran backed away from purchasing shares in Occidental and Pan Am partly because of the bad publicity it received when news of the proposed deals surfaced.[96] Finally, the OPEC countries feared that more permanent forms of investment would become politically hostage.

To minimize repercussions, the OPEC countries had an informal understanding with the Ford administration to consult the United States before making important investments,[97] and Saudi Arabia maintained a policy of making only modest investments in corporate stocks and never purchasing more than 5 percent of a company's capital.[98] In addition, the Arab "surplus countries" have preferred to make investments in productive capacity at home rather than overseas. Consequently, surplus funds are "put away" overseas with the expectation that they will be recalled when needed for use at home. When the OPEC countries *did* make direct investments, it was often to gain access to the skill a company had that the purchaser believed would be useful in his home country. For example, Iran's principal motive in purchasing Krupp stock was to gain access to Krupp technology.[99]

From 1974 through 1978 the OPEC surplus was much less a problem than initially feared. This was due to a surplus that was much smaller than first envisioned, a private banking system that mediated successfully between the surplus, exporting countries and the deficit, consuming countries, and a series of ad hoc responses to crises by the consuming countries. Yet the process was not without its problems: Third World countries, deeply in debt; repeated currency crises; and increased speculation. Moreover, the failure of the consuming countries to work out more durable long-term recycling mechanisms, or grant the OPEC countries a place in the international financial system—as measured in IMF voting rights, for example—commensurate with their financial resources, may lead to major problems in the future.

THE WORLD ECONOMY AFTER THE 1973–74 OIL PRICE RISE

The rise in oil prices posed other problems for the consuming countries as well, for the economic growth of the developed countries had been premised on low-price oil and the productivity of capital plant, dependent upon low-price energy, was reduced by the rise in energy prices. Similarly, a pattern of development premised upon cheap oil and the automobile was also threatened by high-price oil.

In theory, new capital equipment and patterns of living could be made more energy efficient; in practice, these developments were plagued by the suddenness of the OPEC price rises and the uncertainty that surrounded them. Would oil prices stay up? If not, why trade in your gas guzzler and move back to the city? And why, then, should business make the enormous capital expenditures needed to reduce the energy-intensive character of production?

Even if everyone was convinced that high-price oil was here to stay, the suddenness with which it arrived caused problems. Had energy prices gone up slowly and steadily, business, labor, and consumers could have adjusted, but with prices skyrocketing in a mere three months, there were bound to be substantial transitional costs, with business suddenly discovering that much of its energy-intensive plant was now obsolete, workers that their skills were no longer needed, and consumers that their appliances and life styles required too much energy. The rise in energy costs, the uncertainty that surrounded it, and the need to develop less-energy-intensive technologies have contributed to the lag in capital spending that has characterized the world economy since 1973, despite the fact that the OPEC surplus represented a rise in world savings that could have been used to increase capital spending.

The rise in oil prices and the fear of shortages also shifted world concern from maintaining aggregate demand, the principal concern of economic policy makers in the postwar period, to maintaining adequate supplies. Since 1974, access to raw materials and inflation have rivaled unemployment as areas of economic concern.

The OECD estimated that in 1974 the rise in world oil prices directly added about 1.5 percent to the OECD-wide inflation rate of roughly 11.5 percent (for Western Europe the figure was 2.3%, for Japan 2.6%, and for the U.S. 0.4%). According to most estimates, if the secondary effects of the rise in oil prices, in pulling up the price of other energy sources and on the wage-price cycle, are included, the rise in oil prices was responsible for adding 2 to 4 percentage points to the inflation rate in most countries in 1974.[100] Thus even when the secondary effects are taken into account, the rise in oil prices accounted for less than a third of the OECD inflation rate.

Moreover, unlike the effect of higher oil prices on the balance-of-payments or on the transfer of income to the OPEC countries, the effect on inflation was nonrecurring. Once oil prices stabilized, as they did from 1974 to 1978, their

impact on inflation declined sharply. The secondary effects had to work themselves out, and the high energy price was partly responsible for structural
changes, which resulted in bottlenecks and inflationary pressures at a lower level
of economic activity than in the past. In addition, when the United States reduced
the real cost of oil by printing more dollars and eroding their value, one effect of
this increase in world monetary reserves was to increase inflationary pressures.
But once the initial jolt passed, the impact of the oil-price rise on inflation in the
OECD countries was small. In contrast, inflation in the OECD countries, which
continued throughout the 1974–78 period, added several points each year to the
rate of inflation in the OPEC countries.[101]

The most serious problem that the rise in oil prices posed for the consuming
countries was the new tradeoff they faced between high economic growth and
adequate/affordable oil supplies. If economies expanded rapidly, oil consumption would increase, oil prices would go up, and shortages might well emerge,
bringing growth to a halt; but the only near-term alternative was slow economic
growth.

The impact of the price rise on employment was less clear. While energy and
capital tend to be complementary, energy and labor tend to be substitutable. A
less-energy-intensive economy should therefore use less capital and more labor,
but offsetting this employment-boosting effect was the general decline in economic activity that the price rise contributed to. A less-capital-intensive economy
would also be one where the productivity of labor and, correspondingly, labor's
wage were likely to be reduced. Finally, the rise in oil prices was likely to shift
income from oil consumers to oil producers in the consuming countries.

While these developments were likely, each was profoundly affected by policy
in the consuming countries. Confronted by higher oil prices, each consuming
country had to decide the extent to which it would

1. Go into debt—running balance-of-payments deficits—to pay for oil imports;
2. Reduce its oil consumption, preferably through energy conservation measures
   but probably, at least in the short term, through recession;
3. Attempt to pay for its oil imports by boosting its exports.

Concerned about accelerating inflation, U.S. policy makers responded to the
rise in oil prices by adopting extremely restrictive macroeconomic policies. As a
result, the United States suffered its most severe recession since the Great Depression in 1974–75. Particularly hard hit was the U.S. automobile industry. By
the end of 1974 higher oil prices had added roughly 1 percentage point to the
unemployment rate and roughly 3.5 percent to the consumption price deflator.[102]

The United States also ensured that income would be transferred from consumers to domestic producers by allowing "new" oil to rise to the OPEC level
and by boosting the price of "old" oil from $4.25 to $5.25 in December 1973.
The rise in OPEC prices also had an effect on the price of other fuels sold in the
United States. When "new" oil went from $3 a barrel to $12, natural gas, sold
in the uncontrolled intrastate market, went from 45¢ per thousand cubic feet
(mcf) to $1.75, and steam coal went from $7 a ton to $28. However, by main-

taining price controls, which kept average U.S. oil prices below the OPEC level, the United States avoided many costly adjustments to energy-saving plant and equipment that Europe and Japan had to make.[103]

Like their counterparts in the United States, when the oil crisis hit, Japanese policy makers feared substantial acceleration of already high inflation and consequently adopted restrictive monetary and fiscal policies. But in sharp contrast to the United States, Japan attempted to boost exports to pay for its oil imports. While production in the United States and Japan reached a cyclical peak in the final quarter of 1973, in Western Europe industrial production continued to rise throughout the first half of 1974, and the recession began after that. In general, economic policy in Western Europe, in response to the oil crisis, followed a course broadly similar to that in the United States and Japan, but on a smaller scale and after a lag of about six months.[104]

Contrary to the fears of many, the 1973–74 oil crisis and the recession that followed did not lead to the kind of competitive currency devaluations and beggar-thy-neighbor policies that characterized the 1930s. No major trading nation adopted full-blown protectionism. The success of private bankers in recycling funds, floating exchange rates (in effect since 1973), and the willingness of countries to accept deficits in their balance-of-payments all worked to prevent this. However, in response to the balance-of-payments crisis brought on by the oil price rises, many countries depreciated their currencies and imposed restrictions on imports as they attempted to pay their oil-import bills and "export" their way out of the 1974–75 recession. As *Business Week* stated in October 1977, "The floating-rate system is today being subverted by degrees of government intervention in the currency markets that dwarf anything seen under the fixed-rate Bretton Woods system, when nations were required to intervene."[105] This was true despite repeated pledges of the consuming countries to avoid actions that would shift the balance-of-payments burden of higher oil prices onto their neighbors and to allow their currencies to float "clean," without government intervention to manipulate exchange rates.

The Japanese were the most notorious export boosters. In 1974 they increased exports by 34 percent, bringing their balance-of-payments back into surplus by the end of the year, despite Japan's enormous oil-import bill. Then, in 1976, the Japanese government intervened in the currency exchange markets to keep the yen from appreciating in value, despite the sharp upsurge in Japan's trade and current account surpluses.[106]

The Japanese export surge provoked a protectionist backlash in Europe and the United States. Japan was attacked for exporting its unemployment to the rest of the world. West European countries placed Japanese TV sets, radios, and tape recorders under "voluntary" import restrictions. The EEC negotiated import quotas with Japan's steelmakers and Britain imposed limits on Japanese cars. In the United States, demands mounted for limitations on the importation of Japanese cars, TV sets, steel, and other products. This led to several "orderly marketing agreements" limiting the importation of Japanese textiles, shoes, and color TV sets. In addition, the United States and the EEC instituted "trigger price" systems for steel, designed to prevent the importation of steel priced below a reference level. But in 1976, with the Japanese government under internal attack, Japan's economic policy makers saw massive exports as the only means of maintaining domestic employment.[107] Nor was Japan alone in this.

Early in 1976, weak governments in Italy and Great Britain allowed their currencies to depreciate sharply rather than take deflationary steps that would reduce domestic employment. With capital spending stalled, export-led growth provided the major stimulus for recovery in many countries. In response to the British devaluation, France saw no alternative but to let its currency float downward.[108] The British, French, and Italian floats were a sharp setback for the Rambouillet summit agreement of 1975,[109] which was supposed to have smoothed out currency fluctuations. In 1976 *Business Week* warned that "if Japan and other countries try to hold their currencies at bargain-basement rates, they eventually will set off a series of competitive devaluations and the whole system will break down."[110]

While the strongman of Europe, West Germany, might have eased the balance-of-payments problems of its European partners by allowing its currency to appreciate, West Germany also intervened to keep the mark down in value. The explanation for Germany's behavior is not hard to find. German economic growth was not what it was; Germany was heavily dependent upon exports; and German federal elections were scheduled for 1976.[111]

Besides manipulating their currencies, countries resorted to export subsidies and an array of nontariff barriers, ranging from quotas to packaging regulations, to hold imports down. As the IMF concluded, the instruments of protectionism—import surcharges, advance deposits, quantitative controls, tariff and nontariff barriers—were more widespread in 1977 than in 1974, before the recession began. The Fund stated: "A large number of member countries and a greater proportion of world trade became subject to more restrictive policies—especially nontariff barriers to imports, which were supported to an increasing extent by the negotiation of export restraint agreements."[112]

Once the recovery was under way, a new dispute emerged in 1977. The United States began expanding its economy faster than any other country. As a result, it pulled in massive levels of both oil and non-oil imports, running huge balance-of-payments deficits. With the dollar still accepted as the world's reserve currency and OPEC generally insisting on payment in dollars, the United States could pay for its imports by simply printing more dollars—an option no other country had. However, other countries feared that as the dollar declined in value, it would lose acceptance as a reserve currency, undermining the system of international payments.

The United States maintained that by rapidly expanding its economy it was performing a service for other countries, boosting demand for their products and enabling them to pay their oil bills by selling products to the United States. However, the United States argued that it should not have to assume this burden alone, but should be joined by the other strong capitalist economies, West Germany and Japan. Consequently, the United States urged these countries to expand more rapidly and to reduce their trade surpluses by increasing their imports. By so doing, the United States argued, West Germany and Japan would act like locomotives, pulling the weaker economies out of recession.

However, Japan and West Germany resisted the U.S. entreaties, fearing the consequences that rapid growth would have on inflation. As a country almost totally lacking in fossil fuel reserves, Japan viewed its trade surpluses as a cushion, needed to provide financial protection against further oil price increases. The Japanese also believed they were victims of racism—that the United States took a tougher line with them than with its other trade partners—and that they were being penalized for working hard and penetrating U.S. and world markets.[113]

In May 1977 the leaders of the major industrialized countries committed themselves to a joint 5 percent growth for the year, but it soon became clear that West Germany and Japan were not going to meet their targets. Consequently, in the summer of 1977 the United States attempted to force West Germany and Japan into greater reflation by pushing down the value of the dollar. The effect of the U.S. action was to cut German and Japanese exports, lower their production, and raise their unemployment. But the U.S. hoped that, in reaction, Japan and West Germany would reflate. The Germans and Japanese were furious with the United States. They argued that the main problems confronting the world economy were excessive U.S. oil imports; excess dollars on the world market, which was undermining confidence in the world's leading reserve currency and creating pressures for another oil price increase; and inflation, which U.S. policies were encouraging. The United States replied that the way to improve the value of the dollar was for Europe and Japan to expand more rapidly, pulling in more U.S. imports. Moreover, the Carter administration refused to take direct action to limit oil imports, relying instead on congressional action on its proposed National Energy Plan. As this conflict between the world's leading capitalist powers continued, Japan reported that for the fiscal year ending March 31, 1978, it had a trade surplus of $20.5 billion—the highest ever recorded by any nation. Of the total, $9 billion was in trade with the United States.[114]

In 1978 something approaching a modus vivendi was worked out. Early in the year the U.S. Federal Reserve joined other central banks in an effort to stabilize the value of the dollar. Japan imposed curbs on its exports of autos, steel, ships, and TV sets—products that accounted for roughly a third of Japan's exports. It expanded its economy somewhat more rapidly, allowed the yen to appreciate (a development that began in 1977) and its trade surplus to decline.[115] The United States backed away from the "locomotive" theory and supported the idea that the burden of reflation should be spread over many countries. Then, at the Bonn summit meeting in July, Japan pledged to freeze its 1978 export volume at 1977 levels and to increase its imports. The United States promised to strengthen the dollar by saving oil and fighting inflation. It agreed that, by year end, it would take measures to reduce its oil imports by 2.5 mb/d by 1985, and the Carter administration reaffirmed its desire to raise U.S. oil prices to the world level by 1980. West German Chancellor Schmidt agreed to propose stimulative legislation that would add "up to" 1 percent to West Germany's GNP.[116]

Nonetheless, the limited nature of the consensus is evident. For Japan to freeze its exports at their 1977 level was to keep them quite high; the German commitment to reflationary measures was also limited; nor did the United States actually agree to raise its oil prices to the world level or to reduce its oil imports in the near term. Somewhat more significant was the energy legislation the United States passed later that year and the $30 billion plan to rescue the dollar that it launched in November in coordination with authorities in West Germany, Japan, and Switzerland.[117]

In any case, following the Bonn summit, West Germany and Japan increased domestic demand. In 1978, moreover, U.S. economic growth fell from 5.5 percent to 4.8 percent, while West Germany's rose from 2.8 percent to 3.6 percent. Consequently, both the U.S. trade deficit and the surpluses of West Germany and Japan began to shrink substantially during the first quarter of 1979.[118] Also, in December 1978 the Geneva talks on world trade reached agreement to limit nontariff barriers to imports. But as a U.S. official said, "What we are doing is not negotiating agreements to free trade so much as a 'Geneva convention' defining gentlemanly rules of trade war."[119]

By 1978 there were also distinct movements toward formation of regional currency blocs. Eight European nations (the EEC partners minus Britain) agreed to proceed with plans for a European Monetary System.[120] The EEC countries hoped to achieve exchange stability by reestablishing a fixed-exchange-rate system similar to the Bretton Woods system that collapsed in 1971—but the effect is likely to be intensification of trade among members of the bloc and exclusion of trade with members outside the bloc. U.S. officials also fear that the EMS will become a mark-dominated competitor to the dollar-dominated International Monetary Fund. A similar currency bloc, built around the yen, has been discussed in the Far East.[121]

Protectionist sentiments have also intensified, and this has led to a proliferation of "orderly marketing agreements" in which countries agree to limit importation of a particular product. The agreements have affected textiles and garments, steel, TV sets, radios and calculators, ships and shoes.[122] Despite this, protectionist sentiments in Western Europe and the United States remain strong, and the danger is still very real that, as the economic crisis intensifies, one or more countries will shift to full-blown protectionism, pulling others in their wake.

So far, there has been no breakdown of world trade. The growth in world trade has slowed from 8 percent a year in real terms between 1955 and 1973 to 4 percent a year since 1973,[123] but this reflects the slowdown in economic growth rather than any diminution in the importance of trade. Since 1973, in fact, both imports and exports have increased as a percentage of GNP (see table 9–4).

TABLE 9–4. IMPORTS AND EXPORTS AS A PERCENTAGE OF GNP/GDP, 1973–80

	Imports as % of GNP				Exports as % of GNP			
	1973	1978	1979	1980	1973	1978	1979	1980
U.S.	5.6	8.6	9.2	9.6	5.4	6.8	7.7	8.4
Japan	7.3	8.4	10.7	12.9	7.0	10.3	9.9	11.9
U.K.	23.8	22.6	26.1	23.6	18.9	20.7	23.1	22.6
France	14.6	16.6	18.8	20.4	14.2	16.1	17.7	17.6
W. Germany	11.0	17.4	21.0	22.7	13.5	20.3	22.6	23.3
Italy	25.7	21.2	24.5	26.4	20.5	21.1	22.6	20.6

	Imports as % of GDP			Exports as % of GDP		
	1973	1978	1979	1973	1978	1979
Developed market economies	13.2	15.4	17.2	12.5	14.6	15.7
Developing market economies	16.5	20.3	19.9	18.4	21.4	24.3

All figures for countries computed from CIA, *Handbook of Economic Statistics, 1980* and *1981*, pp. 24, 25, 66, 68, and 26, 66, 68. Other figures computed from data in U.N., *Yearbook of National Accounts, 1976*, part 2, table 1A; *1980*, vol. 2, table 1A; and U.N., *Yearbook of International Trade Statistics, 1980*, 1: 1080–81.

Much of the reason for this has been the increase in the cost of imported oil and the increase in exports to the OPEC countries. Indeed, in 1972–73 the OECD countries sent 4.1 percent of their exports to the OPEC countries, but by 1978 the figure had risen to 9.3 percent, enabling the OECD countries to reduce their balance-of-trade deficits with the OPEC countries. Moreover, this pattern has been fairly general, with no major shifts in the respective OECD countries' share of the OPEC market in this period (see appendix table A7).

Though substantial, the effects of the 1973–74 rise in oil prices were hardly devastating. Ironically, the "manageability" of the crisis proved a problem, for it reduced the commitment of the oil-consuming countries to dealing with the energy problem that *did* exist. In any case, with both real oil prices and oil imports falling between 1974 and 1978, the cost of oil imports as a percentage of GNP generally declined (see table 9–5). The main exception among the advanced capitalist countries was the United States, where the large rise in oil imports boosted the share of GNP that went to pay for oil imports from 1.66 percent in 1974 to 1.77 percent in 1978. Substantial as the world recession of 1974–75 was, only half of the decline in output can be attributed to the effects of higher oil prices.[124] Indeed, the decline in output was generally aggravated by the restrictive policies pursued by the consuming countries.

Between 1973 and 1978, growth in the advanced capitalist countries was only half as fast as during the previous five years (see table 9–6). Most countries plunged into recession in 1974–75. Then, after a brief recovery in 1976, most industrial countries failed to sustain the rates of economic growth that had characterized them between 1963 and 1973 (see appendix table A8). The main exception was the United States, which had a sub-par performance in the earlier period and enjoyed the advantages of substantial domestic energy supplies.

The falloff was sharpest in Japan, where the rise in oil prices reinforced shifts in the pattern of Japanese economic growth. Japan's export-led growth slowed down in response to protectionist reactions in Western Europe and the United States, and Japan's system of lifetime employment came under attack, with companies resorting to temporary layoffs, early retirement, and transfers to subsidiaries (usually at lower pay).[125] Similarly, the slowdown in world trade put a damper on Germany's export-oriented economy.

The trends in the oil-exporting countries were similar to those in the industrial countries (see appendix table A8). However, the non-OPEC developing countries fared surprisingly well, relative to the industrial countries and to their previous economic performance. Between 1973 and 1978 the non-OPEC LDCs had a higher average economic growth than the industrial countries and their rate of growth, relative to its previous level, did not deteriorate as much as the industrial countries' rate. This was true despite the fact that the oil-price increase took 2.5 percent of the non-OPEC LDCs' GDP in 1974, as opposed to only 1.97 percent of the combined GDP of the developed market economies. Nonetheless, to sustain this performance, the non-OPEC LDCs had to increase the proportion of their GDP that they exported.

The non-OPEC LDCs were also hurt in other ways by the rise in oil prices. Their rates of economic growth declined over their pre-1973 levels while they had to devote a larger share of their export earnings to paying for oil. Indeed, in the year immediately following the big rise in oil prices, the increase in the non-OPEC LDCs' oil bill was roughly equal to all the official aid they received from the OECD countries.[126] In addition, the problems in the developed countries reduced their willingness to extend aid to the LDCs, and as we have seen, the recession that the rise in oil prices contributed to in the developed world led to restrictions on imports from the Third World.

Moreover, aggregate data tend to hide the situation of particular countries, some of which experienced severe problems, as a result of the rise in oil prices. Increasingly, the non-OPEC LDCs appear to be divided into two groups. The first group includes such countries as Brazil, South Korea, and Taiwan and is characterized by dynamic, rapidly growing export-oriented economies with ready access to the international financial markets; while it is highly dependent upon imported oil, it is able to export to pay for it. The second group—including such countries as India, Pakistan, and Bangladesh—is densely populated and has relatively stagnant economies and little access to foreign capital. Lacking the means to pay for badly needed oil supplies and having little scope for conservation, these countries are often forced to choose between food and fuel.[127] Indeed, the IMF found that from 1976 to 1978 thirty-nine countries in the non-OPEC LDC group, whose per capita GDP did not exceed $300, had an annual

TABLE 9–5. COST OF OIL IMPORTS AS A PERCENTAGE OF GNP/GDP AND ALL IMPORT COSTS, 1970–80

	1970	1973	1974	1978	1979	1980
U.S.						
Oil imports*	3,419	6,256	6,088	8,364	8,411	6,793
Cost of oil imports†	2.3	7.0	23.4	37.7	56.0	69.0
Cost as % of GNP	.23	.54	1.66	1.77	2.36	2.63
Cost as % of all import costs	5.4	9.5	21.7	20.6	25.6	27.3
Japan						
Oil imports*	4,206	5,576	5,460	5,347	5,635	5,091
Cost of oil imports†	2.7	6.7	20.9	25.5	38.0	57.9
Cost as % of GNP	.80	1.27	3.35	2.67	3.69	5.27
Cost as % of all import costs	14.3	17.4	33.7	31.9	34.6	41.0
W. Germany						
Oil imports*	2,676	3,046	2,796	2,848	2,972	2,692
Cost of oil imports†	2.0	5.1	11.2	14.7	24.5	32.1
Cost as % of GNP	.54	1.02	2.09	2.09	3.22	3.88
Cost as % of all import costs	6.7	9.3	16.1	12.1	15.3	17.1
France						
Oil imports*	2,146	2,875	2,742	2,494	2,762	2,519
Cost of oil imports†	1.6	3.3	9.7	11.5	16.2	26.6
Cost as % of GNP	.88	1.28	3.26	2.33	2.84	4.03
Cost as % of all import costs	8.4	8.8	18.3	14.1	15.1	19.7
U.K.						
Oil imports*	2,487	2,738	2,585	1,596	1,471	1,158
Cost of oil imports†	1.8	3.3	9.0	4.4	2.3	0
Cost as % of GNP	1.60	2.02	4.95	1.27	.58	—
Cost as % of all import costs	8.3	8.5	16.4	5.6	2.2	—

GDP growth of only 4 percent, as opposed to the non-OPEC LDC average of 5.1 percent.[128]

The non-OPEC LDCs have benefited from aid from the OPEC countries. Many OPEC countries have established funds for assistance to Third World countries, and in January 1976 OPEC created an $800 million special aid fund to provide interest-free loans to developing countries.[129] Yet, despite these efforts, OPEC aid has never come close to matching the increase in the non-OPEC LDCs' oil bills. According to one estimate, the oil-price hikes cost the non-OPEC LDCs about $13 billion a year whereas OPEC aid totaled about $5 billion a year.[130] And the OPEC countries have generally been unwilling to sell oil to non-OPEC countries on concessional terms. Still, in comparison with the OECD countries, the OPEC countries consistently contributed a higher proportion of their GNP in aid.[131] However, a very high percentage of OPEC aid went to non-OPEC Arab or Islamic countries, much of it to pay for armaments or war relief.[132]

TABLE 9–5.—*Continued*

	1970	1973	1974	1978	1979	1980
Italy						
Oil imports*	2,345	2,669	2,516	2,363	2,435	1,883
Cost of oil imports†	1.2	2.4	8.0	8.7	11.9	20.5
Cost as % of GNP	1.57	2.22	6.08	3.27	3.73	5.45
Cost as % of all import costs	8.0	8.6	19.5	15.4	15.3	20.6
Developed Market Countries						
Oil imports*	21,800	28,585	27,625	27,660	28,085	24,545
Cost of oil imports†	19.9	44.2	119.7	155.1	231.0	323.6
Cost as % of GDP	.9	1.36	3.33	2.59	3.37	n.a.
Cost as % of all import costs	8.4	10.3	19.6	16.8	19.5	22.5
Non–OPEC LDCs						
Oil imports*	2,860	5,160	5,305	5,965	6,605	6,915
Cost of oil imports†	3.9	9.1	26.4	34.5	37.1‡	n.a.
Cost as % of GDP	1.2	1.9	4.4	n.a.	n.a.	n.a.
Cost as % of all import costs	8.5	11.7	20.8	17.9	15.4‡	n.a.

*Thousands of daily barrels.

†Billions of current U.S. dollars.

‡Does not include residual petroleum products that cost .36 billion in 1978.

Figures for countries from CIA, *Handbook of Economic Statistics, 1980*, pp. 24, 25, 68, 86, and 127, and *1981*, pp. 26, 68, 82, and 107. Computations by author. For individual countries cost is less earnings of exports of these items. Figures for non-OPEC LDCs and Developed Market Countries on Cost of Oil Imports from U.N., *Yearbook of International Trade Statistics*, vol. 2 (various issues). GDP figures from U.N., *Statistical Yearbook, 1979–80*, p. 646, and U.N., *Yearbook of National Accounts, 1976, 1977* and *1980*, vol. 2, table 1A. Figures on volume of Oil Imports from BP, *Statistical Review of the World Oil Industry* (various issues), on Cost of All Imports from U.N., *Yearbook of International Trade Statistics, 1980*, 1:1080. Figures on Oil Imports include crude and products. Percentages and computations by author.

TABLE 9–6. AVERAGE ANNUAL GROWTH OF REAL GNP/GDP, 1968–80

	(1) 1968–73	(2) 1973–78	Ratio of 2/1	1979	1980	1981
Real GNP						
U.S.	3.3	2.3	.70	3.2	−.2	2.0
Japan	9.5	3.7	.39	5.5	4.2	3.8
European OECD	5.1	2.1	.41	3.2	1.4	−0.3
Total OECD	5.0	2.5	.50	3.6	1.1	1.4
Real GDP						
Developing market economies	6.9	5.5	.80	4.4	n.a.	n.a.

Figures for OECD countries from U.S. Dept. of State, Bureau of Intelligence and Research, *Economic Growth of OECD Countries, 1968–78*, p. 9, and *1971–81*, p. 7. Figures for Developing Market Economies from U.N., *Yearbook of National Accounts, 1980*, 2:253.

While it was widely believed in Western Europe and Japan that the United States benefited from the oil-price rise and that, for this reason, the United States secretly conspired to keep prices up, the evidence fails to support this claim. Initially, the relative economic position of the United States improved as a result of the OPEC price rise. The dollar, which was devalued twice during the early 1970s, rose in value after the price rise, regaining its preeminence as the "numeraire" reserve currency, for with oil contracts generally denominated in dollars, consuming countries needed dollars to pay for oil. In addition, because of its lesser dependence upon foreign oil, its extensive domestic energy resources, and its close ties with Iran and Saudi Arabia, investors expected the United States to weather the oil crisis far better than any of the other advanced capitalist countries. In fact, relative to its performance in the preceding five years, between 1973 and 1978 the United States had a better economic performance than either Western Europe or Japan (see table 9–6), which was largely due to the fact that, of the major consuming countries, the United States devoted the smallest percentage of its GNP to paying for imported oil (see table 9–5). And partly because price controls kept U.S. energy prices below world prices, U.S. exports, which had declined steadily from 23.5 percent of all OECD exports in 1960 to 17.5 percent in 1973, began to rise in 1974, reaching 18.7 percent in 1975. In addition, in 1974 and 1975 the United States was able to cover its deficit with the OPEC countries by its ability to attract OPEC surplus funds (see table 9–7).

However, by 1978 these advantages had been dissipated, largely because the United States had boosted its demand for oil imports while other countries had reduced theirs. Between 1974 and 1978, most consuming countries substantially reduced the proportion of GNP they spent on imported oil. In sharp contrast to this pattern, of the countries listed in table 9–5, the United States was the only one that *increased* the proportion of GNP that it spent on imported oil. By 1978 the U.S. share of OECD exports had fallen to 16.5 percent, a full percentage point below its 1973 level.[133] By 1977 the OPEC surplus funds deposited in the United States were far less than the U.S. trade deficit with the OPEC countries,

TABLE 9–7. U.S. BALANCE OF PAYMENTS WITH OPEC, 1974–80 (BILLIONS OF CURRENT U.S. DOLLARS)

	U.S. Balance of Trade with OPEC	U.S. Receipts of OPEC Surplus	U.S. Balance with OPEC
1974	−10.05	11.5	1.45
1975	− 7.93	7.9	− .03
1976	−14.60	11.1	− 3.5
1977	−21.58	7.4	−14.18
1978	−16.32	.4	−15.92
1979	−30.14	7.1	−23.04
1980	−37.02	14.0	−23.02

Figures for U.S. Balance of Trade with OPEC from CIA, *Handbook of Economic Statistics, 1981*, p. 72. U.S. Receipts of OPEC Surplus are from table 9–3.

and the dollar had come under renewed attack, a situation made worse by the OPEC countries' threat to price oil in terms of a "basket" of currencies rather than in terms of the dollar.

Since 1974, the Swiss franc, the Japanese yen, and the German mark have grown in importance as reserve currencies, to the detriment of the dollar, and the European Monetary System is a threat to the predominance of both the dollar and the U.S.-dominated IMF in international monetary affairs.[134] Finally, while the Washington Energy Conference and creation of the International Energy Agency marked a reassertion of U.S. power vis-à-vis Europe, much of this gain was dissipated in subsequent years, as the United States struggled to formulate an energy policy and the IEA became largely a forum in which the other members criticized the United States for its failure to limit its oil imports. In short, when oil prices rose in 1973–74, many believed the United States could take advantage of this development to reestablish a dominant position within the world economy, but by 1978 there was little evidence that this had occurred.

MIDDLE EAST POLITICS AFTER THE 1973–74 OIL PRICE RISE

For all their negative economic consequences, high oil prices were not nearly so devastating to the world economy as another loss of supplies would have been. Yet the Arab oil-exporting countries warned that if there was another Arab-Israeli war, the oil weapon would be used again, and probably on a larger scale than in 1973–74.[135] Even in the absence of war, the oil weapon might be deployed as a way of putting pressure on the United States to extract concessions from Israel. In addition, political instability in any of the volatile oil-exporting countries could also lead to a serious loss of supplies. Indeed, as a result of their wealth, the OPEC countries became increasingly attractive targets for the poorer groups in the Middle East. Moreover, the interest of the consuming countries in the stability and good will of the exporting countries greatly limited their ability to bargain for lower prices, for if, in an effort to bring prices down, the consuming countries were to exert leverage against the exporting countries, the result might be political instability in the exporting countries. As Senator Frank Church stated, prior to the Iranian revolution, U.S. policy had been premised on the assumption "that Saudi Arabia and Iran are so vital to U.S. strategic interests that we dare not put those interests at risk over the price of oil."[136]

Former Federal Reserve Board Chairman Arthur Burns told *Business Week* he believed that by delaying export of certain machinery, planes, and military equipment to the OPEC countries, "something significant could be achieved."[137] Several times between 1973 and 1976, Burns indicated, he had urged that the United States adopt a tougher line with OPEC and that, as the first step toward such a policy, after the 1976 election he had recommended to President Ford that he send Vice President Nelson Rockefeller "to carry on some realistic economic and political conversations with the OPEC countries." He said that President Ford took his suggestion seriously, but Secretary of State Henry Kissinger "talked him out of it."[138] Similarly, a memo written by James Akins while he was ambassador to Saudi Arabia states that "the Saudis had urged us on numerous occasions to put pressure on the Shah to cooperate with Saudi Arabia and reduce the oil prices, yet we had refused to do this."[139] Akins has also said that, at his meeting with the Shah in February 1975, Kissinger was urged to pressure the Shah on the need for lower prices, but the secretary failed to do so. Akins now believes that at this meeting Kissinger told the Shah "the United States understood Iran's desire for higher oil prices."[140]

If Akins' allegations are accurate (Kissinger denies them), the question remains: Did the secretary fail to pressure the Shah on oil prices because he wanted oil prices to stay up, or because he felt the United States could exert little leverage on the issue and would only antagonize the Shah by bringing it up? Kissinger told *Business Week* in December 1974 that "if you bring about an overthrow of the existing system in Saudi Arabia and a Qaddafi takes over, or if you break Iran's image of being capable of resisting outside pressures, you're going to open up political trends that could defeat your economic objectives."[141]

In any case, the Shah later told the Saudis that Kissinger had not broached the issue of oil prices with him. The Shah also told the Saudis and oil industry executives that the United States was indifferent to further increases in the price of oil; and on September 3, 1975, Yamani wrote Treasury Secretary William Simon: "I would like you to know that there are those amongst us who think that the U.S. administration does not really object to an increase in oil prices. There are even those who think that you encourage it for obvious political reasons, and that any official position taken to the contrary is merely to cover up this fact." Yamani also warned that if the United States did not use its influence with the Shah, "It can only lead to Saudi Arabia giving up its present position on crisis and joining its OPEC colleagues in their uncompromising stand."[142]

Because of the fragmentary nature of the public record, it is impossible to draw definitive conclusions about these episodes, but two things should be remembered. First, for every allegation of U.S. officials conspiring to keep prices up, there are many public statements in which officials of comparable rank (sometimes the same official) called for price reductions. Also, many policies of the U.S. government were designed to bring prices down. Consequently, support for high prices within the U.S. government was at most partial and appears to have been confined primarily to officials involved in foreign-policy making. Second, the main reason for U.S. acquiescence in higher prices appears to have been its interest in maintaining the political security and the good will of the oil-exporting countries, and not its interest in improving its economic position vis-à-vis Western Europe and Japan, as is often alleged.

In its efforts to stabilize the situation in the oil-exporting countries, the United States pushed toward a settlement of the Arab-Israeli conflict. Indeed, U.S. officials believed that if progress toward a Middle East settlement did not continue, pressures in the Arab world for another war would mount, and with war would come another cutback in oil supplies. In the summer of 1974, having concluded Israeli-Egyptian and Israeli-Syrian disengagement agreements, Kissinger turned to the possibility of a Jordanian-Israeli settlement; but Israel was reluctant to pull back from the Jordan River and Hussein would accept nothing short of that. Then, in October, the Rabat summit conference of Arab leaders unanimously endorsed the PLO as the sole legitimate representative of the Palestinian people, which ended Hussein's right to negotiate for the Palestinians on the West Bank.

Rather than negotiate with the PLO, Kissinger shifted his attention to the Sinai, where the issues dividing the parties seemed far less intractable than those involving the West Bank. In return for a second agreement with Israel, Sadat demanded Israeli withdrawal from the Mitla and Giddi passes and the oil fields at Abu Rudeis and Ras Sudr. Israel sought to split Egypt from Syria, thereby reducing prospects for a combined Arab offensive. As a result, Israel demanded that Egypt renounce the state of belligerency between the two countries and said that Israeli withdrawal would not include the passes or the oil fields. In March 1975 the negotiations deadlocked on Israeli insistence on a declaration of non-belligerency and on the extent of Israeli withdrawal in the passes and the oil fields.

Following heavy pressure from the United States and resumption of Kissinger's shuttle diplomacy, in September 1975 a second Sinai agreement was reached. Egypt and Israel agreed to resolve conflicts between them by peaceful means, and Israel agreed to withdraw from the passes and the oil fields on the west coast of the Sinai. In return for these concessions, the United States made a series of pledges to Israel: to provide Israel with roughly $2 billion worth of defense equipment each year for the next ten years; to compensate Israel for its increased oil costs as a result of the return of the oil fields[143] and to supply Israel with oil for five years, if necessary; to refuse to negotiate with the PLO until it recognized Israel's right to exist and U.N. Resolutions 242 and 338; and to drop the idea of an interim agreement on the Israeli-Jordanian front and accept only "cosmetic" changes on the Golan Heights.[144] The United States also agreed to establish electronic listening stations, staffed by U.S. soldiers, to monitor military moves on both sides of the truce lines. In addition, the United States agreed to sell arms to Egypt, for the first time in twenty years. The agreement was to remain in force until it was superseded by a new agreement.

With the conclusion of Sinai II, Egypt took a big step toward signing a separate peace agreement with Israel, but Syria, not surprisingly, denounced the Sinai II accord and broke relations with Egypt when it was concluded. Syria objected to the accord because it amounted to a declaration terminating the state of war between Egypt and Israel, without securing the return of most of the Sinai or doing anything to recover the other occupied Arab lands. In addition, Syria feared that the accord would tend to freeze the status quo and allow Israel to mass the bulk of its military strength against Syria.

U.S. policy makers saw the Sinai II agreement as considerably reducing the prospects of another Arab-Israeli war and, with it, another Arab oil embargo, but the next step in Kissinger's much heralded step-by-step diplomacy was far from clear. The commitments to Israel and Syria's hostility to the Sinai II accord seemed to preclude interim agreements with either Syria or Jordan, and the prospect of convening a multiparty Geneva peace conference seemed stymied by the split between Syria and Egypt and the insistence of the Arab states that the PLO be represented at Geneva, a condition that Israel refused to accept.

In the context of a still highly volatile situation, high oil prices seemed to contribute to stability in the Middle East, consolidating a pro-Western axis in Teheran, Riyadh, and Cairo, for the immediate effect of higher prices seemed greatly to strengthen both the internal stability and the international position of the U.S.-designated regional powers, Saudi Arabia and Iran. Between 1972 and 1978 Iran spent over $19 billion on U.S. arms[145]—expenditures it could not have afforded without the oil-price rises. Iran used its military might to take responsibility for controlling the air and the sea lanes at the Strait of Hormuz; the Shah maintained troops in Oman until 1977, after the Dhofaris were defeated; and in 1977 the Shah gave aid to Somalia in its war against Soviet-backed Ethiopia.

Saudi Arabia played a lesser military role than Iran, but it managed to become the third largest purchaser of U.S. armaments, behind Iran and Israel. But more important than the Saudi military role was the use of Saudi money to push the Arab world in a conservative direction.[146] At the Rabat summit of Arab leaders in October 1974, Saudi Arabia emerged as the dominant power in the Arab world. Use of the Arab oil weapon and the enormous growth in Saudi wealth as a result of the price rise had contributed to Saudi prestige.

Moreover, Saudi Arabia was prepared to use its wealth to push the Arab states in a more conservative, pro-Western direction and to help resolve the Arab-Israeli conflict. At the Rabat conference, Arab oil-exporting countries had agreed to provide the Arab "front line" states with $2.35 billion in aid, and though the largest portion went to Egypt, the aid included $700 million for Syria and $50 million for the PLO, which encouraged both Syria and the PLO to moderate their positions. Indeed, Saudi Arabia urged them to accept Israel's existence and agree to creation of a Palestinian state in the West Bank, and following the October War, both Syria and the PLO began to express greater interest in a negotiated settlement with Israel. Saudi Arabia also financed Jordanian purchases of U.S. arms and headed the effort to put together a $400 million aid package that induced South Yemen to ease its ties to the Soviet Union.[147]

Saudi aid played its most crucial role in consolidating Egypt's alliances with the conservative Arab countries and the Western world, for Sadat, in shifting toward the West, had hoped to see a boom in foreign investment that would propel the Egyptian economy forward. But the boom turned out to be a fizzle, because Egypt attracted only $250 million in foreign investment between 1974 and 1977. Consequently, to feed the Egyptian people, the Sadat government became dependent upon aid from Saudi Arabia and the other oil-rich Gulf sheikdoms. Indeed, Arab oil producers contributed two-thirds of the $8 billion that flowed into Egypt between 1973 and 1977, with Saudi Arabia contributing more than half the total.[148] At the same time, the Egyptian–Saudi Arabian alliance became the primary alignment in the Arab world.

Saudi Arabia's most stunning diplomatic triumph occurred in the fall of 1976. Early in 1975 a bloody civil war erupted in Lebanon, with Moslem leftists and Palestinians fighting right-wing Christians, who were backed by the Israelis. The Syrians feared that a left-wing victory in Lebanon might pull them into another costly war with Israel; consequently, in the spring of 1976 the Syrians sent troops into Lebanon to counter the success of the Palestinians and left-wing Moslems. In October, with the Palestinians near defeat, Saudi Arabia requested a cease-fire and summoned the leaders of six Arab nations and the PLO to a summit meeting in Riyadh. With Syria and the Palestinians dependent upon the Saudis for financial support, neither party could resist the Saudi request. In fact, because of the costs of their intervention in Lebanon the Syrians were more dependent upon Saudi aid than ever. At the Riyadh conference, Saudi Arabia got the other Arab states to agree on a peace plan for Lebanon; it provided for an immediate cease-fire and creation of a 30,000-troop Arab force to supervise withdrawal of the warring factions. However, the peace-keeping force was dominated by the Syrians, leaving the Palestinians in a subordinate position but not destroying them altogether. In separate talks at the Riyadh conference, Saudi Arabia also got Syria and Egypt to agree to normalize relations.

By the end of 1976, therefore, Syria, Egypt, and Saudi Arabia had aligned their policies and were ready to resume negotiations with Israel. Indeed, Egypt, Syria, and Saudi Arabia were on record as favoring resumption of the Geneva peace conference and were reported to be studying ways of getting around the U.S.-Israeli veto against the presence of the PLO at the conference.[149] They also supported creation of a Palestinian state on the West Bank and Gaza. Moreover, as a result of their weakened position in Lebanon and their increased dependence upon the Saudis, the dominant factions in the PLO expressed greater interest in a negotiated settlement that would result in a Palestinian state in the West Bank and Gaza—a sharp departure from their previous insistence on a secular state in all of Palestine for both Arabs and Jews.

In addition, Arafat promised the Syrians that, in return for adequate military strength in the refugee camps and certain areas of southern Lebanon, the PLO would be flexible on negotiating tactics.[150] And with Syrian forces dominating Lebanon and the Palestinians forced to abandon their positions along the Israeli border, the rejectionist elements in the PLO would have a hard time disrupting the negotiating process through attacks into Israel. In short, Saudi Arabia had created the greatest opportunity for a comprehensive settlement of the Arab-Israeli conflict since the creation of the state of Israel. Yet, as we shall see (in chapter 13), the failure to exploit this opportunity was to have damaging consequences for both the price of oil and the stability of the Middle East; nonetheless, the immediate effect of these developments was to greatly weaken the force of Arab radicalism.

Iraq, Libya, and the leftist factions of the PLO were isolated from the Arab mainstream. In addition, to secure Saudi money, South Yemen adopted a more conciliatory attitude, and early in 1976 the Sultan of Oman declared final victory in his war against the PFLOAG. Oman had used oil revenues to strengthen its military, while economic troubles in oil-less South Yemen forced this radical Arab state to cut back its support for the PFLOAG in return for economic aid from Saudi Arabia and the other Arab states.[151]

Similarly, Soviet influence in the Middle East declined. As we have seen, Egypt strengthened its alliance with the West, and Soviet influence in the country dissipated. In fact, in 1976 Sadat formally repudiated the fifteen-year Treaty of Friendship signed with Moscow in 1971. Though still aligned with the Soviet Union, Iraq and Syria greatly expanded their trade with the West. Iraq, newly enriched by oil wealth, was particularly anxious to secure technology and delivery reliability that the Soviet Union could not provide.[152]

The civil war in Lebanon, in which Syrians and Palestinians (both of whom the Soviets backed) fought each other with Soviet-supplied weapons, was also a setback for Soviet influence in the Middle East. In November 1977 the Soviets suffered another reversal when the lure of Saudi money led Somalia to oust Soviet advisers and halt Soviet use of Somalian air and naval facilities. Similarly, Sudan broke all ties to Moscow in exchange for Saudi aid. In response to these developments, the Soviet Union sought new allies in Libya and among the more radical factions of the PLO, and was partly successful, with Libya shifting from Islamic-motivated anti-Sovietism toward friendly relations with the Soviet Union, which began pouring arms into Libya.

The rise in oil prices also led the OPEC countries to resolve several longstanding disputes in order to reduce the possibility that these conflicts among members would weaken the organization. In July 1974 Abu Dhabi and Saudi Arabia resolved their dispute over the Buraimi Oasis, with the Saudis dropping their claim to the oasis and other oil-rich portions of Abu Dhabi in return for access to the Gulf between the UAE and Qatar. In March 1975, at the first meeting of OPEC heads of state, Algerian President Houari Boumedienne helped Iran and Iraq settle their disputes over Kurdistan and the river frontier along the Shatt al-Arab. Iran, which in 1972 had begun to aid the Iraqi Kurds in their struggle against the Iraqi government, agreed to close its borders to the Kurds, enabling Iraq to crush the Kurdish rebellion. In return, Iraq made concessions on its boundary on the Shatt al-Arab, a waterway flowing into the Gulf, where Iraq wanted to establish port facilities. The agreement was motivated by recognition that continuation of the dispute could lead to a major war between Iraq and Iran, which would damage the oil fields on both sides of the waterway and worsen Iran's relations with the Arab world. In addition, Iraq came to an understanding with Saudi Arabia over partition of the disputed Neutral Zone between the two countries.[153]

From the perspective of the oil-consuming countries, the world appeared much safer in mid-1978 than in 1974. Petrodollars were recycled and the OPEC surplus was shrinking. Though significant, the economic consequences of the 1973–74 oil-price rise had proved manageable, and under the guidance of the U.S.-appointed guardians, Iran and Saudi Arabia, the Middle East appeared to have stabilized. But appearances can be deceiving. The basic problems of dependence upon Middle East oil, rivalry among the oil companies, and consuming-country disunity had not been resolved; nor had the force of Middle Eastern nationalism been permanently moderated. These factors would combine to produce an oil crisis in 1979, just as they had in 1973–74.

Keeping the Price Up [I]: The Structure of the Cartel and Consuming-Country Energy Policies

As we have seen, in the crisis atmosphere brought on by the Arab oil embargo and production cutbacks, the oil-exporting countries were able to boost the world oil price from about $2 a barrel to more than $8; but raising prices is one thing and keeping them up is quite another. How were the oil-exporting countries, which lacked such rudimentary aspects of a cartel structure as agreements on production quotas and market shares, able to keep prices more than thirty times higher than the cost of production—something no other cartel had come close to doing for anything like as long? Typically, cartels break up as a result of rivalry among members, competition from outside the cartel, and the development of substitutes for the product of the cartel. Indeed, the more the cartel raises prices, the greater the temptation for members to "cheat" on their agreement and sell more than their allotted shares. Similarly, the higher the cartel's prices, the greater the incentive for others to enter the industry or develop substitutes for its product. The improved prospects for doing this was, in fact, the opportunity that the rise in oil prices presented to the consuming countries.

Yet several factors combined to enable the exporting countries not only to maintain the cartel price they established in 1973–74 but to raise it further. One factor was the failure of the consuming countries and the international oil companies to respond adequately to the opportunity that the rise in oil prices opened. Consuming countries failed to develop effective energy policies and oil companies failed to develop enough new oil sources to put pressure on OPEC's price. Equally important was that, as oil prices rose, individual oil-exporting countries found they could meet their revenue needs at lower levels of production. As a result, they were willing to hold back their production, which greatly reduced the exporting countries' vulnerability to internal rivalry, and as oil prices rose, powerful groups within and among the consuming countries came to have an interest in high oil prices. Finally, the exporting countries would never have been able to charge $8—or $30—for a barrel of oil if consumers were not willing to pay it. The inelasticity of demand for oil continued to provide a strong basis for its high price.

Once oil prices went up, a constituency emerged in the consuming countries that helped keep them up. This was partly because, while, from the perspective of maintaining economic growth in the consuming countries, high oil prices were a problem, from the perspective of ending dependence upon OPEC, high oil prices were part of the solution, for high oil prices encouraged conservation and made development of alternative energy sources possible.

Moreover, the greater the efforts at conservation and developing alternative energy sources, the greater the high-oil-price constituency in the consuming countries. As these prices became a fact of life, projects were planned on the assumption of high oil prices, and the success of these projects depended on maintenance of such prices. The development of North Sea and Alaskan oil, the expansion of the nuclear and coal industries, and the development of powerful incentives for energy conservation were premised on high oil prices, and the groups involved in these projects—the U.S. and British governments; the nuclear, coal, and oil industries; and the environmental community—came to have an interest in maintaining high oil prices.

In addition, the Western companies that benefited from high oil prices—energy companies, companies that sold goods to the exporting countries, and banks involved in financing these activities—tended to lobby on behalf of the exporting countries and, indirectly, in support of high oil prices. As we saw in the previous chapter, U.S. foreign-policy makers came to see high oil prices as contributing to the stability of the Middle East. None of this denies the negative economic impact that high oil prices had on the consuming countries, or suggests that the consuming countries, as a group, did not favor a reduction in oil prices, but because of these other factors their commitment to this goal was far more ambivalent than it would otherwise have been.

Equally important in maintaining the high price was the willingness of individual exporting countries to accept reductions in their oil production. The desire of any oil-exporting country to produce more oil depends upon its revenue needs, the extent of its oil reserves, and its assessment of the future market for oil. These factors point to the crucial role that expectations play in shaping production and pricing policy. If an exporter expects prices to rise rapidly in the future, the exporter will be inclined to hold back on present production so that future production can be greater; but if he expects prices to be lower tomorrow than they are today, it will be in his interest to maximize present production. Similarly, if an exporting country believes its proven reserves will grow over time, it will be more inclined to boost production than if its reserves are destined to decline.

These expectations can be greatly influenced by the actions of the consuming countries and the oil companies. If the consuming countries appear to be forging ahead with new energy sources and the oil companies are pushing ahead with the development of newly discovered oil reserves, the prognosis is for lower oil prices. But if the consuming countries are bumbling along and the oil companies are making only modest efforts to develop non-OPEC oil resources, the outlook is for higher oil prices. And the exporting countries' attitude toward their oil-resource potential can be greatly influenced by the interest oil companies show in exploring for more oil in their territories. Consequently, because they shape expectations, the actions of the consuming countries and the oil companies in developing new energy resources have an important effect on immediate pricing and production decisions. This is in addition to their direct effect on the future energy market.

The actions of the consuming countries are also significant in another respect, for the decision of oil-exporting countries that have balance-of-payments surpluses to produce more oil depends in part on their assessment of whether they can earn more from producing more oil and investing the proceeds or from deferring production and waiting for their oil to appreciate in value. But that assessment depends on secure, profitable investment outlets in the consuming countries. If the consuming countries are willing to provide these countries with an inflation-proof, exchange-rate-free bond, as has been suggested, the exporting countries would be more inclined to boost production. If, instead, the exporting countries' investments in the consuming countries are vulnerable to inflation, exchange-rate losses, and confiscation, they are likely to conclude that "oil in the ground is worth more than money in the bank."

Similarly, as the economies of the oil-exporting countries develop, their capacity to absorb more revenue should increase, but if their development programs falter and they continue to lack mature economic infrastructures and skilled workers, their revenue needs will lag behind their oil receipts and they will think twice about expanding production. In addition, the production and pricing decisions of the OPEC countries are influenced by the effect their actions will have on both the world oil market and the world economy, as well as by their own political concerns.

OIL POLICY IN THE OPEC COUNTRIES

Of course, the OPEC countries vary in their concerns, their assessments of the factors that affect pricing and production policy, and the importance of these factors to them. They also are widely different in terms of petroleum reserves, wealth, population, and the ability of their economies to absorb additional revenue (see table 10–1).

Basically, the OPEC countries can be categorized according to their revenue needs. At one extreme are the "rich" OPEC countries, or "low absorbers": Saudi Arabia, Kuwait, the United Arab Emirates, Qatar, and Libya—countries with small populations, high per capita GNPs, and high reserves-to-production ratios. Since their oil revenues greatly exceed their internal capacity to absorb funds, these countries have the least interest in expanding production and generally bear the burden of production cutbacks in periods of slack demand.

In contrast, the "high absorbers"—Indonesia and Nigeria—are characterized by large populations and small per capita GNPs. Since these two countries are badly in need of additional revenue, they have an interest in maximizing production and are unlikely to voluntarily restrict it. While somewhat better off economically, Algeria, Gabon, and Ecuador also tend to be badly in need of additional revenue. In fact, throughout the 1970–78 period Indonesia, Algeria, Gabon, and Ecuador ran balance-of-payments deficits, and Nigeria was in deficit for most of those years.[1] Between this group and the "rich" OPEC members are Iran, Iraq, and Venezuela—OPEC countries of moderate wealth. Since these three countries have moderate-size populations and substantial oil revenues, they, of all the OPEC countries, probably have the greatest possibilities of industrializing.

While the eight "non-rich" OPEC countries generally seek to boost production, they are constrained by their limited oil reserves. In fact, since they will have substantial financial needs in the future and their resources are limited, they are often inclined to conserve them despite their immediate revenue needs. In contrast, the reserves of the "low absorbers" are large enough to enable them to greatly expand production, but because they have limited immediate revenue needs, they have generally chosen not to do so. Indeed, the fact that the countries with limited revenue needs have the greatest capability of expanding production stabilizes the high oil price, for when demand slackens, these countries can accept the bulk of production cutbacks, often enabling the other exporters to continue to produce at or near capacity. However, there is a point at which even these "low absorbers" are not willing to cut their production further, and when that point is reached the OPEC price is in jeopardy.

These "low absorbers" account for less than 5 percent of the OPEC countries' population, but so long as they are able to expand and contract production, they are the dominant powers within OPEC. More than any other factor, the sum of their individual decisions to increase or decrease production determines the world oil price. Moreover, these countries could exercise this power even if OPEC did not exist, but when the market tightens and the "low absorbers" lose their spare capacity, the other exporting countries are free to charge as much as the market will bear.

Saudi Arabia. Towering over the others is the power of one country, Saudi Arabia, the largest producer in OPEC and the largest exporter in the world. Its proven reserves are at least twice as large as those of any other country,[2] and it has substantial prospects of finding new reserves. In the 1970s the consuming countries increasingly looked to Saudi Arabia to become the residual supplier that would expand production as needed in the 1980s to fill the gap created by a world oil demand that was expected to grow more rapidly than non-Saudi oil supplies.

Saudi Arabia also generally has more spare capacity than any other OPEC country, enabling it to expand production sharply, but because of its huge currency reserves and limited revenue needs, Saudi Arabia can also reduce production. Even before the 1979 oil-price increases, many Saudis insisted that it would be in their economic interest to cut back to 5 mb/d.[3] Consequently, Saudi Arabia has a far greater range of production levels than any other country. If it chooses to

TABLE 10–1. OPEC COUNTRIES' CHARACTERISTICS IN 1976–77

	Oil Reserves*		Productive Capacity[†]	
	Total	% OPEC	Total	% OPEC
Saudi Arabia	170	37	10.0	27
Kuwait	70	15	3.5	9
U.A.E.	31	7	2.4	7
Qatar	6	1	.7	2
Libya	26	6	2.5	7
Iran	63	14	6.7	18
Iraq	35	8	3.0	8
Venezuela	14	3	2.6	7
Algeria	7	2	1.0	3
Gabon	2	<1	.3	<1
Ecuador	2	<1	.2	<1
Nigeria	20	4	2.3	6
Indonesia	14	3	1.7	5

*Billion barrels.
[†]Mb/d.
[‡]U.S. dollars.

Figures on oil reserves, productive capacity, and 1976 production from Comptroller General of the U.S., *More Attention Should Be Paid to Making the U.S. Less Vulnerable to Foreign Oil Price and Supply Decisions* (Washington, D.C.: General Accounting Office, 1978), p. 82, with the figure on Saudi Arabia's productive capacity adjusted as described below. Figures on population and per capita GNP from CIA, *Handbook of Economic Statistics, 1977*, p. 20, and *PE* (Oct. 1979), p. 427. The reserves-to-production ratio was computed by author. Figures on reserves and productive capacity are as of Apr. 1977. Figures on productive capacity must be interpreted with skepticism. Published capacity figures are estimates of production sustainable for 90 days and may overstate the rates that could be sustained over longer periods. Even for a 90-day period, most nations cannot produce at capacity because of technical considerations: equipment delays, transportation bottlenecks, etc. In practice, most nations require a small margin of "spare capacity." In addition, countries often do not have accurate estimates of their capacity. For example, in Nov. 1976 Saudi Arabia believed Aramco's capacity was 11.2 mb/d on a sustained basis, yet subsequent experience revealed it was no more than 10 mb/d (U.S. Senate, Committee on Foreign Relations, Subcommittee on International Economic Policy, *The Future of Saudi Arabian Oil Production* [Washington, D.C.: Government Printing Office, 1979], p. 13). Even when this is not a problem, countries often have an interest in misrepresenting their capacity figures in order to gain political leverage. For example, the more spare capacity Saudi Arabia can persuade others to believe it has, the greater its power in OPEC and the more it has to offer the consuming countries in terms of increased production. Not surprisingly, then, estimates of a nation's productive capacity vary with the organization that makes the estimate.

maximize production, it can bring the world oil price down; alternatively, if it chooses to cut back sharply, prices will skyrocket and the consuming countries may face serious shortages. In either case, Saudi Arabia's total revenues might rise. In the first case, it sells more oil; in the second, it earns more from each barrel it produces. But the consequences of Saudi Arabia's decision for other countries would not be nearly so inconsiderable. As Yamani once boasted, "To

1976 Production[†]		Reserves/Production	1976 Per Capita	1976 Population
Total	% OPEC	Ratio	GNP[‡]	(Millions)
8.5	28	20.0	8,430	5.8
2.2	7	31.8	13,960	1.0
1.9	6	16.3	9,570	.7
.5	2	12.0	26,580	.2
2.0	7	13.0	5,380	2.6
5.9	17	10.7	2,060	33.4
2.1	7	16 7	1,390	11.5
2.3	8	6.1	2,600	12.4
1.0	3	7.0	880	17.3
.2	<1	10.0	3,400	.5
.2	<1	10.0	680	7.3
2.1	7	9.5	470	64.7
1.5	5	9.3	250	134.3

ruin the other countries of the OPEC, all we have to do is produce to our full capacity; to ruin the consumer countries, we only have to reduce our production."[4] And the Saudis have used this power. In April 1977, when Saudi Arabia was trying to force prices down, its production went to 10.2 mb/d, but in August 1978, when a glut of oil threatened the OPEC price level, Saudi Arabia cut its production to 7.15 mb/d.[5]

Saudi Arabia is clearly the most powerful member of OPEC, able to significantly affect the world oil price on its own, but Yamani's claim is an exaggeration. Saudi Arabia cannot single-handedly make or break the cartel. While Saudi Arabia's spare capacity is large, its significance could be offset by cutbacks in the other OPEC countries. If Saudi Arabia cuts back production, other countries can usually increase production. Still, to understand world oil pricing, the place to begin is Saudi Arabia.

What determines Saudi oil policy? First, Saudi Arabia, like all OPEC members, has a strong interest in maintaining the power the oil-exporting countries have achieved. While it has generally advocated prices below those favored by the other OPEC members, it has no desire to see prices fall back to the levels that prevailed before October 1973. Consequently, the Saudis have no intention of flooding the market with oil and, in fact, recognize that it is generally in their interest to limit production in order to keep prices up. In addition, the Saudis want to keep OPEC together, and for this reason (all other things being equal) they would like to see all OPEC members maintain a common price, with adjustments only for differences in crude quality and location.

As a country with substantial oil resources, discovered and undiscovered, Saudi Arabia is far less concerned about the immediate prospects of becoming an "oil-less" country than most other OPEC members. In fact, the argument has frequently been made that the Saudis are afraid that if the price of oil goes too high, it will encourage the consuming countries to shift to alternative sources, leaving the Saudis with unsellable oil some twenty years or so from now. This is a difficult claim to evaluate; to do so, one would have to know when these alternative sources will be developed, what they will cost, how much they will contribute to world energy supplies, what world demand for energy will be, and how large Saudi Arabia's ultimately recoverable reserves of oil actually are. Since each of these variables can only be guessed at, there is no way of definitively resolving the issue.

But few people in Saudi Arabia take the claim seriously. The Saudis have long held that they can continue to sell their oil far into the future, if not as energy, then as a feedstock for petrochemicals. Since 1974 this view has been reinforced, as the Saudis have seen the consuming countries' lack of success in formulating comprehensive energy plans and developing alternative energy sources. Consequently, rather than believe that oil prices would fall, after 1974 the Saudis maintained that real oil prices were destined to rise further, probably in the early 1980s, when they expected the growth in world energy demand to outpace the growth in world energy supplies.[6]

One might argue that, economically, it is in the Saudi interest to sell as much oil as possible today, for the long-term value of that oil to the Saudis is equal to the sum of what they obtain directly from its sale and what they get from investing the proceeds. But again, the Saudis are not convinced that the benefits they would derive from this are greater than those they would obtain from simply leaving the oil in the ground to appreciate in value. Their investments in the West have been plagued by inflation-related and exchange-rate losses, the result being that, since 1973, the Saudis have earned a negative real return on their foreign investments.[7] These investments have also provoked a backlash in the consuming countries, leading the Saudis to fear confiscation. Their longer-term investments have necessitated a loss of liquidity, and a number of governments place restrictions on Arab investments in their countries. Also, by deferring oil production, Saudi Arabia can wait until it has the capacity to absorb more of its oil revenues in domestic investments. Consequently, the Saudis have increasingly come to prefer oil in the ground to money in the bank.[8]

While not afraid of being oil-less any time soon, the Saudis are very much concerned about how long they will be able to sustain a given level of production, and this concern has intensified in recent years as the Saudis have seen their grandiose development plans fail to materialize. It is one thing to become oil-less if one has other sources of wealth and productivity, but quite another if oil is all one has; and, of course, the lower the level of production, the longer it can be sustained. Moreover, if Saudi Arabia cuts back on its production, it is likely that prices will rise, possibly enough to enable Saudi Arabia to derive as much revenue at the lower production level as at the higher level.

These considerations help to dispel another argument frequently put forth as an explanation for Saudi oil policy. According to this view, since Saudi Arabia bears the burden of OPEC production cutbacks, it has an interest in lower oil prices that the other OPEC members lack. As the following hypothetical example shows, if one assumes that a 50 percent increase in price leads to a 10 percent reduction in demand for OPEC oil, and that the entire production decline is borne by Saudi Arabia, then Saudi Arabia's total revenues would decline as a result of a price increase that the other OPEC members would benefit from. (see table 10–2).

As an explanation for Saudi behavior, this argument fails to stand up under scrutiny. It is extremely unlikely that Saudi Arabia would have to accept the entire cutback in OPEC output. It certainly did not do this during the slump in demand from 1974 to 1976. Moreover, implicit in the idea that Saudi Arabia accepts the entire production cutback is an oversimplified notion of how OPEC operates. This view places Saudi Arabia, and Saudi Arabia alone, in the role of "swing supplier," adjusting its production to the level of demand. In reality, the workings of the cartel are more complex, with the oil companies allocating production cutbacks among the various OPEC nations.

In addition, the 20 percent price elasticity in the foregoing example is probably high by at least a factor of two, and even in the unlikely event that a price increase would lead to a decline in Saudi revenues, it is doubtful that the Saudis would object to this, so long as their total revenues remained greater than their current expenditures. So long as they believe that real oil prices are going to rise, they would value the oil conserved more highly than the immediate revenue forgone.

If all these considerations point toward lower Saudi production levels and higher prices, why has Saudi Arabia consistently argued for lower OPEC prices and generally been willing to raise its production level? Like all OPEC members, Saudi Arabia needs oil revenues sufficient to cover its expenditures.[9] In 1974 it hardly seemed that this would become a problem, but between 1974 and 1978 real oil prices declined and Saudi expenditures increased. Consequently, in both 1977 and 1978 Saudi Arabia ran a budget deficit, and to meet their budget needs, the Saudis drew on their reserve assets.[10]

TABLE 10–2. HYPOTHETICAL EXAMPLE: EFFECT OF 50% PRICE INCREASE ON SAUDI ARABIAN REVENUES

	Before Price Increase			After Price Increase		
	Production	Price	Total Revenues*	Production	Price	Total Revenues*
Saudi Arabia	8.5 mb/d	$12.70	107.95	5.5 mb/d	$19.05	104.775
Other OPEC Countries	21.5	$12.70	273.05	21.5	$19.05	409.575
Total	30.0 mb/d	$12.70	381.00	27.0 mb/d	$19.05	514.350

*Millions U.S. dollars per day.

However, there are limits to this process. Not all reserves are in readily liquidable form, and the Saudis have been reluctant to draw upon them to pay for current expenditures. For example, early in 1978 a surplus emerged on the world oil market, forcing Saudi Arabia to cut back its production from 9.1 mb/d in the second half of 1977 to 7.6 mb/d in the first half of 1978. As a result, Saudi Arabia was confronted with a "cash squeeze" that resulted in a 30 percent cut in its government budget. Yet to fully absorb the world oil surplus, Saudi Arabia would have had to go down to a production level of 6 mb/d, something the kingdom apparently was not willing to do. As it was, from June through August 1978 Saudi Arabia ran a current-account deficit, a situation that was rectified in September when demand for oil increased, allowing Saudi Arabia to boost production.[11]

Of course, rather than raise more revenue by boosting production, Saudi Arabia could decide to reduce its spending, and many people in Saudi Arabia favor this course. They argue that much of the government's massive spending has been wasteful, inflationary, and that it disrupts the traditional patterns of Saudi life, which they would like to preserve.

Fortunately for the consuming countries, since 1974 those opposed to industrialization have not been able to determine Saudi policy; but as a result of the Iranian revolution and the disappointing results of the Saudi development program, this position is gaining support. If it becomes the dominant position within Saudi Arabia, the kingdom will be much less likely to be willing to maintain high oil production levels. If this happens, Western companies and consuming-country governments will be partly responsible, for to help solve the recycling problem they encouraged the Saudis to make massive expenditures at inflated prices, which has led to widespread disillusionment within Saudi Arabia.

As important in shaping Saudi oil policy as its revenue needs is Saudi Arabia's interest in the economic and political stability of the capitalist world. "From each according to his ability, to each according to his needs" is not a slogan likely to be raised by Saudi Arabia or any of the other oil-rich sheikdoms. As a holder of vast wealth—most of it in investments in the advanced capitalist countries—Saudi Arabia has a direct interest in the health of the world economy. If the dollar declines in value, if inflation in the consuming countries increases, or if the capitalist countries are plagued by recession, the real value of Saudi Arabia's assets declines.

The Saudis also understand that a serious long-term recession/depression in the consuming countries would nullify their predictions of a rising real oil price, and probably destroy OPEC as well. In addition, as fervent anti-Communists the Saudis are concerned about the danger that economic instability in the advanced capitalist countries will lead to political instability. Consequently, while other OPEC members can set oil prices simply to maximize their revenues, Saudi Arabia is forced by its position in the world economy to consider the overall effects of high oil prices on the capitalist world.

Other factors that are frequently cited in explaining Saudi Arabia's price restraint include the kingdom's (1) need for Western aid in its industrialization program, (2) desire to maintain good relations with the Third World, and (3) dependence upon the consuming countries, and particularly the United States, for its political and military security. Of these factors, only the last has much effect on Saudi Arabia's oil pricing policy, and even its role is generally quite limited.

The companies that aid the Saudi industrialization program are not doing this as a favor to Saudi Arabia. Rather, it is very much in their interest that they do it, and it is in the interest of their home governments, since it eases the petrodollar recycling problem. Moreover, by raising prices Saudi Arabia could buy more of this assistance—far more than it would get from the good will shown to it by companies appreciative of its actions in keeping prices down. Nor has Saudi Arabia's solicitude for the Third World ever led it to be especially generous on the issue of oil pricing.

The Saudi regime's dependence upon the United States for its political and military security is a more significant factor, but it is increasingly unlikely that the United States would withdraw that support because of a dispute over small changes in oil prices—the difference between, say, a price freeze and a 10 percent increase. The consuming countries' dependence upon Saudi oil is too great and the alternatives to the existing Saudi regime too threatening (from the West's perspective) for the United States to adopt any other course. Still, on a particular issue—say the sale of U.S. armaments to the Saudis—the position that Saudi Arabia adopts on oil pricing and production can be decisive. Moreover, if the Saudi regime were to stray too far from policies advocated by the United States, Washington might well begin looking for a more pro-Western Saudi leadership. In the current political context, that is a highly risky course to pursue, and as a result, the Saudi regime has considerable leeway. In addition, the Saudi regime must weigh the benefits of improved relations with the United States against the hostility that is likely to be aroused in the Arab world from appearing too conciliatory toward U.S. interests.

The other important factor that affects Saudi oil policy is the Arab-Israeli conflict. The Nixon, Ford, and Carter administrations have all denied "linkage" between this conflict and the price of oil. As Kissinger stated, "I don't believe it is wise for us to try to sell the Israeli concessions for a reduction in oil prices, because this would create the basis for pressures in the opposite direction during a stalemate. Everytime [sic] the OPEC countries want something from us politically, they could threaten to raise the prices again."[12] Nonetheless, since 1973 there has been an implicit link between the price of oil and the Arab-Israeli conflict. Indeed, at the same time that he publicly disavowed any linkage between the Arab-Israeli conflict and the price of oil, Kissinger insisted in private that the behind-the-scenes influence and money of the Saudis were decisive in keeping Sadat interested in negotiations and in persuading Assad to go through with the disengagement agreement in May 1974.[13] As a U.S. government official stated, "No administration will ever say: 'Yes, if oil prices are low we will push the Israelis.' But it will be on everyone's mind anyway."[14]

Saudi Arabia greatly desires resolution of the Arab-Israeli conflict, not so much because of its concern for the Palestinians but because of the stabilizing effect a settlement would have on the Middle East and on the security of the Saudi regime itself. Indeed, this would be worth several dollars on the barrel to the Saudis. However, this is not to say that if a settlement were reached, the Saudis would reward the West by maximizing production and bringing prices down as much as they could. Unless a deal had been made in advance, in the event of a settlement there would be no need for the Saudis to do this, because their goal would already have been achieved.

What the Saudis have done, and will do, is use concessions on oil pricing and oil production to cajole the United States into putting greater pressure on Israel to make the concessions necessary for a settlement to be possible. Alternatively, if the United States fails to be responsive to the Saudis' Mideast concerns, the Saudis will use the oil weapon to put pressure on the consuming countries. In the event of another Arab-Israeli war, the Saudis would probably impose production cutbacks and embargo the United States, as they did in 1973, and with their enormous currency reserves, they would be able to sustain such an action for quite some time. In this situation their political motives would override whatever interest they might normally have in higher production levels. Nor could they easily avoid such action: if they failed to act, others in the Arab world would probably stop the flow of oil by blowing up oil fields or blocking tanker routes.

Even in the absence of such a war, the Saudis may cut back production and raise prices in an effort to get the United States to put pressure on Israel—and the Saudis might not have much choice about this either, for if the Arab countries fail to make progress toward resolution of the Arab-Israeli conflict, the resentments in the Arab world could well turn inward, against the conservative Arab regimes that have failed to secure a settlement.

Other political factors also influence Saudi production and pricing policy. Until 1978 the Saudis feared that the more prices went up, the stronger Iran was likely to become, enabling the Shah to dominate the Gulf. In 1979, rather than face the political consequences of appearing hostile to the new Iranian regime, following the Iranian revolution, Saudi Arabia cut back production to accommodate resumption of Iranian production.

These concerns—interest in the health of the world economy, desire to conserve resources, and sensitivity to political developments—are evident in the evolution of Saudi oil policy. As we have seen, the Saudis opposed the large rise in oil prices that was announced in December 1973 and they sought to get the price down. When they were unable to do this, they held out (more successfully) for a series of price freezes. Their concern about the effects of high oil prices on the world economy led the Saudis to seek to hold prices down. At the same time, to boost their revenues and conserve their resources, they favored gradual and steady price increases.

Since 1974 Saudi Arabia has maintained an official ceiling on production, generally 8.5 mb/d; however, until 1979 the ceiling had little real effect, since production would have remained below the ceiling in any case.[15] Saudi Arabia made no direct threats to cut back production in this period, but it held out the promise of additional future production as a means of exerting pressure on the United States on such issues as the Arab-Israeli conflict and U.S. arms sales to the Saudis.

On the other hand, Saudi Arabia's concern with conserving its resources led the kingdom to reduce its plans for building additional capacity. In the early 1970s Aramco planned to build capacity as high as 20 mb/d by the early 1980s, but following the 1973–74 rise in oil prices and the slowdown in the demand for oil, this target was reduced to 16 mb/d, which was to be reached by 1983. As late as May 1977, Aramco Chairman Frank Jungers said that Saudi Arabia was "headed for 16 million barrels a day of capacity by 1982." However, Jungers spoke without the authorization of the Saudi government. At the end of 1977 Saudi Arabia lowered the target to 14 mb/d of facility capacity, or 12 mb/d of sustainable capacity,[16] and they did not plan to attain this level until after 1986. By 1983 their maximum sustainable capacity was expected to be only 10.8 mb/d, compared with about 10 mb/d at the time the decision was made.[17]

There appear to have been several motives for the 1977 Saudi decision. At the time it was made, demand was weak and the Saudis questioned whether a capacity higher than 12 mb/d would be needed in the foreseeable future. The Saudis were also concerned about the cost of installing additional capacity, particularly since it might be used for only a few years.[18] In addition, by holding down their rate of production, the Saudis could maximize the amount of oil they would ultimately recover and extend the period during which their peak production rate could be maintained. This concern became especially important in 1977, when it was discovered that the Saudi oil fields had been seriously damaged by salt-water corrosion in the pumps and pipelines and by chronic drops in oil field reservoir pressure.[19] The Saudis recognized that in holding down their spare capacity, they would reduce their power within OPEC, but in 1977 this concern appears to have been more than counterbalanced by their fear that if they added the capacity, the consuming countries would pressure them into using it.

Following the Iranian revolution and the 1979–80 decline in Saudi influence within OPEC, the Saudis reversed course and sought to rapidly boost their capacity. But as a result of the 1977 decision to slow the expansion of capacity, the Saudis' ability to make up for the loss of Iranian production in 1979 was limited. A second consequence is that it will be several years before Saudi Arabia can boost its capacity significantly. In the spring of 1979 a report by the Senate Subcommittee on International Economic Policy estimated that by drilling more wells (in any year) from 1980 to 1983, Saudi Arabia will be able to add a one-time-only increase in sustainable capacity of from 0.8 to 1 mb/d. The report concluded that increases beyond this amount would require additional equipment that would take two to four years to install, after the decision was made.[20]

For the next few years, therefore, Saudi Arabia will have only limited ability to expand production beyond a level of about 10 mb/d. If the market remains soft, this may be more capacity than the kingdom can use. But if, on the other hand, demand picks up and a major loss of supplies occurs in another exporting country, Saudi Arabia is likely to find that it lacks the capacity to prevent serious shortages from occurring in the consuming countries or to keep prices from taking off again.

Other OPEC Countries. After Saudi Arabia, Kuwait is the OPEC country with the largest reserves; but in contrast to Saudi Arabia, Kuwait has a much smaller population—about a million people—and consequently much smaller revenue needs. While Saudi Arabia is attempting to industrialize, Kuwait has been far more wary of the social consequences of industrialization. Because the average Kuwaiti citizen is highly privileged, most of the work in Kuwait is done by non-Kuwaitis; consequently, as Kuwait has developed, non-Kuwaitis have poured into the country. Already, less than half of the roughly one million people who live in Kuwait are Kuwaiti citizens, and perhaps a quarter are Palestinians,[21] and Kuwaiti citizens feel threatened by this trend. They recognize that further industrialization will mean an influx of even more foreigners and will require the Kuwaiti treasury to increase its expenditures on services and infrastructure to accommodate these foreigners, and the cost of this may outweigh the benefits of the industrial projects. Consequently, rather than a full-blown industrial country, Kuwait has opted to become a lightly industrialized, rentier society. This policy has reduced Kuwait's immediate revenue needs and encouraged the country to stretch out its life as an oil producer. Also, in contrast to Saudi Arabia, Kuwait has little prospect of finding additional oil reserves.[22]

Kuwait has been far more successful than Saudi Arabia in investing its surplus oil revenues, consistently earning a positive real rate of return.[23] This has made Kuwait's choice between money in the bank and oil in the ground more difficult. In practice, the sheikdom appears to be hedging its bets—producing more oil than it needs to meet its revenue requirements, but far less than it might. From July 1975 until April 1980, Kuwait's production ceiling had been only 2 mb/d, whereas its estimated potential is between 5 and 6 mb/d. However, since 1972 investment in petroleum development in Kuwait has been negligible, as the government has chosen to allow the nation's capacity to gradually decline.[24] Indeed Kuwait, which wants to remain an oil exporter as long as possible, has the highest reserves-to-production ratio of all the OPEC countries.

Still, if it wanted to, the Kuwaiti government could probably boost its sustainable productive capacity from 2.5 mb/d to 3 mb/d within a year,[25] but like the Saudis, the Kuwaitis recognize that it is in their interest to limit production in order to keep prices up. Kuwait's oil policy is also influenced by its fear of offending the Palestinians who live in the country, which leads Kuwait to take a harder line on pricing and a more militant stance in general. Also, in contrast to the Saudis, the Kuwaitis have shown less concern about the Arab-Israeli conflict or the effects of their oil policy on the stability of the world economy.[26]

Saudi Arabia's production level is extremely flexible whereas Kuwait's is comparatively rigid. Since Kuwait produces a relatively heavy crude, for which there is only limited demand, it generally cannot produce much more than 2 mb/d without eroding the price of this crude. On the other hand, since it needs nearly all of the associated gas produced at its ceiling level of oil production (now 1.5 mb/d) to fuel its internal economy, it cannot easily reduce its production much below this level. Indeed, Kuwait has protested vigorously whenever its production has fallen significantly below its policy-stipulated level.[27] This rigidity also reduces Kuwait's power in OPEC and in international politics, for with its production level relatively fixed, it cannot exert much leverage. In fact, given its natural gas requirements, it is questionable whether Kuwait could significantly reduce production in the event of another Arab-Israeli war. And since hardly any of its oil goes to the United States, an embargo by Kuwait would not have much effect.

The fact that Kuwait is much smaller than Saudi Arabia in terms of population and oil production makes it almost inevitable that it would play a lesser role in both inter-Arab and world politics—positions which these other factors tend to reinforce. Conceivably, this could change, if Kuwait showed interest in boosting its productive capacity toward its potential, but so far it has not. Within OPEC, Kuwait has often assumed the role of a moderate, trying to work out a compromise between price hawks and doves.

Like Kuwait, Qatar and the United Arab Emirates[28] have tiny populations and both maintain ceilings that keep their oil production well below its potential capacity. Also like Kuwait, Qatar and the U.A.E. are concerned whether the "costs" associated with an influx of foreigners, needed for industrialization, are worth the benefits.

The U.A.E. has enormous oil reserves and could probably boost its production substantially, if it had any economic interest in doing so. In the past, it has exhorted the companies to increase their exploration and development efforts; however, the fact that it has maintained strict limits on the companies' production levels, frequently forcing them to cut back, has been a deterrent to further development of its resources. In recent years it has limited production to 80 percent of capacity. Nonetheless, like all OPEC countries, the Emirates are concerned about meeting their current revenue needs. Consequently, in 1975, when production fell below 1 mb/d, Abu Dhabi discounted its prices in order to boost sales.[29]

Qatar, on the other hand, has only limited reserves and limited prospects of discoveries, making it likely that this sheikdom will become the first of the "rich" OPEC countries to become "oil-less." To delay this, Qatar has maintained strict limits on production, keeping it fairly static during the past several years. Like Kuwait and the Emirates, Qatar has only limited prospects of industrializing and is concerned about the impact on its society of an influx of additional foreigners. Nor has Qatar been as successful as Kuwait in investing its surplus revenues. Consequently, although Qatar could probably boost its capacity from 650,000 b/d to 1 mb/d within a year it is unlikely to do so. In any case, its current and its potential production are too small to enable it to play much of a role in OPEC.[30]

Like Kuwait, Libya has maintained a production ceiling of 2 mb/d and, again like Kuwait, has protested vigorously whenever its production falls significantly below this level, discounting its oil to get sales back up.[31] But there the similarity between Libya and the other "rich" OPEC countries ends. While Libya has substantial potential for expanding its reserve base and boosting its capacity, it is unlikely to be an oil producer nearly as long as Saudi Arabia, Kuwait, or the U.A.E. In addition, having had a far smaller balance-of-payments surplus since 1973 than either Kuwait or Saudi Arabia, Libya has far fewer investments in the developed countries, and since its revolution in 1969, Libya has been ideologically hostile to the West.

All of these factors make Libya far less concerned than the other "rich" OPEC countries about the possible negative effects its actions with regard to oil will have on the capitalist world economy. Consequently, unlike the other "rich" OPEC countries, Libya, which is not as "rich," has generally aligned itself with the price hawks in OPEC.

Until the middle of 1977, the OPEC countries that took the lead in opposing Saudi Arabia's call for price moderation were Algeria, Iran, and Iraq. While Saudi Arabia correctly saw itself as ensconsed in the capitalist world economy, Algeria advocated transformation of that economy. In contrast to Saudi Arabia, Algeria's oil production is far smaller, and because of its limited resource base it will have a much shorter future as an oil producer. Nor can it afford to defer its oil production until prices rise.

Consequently, Algeria has wanted higher oil prices *today*, regardless of the consequences on the economies of the advanced countries. It has also advocated indexing oil prices to the increase in the cost of OPEC imports, and it has been willing to link oil prices to the price of Third World commodity exports, partly because, as a small oil exporter, it has not had much to lose by pursuing this strategy. Probably the main reason why Algeria sought higher oil prices from 1974 to 1978 was that it needed such prices to make development of its enormous natural gas resources economically viable. Since the cost of liquefying and transporting natural gas, so that it could be sold in the United States and Western Europe, was extremely high and very capital intensive, this would become feasible on a large scale only if the gas were to compete with high-price oil.[32]

Like Algeria, Iran has extensive reserves of natural gas and a relatively short future as an oil exporter. Even before the Iranian revolution, Iran's production was expected to peak in the late 1970s at about 7 mb/d.[33] Yet none of these factors has been as important in the determination of Iran's oil policy as in Algeria's, for Iran's future as an oil exporter is not as limited as Algeria's. The Shah took advantage of the fact that Iran adjoins the Soviet Union and worked out an agreement whereby its gas would be sent via pipeline to the Soviet Union, which would then export its own gas to Western Europe—a much cheaper arrangement than liquefaction.

Nor did prerevolutionary Iran share Algeria's hostility toward the West. Iran's demand for higher prices was rooted in the huge, immediate revenue needs it had as a result of the Shah's grandiose plans for economic and military development. Consequently, Iran advocated indexing the price of oil to the cost of major industrial products and important raw materials. The Shah also argued that the price of a barrel of oil should correspond to the cost of obtaining the same amount of energy from an alternative source.

In contrast to the other price hawks, Iran and Algeria, Iraq had a much higher reserves-to-production ratio and substantial prospects for expanding its reserve base. In fact, a British estimate puts Iraq's potential reserves at 95 billion barrels.[34] Consequently, prior to the Iranian revolution Iraq was the only OPEC country with high immediate revenue needs that also had substantial prospects of boosting production. Its policy has been to allow its oil production to vary according to what was necessary to cover the government's revenue needs. In the early 1970s, when prices were low, that meant seeking to expand production rapidly; then in 1974–75 when demand slumped, Iraq cut its prices in order to boost sales. Then, toward the end of the 1970s, Iraq adopted a more "conservationist" stance. In the early 1970s Iraqi officials spoke of capacity goals as high as 6 mb/d, but Iraq's recent plans call for only 4 mb/d by the mid-1980s.[35]

As a supporter of planning, Iraq has opposed allowing the market to determine the level of OPEC production, the price charged for OPEC oil, or the distribution of production shares among the OPEC countries. Within OPEC, consequently, despite its own price cutting, Iraq has advocated a prorationing scheme, based on a country's need for revenue and designed to keep prices rising even in periods of slack demand. However, as a result of its relative isolation and its differences with other OPEC countries (its territorial demands on Iran and Kuwait and its public attacks on Saudi Arabia), Iraq, until recently, has not had much influence in OPEC. Lacking extensive investments in the capitalist countries and (until recently) politically aligned with the Soviet Union, Iraq regards Saudi oil-pricing policy as subservient to the United States. Saudi Arabia, for its part, resents the fact that while Iraq calls for higher prices within OPEC, it discounts prices on its own. In response to Saudi attacks, Iraq has denied that it cut prices, but argued that it had a right to do so, especially since the other OPEC countries did worse in granting discounts to the international oil companies that had equity in their producing operations.[36]

Like Iraq, Venezuela has long supported proposals for production prorationing in OPEC in order to boost its per barrel revenues while conserving its resources. The main problem confronting Venezuela as an oil producer has been the decline in its production, from 3.76 mb/d in 1970 to 2.24 mb/d in 1978,[37] and to conserve its resources, the Venezuelan government has imposed a production ceiling of 2.3 mb/d. Since its nationalization of the oil industry in 1976, the Venezuelan government has also attempted to boost the country's proven reserves. Within OPEC, Venezuela has generally aligned itself with the OPEC price hawks, though it frequently finds itself in a mediating role between hawks and doves. Venezuela has also supported Iran's demand that oil be priced at the cost of alternative energy sources.[38]

With its large population and small per capita income, Nigeria badly needs additional revenue, but because its proven reserves are small, the Nigerian government has expressed interest in limiting production. In addition, since its oil revenues went up so suddenly, in 1974–75 the country had trouble utilizing its new wealth.

In 1975 Nigeria ordered 16 million tons of cement, to be delivered within a year, but this was almost four times as much as could be unloaded in Nigerian ports. As a result, by the middle of 1975 more than 260 ships, carrying cement, lay offshore awaiting berths. The situation got so bad that, in the end, the Nigerians refused to pay for either the cement or the ships' waiting time.[39] This episode showed that when revenues rise suddenly, as they did in 1974 and again in 1979, even the OPEC countries most badly in need of additional revenue can encounter bottlenecks and other problems, which prevents them from absorbing all their new wealth. At such points, it appears attractive to defer production until one's infrastructure is better developed and one's reliance upon imports is reduced.

Still, Nigeria has substantial prospects for discovering additional reserves and the government has been anxious to pursue them. However, since its oil fields are small, with short productive lives, it tends to be expensive to maintain, let alone expand productive capacity. Consequently, with world demand lagging from 1974 through 1978, the companies were reluctant to expand capacity in Nigeria, and the effect was to reduce both Nigeria's ability to expand production and the government's commitment to do so.

Nigeria has not played a very active role within OPEC, partly because it is not a major exporter but also because its population is split between Christians and Moslems. It has therefore been reluctant to align itself with the Arab OPEC states.[40]

Indonesia is OPEC's most populous country. Like Nigeria, it is badly in need of additional oil revenues, and has substantial prospects for expanding production, but its oil fields also tend to be small, making it expensive to find and develop reserves. In addition, Indonesia has wasted much of its oil revenues on showy, uneconomical industrial projects, nonessential imports, and mismanagement and corruption in state agencies. (The most extreme case involved Pertamina, the government petroleum monopoly, which ran up a $10 billion foreign debt in 1975.)[41] Isolated from the Middle East countries, Indonesia has played only a minor role in OPEC, frequently deviating from OPEC decisions while benefiting from the OPEC price increases.

OPEC's newest members, Ecuador and Gabon, are minor producers. Both became associate members late in 1973, with Ecuador becoming a full member in 1974 and Gabon in 1975. Ecuador's production peaked at 200,000 b/d in 1973; Gabon's at 225,000 b/d in 1975 and 1976.[42] Both countries would like to boost production, but this remains questionable.

Unlike the other African OPEC members, Gabon does not have light, low-sulfur crude. Along with Gabon's location, this makes for somewhat lower prices, but it insulates Gabon from the boom-and-bust fluctuations in output and the price cutting that characterize other African countries. Ecuador, on the other hand, is the country most vulnerable to competition from Alaskan crude. However, because of their modest levels of production, neither Ecuador nor Gabon is able to exert much influence either within OPEC or in the world oil market.

A Cartel of Nation-States. The foregoing analysis points to the importance of individual decisions by individual OPEC members in shaping the world oil market. Every OPEC member has a level of current revenue needs, which it feels it must meet,[43] but once it attains this level, the incentives for limiting production grow enormously. Moreover, if prices rise rapidly, even the moderate and high absorbers may have difficulty absorbing the additional revenue and find it is in their interest to conserve their resources. As a result, production is restricted and the price level is maintained, not through any elaborate collaborative mechanism but through the actions of individual countries pursuing what they believe to be in their best interest. Indeed, since it is based on the self-interest of individual OPEC members, the high price level is far more secure than if it resulted from a series of agreements based on compromises among the OPEC countries. So long as the exporting countries, with the ability to expand production, have no interest in doing so, the cartel price holds.[44]

Conversely, when countries decide it is in their interest to produce more oil, the price level is jeopardized by the threat of a competitive scramble of countries seeking to expand their market share. Yet the structure of the world oil industry provides many safeguards against this possibility. The countries with the greatest interest in expanding production generally lack the capacity to do so. In addition, as the price goes up, countries can attain the same level of revenue at a lower production level, which gives them an interest in further restrictions on production, which in turn provides additional protection for the newly raised price level. For example, Kuwait would have a hard time surviving on 2 mb/d at a price of $4 a barrel, but at $26 a barrel, it could easily reduce production to 1.5 mb/d.

Moreover, the market for crude tends to be segmented rather than homogeneous, and this gives the exporting countries additional protection against competitive price cutting. Given sufficient time and investment in conversion processes, most crudes can be substituted for one another, but, in the short term, buyers demand particular products, and to make those products refineries require particular crudes. In addition, as a result of locational differences, the crudes from different countries tend to form semiseparate markets. The supply bloc in light crudes—Libya, Algeria, and Nigeria—and the bloc in heavy crudes—Iran, Kuwait, and Saudi Arabia—are particularly important. There is also a "stream" in heavy crudes and fuel oil from Venezuela and the Caribbean to the United States, and another in low-sulfur, light crudes from Indonesia and other Southeast Asia countries to Japan. Altogether, the OPEC countries are involved in about sixteen major crude oil streams.[45]

The crudes in any of these streams are somewhat insulated from the pressure of price cuts in the other streams. For example, a slight decline in the price of Venezuelan heavy crudes is not likely to have an effect on the demand for North African light crudes; consequently, it is not likely to trigger an OPEC-wide competitive price scramble. Similarly, the oil companies with ties to particular exporting countries are not likely to jeopardize those ties by shifting their purchases dramatically in response to small changes in price. In fact, in many instances they are legally committed to obtain their oil from a particular supplier.

Within these limits, it is still the companies as a group that make the decisions about where they purchase their oil; so when demand weakens and production cutbacks must be made, the international oil companies allocate those cutbacks through their decisions about where to purchase their crude supplies. In doing this, the companies greatly ease the exporting countries' burden, for if the OPEC countries had to allocate the cutbacks, tensions would undoubtedly develop and individual countries might choose to break from the group, lowering prices in the process. If Saudi Arabia were to assume the role of "swing supplier," accepting the full burden of the production cutbacks, these problems could be avoided, even without the companies, but Saudi Arabia has generally not been willing to assume this role and, as a result the task has been left to the companies.[46]

The other factor important in maintaining exporting-country solidarity is OPEC's success. Since the members recognize that they have benefited from OPEC's gains, they are generally inclined to go along with group decisions; and no member wants to set off a spiral of price cutting if it can avoid it. In addition, because OPEC has been so successful, the richer OPEC members are now in a position to cut back production and to lend money to the poorer members, enabling them to avoid resorting to competitive price cuts.[47] Finally, because they have the bulk of OPEC's spare capacity, consultation among OPEC's "rich" members can effectively limit production.[48]

Still, if the key decisions that shape the world oil market are made by individual exporting countries, what is the significance of OPEC as an organization? Basically, OPEC is an association of sovereign governments that get together periodically to fix prices. The price agreed to by the OPEC countries, when they agree, is typically less than the price the OPEC economic commission indicates would be justified on the basis of strictly economic factors, for example, the impact of inflation on the cost of OPEC imports, the state of the world oil market, etc.

Moreover, the arrived-at price is generally a compromise between Saudi Arabia and the price hawks, usually Iran, Algeria, Libya, and Iraq. The OPEC countries frequently attempt to work this compromise out before the conference but are often unable to do so. The process of arriving at a price also usually involves a good deal of posturing, with countries "leaking" exaggerated estimates of their "minimum" acceptable demands to the press before OPEC deliberations begin. This is intended not only to influence the final OPEC decision but to win political points with non-OPEC countries. For example, Saudi Arabia might go into an OPEC meeting publicly insisting on a price freeze, not so much because it insists on keeping prices frozen but because it wants the United States to think it does.

OPEC's price-setting function is far more significant when the market is slack than when the market is tight, for, in a slack market, the established price indirectly sets a limit on OPEC's total production, that is, the amount demanded at that price. But when the market is tight and countries are already producing at or near capacity, the OPEC-set price has no effect on production and countries are free to get what they can for their oil. Then, OPEC often ratifies increases that individual OPEC countries have already put into effect.

In periods of rapidly rising prices, the pattern is for prices to go up in the spot markets, then spread to the non-OPEC countries, and then to the individual OPEC members, with the official OPEC price going up only at the end of the process. From the perspective of the conservative exporting countries that sell most of their oil through the international companies, there is a defensive element to this. As market prices rise, the first to benefit are the companies and the exporting countries that sell oil directly. It is only by raising the official price that the conservative exporting countries are able to bring the companies' margins back down and recoup the windfall profits for themselves.[49] However, once the official price goes up, all OPEC members have an interest in keeping it up, since a decline would be unsettling to the organization. In fact, while OPEC countries have frequently cut back production to maintain a price, they have never cut back production with the explicit aim of raising the price.

At its regularly scheduled meetings, OPEC, by unanimous agreement of its thirteen members, sets the price of the "marker" crude—Saudia Arabia's 34 degree Arabian light, by far the largest-volume crude in the world. Countries are then supposed to set the price of their crudes in relation to the price of the marker, adjusting only for differences in quality and location. However, the OPEC countries are frequently unable to agree on a common price for the marker crude, with different countries then applying different increases to the prices of their crudes.

Nor is there agreement within OPEC on the appropriate differentials between crudes. In the past, there was pressure on countries to adjust their crude prices to conform to the way in which the market evaluated their crudes in relation to the marker, since, if they failed to do so, companies could substitute Arabian light for their crude, but since Saudi Arabia placed a ceiling on production of Arabian light at the beginning of 1978, it no longer serves as a genuine substitute for other crudes. This has given countries greater leeway in determining the prices they charge. Iraq generally conforms with the percentage changes in the marker crude but does not generally announce its prices, which irritates some other OPEC members, who claim it enables Iraq to boost its production by giving the companies hidden discounts. Still, in general, market pressures force the Middle East countries to stay fairly close to the marker crude.

In contrast, Venezuela has had greater flexibility in its pricing policies because it sells mainly petroleum products and heavier crudes that tend to follow the price of fuel oil. As a result, whether the marker price changes or not, Venezuela adjusts both its crude and its product prices on a quarterly basis (monthly in the case of fuel oil). Similarly, because the value of their quality and locational advantages shifts with change in the market, the main African producers—Nigeria, Libya, and Algeria—alter their prices every quarter, and Indonesia, insulated by its distance from the Gulf, shifts its prices from time to time as the need arises.

Still, the OPEC-set marker price is something of a reference point. Until 1979, the prices of all the various crudes were generally within $2 a barrel.[50] But the fact remains that the individual governments set their prices, not OPEC.

In periods of slack demand, countries frequently shade prices by altering differentials. This has often been seen as a weakness, but it gives the OPEC structure flexibility, for any OPEC country that is producing below capacity and needs additional revenue can boost its sales by reducing its price through alterations in its differentials. Other OPEC members may protest its actions, but the price cutter has broken no OPEC rules and remains a member of the organization. Nor is its action likely to do any long-term damage to the cartel's structure. In contrast, if the only way a country could raise additional revenue were by taking actions that violate the cartel agreement (as is the case in more formally structured cartels), the cartel would be much more vulnerable to disintegration.

Despite this, the fear that lack of agreement on differentials will lead the exporting countries into a series of competitive price reductions has led the OPEC members to numerous attempts to establish a fixed system of differentials. These efforts date to at least 1975, but very little progress has been made and no solution is in sight. Nor is this surprising. With debate over the price of the marker crude typically taking up most of the OPEC conferences, there is not much time for dealing with the issue of differentials, and the technical problems in working out a valid system of differentials are extremely complex.

Basically, three factors determine a crude's value: its specific gravity, which determines its yield of products; its sulfur content; and its location. Yet the importance of each of these factors is constantly changing. For example, when world demand for gasoline is up, light crudes, which yield proportionally more gasoline, go up in value, but when demand for gasoline falls off, so does the value of light crudes. Similarly, when environmental regulations increase, low-sulfur premiums increase, but once refineries add desulfurization facilities, they go down.

And the value of a favorable location shifts with changes in tanker rates. In addition, there is no way of establishing a freight differential that will equate the value of North African and Persian Gulf crudes in the United States and Western Europe. Changes in economic activity in the consuming countries and development of new oil sources can also affect the value of crudes. For example, when North Sea oil (mainly light crude) came on stream, it reduced the market for the light crudes produced in North Africa and Nigeria.

Even if a valid series of indexes (as Algeria has proposed) could be devised, it is not likely that OPEC would adopt them, for a firm agreement on differentials is implicitly an agreement on market shares and a transfer to OPEC from the sovereign governments of the power to set specific crude prices. It is extremely doubtful that the countries that comprise OPEC would be willing to yield this much power to the organization, and equally doubtful that they could agree on a system of market shares. For similar reasons, the OPEC countries have been unable to agree on a permanent system of production prorationing. The opposition to such a system by Saudi Arabia effectively vetoes it. The Saudis adamantly oppose any system that gives anyone other than the Saudi government any say over Saudi production levels. As Yamani stated in March 1979, "We refuse to talk about levels of production of Saudi Arabia with OPEC member countries. It is not their affair; it is our affair. It was our policy since the early sixties to avoid any production program. Nothing has changed."[51]

In submitting to a permanent system of production prorationing, Saudi Arabia would yield its enormous power in the world oil market by virtue of its ability to shift production up or down. Nor has Kuwait shown much interest in prorationing schemes. While other OPEC countries—especially Iraq, Algeria, Libya, and Venezuela—have favored prorationing, whether they would actually be able to agree on such a system and abide by it, if it were instituted, is questionable. In fact, in 1977–78 the three major African producers—Libya, Algeria, and Nigeria—attempted to develop a miniprorationing scheme of their own, but nothing has come of it.

Unable to control its members' production or prices, OPEC as an organization falls far short of its powerful image in the Western media. Even in the absence of OPEC, most oil-exporting countries would behave much as they do, and the world oil price would in all probability be as high. Nor does it make much difference whether such new oil-exporting countries as Mexico or Great Britain join OPEC. In fact, these countries often charge prices that are even higher than those of OPEC members.

Basically, OPEC provides a forum for members to consult one another. As such, it tends to smooth out price fluctuations, but it does not fundamentally affect the price. It provides expert staff services to member countries, but the absence of a strong secretariat tends to lessen the significance of this role. Yet it was individual OPEC members, not OPEC as an organization, that were responsible for the major gains of the early 1970s. Therefore it is not surprising that it is not to OPEC, but to OPEC members, that power has accrued.

So far, the analysis in this chapter has attempted to demonstrate that what supports high oil prices is that countries with the ability to expand production sharply have not had an interest in reducing prices to do so. Yet this could change dramatically if these countries find that their revenues do not meet their needs. They would then be tempted to boost their total revenues by cutting prices and boosting their market share, which could trigger a competitive wave of price cutting as other exporting countries are forced to match the price cuts in order to protect their market shares.

Three factors could bring about such a situation:
1. An increase in the revenue needs of exporting countries that have the ability to expand production,
2. A decline in world oil demand, and
3. An increase in world energy supplies, especially non-OPEC supplies that cost less than the price of OPEC oil.

Since 1974, however, developments in these areas have been disappointing.

OPEC Countries' Development Efforts. Following the 1973–74 rise in oil prices, most of the major oil-exporting countries announced ambitious new development programs. Not surprisingly, the biggest were announced by the biggest oil exporters, Iran and Saudi Arabia. In January 1974 Iran doubled its five-year development plan, to $70 billion. Similarly, in 1975 Saudi Arabia revealed a $142 billion, five-year plan, aimed at diversifying the economy through agricultural and industrial development. Iraq, Libya, Nigeria, and Venezuela also embarked on far-reaching investment plans. One effect of these plans was to greatly increase the exporting countries' revenue needs, and they were encouraged by Western companies, anxious to find new markets in the exporting countries, and by the consuming-country governments, which saw the plans as greatly easing the recycling problem. As we saw in chapter 9, the growth in OPEC imports was far greater than the consuming countries expected and it made a major contribution to resolving the recycling problem.

The major oil companies found a new role as managers of and contributors to the exporting countries' development programs. The clearest example involves Aramco, which has taken responsibility for managing Saudi Arabia's $15 billion gas utilization project, the largest industrial project in history. It is aimed at using the country's associated gas to diversify into such related industries as petrochemicals and iron ore processing. Yet the conditions under which many of these exporting countries have been attempting to modernize are extremely unfavorable: inhospitable climates and a lack of arable land, water, and other nonenergy resources. They have poor infrastructures, high rates of illiteracy, and shortages of both skilled and unskilled workers. In Saudi Arabia, Kuwait, the United Arab Emirates, and Qatar, much of the native population, which has benefited from enormous oil revenues, has little interest in engaging in hard labor.

Not surprisingly, then, the exporting countries' development programs have been plagued by problems: high inflation, urban congestion, an upsurge in crime, lopsided distribution of wealth, and enormous corruption. Commissions are frequently paid on inflated government contracts to friends and relatives of rulers who serve as agents of foreign companies. These societies have also been disrupted by an influx of foreign workers and erosion of traditions and customs. In Saudi Arabia, this has been particularly upsetting to the country's powerful religious leaders, and in many OPEC countries agricultural and other traditional industries have declined, forcing them to import food. There is also an enormous amount of waste. Port congestion is a continual problem, increasing transportation costs and leading to delays of several months in unloading construction materials and consumer goods. Similarly, roads and telecommunications are generally inadequate.

Nor are these countries getting reasonable value for their money. Projects cost much more than estimated. For example, by 1976 the annual cost of Saudi Arabia's five-year plan, begun a year earlier, had doubled.[52] This systematic underestimation of costs has been due primarily to administrative costs and infrastructure bottlenecks that resulted when a number of projects were started at once. As economist Walter Levy has pointed out, between 1974 and 1978 OPEC countries spent roughly $400 billion on goods and services, but the value of what they got, in terms of what it would cost in the OECD countries, was between $200 billion and $300 billion. Similarly, capital projects in the OPEC countries typically cost two to three times what they cost in the developed countries, and sometimes four to five times as much.[53]

Also, many OPEC countries have tried to take advantage of their oil wealth by building refineries, tanker fleets, and petrochemical plants.[54] While this may seem quite sensible, the problem with it as a development strategy is that since 1974 all of these industries have been plagued by worldwide overcapacity, due largely to the falloff in demand as a result of the rise in oil prices.[55] Consequently, most of these OPEC facilities are not profitable to operate, and are particularly burdensome in OPEC countries that lack a large internal market.[56]

As a result of the problems the exporting countries have experienced in their development programs, opposition to these programs has been growing in many countries. The most dramatic example, of course, is Iran, where the government was overthrown by forces opposed to the development program pursued by the Shah. Yet in Venezuela, the Acción Democrática government led by President Carlos Andres Perez, was voted out of office in December 1978 as a result of popular disapproval over the way it had used the country's oil revenues. Instead of rising living standards, Venezuelans' wage gains were eroded by inflation and they endured food shortages resulting from surging demand; corruption and urban and rural crime were also of growing concern. As dependence upon foreign goods increased, Venezuela ran its largest balance-of-payments deficit in history in 1978, and between 1974 and 1979 Venezuela's external public debt increased from $767 million to $12.2 billion.[57]

In other exporting countries, Saudi Arabia among them, disenchantment with the development programs is spreading to large segments of the population. Dissatisfaction is intensified as the masses observe Arab potentates who impose puritanical standards of behavior at home while pursuing free-wheeling lives abroad. Public dissatisfaction has led the exporting countries to slow the pace of growth, with many projects being canceled and others "stretched out." Overall plans for building a non-oil-industry base are being reassessed.[58] Exporting countries are also backing away from plans to move "downstream" by adding refineries and petrochemical plants.[59]

Yet as growth slows, the exporting countries' revenue needs diminish, and as countries become disillusioned with developing non-oil-based economies, they are increasingly committed to conserving their oil resources. Yet the real danger to the consuming countries is not that the regimes in the exporting countries will reverse course, abandoning their development programs; rather, failure to change course may lead to their downfall, ushering in new regimes much less committed to a development strategy based on massive imports. Indeed, this has already happened in Iran.

CONSUMING-COUNTRY ENERGY POLICIES

Mirroring the failure of the oil-exporting countries to establish viable economic development programs has been the failure of the consuming countries to adopt effective energy policies. Five problems stand out: the rise in U.S. oil imports; the lack of consuming-country cooperation; overemphasis on nuclear power, despite its inability to keep pace with the expectations of energy planners; the corresponding neglect of alternative energy sources; and inadequate effort to find and develop additional sources of oil and natural gas.

Following the 1973–74 rise in oil prices, most consuming countries took steps to limit their consumption of oil. Almost all the OECD countries shifted funds from highway construction to public transport, encouraged greater efficiency in buildings through insulation, etc.[60] The most ambitious effort to reduce oil consumption was made by France, which early in 1974 announced it would hold its imports for the year below their 1973 level. Later in the year, France decided to limit the amount that could be spent on crude oil imports; for 1975 the figure was set at 51 billion francs—what it would cost to keep imports 10 percent below their 1973 level. To reduce consumption, France raised the price of gasoline and other oil products, imposed lower speed limits, mandated various conservation measures (e.g. temperatures had to be set 2 degrees below normal), and loosened credit for energy-saving investments.[61]

In contrast, West Germany has relied almost exclusively on higher prices, allowing all its energy prices to rise to world market levels. Other countries fall in between, relying on a mix of government regulations and higher prices to reduce oil consumption. For example, in 1974 Britain increased taxes on gasoline and imposed a speed limit of 50 miles an hour on most roads, while allowing the price of domestically produced fuels to rise, but not all the way to the OPEC level.[62]

For the first time in the post–World War II period, in 1974–75 the consuming countries succeeded in reducing their demand for oil;[63] however, the impact of the recession, rather than the efforts of consumers to use energy more efficiently, was primarily responsible. In fact, at least three quarters of the decline in oil consumption was associated with reduced economic activity rather than improved efficiency.[64] Once the recovery got under way, oil consumption was back up, though it did not rise as rapidly from 1976 to 1978 as it had in the period preceding the 1973–74 increase in oil prices. Partly as a result of this, in 1978 demand for OPEC exports was 5.4 percent below the 1973 level,[65] a considerable achievement.

If non-Communist demand for oil had continued to increase at its pre-1974 rate of 7.3 percent per annum, demand for OPEC exports in 1978 would have been 50 percent above its 1973 level.[66] Clearly, the slackened demand for oil had reduced the pressure on world oil markets, but at the cost of reduced economic growth; the improvement in energy efficiency was quite modest.[67] Indeed, the 1979 review by the IEA concluded that, apart from Denmark, the Netherlands, and Sweden, the IEA countries had failed to make substantial progress in developing and implementing new conservation measures.[68]

Several factors combined to limit the effect of higher oil prices on energy conservation. First, there is no direct relationship between the price of crude oil and the price of petroleum products. Despite the 1973–74 OPEC price hikes, the cost of crude oil still accounted for less than half of the final cost of most petroleum products.[69] Second, the short-run price elasticity of crude oil consumption is low, about 0.1 during the first year and only about 0.3 over a four-year period. On the other hand, the income elasticity is much higher, about 1.0.[70] Demand for oil is also highly sensitive to nonprice government policies. In Western Europe and Japan, moreover, oil consumption and oil imports were less in 1978 than they had been in 1973, but in the United States, oil consumption and oil imports were greater in 1978 than they had been in 1973 (see table A4). This was partly because energy consumption grew more rapidly in the United States than in Western Europe and Japan—despite the fact that in 1973 the United States used almost twice as much energy per unit of GNP as either Western Europe or Japan. Between 1973 and 1978 per capita U.S. energy use declined slightly in the industrial sector, and increased by only 1 percent in both the residential and commerical sectors, but in the transportation sector it increased by 4 percent.[71] The average fuel efficiency of U.S. cars increased from 13.1 miles per gallon for 1973 models to 18 miles per gallon for 1978s. But with real gasoline prices falling from 1974 to 1978, driving increased. As a result, gallons consumed per car were about the same in 1978 as in 1973.[72]

While transportation accounted for about 25 percent of oil requirements in Western Europe and Japan, in the United States it accounted for more than 50 percent. This meant that Western Europe and Japan could reduce oil consumption by substituting other fuels for oil in sectors of the economy where liquid fuels are not essential, but in the United States, oil savings had to focus more on the transportation sector. Even so, consumer-country taxes accounted for at least half the price of gasoline throughout Western Europe and for about 30 percent in Japan; in the United States the figure was only 20.5 percent.[73]

Still, a more important reason for the rise in U.S. oil imports between 1973 and 1978 was the decline in U.S. oil and natural gas production. With its domestic energy production declining, the United States resorted to larger oil imports to satisfy its growing appetite for energy. In contrast, Japan limited its oil imports by increasing its imports of LNG, and in Western Europe slower economic growth and the development of North Sea oil reduced demand for imported oil.[74] Had the United States reduced its demand for imported oil, the ability of the oil-exporting countries to maintain their high price would have been severely tested. Of all the consuming countries, the United States had the greatest potential to affect the world oil price since it was the largest oil importer and the consuming country with the greatest potential to boost its domestic energy production. But even with its extensive reserves of coal and shale oil, its enormous conservation potential,[75] and its favorable climate for solar energy, the United States did not reduce its demand for imported oil in this period, despite the continual pleading of other consuming countries and the repeated efforts of Presidents Nixon, Ford, and Carter.

U.S. Energy Policy. As early as October 11, 1973, President Nixon stated: "Our goal must be self-sufficiency—the capacity to meet our energy needs with our own resources. I intend to take every step necessary to achieve that goal. A great nation cannot be dependent upon other nations for resources essential to its own social and economic progress."[76] Then, after the Arab oil embargo had begun, on November 7, 1973, President Nixon announced Project Independence and said: "Let us pledge that by 1980, under Project Independence we shall be able to meet America's needs from America's own energy resources."[77]

In an energy message in January 1974, Nixon described Project Independence as entailing three concurrent tasks: rapidly increasing domestic energy supplies, reducing demand by conserving energy, and developing new technologies through a massive new research and development program. However, a month later the top U.S. energy official, William Simon, explained that Project Independence did not "mean that the United States will terminate all imports. Rather the U.S. objective is to be [in] a position by 1980 where it can go without imports, if necessary, without serious damage to the U.S. economy."[78]

A presidential task force was established to devise ways of meeting the president's goals. The Project Independence Report, released in November 1974, showed that any substantial reduction in U.S. dependence upon imported oil would be extremely difficult to achieve in the short term, by 1980. However, the report concluded that energy "independence" was feasible in the long term, by 1985. Nonetheless, when the report was released, FEA chief John Sawhill said he considered reduction in U.S. dependence upon imports to 25 percent of its consumption by 1985 "a reasonable goal" (the figure was 38% in 1974).[79]

To reduce oil imports, Presidents Nixon, Ford, and Carter sought to raise U.S. oil prices, reasoning that this would reduce domestic consumption and boost domestic production, but their efforts were opposed by a Democratic-controlled Congress, which maintained that gains from higher oil prices would not justify the burden that higher costs would place on consumers. Stalemate on this issue has continually impeded U.S. efforts to formulate an energy policy and reduce its dependence upon imported oil.

In March 1974 President Nixon vetoed the Energy Emergency bill, which he had proposed, because Congress had added a provision that set a ceiling price on domestically produced oil. The bill would have held the price of "old" oil at $5.25 and authorized the president to raise the price of "new" oil and stripper crude to as much as $7.09. However, at the time the bill was passed, the price of uncontrolled oil (new oil and stripper crude) had risen to $10.35 a barrel.[80] Congress failed to override the president's veto and by summer was preoccupied by the Watergate hearings, so that no energy legislation of significance was passed in 1974.

In October 1974 President Ford committed the United States to reducing its oil imports by 1 mb/d by the end of 1975 and by 2 mb/d by the end of 1977—the reduction that Kissinger had pledged to IEA. In January, to achieve this goal, President Ford proposed that old oil (still about 60% of domestic crude) be decontrolled on April 1, which would raise its price from $5.25 a barrel to about $14, and that a $2 per barrel excise tax (or import fee) be placed on all oil consumed in the United States. These proposals would have equalized the prices of all crude oil sold in the United States and raised the average price from about $9 to about $13.[81] The president also proposed a "windfall profits tax" on any additional earnings that the industry failed to reinvest.

Ford asked Congress to deregulate the price of newly discovered natural gas and to impose an excise tax of 37¢ per thousand cubic feet (mcf) on all gas production. He called on Congress to defer auto emission control standards for five years in exchange for a pledge by automakers to design cars that would get 40 percent better gas mileage. The president also proposed that, to encourage development of alternative energy sources, Congress establish a price floor for domestically produced oil. Yet Congress was reluctant to go along with the president's plan for higher energy prices. In July it passed a bill that would have continued price controls on old oil and rolled back the price for new oil from $12.75 to $11.28. Ford vetoed the bill.

However, the president did not want to stand for election in 1976, having sharply boosted oil prices despite congressional protests. Thus he proposed a compromise: rather than immediate price decontrol, he would agree to a phased decontrol program over the next two and a half years. In addition, he proposed that a ceiling of $13.50 be established for uncontrolled oil, then selling at roughly $12.75, to insulate U.S. prices from future OPEC increases. Finally, in November the president and Congress reached agreement. "New" (or upper tier) oil, which had been selling between $13 and $14, was placed under controls and brought down to $11.28, and controls were maintained on "old" (or lower tier) oil. The effect was to roll back the average price for domestic crude from $8.75 to $7.66. The average price would be allowed to rise at an annual 10 percent for forty months, at which time all controls would be removed (unless new legislation was enacted). The president was given considerable authority to set higher prices for some oil and lower prices for other oil, as long as the average increase did not exceed the stipulated level. The president was also authorized to provide special incentives for Alaskan oil and to exclude it in calculating the overall domestic average price.[82]

Beginning with the 1978 model year, the bill set mandatory fuel efficiency standards for automobiles. By 1980 a manufacturer's "fleet" had to average 20 mpg and by 1985, 27.5 mpg. The bill also authorized the president to begin a "strategic petroleum reserve," with a goal of 150 million barrels in three years and 550 million in seven—enough to replace slightly more than ninety days' crude oil imports at the 1975 rate. However, among the issues the bill failed to resolve were "new" natural gas pricing, federal incentives for development of synthetic fuels, and federal standards for thermal efficiency.[83]

Oil industry officials and conservative Republicans were outraged that, after a year of seeking higher oil prices, the president agreed to a compromise that reduced oil prices, at least in the short run. They maintained that this would increase U.S. oil consumption and reduce domestic production, but the administration indicated that it was bowing to unavoidable political pressures and that the compromise was better than no legislation at all. Nor was the bill especially injurious to the interests of the large oil companies. While the price rollback would cost the industry $3.5 billion in the short run, the legislation held out the strong possibility of eventual removal of all price controls. A few independents with a high proportion of new oil would be hurt by its reduction in price, but this would not have a major effect on most companies. Nor did the final legislation include provision for a windfall profits tax. In addition, it was hoped that the price rollback would deflect the growing sentiment for divestiture of the oil industry.

Despite the attention the energy issue received and the legislation that had been enacted, in November 1976, when Jimmy Carter defeated Gerald Ford, the U.S. energy situation was more precarious than it had been three years before, just prior to the Arab oil embargo. Imports had increased from 33 percent to 42 percent of U.S. oil consumption and were still rising. While in 1973 the United States relied on Arab oil for 11 percent of its oil needs, in 1976 Arab oil accounted for 18 percent. Domestic oil production had fallen from 9.2 mb/d in 1973 to 8.04 mb/d in 1976. Oil from shale and tar sands and gasification and liquefaction of coal seemed at least as far from realization in 1976 as in 1973.

In the fall of 1976 the International Energy Agency released a study that concluded the United States had the worst postembargo conservation record of any country in the seventeen-nation group, despite the fact that the United States had the greatest conservation potential and had sought to play a leading role in the organization. Moreover, the U.S. nuclear program was stagnating and the use of coal had increased only modestly.[84]

The most immediate problem involved natural gas supplies. Like U.S. oil production, U.S. natural gas production declined steadily after 1973. Producers complained that federal price controls made it unprofitable for them to find and produce more gas while critics charged that they held back production to boost prices. But one thing was clear: on a BTU basis, natural gas was the cheapest fuel in the United States. In 1975, natural gas at the wellhead cost about 40¢ per million BTUs; in contrast, the same amount of energy from coal cost 80¢, and from imported oil the cost was $2.30.[85]

Yet rather than husband natural gas for uses in which it is hardest to replace, as a feedstock for fertilizer and ammonia plants and as a fuel in glass and some metal and textile processes, the United States substituted natural gas for other fuels. To meet environmental standards, natural gas replaced coal as a boiler fuel for large plants and electric utilities; and as oil prices rose, residential and commercial customers shifted to natural gas. The situation was made much worse by two markets for natural gas, interstate and intrastate. Gas sold across state lines was subject to federal price controls, but gas sold within the state in which it was produced was free of price controls. Early in 1976 federal controls held the price of gas newly committed to the interstate market at 52¢ per mcf, but the intrastate price rose as high as $2 per mcf. Consequently, producers diverted as much gas as they legally could to the intrastate market. In 1975 only 16 percent of the new gas sold by producers went to the interstate market, and most of it came from offshore fields in federal waters, which was legally bound to the interstate market. Exploration and development were channeled into increasing onshore supplies for local markets while high-cost (mostly offshore) fields that could supply the interstate market went undeveloped.[86]

In the mid-1970s the United States consumed roughly twice as much gas as it found. Even so, in the winter of 1974–75 supply was 14 percent below demand (at the controlled price), and in the winter of 1975–76 it was 18 percent below demand. Had these winters not been mild, serious dislocations would have resulted. As it was, plants were forced to shut down and jobs were lost as natural gas supplies were shifted from industry to residential consumers, and to make up for the shortfall, more oil had to be imported. Yet, at the same time the country (as a whole) suffered from natural gas shortages, Texas—the largest producing state—had a surplus, with most of its gas locked in by higher intrastate prices.[87]

In an effort to boost gas supplies and pull more of those supplies into the interstate market, in 1976 President Ford proposed that new gas be freed from price controls. However, Congress refused to go along with the proposal. Then, in July 1976, the Federal Power Commission raised the price of new gas, defined as gas discovered or committed to the interstate market since January 1, 1975, from 52¢ per mcf to $1.42. Gas discovered between January 1, 1973, and December 31, 1974, was raised from 52¢ to $1.01.[88] In addition, the FPC began allowing producers to raise the price of old gas (discovered before Jan. 1, 1973) from 29.5¢ to 52¢ when a contract expired. The FPC estimated that these higher rates would cost consumers $1.5 billion a year, or $15.60 per consumer, an increase of 5–6 percent.[89]

Yet these decisions did not avert a natural gas crisis in the winter of 1976–77. With gas supplies unavailable, more than a million workers temporarily lost their jobs; schools and public buildings were forced to close; and in a few areas residents were close to losing their fuel supplies. The crisis eased only with the arrival of spring.[90]

Two factors provoked the crisis: the winter of 1976–77 was much colder than the three that preceded it, and the oil companies withheld supplies from the market. Several reports confirmed this. For example, congressional investigators found that Texaco had reserves in the Gulf of Mexico of more than 500 billion cubic feet of natural gas, but the company did not produce from these reservoirs because of its "desire to maximize its profits." Committee investigators said Texaco was just one of many companies with large gas reservoirs that were withheld from production.[91] A report commissioned by leading gas utilities concluded that gas producers also failed to bring to market reserves in the Gulf of Mexico that would have been equal to much of the cutbacks during the winter of 1976–77.[92]

In the aftermath of the natural gas crisis, in April 1977 President Carter presented his National Energy Plan to Congress. The thrust of the Carter plan was to reduce oil imports by greater reliance upon conservation and coal consumption. Deeming the U.S. energy problem "the moral equivalent of war," the president announced three objectives:

a. In the short-term, to reduce dependence on foreign oil and to limit supply disruptions.
b. In the medium-term, to weather the eventual decline in the availability of world oil supplies caused by capacity limitations.
c. In the long-term, to develop renewable and essentially inexhaustible sources of energy for sustained economic growth.

He asked Congress to commit the United States to six goals by 1985:

Reducing annual growth of United States energy demand to less than 2%.
Reducing oil imports from a potential level of 16 million barrels a day to less than six million barrels, about one-eighth of total energy consumption.
Achieving a 10 percent reduction in gasoline consumption.
Insulating 90 percent of all residences and other buildings.
Increasing coal production on an annual basis by at least 400 million tons.
Using solar energy in more than two and a half million homes.[93]

To achieve these goals, the president proposed a comprehensive energy plan whose centerpiece was the crude-oil equalization tax. According to the plan, the ceilings of $5.25 and $11.28 would remain in effect for previously discovered oil, subject only to escalation at the general rate of inflation. However, a tax to encourage conservation would be placed on the oil, raising the price to the consumer to the level of world oil prices, about $13.50 (the average price of U.S. crude at the time was about $9).

It was estimated that one effect of this would be to raise the price of gasoline by 7¢ a gallon; however, all proceeds from this tax would be rebated to consumers on a per capita basis. In addition, families that heated with oil could claim a tax credit equal to the amount the tax added to their heating bills. While the federal government would have to administer the system of tax and rebates, one advantage of raising U.S. prices to the level of world oil prices was that it would enable the federal government to abolish petroleum-product price and allocation controls, doing away with the cumbersome entitlements program. The price of newly discovered oil would be allowed to rise over a three-year period to the 1977 level of world prices (adjusted for inflation). After that, its price would increase only with increases in the general rate of inflation.

To encourage conservation and conversion to coal, the president proposed heavy and progressively rising taxes on the use of oil and natural gas by industry and the utilities (the user's tax). He recommended graduated taxes on fuel-inefficient cars, with the proceeds rebated, on a graduated basis, to purchasers of fuel-efficient cars. On the controversial issue of natural gas pricing, the president's plan called for raising the price of newly discovered gas, and gas newly committed to the interstate market, from $1.45 per mcf to $1.75—the BTU equivalent of the average refiner cost (before tax) of all domestic crude. The president also asked Congress to extend federal price controls to the intrastate market. However, as a concession to the oil industry, the president indicated that consideration of both vertical and horizontal divestiture could be put off for the time being.

On nuclear power, the president called for indefinite deferral of the commercial reprocessing and recycling of spent fuel produced in nuclear power plants. The president wanted to redirect efforts toward evaluation of alternative "breeders," with emphasis on nonproliferation and safety concerns. The plan did not say much about conventional nuclear reactors, but administration officials privately admitted the need for expansion of nuclear power.

Other measures proposed by the president included

A standby gasoline tax of 5¢ per gallon to be added each year that gasoline consumption exceeded the target set by the president. The cumulative tax was not to exceed 50 cents.

A home insulation tax credit equal to 25% of the first $800 spent and 15% of the next $1,400.

A 10% tax credit for businesses that installed either solar or energy conservation equipment, including "co-generation" of electricity and usable steam heat.

Either a 10% tax credit for industrial conversion to coal or other fuels or a dollar-for-dollar rebate on any oil and gas user tax paid.

A prohibition on the burning of oil or gas by new industrial facilities or utilities, with only "limited exceptions". A ban on the burning of natural gas by all utilities after 1990, with authority for the federal government to prohibit oil and gas burning in other facilities.

Restructuring gas and electric utility rates to encourage less energy use.

A 40% tax credit for homeowners on the first $1,000 spent on solar equipment and a 25% credit on the next $6,400 spent.

An increase in the size of the strategic petroleum reserve from the projected level of 500 million barrels to one billion barrels.[94]

The administration estimated that the program would result in 100,000 additional jobs by 1985, would have no net effect on GNP, and would add only 0.4 percentage points a year to the inflation rate between 1978 and 1985.[95]

Carter's energy program differed from that of his Republican predecessors in several respects. First, there was much greater emphasis on conservation in the Carter program than in the proposals put forth by either President Nixon or Ford. At the same time, the Carter program placed much less emphasis on boosting domestic oil and natural gas production. While Nixon and Ford had sought to stimulate domestic production by removing price controls, Carter argued for their maintenance, but advocated taxes to discourage consumption.

The Carter plan placed little emphasis on development of synthetic fuels— shale oil and coal gasification and liquefaction—or on liquified natural gas, nor did it advocate major cutbacks in environmental standards. At the same time, it did not seek a great boost from solar energy and other renewable resources to U.S. energy supplies. The Carter plan was far more comprehensive than the proposals by Nixon and Ford, but still there were omissions, the most important being an initiative on mass transit; nor did the plan say much about the international aspects of the energy problem.

The plan provoked a storm of opposition. The oil industry wanted greater incentives for boosting U.S. oil and gas production, not continuing price controls; and if prices to the consumer were going to rise, as the president proposed, the industry wanted part of this revenue. The oil companies also opposed placing price controls on natural gas sold in the intrastate market, which would reduce their revenues.

The nuclear industry objected to the president's deferral of reprocessing and the breeder, and wanted stronger federal promotion of conventional nuclear power plants. Utilities that operated on oil and gas did not want to switch to coal, or be penalized for not switching. The coal industry liked the president's stress on coal, but it maintained that to get the increases in production that he was looking for, strip mine and clean air regulations would have to be eased—which the president opposed. The automobile industry, in the midst of a record year, based primarily on renewed sales of big cars, objected to the president's automobile tax and rebate program; taxes on large cars would discourage their sale while rebates on small cars would be a boon to foreign-car sales in the United States.

The major oil and gas producing states—Texas, Louisiana, Oklahoma—also opposed the plan. They did not want to lose the gas that would flow across their borders once federal price controls were imposed on the intrastate market, nor did they want their electricity rates to rise as their utilities were forced to convert from natural gas to more costly coal. The governments in these states had been counting on higher energy prices to increase the revenues they derived from wellhead severance taxes on the sale of oil and natural gas, but under the Carter plan the federal government, not the oil companies or the producing states, would receive this revenue. There were also numerous criticisms that the plan would not do what the president said it would, that is, reduce oil imports by 4.5 mb/d in 1985, etc.[96] Questions were also raised about how much of the increase in the crude oil wellhead tax would actually be passed on to consumers and, consequently, how much impact it would have on reducing consumption.[97]

The plan had a very small constituency. Consumers and consumer groups generally opposed its high price provisions, despite the president's promise to rebate the proceeds from the crude oil equalization tax.[98] This was particularly true of those who lived in rural areas and lacked access to mass transit, for they would have to pay more for the energy they used, would have a hard time cutting back, and would get the same rebate as those who consumed far less energy. While some environmentalists strongly supported the plan, others objected to it as not doing enough to promote renewable sources and being secretly "pro-nuclear."[99]

If the plan had a constituency, it was the Northeast. Because this region relied most heavily on home heating oil, its residents would be the main beneficiaries of the special tax credit for those who heated with oil. And while they consumed mainly imported oil, whose price was high and probably rising, in any case, they would share in the rebates from the tax on domestic crude oil. The Northeast would also benefit from the freeing of natural gas from the intrastate market.

With Speaker Tip O'Neill, a Democrat from Massachusetts, guiding the way, the president's plan emerged from the House of Representatives largely intact, but in the Senate it was torn to pieces. The plan was opposed by liberals, who saw it as too generous to the oil industry and by conservatives, who saw it as not doing enough for the industry. Support for the plan came mainly from moderates, led by Majority Leader Robert Byrd and Energy Committee Chairman Henry Jackson, but the opponents of the plan were strategically located. Finance Committee Chairman Russell Long, a Democrat from Louisiana, the nation's number two oil- and natural gas-producing state, refused to approve a wellhead tax that did not contain provisions for diverting some or all of its revenues to energy development programs, rather than rebate them to consumers, as the president proposed. Long's insistence on such changes led liberal senators to oppose the tax altogether. The other Louisiana senator, Bennett Johnston, chairman of the Subcommittee on Conservation and Regulation, blocked the proposals for utility rate reform.

The most controversial issue was natural gas pricing. A coalition of pro-industry Republican and oil-producing-state Democrats emerged in favor of total deregulation of new gas prices and opposed to federal controls over intrastate gas pricing. They were opposed by a group of liberal Democrats who favored federal control of the intrastate market and believed the Carter pricing proposals were far too generous to the oil industry. The conflict between these groups resulted in a filibuster and led to the first all-night session of the Senate in thirteen years. It also delayed passage of any part of the Carter energy program for seven months. The key question in the debate was the effect that price deregulation would have on natural gas supplies. Both sides produced a wide array of studies, but even the most optimistic doubted that U.S. natural gas production would ever again reach the 1973 peak.[100]

In April 1978 a compromise was reached. Federal price controls were extended to the intrastate market. However, when the law went into effect on December 1, 1978, new gas was to be priced at $2.08 per mcf—about as much as it had brought at its peak on the intrastate market.[101] The controlled price would escalate gradually until 1985, when all price controls on new gas would be removed. Gas from wells that had been shut down could be sold on the national market at $1.63 per mcf, almost equal to the average price of $1.67 for gas on the intrastate market at the time the law went into effect. All prices would be adjusted annually to make sure they kept pace with inflation, plus an additional 3.7 percent per year during the first four years and 4.2 percent during the next four years.[102]

By the time the compromise was reached, President Carter badly needed passage of an energy bill in order to save face domestically and internationally. Consequently, the president claimed that the compromise was a major victory for his energy program. In reality, the price agreed to for new gas, $2.08, was a far cry from the $1.75 he had proposed. However, the compromise paved the way for enactment of national energy legislation in November 1978, eighteen months after the president had proposed his plan.

However, the enacted legislation bore only a pale semblance to the president's program. There was no crude oil equalization tax, no users' tax on firms that burned oil and natural gas, no mandatory utility rate restructuring, no tax on "gas guzzlers" or rebates for fuel-efficient automobiles, and no standby gasoline tax. The legislation also failed to deal with the licensing of nuclear power plants and the treatment of nuclear wastes.

Congress provided generous tax credits to homeowners and businesses that installed energy-saving or solar equipment and similar credits for companies that shifted from oil and gas to coal. To further encourage the purchase of conservation equipment, Congress established a $3 billion federally subsidized loan program for those below the median income and a $2 billion program of unsubsidized loans for those above the median. Congress also permitted public utilities to make loans to customers of up to $300 for the installation of energy conservation equipment, and loans for solar energy were federally subsidized.

The legislation established mandatory efficiency standards for home appliances; it prohibited new plants from burning oil or natural gas, except where this was necessary to meet environmental regulations, and gave the federal government greater power to force existing plants and utilities to shift to coal; and it required public utility commissions to consider plans for lower rates for customers who used electricity during off-peak hours. Finally, Congress authorized the president to boost the strategic petroleum reserve to 250 million barrels by the end of 1978, rather than the 150 million barrels originally sought by that date, and to 1 billion barrels, rather than 500 million, by 1982.[103]

Besides the opposition of interest groups to the proposals, the weakness of the final legislation was due to loss of a sense of urgency on the part of Congress and the public.[104] The president's program was announced just after the gas crisis of 1976–77, but by the time it was acted upon there was a surplus of crude on the world oil market, and Alaskan oil had come onstream, easing the U.S. energy problem, at least in the short term. The plan's passage through Congress was also hurt by the fact that it was formulated in secret, with little effort to consult members of Congress prior to announcement of the program. Administration lobbying for the plan was also poor.

The administration claimed that the legislation enacted would save from 2.4 mb/d to 3 mb/d of oil imports by 1985; however, increased gas production was counted on for nearly half of the savings.[105] Yet many feared that the complexity of the new gas bill, with its seventeen-odd categories of natural gas, would be expensive to administer and lead to costly delays in production.

In any case, by the time the legislation had passed, a surplus of up to 1 trillion cubic feet of natural gas had accumulated on the intrastate market, with producers unwilling to sell it at the lower prices that had prevailed until then on the interstate market. And their refusal to sell on the interstate market was encouraged because they knew that, with passage of national energy legislation, prices on the interstate market would go up. But once the legislation was enacted, gas started flowing from the intrastate to the interstate market. The Carter administration sought to take advantage of this by encouraging homeowners and companies to switch to natural gas, despite the administration's previous position, which had sought to get industry to abandon natural gas and switch to coal. Yet, by the end of 1978, increased consumption of natural gas was seen as the most immediately feasible way of reducing oil imports; but with U.S. natural gas production continuing to stagnate and the United States consuming more than twice as much gas as it was adding to reserves, whether this was a viable long-term strategy was questionable.[106]

As a result of the failure to develop an effective energy policy, U.S. oil imports continued to increase. While in January 1975 President Ford had pledged to cut U.S. oil imports by 2 mb/d, by 1977 U.S. imports had *increased* by 2 mb/d.[107] With the onflow of Alaskan oil, imports declined slightly in early 1978, but by the end of the year they were back up and showed every indication of rising.

Consequently, when Iranian oil exports ceased at the end of 1978, the United States was more vulnerable to a loss of supplies from the Middle East than in 1973. Between 1973 and 1978, U.S. oil and natural gas production had declined

TABLE 10–3. U.S. ENERGY PRODUCTION AND CONSUMPTION, 1973–81 (QUADRILLION BTUs)

						Production			
							Percent Change		
	1973	1978	1979	1980	1981	1973–78	1978–79	1979–80	1980–81
Coal	14.37	15.04	17.65	18.75	18.25	4.7	17.4	6.2	−2.7
Oil	22.06	20.68	20.39	20.53	20.42	−6.3	−1.4	.7	−.5
Natural gas	22.19	19.49	20.08	19.75	19.99	−12.2	3.0	−1.6	1.2
Nuclear	.91	2.98	2.75	2.70	2.91	227.1	−7.7	−1.8	7.8
Hydroelectric	2.86	2.96	2.95	2.91	2.72	3.6	−.3	−1.4	−6.5
Other	.05	.07	.09	.11	.13	47.8	30.9	28.1	18.2
Total	62.43	61.20	63.91	64.76	64.41	−2.0	4.4	1.3	−.5
						Consumption			
Coal	13.30	13.85	15.11	15.60	16.12	4.1	9.1	3.2	3.3
Oil	34.84	37.97	37.12	34.30	32.12	9.0	−2.2	−7.6	−6.4
Natural gas	22.51	20.00	20.67	20.50	20.22	−11.2	3.4	−.8	−1.4
Nuclear	.91	2.98	2.75	2.70	2.91	227.1	−7.7	−1.8	7.8
Hydroelectric	3.01	3.16	3.17	3.13	2.94	5.0	.3	1.3	−6.1
Other	.05	.07	.09	.11	.13	47.8	30.9	28.1	18.2
Total	74.61	78.15	78.97	76.30	74.42	4.7	1.0	−3.4	−2.5

All figures from U.S. Dept. of Energy, *Monthly Energy Review* (Feb. 1982), pp. 6 and 8. Figures on "Oil" include natural gas petroleum liquids; "Other" includes solar, geothermal, and electricity from wood waste.

(see table 10–3). During this period, nuclear power continued to expand as plants, ordered years before, came into operation; however, since 1975 the nuclear industry had been plagued by a sharp decline in orders for new plants and coal production had been constrained by a lack of demand and serious concern about the stability of labor-management relations. Furthermore, after a burst of activity in 1974–75, efforts to develop synthetic fuels had largely fizzled out, with no substitute for conventional oil in sight.

Consumer-Country Cooperation. The failure of the United States to develop an energy policy was paralleled by the failure of the consuming countries to develop an effective, collaborative response to the oil crisis. In a move that complemented President Ford's proposal to Congress, that it establish an oil-price floor, in February 1975 Kissinger asked the consuming countries, acting through the International Energy Agency, to establish a minimum safe-guard price (MSP) to encourage development of new energy sources.

The rationale for this proposal was as follows. The consuming countries have substantial domestic energy resources, including shale oil, tar sands, and coal, which could be liquified and gasified, and conventional oil. Yet under the most optimistic scenarios, these resources would cost considerably more than it costs to produce oil in the OPEC countries. However, after some development work, they might well cost less than OPEC's current price. But companies are reluctant to do this development because they fear that if they develop resources that can be profitably sold for less than the OPEC price, OPEC will simply reduce its price, making the new sources uncompetitive once again. Consequently, Kissinger reasoned, by guaranteeing private companies that oil would not be traded on the world market below a minimum price, this obstacle would be overcome and development of non-OPEC-controlled energy resources would be encouraged. Initially, the United States advocated a minimum safeguard price of $9 a barrel.[108]

Consuming countries with substantial domestic energy resources tended to support the Kissinger plan. In fact, the United Kingdom, Norway, and the Netherlands favored a higher price floor than the United States. Countries without substantial energy resources feared that the resource-rich countries, particularly the United States, would derive most of the benefits from the scheme. In contrast, the resource-poor countries would be locked into paying high prices for energy, even if world oil prices fell. Yet, rather than oppose the plan outright, they argued for a lower safeguard price.

Dispute over this issue was the main IEA activity during 1975. In January 1976 a $7 minimum safeguard price was agreed to but the details were not worked out until September 1976. At the time this agreement was reached, the OPEC price was $11.51 and the cost of alternative energy sources was expected to be at least $10.[109] Consequently, the $7 MSP could do little to stimulate development of alternative energy sources. Moreover, at the time the MSP was adopted, Canada and the United States were selling domestically produced oil for less than $7 a barrel.

The MSP agreement yielded no tangible benefits; but it divided the IEA members. In exchange for the agreement of the energy-poor consuming countries to the MSP, the energy-rich countries had to agree that nationals from all countries would have an equal right to participate in the development of all energy resources in the IEA countries and that no trade restrictions (tariff barriers, etc.) would be placed on the sale of these resources. Rather than agree to this, Norway became an associate member of IEA, and Canada, while it signed the agreement, maintained it was not bound by the equal-access provision.

In the unlikely event that MSP would cause the OPEC price to fall below the consumers' price floor, the division between the consuming countries would probably increase, for the temptation for resource-poor countries to opt out of the MSP agreement and purchase cheaper OPEC oil would be almost irresistible. Alternatively, the resource-rich countries, or perhaps the United States alone, might make a deal with the OPEC countries to keep the world oil price at the MSP level. The IEA has no understanding of how this situation would be dealt with[110]—but at the existing MSP level, it is not likely to occur.

To promote development of new energy sources, in 1975 the IEA established a Committee on Research and Development; however, the work of the committee has been plagued by the different interests and capabilities of IEA members and by their reluctance to share their technical knowledge, each country fearing that it will give up more than it receives. As a result, the most important energy research and development projects are still national projects, and the IEA accounts for only about 5 percent of its members' research and development spending. Since participation in particular IEA R&D projects is voluntary, many of them are essentially U.S.-German projects that could easily proceed on a bilateral basis in the absence of IEA.[111]

The IEA has also established annual reviews of member countries' national energy policies. Through this system, IEA seeks to persuade the consuming countries to make greater efforts to conserve energy and to develop new energy sources, and in April 1977 IEA adopted a group target of 26 mb/d of oil imports by 1985. This was more than the 22–23 mb/d then imported, but less than the 30 mb/d projected at the time. However, while the United States supported adoption of national targets, most IEA members objected and they were not established. Then, in June, IEA agreed on twelve principles to guide the energy policies of member governments, but these have no legal force. IEA's ability to affect its members' energy policies is greatly limited by its lack of authority. At most, it therefore tends to create a transnational constituency that is concerned about energy issues and seeks to put pressure on individual governments.

Ironically, while the United States pushed for creation of IEA and has played the leading role in urging greater IEA activity, the IEA has increasingly become a forum for criticism of U.S. energy policies—its extravagant use of energy, its failure to develop its enormous energy potential, and consequently its high oil imports. Moreover, the United States' failure to reduce its oil imports to reasonable levels in the 1970s has undermined its claim to leadership within IEA. In fact, the countries of Western Europe and Japan feared that their efforts to reduce dependence upon foreign oil and the world oil price were undermined by the United States' seemingly insatiable appetite for imported oil.

The IEA also has responsibility for gathering information on the world oil market and the activities of the international oil companies, and its most widely heralded achievement is the emergency energy sharing plan that it established in the fall of 1974. The plan requires all IEA members to hold stockpiles equivalent to ninety days' oil imports and to have plans that would enable them to reduce consumption in an emergency by 7 percent immediately and 10 percent subsequently.[112] If any country is faced with more than a 7 percent shortfall, it has the right to trigger emergency sharing. In a highly unusual arrangement for an international organization, the scheme does not require the unanimous support of IEA members but goes into effect automatically, once the IEA secretariat confirms such a shortage. Nor can the scheme be blocked by the EEC countries' or the United States' acting alone, though it can be blocked by the EEC or the United States with the support of one to four other IEA members.

Once the sharing mechanism goes into effect, any shortfall beyond 7 percent is shared equally among the IEA members. If the shortfall reaches 12 percent, countries must reduce their consumption by 10 percent, and a further reduction is required when stock levels decline by 50 percent. Sharing is on the basis of oil consumption, not energy consumption, as the Europeans and Japanese advocated, nor on the basis of oil imports, as the United States preferred. The United States has agreed that its domestic oil production would be subject to the scheme, but given its import dependence, it is unlikely that the United States would have to ship domestically produced oil elsewhere. Norway, on the other hand, refused to join the sharing agreement because it feared that, were it to do so, it would be forced to share its North Sea supplies in an emergency. Consequently, Norway became an associate member of IEA.[113]

Still, there are several reasons for believing that, in an emergency, the sharing agreement might not work. The amount of oil that could be drawn from the stockpiles is much less than the stipulated ninety-day supply, since for most countries this includes working inventories, which could not be withdrawn for technical reasons.[114] However, if imports decline about 15 percent, as they did in 1973, stocks equivalent to forty-five days' imports could last for more than six months.

But there are other problems with the sharing scheme as well. Countries are unlikely to be willing to use up their stockpile the first time an emergency occurs, particularly since in such a period it usually appears that the situation will get worse. In fact, in 1973–74 most countries did not use their stocks to make up for the decline in imports. While the "automaticity" of the scheme is claimed as a virtue, ambiguities in the agreement leave considerable room for debate, delay, and acrimony. In addition, it is doubtful that most countries can reduce demand by 7 percent without drastically slowing their economies. For example, in the United States the Federal Energy Administration indicated that demand restraint beyond 3 percent would be difficult to achieve without severe economic impacts; and the United States is the least efficient energy user in the IEA.[115]

Rather than accept severe reductions in consumption and sharp economic declines, in the event of an embargo or production cutback that impacts primarily on a single country, other consuming countries are likely to opt out of the sharing agreement, especially if the exporting countries threaten retaliatory action. In this situation, compliance with the emergency sharing scheme would likely lead to escalation of the cutbacks. Also, rather than reveal their inability to comply with the plan, nations are likely to refrain from invoking it. In an actual emergency, consequently, ad hoc measures are likely to be devised (as happened in 1979).

The plan also suffers from its failure to make arrangements for the prices at which supplies will be transferred among countries. Nor do the consuming countries have the power to force the oil companies to violate strictures that may be imposed by the exporting countries. Yet without the companies' cooperation in shifting supplies, the plan could not work, and even with the companies' cooperation, technical problems in getting oil to the consumer are likely. The importance of the oil companies' role also gives the United States a veto over the sharing system since the United States would have to apply sanctions against companies that refuse to comply with the system.

Moreover, the plan could not protect the consuming countries against a major cutback of long duration, nor could it prevent nonparticipating countries from bidding up prices. Still, IEA officials believe that the plan is a deterrent to an embargo and would reduce the likelihood of competitive bidding by consuming countries in the event of another oil crisis.

The EEC was no more successful than the IEA at getting its members to cooperate on measures aimed at alleviating the energy crisis. In the spring of 1974 there was discussion of establishing an EEC energy agency, but by the fall this idea had been abandoned. Then, in September 1974, the EEC Council of Ministers adopted energy guidelines, proposed by the commission, for decreased oil imports, increased efficiency of energy use, a coordinated plan to deal with shortages, and efforts to encourage energy research and development (especially in the nuclear field). However, these guidelines are little more than target figures to guide national policies.

The EEC commission had advised the EEC to limit energy import dependence to 50 percent by restricting oil imports to 500 million tonnes in 1985, substitute natural gas for oil, adopt proposals for hydrocarbon exploration and refining, prevent further declines in coal production and consumption, strengthen its nuclear program, provide incentives for conservation, encourage development of new energy sources, coordinate member states' energy policies, and ensure a favorable climate for private investment in Community energy resources. Yet little Community action has been taken on any of these recommendations.[116]

As in the IEA, in the EEC the conflict between resource-rich and resource-poor countries has been a major barrier to a common program. Indeed, this conflict is similar in both origins and effects to the conflict between energy-rich and energy-poor states in the United States. Each EEC nation with domestic resources has been quick to assert its national right to control those resources. While Britain has sought an EEC minimum safeguard price to protect its North Sea oil, France has resisted such a move as an unwarranted subsidy for resource-rich countries. France, which lacks significant fossil fuel reserves, has supported greater EEC financing for the Euratom nuclear program. In retaliation for France's opposition to an MSP, in December 1976 Britain indicated that it would block the scheme for Euratom loans favored by France.[117]

In general, Britain has resisted any proposal that would infringe on its control over North Sea oil. Until the end of 1977, this prevented adoption of a Community-wide emergency sharing scheme.[118] Similarly, Norway has refused to join EEC, fearing that if it did, its control over North Sea oil would be reduced. Also, while West Germany and Great Britain, the leading EEC coal producers, backed EEC proposals for greater coal production, other EEC members opposed this. Proposals for financial aid to encourage greater use of coal in electric power generation were not approved, partly because Germany, the United Kingdom, and France have feared that this might benefit third countries that export coal more than it would help employment in the EEC countries.[119]

In addition, conflicts over nonenergy issues have impeded progress on energy issues within EEC. Britain obstructed a common EEC energy policy in order to win more generous treatment within EEC, eventually seeking to renegotiate the terms of its EEC membership. Domestic political pressures led France to keep its distance from the United States and to push for a strong European energy policy. But the Netherlands, Denmark, Germany, and Great Britain refused to agree to anything that would limit their freedom of action or impair their relations with the United States.[120]

Nuclear Power. The consuming countries' response to the oil crisis was also weakened by their overemphasis on nuclear power and the subsequent failure of nuclear power to meet the goals that had been set for it. Immediately after the 1973–74 rise in oil prices, most consuming countries announced ambitious new goals for nuclear power. Member countries of EEC planned to boost nuclear's share of their energy needs from 2 percent in 1974 to between 13 and 16 percent by 1985, or up to half of all electricity generated within EEC. Over the same period, Japan planned to boost nuclear's share of its generating capacity from 6.2 percent to 17 percent. In the United States, in January 1975 President Ford called for the United States to add 200 nuclear power plants by 1985 (only about fifty reactors were operating at that time). The main exception to this pattern was Great Britain, where, with North Sea oil coming onstream, the government made a decision in the summer of 1974 to go slow on nuclear power.[121]

In 1974 a record fifty-six nuclear power plants were ordered in the non-Communist world (see table 10–4), but by 1975 nuclear orders had fallen to half the level of the previous year, and they kept falling for the next two years. In the United States since mid-1974, more reactors have been canceled than ordered and over a hundred more have been deferred.[122] Moreover, as table 10–4 shows, projections of nuclear generating capacity in 1985 have fallen continuously.

There were several reasons for the slowdown in nuclear power. The most important was that the slowing of economic growth, due in part to the rise in oil prices, led to reduction in the growth in demand for electricity. This lessened the immediate need for new power and made it hard for utilities to project demand. It also plunged many utilities into a financial crisis that made them hesitant about committing the huge capital required for a nuclear plant. The uncertainty of demand was especially disadvantageous to nuclear power plants because their construction takes far longer than construction of fossil fuel–fired plants,[123] and as concern over nuclear safety mounted, the cost of building nuclear plants escalated sharply. Finding acceptable sites for nuclear reactors was another barrier, particularly in densely populated Japan.

Public opposition to nuclear power also played a role in slowing its develop-

TABLE 10–4. NUCLEAR REACTOR ORDERS IN NON-COMMUNIST WORLD (1970–78) AND ESTIMATES OF YEAR-END 1985 NUCLEAR GENERATING CAPACITY

	1970	1971	1972	1973	1974	1975	1976	1977	1978
Orders	27	37	39	54	56	28	18	14	22

Estimates of Nuclear Electric Generating Capacity, Year-End 1985 (Thousand Megawatts)

(Dates of Estimates)	Sept. 1970	Aug. 1973	Jan. 1974	Apr. 1975	Dec. 1975	Feb. 1976	Aug. 1976	Jan. 1977	Dec. 1977	Dec. 1978
U.S.	277.0	280.0	260.0	204.5	185.0	180.0	147.0	145.0	115.0	100.0
Japan	60.0	60.0	60.0	60.0	49.0	41.0	30.0	35.0	27.0	18.0
Western Europe	202.5	184.3	175.0	202.7	211.6	166.8	140.8	125.0	106.8	84.0
Total OECD Nations	562.6	542.3	513.0	486.4	464.0	399.8	330.6	318.0	258.8	213.9

CIA, *The World Oil Market in the Years Ahead*, pp. 52–53. For the agencies that made the estimates, see ibid.

ment. In September 1976 the Center Party made its opposition to nuclear power the leading issue in Sweden's election campaign and succeeded in ousting the Social Democratic Party from office for the first time in forty-four years. While the coalition that took office (which included pronuclear parties) did not phase out the Swedish nuclear program, as the Center Party had promised, it slowed it down. Opposition to nuclear power from environmentalists and citizen action groups forced a de facto moratorium on West Germany's nuclear industry in 1977–78 and led the German government to give greater emphasis to coal and less to nuclear in its long-range planning.[124]

There was also major opposition to nuclear power in France. Ecologists, campaigning on a platform of green trees and no nuclear power plants, secured 10 percent of the vote in Paris's municipal elections in March 1977. In July, more than 30,000 people, many of them from other West European nations, demonstrated at Creys-Manville, site of the non-Communist world's first commercial breeder reactor.

In Spain, 200,000 people gathered in Bilbao on July 13, 1977, to protest nuclear power. Because of public opposition, the Spanish government placed a moratorium on construction of nuclear reactors. In Switzerland, by collecting 125,000 signatures, environmentalists forced a nationwide referendum on nuclear power and got the Swiss government to halt the licensing of new plants until the referendum was held. Public opposition also delayed the first nuclear reactors in Denmark and Norway and slowed nuclear programs in Italy, the Netherlands, and Great Britain. In November 1978, in the first national referendum on nuclear power, Austrian voters opposed activation of their nation's first nuclear power plant, completed in 1977; and in Japan, public opposition to nuclear power held up construction of thirteen reactors, scheduled to be in operation by 1980.

In the United States in May 1977, over 2,000 people, organized into the Clamshell Alliance, occupied the site of the nuclear generating plant proposed for Seabrook, New Hampshire. Then, on August 6, in commemoration of the thirty-second anniversary of the atomic bombing of Hiroshima and Nagasaki, antinuclear demonstrations were held in thirty-five states. Altogether, tens of thousands of people had been involved in antinuclear demonstrations in the United States by 1978 and more than half a million had signed a petition calling on the government to "phase out the operation of nuclear power plants as quickly as possible." By getting state legislatures and federal regulatory agencies to require stricter safety standards and satisfactory waste disposal programs before more nuclear plants could be built, by creating a public climate hostile to further development of nuclear power, and by preventing passage of laws (i.e. licensing reform) to accelerate the U.S. nuclear program, the antinuclear movement has helped to stall development of nuclear power in the United States.

Despite these opposition movements, the governments in West Germany, France, and Japan have remained firmly committed to nuclear power as their only long-term hope of substantially lessening dependence upon foreign oil. Consequently, in 1977 they were jolted by the United States when President Carter announced his antiproliferation strategy: the United States would not use plutonium to fuel reactors and, accordingly, would indefinitely defer commercial reprocessing of nuclear fuels. Carter also asked Congress to halt work on the Clinch River breeder reactor demonstration project. The president called on countries that did not yet have them to follow the U.S. lead and defer both reprocessing plants and breeder reactors. Carter objected to these technologies because they involve the separation of plutonium (the fuel used for nuclear weapons) from nuclear waste material and thereby make it easier for a country or terrorist group to obtain plutonium and develop a weapons capability.[125]

Administration officials indicated that they hoped the countries that already had commercial reprocessing plants in operation—France and Great Britain—would stop using them. The United States also wanted France to halt its planned sale of a reprocessing plant to Pakistan, and West Germany to call off its sale of a reprocessing plant and a uranium enrichment plant[126] to Brazil. However, while Carter opposed the near-term commercialization of reprocessing and the breeder, he remained committed to the expansion of nuclear power.

Carter's policy was motivated by concern about the dangers of nuclear weapons proliferation. In 1974 India had become the world's sixth nuclear power, after diverting plutonium from a research reactor supplied by Canada. With Brazil, Argentina, Pakistan, Iran, Iraq, South Korea, Taiwan, and South Africa acquiring nuclear technology, fear grew that if their civilian nuclear power programs gave them direct access to plutonium, the likelihood of their acquiring nuclear weapons would increase since they would then have the fuel needed for weapons manufacture. While Carter might have sought to prevent the supply of reprocessing plants and breeders only to countries thought to be proliferation risks, a discriminatory policy of this nature would have provoked enormous opposition from the Third World and would have had little likelihood of success. As it was, Third World countries charged that the Carter policy was discriminatory because it tolerated reprocessing plants in the developed countries that already had them.

Still, most countries of Western Europe and Japan saw reprocessing and the breeder as their principal long-term hope of reducing dependence upon foreign energy supplies. With conventional reactors, most of these countries still had to import uranium; and in any case, the supplies of the fuel used in conventional reactors (uranium 235) were limited and probably would not last more than another fifty years. But by reprocessing the spent fuel from conventional reactors, fuel supplies could be stretched out, and the breeder reactor, drawing upon the more abundant uranium 238, promised nearly unlimited supplies.

Moreover, many people in Europe and Japan suspected that by getting them to forgo reprocessing and the breeder, Carter was trying to keep the Europeans and the Japanese permanently dependent upon the United States for their supplies of enriched uranium. They also feared that the United States might use its position as a major supplier of enriched uranium to put pressure on them to accept the U.S. position.[127] Indeed, members of Congress and some administration officials spoke of this. In addition, France, West Germany, Sweden, and Canada saw nuclear reactor sales as offering a lucrative market for the future, and with the slump in demand for reactors, they saw nuclear exports as essential for maintaining the economic viability of their nuclear industries. Consequently, they did not want to do anything (i.e. cancel reprocessing deals) that would jeopardize these export sales.

Western Europe and Japan also feared that in calling for a halt to reprocessing and the breeder, the United States was trying to gain an advantage over its competitors in international markets. Since it had far more abundant nonnuclear fuel resources and more substantial uranium 235 supplies, the United States had less need for reprocessing and the breeder than these other countries did. In addition, the United States lagged behind several countries, especially France, in breeder technology, and many suspected that it may have been urging a moratorium on Europe so that it could "get ahead." While Carter proposed to cancel the Clinch River project, he approved research and development on the liquid metal fast-breeder reactor, the mainstay of the nuclear R&D program, and investigating alternative breeder concepts as well.

If European nuclear suppliers lost export sales, U.S. companies might well gain them. In fact, in 1975 West Germany's Kraftwerk Union had won out over suppliers from other countries, securing the contract to supply eight nuclear reactors to Brazil, mainly because it had agreed to supply Brazil with an enrichment and a reprocessing plant.[128] U.S. manufacturers could not match the offer because they were not allowed to export enrichment and reprocessing technology.

From the outset, Western Europe and Japan showed little readiness to go along with Carter's proposals. In a sharp rebuff to the president, three months after his policy was announced, France, West Germany, Italy, Belgium, and the Nether-lands signed a series of accords calling for joint research and development of breeder reactors and for their eventual sale abroad. Similarly, Japan's Prime Minister Takeo Fukuda told President Carter that Japan needed the breeder to free itself from costly, insecure dependence upon foreign energy sources. At a conference of forty nations in Washington in October 1977, not a single country expressed willingness to cancel or defer projects to enrich uranium or reprocess plutonium.

At the London economic summit in May 1977, to defuse the tensions over this issue, the leading capitalist countries agreed to study the relationship between nuclear power and nuclear weapons proliferation. To do so, they established the two-year International Fuel Cycle Evaluation (INFCE). Then, in January 1978, fifteen nations that export nuclear technology agreed on a code of safeguards to ensure that their exports would not be used for construction of nuclear weapons. However, as a result of French and German opposition, the code did not require nations to accept "full-scope" safeguards or to allow all their nuclear facilities to be inspected by international teams before they ordered new equipment. The supplier nations agreed not to export reprocessing equipment that could be used to produce plutonium for weapons in the future.

While this agreement did not put a halt to either the West German–Brazilian or the French-Pakistan deal, France, in August, backed out of its agreement to provide Pakistan with a reprocessing plant. Also, in 1978 the United States enacted the Nuclear Non-Proliferation Act, barring the export of uranium to countries that refused to accept "full-scope" safeguards against diversion of nuclear fuel for weapons purposes. However, the Act authorized the president to continue such shipments for two years, while he sought an agreement with the recipient country on "full-scope" safeguards.

In November 1979 the International Nuclear Fuel Cycle Evaluation released its final report. It concluded that enormous expansion in the number of nuclear power plants in the industrialized and developing countries in the next twenty years would result in a dramatic, unavoidable increase in supplies of bomb-grade nuclear material and that there *is* no proliferation-proof nuclear fuel cycle. The report also assessed the proliferation dangers posed by breeder reactors as no greater than those of existing plants, a position contrary to that of the Carter administration. INFCE advocated continued development of nuclear power and specifically endorsed plutonium-based energy systems, warning that, without the breeder reactor, there would be a shortage of uranium fuel by the end of the century.[129]

While INFCE defused the tensions that existed in 1977, it failed to reconcile national viewpoints about the role of nuclear power. Consequently, the problems that President Carter raised in 1977 are no closer to resolution today. Indeed, as President Carter stated in October 1979, "There are about 10 or 12 and perhaps more nations who have the technical capability and the national means to develop nuclear explosives without delay."[130] In addition, several countries have side-stepped the 1978 agreement to ban the export of sensitive technologies. For example, early in 1980 Switzerland agreed to sell Argentina a heavy-water plant, capable of producing bomb-grade material, despite the fact that Argentina has not agreed to allow international inspection of all its nuclear facilities.[131]

Nor do countries such as Pakistan,[132] South Africa, or Iraq[133] appear to be less intent on acquiring weapons capability today than they were in 1977. If they are denied reprocessing facilities, they can follow other routes to acquiring such capability, that is, small-scale, clandestine facilities. Moreover, since the Carter antiproliferation policy raised concerns about the reliability of the United States as a nuclear supplier, European countries are more determined to obtain their own enrichment and reprocessing facilities and breeder reactors, a development likely to aggravate the proliferation problem. Indeed, rather than reduce the risks of proliferation, the main effect of the president's initiative appears to have been to further erode the prospects for consumer-country cooperation on energy.

Alternative Energy Sources. With nuclear power stalled, many countries looked toward coal as a means of reducing dependence on foreign oil. Despite this, between 1973 and 1978 coal consumption declined in both Western Europe and Japan (see table 10–5). The main reasons for this were that the quality of coal reserves in Western Europe and Japan are generally quite poor and the coal industry in these areas had suffered from years of decline, which were difficult to reverse.

In the United States, where coal reserves are much better, coal consumption grew only modestly in this period. Since 1974, coal has been a much cheaper source of fuel and electric power than oil;[134] however, questions have been raised about the adequacy of the nation's supply of skilled coal miners and the ability of the railroad system to handle substantially increased coal production. Uncertainty about passage of a bill to control strip mining and objections to the reclamation standards eventually established have also hindered coal production.[135] In addition, a wave of wildcat strikes in 1977 and then a four-month

TABLE 10–5. COAL CONSUMPTION, 1973–81 (MILLION-TONNES OIL EQUIVALENT)

	1973	1978	1979
U.S.	335.0	348.9	380.7
Japan	53.7	46.5	50.4
Western Europe	253.6	246.5	259.8
Non-Communist World	825.9	872.2	943.3
Total World	1,668.4	1,863.3	1,975.8

BP, *Statistical Review of the World Oil Industry, 1981*. Changes computed by author.

nationwide coal strike in the winter of 1977–78 hampered production and discouraged investors from making a long-term commitment to coal.

But of all the problems in supplying coal, the most significant constraint on U.S. production has been lack of demand. During the past several years, between 10 and 20 percent of the country's coal capacity has generally gone unused for lack of demand.[136] Utilities have been reluctant to switch to coal because of uncertainty about the emission control standards they will be held to and objections to pollution control devices, where they have been mandated. And Congress's failure to pass the oil and gas users' tax that President Carter recommended has left utilities and industrial plants without strong incentives to convert to coal.

Ultimately, demand for coal will increase substantially only when economically competitive ways of liquifying and gasifying it are found. Following the 1973–74 rise in oil prices, corporate and government officials envisioned development of a major synthetic fuels industry. The Project Independence Report, released in November 1974, estimated that if an accelerated effort were made, shale oil could supply the United States with a million barrels of oil a day by 1985.[137] Early in 1975, President Ford announced a goal of 1 million barrels a day of synthetic oil and gas from coal and oil shale by 1985.[138]

In January 1974, Standard Oil of Indiana and Gulf Oil made a joint bid of $210 million for one of six Western shale-oil tracts offered for lease by the federal government. The companies planned to produce 75,000 barrels of shale oil a day by 1980. A month later, the partners in Colony Development Operation—Shell, Atlantic Richfield, Ashland Oil, and Shale Corporation (TOSCO)—bid $117 million for another rich Colorado tract. Within the next year, two Utah tracts were purchased by consortiums involving Phillips, Sun, and Standard Oil of Ohio.[139]

Similarly, in the early 1970s a number of natural gas transmission companies, including Texas Eastern, El Paso, and American Natural Resources, planned commercial coal gasification projects. These projects, as well as the shale pro-

		Percent Change			
1980	1981	1973–78	1978–79	1979–80	1980–81
393.2	406.3	4.1	9.1	3.3	3.3
57.6	63.2	−13.4	8.4	14.3	9.7
265.5	264.4	− 2.8	5.4	2.2	−.4
986.7	1,018.2	5.6	8.2	4.6	3.2
2,006.5	2,007.2	11.7	6.0	1.6	<.1

jects, were supposed to come onstream by 1980. If they had, they would be capable of producing the equivalent of 365,000 barrels of oil a day, and the United States would be well on its way towards development of a major synthetic fuels industry, enabling it to substantially lessen its dependence upon foreign oil.[140]

However, by October 1974 Colony Development had announced that its commercial shale plant was postponed indefinitely. By the end of 1975, Arco and TOSCO had pulled out of the Colony project and the remaining partners—Shell and Ashland— said they would carry on experimental work at a reduced rate for the time being. Then, in 1976, the Colony partners, the Gulf/Indiana Standard joint venture, and the companies that held the two Utah shale tracts asked the secretary of the interior to suspend their permits. The companies maintained that they could not proceed without federal loan guarantees, cost-sharing grants, or price supports. The secretary agreed to a one-year suspension, freeing the companies from further payments to the federal government and halting work on the projects.[141]

After the suspension was up, Shell dropped out of the Colony venture and the remaining partner, Ashland, teamed up with Occidental on a five-year experimental program using the *in situ* process developed by Occidental, rather than the conventional mining and aboveground retorting process. However, in November 1978 Ashland wrote off its oil-shale investment altogether, and in March 1979 Gulf and Indiana Standard paid Occidental $6 million for the right to use its *in situ* process, which indicated that the Gulf/Indiana Standard process was not working out. Similarly, the various coal gasification projects had either been scaled back to experimental projects or canceled altogether.[142]

By 1980 there was not a commercial synthetic fuels plant of any kind operating in the United States and only one commercial plant was being built: Occidental's *in situ* shale-oil plant, which was expected to be in operation by 1985. Other projects were still in some phase of development, but none was expected to produce commercial quantities before the mid-1980s. Nor has any process been shown to be commercially feasible. At most, energy experts estimated, by 1990 the United States would have a "synfuels" industry capable of producing the equivalent of 2 million barrels of oil a day. Construction of such an industry would cost $60 billion in 1979 dollars—roughly twice the amount spent on all plant construction in 1978.[143]

There were several reasons for nondevelopment of synthetic fuels. While estimates of the cost of various synthetic fuels varied, they rose steadily, and at least until 1979 they were consistently well above the price of OPEC oil.[144] In addition, synthetic fuel plants involve long lead times—about ten years—and huge capital costs—at least $1 billion for a 100,000 b/d plant.[145] Consequently, with the future price of OPEC oil highly uncertain, companies have been reluctant to make the investments necessary for development of a commercial synthetic fuels industry.

Development was also hindered by environmental problems. Shale oil, coal gasification, and coal liquefaction processes require huge quantities of water, yet in the western United States, where nearly all U.S. shale and important coal reserves are located, water is scarce. Production of synthetic fuels also emits considerable pollution, and some of the released particles are believed to be carcinogenic. Synthetic fuel projects also give rise to rapid population movements, creating undesirable "boom town" effects, and mining coal and shale oil "insults" the landscape.

In addition, after shale oil is retorted, the leftover material is greater in volume than the material one began with, creating enormous waste disposal problems. The advantages of the *in situ* process are that it uses less water than conventional mining and retorting and it minimizes the problem of waste disposal, since 80 percent of the material is left in place; however, while Occidental has claimed that its *in situ* process is capable of producing oil at a price competitive with the OPEC price, most industry observers disputed this.[146]

These problems pointed to the need for government action to resolve the environmental issues and provide assistance for technologies that were not yet commercially viable. As a 1976 report by Inform concluded, after surveying the efforts of private corporations to develop seventeen alternative energy technologies, "With a few exceptions, corporations are waiting for the Government to take the lead in deciding whether and how to pursue them."[147] In 1974, in an effort to stimulate development of new energy sources, Congress created the Energy Research and Development Administration (ERDA). While most of ERDA's funds were devoted to development of nuclear power, the agency gave top priority to development of a synthetic fuels industry by the mid-1980s. Indeed, much of the work by private industry on synthetic fuels has been done with funds from ERDA.[148]

In September 1975 President Ford asked Congress to create a $100 billion Energy Independence Authority to encourage development of new energy sources. According to the president's plan, EIA would raise $25 billion through bond sales to the U.S. Treasury and $75 billion through bond sales to the public. It would then lend this money for energy projects that could not be built without government help. However, the authority would not own or operate any energy facility, unless it had to foreclose a loan or was planning to sell or lease the facility as soon as it was in operation.[149]

The plan, originally proposed by Vice President Nelson Rockefeller, met tremendous opposition. Conservatives viewed it as giving too much power to the federal government and feared the impact of such massive federal borrowing on financial markets. Liberals saw it as a subsidy to big business, while energy companies were afraid it would lead to government interference with their activities. Representatives from oil-producing states were uneasy about assisting energy competitors, and environmentalists saw it as encouraging environmentally destructive technologies. Consequently, the plan died in Congress.

As in the United States, Western Europe's and Japan's interest in synthetic fuels increased after the 1973–74 oil-price rise. West Germany, Great Britain, and Belgium, Western Europe's leading coal producers, did experimental work on coal gasification, and Japan, the country most dependent upon imported oil, has maintained a coal liquefaction program.[150] However, in Western Europe and Japan there was generally less effort to develop a synthetic fuels industry than in the United States. The main reason was that Western Europe and Japan had only modest coal reserves and no significant shale resources.[151]

In the United States, pressure for coal gasification came from the fact that the United States was highly dependent upon natural gas consumption and had a large domestic natural gas industry whose production was declining. Coal gasification was seen by both the government and the natural gas industry as a source of badly needed new supplies, but neither Western Europe nor Japan has been as dependent upon natural gas consumption as the United States. Also, between 1973 and 1978 natural gas production increased in Western Europe, while in Japan the natural gas industry was virtually nonexistent. As a result, there was less pressure from consumers and producers for coal gasification in these countries.

Just as interest in synthetic fuels increased after the 1973–74 oil-price rise, so did interest in solar energy and other renewable sources. In the United States, federal funding for solar and geothermal energy increased by a factor of ten between fiscal 1974 and fiscal 1976.[152] In April 1974 Japan launched its "Sunshine Program," aimed at broad-scale utilization of solar energy, geothermal power, and hydrogen as a secondary source. In Europe, the most ambitious program was begun by France, which began building a solar power plant, subsidizing flat-plate solar collectors for both water and space heating, and supporting three companies that started work on prototypes of a 1 kilowatt solar generator designed to replace costly diesel-fired generators in remote areas. West Germany also has a large solar heating program.[153]

While the United States spent over $100 million on solar energy in 1976, no other country spent more than $10 million.[154] This difference was due to the greater wealth of the United States and to the fact that its climate is more suitable to utilization of solar energy than most European countries or Japan. Also, spending on solar energy was only a small fraction of spending on nuclear energy. For example, in the United States in fiscal 1976, the government spent more than 6.5 times as much on nuclear power as on solar energy.[155] Nor were the results of solar programs encouraging. Early in 1979 the U.S. Department of Energy concluded that solar heating technology was not yet ready, in cost or in technical terms, for major marketing. At the same time, the department concluded that government purchases, by stimulating mass production, would not bring down the cost of solar photovoltaics enough to make them commercially viable.[156] Similarly, the centerpiece of France's solar program, the 2 megawatt Themis solar thermal-electric generator, was scrapped in 1979. It was estimated that electricity from Themis would have cost about thirteen times more than that produced by France's almost completed Super-Phenix nuclear breeder reactor.[157]

With development of solar energy lagging, by the end of the 1970s none of the developed countries received more than 1 percent of its energy supplies from solar energy, and no "renewable" technologies were likely to meet a major share of the industrial countries' energy needs before 1990.[158]

With the 1973–74 rise in oil prices, prospects improved for the development of many new energy sources, yet the failure of the consuming countries to take adequate advantage of these new opportunities—their inability to develop a commercially viable synthetic fuels industry, their limited efforts in terms of energy conservation and renewable resources, their continual emphasis on nuclear power and its disappointing progress and the rise in U.S. oil imports—contributed to the exporting countries' ability to keep prices up and even increase them. Indeed, with the consuming countries making little progress on the development of alternative energy sources, the exporting countries did not have to confront serious immediate declines in the demand for their oil or the prospect that, in the foreseeable future, they might have trouble selling it because substitutes were available.

The consuming countries' efforts to develop effective energy policies were hindered by lack of cooperation with one another, which prevented them from developing an effective emergency sharing scheme. As a result, when another loss of supplies occurred, they panicked, again driving up prices. Yet the failure of the consuming-country governments to develop effective energy policies was only part of the inadequacy of the consuming countries' response to the 1973–74 rise in oil prices. Equally important was the lack of effort by the international oil companies to develop new sources of oil and natural gas.

11

Keeping the Price Up [III]: The Fallowing of the World's Oil and Gas Resources

Of all shortcomings of international energy policy, none is more serious than the failure to find and develop the world's remaining oil and natural gas resources. Aside from certain investments in energy conservation, no energy source is likely to be less expensive to produce than conventional supplies of oil or natural gas. Although oil currently sells for more than $30 a barrel, the exploration and development cost of even the high-priced North Sea oil is estimated at no more than $12. Exploration and development costs in the prolific Persian Gulf fields still run at about 50¢,[1] and experts have estimated that most of the world's ultimately recoverable oil resources could be produced for less than $12 (in 1976 dollars).[2]

While it takes at least three to five years from the time a new oil field is discovered until it is brought into production, this is shorter than the ten years it takes to develop a new coal mine, the ten to twelve years it takes to build a nuclear power plant, and the ten to fifteen years it would take to develop a synthetic fuels industry. Moreover, as we saw in chapter 2, there are substantial prospects for finding additional reserves of oil and natural gas. Writing in the American Association of Petroleum Geologists' *Bulletin* in May 1978, Michel T. Halbouty concluded that as much oil and slightly more gas remains to be found as has been discovered so far.[3] Moreover, new sources of oil and gas would put downward pressure on the cartel price.

From 1920 to 1970, oil discoveries averaged 20 billion barrels a year, but during the 1970s they averaged only 10 billion barrels.[4] With oil consumption averaging about 20 billion barrels a year,[5] proven reserves have fallen. While between 1947 and 1974 the world's proven reserves of oil increased by a factor of ten, in 1975 reserves declined and since then they have remained essentially stagnant (see table 11–1).

The situation with natural gas is only slightly more encouraging; after increasing steadily, noncommunist world reserves have been essentially stagnant since the end of 1974 (see table 11–2). While world reserves of natural gas are more than forty-five times world consumption,[6] problems in the delivery system prevent consumers from utilizing much of the gas that is available. In fact, because they have no market for it, each day the OPEC countries "flare off" half the gas that is produced with the oil they pump.[7] If this gas could be utilized, it would provide the energy equivalent of 4 mb/d of oil—more than any OPEC country, aside from Saudi Arabia, currently exports.[8]

Of the world's 600 petroleum basins, 200 have had little or no exploration for oil and gas. However, their dimensions, the amounts and types of their sediment fill, and their gross structural properties are known. About half of these unexplored basins are small and not likely to yield large quantities of hydrocarbons; of the remaining unexplored basins, most are in harsh physical environments, either deep offshore or in polar areas, where drilling is likely to be slow and expensive. Moreover, potential for significant reserves of hydrocarbons is thought to exist in only twenty of these basins, and of these twenty, most have been bypassed because they are too remotely located (i.e. deep within the interior of continents) or because political disputes have prevented access to them.[9]

Two hundred forty of the remaining 400 basins have been explored to some extent, but have not yielded commercial discoveries. Of the remaining 160, only twenty-five have the equivalent of at least 10 billion barrels of oil or gas. These twenty-five basins contain 86 percent of the hydrocarbons discovered to date. Only six basins have more than 50 billion barrels, and these account for 65 percent of the discovered petroleum. The Arab-Iranian Gulf Basin alone contains 40 percent of all discovered hydrocarbons.[10] Moreover, geologists Moody and Halbouty estimate that half of the world's undiscovered resources are likely to be found in areas currently producing or known, with most of the remainder in harsh, higher-cost environments.[11]

With "both sides" acknowledging these basic facts of geology, there is a pessimistic and an optimistic view of the potential for finding additional hydrocarbon resources. The pessimists, who include most oil companies and the CIA, argue that 50 percent of the recoverable oil discovered so far is in thirty-three "supergiant" fields[12] and 25 percent has been found in relatively few "giant" fields.[13] But giant and supergiant fields tend to be discovered early in the exploration process in any given petroleum basin because they usually occur in large, identifiable structures.[14] Consequently, the prospects for finding more giant and supergiant fields grow increasingly dim, reducing the likelihood of major discoveries.

While in the early 1960s thirteen recognized or potential supergiant fields were found, in the early 1970s only two potential supergiants were found.[15] Similarly, of the fifty-seven giants in the continental United States, fifty-three were found before World War II. Total reserve discoveries in giants and supergiants have been fewer in the 1970s than in any decade since 1920. While moderate amounts of oil may still be found in smaller fields, it is sure to be more costly than oil from the giants, and in recent years the discovery rate has been falling throughout the non-Communist world.[16]

This pessimistic view may be questioned on several grounds. Whether giant and supergiant fields are readily discovered is far from clear; the historical record suggests that this may not be the case. It took more than six years' exploration

TABLE 11–1. ESTIMATED PROVEN RESERVES OF CRUDE OIL, 1947–81 (BILLION BARRELS)

Year-End	United States	Canada	Latin America	Western Hemisphere	Middle East
1947	21.5	0.1	10.1	31.7	28.6
1959	31.7	3.5	24.4	59.7	181.4
1969	29.6	8.6	29.2	67.4	333.5
1973	35.3	7.7	31.6	74.6	350.2
1974	34.2	7.2	40.6	82.0	403.9
1975	32.7	6.7	35.4	74.7	368.4
1976	30.9	6.3	29.6	66.8	367.7
1977	29.5	6.0	40.4	75.8	366.2
1978	27.8	6.9	41.2	75.9	370.0
1979	27.1	6.8	56.5	90.3	361.9
1980	29.8	6.4	69.5	105.7	362.1
1981	29.8	7.3	85.0	122.1	362.8

Basic Petroleum Data Book, vol. 2, no. 2, sec. 2, table 1.

before oil was discovered in Iran in 1908 and more than five years of drilling, plus a number of years of reconnaissance and survey work, before Nigeria's first commercial oil find in 1956.

Even if giant and supergiant fields *are* more easily discovered, it seems premature to dismiss their existence in the 240 basins that have been explored "to some extent," without commercial finds, or the 200 that have not been explored. Indeed, many geologists have a far more optimistic view of the world's undiscovered potential. For example, in 1978 officials from the U.S. Geological Survey told the Energy Subcommittee of the Congressional Joint Economic Committee that the world's supply of recoverable oil might well be two or three

TABLE 11–2. ESTIMATED PROVEN RESERVES OF NATURAL GAS, 1966–81 (TRILLION CUBIC FEET)

Year-End	United States	Canada	Latin America	Western Hemisphere	Middle East
1966	289.3	43.5	64.6	397.3	215.1
1969	275.1	52.0	163.2	490.2	235.3
1973	250.0	52.5	91.3	393.7	413.3
1974	237.1	56.7	100.2	394.1	672.7
1975	228.2	57.0	90.5	375.7	538.6
1976	216.0	58.3	90.3	364.6	536.5
1977	208.9	59.5	108.5	376.8	719.7
1978	200.3	59.0	113.0	372.3	730.7
1979	194.9	85.5	144.5	424.9	740.3
1980	199.0	87.3	159.8	446.1	752.4
1981	198.0	89.9	176.3	464.2	762.5

Basic Petroleum Data Book, vol. 2, no. 2, sec. 13, table 1.

Africa	Asia	Western Europe	Non-Communist World	Communist	Total World
0.1	1.3	0.1	61.7	6.5	68.2
7.3	10.2	1.5	260.0	30.0	290.0
54.7	13.1	1.8	470.5	60.0	530.5
67.3	15.6	16.0	523.7	103.0	626.7
68.3	21.0	25.8	601.0	111.4	712.4
65.1	21.2	25.5	554.9	103.0	657.9
60.6	19.4	24.5	539.0	101.1	640.1
59.2	19.7	26.9	547.8	98.0	645.8
57.9	20.0	24.0	547.8	94.0	641.8
57.1	19.4	23.5	522.2	90.0	642.2
55.1	19.6	23.1	565.6	86.3	651.9
56.1	19.2	24.6	584.9	85.8	670.7

times larger than previous estimates (in the 2,000-billion-barrel range) suggested.[17]

There is also a strong possibility that the official estimates of "proven" reserves have been underestimated. Rather than estimates of the amount of oil in a given field, "reserve" estimates are estimates of the amount of oil that can be produced economically at prevailing price levels. Therefore reserve estimates should have increased substantially as companies reassessed the percentage of oil that could be produced economically following the 1973–74 oil-price increase. However, the officially reported increases in both the year-end 1974 and the year-end 1980 reserve estimates were quite modest (see table 11–1), which

Africa	Asia	Western Europe	Non-Communist World	Communist	Total World
158.2	32.5	88.6	891.6	150.0	1,041.6
197.1	67.5	150.8	1,140.9	350.0	1,490.9
187.7	114.2	193.8	1,302.8	735.4	2,038.2
315.0	115.9	202.8	1,700.4	846.0	2,546.4
207.2	111.6	180.9	1,413.9	835.0	2,248.9
209.1	120.0	141.9	1,372.1	953.0	2,325.1
207.5	122.7	138.2	1,564.9	955.0	2,519.9
186.3	119.9	143.3	1,552.3	945.0	2,497.3
210.4	128.8	135.4	1,639.2	935.0	2,574.2
208.5	126.3	159.3	1,692.6	953.9	2,646.5
211.7	127.6	150.7	1,716.6	1,194.7	2,911.3

suggests that, rather than a decline in reserves, there is systematic underreport-ing.[18] Indeed, official reserve figures have grossly understated the producible reserves in the Middle East for more than forty years.[19]

Because nearly all reserve estimates originate with the oil industry, it is not difficult to imagine a motive for underreporting. Also, reserve estimates are likely to be unreliable for countries in which companies are not currently operat-ing. Furthermore, reserve estimates for fields discovered in recent years are likely to increase substantially in the future, for with continued drilling, reservoir characteristics become better known, making it possible to substitute more realis-tic estimates for reserves. In the past, this has generally led to increases in reserve estimates.

In the future, proportionally more oil may come from smaller fields, but improved recovery technology may keep its cost down. Also, as technology improves, the recovery rate should increase, boosting reserves.[20] Even most pessimists recognize this, to some extent. In the Middle East, in particular, the allowance for increased recovery by secondary methods is assessed with consid-erable overcaution.[21] Improved technology should also make it possible to find and economically produce oil in areas previously considered too difficult to make exploration worthwhile. Indeed, while offshore production accounts for about a sixth of the oil produced today, offshore drilling began only in 1947.[22] Since then, companies have learned to drill in deeper and deeper waters.

The history of "expert opinion" about the future of oil reserves should also make one skeptical about predictions of imminent shortages. In 1930 Dad Joiner, a seventy-year-old wildcatter, without a nickel to his name, discovered oil in East Texas after the leading geologists and major oil companies of the day had opined against the possibility of oil in the area. Prior to Socal's 1932 discovery of oil in Bahrain, experts had said there was no oil in the Persian Gulf area outside Iraq.

In 1917 the director of the U.S. Bureau of Mines recommended that shale oil be considered the principal basis of future petroleum products "because of the threatened shortage of petroleum from oil fields in this country." Throughout the 1920s, experts in and out of government warned of a severe scarcity that never materialized.[23] In 1939 the Department of Interior predicted that U.S. oil sup-plies would last only another thirteen years, and in 1949 Interior Secretary Julius A. Krug warned that the end of the U.S. oil supply was almost in sight.[24]

Another big question mark is the hydrocarbon potential of the non-OPEC LDCs. The conventional estimate of the world's ultimately recoverable potential is about 2,000 billion barrels, but in recent years this figure has been challenged by Bernardo Grossling, senior scientist at the U.S. Geological Survey, who maintains that the ultimately recoverable potential could be as high as 6,000 billion barrels, with most of the big, undiscovered fields in the poorer countries that have been only lightly explored.[25]

Grossling points out that, through 1975, the Soviet Union, the continental United States, and the Middle East accounted for 72 percent of the world's production and proven reserves of oil, but only 28 percent of the world's prospective area. Latin America, Africa, and South Asia–Pacifica accounted for less than 20 percent of the world's production and proven reserves of oil, but for nearly 50 percent of the prospective area. While drilling density averaged 0.96 well per square mile of prospective territory in the United States and 0.15 in the Soviet Union, in Latin America the average was less than 0.05 and in the South Asian-Pacifica less than 0.01. Consequently, while Moody estimates the remaining undiscovered potential of the Third World at slightly over 200 billion barrels (see table 2–6), Grossling estimates it at between 465 billion and 1,715 billion barrels.[26] Moreover, a 1978 report to the Joint Economic Committee maintained that production in Third World countries outside the Middle East could be boosted by 4 mb/d by 1990 and by twice that by the year 2000.[27]

Even if one accepts the conventional view, as represented by Moody, there is considerable scope for finding and developing additional oil and gas reserves. According to Moody's calculations, for every barrel of oil consumed during the 121-year oil era, four barrels of oil—discovered and undiscovered—are still in the ground. And as Exxon Chairman Clifton C. Garvin told company stockholders in May 1977, "Look, we're not running out of oil. That's not the consideration. We're not going to run out in your lifetime or mine. I don't know when the transition period is as to when we will no longer have as much oil as we want, to use in any form that we want."[28]

The prospects for natural gas are even better. While worldwide consumption of natural gas is equal to about 27 mb/d of oil, proven reserves of natural gas, at a reserves-to-production ratio of 20:1, would support production equivalent to 75 mb/d (world consumption of oil is currently about 60 mb/d).[29] And according to *Petroleum Intelligence Weekly,* reserves of natural gas are "seriously understated."[30]

While the ultimately recoverable reserves of natural gas are estimated to be about equal to the ultimately recoverable reserves of oil, roughly 60 percent of the oil has already been found but only about 30 percent of the gas. This is partly because at low drilling depths there is a better chance of finding oil than gas, but at deeper depths the reverse is true. Since most drilling has been at relatively modest depths, more oil has been found. In fact, it is only as drilling technology has improved that deeper drilling has become possible.

Equally significant is that, outside the developed countries, there have been hardly any efforts to find natural gas, most gas being discovered accidentally in the search for oil. Nonetheless, only 10 percent of the giant hydrocarbon fields discovered around 1955 were gas fields, but between 1970 and 1975, 72 percent were gas fields. A 1975 OECD report expressed the hope of finding much more gas in the industrialized countries.[31] Moreover, while one may object to LNG as dangerous and overly expensive, there are many markets to which natural gas could be supplied by pipeline, and the possibility of substituting natural gas for oil in domestic markets, thereby freeing oil for export, is worthy of far more consideration than it has received.

WORLDWIDE EXPLORATION AND DEVELOPMENT

What has been lacking has been a sufficient commitment to develop these potentials. Since 1973, real expenditures on exploration and development have increased substantially (see appendix table A5), especially by historic standards; however, this increase has not been commensurate with the world's increasing expenditures on oil and natural gas. Nor has it substantially boosted the world's proven reserves of oil and natural gas or created enough productive capacity to force the nominal world oil price to fall (as it did from 1957 to 1970). As Adelman stated, "We are getting the worst of both worlds—high prices and lagging investment."[32]

As in the period prior to 1973–74, there has been continuing overemphasis on exploration and production expenditures in the United States, the world's most heavily explored area, which still accounts for roughly half of all exploration and production expenditures. Between 1973 and 1978, an increasing percentage of all wells drilled in the world were drilled in the United States, a reversal of the pre-1973 trend (see table 11–3). Correspondingly, prospects for expanding production in the Third World continued to be neglected. In 1978, Latin America, Africa, and the Far East accounted for only 20 percent of all noncommunist world expenditures on exploration and development. While 48,513 wells were drilled in the United States in 1978, only 2,668 were drilled in all the non-OPEC LDCs, despite the fact that, on average, wells in non-OPEC LDCs yield about 300 barrels per foot drilled versus only 15 to 20 barrels per foot drilled in the United States.[33]

A study by the World Bank, published in 1978, found that "vast sedimentary

TABLE 11–3. WORLDWIDE OIL EXPLORATION, 1973–78

	Total Wells Drilled			Total Wildcats Drilled		
	1973	1978	% Increase 1973–78	1973	1978	% Increase 1973–78
Non-Communist world	36,586	61,122	67.1	10,974	15,248	38.9
U.S.	27,602	48,513	75.8	7,466	10,677	43.0
Canada	4,621	7,170	55.2	2,219	3,144	41.7
Other Developed nations	522	789	51.1	319	395	23.8
OPEC countries	1,925	1,982*	3.0	363	364	.3
Non-OPEC LDCs	1,916	2,668	39.2	607	668	10.0
African non-OPECs	156	208	33.3	80	102	27.5
Latin American non-OPECs	1,572	1,982	26.1	417	349	−16.3
Asian non-OPECs	74	310	318.9	70	150	114.3
U.S. as % of total	75.4	79.4		68.0	70.0	

*Figures for Iraq not available.

All figures from *Oil and Gas Journal* (various issues); percentage increases computed by author. "Wildcats" are wells drilled in previously unexplored areas.

areas that probably contain 75 percent of all potential petroleum resources of Latin America, 80 percent of those of Africa and 95 percent of Asia and the Far East, are yet to be intensively prospected and developed."[34] The Bank estimated that while the oil-importing developing countries have only 2 percent of the world's proven reserves, they may account for as much as 15 percent of the world's ultimately recoverable reserves. According to the Bank, while twenty-two oil-importing developing countries produce *some* oil, thirty-eight others have reasonable prospects of finding significant quantities. Of these thirty-eight countries, the Bank concluded that only seven had been explored on a more or less adequate scale while another seven had been explored on a moderate scale.[35]

Similarly, in 1979 the CIA concluded that while finding fields of Persian Gulf size appears possible only in Mexico and, perhaps, Egypt, more work is needed to prove and expand reserves in the Upper Amazon Basin and offshore areas of Brazil. The agency indicated that the Bay of Bengal, onshore Burma, the Andaman Islands, and the South China Sea also show promise, and the coast of East Africa was found to be almost entirely unexplored.[36]

Few non-OPEC LDCs are likely to become major oil exporters, but even if they do not export oil, development of their oil resources would reduce their demand for oil imports, which could be important in lessening pressure on world markets. Of course, as countries develop their oil industries, they are likely to increase their consumption of oil, which would offset the gains the consuming countries would realize vis-à-vis OPEC from increased oil production. However, if natural gas consumption in non-OPEC LDCs could also be boosted, oil would be freed for export. In addition, most non-OPEC LDCs have undeveloped hydro potential.[37]

Several factors have combined to limit exploration and development. Rather than to the oil industry, the bulk of increased revenues from the sale of oil went to governments, which used most of the money for purposes other than expanding oil supplies. In addition, a multinational corporation can choose between countries, seeking the most favorable opportunities for new investment and spreading risks by investing in several countries. But a producing-country government lacks these advantages since it is not likely to invest in another country's oil industry. Producing-country national oil companies also lack the majors' experience in exploration, and do not have data on exploration prospects comparable to the majors'.

The principal barrier to expansion of natural gas use has been the difficulty of transporting it from where it is produced to where it is needed.[38] In 1975 the OPEC countries accounted for 60 percent of the non-Communist world's natural gas reserves but only 8 percent of its marketed production.[39] Lacking large populations, industries that could utilize this gas, and internal distribution systems, these countries have been unable to absorb the bulk of the gas they produce along with oil. On the other hand, exporting the gas requires costly investments in pipelines, liquefaction plants, cryogenic tankers, etc. The required investments can often take twenty to twenty-five years to pay off and the lead times are substantial, roughly five years for an LNG project. Yet with natural gas pricing policy in the consuming countries uncertain, both exporting countries and private companies have been reluctant to make such extensive, long-term investments.

Moreover, the magnitude of the OPEC countries' per barrel revenues on oil is also a barrier to marketing their enormous natural gas resources. It costs much more to deliver natural gas to consumers, because liquefaction and transport are very expensive.[40] Therefore, if natural gas and oil are sold for the same price to consumers, the OPEC countries net much less on natural gas. Thus in 1979, on gas sales, Algeria netted $1.25 per million BTUs, or the equivalent of $7 per barrel of crude oil[41]—a nice profit, but not nearly so much as the OPEC countries were then earning by selling 50¢ oil for more than $20. Recognizing this, OPEC countries have been afraid that, by selling natural gas, they would reduce their total oil sales and that, as a result, their total revenues would decline. Partly because of this, half of the associated gas produced in the OPEC countries continues to be flared.[42] However, if countries continue to lack markets for the natural gas they produce, they may cut back on oil production rather than continue to flare the associated gas.

With production from Europe's principal source of natural gas—the Groningen fields in the Netherlands—declining and with gas supplies from the North Sea unable to make up for the entire decline, Western Europe has been looking for new sources of supply.[43] Similarly, Japan plans to increase greatly its LNG imports in the future. But meeting this demand will only be possible if the necessary investments in new facilities are undertaken, and so far the uncertainty about natural gas pricing has hindered new investment. In an effort to resolve the issue of natural gas pricing, Abu Dhabi has taken the leadership in pushing for natural gas to be priced at parity with the landed cost of imported crude oil. So far, Japan has accepted this principle, but Western Europe and the United States, both of which have not paid such high prices for natural gas in the past, have been reluctant to do so.[44] Moreover, even if this principle is accepted, as increasingly it is, uncertainty about the future price makes rational decision making on LNG difficult. The technical difficulties of building an LNG plant and the uncertainty of consuming-country energy policies have also led to delays in building LNG plants.

Investment in new oil and gas resources has also been hindered by the transformation of the concession system. When oil companies had twenty-five- to sixty-year concessions, they could make investments and feel confident they would be around to reap the rewards, but as a result of the changes in the early 1970s, the companies have lost that security. With the OPEC countries tearing up one agreement after another, sanctity of contracts has become a thing of the past for the international oil industry. Third World countries can still invite the companies in on highly favorable terms, but, in view of the OPEC revolution, the durability of commitments lacks credibility for the companies. This has been particularly true in countries where the regimes have been politically unstable.[45]

Territorial disputes between countries, particularly in Southeast Asia, have also been an important obstacle to the development of oil and gas resources.

Since prices rose, neither the oil-exporting countries nor the oil companies have had any interest in bringing them down. For the companies, falling prices would reduce the value of their oil reserve holdings throughout the world, transforming the huge inventory profits of 1974 into inventory losses. The majors would certainly want to secure their position in a new oil producing area, and they would want to make sure they have enough crude to meet their marketing needs, but to expect them to make a vigorous exploration effort in an unproven, politically risky area, in an effort to drive prices down, is to fail to recognize that the companies are private, profit-maximizing organizations and not promoters of the public welfare. Consequently, with the market soft from 1974 to 1978 and with real oil prices falling, it is not surprising that the companies showed considerable restraint in searching for and developing new oil supplies. Moreover, companies have never been eager to develop new sources of oil before they have refining and marketing outlets for it.

The major international oil companies also have several reasons for favoring the continued production of OPEC oil rather than oil from non-OPEC LDCs. Through the participation agreements, the major companies have carved out a lucrative role for themselves as service agents to the OPEC countries. Yet this role might be jeopardized if they took actions that threaten the OPEC price level. While smaller companies generally lacked ties to the OPEC countries and therefore have not had to worry about antagonizing them, these companies have also lacked the capital required to undertake exploration in remote and unproven areas.[46]

Moreover, so long as an OPEC country charged a company a specially low price for equity oil, that company had an interest in boosting the country's total production, since the more oil that was produced, the more equity oil the company received. Also, companies were often paid in crude for their loss of equity in the producing concessions in the exporting countries, further committing them to crude purchases in the OPEC countries. Furthermore, as the exporting countries increased their participation share, they assumed increasing responsibility for providing the investment capital needed to expand production in their countries. This meant that, with little or no investment, the companies could secure the oil they needed for their refining and marketing needs from the OPEC countries. Indeed, even companies that were not former concessionaires could generally purchase oil from the OPEC countries.

In contrast, to secure oil in a non-OPEC LDC, the companies would have to make extensive investments that are politically and geologically risky,[47] and unlike the situation in the OPEC countries, the non-OPEC LDC host countries are not likely to provide any initial investment capital. The companies' disinclination to invest in the non-OPEC LDCs is accentuated by the fact that their oil fields are likely to be smaller and the costs of production (between $3 and $6 a barrel)[48] higher than in the Persian Gulf. Exploration and development in the non-OPEC LDCs has also been hampered by inadequate analysis of data and shortages of skilled personnel. In addition, it is much more expensive to drill in a new territory than in an established one.

By raising prices and making production of U.S. oil so profitable, the United States reduced the likelihood of development occurring in other parts of the world where geologic conditions are more favorable, for the effect of U.S. policy was to divert capital, equipment, and skilled labor to the United States. Favorable financing arrangements have also made investments in the United States extremely attractive. Furthermore, by guaranteeing refiners a supply of crude oil and assuring that all U.S. refiners paid the same amount for it, the U.S. entitlements program greatly reduced the incentives that companies would otherwise have had for finding their own oil.

The oil industry's limited exploration and development was also due to an increasingly unfavorable financial situation. Figures compiled by Chase Manhattan Bank on twenty-six leading oil companies show that from 1973 to 1978 the ratio of their combined cash flow to their capital expenditures declined.[49] Still, it would be wrong to view the industry as "cash starved." With these highly creditworthy companies able to borrow funds, capital availability was not an immediate constraint on further increases in spending.[50] Indeed, the White House's Office of Energy Policy and Planning found that the top eighteen U.S. oil companies had $4.9 billion on hand at the end of 1975, versus $1.9 billion at the end of 1973,[51] and in 1977 Exxon President Howard C. Kauffman told Dallas security analysts that Exxon's problem was not lack of cash but lack of opportunity.[52]

To encourage development of oil resources in the non-OPEC LDCs, in 1977 the World Bank reversed its longstanding policy against making loans for petroleum projects in Third World countries and lent $150 million to India for development of its offshore Bombay oil fields. Yet, the Bank was still not willing to make loans for oil exploration, its funds being limited to projects for development of proven reserves. Then in 1978 the Bank's staff proposed a $500 million plan to finance oil exploration in the world's poorest countries as a means of helping them cope with soaring oil prices. The plan ran into opposition from the international oil companies and various U.S. government officials.[53] They feared that the Bank's policy would encourage the growth of national oil companies and impinge upon the traditional role of the private sector.

As a result of this opposition, in January 1979 the Bank announced a scaled-down plan for expansion of its lending program and a new willingness to consider loans for exploration. To accelerate production in the non-OPEC LDCs, the Bank planned to lend $3 billion between 1979 and 1983.[54] For 1979–80, however, only $40–50 million was allocated for exploration, about one-tenth the amount originally envisioned.[55]

Nonetheless, Exxon opposed even this scaled-down program. An Exxon executive, who was planning to leave the company to work in the World Bank's energy section, explained the reasons for Exxon's opposition: "We only take exception to lending for exploratory drilling to generally inexperienced national oil companies. If you had the bank supporting a national oil company with 7 percent money it would take out of the picture the established oil companies, which require a larger return. If a field looks good, let us do it ourselves—that's what's bad about the bank loans for exploration."[56] But the World Bank staff maintained that drilling has lagged in the non-OPEC LDCs primarily because the major oil companies are not interested in small or medium-size fields outside politically stable areas like the United States. Nor can smaller national and private oil companies generally raise capital for expensive and risky exploration projects in the non-OPEC LDCs.[57]

In addition to the World Bank program, in 1977 the Overseas Private Investment Corporation began offering political-risk insurance to companies investing in exploration, development, and production in non-OPEC LDCs (contracts have been signed covering exploration in Jordan and Ghana). However, like the World Bank's program, OPIC's program is quite small, being limited to a maximum 20 percent of its portfolio. Nor does the program overcome the basic obstacles to exploration and development in non-OPEC LDCs, for while it protects companies against losses due to confiscation, it does not insure their right to continue to operate and earn a profit once oil is discovered; nor does it protect them against financial or geologic risks.[58] Aside from these limited programs, neither the United States nor the other developed countries have any policy to encourage development of oil and gas in the non-OPEC LDCs. Nor, as we shall see, have their efforts to develop their own hydrocarbon resources been particularly successful.

In the pages that follow, we will briefly examine the efforts to develop oil and gas resources in the various areas of the world (see tables 11-4 and 11-5). This survey is intended to demonstrate and highlight many of the points already made. It should also provide an overview of both exploration and development in the 1974–78 period and the prospects for further oil and gas development in the immediate future.

From this survey, the following conclusion should become clear. Throughout the 1970s there have been substantial prospects for developing additional oil and gas resources; yet the opportunities were not adequately exploited because of political and economic obstacles and a lack of commitment by the international oil companies.

The United States. Despite record drilling between 1973 and 1978, reserves of oil and natural gas continued to decline in the United States. In this period drilling increased from 136.4 million to 226.6 million feet, but the "finding rate" in barrels-of-oil equivalent per foot drilled declined from 24.8 to 14.[59] In 1973 the United States added 2.6 billion barrels to its reserves, but from 1975 through 1978 the yearly discovery rate averaged only 1.8 billion barrels.[60]

TABLE 11-4. WORLD OIL PRODUCTION, 1973-81 (TB/D)

	1973	1978	1979	1980
U.S.	10,950	10,270	10,135	10,170
Canada	2,115	1,575	1,770	1,725
Norway	35	350	385	525
U.K.	*	1,095	1,600	1,650
Total Western Europe	440	1,820	2,380	2,560
Saudi Arabia	7,440	8,315	9,555	9,990
Iraq	2,020	2,560	3,475	2,645
Kuwait	2,810	1,945	2,270	1,425
Neutral Zone	535	470	570	535
United Arab Emirates	1,525	1,830	1,830	1,705
Qatar	570	485	510	470
Iran	5,895	5,275	3,175	1,480
Algeria	1,095	1,230	1,225	1,105
Libya	2,180	1,985	2,090	1,790
Nigeria	2,055	1,895	2,300	2,055
Gabon	150	210	205	175
Ecuador	210	205	215	210
Venezuela	3,460	2,235	2,425	2,240
Indonesia	1,335	1,635	1,590	1,580
Total OPEC	31,280	30,275	31,435	27,405
Soviet Union	8,685	11,595	11,870	12,215
China	1,100	2,090	2,130	2,125
Total Communist	10,170	14,115	14,410	14,725
Mexico	550	1,330	1,630	2,155
Egypt	255	480	525	590
Total Non-OPEC LDCs	3,155	4,560	5,165	5,710
Total Non-Communist	48,340	48,960	51,350	47,980
Total World	58,510	63,075	65,760	62,705

*Less than 5,000 b/d.

BP, *Statistical Review of the World Oil Industry, 1981*. Figures for U.S. include natural gas liquids. Average annual increases computed by author.

Because of the extent to which the continental United States had already been drilled, this was not surprising. As Robert Stobaugh, director of the Energy Project at Harvard Business School, has pointed out, four times as many wells have been drilled in the United States as in all other non-Communist nations combined.[61] Dr. H. Williard Menard, director of the U.S. Geological Survey, recently stated that the chances of finding a new giant oil field in the United

1981	Average Annual Increase (Percent)			
	1973–78	1978–79	1979–80	1980–81
10,150	− 1.3	− 1.3	.3	− .2
1,565	− 5.7	12.4	− 2.5	− 9.3
505	58.5	10.0	36.4	− 3.8
1.845	—	46.1	3.1	11.8
2,735	32.8	30.8	7.6	6.8
9,990	2.2	14.9	4.6	—
900	4.9	35.7	−23.9	−66.0
965	− 7.1	16.7	−37.2	−32.3
370	− 2.6	21.3	− 6.1	−30.8
1,510	3.7	0	− 6.8	−11.4
405	− 3.2	5.2	− 7.8	−13.8
1,315	− 2.2	−39.8	−53.4	−11.1
1,010	2.4	− .4	− 9.8	− 8.6
1,120	− 1.9	5.3	−14.4	−37.4
1,445	− 1.6	21.4	−10.7	−29.7
150	7.0	− 2.4	−14.6	−14.3
220	− .5	4.9	− 2.3	4.8
2,170	− 8.4	8.5	− 7.6	− 3.1
1,605	4.1	− 2.8	− .6	1.6
23,175	− .7	3.8	−12.8	−15.4
12,370	5.9	2.4	2.9	1.3
2,035	13.7	1.9	− .2	− 4.2
14,760	6.8	2.1	2.2	.2
2,585	19.3	22.6	32.2	20.0
690	13.5	9.4	12.4	16.9
6.290	7.6	13.3	10.6	10.2
44,340	.3	4.9	− 6.6	− 7.6
59,100	1.5	4.3	− 4.6	− 5.7

States mainland are just about zero.[62] Nonetheless, federal policy continues to encourage development of domestic sources of oil and gas.

One effect of this has been to leave producers with very high profits on domestic production. For example, figures released by Exxon show that while between 1975 and 1978 its return on "employed capital" (both equity and long-term debt) averaged 22.0 percent in domestic exploration and production, its

TABLE 11–5. WORLD MARKETED PRODUCTION OF NATURAL GAS, 1973–81 (TB/D OF OIL EQUIVALENT)

	1973	1978	1979	1980
U.S.	11,134	9,796	10,073	9,886
Canada	1,398	1,406	1,508	1,384
Netherlands	1,076	1,348	1,422	1,380
U.K.	510	677	687	641
Norway	—	269	390	471
Total Western Europe	2,364	3,079	3,273	3,190
Saudi Arabia	82	171	211	264
Kuwait	94	113	157	124
Abu Dhabi	22	90	113	104
Iran	358	351	362	150
Total Middle East	651	852	1,036	841
Algeria	86	251	470	387
Libya	56	92	123	94
Nigeria	6	6	24	20
Indonesia	92	197	285	335
Venezuela	235	267	295	300
Mexico	277	442	470	545
Soviet Union	4,276	6,513	7,101	7,614
China	133	249	251	244
Total Communist	5,229	7,730	8,280	8,764
Developed Market Economies	15,038	14,507	15,096	14,718
Developing Market Economies	1,992	2,900	3,528	3,391
Total Non-Communist	17,030	17,407	18,624	18,109
Total World	22,259	25,137	26,904	26,873

BP, *Statistical Review of the World Oil Industry, 1981.* Tb/d conversions and average annual increases computed by author.

return on domestic refining and marketing averaged only 10.5 percent.[63] The earnings of independent oil companies, engaged primarily in U.S. production, confirms the tremendous profitability of U.S. oil production.

By providing huge incentives for domestic production, U.S. policy has tended to drive the cost of production up. Indeed, since 1973 drilling costs have doubled. With companies eager to get the high profits obtainable on newly discovered oil, they bid up the price of supplies, skilled labor, and oil-field equipment and they pursued leads of questionable viability. As a study done for the Joint Economic Committee stated, "High costs are a consequence of high prices and profits."[64]

While the start-up of Alaskan oil production in 1977 temporarily reversed the

	Average Annual Increase (Percent)			
1981	1973–78	1978–79	1979–80	1980–81
10,025	− 2.5	2.8	− 1.9	1.4
1,366	0.1	7.3	− 8.2	− 1.3
1,305	4.6	5.5	− 3.0	− 5.4
641	5.8	1.5	− 6.7	—
456	—	45.0	20.8	− 3.2
3,165	5.4	6.3	− 2.5	− 0.8
265	15.7	23.4	25.1	0.4
104	3.6	38.9	−21.0	−16.1
108	32.5	24.4	− 8.0	3.8
115	− 0.4	3.1	−58.6	−23.3
763	5.5	21.6	−18.8	− 9.3
394	23.8	87.3	−17.7	1.8
58	10.5	32.6	−23.2	−38.2
14	—	300.3	−17.0	−29.5
339	16.3	44.7	17.5	1.2
311	2.6	10.5	1.7	3.7
645	9.8	6.3	16.0	18.3
8,270	8.8	9.0	7.2	8.6
233	13.4	0.8	− 2.8	− 4.5
9,433	8.1	7.1	5.8	7.6
14,833	−0.7	4.1	− 2.5	0.8
3,418	7.8	21.7	− 3.9	0.8
18,251	0.4	7.0	− 2.8	0.8
27,683	2.5	7.0	− 0.1	3.0

decline in U.S. oil production, up until 1979 production in the continental United States continued to decline at an annual rate of 200,000–300,000 b/d[65] and U.S. production of natural gas remains well below its 1973 peak (see tables 11–4 and 11–5). While these basic production trends were probably unavoidable, the federal government, by decontrolling prices in stages, encouraged companies to hold back production until prices rose further.

With the continental United States heavily explored, the main prospects of boosting U.S. reserves of oil and natural gas are in increased recovery rates through the use of secondary and tertiary recovery methods, exploration of the continental shelf, and development of Alaskan oil and gas resources. Yet since 1974 the results in each of these areas have been disappointing.

A 1976 study by the Washington consulting firm of Lewin and Associates projected that by 2000, under optimum conditions, tertiary oil recovery could nearly double the United States' proven reserves of 32.7 billion barrels. However, the cost of tertiary recovery has risen steadily, and at least until 1980 it exceeded the world oil price.[66] At most, consequently, tertiary oil is expected to add 1 million b/d to U.S. production in 1990.[67]

Because only about 3 percent of the U.S. continental shelf has been drilled, many of the best prospects of finding more oil and gas in the United States are in the offshore areas.[68] So in January 1974 President Nixon called for an accelerated offshore leasing program under which 10 million acres a year would be leased to private companies, but lawsuits, brought under the National Environmental Policy Act, held up the first sale under the new program until December 1975. Since then, the government has leased roughly 19 million acres on the outer continental shelf, four times the amount leased from 1970 to 1974.[69] But the results have not been encouraging. In 1974 Exxon, Mobil, and Champlin spent almost $1 billion drilling off the Florida coast, and in 1977 five companies spent nearly $1 billion on leases for drilling in the Gulf of Alaska. Little of significance was found, and most of the drilling in these two areas has been abandoned. While $438 million was bid in 1975 for acreage off southern California, the area has yet to produce evidence of significant amounts of oil.[70]

Similarly, in 1976, when the government began leasing areas in the Atlantic Ocean off the coast of New Jersey, companies bid heavily on ninety-three tracts of about 5,760 acres each. Successful bids totaled $1.13 billion. Government geologists estimated the area's potential at 800 million barrels of oil and 13.3 trillion cubic feet of gas, but in February 1979, after spending about $90 million as its share of the cost to drill three dry holes in the Baltimore Canyon, Shell announced that it was abandoning efforts to find hydrocarbons in the area. Later that month a second lease sale in the area drew only $42 million in successful bids, as companies began to give up on finding significant resources in Baltimore Canyon. By the middle of 1979, seven oil companies had abandoned the area, but between May and November 1979, Tenneco and Texaco announced natural gas finds in the area, reviving hope in the region and indicating that the other companies might have given up too soon.[71]

The development of Alaska's oil resources has been held up because of problems in transporting and marketing Alaskan oil and natural gas. Since 1978, roughly 1.2 mb/d have been piped southward from Prudhoe Bay via the $8 billion Trans Alaska Pipeline System (TAPS). But the capacity of TAPS is 2 mb/d, a level that Alaskan production could easily attain. However, since Alaskan oil is heavy and high in sulfur, many refineries on the U.S. West Coast have been unable to handle it. Also, since Alaskan oil came onstream in 1978, there has generally been a surplus of crude on the West Coast. While Alaskan oil would find a ready market in the Midwest, the problem is getting it there. First, the oil companies were slow to submit plans for new pipelines to ship the oil to the

Midwest;[72] then, when they submitted plans, they ran into a maze of environmental opposition and governmental regulatory delays.

Sohio, which owns slightly more than half of the Alaskan crude, but has no West Coast refineries, proposed shipping the oil by pipeline from Long Beach to Texas; the oil would then be transported from Texas to the Midwest through existing pipelines. Sohio planned to ship the oil through the El Paso Natural Gas Company pipeline, which runs from California to Texas (but was not then in use). In addition, a relatively short pipeline would have to be built from Long Beach to the El Paso line, but California regulatory agencies objected to the plan because landing the oil at Long Beach would increase pollution in the area and risk oil spills. California officials were also concerned about the possibility that the unused pipelines by which Sohio proposed to ship the oil to Texas would soon be needed to bring natural gas to California, possibly from Mexico.

After more than a year of squabbling, the California Air Resources Board gave its approval when Sohio agreed to build new air control facilities for Southern California Edison Company to offset the pollution that landing the oil in Long Beach would create. But with other approvals still required, in March 1979 Sohio unexpectedly announced that it was abandoning the plan. Sohio Chairman Alton W. Whitehouse explained that the decision was due to fears of further regulatory delays, environmental lawsuits, and concern that new supplies of gas might make it impossible to convert the El Paso Natural Gas Company pipeline to carry oil.[73]

Without a pipeline from the West Coast, Alaskan oil has to be shipped by tanker through the Panama Canal, landed in Texas, and then sent by pipeline to the Midwest. But this circuitous route greatly increases the landed cost of Alaskan oil; so demand for it has been limited. A possible solution would be to ship the oil to Japan, but in 1973, when it authorized the Alaskan pipeline, Congress stipulated that no Alaskan oil could be sold outside the United States.

The situation with Alaskan gas is similar. At present, there is no way of bringing it to markets in the continental United States. An Alaskan pipeline through Canada has won the approval of both the U.S. and Canadian governments; however, the multi-billion dollar pipeline is by far the most costly project ever attempted without government backing, and financing remains a problem. The pipeline, originally scheduled to be completed by 1985, is now not expected to be finished until 1989, if at all. If completed, it will bring 2.4 billion cubic feet of natural gas into the continental United States—the equivalent of about 5 percent of today's natural gas consumption, or enough to replace more than 10 percent of U.S. oil imports.[74]

With transportation links impeded and federal policies often unclear, since 1971 more than twenty companies have abandoned their exploration and development programs in Alaska, despite the fact that, according to U.S. Geological Survey estimates, there are 30 billion barrels of undiscovered oil and 76 trillion cubic feet of undiscovered natural gas in Alaska.[75]

Canada. As in the United States, oil reserves in Canada have declined since 1973. However, while the continental United States is a heavily explored area, with more than half its ultimately recoverable reserves of oil already discovered, most of Canada's oil resources remain to be discovered. According to Moody's figures, Canada's ultimately recoverable reserves of conventional oil total 86 billion barrels; but as of 1974, only 16 billion barrels had been found. Similarly, its ultimately recoverable reserves of conventional natural gas total 516 trillion cubic feet, with only 106 trillion cubic feet discovered as of 1974.

Despite Canada's favorable geologic prospects, after the 1973–74 rise in prices oil companies in Canada began moving their rigs to the United States, where prices and company profits on newly discovered oil were higher. As a result, Canada was the only major oil-producing country to show a decline in drilling in 1974. In 1974, active rigs increased by 23 percent to 1,472 in the United States, but in Canada they declined by 13 percent, averaging only 152.[76]

In an effort to boost Canadian reserves and end dependence on foreign oil, following the 1973–74 increases, the Canadian government established a policy of gradually boosting oil prices to the world level. Canadian prices rose from $6.50 a barrel in 1975 to $11.75 in 1978. However, the bulk of this increase was absorbed by provincial and federal government taxes and royalties.[77] (Oil exported from Canada carries an export tax designed to raise its price to the world level.) Gas prices were also allowed to rise gradually, until the price of natural gas (on a BTU basis) equals the price of imported oil on Canada's east coast. As a result, gas prices went from 54¢ per mcf in 1974 to $2.25 in the summer of 1977.[78]

In November 1974 the Canadian government announced that crude oil exports to the United States would be reduced by 100,000 b/d, effective January 1, 1975, and phased out entirely by 1982. Rather than have the western Canadian provinces continue to export oil to the United States, while the eastern provinces relied on imported oil, the government extended the Interprovincial Pipeline east from Sarnia into Montreal, enabling Canadian oil produced in the West to be sold in the East.

In 1975 Canada created a national oil company, PetroCanada, which was charged with exploring for and developing oil resources in areas neglected by private companies. The company's first priority was to assure that frontier areas off the east coast and in the Arctic regions were explored sufficiently to delineate their reserves. PetroCanada took over the government's holdings in various projects and brought state support to projects that would not have been fully financed by private capital. In 1976 the Canadian government ruled that all oil ventures on government-owned frontier lands must be at least 25 percent Canadian owned, and the parties must make an additional 25 percent available to PetroCanada upon request.[79] Initially, Canada planned to phase out natural gas (as well as oil) exports, but the reclassification of gas reserves as "economic" (as prices increased) and the discovery of additional reserves in Alberta created a Canadian gas surplus by the late 1970s. As a result, Canada increased gas exports to the United States (on a "temporary" basis) and in early 1979 the Canadian National Energy Board certified that Canada's gas reserves were sufficient to meet domestic demand plus authorized exports until 1992.[80]

Aside from its considerable resources of conventional oil and natural gas, Canada has two important but unconventional sources of hydrocarbons: the Athabasca tar sands and the Arctic supplies of oil and natural gas. If they could be mined and processed economically, the Canadian tar sands could yield 600 billion barrels of oil—more than the reserves of all the OPEC countries.[81] Since 1967, crude-poor Sun Oil Company has been mining the tar sands, producing 45,000–50,000 b/d. However, it was not until the 1973–74 rise in prices that its plant emerged from the red, and even then its profits were quite modest. The project has been plagued by technical foul-ups and equipment failures.[82]

A second tar sands project, Syncrude Canada Ltd., was begun by several oil companies in 1974, but by the end of the year two of the partners, Arco and Shell, had withdrawn, throwing the project into financial crisis. The project was rescued in early 1975 when the remaining partners agreed to put more money into it, and the Canadian government agreed to invest $600 million. Syncrude Canada Ltd. came onstream in the summer of 1978 with production costs of about $17 a barrel, or nearly twice the cost of oil from the Suncor plant—built in a period when construction costs were cheaper. In the early 1980s Syncrude's capacity reached 120,000 b/d, but the plant would not be profitable were it not for the 1979 rise in world oil prices.[83] Also, until April 1979, oil from the tar sands was subject to Canadian price controls.

At the end of 1978 the Alsands Project Group, a consortium of oil companies, applied for approval to start a third Athabasca project. In the summer of 1979 the Alberta Energy Resources Conservation Board gave preliminary approval to both the Alsands project and a tar sands project proposed by Exxon. Had these projects proceeded as scheduled, they would have produced at least 500,000 b/d by 1990. However, as a result of disputes over Canadian energy policy (see chapter 14), both projects were delayed, and then, as a result of the softening of the world oil market in 1981–82 and rising construction and financing costs, they were terminated.[84]

Canada's other potential bonanza is the resources of the Canadian Arctic, which many experts believe could become another Middle East.[85] To exploit the resources under the High Arctic islands, in 1967 Ottawa formed Panarctic, with a 45 percent government equity. The new company was given 35 million acres to explore (later increased to 85 million) in an area believed to contain 40 billion barrels of oil and 250 trillion cubic feet of natural gas. (The government's share has been taken over by PetroCanada.) By the winter of 1972–73 Panarctic had discovered five major gas fields, but during the next two years results were disappointing, so that many private companies in the project gave up hope. Then, late in 1975, Panarctic made a commerical discovery of oil in the area, keeping activity alive. But despite its substantial prospects, the companies involved in Panarctic have been reluctant to put much money into development of the area. High costs and uncertainty about Canadian government policy have been cited as factors in their hesitancy.[86]

The other area of the Arctic that has received attention is the Beaufort Sea, where experts estimate there may be as much as 400 trillion cubic feet of gas and 40 billion barrels of oil.[87] So far, development has been impeded by the difficulties of operating in Arctic waters, covered by heavy ice for much of the year. Aside from Dome Petroleum, a middle-size company that has been exploring the area, oil companies have not shown much interest in the Beaufort Sea.[88]

Europe and the North Sea. Between 1974 and 1978 the most encouraging development in the European energy picture was the onflow of North Sea oil. Britain, a nation of 50 million people, badly in need of additional revenue, had encouraged rapid development of its North Sea resources. While Britain's terms would ultimately give the government 70 percent of the proceeds from the sale of British oil, to encourage the companies to begin finding and producing oil as soon as possible, they were offered generous concessions in the early years of production. Companies were allowed to write off 175 percent of their investments before paying the government's 45 percent revenue tax. As a result, in the early years of production from a given field, the British government received only 10 to 15 percent of the revenues.[89]

Yet exploration in the North Sea has declined. While 116 wells were completed in 1975, only sixty-seven were completed in 1978. A survey by the UK Offshore Operators' Association found that companies operating in the British North Sea attributed the decline in drilling to the lack of new acreage offered for lease by the British government and to insufficiently attractive financial terms. Between 1977 and 1981 there was a progressive toughening in British North Sea tax rules.[90]

British North Sea oil began flowing in June 1975, and despite technical delays, by 1978 production was up to 1 mb/d. By 1980 Britain was exporting more oil than it was importing and producing enough to meet roughly 20 percent of EEC's oil needs (however, by the mid-1980s production is expected to level off). The British sector of the North Sea accounts for about 90 percent of EEC's reserves and production.[91]

In contrast to Britain, Norway, with a population of only 4 million, has held production close to the level of internal demand. The government takes roughly 80 percent of the profits from the sale of the oil and provides no special incentives to encourage early production. Norway's policy is rooted in the fact that even before the advent of North Sea oil, it had been a prosperous and relatively egalitarian society, and the government feared that huge increases in oil revenues would lead to inflation, structural imbalances in the economy, and social inequality. It also sought to conserve its resources. Consequently, while unofficial estimates of Norwegian reserves run as high as 100 billion barrels, by 1979 production still remained below 400,000 b/d.[92]

Paradoxically, the differences in Norwegian and British policy reveal that when developed countries become major oil producers, they tend to act very much like the OPEC countries. Norway, rich in oil resources, but concerned about their conservation and the social consequences of too rapid production, acts very much like Kuwait and for very similar reasons. Britain, with a much larger population and more immediate revenue needs, has an oil policy very similar to that of Iran under the Shah: it seeks to maximize revenue by boosting production, with conservation a secondary matter.

Both Britain and Norway have created national oil companies to facilitate development of their resources. Though the British government held a majority share in British Petroleum, in 1976 it created the British National Oil Company (BNOC) to further the government's interests in North Sea oil. In all fields leased after BNOC's creation, the government mandated that BNOC be given at least a 51 percent share. For fields leased before the national oil company's creation, BNOC was given access to information about their development, a voice in the leaseholders' policy-making committees, and the right to take up to 51 percent of the fields' production at agreed-upon "market prices." BNOC owns a number of leases in entirety, and all of Britain's North Sea gas is sold to its nationalized gas industry at controlled prices.

BNOC has worked out cooperation agreements with BP, Shell, and Exxon under which the majors provide BNOC personnel with training and involve the national oil company in planning their United Kingdom production, refining, and marketing operations. In return, BNOC has given the majors the right to buy back BNOC's share of production. Yet with BNOC lacking both downstream facilities and wholly owned fields in current production, its role has been primarily that of a purchaser and reseller of North Sea oil. Moreover, since it buys the oil it purchases at market prices, its profits have not been great. (In the fall of 1982 the British government put 51 percent of BNOC's exploration and production interests up for sale.)[93]

In a policy quite similar to Great Britain's, up until 1982 Norway required that its national oil company, Statoil, be given a 50 percent interest in all of Norway's North Sea fields and as much as 75 percent, depending upon the size of the discovery. Moreover, while Britain did not mandate BNOC's participation until 1977, Norway required Statoil's participation in all Norwegian fields since the beginning of Norway's North Sea oil development—a further factor in the slow pace of that development. Also, while the United States, Canada, and Australia maintained price controls on domestic production, Great Britain and Norway allowed prices to rise to the world level, imposing wellhead taxes on the companies' production.

Soviet Oil.   In 1977 the CIA caused a storm of controversy by predicting that by 1985 the Soviet Union and Eastern Europe would need to import from 3.5 to 4.5 mb/d and that this would put great pressure on world oil markets, intensifying international competition for scarce supplies.[94] The idea that the Soviet bloc, long a net exporter of oil to the West, would become a net importer seemed to run counter to both historical experience and the geologic potential of the Soviet Union's vast resource endowment. Since 1976 the Soviet Union has been the world's largest producer of oil. Its proven reserves, 63 billion barrels, are exceeded by only Kuwait (64.5 billion) and Saudi Arabia (164.6 billion). Its proven reserves of natural gas, 1,160 trillion cubic feet, are more than twice as large as those of any other country. It also has the world's largest reserves of coal and vast, untapped hydro potential. As geologists Moody and Geiger have stated, "If there is another Middle East in the world, the chances are it is in Western Siberia."[95] There are also great prospects for the Soviet Union's vast northern fringe and along the Arctic continental shelf.[96]

Despite this natural wealth, the Soviet Union's energy supply is in crisis, as is the energy supply of the non-Communist world. The basic problem is that most Soviet resources are in remote areas and difficult to exploit; the Soviet Union has aggravated its problems by neglecting exploration drilling and exploiting established reservoirs too quickly. As a result, where resources have been developed, they are rapidly exhausted, and the rate of growth in Soviet oil production is falling. While Soviet oil production grew at 8 percent per year from 1965 to 1970, it grew at 6.6 percent from 1970 to 1975, at 6.3 percent from 1975 to 1978, and at only 2.2 percent from 1978 to 1981.[97] In both 1978 and 1979 the Soviet Union failed to meet its planned levels of production.[98]

Initially, most Soviet oil production came from the western part of the country, but as the fields in this area became exhausted, production declined in the mid-1970s. Since 1964, most of the growth of Soviet oil production has been due to the rapid (perhaps overrapid) exploitation of western Siberian reservoirs. Yet despite its great potential, there had not been a major find in this area between 1965 and 1980, and it is now threatened with declining production and rising costs. The Soviets themselves said that by 1980 half the fields in this area would be in decline.[99]

The development of western Siberia has lagged for several reasons. It is difficult to develop resources in the harsh, subarctic environment of western Siberia, where prospective fields are widely scattered in swampy forest. The Soviet Union also lacks facilities for transporting oil to markets in the industrialized parts of the country, and the difficulties of building them in the wilderness are formidable. In addition, the Soviet Union puts extreme pressure on existing wells, forcing them to overproduce through water-injection techniques that damage deposits, require extra drilling, and thereby divert drilling crews and equipment from exploration. These methods create high productivity rates in the early years of an oil field's life, but they lead to problems as fields age. While there are also great prospects east and north of western Siberia, little exploration has been carried on in these areas because of the hazardous conditions they present. The Soviet Union has also neglected its offshore areas, partly because it has had promising onshore prospects and partly because its offshore technology is backward.[100]

With the Soviet Union relying on oil exports for 40 to 60 percent of its hard-currency earnings, the slowdown in oil production has posed a threat not only to its energy outlook but also to its ability to pay for imports from the West. The limits on Soviet oil production also prevented the Soviet Union from attempting to win friends in the Third World with offers of cheap oil after the 1973–74 rise in oil prices. The Soviet Union has attempted to respond to this situation in various ways, notably by enlisting the support of Western oil companies in development of its oil and gas resources. In 1972 President Nixon granted the Soviet Union access to U.S. oil equipment, prohibiting only those deals that were judged to have direct military application. Then, in 1973–74, the increase in world oil prices greatly increased Soviet hard-currency earnings and enabled the Soviet Union to increase its purchases of Western equipment and technology.[101]

However, as the Soviet Union's ability to make purchases from the West increased, its interest in pursuing joint ventures with Western companies lessened. Still, the Soviet Union remained interested in concluding deals for development of the Yakutsk and North Star gas reserves in Siberia, for assistance in secondary and tertiary recovery, and for aid in offshore operations. In response to the Soviet interest, the Western oil companies indicated that they were eager to work with the Soviet Union if the terms were right, but the unfolding of the U.S./Soviet detente policy put a damper on the program.

In 1974 Congress made the granting of most-favored-nation status and Export-Import Bank credits conditional on the Soviet Union's agreeing to remove restrictions on emigration. The Soviet Union refused, though it appears to have made some concessions on emigration. As a result, Congress and the administration reached a compromise, allowing the president to extend trade privileges to the Soviet Union for a trial period of eighteen months. Yet so far as oil trade is involved, whether the Soviet Union has MFN status or not makes little difference, since the United States levies no tariff on liquified natural gas and only minimal tariffs on some oil products. However, the compromise between Congress and the administration placed severe restrictions on Ex-Im credits, limiting them to $300 million over a four-year period, placing a $40 million ceiling on credits for oil and gas exploration, and denying credits for oil and gas production. This greatly reduced the willingness of U.S. companies to conclude deals with the Soviet Union. With both the Yakutsk and the North Star projects dependent upon Ex-Im financing, negotiations broke off.[102]

In 1975 Japan and the Soviet Union concluded an agreement for joint exploration and development of oil and gas resources on Sakhalin island. In 1976, after two years of on-again, off-again negotiations, the Soviet Union signed an agreement under which the Bank of America, Japan's export-import bank, and twenty-three Japanese commercial banks would put up $50 million, split evenly between the American and the Japanese, for exploration and development of gas in the Yakutsk region. The sum was reduced from the original $200 million, partly because the Soviets had already done some exploration in the area and partly because they balked at paying commercial interest rates in the absence of low-cost U.S. Export-Import Bank financing. Soaring production costs and problems in financing have continued to delay the project.[103]

A second Soviet response to the slowdown in oil production was to seek to boost the contribution that other fuels, especially nuclear power, could make to the Soviet energy supply. In 1975 the Kremlin decided to go "full steam ahead" on development of nuclear power, boosting nuclear's share from 3 percent to 7 percent of Soviet electric generating capacity by 1980, but the Soviet program fell far behind schedule. Western analysts attributed the Soviet nuclear lag to pervasive inefficiencies in its machinery industry, shortages of skilled labor, and a scarcity of equipment to turn out the massive, precision-tooled steel parts of nuclear reactors.[104] Similarly, since 1975, as output from the Donets Basin, the nation's largest coal producing area, declined, Soviet coal production has remained essentially stagnant.[105] And in contrast to the West, the Soviet Union has much less scope for conservation.

The brightest spot in the Soviet energy picture has been the growth of natural gas supplies, which has consistently exceeded the levels stipulated in the Soviet plan. Yet the fact that it takes five times as much pipeline capacity to transport natural gas as it does to transport equivalent amounts of oil is a substantial drawback to increased reliance on natural gas, especially given the inhospitable terrain and distances involved. Also, in an effort to boost its hard-currency earnings, in December 1975 the Soviet Union worked out an arrangement with Iran whereby Iran would ship natural gas by pipeline to the Soviet Union and the Soviet Union would then export a comparable quantity of natural gas to Western Europe. Deliveries were to begin in 1981 and continue for twenty years. It was believed to be the largest gas deal in history, and the pipelines were estimated to cost $7 billion. The Soviet-Iranian cooperation on energy was particularly valued by the Soviets since, while the Arab countries insisted on payment in hard currency, Iran was willing to accept barter terms. However, following the Iranian revolution, the Soviet-Iranian gas deal was canceled.[106]

In 1975 the Soviet Union, which had provided Eastern Europe with unlimited oil supplies, decided to greatly reduce the rate of growth in its shipments of oil to Eastern Europe. The decision was intended to hold Eastern Europe's share of Soviet oil production at a steady 13 percent between 1975 and 1980. The Soviets also began increasing the "friendship prices" they charged the East Europeans for oil and gas. Prices were linked to a rolling three-year average of Western prices, particularly those charged by OPEC members. Consequently, in 1975 prices were boosted by 50 percent. After this increase, prices to Eastern Europe still trailed world prices by several dollars, but by early 1978 the "friendship price" was only 25 percent below the OPEC level.[107] As a result of these changes in Soviet policy, East European countries stepped up their purchases of Middle East oil. Moreover, by the close of the 1970s the deteriorating Soviet energy outlook threatened to change the Soviet Union from a net oil exporter to a net oil importer, which would put substantial upward pressure on the world oil price.

China and Southeast Asia. Like the Soviet Union, China has a vast, untapped hydrocarbon potential. According to CIA estimates, China's ultimately recoverable onshore reserves of oil probably total 40 billion barrels—even as much as 100 billion barrels. Offshore reserves are probably on the same order of magnitude.[108] And no more than 5 percent of the total has been produced so far.[109]

From 1970 to 1975 China's oil production grew at 20 percent a year, but since then it has increased at less than 15 percent a year.[110] In 1978 production totaled 2.1 mb/d. Both the falloff in the recovery rate in several oil fields and a June 1976 earthquake played a role in the slowdown in growth of production. The so-called Gang of Four, which gained ascendancy during 1975–76, criticized the faction led by Deng Xiaoping for increasing production too rapidly and deviating from China's policy of self-reliance. Then, as Deng gained control, oil production increased more rapidly and China began negotiating with foreign companies for aid in development of its oil resources.

As in the Soviet Union, many of China's onshore hydrocarbon resources are remote from industrial and coastal regions and difficult to exploit, and partly as a result, much of China's prospective onshore territory has never been explored for oil. Nor does China have the capital or the transportation system that would permit extensive development in these areas. (China still relies heavily on railroads to transport oil.) While China's *offshore* prospects are close to markets in both China and Japan, China lacks the technology to drill offshore on its own. Yet, as a result of the Maoist emphasis on self-reliance, China has been reluctant to allow foreign companies to operate in Chinese territory and to become dependent upon foreign technology.

However, in the late 1970s China began to purchase drilling equipment from the West. In 1978 the Chinese welcomed foreign development loans and the participation of foreign capital in joint ventures, provided the Chinese retain 51 percent. Also in that year, an agreement with Japan was concluded for joint exploration in the shallow Pohai Bay, and in 1979, following U.S. recognition of China, agreements were reached permitting twelve U.S. oil companies to do preliminary exploration work in China's offshore territories (a second stage of lease agreements was expected in 1981). Late in 1979 China also invited Western companies to participate in development of its onshore fields. As a result of its purchases of foreign technology and its agreements with foreign firms, China's offshore areas began to be explored in the late 1970s, and already there have been potentially important finds. However, significant production is not expected until the late 1980s.

China's first significant oil exports came in 1973, when it signed an agreement with Japan, but since then, China's exports have remained small. Whether they will grow in the future depends primarily upon China's success in finding and developing new reserves and on the economic policies that China adopts. With oil exports already China's leading source of foreign-exchange earnings, exports will probably increase substantially in the future, if China expands its links with the world economy and increases its imports of Western goods and services. Alternatively, China might opt for a policy of self-reliance, consuming the bulk of whatever oil it produces at home. In either case, as China develops, and particularly as its automotive and petrochemical industries grow, increasing quantities of Chinese oil will be consumed at home, limiting exports.[111] Nor is China likely to accept the role of raw materials exporter, preferring, instead, to industrialize and export finished goods. And even while China moves toward greater integration into the world economy, the Maoist emphasis on self-reliance is likely to persist and to militate against China's ever becoming a major oil exporter—and correspondingly, a major importer of foreign technology, foreign exchange, etc. (The high wax content of China's oil is also likely to limit its exports.)

The principal purchaser of whatever oil China exports will almost certainly be Japan. In 1978 China agreed to begin exporting 100,000 b/d to Japan and to increase this amount gradually to 1 mb/d by 1985.[112] One consequence of Japan's interest in China's oil has been to lessen its interest in concluding deals for the development and importation of Soviet oil.

In April 1976 the *Petroleum Economist* estimated that, in the area extending south from Japan to Australia, oil production might be increased from 2 mb/d in 1974 to 4 mb/d in 1980, and to 7 mb/d by 1985, if the necessary exploration and development work were undertaken. While this area does not appear to have petroleum reserves on the order of the North Sea or Alaska, it has a multitude of commercially attractive small fields, most of them offshore, and since 1974 the countries in this area have generally been eager to have the international oil companies come in and undertake operations.[113] After the 1973–74 price hikes, the international oil companies' interest in this area picked up, but by 1975 interest had waned and exploration had slowed down. Development in this area has been hampered by territorial disputes and political conflicts.

China claims areas of the continental shelf off the South China Sea that, under normal rules of international law, would belong to the Philippines, Malaysia, Brunei, or Vietnam. China bases its claim on the grounds that the sediments in the areas were washed into the sea by Chinese rivers and by claims to various islands and atolls in the area. China also has territorial disputes in prospective offshore areas with South Korea and Taiwan, and Japan and China dispute large parts of the East China Sea. Moreover, since late 1970 the position of the U.S. government has been that no protection could be given U.S. companies operating in Chinese-claimed waters. The U.S. government has also tried to prevent U.S. companies from operating in these areas by banning U.S.-registered rigs and the employment of U.S. citizens from the territories in question.

Both Taiwan and South Korea have awarded exploration concessions to various U.S. companies, but exploration has been reduced because of territorial disputes with China and the unwillingness of the U.S. government to support the companies against China.[114] In fact, since 1975 there has been no drilling by

U.S. companies in offshore areas claimed by Taiwan because the companies fear that the U.S. government will back China's claims to the area. To appease China, Japan, which wants to increase its purchases of China's oil, has refrained from authorizing offshore exploration in the East China Sea, except on a minor scale near the Japanese mainland.[115]

In 1974 Japan and South Korea concluded an agreement for joint development of a border zone between their offshore areas. However, as a result of Chinese protests, territorial disputes, political hostilities, and domestic scandals in Japan and Korea, its final ratification was delayed five years. When it was approved in 1978, China called it an infringement on her sovereignty. Also, in an effort to improve relations with the West, in 1977–78 China appeared to be backing away from some of its territorial claims; however, following the Chinese/Vietnamese split in July 1978, China reverted to a tougher line.[116] Large oil deposits are also believed to exist in the Yellow Sea, but development has been impeded by territorial disputes among Japan, the Philippines, and Vietnam.

In Vietnam in 1973–74, seven groups of mainly U.S. companies leased thirteen offshore tracts in ten-year concession arrangements. Four wildcats were drilled before the Communist victory in 1975, and all four showed signs of oil. Industry experts estimated that Vietnam might eventually produce as much as 1 mb/d[117] However, once they took control of the south, in April 1975, the Communist regime canceled all the concessions; but the new government lacked the technology to drill offshore, and so did its ally, the Soviet Union. Consequently, almost as soon as the old concessions were terminated, the new government called for bids by foreign companies on offshore territory. Because the United States has the world's best offshore technology, the Vietnamese government was prepared to welcome back the same companies that had already drilled in the area, provided that new terms could be worked out.[118]

But the U.S. government made it illegal for U.S. companies to operate in Vietnam and banned the sale of U.S. technology to Vietnam. Expecting relations with the United States to be normalized and wanting the U.S. companies to come back, Vietnam held off exploration in the areas in question for three years. Finally, in 1978 it gave permits to explore for oil in the areas to three groupings of non-U.S. companies, which Shell challenged on the grounds that it amounted to expropriation without compensation.

These non-U.S. companies have had difficulty finding replacements for U.S. drilling technology and they lack the U.S. companies' experience in the area. As a result, little activity has occurred in the area since the U.S. companies left. The U.S. companies would like to return, and Communist Vietnam would like to have them back, but with the United States trying to woo China, China having broken relations with Vietnam, and Vietnam having invaded Cambodia, the prospects for normalization of U.S./Vietnamese relations seem remote. Consequently, Vietnam is unlikely to achieve its goal of oil self-sufficiency by 1990.[119]

Historically, India, Pakistan, Bangladesh, and Sri Lanka sought to build indigenous oil expertise with Soviet technical aid, but since 1974 they have turned to the international oil companies for aid in exploration and development; however, the companies have been reluctant to make investments in these countries. For example, experts estimate that twenty-five to fifty wells should be drilled yearly, if Pakistan's oil potential is to be properly explored, and more than ten international oil companies hold exploration permits in the country. But on the average, only 9.2 wells were drilled in Pakistan between 1974 and 1978.[120]

Mexico, Latin America, and Africa. Since 1974 the most encouraging development in international energy policy has been the increasing estimates of the size of Mexico's reserves of oil and gas. Early in 1977 the Western press reported that, rather than the conservative official figure of 11 billion barrels, Mexico's oil reserves total 60 billion barrels—roughly twice the level of U.S. reserves and almost as much as Kuwait's.[121]

The oil industry has long known that Mexico has the potential to be a major oil producer. In 1955 the *Petroleum Press Service,* an industry periodical (now the *Petroleum Economist*), stated:

There is no doubt that Mexico possesses great oil wealth. She has sedimentary areas which, in total, are as extensive as those of Texas, and she is likely to be as well endowed with oil resources as any other country in Latin America, not even excepting Venezuela. And even bigger resources may lie within her large continental shelf which stretches out into the Gulf of Mexico.[122]

Yet between 1960 and 1974 Mexico was a net importer of oil.

Until 1972, Mexico's situation was similar to that of other Latin American countries: it had a large number of small, mainly shallow fields. However, in 1972 major discoveries were made in the Reforma area of southern Mexico, but the magnitude of these discoveries was kept quiet until late in 1976. The reasons for this are not entirely clear, but since its founding in 1938, when the foreign oil companies were nationalized, Pemex, the state oil company, has had a long tradition of hostility to foreign capital in general and the United States in particular. It has viewed its role as supplying cheap Mexican oil to Mexicans. Consequently, there were undoubtedly people in Pemex who feared that if news of the discoveries leaked out, the pressures on Mexico to export would increase and the international oil companies would seek to participate in the development of Mexican oil.

Official acknowledgment of the size of Mexican reserves came late in 1976, when José López Portillo became Mexico's new president. In contrast to Luis Echeverria Alvarez, whom he succeeded, Portillo is much less hostile to foreign capital. He also recognized that with Mexico's long-term foreign public debt approaching 20 percent (it was only about 5 percent in 1973), something had to be done to boost Mexico's international credit rating. Consequently, Portillo sought to develop Mexico's oil industry as rapidly as possible. Yet Mexican officials insist that he would not have done this if he had not been convinced of the magnitude of Mexico's reserves.[123]

Upon taking office, Portillo appointed a task force to determine the size of Mexico's reserves. Within a month the task force reported that Mexico's reserves were not 6.3 billion barrels, as reported by Pemex, but 11.1 billion barrels. This public recognition of the size of Mexico's reserves came nearly five years after the first Reforma discoveries. Moreover, by boosting spending on exploration and development the Portillo administration was able to further increase Mexico's proven reserves. Pemex boosted its official estimate of Mexico's proven reserves from 11.2 billion barrels at the end of 1976 to 16.8 billion barrels at the end of 1977, with another 30 billion barrels in "probable" reserves and 120 billion barrels in "potential" reserves.[124]

While various claims by the Mexican government have probably been exaggerated to win the confidence of private lenders, many Western analysts believe that Mexico's proven reserves of oil and natural gas liquids will reach 60–100 billion barrels in coming years. In 1978 the CIA estimated Mexico's proven reserves at 50 billion barrels, with probable reserves at 157 billion. *Oil and Gas Journal* put Mexico's proven year-end 1981 oil reserves at 57 billion barrels, a level exceeded only by Iran (57 billion), the Soviet Union (63 billion), Kuwait (64.5 billion), and Saudi Arabia (164.6 billion). Mexico's reserves of natural gas—75.4 trillion cubic feet at year-end 1981—place it behind Canada (89.9 trillion), Saudi Arabia (114 trillion), Algeria (130.9 trillion), the United States (198 trillion), Iran (484 trillion), and the Soviet Union (1160 trillion), but ahead of the Netherlands (55.7 trillion) and Norway (49.4 trillion).[125]

To encourage development of Mexico's oil and gas resources, the Mexican government has encouraged private capital to operate in the country under a law that requires majority domestic shareholding of private companies. While the official Pemex monopoly has been maintained, U.S. firms supply services to Pemex.

Between 1973 and 1978 Mexican oil production increased from 550,000 b/d to 1.3 mb/d, and by 1980 Mexico was producing more than 2 mb/d. Exports, which began in 1975 on a modest level, reached 360,000 b/d in 1978 and were up to 1.2 mb/d by spring of 1981.[126]

The idea of Mexico's joining OPEC has been discussed, but Washington has attempted to dissuade Mexico from doing so. Under provisions of the U.S. Trade Reform Act of 1974, Mexican exports would no longer be eligible for duty-free treatment from the United States if it joined OPEC. Since Mexico has generally charged prices at least as high as those of OPEC countries,[127] it is doubtful that the benefits of OPEC membership to Mexico would outweigh the penalties it would incur as a result of U.S. policy. Moreover, as a growing producer, Mexico would not want to be bound by any prorationing scheme that OPEC might impose on the basis of historic shares.[128]

Despite Mexico's enormous growth and its vast potential—much of the country remains unexplored—there is considerable uncertainty about its future as an exporter. Heavily in debt, Mexico may have difficulty raising the capital it needs for maximum development of its oil and gas resources, particularly if the world oil market remains slack. The Mexican oil industry is already experiencing shortages of skilled crews and bottlenecks in transportation, materials, and support services, such as water and electricity, and these are likely to get worse as production increases.[129]

There are many powerful factions in Mexico that believe that Mexican oil should be reserved for Mexicans; others believe it is not in the country's interest to boost production too rapidly. Part of the concern stems from the fact that rapid oil production is likely to benefit only certain groups within Mexico, thereby worsening social inequality. This could lead to greater social unrest in Mexico. In this respect, Iran becomes a worrisome precedent for the Mexican leadership.

In any case, following a series of U.S. intelligence reports that Mexico could export as much as 5 mb/d to the United States by 1985, President López Portillo said production would be held at 2.75 mb/d between 1980 and 1982, when he would leave office. Portillo also said that Mexico's oil production should be determined by the pace of domestic development rather than the size of its reserves and the pressure of foreign demand. Mexico would rather export finished goods, petroleum products and petrochemicals, than raw materials. Moreover, as the Mexican economy grows, more oil will be consumed at home. With relations between the United States and Mexico no better than "mixed" and Mexico fearful of overdependence on a single market, there is strong opposition in Mexico to increasing sales to the United States.[130]

Oil can be exported to many markets,[131] but if Mexican natural gas is to be exported, it must go by pipeline to the United States (the cost of liquefaction rules out exports to other countries). Yet the United States has done little to encourage the export of Mexican natural gas. In 1977 Mexico and a consortium of six U.S. companies agreed that a $1.5 billion, 758-mile pipeline would be built to enable Mexico to export 2 billion cubic feet a day in 1980—equal to 3 percent of the anticipated level of U.S. natural gas demand at that time. The price of the gas was to be equal on a BTU basis to the landed imported cost (in New York) of No. 2 light fuel oil, about $2.50 per mcf. However, this price was higher than the price Canada charged for its natural gas exports ($2.16 per mcf), which was linked to the cost of imported crude oil, and the $1.75 that President Carter had proposed as the price for new supplies of natural gas in the United States. Consequently, in December 1977 the Energy Department blocked the Mexican deal on the grounds that the price was too high.[132]

Mexico, angered by Washington's move, decided to use more of its natural gas domestically, substituting gas for petroleum products and increasing its exports of petroleum. The United States believed that Mexico's need for Export-Import Bank financing to pay for the steel for the pipeline would force it to back down and accept Washington's terms. But Mexico secured both steel and financing from Europeans. In the fall of 1978, when Washington suggested that negotiations on a gas deal be resumed, Mexico replied that no gas was available. The

Carter administration then took the position that the United States could get along without Mexican gas, but Governor Edmund G. Brown Jr. of California and Governor William P. Clements of Texas made journeys to Mexico City to express interest in buying Mexican gas.[133]

In 1979, after the passage of U.S. energy legislation, the United States and Mexico resumed negotiations on natural gas. Mexico again sought to link its price to the price of light fuel oil while the United States insisted on linking it to lower-priced heavy fuel oil. Finally, in September 1979, a compromise was reached, linking the price of Mexican natural gas to the landed price of a composite of various crude oils. However, while they might increase in the future, the quantities in the initial agreement were to total just 300 million cubic feet a day, as opposed to the 2.2 billion agreed to by Mexico and the U.S. companies that made the original deal in 1977.[134] Had Mexico not agreed to sell gas to the United States, it is doubtful that it would have been able to expand its oil production (as planned) without flaring gas. While the United States got a lower price in the end, it is doubtful that this was worth the reduction in the size of the deal, the ill will it engendered, and the effect this had in reducing Mexico's readiness to export to the United States.

Regardless of the policy followed by the Mexican government in the future, its success in boosting its proven reserves is of major international significance. It pushes back the heralded "doomsday" of declining world oil supplies. It also raises serious questions about the validity of official reserve figures and about the prospects of finding major oil supplies in countries not generally regarded as having the potential to be major oil exporters. For as recently as 1976, few people saw Mexico as having this potential.

According to a 1975 study by Bernardo Grossling, Latin America as a whole has 19 percent of the world's prospective petroleum area, but has accounted for only 9 percent of world production. In much of Latin America the drilling density was .01 well per square mile, versus 1.17 in the United States.[135] Since 1974, non-OPEC countries in Latin America have been seeking to attract the aid of the international oil companies in the development of their oil resources, but the companies have shown only limited interest in these areas. Brazil, after excluding foreign oil companies for twenty-two years, in 1976 announced that it was opening up areas for exploration by foreign companies operating under service contracts. While 83 percent of the country's sedimentary basins have been made available to the private sector, the companies have shown little interest in the area and had made only one significant oil find by the spring of 1982. The companies have claimed that the terms offered by Brazil have not been attractive enough to encourage exploration in a new area and in an effort to conciliate the companies Brazil has progressively eased contract terms.[136]

Also in 1976, Argentina ended its state oil company's monopoly and granted new exploration areas to private companies, for the first time since 1964. Argentina was particularly anxious to enlist the aid of the companies in boosting the recovery rate of its oil fields through secondary recovery techniques.[137] Petroleum geologists believe that Argentina's offshore sedimentary areas hold a production potential comparable to the North Sea fields of Britain and Norway. Yet the drilling rate in Argentina is only about 4 percent of the rate in the United States.[138] To reverse this situation, late in 1977 Argentina began leasing offshore areas to foreign companies.

Argentina's new openness to investment by foreign companies has boosted its oil production, but the gains have come mainly from intensified output from existing fields, with few new discoveries made to date. Nor is this surprising, given that the number of wildcat wells drilled in Argentina declined between 1973 and 1978.[139] Part of the problem is that some of Latin America's best prospects are in a disputed area near the Falkland Islands, known in Argentina as the Malvinas Islands.

Another factor hindering exploration in Latin America is the lack of good maps and geologic knowledge. The best information about the area's potential is held by the international oil companies, and they have not been liberal in offering it to others. Also, because of the lack of roads, many onshore areas are difficult to reach.

According to Grossling's calculations, Africa is the least explored continent (aside from Antarctica);[140] nor has there been much increase in drilling in the non-OPEC African countries since 1973 (see table 11–3). As in Latin America, in Africa the difficulty of reaching much of the continent and the lack of facilities for transporting oil to markets have hindered exploration and development.

Ironically, in the few places where there has been activity, it has been interrupted by political conflicts. The prospects in West Africa are believed to be good, but the oil companies have confined most of their work to areas with proven hydrocarbon potential, mainly Nigeria and Gabon. Development has also occurred in Angola, West Africa's third largest producer, but the companies' activity in Angola was interrupted in 1975–76 as a result of the country's civil war.[141] Since the victory of the MPLA, activity has resumed, with Gulf and Texaco signing agreements with the radical government.

Egypt is another area of significant activity. After the October War in 1973, the Egyptian government began granting leases to Western oil companies. Within a year, more than fifteen companies, including some majors, had signed exploration agreements. Then, in 1975, production increased significantly when Israel returned the Abu Rudeis field in the Sinai. By 1976 production was up to 325,000 b/d (from 255,000 b/d in 1973), and Egypt had shifted from a net importer to a net exporter of oil. (Currently, only Mexico exceeds Egypt as a non-OPEC oil exporter.)[142]

While production increased in subsequent years, full development of the nation's resources had to await return of portions of the Sinai, occupied by Israel until April 1982. Standard Oil of Indiana has played a particularly important role in the development of Egypt's oil resources. Following the peace treaty with

Israel in 1979, Egypt hoped to boost its production from the 525,000 b/d level of 1979 to 1 mb/d by 1982.[143]

The limited efforts to develop new oil and gas resources in the non-OPEC LDCs, the success that has occurred in a few of them (notably Mexico and Egypt), and the geologic estimates suggest that there is considerable potential for greater production in these countries. If it were to materialize, it would help to alleviate the desperate economic situation of many of these countries and put downward pressure on the world oil price.

OPEC Oil. Many of the best prospects for expanding reserves of oil and gas are in the OPEC countries themselves. Development of these resources would benefit the consuming countries in two ways. First, it would expand world energy supplies and stretch out the period during which consumers can rely on oil and natural gas. But more immediately, an increase in the reserves of any OPEC country is likely to increase that country's willingness to produce, and in so doing put downward pressure on the world oil price. This will be particularly true of OPEC countries that already attempt to maximize production.

Yet since 1974 investments in exploration, development, and improved recovery in the OPEC countries have not been timely.[144] The uncertain status of the Western oil companies in these countries and their idle capacity have served to deter investment. While this lack of investment may have been completely rational, from the perspective of both the international oil companies and the exporting countries, its effect was to keep the world's idle capacity just slightly above the peril point. Consequently, when a major loss of supplies occurred in 1979, the consuming countries were unable to find suitable alternatives.

Reserves in the OPEC countries are likely to increase both from genuine new discoveries and the reevaluation (or "proving up") of existing fields. Indeed, according to Z. R. Beydoun and H. V. Dunnington in *Petroleum Geology and Resources of the Middle East,* increases in the recovery factors for large volumes of discovered oil-in-place could produce future increases in the total proven reserves of the Middle East commensurate with those from 1955 to 1975. In addition, substantial quantities of heavy and sulphurous oils in the Middle East await the application of current technology to make them economic. Beydoun and Dunnington believe this oil could assume large proportions in the proven reserves of Syria, Iraq, Kuwait, Iran, and Saudi Arabia.[145]

The best prospects for the "proving up" of reserves and genuine discoveries in the OPEC countries are in Saudi Arabia and Iraq. While the *Oil and Gas Journal* estimates Iraq's reserves at 29.7 billion barrels, many industry officials believe Iraq's reserves are close to 60 billion barrels. Similarly, Saudi Arabia's reserves have long been officially understated, and are probably 200–300 billion barrels rather than the 164.6 billion reported by *Oil and Gas Journal.* Also, of thirty-seven fields discovered in Saudi Arabia, only fifteen have been put in use.[146] In addition, both Iraq and Saudi Arabia possess vast, unexplored areas of great promise. In fact, all the oil fields discovered so far in Saudi Arabia are in the eastern part of the country; the northern, center, and western parts have been only lightly explored. In Iraq, much of the middle part of the country remains unexplored.

While the Iraqi government does not make drilling statistics or reserve figures available,[147] indications are that, even before the war with Iran, its exploration and development program had fallen behind schedule. In the early 1970s Iraqi officials spoke of a production target of 6.5 mb/d by 1980, but by August 1975 this had been reduced to 4 mb/d in 1982. Iraq's main fields, Kirkuk and Rumailia, are experiencing problems and have probably reached their peak production. Since mid-1974, responsibility for exploration has rested with the Iraq National Oil Company (INOC); however, while the state oil company does much of the exploration itself, it also contracts out to foreign companies. Iraq also has a large, unexplored natural gas potential, and although the Iraqi government has begun evaluating its gas resources, their magnitude is not well known. At present, Iraq flares about 85 percent of the gas it produces, but plans are under way for Mitsubishi to construct an export-oriented liquified petroleum gas plant.[148]

In contrast to Iraq, Saudi Arabia is almost totally dependent upon the Western oil companies for exploration and development. The Saudi government, long anxious to determine the magnitude of its resources, has urged the companies to undertake exploration in hitherto untapped areas, and in the mid-1970s repeatedly emphasized its desire to develop as many fields as possible. But with little immediate need for additional reserves in Saudi Arabia, the companies have been slow to respond. In fact, from 1973 to 1978 the total number of wells drilled in the country declined from 323 to 145, and the total number of wildcats drilled in the five-year period is miniscule: 66.[149]

Unlike most OPEC countries, Saudi Arabia does not plan to enter the LNG trade; it plans to use its natural gas at home. Indeed, when its gas-gathering network is completed in the 1980s, Saudi Arabia expects to process and use all the gas it produces, ending flaring. (Before the system was begun, in 1976, Saudi Arabia flared more than three quarters of the 4.4 billion cubic feet it produced each day.) However, Saudi Arabia plans to export liquified petroleum gas and natural gasoline, giving it an important place in the international trade by the mid-1980s.[150] Also, it is likely that when the gas-gathering system comes into full operation (in the mid 1980s), the Saudi industries it is intended to serve will not be ready to absorb all its output, in which case Saudi Arabia may end up exporting LNG.[151]

While the prospect of new discoveries is not nearly as great in the other OPEC countries as in Saudi Arabia and Iraq, it is substantial in many of these countries. In Libya, all commercial fields currently in production are in the Sirte Basin, in the north-central part of the country. Since 1976, however, Libya has been exploring its offshore area and the western part of the country, and several important discoveries have been reported. From 1976 until 1979, the Libyan government had indicated it would like to boost production, but only if additional reserves were found. To encourage exploration and development, RCC has required companies that retain an equity share in Libyan concessions to make reinvestments in the country, and it has concluded new production-sharing agreements with Western companies that involve sizable exploration commitments. The RCC acknowledges that it needs the companies for assistance in enhanced recovery and exploration.[152]

Despite all this, Libya's productive capacity has declined as a result of insufficient investment and maintenance, and the Libyan development program has fallen behind schedule. Capacity and production were to reach 2.7 mb/d in 1980, but thus far capacity is only 2.1 mb/d[153] The delay has been due in part to the outbreak of hostilities with Egypt in 1977, as a result of which Libya decided to reroute a pipeline, making it less vulnerable to attack. In any case, between 1979 and 1985 Libya's capacity will probably decline slightly, despite its potential.[154] Libya has one LNG export plant in operation and is investing in "gas gathering" so that its associated gas can be used in local industry.

In 1974 it was predicted that by 1976 Nigeria would be producing 3–4 mb/d. In fact, Nigerian production, which was 2.26 mb/d in 1974, has never surpassed the 2.3 mb/d that it reached in 1979; and large areas of the Niger delta, Nigeria's main oil-producing region, have yet to be fully explored.[155]

Since Nigerian fields are small, with short productive lives, large-scale exploration is required simply to maintain productive capacity. Yet drilling declined steadily after 1974. The main reason was lack of immediate demand for Nigerian oil as a result of the general softening in demand for world oil and the increase in North Sea production. (Since both areas produce light crudes, Nigerian and North Sea oil are direct competitors.) The companies also claimed that their profit margins on Nigerian oil were too low to justify new capital investments.

To reverse this situation, in 1977 the government introduced a package of incentives to encourage greater exploration and production in Nigeria. Following this move, exploration increased somewhat, but total drilling continued to decline. Exploration in Nigeria has also been hampered by the fact that while Nigeria reserves many areas for the Nigerian National Petroleum Company, the state oil company, it has limited capital resources and shortages of personnel and technology. Nigeria also has extensive gas reserves, but most of the gas it produces is flared. With the assistance of Western companies, Nigeria had been planning to build a gas liquefaction plant but in 1982 the companies abandoned the project, putting its future in doubt.[156]

As in Nigeria, Indonesia's oil fields tend to be small and widely scattered, requiring a good deal of exploration simply to maintain production. Also like Nigeria, Indonesia has the potential to expand production, but as of 1976, less than 10 percent of Indonesia's prospective petroleum area had been properly tested. Prior to his ouster as head to Pertamina in 1975, General Sutowo talked of producing 3 mb/d by 1980; in fact, Indonesia's production has never exceeded the 1.69 mb/d it reached in 1977, and in the immediate future it is likely to continue to decline as the Minas field, the country's major producer, reaches maturation. And if domestic oil consumption continues to increase as rapidly as it has in recent years, Indonesia could become a net oil importer by 1990.[157]

To encourage exploration and development, Indonesia had permitted the companies to earn as much as $2.30 a barrel on their Indonesian production (as opposed to the 22¢ the companies officially earned on their Middle East production). However, in 1976, after Pertamina ran into serious financial difficulties, it boosted its profit share from 65–72.5 percent to 88 percent, which reduced the companies' profits by about $1 a barrel. Indonesia also reduced its generous cost recovery provisions. As a result of these moves, the companies' interest in exploration and development was greatly reduced. Also, in 1976 the U.S. Internal Revenue Service ruled that payments under Indonesia's production-sharing system were actually royalties and that, therefore, the companies should no longer be permitted to receive foreign-tax credits for these payments. The companies got a one-year reprieve from Congress, during which time they modified their legal arrangements with Indonesia to continue to take advantage of the foreign-tax credit. However, the immediate effect of the ruling was to further reduce corporate exploration in Indonesia.[158] With little exploration and few discoveries, Indonesia's oil reserves have declined in recent years.[159]

Indonesia has been exporting LNG to Japan, and in 1973 two California utilities agreed to import Indonesian LNG. However, because of opposition to both the pricing of gas and the siting of the receiving terminal, the deal did not receive regulatory approval until late in 1979, and the gas is not expected to flow until at least 1984. In the event the deal did not go through, Japan indicated its willingness to take whatever gas was available.[160]

Venezuela is generally regarded as a declining oil producer. Between 1970 and 1978 its production fell from 3.76 to 2.24 mb/d. While investment lagged in the early 1970s because of the oil companies' fear of nationalization, since 1976 Petroven, the Venezuelan national oil company, has attempted to boost reserves. But intensive exploration in traditional producing areas has yielded only small payoffs. And unlike most OPEC countries, Venezuela already makes fairly intensive use of secondary and tertiary recovery methods.[161]

However, two "nontraditional" areas in Venezuela have potential for substantial production. One is the offshore area where Petroven believes there may be as much as 30 billion barrels of oil. Yet, despite its potential, drilling did not begin until late in 1978. Moreover, Venezuela still lacks the infrastructure and technical expertise for development of this area.[162] Its other prospect for greatly expanding output is the Orinoco heavy-oil belt; estimates are that as many as 150 billion barrels of recoverable oil may be found in this area. Since the oil is extremely heavy, ranging from 9° API to 14° API, most of it may have to be produced by steam injection, and once produced, it will require upgrading by one of several methods currently being investigated. Nonetheless, estimates by Petroven are that total costs will range from $13 to $15 a barrel—less than synthetic fuels, solar energy, and oil from Canada's Athabasca tar sands.[163]

In 1976 Venezuela signed a technical cooperation agreement with PetroCanada to develop suitable methods of extraction in the Orinoco Belt. Venezuelan officials believe that the Canadian experience in the Athabasca tar sands will prove helpful in development of Orinoco. Technical aid agreements have also been signed with France and West Germany, but so far Venezuela has stopped short of permitting direct investment by foreign nationals in Orinoco. As of 1979, only about 15,000 b/d were produced in the Orinoco Belt, but Petroven hopes for an eventual output of 1 mb/d.[164]

In Ecuador, Latin America's other OPEC member, conflicts between the government and the international oil companies have impeded exploration. While Ecuador has been an oil producer for more than sixty years (longer than most OPEC countries), it became an oil exporter only in 1972, after Gulf and Texaco launched an exploration program in the country. However, in the mid-1970s Ecuador's government imposed increasingly strict terms on the companies, so that the drilling of wildcats, which had averaged fourteen a year from 1967 to 1973, fell to an average of five a year from 1973 to 1978. At the end of 1976, Gulf, one of the two leading producers in the country, announced that it would abandon operations in Ecuador effective January 1, 1977. In addition to stiffened terms, the companies are worried about the popularity of Ecuador's left-wing populist Aguilera Party.[165] With the companies pulling back, Ecuador's reserves have dwindled and its output and exports have been erratic.

Of all the OPEC countries, Ecuador is most vulnerable to competition from Alaskan oil. Also, domestic oil consumption has grown rapidly, threatening the country's position as an oil exporter. Its gas reserves remain undeveloped.[166]

Similarly, exploration in Abu Dhabi has been deterred by conflicts between the government and the oil companies. While the government has frequently exhorted the companies to step up their search for additional reserves, the companies have been reluctant to do so as long as Abu Dhabi maintains a ceiling on production. In April 1977 Abu Dhabi became the first Middle East country to enter the LNG trade.[167]

Algeria, since the nationalization of the foreign oil companies in 1972, has maintained one of the most extensive exploration and development programs of all the OPEC countries. This has involved work by the Algerian national oil company, Sonatrach, and by foreign oil companies operating as minority partners in joint ventures with Sonatrach. Despite these efforts, no oil finds of consequence have been made in Algeria in more than a decade. However, increases in production of natural gas liquids are expected to more than offset declines in crude production through the mid-1980s.[168]

As explained previously, Algeria's growth potential is as a producer of natural gas, not as a producer of oil. Consequently, Sonatrach has taken an active role in promoting natural gas sales. To transport natural gas to Europe, a trans-Mediterranean pipeline has been built, from Algeria to Italy, and a second is being considered. Algeria, the world's first LNG exporter, also concluded LNG deals with El Paso and Tenneco for export to the United States, but after the FPC held up approval of the deals for several years, in 1978 Algeria announced that it would offer the gas elsewhere.[169] It began signing up European LNG customers, but has recently been looking at increased sales to Europe through pipelines.

Prior to the 1979 revolution, Iran's growth as a hydrocarbon producer appeared to rest on natural gas, not oil. When the new agreement with the Consortium was reached in 1973, the Consortium agreed to increase Iran's capacity from 5 mb/d to 8 mb/d by October 1976, "provided that this is technically feasible and economically justifiable." This proved not to be the case. Production declined in some Consortium fields much more rapidly than expected while other fields, rated very highly in 1973, proved disappointing. As a result, in October 1976 the National Iranian Oil Company announced that capacity would be held at 6.5 mb/d, with only about 6 mb/d coming from the former Consortium area. Consequently, before the revolution, Iranian production was expected to level off between 6 and 7 mb/d. It was hoped that this level could be sustained for about ten years, at which point production declines would probably be inevitable.[170]

On the other hand, Iran, with the world's second largest gas reserves, planned to make increasing use of this fuel in the future. While it planned to reinject all its associated gas in order to boost oil production, Iran has extensive supplies of nonassociated gas. As indicated, part of this was to be exported to the Soviet Union, with the Soviet Union then exporting natural gas to Europe. Prior to the fall of the Shah in late 1978, Iran expressed interest in making LNG sales to the United States, but these plans have been abandoned.

Gabon's production is widely believed to have peaked at 225,000 b/d in 1975–76. While OPEC's remaining members, Qatar and Kuwait, could easily expand production if they were so inclined, this appears unlikely, for reasons already discussed. Neither country offers much prospect of new discoveries, and there is virtually no exploration or major new development in either of them. However, Qatar has significant untapped reserves of nonassociated natural gas, and three gas processing plants are being built. While Kuwait plans to use most of its gas at home, it also plans to become a significant exporter of natural gas and petroleum products.[171]

THE EVOLUTION OF WORLD OIL PRICES FROM 1974 TO 1978

Despite the limited conservation efforts by the consuming countries, the decline in world oil consumption that resulted from the 1974–75 recession greatly weakened the demand for OPEC oil. From 1975 through 1978, demand increased, but the growth in non-OPEC oil production kept demand for OPEC oil in check—despite the limited efforts to develop new sources. These developments led to a softening of the world oil market. Moreover, the political forces at work in this period, chiefly Saudi Arabia's interest in encouraging an Arab-Israeli settlement and its desire to solidify its ties with the United States, tended to reinforce price moderation. As a result, between year-end 1974 and year-end 1978, the real world oil price declined.

While the consuming countries could regard this as a success of sorts—indeed, it led to widespread complacency—in reality they missed an opportunity and left themselves exposed to a danger. The opportunity was the possibility of reducing demand for OPEC oil enough to provoke competitive price cutting that would lead to a sharp reduction in the nominal OPEC price and weaken the power of the exporting countries. The danger was their continued vulnerability to a major loss of supplies from the OPEC countries because of a lack of alternatives that could be used in an emergency.

By the beginning of 1974 the oil market had already weakened. In December 1973 the Arab states had begun to restore production, and both the rise in prices and the recession reduced demand for oil. Several oil-exporting countries held auctions early in 1974 but failed to realize prices as high as a few months before. In February, Tunisia received bids in the $14–15 range; Iranian oil that had been bought for $17 in November was reselling at $13; and Kuwait received bids of about $9 a barrel. Also, companies were backing away from deals negotiated earlier but not finalized.[172]

With the end of the Arab oil embargo in March, most Arab oil-exporting countries attempted to boost production further. By May, Saudi production had risen above its September 1973 levels, and during the second half of 1974 Saudi production averaged 8.8 mb/d. Of the major Arab oil-exporting countries, only Kuwait and Libya attempted to hold production below the pre-embargo September 1973 levels, but these two countries had been reducing production to conserve supplies even before the October War. In contrast, Saudi Arabia, Iraq, Algeria, and Iran were seeking to boost production as rapidly as possible. As a result, by the summer of 1974 there was a surplus of about 2 mb/d on the world market.[173]

When the OPEC countries raised prices in December 1973, they widened the gap between the prices of participation and equity oil to as much as $3.72. This resulted in windfall profits for oil companies with access to equity oil. Throughout 1974 the companies' excess profits were an issue among the OPEC countries. Then, in the summer of 1974, in a weak market, the companies began cutting into their profit margins in order to reduce prices to sell crude and thus were often able to undersell the OPEC countries' national oil companies. That summer, Kuwait, Iran, Tunisia, and Ecuador attempted to auction state-owned participation crude, but failed to attract the kind of offers they hoped for.[174]

When the OPEC countries met in September, they agreed that, to prevent the international oil companies from underselling their national oil companies, the gap between the prices of equity and participation oil should be reduced. However, Saudi Arabia still advocated a decline in the average OPEC price. It proposed that the price of participation oil be reduced while the price of equity oil was raised, so that the two prices would meet at a point below the companies' average tax-paid cost. But the other OPEC countries, led by Iran, favored an overall price increase to compensate for the decline in their per barrel revenues as a result of inflation. Their position was buttressed by a recommendation from OPEC's economic commission that, to compensate the OPEC countries for inflation, the average cost of crude to the companies should rise by 14 percent. The Commission also recommended that, to mop up the crude surplus, there be across-the-board production cutbacks by all countries.

Following strong objections by Saudi Arabia and others to the economic commission's proposal for production controls, the conference agreed to have the OPEC secretary general carry out a "study on the subject of supply and demand." On pricing, the OPEC countries decided to leave the price of participation oil alone, but raised the cost of equity crude to the companies enough to boost their average tax-paid cost from $9.41 to $9.74. This reduced the gap between the cost of participation oil and the cost of equity oil, but did not eliminate it. It was announced that the increase was to compensate the OPEC countries for inflation in the industrialized countries—and on an annual basis, the increase was in fact equal to the 14 percent increase the economic commission recommended. However, Saudi Arabia refused to accept the OPEC decision and did not raise prices in accordance with it. Yet there were reports that the Saudis were growing uneasy with their isolation from the rest of OPEC. At the same time, the softening of the world oil market was weakening Iran's drive for higher prices. The September OPEC conference also established a working committee "to study and recommend a new system for long-term oil pricing."[175]

Before OPEC could consider the recommendations of this committee, a surprise meeting of the Gulf exporting countries was held in Abu Dhabi on November 9–10. At this meeting, Saudi Arabia, the United Arab Emirates, and Qatar agreed to implement, retroactive to November 1, a Saudi proposal that raised the price of equity oil and reduced the price of participation crude. (Kuwait and Iran believed that no decision should be taken until the OPEC meeting in December, while Iraq opposed any reduction in the price of equity oil.) The effect of this proposal was to raise the companies' average cost about 55¢ a barrel but to reduce the difference between the price of equity and participation crude from $2.46 to 75¢.[176]

Saudi Arabia had several reasons for supporting this proposal. By reducing the price of participation oil (and the price of government-sold oil), Saudi Arabia could claim to have achieved the reduction in the market price that it had promised consuming countries. Yet, since the overall effect of the Saudi move was to raise prices, Saudi Arabia hoped that the other OPEC countries would accept it at their meeting in December, thereby reestablishing OPEC price unity. It also hoped that by presenting the new system to the OPEC meeting as a *fait accompli*, it would preempt proposals by Iran for a single pricing system that would eliminate the distinction between participation and equity crude and by the OPEC commission for the indexing of oil prices so that they would rise automatically with inflation in the industrialized countries. (Iran wanted a single pricing system to aid in detection of price cutting.) By reducing the companies' profit margins on equity oil, the Saudi move eliminated their windfall profits and the danger of their taking business away from OPEC national oil companies by price cutting. Overall, the Saudi move reduced the companies' average profit margin on crude from about 80¢ a barrel to about 22¢.

Most importantly, Saudi Arabia saw the move as a way of resolving its demand for 100 percent participation. Since June, Saudi Arabia had been demanding this and the companies had resisted it. Consequently, by instituting these fiscal changes Saudi Arabia gave itself the financial benefits of 100 percent participation and reduced the companies' interest in maintaining an equity stake in Aramco, since their profits on equity oil were no longer so great. Still, to force the companies to capitulate to 100 percent participation, after the Abu Dhabi meeting Saudi Arabia threatened to sell 3 mb/d to independent companies at a price below Aramco's weighted average tax-paid cost. Finally, in December the Aramco partners accepted the principle of 100 percent participation.[177] Following the Abu Dhabi meeting, Saudi Arabia ceased advocating price reductions and appeared content to allow the real price level to erode through inflation, while holding the nominal price constant.

When the OPEC countries met in December, they basically ratified, on an OPEC-wide basis, the changes that Saudi Arabia had initiated. The December conference also decided that, from then on, OPEC would set prices by fixing the average take on the marker crude rather than by fixing the posted price, as it had in the past.[178] This decision greatly reduced the importance of posted prices. As of January 1, 1975, the average government take was set at $10.12—about the level that Saudi Arabia had effectively established in November. With a cost of 12¢ a barrel and a company margin of 22¢ a barrel, the official market price was $10.46.

While the 22¢ margin permitted the former concessionaires to earn a profit on their production of OPEC oil, it would not enable them to undersell the OPEC national oil companies in third-party markets. Moreover, while the former concessionaires could still secure crude for 22¢ less than other companies, this was considerably less than the 94¢ advantage they had enjoyed for most of 1974. In addition, the companies were afraid that the state oil companies might reduce their margins by selling crude for less than $10.46, especially since no decision on the price that the state oil companies would charge had been reached at the December meeting.[179]

In a departure from the decision implied in September, the new pricing system contained no automatic inflation escalator, as Iran had sought. Instead, OPEC announced that it was freezing prices for nine months—a decision certain to erode real price levels in view of the expected inflation. Nonetheless, the increase in the average per barrel take that OPEC achieved during 1974, from

$8.20 to $10.12, was quite an achievement in view of the softness of the world oil market.[180] According to the 1971 Teheran Agreement, between 1970 and 1975 the government's average per barrel take was supposed to rise by a total of about 70¢. Instead, it rose from 96¢ to $10.12.

With world demand declining, OPEC production, which had begun to fall in the third quarter of 1974, continued to sink until it reached a low of 26.15 mb/d in the second quarter of 1975. At this level, OPEC's production was 20.7 percent below its September 1973 pre-embargo level. Nearly a third of OPEC's capacity was unused, with spare capacity totaling 11.95 mb/d (see table 11-6).

This decline in production threatened to undermine the world oil price as countries resorted to price cutting to boost sales. Indeed, price "cheating" became widespread as countries offered occasional secret discounts, generous credit terms, and reduced differentials and resorted to bartering crude, all in an effort to disguise price cuts. But for the most part, these reductions were modest, generally no more than a dollar a barrel. More importantly, they did not lead to reduction in the official price of the OPEC marker crude. Countries recognized that it was not in their interest to take actions that would lead to reduction in the marker price; so the problem became allocation of production among the member countries at the fixed price. At their meeting in March 1975, the OPEC countries considered a formal prorationing system, but, as always, Saudi Arabia opposed prorationing and succeeded in killing the proposal, despite the fact that all other OPEC members supported it.[181]

In the absence of formal prorationing, the international oil companies allo-

TABLE 11–6. ALLOCATION OF OPEC PRODUCTION CUTBACKS IN SECOND QUARTER, 1975 (MB/D)

	Sept. 1973 Production	Second Quarter, 1975	
		Production	Capacity
Saudi Arabia	8.57	6.59	10.3
Kuwait	3.53	2.10	3.8
United Arab Emirates	1.67	1.78	2.28
Qatar	.60	.44	6.5
Libya	2.29	1.28	3.0
Algeria	1.10	.80	1.1
Iraq	2.11	2.33	2.6
Iran	5.83	5.23	6.5
Nigeria	2.14	1.59	2.5
Gabon	.19	.21	.2
Indonesia	1.42	1.19	1.6
Venezuela	3.39	2.45	3.3
Ecuador	.12	.16	.26
OPEC Total	32.96	26.15	38.10

Figures on production from Rustow and Mugno, *OPEC: Success and Prospects*, pp. 136–37; figures on capacity from *PIW*, July 28, 1975, p. 7. All other calculations by author.

cated crude supplies by responding to the adjustments that individual OPEC countries made for the prices of their crudes. Initially, as tanker rates fell, short-haul crudes—those produced in Libya, Algeria, and Nigeria—became uncompetitive and their production declined sharply. To stem this decline, these countries reduced the premiums they had imposed in 1973–74.

Libya is the most extreme case. In January 1974 Libya was producing 2.032 mb/d and selling its oil for $16 a barrel, with some of its "undisputed" oil fetching as much as $20 a barrel. But when tanker rates fell, so did Libyan production, to a low of 863,000 b/d in February 1975. To restore production, between October 1974 and June 1975 Libya cut prices five times. By June 1975 its price was down to $11.10 and its production up to 1.51 mb/d.[182]

Similarly, Abu Dhabi's production fell from 1.212 mb/d in December 1974 to 0.728 mb/d in February 1975. Abu Dhabi accused the companies of trying to break OPEC and complained publicly about OPEC's failure to avoid surpluses by coordinating its members' production. In March, however, Abu Dhabi's production was up to 1.154 mb/d, after the sheikdom agreed to reduce the price of its crude about 55¢ a barrel by virtually eliminating the low-sulfur premium it had previously charged.[183]

With Saudi Arabia refusing to implement the OPEC price increases of June and September 1974, its production increased steadily, reaching 9.35 mb/d in October 1974. But once it boosted prices in accordance with the November Abu Dhabi agreement, its production declined rapidly, reaching a low of 5.919 mb/d in April 1975. This change in Saudi financial terms and a lowering of prices by

Second Quarter, 1975		% Change in Production
Spare Capacity	Spare Capacity as % of Total Capacity	Sept. 1973 to Second quarter, 1975
3.71	36.0	−23.1
1.70	44.7	−40.5
.50	21.9	6.6
.21	32.0	−26.7
1.72	57.3	−44.1
.3	27.3	−27.3
.27	10.4	10.4
1.27	19.5	−10.3
.91	36.4	−25.7
0	—	10.5
.41	25.6	−16.2
.85	25.8	−27.7
.10	37.3	33.3
11.95	31.4	−20.7

the short-haul producers meant that, increasingly, more of the decline in total production was shifted onto Saudi Arabia.[184]

This ad hoc move and countermove by the exporting countries and the companies had one great advantage over formal prorationing: it gave the exporting countries great flexibility and thereby enabled adaptations to the needs of particular countries, which probably, OPEC would never have agreed to as part of a formal prorationing system. For example, if an official OPEC prorationing scheme had been in effect, it is doubtful that the OPEC countries would have allowed Iraq to increase production while OPEC production, as a whole, declined by more than 20 percent; but by cutting the price of its crude slightly below the price of the marker crude, Iraq achieved this result. (Iraq denied that it cut prices, but its per barrel revenues for 1975 were 53¢ below the OPEC average.)[185]

Nonetheless, this de facto system of "tolerated cheating" would probably have led to the undermining of the world oil price, were it not for the fact that, because of their financial gains the previous year, most OPEC countries could "accept" the production declines and consequent revenue losses. This was particularly true of the "rich" OPEC countries. Indeed, OPEC's solidarity was enhanced by the fact that the countries that suffered the largest production declines (proportionally) and had the highest spare capacity (in relation to their capacity) were in this group—Kuwait and Libya. So was Saudi Arabia, which experienced the largest production cutback in absolute terms and had the most spare capacity. Still, these "rich" OPEC countries did not absorb the entire decline. As table 11–6 shows, the decline was shared with Algeria, Nigeria, and Venezuela, which accepted slightly more than their proportionate reductions. This general sharing of cutbacks, uneven though it was, reduced the pressure a single revenue-maximizing country would have felt had it borne a grossly disproportionate share of the cutback. Libya and Kuwait were able to do this without cutting prices below the marker level, but it is doubtful that Iran or Indonesia (for example) would have been able to do the same.

As it was, their modest revenue losses caused major problems for these two countries. Iran's revenues fell far short of its budget needs, and it was forced to scale down its five-year plan;[186] and the decline in demand produced a crisis in Indonesia. As its oil revenues rose, Pertamina, the state oil company, had diversified into steel, air transport, petrochemicals, fertilizer, liquefied natural gas, insurance, rice farming, roadbuilding, and construction, ranging from housing and hospitals to golf courses. To finance this program, Pertamina had borrowed heavily, expecting to pay its debts as its oil revenues mounted; but when demand for Indonesian oil slumped, Pertamina was unable to repay.

With its borrowing at $10 billion and cross-default clauses stipulating that once one loan was declared in default, its other loans were in default, the threat to Pertamina also threatened the Indonesian government and the international financial system. But the U.S. government urged Indonesia's creditors not to panic, a rescue plan was worked out, and the Indonesian central bank assumed responsibility for $4 billion worth of Pertamina's debt. Other debts were refinanced with long-term rescue loans syndicated by Morgan Guaranty Trust Company, which had not been involved in the earlier lending to Indonesia. A report by the Senate Subcommittee on International Economic Policy later concluded that, in showering Pertamina with credit, the international banks had ignored warnings by the IMF, the U.S. government, and segments of the Indonesian government. The banks had persisted in lending to Pertamina largely because they were confident that neither the Indonesian government, nor their home governments, would permit default, an assumption that turned out to be correct.[187]

In the latter part of 1974, as the U.S. economy began to recover, demand for OPEC oil began to increase. Demand was particularly strong for the light crudes produced in Libya, Algeria, Nigeria, and Indonesia, mainly because they were the crudes that U.S. refiners needed. On the other hand, demand for the heavy crudes produced in Venezuela, Iran, and Kuwait continued to languish. This was the context when the OPEC countries met in September 1975, at the end of their nine-month price freeze, and the meeting proved to be one of their most acrimonious encounters. The *Middle East Economic Survey* described the meeting as the "worst bout of international tension the Organization had experienced since the royalty expensing drama of 1964."[188]

The price hawks, led by Iran and Iraq, went into the meeting concerned about the impact of worldwide inflation on the purchasing power of their oil revenues; initially they demanded an increase of about 30 percent.[189] Saudi Arabia was concerned about the impact of another price increase on a world economy still teetering near disaster. In 1975 the regimes in Portugal, Spain, Italy, and Greece were challenged by leftist movements, and the Saudis were told that if oil prices were raised, small European countries would become vulnerable to Communist takeovers.[190] In addition, in September 1975 Secretary of State Kissinger had just concluded a disengagement agreement for the Sinai, which was confirmed and approved by the Saudis. In return, the United States expected the Saudis to show moderation on oil pricing. Consequently, Yamani asked the meeting for an increase of no more than 5 percent and indicated that "10% is not an increase we could accept."[191]

During the meeting, Saudi Arabia threatened to freeze its prices and to flood the market with oil, if the demands by the hawks for a 15–20 percent increase were accepted. Yamani even walked out of the Vienna meeting at one point, flew to London, and then returned. With Venezuela, Kuwait, the UAE, and Algeria mediating between Saudi Arabia and the OPEC price hawks, a compromise was reached after four days of heated debate. Starting October 1, the price would be increased 10 percent, from $10.46 a barrel to $11.51, and would remain in effect until June 30, 1976, when it would be reviewed. While the 10 percent increase was more than Saudi Arabia had indicated it would accept, in keeping with Saudi desires the compromise contained no provision for linking the future price of oil to inflation in the West, as several OPEC countries had sought.[192]

At the September meeting Saudi Arabia and Algeria also accused Iraq and Libya of underpricing their oil. Moreover, after the meeting, Indonesia increased its prices only 1.6 percent, rather than the 10 percent OPEC increase. This was the first time since late 1973 that Indonesia had failed to match an OPEC price increase with a comparable increase of its own, but, given its precarious financial situation, it had to take measures to assure that its production would increase.[193]

When OPEC next met, in December 1975, little was expected. The price freeze announced the previous September was to continue until June 30, and the meeting was to focus primarily on the complex question of appropriate price differentials, but the meeting made headlines when eleven of OPEC's thirteen ministerial delegates, including Yamani and Amouzegar, were taken hostage. Their captors demanded renunciation of the Israeli-Egyptian Sinai agreement and a more aggressive attitude toward Israel. The OPEC ministers were soon freed, but the episode underscored the close connections that had developed between oil pricing and international politics.

When the OPEC countries met in May 1976 to review the price freeze, the same split that had characterized their September meeting reappeared. Iraq sought a 20 percent increase to compensate the exporting countries for inflation in the West, while Saudi Arabia again threatened to flood the market if its demand for extension of the price freeze was not met. This time the other OPEC countries went along with Saudi Arabia, extending their price freeze another six months. As a result of the recession in the West, demand for oil was still lagging, there were about 10 mb/d of spare capacity in the OPEC countries, and the price of OPEC imports had not risen much since the last OPEC price increase in September.[194] Moreover, the OPEC countries believed they were better off deferring price increases until the Western recovery was well under way, when demand for oil would increase enough to make a hefty price increase possible.

But when that time came, Saudi Arabia again demurred. Several months before the Decembr 1976 OPEC meeting, Iran came out in favor of a 40 percent increase. By the time the meeting began, Iran had moderated its position, publicly insisting on at least a 15 percent increase on the eve of the conference.[195] But Iraq was still calling for a 25 percent increase. In November, Yamani had said that Saudi Arabia would accept "nothing above 10 percent"; then, as the meeting began, Yamani announced that because the recovery in the West was not as strong as initially believed, Saudi Arabia wanted another six-month price freeze.[196]

In the meetings, three positions emerged: a six-month freeze, which the Saudis alone demanded; an immediate 15 percent increase, which the majority, including Iran, demanded; and a 10 percent rise, which a few would-be moderates—Kuwait, Venezuela, and Indonesia—proposed as a compromise. However, the OPEC countries were unable to reach a compromise acceptable to all. Consequently, the majority decided that as of January 1, 1977, they would raise prices by a little over 10 percent, from $11.51 to $12.70, with another 5 percent increase on July 1, 1977. But Saudi Arabia and the United Arab Emirates announced that on January 1 they would raise prices by only 5 percent, from $11.51 to $12.08, and would schedule no further increase for 1977. Yamani indicated that, to force the "ten percenters" to reduce their prices to the Saudi level, Saudi Arabia would increase its production sharply. At the same time, Yamani warned the West that if progress was not made in the North/South talks, and if the Arab-Israeli conflict did not move toward a resolution, Saudi Arabia would reconsider its moderation on pricing.[197]

Many Western analysts pooh-poohed the official Saudi statements and argued that the Saudis kept the price down to boost their sales, but this contention does not stand up to analysis. Saudi Arabia could probably have increased its revenues as much by increasing its price 10 percent as by boosting its sales at the lower price, and it would not have had to sell as much oil to get the same amount of revenue.[198] Consequently, Saudi Arabia's actions can be explained as those of a "revenue maximizer" only if one assigns negative value to the oil that Saudi Arabia would have saved by producing less at a higher price—a dubious proposition.

The Saudis had two basic concerns. One was the fragility of the developed world's economic recovery. When the OPEC countries met in December, the recovery was already losing momentum in the United States and OECD economists were revising their forecasts downward.[199] Moreover, the Saudis were afraid that continued economic weakness would lead to political instability, particularly in Western Europe, where Communists were gaining support.[200] The other major Saudi concern was the Arab-Israeli conflict. As will be recalled from chapter 9, in the fall of 1976 Saudi Arabia had intervened in the Lebanese conflict and had brought Egypt and Syria into a common bloc that was prepared to go to Geneva and negotiate a resolution of the Arab-Israeli conflict. And because of its increased dependence upon Saudi Arabia, the PLO was showing more willingness to reach a negotiated settlement with Israel. Israel also had endorsed the idea of a conference, though it was still unwilling to negotiate with the PLO. But a new president had just been elected in the United States, and the Saudis believed he could exert leverage on the Israelis. In this context, moderation on oil pricing was a carrot the Saudis held out to a new U.S. president in order to put pressure on Israel.

Despite the lower prices charged by the Saudis and their commitment to increase their production, only the other Gulf countries suffered significant production declines in the first half of 1977, compared with the second half of 1976.[201] There were several reasons for this. Demand for the light crudes produced in Algeria, Libya, Nigeria, and Indonesia remained strong throughout this period, and since Saudi Arabia's spare capacity was mainly in heavy crudes, it could not be substituted. Cold weather in the United States and Europe, the United States' natural gas crisis, continued growth in U.S. imports, and U.S.

refiners' dependence upon light crudes all contributed to the strong demand for oil from Algeria, Libya, Nigeria, and Indonesia. In addition, while officially Indonesia went along with the ten percenters, it raised its prices only seven percent. In the aftermath of the Pertamina crisis, Indonesia did not want demand for its crude to decline again.[202]

Saudi Arabia, also, had trouble raising its production substantially. Yamani stated that Saudi Arabia would allow it to rise from 9.188 mb/d in December 1976 to 10 mb/d during the first quarter of 1977, but production during the first quarter averaged only 9.306 mb/d. While there are always technical problems in raising production sharply, it is doubtful that Saudi Arabia had the 11.8 mb/d capacity it claimed.[203] In addition, stormy weather in the Gulf put the Ras Tanura loading facility out of operation for most of January and part of February, greatly reducing Saudi Arabia's ability to ship its oil to market. After the terminal was repaired, Saudi Arabia's production increased from 8.484 mb/d in January to 10.21 mb/d in April.[204] But in May a fire in the Abqaiq field (south of Ras Tanura) reduced capacity in both the Ghawar and Abqaiq fields.[205] As a result, production fell back to 8.462 mb/d in May. While the Saudi government denied that the fire was due to sabotage, many Saudis (and other observers) believe this *was* the cause of the fire. (As a result of the fire, the Saudi elite's perception of its vulnerability increased.)[206]

In contrast to the Saudis, the UAE did not permit its allowable production to rise during the period of split pricing. The UAE oil minister, Mana Saeed al-Otaiba, said that while the UAE had the potential to boost its production by 300,000 b/d immediately and by 1 mb/d by the end of 1977, it would not do so for fear of hurting "our OPEC colleagues."[207] Even with the Saudis raising their price by only 5 percent, Abu Dhabi could probably have sold all its allowable production if it had raised prices by 10 percent.[208] Its restraint stemmed from its acute sense of vulnerability and its consequent desire to offend neither the Saudis nor the other OPEC members.

Another reason for the ten percenters' success in selling their oil, despite the lower price charged by the Saudis and the UAE, was the fact that the international oil companies were not about to jeopardize their relationships with the ten percenters in order to gain a slight and probably temporary advantage by increasing their purchases of Saudi crude. Moreover, many of these companies had long-term contracts that committed them to purchase a particular crude. Similarly, while over the long term refineries could be adapted to run on practically any crude, refiners had demands for particular, not "anonymous," crudes.

In the first half of 1977 Kuwait and Qatar experienced the largest-percentage production declines, but their wealth and their limited revenue needs made it relatively easy for them to endure these cutbacks. In contrast, Iran and Iraq were probably most badly damaged by the Saudi actions. Indeed, one of the reasons for the Saudi insistence on lower prices may have been to weaken its principal rivals for leadership in the Gulf, both of whom needed additional revenue far more than the Saudis did. In particular, the Saudis may have sought to slow the Iranian arms buildup.

Iran, which had been hurt by both the 1974–75 slump in demand and the weakening in the market for heavy Gulf crudes in the latter part of 1976, particularly resented the Saudi action. The Iranians were especially vulnerable because their agreement with the Consortium imposed no minimum lifting requirement upon the companies. Early in 1977 the Shah said that, as a result of the decline in its production, Iran faced a budget deficit of $7 billion. He indicated that this would necessitate a cut in foreign aid, lower defense expenditures, and reappraisal of Iran's foreign policy. Any increase in Saudi or UAE production, he declared, would be "an act of aggression against Iran."[209] *Rastakhiz,* the newspaper of Iran's only legal political party and a pillar of the Shah's political system, declared in a December editorial that "the Third World and all progressive nations everywhere are angry and detest Sheikh Yamani for having sold the real interests of his country and of OPEC to imperialism." However, the Iranian news media concentrated on Yamani and did not criticize Saudi Arabia in general or the Saudi monarch, King Khaled.[210] The Iraqi oil minister hinted that Iraq would support a campaign of propaganda and sedition against Saudi Arabia, and he accused the Saudis of acting in "the service of imperialism and Zionism."[211]

In any case, with Venezuela acting as mediator, the OPEC countries reached a compromise in May.[212] The ten percenters agreed to cancel the 5 percent increase they had scheduled for July 1. In return, Saudi Arabia and the UAE agreed that, at the beginning of July, they would raise their prices to the level of the other OPEC countries, and Saudi Arabia reimposed its production ceiling of 8.5 mb/d. This compromise had been proposed soon after the split emerged, but Saudi Arabia and the UAE had rejected it initially, hoping to force the other exporting countries to lower their prices. While the ten percenters resisted this, they had little choice but to accept the compromise since worldwide demand had slackened, and with the damage caused by the May fire soon to be repaired, Saudi Arabia was in a position to boost production again.

The episode indicated that neither Saudi Arabia nor the other OPEC countries could set the price on its own. A clear beneficiary was the Aramco partners, who in theory could pocket the difference between the Saudi price and that of the other OPEC countries. The Saudis attempted to prevent this, requiring the companies to sell at the official Saudi price, but it is doubtful that the Saudi government's efforts were fully successful, especially since most of the Aramco partners' crude moved through their own refining systems and was never sold as such. In addition, the Aramco partners benefited from the increase in Saudi production that resulted from the kingdom's actions.

As soon as the split-pricing episode was resolved, Saudi Arabia and Abu Dhabi began campaigning for OPEC to extend the price freeze at its next conference, in December 1977, and they were greatly aided by the weak world demand for OPEC oil during the second part of 1977. Lagging economic growth in the West, energy conservation, and the growth of production in Mexico, the North Sea, and Alaska all played a role in this. Moreover, during the previous year the market in light crudes had been strong while demand for heavy crudes languished, but in the latter part of 1977 the market for light crudes weakened dramatically, for several reasons. U.S. demand let up, as the U.S. economy worsened and U.S. refiners added desulfurization plants, reducing the need for light crudes. In addition, light North Sea oil cut into the market for OPEC light crudes.[213]

With the market soft, prospects for a substantial price increase were dim. Nonetheless, Iraq, Libya, and Algeria came out for price increases of 10–23 percent, and several weeks before the December meeting such OPEC moderates as Kuwait, Venezuela, and Indonesia indicated that an 8 percent price hike was warranted to offset worldwide inflation and the diminishing purchasing power of the dollar, which oil was priced in. In July, however, Iran, until then a leading price hawk, abandoned its longstanding demand for linking the price of oil to the rising cost of the goods the OPEC countries imported, and joined Saudi Arabia in calling for a continued price freeze. Both Yamani and Iran's interior minister, Jamshid Amouzegar, said they feared that another rise in the price of oil might damage the industrial countries' tentative recovery from the deepest and longest recession in over a generation.[214]

Following his visit to Washington in November, the Shah promised to work against any increase in oil prices during 1978, and his motives in adopting this position are not difficult to fathom. He was trying to gain U.S. approval to purchase an additional 140 F-16 fighter-bombers (160 were already contracted for) and was also concerned about the growing closeness of Saudi Arabia and the United States, which threatened to reduce Iran's importance to the United States. Since it would be difficult to raise oil prices in the prevailing market, why not come out for a price freeze in an attempt to curry U.S. favor? Also, in 1977 the Soviet Union was moving toward much closer relations with Libya and had forged an alliance with Ethiopia, which the Shah saw as potentially leading to Soviet dominance of the strategic Horn of Africa. To buttress the security of the Gulf area, Iran sought to improve relations with Saudi Arabia, and ending their rivalry over oil prices was one way of doing that.

Shortly before the OPEC conference began, following intensive lobbying by the United States, Venezuela, Qatar, and Kuwait came out in favor of a continued price freeze. With countries accounting for roughly 70 percent of OPEC's production opposed to any price increase by the time the conference started, it was unlikely that oil prices would rise. Nonetheless, the December meeting was marked by conflict between the remaining price hawks and the OPEC majority. Iraq took the lead in arguing for a 23 percent increase, but in the end the OPEC secretary general announced that the members had reached "an agreement not to disagree, so present prices will continue."[215]

During the first half of 1978 a substantial surplus continued to glut the world market, as Alaskan and North Sea oil supplies increased, and in anticipation of a price increase at the December 1977 meeting, oil companies had increased their stocks. But when the increase did not materialize, they reduced their inventories, adding to the surplus on the world market. Price discounts and special deals became common, with Algeria, Libya, Nigeria, and Iran cutting prices. During this period, Saudi Arabia absorbed nearly half the cutbacks in OPEC production.[216]

In this period the OPEC countries became increasingly concerned about the impact of the declining dollar on the real value of their oil revenues. No major oil-exporting country believed that the world trade could be carried on in anything but dollars; there was simply no other reserve currency in sufficiently wide circulation to support the volume of transactions that the OPEC countries generated. (SDRs can be transferred only among central banks.) But many OPEC countries increasingly questioned whether oil should continue to be priced in dollars,[217] for, as the dollar fell, both the cost of oil to countries other than the United States and the OPEC countries' real per barrel income declined.[218] To avoid this, the 1972 Geneva Agreement had stipulated that oil would be priced according to the weighted average of a "basket" of currencies. However, this system was abandoned in October 1973, largely because, with the dollar appreciating in value, following the Geneva Agreement would have meant reducing oil prices. Then in June 1975 the OPEC countries had stipulated that oil would be priced in SDRs, but this decision was never implemented, largely because, shortly after it was made, the dollar again began to rise in value. However, with the dollar falling, Iraq, Kuwait, Venezuela, Indonesia, Qatar, and the UAE advocated a switch to some other pricing standard (probably the SDR) or an increase in the price of oil to compensate for the decline in the dollar. But switching to another pricing standard posed several problems. Finding an acceptable alternative was not easy: since all OPEC countries had different import mixes, there *was* no basket of currencies that would protect all of them against reductions in their purchasing power because of foreign-currency fluctuations. Nor was it easy to find an alternative standard that was not heavily weighted by the dollar. In addition, when the dollar was falling and interest in switching was greatest, it probably made *least* sense to switch, for by the time OPEC had agreed on an alternative, the dollar was likely to be rising again. Most importantly, any move away from the dollar by OPEC would *reduce* confidence in it, further weakening its value. Thus a country such as Saudi Arabia, which held a large portion of its assets in dollars,[219] would see their value decline. It would also tend to undermine the stability of the international financial system.

Saudi Arabia therefore opposed any effort by the OPEC countries to shift to a different standard, but in return for its commitment to the dollar and its restraint on oil pricing, Saudi Arabia expected the United States to take measures to halt the decline in the value of the dollar. In addition, the Saudis expected Congress to approve the sale of sixty F-15 fighter aircraft to Saudi Arabia. After much controversy, with supporters of Israel on one side and supporters of improved relations with Saudi Arabia on the other, Congress approved the sale in May 1978.[220]

When the OPEC countries met in June 1978, the majority favored a price increase to compensate them for the effects of inflation and decline in the value of the dollar on the purchasing power of their oil revenues.[221] But with the market still weak and both Iran and Saudi Arabia still opposed to a price increase, the freeze was extended another six months. OPEC also decided to continue to price oil in dollars, but to set up a committee to study the effect of exchange-rate fluctuations on oil revenues.

When the "militant" OPEC members maintained that Saudi Arabia and Iran were acting as agents of the United States and other Western nations, Yamani explained that since Saudi Arabia had a huge investment in the dollar, the kingdom did "not want to do anything that might help the deterioration of the dollar's value."[222] Moreover, despite the oil glut during 1977–78, which most observers believed would persist at least another year or two, most oil-exporting countries, including Saudi Arabia, continued to believe that markets would tighten by the 1980s, making it possible to raise world oil prices substantially.

The weakness of the market kept the world oil price at $12.70 a barrel from July 1977 until the end of 1978, but it had several detrimental effects. It created a sense of complacency, which reduced the consuming countries' willingness to adopt strong measures to deal with the "energy crisis." The failure of Congress to adopt most of the Carter energy plan is the most striking example. In addition, it reduced the oil companies' and the oil-producing countries' commitment to developing new sources of oil and gas. As a result, loss of a few million barrels a day was enough to shift the world market from surplus back to crisis.

The Impact of the
Oil Price Revolution on
the International Oil
Companies

In chapter 9 we examined the impact of the rise in oil prices on the consuming countries, and in the previous two chapters we explored the factors that have enabled the oil-exporting countries to keep prices up. But what about the third actor, those pillars of modern capitalism, the international oil companies? How have they fared following the rise in oil prices and the growth of oil-exporting-country power? Have the companies been better off with oil selling for more than $10 a barrel than they were when it sold for less than $2?

The answer is not as clear cut as it may seem. While the companies' revenues have gone up, so have their costs. The oil-exporting countries have taken formal control over their oil producing assets, and the companies have come under widespread attack in the consuming countries. Yet the companies have managed to adapt remarkably well to these new conditions.

Despite the substantial achievements of the exporting countries, their dependence upon the international oil companies has persisted. No OPEC member has been able to operate its oil industry without assistance from the international oil companies, either in the technology required for further exploration and development or in the marketing of its oil. As we have seen, the exporting countries, as a group, still rely on the companies to allocate production among them, which insulates the OPEC members from direct conflicts over market shares. In periods of market weakness, the OPEC countries have found that they need the major international oil companies to market their oil, and individual OPEC countries have been willing to conclude long-term contracts at substantial discounts to assure that the companies continue to purchase at least a minimum amount of the crude they produce. Moreover, the greater the discount offered, the larger the volume involved, and the longer the period contracted for, the greater assurance an exporting country has that its oil will be sold and that the companies will continue to do its bidding. The majors' large market outlets also provide the exporting countries considerable stability in the demand for their crude.

The advantages of vertical integration and the logistical skills of the companies are also still valued by the exporting countries,[1] and the poorer exporting countries still look to the international companies to supply the capital they require for the maintenance and expansion of their oil producing operations. While many exporting countries have developed substantial indigenous capabilities, and many technological services can be supplied by a wide range of Western companies, the majors are the only ones who can perform most secondary and tertiary recovery work and have the technology for the liquefaction of petroleum gases.[2] Consequently, the exporting countries are still dependent upon the majors for work in these areas. In addition, it is generally the former concessionaires[3] who possess the best information about a country's undeveloped oil and gas prospects.

Many exporting countries also look to their former concessionaires for aid in moving into downstream operations and developing LPG and LNG industries. In addition, the oil-exporting countries have sought the oil companies' assistance in their general economic development programs. Finally, the exporting countries rely on the oil companies for political support within the consuming countries.

For their part, the former concessionaires have looked to the exporting countries to assure them of access to the crude supplies they need, preferably at preferential prices but certainly at a price no higher than that charged similarly situated companies. While the companies have sought assured access, they also want as much freedom as possible to reduce their liftings, in the event that this becomes advantageous. Moreover, both the international oil companies and the exporting countries have an interest in maintaining the high price level and the continuity and stability of relationships in the world oil industry.

As a result of their mutual dependence, it is not surprising that the majors and the oil-exporting countries have worked out a *modus operandi* that is highly advantageous to each. While the terms vary with the needs of particular countries, these arrangements have generally provided the former concessionaires a guaranteed minimum supply of oil at a price slightly lower than that which other companies pay. In return, the former concessionaires have generally agreed to meet minimum lifting requirements. These minimum requirements allow the companies some flexibility with regard to how much oil they take, particularly if a country's prices rise to noncompetitive levels.

During 1974–75, when most of these arrangements were being worked out, the companies adopted a conciliatory approach toward the exporting countries in order to secure their position and win the most favorable terms. The companies' vulnerability in these negotiations was increased by the fact that they got no support from their home governments (mainly the U.S.). On the other hand, following State Department and oil company protests, the Ford administration rejected a proposal to give the Federal Energy Administration the right to review the long-term supply arrangements being negotiated between the companies and the exporting countries.[4] The U.S. government, therefore, neither aided nor regulated the companies in the crucial negotiations over their arrangements with the exporting countries. As a result, rather than take a hard line in bargaining over price levels, the companies focused on what they were most concerned with: continued access to crude supplies and making sure that they paid no more than similarly situated companies for the crude they received.

But the consequence of this for consumers was that the group that had the greatest possibility of exerting downward leverage on OPEC prices, through hard bargaining and the maximization of non-OPEC supplies, had little interest in doing so. Indeed, until November 1974, when Saudi Arabia readjusted relative prices, the huge gap between the price of participation and equity crude assured the majors of windfall profits and left them with very little interest in countering OPEC's pricing policies. Even after this, to secure guarantees that no other company would receive oil at lower prices, the companies were generally willing to agree to open price terms, which allow the exporting countries to raise prices unilaterally without voiding the contract.

Still, there has been considerable conflict over the precise terms of the arrangements between the exporting countries and the oil companies. The main issues have been the compensation the companies would receive, the size of their service fees, and their minimum lifting obligations. As we have seen, in November 1974 Saudi Arabia reduced the companies' margins on equity oil and threatened to sell oil to other companies at lower prices to pressure the Aramco partners to accept 100 percent participation. While the Aramco partners acceded in principle to the Saudi demand for 100 percent participation in December 1974, disagreements about the amount of oil the companies would be guaranteed access to, the amount of oil they would be required to lift, and the per barrel fees they would earn persisted until March 1976. At that time it was reportedly agreed that the four Aramco partners would continue to market about 80 percent of Saudi Arabia's oil and that they would receive a service fee of about 21¢ a barrel for the oil they exported.[5] The 21¢ figure included a basic operation fee of 15¢ a barrel and an exploration fee of about 6¢ a barrel.

While the 21¢ service fee was somewhat less than the 22–25¢ the companies were then receiving, the companies' financial burdens were reduced under the new agreement. Saudi Arabia agreed to pay for the development of oil fields already discovered, but it wanted the Aramco partners to invest in exploration to assure that it was pursued in an efficient manner. Consequently, to encourage the companies to undertake exploration with their own risk capital, the agreement provided for bonuses and extra crude entitlements in the event of successful exploration. The service fee concept also did away with the practical significance of the complicated system of equity and participation oil. However, the agreement was not completed until 1980 and has yet to be formally made final, though the Aramco partners appear to have been operating under its terms since 1976, and received payment for their remaining 40 percent interest in 1980. Compensation under the agreement was paid on the basis of net book value.[6]

When Saudi Arabia shifted the relative prices of equity and participation oil in November 1974, it left the companies an average profit of about 22¢ a barrel. In December OPEC recommended that the 22¢ be adopted by its members as the standard profit margin for the companies, but it did not take long for an exporting country to break the new standard. In March 1975, Kuwait surprised its concessionaires, Gulf and BP, by announcing that it was immediately taking over their remaining 40 percent interest in Kuwait Oil Company. By the end of the year,

Gulf and BP agreed to accept compensation on the basis of net book value. They also agreed that, for the next five years, Gulf would be required to lift 500,000 b/d and BP 450,000 b/d. They would get this oil at a discount of 15¢ a barrel. During the five-year period each company would be entitled to purchase 400,000 b/d, but would not receive a discount on it.[7]

Kuwait was able to make this deal because, of all the oil-exporting countries, it had perhaps the least dependence upon the international oil companies. In contrast to Saudi Arabia, there was little scope for exploration in Kuwait, and therefore Kuwait was not dependent upon the companies for exploratory work, and partly because of this, at the time of nationalization Kuwait's oil industry was already heavily managed by Kuwait nationals and the state oil company had already negotiated several long-term sales contracts, further reducing Kuwait's dependence upon the majors. As part of the takeover settlement, Kuwait agreed to sell 300,000 b/d to Shell, a long-established purchaser of part of Gulf's production in Kuwait. (Shortly before this agreement was reached, Shell and Gulf had terminated the long-term sales contract that they had concluded in 1947, which was supposed to run until 2026—the year the Kuwait concession was originally scheduled to expire.) Finally, while the 15¢ fee was less than the 22¢ the companies had been receiving, they were willing to accept it, partly because their financial responsibilities were greatly reduced under the new agreement.[8]

Like Saudi Arabia and Kuwait, in September 1976 Qatar took the remaining 40 percent of the companies' interest in the Qatar Petroleum Company. (Since Qatar lacks the personnel and technical expertise to run the company, it has left managerial control in the hands of its former concessionaires.) The companies agreed to minimum lifting requirements and to continue to provide management and operational services for a per barrel fee of 15¢, figured on Qatar's total production, not just the companies' liftings, as in Kuwait. These fees are indexed to the price of Qatar crudes and therefore become a kind of percentage commission on the total value of Qatar's oil output. The companies also have the right to buy substantial volumes of crude under long-term contracts.[9] The following March, Qatar completed nationalization of its resources by concluding a similar agreement with Shell, which had the concession for Qatar's offshore territory. Since the technical and operational requirements were more difficult in the offshore area, where Shell operated, it received a higher per barrel fee.[10]

In contrast to Qatar and Kuwait, Abu Dhabi has substantial prospects for additional discoveries, both onshore and offshore, and it requires the companies' aid in utilization of its natural gas reserves. Consequently, to keep the companies operating on its behalf, Abu Dhabi has remained committed to the sixty/forty participation pattern.[11] It allowed its concessionaires a 35–40¢ per barrel margin, as opposed to the 15–22¢ that prevailed elsewhere in the Gulf. But with 40 percent of the equity, the companies that operate in Abu Dhabi are required to make substantial investments in development of its resources. These include investments in new expansion and secondary recovery schemes that are costly in comparison to previous industry standards.[12]

As will be recalled, in 1973 Iran concluded an agreement with the Consortium, giving it formal 100 percent ownership of its oil producing assets. The agreement assured Iran of per barrel financial terms equal to those received anywhere else in the Gulf, but unlike nearly all the other agreements between the companies and the exporting countries, the Iranian agreement failed to stipulate any minimum lifting requirement for the companies. (Even the countries that nationalized the companies' operations generally had long-term agreements that committed the companies to purchasing a sizable proportion of the crude they produced.)[13]

As a result, from the mid-1970s through 1978 Iran and the Consortium (renamed the Oil Service Company of Iran, OSCO)[14] argued repeatedly about the level of production, just as they had in the 1960s. For example, in 1978 Iran wanted the Consortium to lift 3.3 mb/d, but the Consortium's liftings totaled only 2.95 mb/d during the first half of 1978.[15] Moreover, while the Iranian agreement stipulated that the companies were to raise Iran's productive capacity to 8 mb/d by 1976, the companies inserted a clause that made this conditional on its being technically and economically feasible. When the companies deemed this was not the case and began cutting back their investments in the country, conflict ensued. In the end, the National Iranian Oil Company accepted reduced capacity and put up more of the money itself, charging the Consortium interest on what it deemed to be its 40 percent share.[16]

Of all the Gulf countries, Iraq has pursued the most independent oil policy. In June 1972 it became the first Gulf country to nationalize a substantial portion of its oil industry; in mid-1974 it gave its national oil company, INOC, control of all exploration in the country; and in December 1975 it completed nationalization of its industry. Yet even Iraq remains dependent upon the international oil companies. It has concluded several long-term sales contracts with the majors. It continues to maintain a special relationship with CFP, selling it crude at prices below those that other large-scale "offtakers" pay. And while it does not enter into joint-venture agreements with foreign companies, it utilizes the services of Western companies on a contract basis.[17]

Like Iraq, Algeria has pursued an independent oil policy. Since the mid-1960s it has sought to develop its indigenous capabilities, and in 1971 it became the first OPEC country to nationalize the companies' producing assets. Yet even though such conservative regimes as Kuwait and Saudi Arabia have moved to 100 percent participation, Algeria maintains the fifty-one/forty-nine arrangements that it initiated in 1971; nor is Algeria particularly interested in reaching 100 percent ownership. As Sonatrach's Executive Vice President Nordine Ait Laoussine explained, "It is control that counts, not ownership. Algeria wants to run its national petroleum industry, not just hold the shares and let the foreign companies go on running the operations."[18] Yet Algeria lacks the skilled labor that would permit it to do this. In contrast to Saudi Arabia or Kuwait, Algeria, as a relatively poor OPEC country, needs the technical aid and capital that international oil companies can provide. Indeed, it is because of this that in recent years Algeria has entered into contracts with foreign companies for hydrocarbon exploration, promising joint development in the event of success.

Libya is considerably richer than Algeria, but its oil capabilities are much less developed and its petroleum potential is much greater. Consequently, it is at least as dependent upon the international oil companies as Algeria. Like Algeria, Libya has retained many fifty-one/forty-nine concession arrangements (with Occidental, Exxon, and Mobil/Gelsenberg), and the companies' 49 percent share requires them to finance a considerable portion of new investment. By January 1, 1974, Libya controlled roughly two-thirds of its oil production, but it does not control much more than this today.[19]

Since 1974, to further exploration and development, Libya has entered into several production-sharing agreements with foreign companies that typically take the form 85/15 percent onshore and 81/19 percent offshore and involve sizable exploration commitments on the part of the companies. Also since 1974, Libya has resolved most of its disputes with the international oil companies. In early 1974 Shell agreed to accept compensation on the basis of net book value for the nationalization of its holdings in the Oasis concession; later that year, BP accepted compensation for the 1971 nationalization of its interest in the Sarir oil field; and the following year Libya and Bunker Hunt resolved their dispute over the nationalization of the other half of the field. In 1977 Libya reached a settlement with Texaco and Socal on the 1973–74 nationalization of their Libyan assets.[20]

Outside the Middle East and North Africa, the pattern has been similar: assertions of national control combined with continued dependence upon the international oil companies. On January 1, 1976, Venezuela nationalized its oil industry. Yet the operating companies remained in place, aiding Petroven, the Venezuelan national oil company in the production, refining, and marketing of Venezuelan oil. (By this time foreigners constituted only about 5 percent of the oil industry's staff.) The companies were compensated for their loss of assets on the basis of net book value, equal to only about a fifth of the replacement value of their assets. They continued to have privileged access to Venezuelan crude oil, and they received a fee of about 20¢ a barrel for the services they performed. As in Qatar, this fee was based on the total production of Venezuelan crude, not simply on what the companies took for their own operations.[21]

In Ecuador, the government acquired a 25 percent participation share in June 1974. Effective January 1, 1977, Gulf sold its 37.5 percent share to CEPE, the state oil company, giving it 62.5 percent ownership. Yet CEPE remains extremely dependent upon Texaco, its 37.5 percent partner, and has backed away from its policy of full nationalization.

In June 1974 Nigeria concluded a 55 percent participation agreement, but day-to-day decision making remained with the operating companies, BP and Shell. It has also concluded joint-venture and production-sharing agreements with other international oil companies. The Nigerian government has sought to market almost a third of its oil directly, but has had trouble selling oil. In August 1979 Nigeria increased its participation share to 60 percent, and in September it nationalized BP's share, giving the Nigerian National Petroleum Company 80 percent ownership. However, at the time of the nationalization Shell had been supplying all of the expatriate staff for the companies' joint venture in Nigeria, and is expected to continue to do so. Nigeria still needs Western technological aid for production and exploration.[22] Of all the OPEC countries, Gabon has the smallest participation share, 25 percent, and little desire to increase it.

In Indonesia, operations are still carried on through production-sharing agreements or with private international oil companies that act as service contractors to Pertamina and receive a fee for their services. As explained previously, in the summer of 1976 the Indonesian government boosted its production share from 65–72.5 to 85 percent, making the actual split (after taxes) 88/12. Pertamina maintains that only the international oil industry can provide the capital and technology necessary for exploration in Indonesia.

As a result of these arrangements with the oil-exporting countries, the major international oil companies have continued to market the bulk of the oil in international trade. Still, the OPEC countries have substantially boosted the amount of oil they market themselves. In 1971 OPEC nations sold about 1 mb/d, or about 4 percent of their annual production, directly to third parties; by 1974 the OPEC countries' direct sales totaled about 3.7 mb/d, or about 12 percent of their annual production, and by 1976 direct sales were estimated at more than 6 mb/d, or about 20 percent of OPEC's production. This greatly reduced the amount of crude the majors had available to sell to third-party purchasers, and their customers therefore shifted increasing proportions of their purchases to the exporting countries.[23]

The major international oil companies have also continued to supply much of the key personnel and strategic thinking for the operation of the oil industries in the exporting countries. They have often retained control over management of day-to-day operations in these countries, and these former concessionaires still have privileged access to substantial quantities of oil at prices less than other purchasers have to pay. One consequence of the majors' favorable position in the exporting countries and their commitments to purchase OPEC oil is that it has reduced their interest in developing oil resources in non-OPEC countries.

THE OIL COMPANIES' POSITION IN THE CONSUMING COUNTRIES

In 1977 Geoffrey Chandler, the head of Royal Dutch/Shell's office of government relations in London, stated that "paradoxically, the threat to the viability of an oil company may today come more from the importing than the exporting governments."[24] Indeed, in the early 1970s the governments in France and the United States launched antitrust investigations of oil companies' activities within their borders. Then, after the 1973–74 rise in oil prices, similar investigations were undertaken in Japan, Belgium, Italy, and West Germany, and in the United States a campaign for both horizontal and vertical divestiture of the oil companies emerged.[25] In contrast, Great Britain and Holland, which are "home" to two of the international majors and have substantial supplies of oil and gas of their own, were more supportive of the companies.[26]

So far, little has come of the actions against the companies. In 1976 the French antitrust commission concluded that the companies had not engaged in illegal anticompetitive practices during the period under investigation. In the United States, the Federal Trade Commission finally dropped the antitrust case against the eight largest U.S. oil companies in 1981, and after making a strong start, the divestiture campaign has languished.[27] With so little accomplished, these actions against the companies have done more to divert public attention than to deal with the real problems posed by the oil crisis.

The consuming countries have also sought to respond to the 1973–74 rise in prices by creating and strengthening their national oil companies, hoping they would serve as a counterweight to the international companies. In 1974 the West German government acquired majority shares in Gelsenberg and brought about a merger of Gelsenberg and Veba, creating the largest business enterprise in West Germany. Its intent was to create a company that would be capable of dealing directly with the oil-exporting countries. The West German government also agreed that to encourage its worldwide exploration efforts, it would provide Deminex 200 million deutschemarks a year from 1975 through 1978.[28]

Similarly, Japan took steps to consolidate its private oil companies and strengthen its national oil company. Immediately after the 1973–74 price rise, MITI sought to encourage greater exploration by Japanese companies; however, after 1974–75 the interest of Japanese companies in exploration waned considerably.[29] In recent years there has also been a trend toward greater contact among the national oil companies, including both consuming- and exporting-country national oil companies.[30]

Of the major consuming countries, only the United States does not have a national oil company.[31] Nor is this surprising. In most consuming countries the oil industry is dominated by foreigners, mainly U.S. corporations, so that the main impetus for creation of national oil companies has come more from nationalism than from any interest in socialism or publicly owned companies per se. But in the United States, the oil industry is populated primarily by U.S. companies, greatly reducing popular interest in creation of a national oil company and creating a powerful domestic constituency opposed to such a company.

Since 1974 the U.S. government has attempted to respond to public resentment of the oil companies by reducing some of their tax privileges. As early as January 1974, President Nixon proposed a reduction in the credits companies could claim against U.S. income taxes and elimination of the "depletion allowance" for foreign oil producers. In March 1975, legislation eliminated the depletion allowance for the major U.S. companies and reduced the benefits that independent producers (producing less than 3,000 b/d) could derive from it.[32] It was estimated that this would cost the industry $1.7 billion in 1975, but in the context of greatly increased prices for U.S. oil and gas, this was hardly a major blow. Indeed, in December, ARCO President Thornton Bradshaw had called for abolition of the depletion allowance, terming it "an albatross around our neck, far more trouble than it's worth."[33] (The depletion allowance was more important to small independent U.S. producers, who used it to attract investors looking for tax shelters.) However, the enacted legislation enabled the independents to retain most of the benefits they had derived from the allowance. Moreover, to compensate the nation's gas producers for loss of the depletion allowance, the Federal Power Commission raised gas prices from 23.5¢ per mcf to 29.5¢ as of July 1, 1976.[34]

The 1975 Tax Reduction Act limited the foreign-tax credits claimed by oil companies to 52.8 percent in 1975, 50.4 percent in 1976, and 50 percent thereafter, regardless of the rate the exporting countries charged. The Tax Reduction Act of 1976 reduced this further, to 48 percent. Yet, despite these changes, the international oil companies still pile up more credits than they can use.[35]

Since 1974 the Treasury Department has issued at least ten rulings modifying the terms of the foreign-tax credit, but so far these regulations have not prevented U.S. oil companies, operating abroad, from continuing to claim foreign-tax credits, and they have had little impact on the taxes paid by these companies. In 1978 the IRS ruled that the companies could no longer claim credits for payments made on the basis of posted prices that were tax-reference rather than realized prices. Had this ruling been imposed several years before, it would have denied the companies most of the benefits they received from the foreign-tax credit, but by 1978 most countries had done away with posted prices, and in response to the IRS ruling they modified their tax laws slightly, so that, legally, they were taxing the companies on the basis of realized prices, greatly reducing the significance of this ruling. (Its main impact has been in Libya, where several 51/49 concession agreements remain.) As a result, since 1974 the foreign-tax credit has continued to cost the U.S. Treasury between $1 billion and $2 billion a year.[36]

More than by any action by consuming-country governments, the profitability of the oil companies' operations was hurt most by the effect the rise in oil prices and the slowdown in economic activity had on demand for oil products. The oil companies had planned additional facilities in the early 1970s on the expectation that demand for oil would continue to grow at 7–8 percent a year. When the rise in oil prices and the slowdown in economic growth falsified that assumption, it was generally too late to stop construction of the new facilities.

From 1975 through 1978, roughly one-third of the world tanker fleet was in surplus, and to deal with the overcapacity, a record number of tankers were scrapped in the first half of 1978. Despite this, tanker capacity is expected to remain in surplus at least until 1985. While some oil companies benefited from the weak demand for tankers, most major oil companies, as owners of almost 40 percent of the world tanker fleet, were hurt by this development.[37] Similarly, the world petrochemical industry, which the oil companies are heavily involved in, has been plagued by serious problems of overcapacity and its growth rates have declined substantially.[38]

Between 1974 and 1978 refineries in Western Europe generally operated at only 60–70 percent of capacity, as opposed to 85 percent from 1963 to 1973. Since their heavy capital costs made it cheaper to run refineries at a loss, rather than leave them idle, the temptation to cut prices was strong and many Western European refineries consistently lost money in this period. To alleviate the situation, in March 1977 the European Commission recommended that, to restore profitable refining utilization, Western Europe take 140 million tonnes of refining capacity a year permanently out of service. Following this recommendation, in 1977 81 million tonnes were retired, but a year later the EEC energy ministers rejected proposals from the commission for further reductions in European refining capacity.[39] Consequently, the problem of overcapacity is expected to persist well into the 1980s.[40]

Moreover, the problems of excess capacity in tankers, refining, and petrochemicals are likely to intensify because of the growth of these facilities in the oil-exporting countries. In fact, if Europe raised its product prices to aid its refineries, it would have to contend with increased competition from sources in the Mediterranean, the Caribbean, the Soviet bloc, etc.

In each of these sectors—refining, tankers, petrochemicals—the situation in the United States was very different from that in Western Europe. The demand for U.S. tankers remained quite strong as a result of government rules that required that all U.S. crude and a high percentage of U.S. imports be shipped in U.S. tankers, despite the fact that U.S. ships cost roughly twice as much to operate as ships registered in other countries. Moreover, the efforts of the U.S. government to encourage enlargement of the U.S. tanker fleet are likely to exacerbate the worldwide problem of overcapacity. Similarly, the U.S. petrochemical industry benefited from access to price-controlled supplies of U.S. oil and natural gas for use as feedstocks.

Most significantly, while Europe suffered from refining surpluses, the United States was plagued by shortages of refining capacity, largely because, by restricting refiners' profit margins, U.S. price controls left little incentive to build new, more efficient refineries—especially since construction costs were rising rapidly. In fact, most of the limited refinery expansion in the United States from 1974 to 1978 consisted of small, relatively inefficient refineries that benefited from the "small refiner bias" (worth about $2 a barrel) that was part of the U.S. government's entitlements program.[41] In addition, companies were hesitant to build new refineries because, as a result of new, government-mandated automobile mileage standards, they expected demand for gasoline in the United States to peak around 1980. Existing refineries should have added desulfurization facilities, so they could handle more of the heavy, "sour" crudes that were becoming increasingly common, but this too was discouraged by the fixed profit margins that the U.S. government maintained on refiners. Why should a refiner invest in facilities that would enable use of cheaper crude, if the government would simply lower the prices the refiner was allowed to charge, so that its profit margin remained fixed?

An obvious solution would have been for European refineries to supply the U.S. markets, but this was greatly impeded by the U.S. system of price controls. With U.S. refiners relying heavily on price-controlled U.S. oil, their average costs were considerably less than those of their European counterparts and, consequently, petroleum products produced in Europe generally were not price competitive with U.S. products. On the other hand, U.S. refiners that imported high-price foreign crude oil received entitlements credit for it; as a result, U.S. refiners that imported crude oil were effectively subsidized.[42] This situation encouraged U.S. refiners to import crude oil, rather than products,[43] and enabled them to outbid their European counterparts, who received no comparable subsidy. Also, since most U.S. refiners lacked desulfurization facilities, they were extremely dependent upon light crudes, and they bid very strongly for them. Thus, again, consuming-country policies served to buttress the world oil price.

OIL COMPANY PROFITS AND DIVERSIFICATION

Any attempt to assess oil company profits runs into problems of data availability and reliability. Oil companies ordinarily do not report profits by industry sector (refining profits, production profits, etc.) nor is the geographical distribution of profits broken down very finely in publicly available sources. In addition, accounting practices vary widely, and are often designed more to reduce a company's tax liability than accurately reflect its financial position.

Despite these problems, the basic trends in oil industry profits seem clear. From 1964 to 1972 U.S. oil company profits lagged behind the profits of all other U.S. industries, but from 1973 to 1975 they were substantially higher (see table 12–1). However, the dramatic rise in oil company profits that began late in 1972 reached its peak in the second quarter of 1974. The tightening of the world oil market in 1972–73 and the rise in world oil prices in 1973–74 led to an enormous increase in the profits earned outside the United States. Part of the 1973 increase was due to the impact that devaluation of the dollar had on the profits of U.S. oil companies. The increase in 1974 profits was due in part to the large gap between the prices of participation and equity oil that persisted until November 1974, enabling companies with access to equity oil to reap large windfall profits. Worldwide, 1974 was also a strong year for petrochemical sales. The 1973–74 rise in OPEC prices also led to increases in the prices the oil companies received on their non-OPEC production. This resulted in a sharp rise in oil profits inside the United States.[44]

By any measure, 1974 was an enormously profitable year for oil companies, both worldwide and within the United States. Nonetheless, rather than representing real improvement in the companies' performance, most of their increased

TABLE 12-1. OIL COMPANY PROFITS, 1947–80

	1947	1948	1949	1950	1951	1952	1953
Net Income as % of Net Worth							
Petroleum companies	15.9	21.6	13.6	15.1	16.7	14.5	14.7
All U.S. industry	18.3	18.2	13.2	14.8	11.5	10.1	9.9
	1964	1965	1966	1967	1968	1969	1970
Petroleum companies	11.6	11.9	12.6	12.8	13.1	11.9	11.0
All U.S. industry	12.1	13.2	13.7	13.2	14.1	13.5	11.7
International Oil Companies' Rates of Return on Average Invested Capital							
Worldwide		10.8	11.3	11.5	11.7	11.0	10.4
U.S.		11.2	12.3	12.6	12.3	10.9	9.9
Rest of world		10.2	9.9	10.1	11.0	11.2	11.0
U.S. Net Income as % of Total Net Income	54.2	57.5	60.8	60.6	58.7	56.3	54.4

Figures on net income as % of net worth from *Basic Petroleum Data Book* (vol. 2, no. 2, sec. 5, table 4A) and are for U.S. companies. All other figures for the 26 oil companies in Chase Manhattan Bank annual study (Energy Economics Division, *Financial Analysis of a Group of Petroleum Companies, 1976*, pp. 22–23, and *1980*, p. 5 and as reprinted in *Basic Petroleum Data Book*, sec. 5, table 5. The companies in this study are the major companies in the worldwide petroleum industry and are the companies referred to in the text. Figures adjusted to account for mergers and acquisitions by and among these companies. Group includes U.S. and foreign companies, but does not include any OPEC-country national oil company.

profits during this phenomenal year were due either to the impact of inflation on nominal profits or the taking of one-time inventory profits. When prices went up, companies could sell the oil they had in inventory for huge profits, but when they turned around to replace those inventories, they had to pay much higher costs, greatly reducing the long-term benefits of the windfall. Indeed, Mobil estimated that without inventory profits, its 23 percent 1974 earnings increase would have been an 11 percent decline.[45]

By 1975 total industry profits were below the level of 1973 and the industry's rate of return had fallen to much more modest levels. The disappearance of inventory profits, the narrowing gap between the prices of equity and participation oil, the decline of demand and the consequent costs of operating below capacity, loss of the depletion allowance, the worldwide falloff in the petrochemical business, and the strengthening of the dollar all hurt industry profits in 1975. Profits recovered in 1976, as the oil companies appeared to enter a new period of stability. Still, from 1976 to 1978 profit rates did not approach the levels of 1974, and in 1977 and 1978 U.S. oil companies again earned less than the average for all U.S. industries. Moreover, while the industry's rate of return appears to be higher in the 1970s than in the 1960s, this mainly reflects the effect of inflation on nominal industry profit rates. Were adjustments made for inflation, it is likely that the industry's real rate of return would be seen to have declined, as has the real rate of return for U.S. industry in general.[46]

1954	1955	1956	1957	1958	1959	1960	1961	1962	1963
13.8	14.1	14.6	13.7	9.9	10.0	10.3	10.4	10.6	11.5
9.9	10.9	11.4	10.8	10.5	11.9	10.7	10.2	10.3	10.4

1971	1972	1973	1974	1975	1976	1977	1978	1979	1980
11.2	10.8	15.6	19.6	13.9	14.8	14.0	14.5	22.6	24.9
11.7	11.8	12.7	13.5	13.0	14.7	15.0	15.3	15.7	14.1
10.7	9.7	15.5	19.2	12.8	13.8	13.8	13.2	24.0	22.4
9.3	9.6	10.5	14.6	12.9	15.2	14.2	13.8	18.2	18.1
12.5	9.9	20.9	23.9	12.7	12.3	13.4	12.5	30.8	27.7
48.0	53.3	35.4	39.1	51.9	57.5	54.2	55.5	40.5	44.4

From 1969 to 1974 the oil industry's rate of return was higher in the rest of the world than in the United States, but from 1975 to 1978 the reverse was true. Moreover, from 1975 to 1978 the United States accounted for more than half of the combined earnings of twenty-six leading international oil companies.

Perhaps the most significant effect of the 1973–74 price rise on the oil companies was that it greatly increased the value of their assets. When prices rose, the value of the companies' reserves in the United States and overseas increased enormously. Many fields where production had not been economically viable suddenly became valuable properties. Prime examples are the heavy, viscous crude oil reserves in Southern California.[47]

As in the period prior to the oil-price revolution, oil production continues to be the most profitable sector of the industry. Figures released by Exxon show that between 1975 and 1978 the world's largest oil company had an average return on capital employed of 32.2 percent in foreign exploration and production and 22 percent in U.S. exploration and production. But on foreign refining and marketing, Exxon's earnings in this period averaged only 7.4 percent and on U.S. refining and marketing 10.5 percent.[48]

The situations of other companies may differ, but the general picture seems consistent with that of Exxon, for oil production in both the United States and the OPEC countries remains enormously profitable. In October 1973, just before the Arab oil embargo, the average price of U.S. oil was $4.47; by 1978 it had doubled, reaching $9.[49] Since November 1974, most OPEC countries have officially sought to limit the companies' profit margins on production to about 22¢ a barrel, compared with the 35–40¢ the companies earned between 1965 and 1973,[50] but since the companies' investment requirements in the exporting countries have also been greatly reduced, their overall financial position in these countries has not deteriorated substantially and may even have improved. (To tell, we need better data than we have.)

There are also reasons to believe that the 22¢ figure seriously understates what the companies are able to earn as a result of their role as crude producers. The oil companies are well remunerated for their aid in the exporting countries' development efforts. In many instances, the exporting countries' generosity in this respect may involve partial compensation to the companies for carrying on their traditional oil producing operations. At any rate, the oil companies would not have had such an easy time acquiring these lucrative roles were it not for their traditional position as oil producers in the OPEC countries.

Through elaborate transfer pricing schemes the oil companies are often able to substantially boost the revenue they receive from a barrel of oil. For example, Peter R. Odell calculated that throughout 1976 the oil companies achieved a gross profit on crude oil delivered to the refineries in Rotterdam (the most important market for OPEC crude oil) of about 85¢ a barrel.[51] As a result of the foreign-tax credit, the companies still pay little or no taxes on these profits, which makes these gross profits worth considerably more to the companies than earnings in the consuming countries, which are subject to nominal corporate tax rates of about 50 percent in most countries. Similarly, in a lawsuit against an Exxon affiliate a public utility in Nova Scotia produced Exxon documents that showed that, during 1973 and 1974, Exxon disguised increases in profit margins by backdating them to blend, as it were, with price increases tied to OPEC price increases. The oil giant used transactions between subsidiaries (which were not at "arm's length") to justify price increases to other customers. Exxon also used offshore corporations to "launder" and artificially inflate price increases, and, as company executives conceded, to avoid paying millions of dollars in taxes.[52]

There is also evidence that integrated refiners have avoided U.S. controls on crude oil prices by raising product prices.[53] For example, in 1977 the President's Council of Economic Advisers concluded that perhaps one-third of the revenue intended for consumers under price-control policy was not getting to them.[54] In addition, during the Carter administration the Department of Energy charged the nation's fifteen major refining companies with more than $10 billion in possible pricing violations.[55] However, the Reagan administration has not been very aggressive in pursuing these suits, making it unlikely that the full amount of overcharging by these and other companies will ever be recovered.[55]

The companies are often able to earn inventory profits by stocking up before OPEC decides on new price increases, then selling the oil at the higher price; and since OPEC is not likely to decrease prices, the companies face little risk. On the other hand, the surplus in tankers, refining (particularly in Europe), and marketing operations has served to keep these the "poor" sectors of the oil industry. Moreover, price controls in various consuming countries have often created delays between the time crude prices go up and the time that oil companies can recover their increased costs in product prices. This has reduced the companies' profit margins in the interim.[56]

Because of the volatility of their earnings and the uncertainty of their long-term position in the exporting countries, since 1974 the oil companies have intensified their efforts to move into other energy sources and nonenergy fields. In the mid-1960s the oil companies began acquiring coal leases, and eleven oil companies now have control of roughly one-third of U.S. coal resources. In 1978 oil companies accounted for 22 percent of U.S. coal production, and by 1985 they plan to increase this to 50 percent.[57] Moreover, BP and Shell have made large investments in Australian coal.[58] Oil companies also perform a large proportion of the work in synthetic fuels, limited as it is.

Since the 1960s, oil companies have invested more than $2.5 billion in uranium exploration, mining, and processing. Today, oil companies control almost half of all U.S. uranium reserves, and Kerr-McGee owns a quarter of the nation's uranium-milling capacity.[59] Several oil companies have worked on geothermal energy, and Union Oil claims to be the world leader in the field. Exxon, Shell, and Mobil are working on solar energy.[60]

Oil companies have also made major nonenergy acquisitions. In 1974 Mobil began its takeover of Marcor, a department store and packaging conglomerate, best known for its Montgomery Ward outlets, which is estimated to have cost the company nearly $2 billion. In May 1975 Standard Oil of California spent $333 million to acquire a 20 percent share of Amax Inc., a company that mines, processes and markets aluminum, copper, nickel, and coal. In November 1974, ARCO announced that its chemical division had undertaken a billion-dollar, five-year capital expansion program, and early in 1977 it merged with Anaconda, a copper company.[61]

Meanwhile, Exxon has been developing a chain of small computer-related companies with the aim of becoming a leader in data processing and office automation. In 1977 Gulf spent $446 million to secure control of Kewanee, a company that derives three-fourths of its income from chemical sales. Gulf had previously attempted to purchase CNA Financial Corporation, a big insurance firm; Rockwell International, a manufacturer of aerospace systems, auto components, and electronic products; and Ringling Brothers–Barnum and Bailey Circus. Aside from Texaco, each of the seven major oil companies now have significant holdings outside the traditional oil, gas, and petrochemical fields. In recent years, many oil companies have also increased their petrochemical operations substantially.[62]

In pursuing this diversification strategy the oil companies have had several motives. With demand for energy in general and oil in particular slowing, the companies have been looking for new growth areas; and to survive, the companies recognize that they have to dominate new energy sources and technologies. In addition, because earnings from oil and gas are highly volatile, the companies have sought to move into areas that would add stability to their earnings.

Given the political risks involved, the companies have also wanted to limit their dependence upon foreign earnings, but since the prospects for investing in

U.S. oil and gas are quite limited, the companies have moved into other fields to increase their U.S. earnings. For example, Mobil claims it knew that Marcor would reduce the company's average return (which it has), but it bought Marcor anyway, because it wanted to increase its U.S.-based earnings and to balance an increasingly risky energy business.[63]

Yet the diversification schemes still account for only a small portion of the companies' total sales. For example, Mobil, a leader in the diversification effort, still derives more than three quarters of its revenues from oil and gas, and in 1978, Exxon's nonpetroleum units accounted for less than 1 percent of its total sales.[64] Similarly, according to the U.S. Treasury Department, oil industry investment in unrelated fields was 10 percent of cash flow (or $4 billion) in 1974 and only 2 percent (or $626 million) in 1977.[65] These nonenergy investments, therefore, suggest a direction in which the companies appear to be moving, but they are not currently a major factor in company operations. Most of the companies' activities have been in fields related to their oil and gas expertise. For example, uranium mining and geothermal energy require many of the same geological skills needed for oil drilling.

Many of these diversification efforts began long before the 1973–74 rise in oil prices. As indicated, the companies began buying uranium and coal reserves in the mid-1960s; they have been involved in the petrochemical industry since its beginnings, largely because petrochemical production is closely related to oil refining; and as early as 1968 Mobil began planning the diversification that led to the 1974 purchase of Marcor.[66]

In addition to acquiring non-oil companies, oil companies have also been acquiring one another, and the most significant takeover of recent years has been BP's acquisition of Standard Oil of Ohio. In 1970 BP agreed to sell Sohio most of its holdings of Alaskan oil in exchange for a 25 percent share of Sohio, with the stipulation that as Alaskan production increased, so too would BP's equity in Sohio. As a result, by 1978 BP owned 52 percent of Sohio. BP's interest in the arrangement was to lessen its dependence on Middle East oil and to acquire a marketing network in the United States. For Sohio, the deal offered an opportunity to end its dependence on other companies for crude supplies. (In the mid-1970s Sohio had been buying 90 percent of its oil from other companies.)[67]

In 1974 Standard Oil of Indiana, the sixth largest U.S. oil company, attempted to purchase Occidental, the eleventh largest, but Occidental resisted and the takeover bid failed.[68] Then in 1978, Occidental attempted to acquire Mead Corporation, a forest products company, and was similarly rebuffed. Successful oil company mergers in recent years include Marathon Oil's 1976 acquisition of Pan Ocean Oil, and Getty's 1977 takeover of both Mission and Skelly Oil.[69]

Another consequence of the rise in oil prices on the oil industry has been to greatly reduce the conflict between domestic and international producers in the United States, for higher prices provide an "umbrella" that both can live under. And with the price of imported oil pulling up the price of domestic oil, the independent producers no longer have to worry about the threat of cheap imports.

But rivalry between the small independent refiners and marketers and the integrated companies has become a major conflict within the industry. The independent refiners feared that, if left to themselves, the majors would cut their access to cheap, price-controlled domestic crude. To prevent this, they turned to the federal government and secured an entitlements program that not only guaranteed their access to crude at prices comparable to what the majors paid, but gave them special benefits. In doing this, they acted very much like the independent producers who protected their interests in the 1950s and 1960s by getting the federal government to limit imports. But the integrated companies have resented having to share supplies and the government's subsidizing of their inefficient brethren. Moreover, between 1973 and 1978 the integrated companies' share of the U.S. gasoline market declined from 70.4 percent to 67.5 percent.[70]

What is most striking in all this is the international oil companies' ability to maintain their position despite major upheavals and continual flux. The oil-exporting countries quadrupled prices and took over the oil fields, yet the oil companies still derive their greatest profits on their production in the oil-exporting countries. Attacked by government officials and popular forces in the consuming countries, the oil companies emerged essentially unscathed. Now, as the companies move into new fields, their pace is slow and steady, as they take care to cover their bets.

On the other hand, the price rise has hardly been the boon to oil company profits that is popularly imagined. Profits went up greatly in 1973–74, but they came down again—falling below the average rate of return in all other industries. The companies could do better buying government bonds than they generally do refining and marketing oil. Yet, for all their troubles, and for all the turbulence of the industry they are part of, the companies will survive. As we shall see in the next chapter, oil-exporting-country governments are not always able to manage as much.

13

History Repeats:
The Oil Crisis of 1979

Just when the consuming countries thought they had OPEC under control, oil prices took off again. From December 1978 to December 1979 the price of the marker crude nearly doubled, from $12.70 a barrel to $24. As in 1973–74, a political crisis in the Middle East led to skyrocketing prices in 1979. Yet the loss of Iranian supplies would not have had such impact on the world oil market were it not for the problems we examined in chapters 10 and 11: failure of the consuming countries to develop effective energy policies and to work out satisfactory arrangements for sharing supplies in an emergency, and the inadequacy of the oil companies' efforts to develop new supplies of oil and natural gas.

The political developments in the Middle East in that momentous year underscored the power of nationalism as a political force. A national liberation movement in Iran deposed the hated Shah and, in the process, undermined the U.S. strategy of relying on regional powers to contain the radical/nationalist movements in the area. In its efforts to conclude a peace agreement between Egypt and Israel, the United States failed to give adequate recognition to the claims of Palestinian nationalism and, as a result, incurred the ill will of much of the Arab world. Both of these political developments had enormous consequences for world oil prices.

As discussed in chapter 9, in the fall of 1976 Saudi Arabia forged a negotiating alliance with Egypt and Syria, but despite their willingness to negotiate a settlement with Israel, attempts to reconvene the Geneva Conference stumbled over the issue of Palestinian representation. Israel refused to negotiate with the Palestinian Liberation Organization, the group designated as the official representative of the Palestinian people at the Arab summit conference in Rabat in 1974. Israel's intransigence was reinforced by the PLO's unwillingness to amend its charter to recognize Israel's right to exist. Nor would the PLO accept U.N. Resolution 242.[1]

Then, in December, in response to a vote of no confidence, Israeli Prime Minister Yitzhak Rabin disbanded his majority government and called for new elections. With a minority caretaker government in power, it was unlikely that a new peace initiative would occur until after the elections, in May. Then, for the first time in Israeli history, the Labor Party was defeated by the right-wing Likud Party, led by Menachem Begin. Begin had long been opposed to any Israeli withdrawal from either the West Bank or the Gaza Strip, and showed no signs of changing his position. He was opposed to any dealings with the PLO, and his administration was expected to take a harder line in negotiating with the Arabs than the Labor regime that it replaced. Begin's election therefore appeared as a major setback to hope of reaching an overall Arab-Israeli settlement.

Yet a continuing impasse was particularly threatening to Egypt's President Sadat, who had told the Egyptian people that his turn toward the West and his efforts to reach an accommodation with Israel would lead to peace and prosperity. The reality was that his policies had achieved little. Foreign investment had been a mere trickle, and the economy continued to falter. Military expenditures remained a burden and rapid gains in population wiped out most increases in economic growth.[2] While funding from the United States and the Arab oil-exporting countries continued, it was increasingly inadequate; moreover, the exporting countries had been reducing their aid to Egypt, and threatened to eliminate it altogether. Nor did Egypt, the leader of the Arab world, relish the prospect of continued dependence upon the oil-rich but politically backward sheikdoms. At the behest of Saudi Arabia and Kuwait, in 1976 Egypt had sought a large loan from the IMF to cover its balance-of-payments deficits; the condition for the loan was that Egypt remove government subsidies on basic commodities. Nor would Saudi Arabia or Kuwait extend further large-scale credits to Egypt until it met the IMF's conditions.[3]

Sadat warned that removal of subsidies would provoke widespread unrest within Egypt; still, he had no choice but to go along with the IMF demands. But as Sadat predicted, when the subsidies were removed, in January 1977, widespread rioting resulted. The subsidies were restored, the IMF agreed to extend the loan anyway, and the rioting subsided.[4] However, by the summer of 1977 Sadat's popularity had reached an all-time low. Sadat had pioneered a policy of negotiation for an Arab-Israeli settlement, but it seemed to be leading nowhere. He had expelled the Soviets and forged an alliance with the United States, but that had brought Egypt neither peace nor prosperity. Nasserites accused him of betraying Nasser's heritage; liberals resented the lack of political freedom in the country; and the Egyptian masses were hurt by the dire state of the Egyptian economy—a hurt that was turning to anger because a few were getting rich as a result of Sadat's "open-door" policies while the living standards of the majority were declining. In addition, there was an underground Egyptian left, consisting largely of students, intellectuals and urban workers, and a Moslem religious opposition, both of which were ready to challenge Sadat's rule, if given the opportunity. Elements of the armed forces, particularly the air force, were also a potential source of opposition.[5]

Nor could Sadat respond to domestic problems by going to war, as he had in 1973, for in 1977 Israel's military superiority was overwhelming,[6] and having once recaptured a few miles of the Sinai Desert, Sadat could hardly hope to become a hero by doing so again. But Sadat found another way to get the Arab-Israeli talks moving again, rekindling the idea that progress was being made toward a settlement. In the fall of 1977, in a move as daring and ingenious as his

1973 resort to war, Sadat launched a "peace offensive." To the world's amazement, in November 1977 he announced on CBS television that he was prepared to address the Israeli parliament within the next week, once he received a formal invitation from Prime Minister Menachem Begin.

Sadat went to Jerusalem proclaiming that he was doing so to break through the psychological barriers that prevented the reconvening of the Geneva peace conference. His dramatic appearance in Jerusalem certainly lent credence to Egypt's claim that it was interested in concluding an agreement with Israel.

Sadat proclaimed that he would never sign a separate agreement with Israel, but other Arab states feared he would. Of the twenty-one other Arab states, only Morocco, Sudan, and Oman formally endorsed Sadat's initiative; the moderate Arab states, including Saudi Arabia, the UAE, and Kuwait, were skeptical about the prospects. They feared that, by going to Jerusalem, he had given Israel the thing it wanted most, Arab recognition, but had gotten nothing in return. They were also afraid that his move would disrupt Arab unity and lead to the signing of a separate peace treaty, which would likely lead to an upsurge of radical opposition movements in the Arab world.

On the eve of Sadat's departure, Saudi Arabia criticized him for failing to consult others in the Arab world. Privately, the Saudis indicated that they hoped Sadat would succeed, but because they feared he would not, they refused to back him openly. They also made clear their opposition to a separate Egyptian-Israeli treaty. Despite their reservations, the conservative Arab oil-exporting countries did nothing to oppose the success of Sadat's efforts, and they continued to provide Sadat's regime with financial aid. Indeed, they had little choice but to continue to give him support, for if he failed, he was likely to be overthrown, signaling a new wave of Arab radicalism.

Finally, the radical Arab states—Libya, Iraq, Algeria, Syria, South Yemen, and the PLO—were utterly opposed to Sadat's move. In early December they met in Tripoli and formed the Steadfastness and Confrontation Front, but, at Syrian insistence, they did not declare themselves opposed to a negotiated Middle East peace settlement. Iraq, which wanted stronger measures, walked out of the conference and refused to join the front.

Syria was the only participant in the conference that accepted U.N. Resolutions 242 and 338 and was still interested in a negotiated settlement. Syria also sought eventual reconciliation with Egypt. But Syria feared that if Sadat signed a separate agreement with Israel, Syria would bear the brunt of Israeli hostility, and with Egypt out of the picture, Syria would have little leverage in bargaining a negotiated settlement with Israel.

For all the controversy that Sadat's move created elsewhere in the Arab world, within Egypt it made him a hero again, and upon his return from Jerusalem he was widely feted within Egypt.[7] Several days after he returned from Jerusalem, Sadat invited all the parties in the Middle East conflict, including Israel, the United States, and the Soviet Union, to send representatives to talks in Cairo to try to remove the obstacles that still stood in the way of resumption of the Geneva peace conference, but only Israel and the United States agreed to attend the meeting. Inasmuch as the other Arab states had just denounced Sadat for his trip to Jerusalem, it was unrealistic to expect them to follow his leadership in moving toward a settlement with Israel. While Sadat claimed he went to Jerusalem to facilitate the reconvening of a Geneva conference, his move made the convening of such a conference unlikely because of the divisiveness it provoked within the Arab world. In addition, Sadat's trip to Israel led the moderates within the PLO to adopt a tougher line. As a result, in December the PLO reversed its earlier position and came out against the reconvening of the Geneva peace conference.[8]

With others refusing to follow his lead, in December 1977 Sadat announced that he was preparing to negotiate with Israel alone. He also said that by endorsing the Tripoli declaration, denouncing Egypt, and refusing to join the negotiations, the PLO had canceled the Rabat decision recognizing it as the official representative of the Palestinians. Sadat said he would continue to honor the Rabat decision for the time being, but he seemed to be laying the basis for exclusion of the PLO.[9] Still, Sadat insisted that he was negotiating on behalf of all the Arab people, not simply the Egyptians, and he indicated that he would continue to insist on the two Rabat demands: total Israeli withdrawal from all territory occupied during the 1967 war and full restoration of Palestinian rights to national sovereignty.

In late December Begin, who had offered Sadat nothing while he was in Jerusalem, revealed his peace proposal. In return for a peace treaty with the Arab nations, granting full recognition to Israel, Begin was prepared to return the Sinai Desert and to grant the Palestinians limited autonomy over their internal affairs in the West Bank and Gaza. Begin made clear that, under his proposal, Israel would maintain both a military and a police presence in the West Bank and Gaza. In addition, Jews would continue to immigrate to the West Bank, but restrictions would be placed on the immigration of Palestinians to the area.

Negotiations between Egypt and Israel at the ministerial level began in January, but because Sadat and Begin had very different positions on the crucial issue of Palestinian autonomy, the talks broke off a day after they started. The prospect of resuming them was seriously set back in March, when a Palestinian guerrilla raid blew up an Israeli tour bus, killing thirty-five Israelis and an American and wounding seventy. The Palestinian action was clearly intended to disrupt Sadat's peace initiative and serve as a warning that the PLO could not be left out of the peace-making process.[10] Israel retaliated by sending troops and fighter-bombers into Jordan, raiding Palestinian camps and carving out a six-mile "security belt" in southern Lebanon. According to Red Cross estimates, at least 250 Palestinians and Lebanese were killed and 350 wounded in the Israeli raids. Several thousand were forced to flee.[11] Israeli troops remained in southern Lebanon until mid-June.

Despite these hostilities, Sadat did not call off his peace initiative, but by the summer of 1978 he had little to show for it. The Egyptian economy was still in shambles, and he was under growing pressure from the Saudis to call off his maverick efforts and rejoin the other Arab states. In addition, in October 1978 the three-year "no war" pledge that Sadat had made at the time of the Sinai disengagement agreement was due to expire, and Sadat indicated that if no tangible progress were made by this deadline, his initiative would be called off.

Fearing another Arab-Israeli war and, with it, another oil embargo, and anxious to salvage something while Sadat was in a conciliatory mood, in September 1978 President Carter summoned Begin and Sadat to meet with him at Camp David, the presidential retreat outside Washington. After thirteen days of difficult negotiations, two accords were signed. One provided for complete Israeli withdrawal from the Sinai Peninsula, to be carried out over the next two to three years. After the first phase of the withdrawal was complete, three to nine months after the treaty was signed, Egypt would grant full diplomatic recognition to Israel. The other accord dealt with the Palestinian issue. Israel agreed to negotiate the issues of sovereignty and withdrawal of its troops from the West Bank and Gaza, but made no commitment.

The key concession was Sadat's willingness to accept an agreement under which the Palestinians were guaranteed neither eventual sovereignty over the West Bank and Gaza nor the eventual withdrawal of Israeli troops from those areas. Neither Jerusalem nor the Golan Heights, two of the most controversial issues, was mentioned in the agreement; nor was anything said about the PLO. The agreement was supposed to lead to the signing of a formal peace treaty within three months. It also contained a provision for a halt to Israeli settlements in the West Bank and Gaza. However, while President Sadat claimed that this halt was to last five years, during which the fate of these areas would be determined, Begin maintained that the halt applied only to the three-month period during which the final treaty was to be worked out.

The fact that Sadat made the key concession was not surprising, for he was in the more vulnerable position. He had risked his political future on the peace initiative he launched in November 1977. In addition, at this time Israel, which had received $8 billion worth of U.S. arms since 1973, had a clear military edge over any combination of Arab forces.[12]

Both the moderate and the radical Arab states denounced the Camp David Agreement as a separate Egyptian-Israeli peace treaty—something Sadat had promised he would never agree to. He insisted that the provisions regarding the Palestinians meant that this was not a separate Egyptian-Israeli treaty but the basis for an overall agreement. However, his critics doubted that the accord on the Palestinians would be implemented.

The Arab states, minus Egypt, gathered in Baghdad in November to denounce the agreement. They offered Sadat $5 billion a year for the next ten years, if he would renounce the agreement. Saudi Arabia agreed to provide roughly half of this amount.[13] The Arab states also declared that they would break political relations with Egypt, if a treaty were signed. Although the radical Arab states wanted the Baghdad Conference to enact tough punitive measures, to be instituted against Egypt in the event it signed the treaty, the moderate Arab states resisted this. They were still torn between their fear of the consequences of a separate agreement and their fear of a radical Egypt. Consequently, they sought a middle course: opposition to the treaty but continued financial support for Egypt. The conference also agreed to provide financial aid to the "confrontation" states, with most of the $3.5 billion allocated for this purpose coming from the conservative Arab oil-exporting countries.[14]

While the conservative exporting countries feared that an Egyptian-Israeli peace treaty would lead to an upsurge in Arab radicalism, in the fall of 1978 the Shah of Iran confronted a broad-based opposition movement that would topple his regime by February 1979. Iran was plagued, in extreme form, by many of the problems that characterized development efforts in the other oil-exporting countries. The country was unable to transform its growing oil revenues into economic development; corruption was widespread; inflation ran at 30–40 percent a year; and inequality increased.[15]

The Shah's economic programs also had adverse impact on agricultural and traditional industries. In fact, during the Shah's rule Iran shifted from a country self-sufficient in agriculture to one that had to import roughly half of its food. Despite land reform programs, in 1978 three out of five rural families were still landless or nearly landless. Peasants flocked to the cities, only to find serious overcrowding, housing shortages, and widespread unemployment.[16] At the same time, the Shah spent lavishly on extravagant construction projects in Iran and on the acquisition of substantial equity positions in such Western companies as Krupp, the German steelmaker, and Eurodif, the West European uranium enrichment project. And of course there were the Shah's enormous arms purchases: $19 billion worth from the United States alone between 1972 and 1978. The Shah bought more tanks than Britain had in its arsenal; he acquired squadrons of advanced fighters and began building a modern navy. Moreover, since 1973 more than 100,000 foreign personnel had entered Iran, aiding in the Shah's military and industrial programs, and their privileged position, living alongside Iranians who had barely enough to eat, provoked tremendous resentment and hostility.[17]

Despite widespread opposition, the Shah maintained his regime by relying upon the armed forces and that small group of individuals who were enriched by his mammoth spending programs. With U.S. support, he also maintained a powerful repressive force, directed by Savak, the Iranian intelligence agency. However, the cutbacks in oil production in 1976 and 1977 seriously hurt the Iranian economy, weakening the Shah's hold on power. Also, in an attempt to curb inflation, in 1977 the Shah imposed credit and price controls, which greatly antagonized Iran's shopkeepers.[18]

Opposition to the Shah came from four sources. The most important was the religious leaders—the mullahs—and their followers. The religious establishment had generally supported the Shah in 1953, but he alienated them in the 1960s by stripping away their large landholdings, as part of his land reform, and by ending their dominant voice in education, marriage, and divorce. Then in 1977–78 the annual state subsidy to mosques and religious foundations was reduced from $80 million to $30 million. The Shah also ignored a provision of the 1906 constitution that gave the religious leaders the right to determine whether legislation was consistent with Islamic laws. The mullahs also objected to the corruption and repression that characterized the Shah's rule. Then in the 1970s, as the Iranian economy grew and Westerners poured in, the religious leaders became concerned about "Western decadence" in Iran—films, night clubs, liquor stores, the alleged moral laxity of the wealthy, etc.[19]

The Shiite Moslem sect, which dominated Iran, had a tradition of opposition to persecution. In addition, while the Sunni Moslems, who formed the majority in most Arab countries, were supported by the state, the Shiite leaders were supported primarily by contributions from their followers. Moreover, since the mosques were the only nongovernmental forums that were allowed to function under the Shah's regime, it is not surprising that they became the centers of opposition. Allied with the Shiite religious leaders were the "bazaar groups," traditional merchants and entrepreneurs who, rather than benefiting from the Shah's modernization, had been hurt by inflation and competition from foreign goods.

After the religious leadership, the next most important opposition group was the secular liberals, represented by the National Front, the same party that Mohammed Mossadegh led in the 1950s. This group consisted primarily of the growing Iranian middle class, that is, intellectuals, professional people, etc.,[20] many of whom had been educated in the West, and their main demand was reestablishment of constitutional rights. The National Front also advocated progressive taxation and the nationalization of large companies. The Iranian left, including the Communist Tudeh Party and various splinter groups, was a much smaller force than the others, but it played an important role in the opposition and had the support of many of the strategically placed oil workers.

The movement that was to lead to the Shah's ouster began in January 1978 with a small demonstration in the holy city of Qum. The demonstration was started by religious militants, angered by a letter, inspired by the imperial palace, that accused Ayatollah Ruhollah Khomeini, exiled leader of the Shiites, of conspiring with Communists. But large numbers of Iranians who were not particularly motivated by religion joined the demonstration. Demands involved opposition to a land reform program that expropriated some property owned by religious bodies and a call for constitutional government. Twenty people were shot by the police during the demonstration, and in accordance with Shiite tradition a forty-day mourning period followed; but at the end of the forty days another demonstration was held, in what became a series of forty-day cycles, with the struggle against the Shah continually mounting.[21]

This was a distinctly Iranian revolution, combining the traditional ideas of the Islamic clergy with the mass technology of the twentieth century. To bypass the Shah's control of the mass media, his opponents brought tape cassettes with the fiery speeches of the exiled Shiite leader, Ayatollah Khomeini, into the country, where they were played on cassette players away from the hearing of the secret police. Leaflets were copied on duplicating machines by sympathetic clerical workers.[22]

From the beginning, the demonstrations and the propaganda that the opposition disseminated were aimed at winning over the strategically placed oil workers. By the end of October, 37,000 oil workers were on strike, demanding higher wages, replacement of all foreign workers, and an end to the martial law that the Shah had imposed to suppress the demonstrators. The strikers succeeded in shutting down Iran's key oil fields and its refineries. During the first half of November production averaged only 1.4 mb/d, as opposed to the normal 6 mb/d. However, by doubling the pay raises of oil workers, ousting those who remained on strike, and arresting the leaders, the Iranian government forced people to return to work in mid-November.[23] Nonetheless, a small group of workers remained on strike and continued to organize; others, who returned to work, made only minimal efforts to produce. As a result, during the second half of November production averaged only 3.5 mb/d, and much of this was due to the efforts of foreign workers.[24]

Then, in an effort to bring down the Shah, Khomeini, who was exiled in Paris, called for renewed strikes in early December. The Ayatollah termed the oil workers' strike an act of "obedience to God."[25] Responding to Khomeini's call, Iranian workers resumed their strike and attempted to intimidate foreign workers, preventing them from maintaining production. By mid-December production was down to 1 mb/d.[26]

Prior to the cutback in Iranian supplies, there was broad consensus that the world oil market would remain soft for at least another year;[27] nonetheless, even in the absence of the Iranian crisis, there probably would have been an OPEC price increase in December 1978. The price of the marker crude had not increased since July 1977, when Saudi Arabia raised its price to a level equivalent to that of the other OPEC countries. With the nominal price fixed, the real price continued to erode because of inflation and decline in the value of the dollar. In fact, according to the OPEC Economic Commission, since the last general OPEC price increase in December 1976 the real OPEC price had declined from 28 to 57 percent, depending upon which inflation and currency indices were chosen to measure it.[28]

In addition, by 1978 only five of the thirteen OPEC members—Saudi Arabia, Kuwait, Libya, Qatar, and the UAE—were still running balance-of-payments surpluses. As a result, there was considerable pressure within OPEC for a price increase. Iraq, Libya, and Algeria publicly called for increases of up to 25 percent, and Iraq threatened to look for an alternative to OPEC if a major price increase did not come about in December. Venezuela and Kuwait sought increases of 10–15 percent. Saudi Arabia, with the support of the UAE, officially came out for another price freeze, but the Saudis indicated that they could envision an increase of about 5 percent. The Shah, preoccupied with the domestic challenges to his rule and anxious to assure U.S. support for his regime, agreed to remain neutral on oil prices.[29]

The Iranian situation greatly strengthened the OPEC price hawks, for in an effort to make up for the decline in Iranian production, Saudi Arabia boosted its production from 8.4 mb/d in September to 10.4 mb/d in December—close to, if not above, the limits of its sustainable capacity.[30] As a result, Saudi Arabia could not put downward pressure on prices, as it had in 1977, by boosting its production higher. In addition, the Saudis were torn between bolstering the dollar and ensuring continued U.S. support for their political and military stability—factors that encouraged price moderation—and their fear of offending popular forces in the Middle East in the wake of the Camp David Agreement and the Iranian crisis—factors that encouraged reaching an accommodation with the price hawks.

The bargaining position of the price hawks was also strengthened by the rise in spot market prices. This had begun in August as companies began stockpiling oil, partly in anticipation of an OPEC price rise but also out of fear that Sadat's peace initiative would fail, leading to another Arab-Israeli war and another cutback in Arab oil supplies. Then, with Iranian production falling, stockpiling intensified, driving spot prices still higher. Finally, the special commission that the oil-exporting countries had established in June recommended that OPEC shift its pricing standard from the dollar to a basket of international currencies—a move that Iraq and Libya and, to some extent, Kuwait supported. However, Saudi Arabia remained opposed to this.[31]

The December OPEC conference reached a compromise. The conferees agreed to table the proposals on pricing in terms of a basket of currencies, as Saudi Arabia wanted, but they decided to increase prices by 14.55 percent, a figure much higher than Saudi Arabia had initially considered acceptable. This increase was to be imposed in four quarterly installments, the first being 5 percent and coming on January 1. On April 1 prices would increase another 3.809 percent, then 2.294 percent on July 1, and 2.691 percent on September 1. This complicated formula was designed to keep the year's average increase below 10 percent, as Saudi Arabia insisted.[32]

The increase was large by the standards of the past few years, but for the consuming countries it was hardly intolerable. Indeed, it failed to compensate the exporting countries fully for the decline in their purchasing power since 1974. Had the increases announced at this December meeting prevailed, as they were intended to, 1979 would have been no more significant in the history of the international oil industry than the four years that preceded it. However, as the oil workers' strike intensified, on December 26 Iranian oil production fell to 600,000–700,000 b/d—below the level of domestic needs—and Iranian oil exports came to a halt. On December 28 shopkeepers shut down, the state airline suspended operations, and employees in the banks and government ministries refused to return to work until the Shah left Iran. That same day, 500 foreign employees of oil concerns operating in Iran left the country.[33]

A day later, in a last-ditch effort to appease the demonstrators, the Shah appointed Shahpur Bakhtiar, a member of the National Front and a long-time opponent of the Shah, to head a new civilian government. Then, on January 16, the Shah left Iran on a "vacation" to Egypt, leaving Bakhtiar and a nine-man regency council to rule in his absence. Two weeks later Khomeini returned to Iran, after fifteen years in exile. Ten days after the Ayatollah's return, on February 11, Bakhtiar abdicated, and Khomeini named Mehdi Bazargan to head an interim government that would lead eventually to creation of an Islamic republic.[34]

As Egbal Ahmad has stated, the Iranian revolution "was unparalleled for its nonviolent but militant character and for its discipline in the face of Government violence."[35] While all Third World revolutions of the twentieth century have been peasant revolutions, the Iranian revolution was primarily urban based. It demonstrated the enormous power that oil workers could wield in an oil-exporting country and it revealed the contradiction in U.S. policy, for by seeking to buttress its position in the Middle East by strengthening the Shah through arms sales and political support, the United States antagonized the Iranian people, to the detriment of its position in the region.

For the consuming countries, the fall of the Shah had several consequences. It gave rise to a government that was much less committed to maximizing Iran's oil production than the Shah had been. Indeed, the Ayatollah was quick to declare that when oil production resumed, it would remain at about half the previous level. Nor would Iran, under the Ayatollah, pursue economic and military policies that led to massive imports of Western goods and Western armaments. In fact, once the Shah was ousted, Iran canceled $7 billion worth of orders for U.S. weapons.[36] Moreover, in recent years the Shah had moderated his insistence on higher oil prices, but the new Iranian government adopted the position of an ardent price hawk.

While the Shah had eagerly assumed the role of guardian of the Gulf and was generally supportive of Western policies in the Middle East, the Ayatollah made clear that he would pursue a more neutralist position on East-West issues and a more pro-Palestinian position in the Middle East. The Shah had been a strong supporter of Sadat's peace initiative, but the Ayatollah supported the Palestinians in their opposition to it. While the Shah had been willing to increase Iran's oil production during the Arab oil embargo, the Ayatollah was likely to support an Arab oil embargo. Most significantly, the loss of the Shah, the U.S.-appointed guardian of the Gulf, created a security vacuum in the area.

THE EGYPTIAN-ISRAELI PEACE TREATY

The most immediate problem created by the Shah's downfall was the obstacles it created for conclusion of the Egyptian-Israeli peace treaty. In response to attacks on the Camp David accords, as tantamount to a separate Egyptian-Israeli agreement, and the charges that Begin had outbargained him, Sadat sought to establish a formal link between the accord on the return of the Sinai and the one dealing with Palestinian autonomy. More specifically, he wanted to establish a timetable that would link the carrying out of the Egyptian-Israeli accord on the Sinai to resolution of the issue of Palestinian autonomy. But the Israelis were afraid that if they agreed to this, the peace with Egypt, which they desperately wanted, would become hostage to the much more uncertain Palestinian autonomy negotiations. They pointed out that Camp David provided no formal linkage between the two accords. Moreover, under Sadat's latest proposal Egypt could recover much of the Sinai, then refuse to establish normal relations with Israel because of a breakdown in the Palestinian talks. A second point of contention developed over Israel's insistence on its right to resume creating new settlements in the West Bank.

The Camp David accords had stipulated that a final Egyptian-Israeli peace treaty was to be signed by December 17, but the dispute over these issues delayed a final agreement until the Iranian crisis was well under way. At that point Israel, which had received more than half its oil supplies from Iran, became increasingly concerned about giving back the Sinai oil fields, source of another 25 percent of its oil supplies. At the time of the Sinai disengagement agreement in September 1975, the United States pledged to meet Israel's oil requirements, if necessary. However, Israel was not satisfied with this, doubting both the reliability and the durability of the U.S. commitment. The pledge would formally expire in 1980; also, by 1978 it had become illegal for the United States to export oil, and even if Israel obtained oil from the United States, it would have to pay the high and apparently rising world price for it.[37]

Besides, following the turmoil in Iran, Israel was reluctant to give up its military bases in the Sinai; similarly, in the wake of the Iranian crisis, Egypt became concerned about its isolation from the rest of the Arab world and the effect that its increasingly close ties to the United States would have on its standing in the Middle East. Moreover, the fall of the Shah heightened the Arab moderates' sense of vulnerability and led them to question whether the United States would come to their aid in the event they were similarly threatened. As a result of these concerns, they were less likely to support the Egyptian-Israeli treaty than they were before.

For the United States, the Iranian crisis made an Egyptian-Israeli peace treaty more important than ever. With the Shah gone, the United States was anxious to cement its alliance with Egypt, and it hoped that a pro–United States Egypt could help fill the security vacuum created by the Shah's ouster. At the very least, by lessening the conflict between Egypt and Israel and reducing Egypt's arms needs, an Egyptian-Israeli treaty would greatly reduce the likelihood of Egypt's realigning itself with the Soviet Union. It would also rule out another large-scale Arab-Israeli war, since, without Egypt, the other Arab states would be no match for Israel.

As a result of these considerations, the United States put enormous pressure on Egypt and Israel to resolve their differences. This effort came to a culmination in early March, when President Carter flew to the Middle East and succeeded in bringing about final agreement. It was essentially a reaffirmation of the Camp David accords, the main substantive change being a stipulation (in the Egyptian-Israeli treaty) that Egypt and Israel would complete negotiations on all aspects of self-rule in the West Bank and Gaza within a year after final ratification of the treaty. This was the formal link between the two accords that Sadat insisted upon. However, as the Israelis wanted, establishment of normal relations between Egypt and Israel was not contingent upon a successful resolution of these autonomy talks. Israel also agreed to Sadat's proposal for the initiation of self-rule in Gaza, even if the West Bank Palestinians refused to participate in the autonomy talks.

On Israeli oil supplies, Egypt agreed to negotiate normal commercial contracts with Israel, and the United States extended until 1990 its commitment to meet Israel's oil needs, if necessary. Israel agreed that within nine months of ratification of the treaty it would pull its troops in the Sinai roughly halfway back from their position and that it would withdraw them entirely by the spring of 1982. In return, it got what it most wanted: formal recognition and acceptance from the most powerful Arab state.[38]

In return for signing the treaty, the United States agreed to provide Egypt with $2 billion worth of weapons and to give Israel $3 billion to cover its expenses in withdrawing from the Sinai. This was in addition to the high levels of U.S. aid that both countries already received.[39] The United States also indicated that it would take a sympathetic attitude toward additional Israeli and Egyptian arms requests; it pledged its continued involvement in the negotiations on Palestinian home rule; and it agreed to operate surveillance flights over the Sinai to check on Israeli and Egyptian compliance with the treaty.[40]

The signing of the Egyptian-Israeli treaty in Washington on March 26 was accompanied by a storm of opposition in the Arab world. Demonstrations protesting the treaty signing were held in the Palestinian camps in Lebanon, in the West Bank, in Gaza, and in East Jerusalem. In Kuwait, where 250,000 Palestinians live, protesters stormed the Egyptian embassy, and in Damascus demonstrators occupied the office of the Egyptian airline, Egyptair. The new Iranian government also condemned the treaty, and thirty Arab students took over the Egyptian embassy in Teheran.[41]

The general Arab view was that, despite Sadat's insistence upon linkage between the two Camp David accords, he had signed what was essentially a separate Egyptian-Israeli peace agreement. While he recovered the Sinai for Egypt, he got nothing for the other Arabs. Israel had not agreed to return any of the other occupied territory. In fact, neither the Golan Heights nor Jerusalem was even mentioned in the final accord, and the prospect of the Palestinians' regaining sovereignty in either the West Bank or the Gaza Strip seemed as far away as when Sadat launched his peace initiative in November 1977. Even the Palestinian autonomy that the agreements contemplated seemed unlikely.

Saudi Arabia generally shared this view. Saudi prodding had been largely responsible for the emphasis the United States had placed on concluding an Arab-Israeli peace agreement, but the Saudis would have been happier with no treaty at all, rather than the one that resulted. They saw the treaty as doing nothing to resolve the Palestinian problem, and resented the fact that it did not even mention East Jerusalem. They saw the treaty as making the region *less* stable. As Prince Fahd told *Newsweek,* "Any peace treaty must be comprehensive—the withdrawal from illegally held territory and a solution to the Palestinian question. Anything short of such a treaty will dangerously destabilize the entire area." He warned that the Egyptian-Israeli agreement would "trigger convulsions in the region."[42] The Saudis feared that if they backed the treaty, radical Palestinian groups, such as the Popular Front for the Liberation of Palestine, would find a pretext to strike at oil installations.[43]

The Saudis were also disenchanted with U.S. Middle East policy. They believed that the United States should have done more to save the Shah and they feared the consequences that his downfall would have on the stability of the region. They were doubly frightened by the close relationship between post-revolutionary Iran and the Palestinians, which portended growing radicalism in the region.[44]

Despite their unhappiness with U.S. policy and their disapproval of the Egyptian-Israeli treaty, the Saudis could not afford to alienate either the United States or Egypt. They needed U.S. support for their political and military security, and they were afraid that if too much pressure was put on Sadat, he would be replaced by a more radical regime, something they did not want to see. At the same time, the Saudis did not want to antagonize the other Arab states. Consequently, they sought to keep a foot in both the Egyptian and the anti-Egyptian camps. Similarly, they sought to maintain good relations with Washington, but also to keep their distance—never appearing to give too much to the West. As part of this policy of balancing forces, the Saudis signed a security agreement with Iraq and put out feelers to the Soviet Union about opening relations.[45]

The clearest indication of the new Saudi policy came at the Baghdad conference of Arab leaders in March, called to determine what actions the Arabs would take in retaliation for the signing of the Egyptian-Israeli treaty. At the November Baghdad conference the Arab states had decided that if a treaty were signed, they would break diplomatic and economic relations with Egypt and Egypt would be expelled from the Arab League. However, most of the measures to be taken against Egypt were only vaguely stipulated, and in stating that no action should be taken that would hurt the Egyptian people, the November resolutions contained an enormous loophole.

Consequently, when they met in March the Arab states had to determine the sanctions that would be invoked[46] and a three-way split emerged. The PLO favored total diplomatic and economic boycott of both Egypt and the United States. According to PLO leader Yasir Arafat, this would include the raising of oil prices by 30 percent, cutting production back by a comparable amount, an Arab oil embargo against the United States and Egypt, and withdrawal of Arab funds from U.S. banks.[47] Syria, Iraq, Libya, Algeria, and South Yemen favored a total diplomatic and economic boycott of Egypt, but not of the United States. But Saudi Arabia, Qatar, the UAE, and Bahrain favored only the November Baghdad summit's sanctions against Egypt. This would mean suspending Egypt from the Arab League and breaking diplomatic relations with Egypt, but it would involve little in the way of direct economic sanctions against Egypt, since these could be interpreted as hurting the Egyptian people. Privately, Sadat had asked the Arab moderates to give him a chance to make progress on the Palestinian issue and thereby blunt the charge that he was selling out the Palestinians for a separate Egyptian-Israeli peace treaty.[48] By the position they took at the conference, the moderates sought to accommodate Sadat.

Debate over the three Arab positions was long and bitter. At one point the head of the PLO's foreign affairs department warned the countries that were pushing for the moderate line: "If you believe that you have reached the limit of what you are prepared to do, then stand warned that the Arab nation will not forgive you, nor will there be anything to prevent us from striking at U.S. interests wherever they are, for we have nothing to lose."[49] Similarly, the PLO, Iraq, and Syria warned the Saudis that they had to choose between Egypt and the other Arab states—that no middle position was possible.[50]

Finally, a compromise was reached. Egypt was suspended from the Arab League, the League's headquarters were moved from Cairo to Tunisia, and all the Arab states agreed to withdraw their ambassadors from Egypt. They also agreed to a total economic boycott of Egypt, including an end to all Arab financial and economic aid,[51] all trade between Egypt and other Arab states, and an Arab oil embargo against Egypt. In addition, Egyptian firms doing business with Israel were to be boycotted by the other Arab countries. No action was taken against the United States, but Iran agreed to cooperate with the Arab states in boycotting both Egypt and Israel. As Israel gained a new friend in Egypt, it lost one in Iran.[52]

In reality, the measures taken against Egypt were far less damaging than they appeared to be. An Arab oil embargo against Egypt was inconsequential since Egypt was capable of supplying all its own oil needs, and less than 10 percent of Egypt's trade was with other Arab countries. While the Saudis refused to pay for the fifty F-5E fighters that Egypt had ordered from the United States, Sadat arranged for reconditioned F-4 Phantoms as part of Egypt's $1.5 billion in U.S. military credits. While the Arab exporting countries terminated the $2 billion Gulf Organization for the Development of Egypt, the fund was practically depleted by this time. Somewhat more significant was the decision by Saudi Arabia, Qatar, and the UAE to shut down the Arab Organization for Industrialization, a $1 billion weapons and industrial consortium with Egypt.[53]

Restrictions on the remittances of Egyptian workers in other Arab countries would have been a far more substantial blow to the Egyptian economy than any of those adopted. Yet the Baghdad conference called for protection of Egyptians working in the other Arab countries, and no restrictions were placed on the money they regularly sent back to Egypt. In addition, Saudi Arabia and Kuwait continued to keep funds on deposit in Egyptian banks—possibly because if they tried to withdraw these funds, they might be refused. Similarly, Algeria and Iraq increased their capital in joint-venture banks that they held with Egypt. Iran also has maintained financial links with Egypt, despite its professed opposition to the treaty.[54]

At the same time, the treaty had substantial economic benefits for Egypt. It got back the valuable Alma oil field in the Gulf of Suez, and it planned major exploration in the reacquired Sinai. As indicated, the United States agreed to provide the country substantial financial aid, and it was hoped that peace would lead to a reduction in military expenditures and finally usher in the long-awaited boom in foreign investment.

The immediate economic consequences of the treaty for Israel were not nearly so favorable. It lost the valuable Sinai oil fields, and the additional aid it received from the United States simply compensated it for the cost of withdrawing from the Sinai. However, like Egypt, Israel hoped to benefit from an increase in foreign investment and a reduction in military expenditures.

THE SECOND OIL SHOCK

From December 27 until March 5 Iran did not export any oil.[55] The loss of Iranian supplies amounted to about 9 percent of the world's total oil production, or roughly 15 percent of the oil in international trade[56]—comparable to the loss of supplies at the peak of the Arab production cutbacks in 1973. Yet, unlike the situation in 1973, in 1978–79 there was a significant amount of spare productive capacity in the other oil-exporting countries—about 3.7 mb/d, and more than half of it in Saudi Arabia, according to Department of Energy estimates (see table 13–1). In fact, increases in the other oil-exporting countries replaced more than half of the decline in Iranian exports.[57] Despite this, the loss of Iranian supplies transformed a slack world oil market, characterized by surpluses of about 1.5 mb/d, into a tight market, characterized by shortfalls of about 1.5 mb/d—the equivalent of about 3 percent of world oil production or 6 percent of the oil moving in international trade.[58] Small though this shortfall was, it was capable of kicking off a big price increase, particularly if the consuming countries failed to take action to prevent it. Initially, consumers were cushioned from the effects of the shortfall by the fact that, in anticipation of a December OPEC price increase, companies had stockpiled crude supplies, and in January they proceeded to reduce their inventories.[59]

Still, in January, two significant developments occurred. Companies with access to crude supplies from the exporting countries cut back on their sales to third parties. There was nothing sinister or conspiratorial about this; since the loss of companies with interests in the Iranian Consortium was roughly equal to their aggregate surplus of crude, these companies simply sought to assure that their own requirements were met by cutting off sales to third parties. But the

TABLE 13–1. OPEC PRODUCTION AND CAPACITY, SEPT. '78–JAN. '79 (MB/D)

	Production		Estimated
	Sept. 1978	Jan. 1979	Capacity
Saudi Arabia	8.6	10.1	10.7
Iran	6.1	.7	6.5
Iraq	2.9	3.1	3.0
Kuwait	2.7	2.6	2.9
Venezuela	2.3	2.4	2.6
Libya	2.1	2.2	2.3
Nigeria	2.1	2.4	2.3
United Arab Emirates	1.9	1.9	2.3
Indonesia	1.6	1.6	1.7
Algeria	1.3	1.3	1.3
Qatar	0.5	0.5	0.6
Ecuador	0.2	0.2	0.2
Gabon	0.2	0.2	0.2
OPEC Total	32.5	29.2	36.6

BW, Mar. 19, 1979, p. 28.

effect of this led companies without crude supplies to go into the spot market and bid up prices to secure supplies, just as they had during the Arab embargo in 1973. There was also considerable speculation, with middlemen buying in anticipation of higher prices. Only small quantities of oil were exchanged in the spot market, but the prices paid received wide publicity in the exporting countries, putting pressure on the OPEC governments to raise their official prices to comparable levels so that they could obtain the full benefits of this transformed market situation. As a "hard-pressed buyer for a large oil company" told the *New York Times,* "This is one of the flaws of the free market system. Some venal, greedy individuals buy these cargoes, then turn around and find someone who has his back against the wall and must pay these exorbitant prices. The producers see that and figure, 'Why should we let others make profits like that on our oil?' "[60]

Also in January, Saudi Arabia, which in December had been producing 10.4 mb/d, announced that it would limit Aramco's production during the first quarter to an average of only 9.5 mb/d. Three possible motives were given for the Saudi move. First, the Saudis may have lacked the sustainable capacity to produce more than 9.5 mb/d. Second, they may have been seeking to send the West a signal regarding the need for energy conservation. Third, the Saudis' motives may have been political: they may have been indicating their disapproval of the proposed Egyptian-Israeli peace agreement and their disenchantment with the United States for its lack of support for the Shah.

In addition, the Saudis reasoned that by producing 9.5 mb/d, rather than their normal official ceiling of 8.5 mb/d, they were selling 1 million barrels a day in the first quarter that they had intended to sell in the future, when higher prices were scheduled to prevail. They therefore decided to charge fourth quarter 1979 prices for this additional 1 mb/d—$14.53 a barrel, rather than $13.34.

While the Saudi action may have been logical enough, it triggered a round of price increases. For if the Saudis could get $14.53 for some of their oil, other countries could get $14.53 for all of their oil, for with the Saudis producing as much as they were going to, buyers had little prospect of finding cheaper oil. Even if they turned to Saudi Arabia, as they often did when other countries raised prices above official levels, they would have to pay $14.53 for the additional supplies. Moreover, if the exporting countries failed to take advantage of this situation by raising prices, the oil companies could increase their own profit margins by raising prices.

The first countries to respond to this situation were Abu Dhabi and Qatar, which on February 15 added from 84¢ to $1.02 (about 7 percent) to the price of their oil. A week later Libya followed with a similar increase, and on February 22 Kuwait added $1.20, or 9.35 percent, to the price of its oil. The countries that raised prices said their increases were aimed at recapturing the profits the international oil companies were earning as spot prices rose. In this period, exporting countries also began cutting back on sales to their regular customers, the international oil companies, and selling oil directly in the higher-price spot market.[61]

The situation was made worse in early March, when Exxon announced that it was eliminating third-party sales entirely. Exxon's decision followed BP's January decision to cancel a longstanding sales contract of 350,000 b/d to Exxon. BP's sales to Exxon were about equal to Exxon's third-party sales. BP, the company most heavily dependent upon Iranian crude, was forced to cut back on its third-party sales (to Exxon and others) when Iran stopped exporting. The timing of Exxon's decision was widely criticized because it led to a renewed scramble for supplies, which put upward pressure on prices at a time when the world oil market was balanced on a razor's edge. Exxon maintained that it acted when it did because its contracts with Japanese customers were scheduled to come up for renewal on April 1.[62]

Altogether, during the first quarter of 1979 the majors cut back sales to third-party buyers by about 1 mb/d. By mid-March, 55 percent of all OPEC oil was being sold at official prices, based on marker crude's $13.34 a barrel; 40 percent was sold at premiums of about $1.25; and the remaining 5 percent was sold on the spot market at premiums of $5 or more. The effect was to raise average OPEC prices about 6 percent over the levels stipulated at the December OPEC meeting.[63]

In an effort to restore a semblance of unity to world oil pricing, OPEC called a special conference for March 26. As *Business Week* stated, it was dominated by "greed and fear." The poorer OPEC countries, particularly those outside the turbulent Middle East, wanted to take advantage of the tight market and boost prices as much as possible. Joined by the revolutionary government of Iran, the OPEC price hawks pushed for an immediate 25 percent price increase. On the other hand, Saudi Arabia, concerned about the effect such a large increase would have on the world economy and anxious to maintain U.S. support for its security, sought to hold the line on prices. However, in the turbulent situation then prevailing in the Middle East, the Saudis did not want to stand apart from their OPEC brethren,[64] and again a compromise was reached. The OPEC members agreed that the marker price would be raised immediately to the level that was supposed to prevail in the fourth quarter of 1979. The price was therefore raised 9.05 percent, from $13.34 to $14.53. However, the conference agreed that individual members would be free to add surcharges to the prices of their crudes.

In return for the agreement of the other OPEC members to keep the marker price down, Saudi Arabia agreed that in the second quarter of 1979 it would reduce its production from 9.5 to 8.5 mb/d. In addition, Saudi Arabia, Kuwait, and Iraq reached an informal understanding that as Iranian production increased, they would make room for it at the existing price levels by cutting back on their production. Saudi Arabia agreed to cut back 1 mb/d, Iraq 500,000 b/d, and Kuwait 400,000 b/d.[65]

The most significant aspect of the March meeting was the ambivalent role played by Saudi Arabia. On the one hand, Saudi Arabia assumed its traditional role in arguing to keep prices down; yet, at this crucial juncture in the history of world oil, Saudi Arabia agreed to cut back production, and in so doing it did much less to prevent prices from rising than it could have. This was in sharp contrast to both the Saudis' traditional opposition to production controls and Saudi behavior in 1976–77, when the kingdom refused to go along with an OPEC price increase and sought to raise production in an effort to hold prices down.

The ambivalence in the Saudi position reflects the contradictions in Saudi interests at the time. As a holder of vast wealth and a country dependent upon U.S. support for its security, Saudi Arabia sought lower prices; but as a country fearful about the consequences the Iranian revolution and the Arab-Israeli peace agreement would have on its security, Saudi Arabia did not want to offend its OPEC partners or appear to be too conciliatory toward the West. Rather than risk having the Ayatollah denounce them for undermining the Islamic revolution in Iran—a charge that would have great impact within Saudi Arabia—the Saudis agreed to cut production back, making room for the expansion of Iranian production, something they had never done for the Shah.

Immediately after the March OPEC meeting, the Gulf countries—with the notable exception of Saudi Arabia—added surcharges of $1.20 to the prices of their crude. By mid-April, these had generally been increased to $1.80. At the same time, the producers of light, low-sulfur crude—Abu Dhabi, Libya, Algeria, and Nigeria—raised their prices $4 above the price of the marker crude. This gave them the highest prices in OPEC, but the difference between the price of their crude and that of the marker was due to a genuine increase in the relative value of their crudes and was not, strictly speaking, a surcharge. Light, low-sulfur crudes sold for $4 more than the marker crude because they were worth $4 more, but the Gulf crudes that carried surcharges of $1.80 were not worth $1.80 more than the marker.[66]

Following the March OPEC meeting, Yamani had warned the consuming countries to reduce their consumption or be prepared to face further price increases. For a while the consuming countries seemed to heed his advice and a brief period of relative stability set in, with Saudi Arabian crude selling at the marker price of $14.53, other Gulf crudes selling for the marker plus a surcharge of $1.80, and light low-sulfur crudes selling for the marker plus a differential of $4. The return of Iranian production—at 3.6 mb/d in April—tended to stabilize the market.[67]

Then in May, following the appearance of long gasoline lines in California in April, U.S. domestic refiners entered the spot market, bidding up prices. Also in May, the U.S. government, which had discouraged U.S. companies from making purchases at high prices in the spot market, reversed its position and encouraged companies to procure supplies however they could. That sent the major U.S. oil companies into the spot market for the first time, and by June spot prices reached highs of $40 a barrel.[68]

On May 24 the U.S. Energy Department announced that it would provide importers of home heating oil a $5 subsidy, payable through the entitlements program.[69] This boosted U.S. demand for imports of home heating oil and put further upward pressure on world oil prices. Europeans protested the Energy Department's action, but the U.S. maintained that, with higher Rotterdam prices diverting supplies to Europe, the measure was necessary to ensure that the United States received its normal seasonal imports of home heating oil. Yet European nations objected to the United States' enlarging its "price-control shield," which protected U.S. consumers from the full effects of high world oil prices and led to higher U.S. oil consumption.[70]

Also in May, with demand increasing and spot market prices rising rapidly, Iran set off a new round of increases by boosting its surcharge from $1.80 to $2.40–$2.51. At the end of May, with spot prices at $30 a barrel, Iran widened its surcharge to $3.50–$3.80. By June, several countries, including Iran and Kuwait, had adopted "most favored seller" policies, guaranteeing them the highest prices paid to any OPEC country (with appropriate adjustments for differentials).[71]

When OPEC met in June, Saudi Arabia sought to reestablish a unified price of about $17 or $18 a barrel—the level that most other OPEC countries were already charging. The Saudis argued that the free-for-all system then prevailing, with each country adding whatever surcharge it felt it could get away with, could backfire once demand declined. At that point, the Saudis warned, prices could spiral downward, just as they had spiraled upward. To maintain both the high world oil price and the power of OPEC, the Saudis argued, a unified price should be agreed upon. They also pointed out that the surcharges hurt the world economy. The Saudis saw reestablishment of a unified price as necessary if they were to regain their dominance over both OPEC and the world oil price level. So long as countries could tack on surcharges as they pleased, setting their own prices, independently of the marker price, Saudi Arabia's power would be eclipsed.

The other OPEC countries resisted this attempt to reassert Saudi power and the idea that prices should be held at $17 or $18. They sought at least $20 for the marker, with Iran the leading advocate of a higher OPEC price. Debate was intense; and at one point Yamani threatened to leave the conference, hold the Saudi price at $14.53, and boost production as much as possible. Yet in June, as a result of water seepage in the Safaniyah field, Saudi capacity had declined by 500,000 b/d and, according to CIA estimates, was only 9.5 mb/d.[72] Since the Saudis were already producing 8.5 mb/d, their bargaining leverage was limited. Nor did they want to isolate themselves from the other OPEC countries. Consequently, a compromise was reached. The OPEC countries agreed on a base price for the marker crude of $18, which both Saudi Arabia and the UAE would charge. However, Saudi Arabia agreed that the other members could charge a $2 "market premium," plus their normal differentials for location, gravity, and quality, so long as their prices did not exceed $23.50. This reduced the differential between Arabian light and the highest-priced OPEC crudes from $6.76 to $5.50.[73]

OPEC's communique warned the international oil companies against "the irresponsible practice of taking advantage of the present situation to reap unwarranted profits."[74] Moreover, in an effort to recapture some of the windfall profits the companies had made on its lower priced crude, Saudi Arabia announced that its new price of $18 would be backdated to June 1. Following the June meeting, the average OPEC price rose to $20, 56 percent above its level of December 1978. Substantial as this increase was, according to OPEC officials it put the real OPEC price just slightly above its fall 1974 level.[75]

In 1979, as in 1973–74, the failure of the consuming countries' energy policies enabled the oil-exporting countries to boost prices so dramatically. Once again, the consuming countries found themselves unable to compensate for what, on a worldwide basis, was a very modest loss of supplies. Nor were they able to prevent the oil companies from bidding prices up. As the *Petroleum Economist* stated, "If buyers are prepared to pay $35 a barrel in the spot market they should not be surprised to find official government selling prices peaking at $23.50."[76]

On March 2 the IEA members met and pledged to reduce their oil demand by 5 percent, about 2 mb/d, from its projected 1979 level. Since demand was expected to increase by 1.8 percent, this meant a reduction of only 3.2 percent from the 1978 level. But of their 5 percent goal the IEA, as a group, reduced demand by only 1 percent in the first half of 1979, when prices spiraled upward. In May, the IEA secretariat warned the members that their measures to conserve energy, taken to date, were inadequate to meet the 5 percent reduction and that the goal itself was probably too low to balance supply and demand and ease the upward pressure on oil prices.[77]

The United States claimed to have met the 5 percent goal during the first half of the year, but its "success" was due to the unavailability of gasoline in the United States, not to any genuine conservation effort, and the gasoline shortage put *more* upward pressure on world oil prices, rather than eased that pressure, as genuine conservation would have done. Most IEA members took few, if any, tough, effective measures to reduce demand in this critical period, nor did any country (aside from the United States) meet its 1979 commitments to the IEA to reduce oil consumption.[78]

The heralded IEA emergency sharing scheme also proved useless during the 1979 crisis. In May, Sweden and Denmark experienced shortages that were large enough to trigger the plan, and both countries requested that it go into effect, but the other members rejected this request. They feared that triggering the plan would encourage panic hoarding and panic buying, raising prices further, and they were uncertain about their ability to carry out the provisions of the plan, especially its stipulation that countries reduce their demand by 7 percent. Consequently, they felt that, rather than protect them, triggering the plan would reveal their vulnerability. Nations also feared that their citizens would object to enduring worsening shortages in order to help other countries.[79]

The more fundamental problem with the plan is that it does nothing to prevent a small loss of supplies from leading to skyrocketing prices. As both the 1973–74 and the 1979 crises demonstrate, this can occur long before the loss of supplies reaches 7 percent of the consuming countries' total consumption—the level required to trigger the plan. Moreover, to prevent the upward price bidding that encourages higher OPEC prices, an emergency sharing plan would have to assure that supplies are evenly divided among oil companies, as well as consuming countries, and of course the plan does not prevent countries that are not IEA members from bidding up prices during periods of shortages.

In June, while the OPEC countries were meeting in Geneva, the leading consuming countries were holding their sixth annual summit meeting in Tokyo, which was dominated by the energy issue. Everyone agreed that oil imports should be reduced, but every country sought to pass the burden of doing so to its partners. The United States and Japan proposed that the countries commit themselves to country-by-country limits on oil imports for 1979 and 1980; however, the Europeans wanted Europe as a whole, Japan, and the United States to freeze imports at the 1978 level through 1985. This followed an EEC decision in March to hold imports at the present level, about 3.5 billion barrels of oil a year, until 1985. France proposed that controls be placed on the spot market, and the Europeans and Japanese wanted President Carter to speed the timetable he had announced in April for decontrolling U.S. crude oil prices.[80]

The seemingly technical dispute over oil-import quotas reflected the different interests of the two groups of countries. With North Sea oil coming onstream, Europe would have little difficulty freezing its import level, but various European countries might. Japan wanted immediate curbs on imports, but it was afraid that, by freezing its imports at their 1978 level, it would put a serious constraint on its economic growth. Finally, the United States objected to using 1978 as the base year. Since Alaskan oil had come onstream in 1978, U.S. imports had been relatively low that year, and, given the likely domestic repercussions, President Carter was unwilling to speed his schedule for decontrolling U.S. crude oil prices.[81]

Eventually a compromise was reached. The Europeans agreed to an overall EEC ceiling on imports for 1979 and 1980; they also accepted the principle of country-by-country limits for 1979 and 1980, but stipulated that they would work out the actual limits at a later date. The United States accepted a ceiling of 8.5 mb/d for 1985—higher than the 1978 level of imports but lower than both the 1977 level and the level projected for 1979. Japan agreed to a 1985 ceiling of 6.5 to 6.9 mb/d, up from its current level of 5 mb/d.[82] The United States also proposed a system to allocate supplies in the event they were not sufficient to meet the import levels that had been agreed to, but this proposal was dropped when the other countries showed no interest in it. The consuming countries agreed to set up a register of international transactions to provide greater ''transparency'' for crude oil pricing, and they decided to seek better data on company profits. They also pledged to discourage their oil companies from buying in the spot markets.[83]

The actions taken at the Tokyo summit were really quite limited and had little effect on the situation in 1979. The 8.5 mb/d ceiling that the United States committed itself to was well above the expected level of U.S. oil imports in 1979 and 1980.[84] Similarly, the limits that the other importing countries committed themselves to were not particularly stringent, and the registering of spot purchases was a far cry from the genuine control of the spot market that France sought. It would do little to prevent upward competitive bidding, for price stability does not depend upon price transparency but upon secure supplies, or the flexibility to restrain demand and substitute other sources in periods of shortages. But as the 1979 crisis revealed, the consuming countries have attained neither secure supplies nor flexibility in their energy consumption.

Allocation of Supplies and the U.S. Gasoline Shortages. In 1979, as in 1973–74, the consuming countries relied on the international oil companies to allocate supplies. Initially, the companies sought to supply the consuming countries on the basis of their normal import levels; that is, each country would get X percent of its normal imports. But by spring the companies were allocating supplies on the basis of normal consumption, as stipulated in the IEA emergency sharing plan.

Of all the consuming countries, only the United States experienced serious shortages in 1979. There were several reasons for these shortages. Because of the loss of Iranian supplies, the United States experienced a small but significant shortage of crude oil.[85] Many have sought to deny this by pointing to the low level of U.S. oil consumption supplied by Iran (about 3 percent in 1978) or to the fact that U.S. oil imports were 3.9 percent higher in the first half of 1979 than in the first half of 1978.[86] Taken in isolation, however, both of these facts are misleading. The amount of oil the United States normally got from Iran is hardly relevant, since the oil companies attempted to redistribute supplies so that all countries suffered the same percentage decline as a result of the Iranian cutoff, irrespective of the amount they normally got from Iran. Comparing 1978 and 1979 import levels is misleading because, in the first half of 1978, U.S. oil imports had been unusually low, partly because Alaskan production was increasing during this period and helping to meet the growth in U.S. oil consumption. Also, early in 1978 oil companies were working off excessive inventories, built up in anticipation of an OPEC price rise in December 1977 that never materialized.[87] With Alaskan oil production leveling off, in the fourth quarter of 1978 U.S. oil imports began to rise again, and they were expected to increase from 8.36 mb/d in 1978 to 9.2 mb/d in 1979. While they *did* go up, they remained significantly below the level they attained in the second half of 1978 and far below demand, which continued to increase.[88] In addition, while crude oil imports rose in the first quarter of 1979, imports of refined products declined, leading to only a slight increase in total petroleum imports.

U.S. oil imports fell short of demand not simply because of the loss of Iranian supplies but also because, for several months, the United States bore a disproportionate share of the shortfall. This was partly because of the U.S. Energy Department's initial opposition to purchases in the high-price spot market by U.S. companies. Also, U.S. refiners were often unable to bid for petroleum product imports because, as a result of price controls on domestic crude, petroleum product prices were generally higher in Western Europe than in the United States. Similarly, because under the entitlements program refiners could recover only the average cost of imported crude, U.S. companies were discouraged from purchasing the highest-priced foreign crude.[89] In addition, with product prices rising in Western Europe, foreign refineries that normally supply the United States diverted part of their product to Western Europe. For example, the *Energy User News* reported that Texaco diverted 65,000 b/d of petroleum products from its Caribbean refineries to the highly profitable European spot market. Finally, because of Iran's hostility to the United States, U.S. companies were at a disadvantage in bidding for Iranian crude.[90]

The other factor contributing to the U.S. crude oil shortage was an unusually large decline in domestic production, from 10.317 mb/d in the second half of 1978 to 10.158 mb/d in the first half of 1979.[91] With at least some of the controls on domestic oil production expected to be removed June 1 and with President Carter announcing his plan for phased decontrol in early April, some domestic producers probably held back supplies in anticipation of higher prices. In any case, the decline in domestic production was modest and would not have been significant, had oil imports been available to compensate for it. But to meet U.S. demand, imports had to average 8.6 mb/d during the first half of 1979; instead, they averaged only 8.2 mb/d.[92]

Altogether, during the first half of 1979 U.S. crude oil supplies, domestic and imported, were between 2 and 4 percent below the level of U.S. demand.[93] In itself, this should not have led to long gasoline lines, but several other factors entered the situation. Gasoline demand in early 1979 grew at about twice the rate that forecasters had predicted for all of 1979,[94] but during the first four months of 1979, U.S. companies were able to keep supplies above year-earlier levels by drawing upon their inventories. By spring, however, inventories were down and the companies were reluctant to reduce them further, especially since the world oil market was still extremely unstable. There is also evidence that refiners may have deliberately held back supplies. As the Department of Energy later charged, some refiners had "been conservative in their use of their stocks."[95] In addition, at the urging of the Energy Department, the oil companies began to build up home-heating-oil supplies for the winter. While this process traditionally began in spring, in retrospect—given the overall levels of crude supplies—it appears to have been pursued to excess in 1979.[96]

The other factor that reduced U.S. gasoline supplies was that many U.S. refiners could not process the heavy crudes that were becoming common, or processed them inefficiently (getting less gasoline) because they lacked "upgrading" equipment. Moreover, as a result of the entitlements program, efficient refiners that had upgrading equipment often had to share their crude supplies with inefficient refiners that lacked such equipment. The increased use of unleaded gasoline, which takes more crude to make, further reduced U.S. gasoline supplies. As a result of these factors, by May 1979 a crude oil shortage of between 2 and 4 percent became a gasoline shortage of about 12 percent,[97] and it was made worse by the Department of Energy's allocation system. According to this system, certain groups—police, farmers, the military, and various local services—were entitled to all the gasoline they needed. After meeting the needs of these priority users, oil companies had to divide what was left among their regular customers, according to the amount they used in the base period, 1978. In addition, areas that had experienced more than 10 percent growth in gasoline demand between October 1978 and February 1979 were entitled to extra supplies.

These provisions led to enormous misallocations, similar to those in 1973–74. Areas that had experienced rapid growth *since* 1978 were disadvantaged by the use of 1978 as the base year. On the other hand, small gas stations in rural communities (especially in winter resort areas) experienced more than 10 percent growth in gasoline demand between October and February and were therefore entitled to extra supplies—despite the fact that they did not experience shortages, though other places did. In addition, many state governments distributed the so-called "state set-aside," equal to 5 percent of their monthly allocation, in a manner that aggravated the shortages. For example, New York distributed a disproportionate amount to rural upstate counties, depriving downstate New York City and its suburbs, where gasoline lines were longest.[98]

The rigidity of the system made it difficult to correct imbalances when they occurred, and once shortages began, motorists started "topping off": filling their tanks at every opportunity to make sure they did not get caught short. This hoarding, of course, aggravated the shortages and the gasoline lines. In addition, once service station dealers saw that they could sell all the gasoline they were allotted in a short time, they reduced their hours, which lengthened the gasoline lines considerably.[99] As early as December 1, 1978, Shell announced that it would ration supplies to its wholesale customers,[100] and other companies soon announced similar moves. As a result, service stations began to limit supplies to customers or close early.

Long gasoline lines did not appear until late April in California. As a result of rapid population growth, gasoline demand in early 1979 grew much more rapidly in California than the national average, but supplies were allocated on the basis of 1978 consumption.[101] In May, oil companies produced 9.8 percent less gasoline than the previous May, the first monthly year-to-year decline since the Iranian crisis began, and with demand up about 2 percent, a 12 percent shortage resulted. As a result, shortly after the California lines disappeared,[102] widespread gasoline shortages occurred in June in the Northeast.

In response to the shortages, on May 21 the Energy Department reversed its position and encouraged refiners to produce more gasoline and less home heating oil, and for the first time the Energy Department encouraged U.S. companies to make purchases in the spot market. By midsummer the gasoline crisis was over, seemingly having vanished as mysteriously as it appeared. In actuality, higher prices, fear of shortages, and "odd-even" buying schedules, which reduced panic, had reduced demand. At the same time, crude oil supplies increased as the world oil market eased and the allocation system was adjusted.[103]

In contrast to the United States, Japan, which had relied on Iran for 17 percent of its oil supplies, avoided shortages by increasing its purchases on the spot market and through direct government-to-government deals,[104] but the Japanese purchases put upward pressure on world prices. Indeed, there was no way around the dilemma: consumption had to be reduced or world prices would rise. Japan chose policies that encouraged higher OPEC prices, the United States chose policies that resulted in serious shortages; yet neither country reduced consumption enough to remove the pressure for additional price increases and equitably and efficiently distributed the supplies that were then available.

EVOLUTION OF THE WORLD OIL MARKET SINCE THE SECOND SHOCK

Following the resumption of Iranian production in March 1979, the world oil market remained tight, primarily because companies sought to rebuild inventories. This rebuilding of stocks was intense because stocks had fallen sharply during the previous winter and there was great uncertainty about the availability of future supplies. Companies feared that Iranian production would be shut down again. Indeed, there was still conflict between the Iranian oil workers and the new Iranian government;[105] in the long run, the withdrawal of foreign personnel was likely to cause problems; and in response to higher prices, other exporting countries, unable to absorb all their revenues domestically, were threatening to cut back production.[106] Despite these concerns, by July the world oil market had softened considerably. In June, the major international companies had pulled out of the spot market, leading to a decline in spot prices. At the same time, higher OPEC prices and a slowdown in world economic growth reduced demand.[107]

Then on July 1, following an appeal by President Carter, Saudi Arabia boosted its production from 8.5 to 9.5 mb/d. The Saudis were concerned that the spot market might take off again, triggering another round of OPEC price increases. While the Saudi move was prompted partly by the kingdom's concern about the effect of spiraling oil prices on the world economy, the Saudis indicated that their action was to encourage U.S. efforts to promote a comprehensive settlement of the Arab-Israeli conflict. Robert Strauss had recently been appointed U.S. special ambassador to the Middle East, and the Saudi action came a week after Strauss's visit to the kingdom.[108] Also, within a week of the Saudi production increase the State Department recommended sale of an additional $1.2 billion in military equipment to the Saudis. While the State Department's recommendation may well have been made without the additional Saudi production, it is doubtful that Congress would have allowed the sale to go through so easily if the Saudis had not boosted production when they did.

Despite the softening of the market, uncertainty about supplies and ad hoc production cutbacks by several exporting countries—Algeria, Iran, Nigeria, Libya, and Kuwait—kept governments' selling prices firm. Prices on the spot market also remained high, primarily because Japan ignored the Tokyo agreement and had turned to the spot market to rebuild its stocks. As the country most dependent upon imported oil, Japan was particularly anxious to build up its inventories so that, in the event of another supply crisis, growth of the Japanese economy would not be impeded.[109]

The price hawks had wanted to hold another OPEC meeting in September to raise prices further, but Saudi Arabia, anxious to keep prices down, refused to attend such a meeting. Nonetheless, with spot prices high, several exporting countries diverted part of their crude from their normal customers, the major international oil companies, and sold it on the spot market, where they got more than the official OPEC ceiling price of $23.50. In October, Libya broke through the $23.50 OPEC ceiling, setting an official government selling price of $26.27 for its light crude. Shortly thereafter, Algeria and Nigeria, the other producers of light African crude, followed with similar increases.[110]

The defection of the African light producers from the OPEC agreement was hardly surprising, for their crude was worth between $4 and $5 a barrel more than the Gulf crudes. Yet, since the June OPEC meeting, Iran and Iraq had been selling their oil for $22 a barrel. In October, Kuwait raised its price to $21.43 and Iran boosted its price to $23.50, the OPEC limit. Consequently, in raising prices above the OPEC ceiling the producers of African light were trying to get a base price comparable to what the other OPEC countries were getting, plus an appropriate differential.[111]

Reluctantly, in November, the Carter administration allowed the Shah into the United States for medical treatment. In retaliation, Iranian students seized sixty-seven U.S. citizens as hostages. The student-militants quickly gained the support of the Khomeini regime and a major diplomatic conflict between Iran and the United States ensued.[112] Eight days after it began, in an effort to dissociate oil from resolution of the crisis, President Carter announced that the United States would suspend all imports of Iranian oil.[113] While politically dramatic, the suspension of imports had little effect on the world oil market, for by this time stocks were high and the market had softened considerably. Buyers had expected another Iranian crisis; consequently, though spot prices went up, there was no panic buying. In addition, Carter's action was not intended to reduce Iranian production or prevent the Iranians from selling oil to other countries. As a result, the United States was easily able to replace the 6 percent of its supplies (imported and domestic) that it had been receiving from Iran, and neither the other consuming countries nor Iran suffered significantly as a result of the U.S. import suspension.[114]

Another big blow to the consuming countries was not long in coming. On December 13, a week before the next OPEC meeting was to convene, Saudi Arabia announced that it was raising its price from $18 a barrel to $24. Venezuela, Qatar, and the United Arab Emirates joined the Saudis at the new price level. In an effort to retrieve some of the excess profits the companies had made by reselling the lower-priced Saudi crude, the kingdom made the increase retroactive to November 1.

The Saudi move, which paralleled its November 1974 action, was intended to preempt the OPEC price hawks, who wanted an official price of at least $30. The Saudi regime also sought to gain credit with the Saudi people for raising prices on its own, rather than seeming to have its price pulled up by the OPEC hawks. Yet Libya responded to the Saudi action by immediately boosting its crude to $30, which implied a price of $26 for the marker. Then, on the eve of the OPEC conference, Iran set a price of $28.50.[115]

At the conference, Iraq and Kuwait indicated willingness to accept the Saudi-established level, and the OPEC economic commission, usually a proponent of higher prices, recommended a benchmark price of $24 or $25. But the price hawks, Iraq, Iran, Algeria, and Libya, refused to go along. A compromise of $26 a barrel was proposed, but Saudi Arabia, standing alone, said that was too high while Iran said it was too low. Iran wanted $35.[116]

The conference was supposed to last two days, but it carried on for four, and in the end no agreement was reached, not even an "agreement" for two-tier pricing. As in December 1973, Iran was again the leading price hawk and Saudi

Arabia the most insistent on keeping prices down. After the meeting, Iran's new oil minister, Ali Akbar Moinfar, said that oil prices should rise to the cost of alternative energy sources, between $35 and $55.[117] This was the same argument the Shah had made following the December 1973 meeting.

Following the meeting, Saudi Arabia kept its price of $24 a barrel but Venezuela, Iraq, Kuwait, the United Arab Emirates, and Qatar boosted their price to $26. Libya and Algeria posted prices of $34.72 and $33 respectively—the Iranian level plus their light-crude differential. Altogether, since December 1978 the average official OPEC price had doubled, and with diversions to the higher-price spot market, it had more than doubled. At the beginning of 1979 the real oil price was 27 percent below its 1974 level; by the beginning of 1980 it was 37 percent above the 1974 level.[118]

The Saudis indicated their intention to keep production at 9.5 mb/d, creating a small surplus on the world market; then, when pressure built up, it would be possible to restore a unified OPEC price. To help achieve a unified price, Iraq, Kuwait, Abu Dhabi, and Qatar agreed to keep their production up as well. However, once order was restored in the world market, these countries planned to adjust their output accordingly, helping to maintain the new price level. As Yamani stated, "We don't want to see [the official price of oil drop]. We just want a one-tier pricing system."[119]

By January 1980, signs of surplus had begun to appear. One consequence was that countries were no longer able to divert crude supplies to the higher-price spot market, and this provided relief for consumers. In addition, several exporting countries began to suffer production declines; yet, given the magnitude of their recent revenue increases, most countries had little trouble absorbing these cutbacks. Indeed, at this point many countries welcomed them.[120]

With the market soft on January 25, Saudi Arabia boosted its price from $24 to $26, retroactive to January 1. The Saudis hoped that by going up to the level of most of the other OPEC countries, they could reestablish price unity, but their bid was quickly foiled. One day later, Iraq, Kuwait, Qatar, and the United Arab Emirates raised their price to $28.[121] In mid-May, with the market even softer, Saudi Arabia tried again, boosting its price to $28 a barrel (this time retroactive to April 1); but again the Saudi move failed. The other OPEC members responded by raising their prices a dollar or two.

Thus for the third time since December the Saudis had raised prices in an effort to bring about a unified OPEC price but, instead, had driven prices higher. By backdating their increases, the Saudis greatly reduced the benefits the consuming countries and the oil companies initially derived from the lower Saudi prices; nonetheless, so long as the Saudi price remained below the level of the other oil-exporting countries', the Saudis would be under pressure to boost prices further, possibly triggering new upward spirals.[122]

Despite the surplus, prices remained firm during the first half of 1980 because consumers continued to build inventories to record levels and because several exporting countries cut back production: Kuwait, Algeria, Libya, and Venezuela voluntarily,[123] and Iran because of technical and marketing problems.[124] While the consuming countries withstood the loss of Iranian production (by spring its exports were only about 500,000 b/d), the fact that Iran no longer sought to export—or was capable of exporting—5 mb/d greatly aided the OPEC countries in their efforts to maintain prices.

When OPEC gathered in June, its members' prices ranged from $28 to $38 a barrel, with the members' weighted average price about $30.50. Saudi Arabia was at the low end of the scale and Algeria, Libya, and Iran at the high end, with other countries in between. Saudi Arabia went into the Algiers meeting still seeking a uniform price, but insisting that it would not raise its price unless OPEC's highest-priced producers reduced theirs. But the OPEC hawks maintained that they would not lower their prices below $35.[125] Iraq, in a mediating role, proposed a compromise of $32, with the Saudis coming up to this level and the price hawks dropping down. For most other OPEC countries, $32 would mean an increase of about $2.[126]

Officially, neither Saudi Arabia nor the price hawks would accept the Iraqi proposal and the meeting adjourned, the only agreement being that the base price would range from $28 to $32, with members permitted to add an allowance of $5 for quality premiums. However, most OPEC countries set their price at the $32 stipulated by Iraq, and though Saudi Arabia held its price at $28, Yamani indicated that the kingdom might soon raise its prices as well. He also said that if prices were "reunified" in September, when OPEC next met, Saudi Arabia would consider reducing its output by 1 mb/d. Other OPEC ministers said it was understood that the Saudis would raise their price to the new level of $32 by September. Libya's Oil Minister Abdussalam Mohammed Zagaar described the June agreement as "a major step toward price reunification."[127] The agreement also seemed to augur a new leadership role for Iraq within OPEC and a decline in Saudi influence.

When the OPEC countries met in September, they were again unable to reach agreement on a uniform price for the marker crude. Stocks in the consuming countries were at record levels and OPEC production was the lowest in nearly five years. Despite this, there was a surplus of 1–2.5 mb/d on the world market. At the conference, Iran attacked Saudi Arabia for stealing markets by overproducing its less expensive oil, and other countries indicated that Saudi Arabia should absorb the bulk of the surplus by cutting its production.

The Saudis went into the meeting proclaiming that, in return for price unity, they would reduce their production by 1 mb/d. But Saudi Arabia did not want to raise its price and the other countries did not want to lower theirs. After considerable conflict, a compromise was reached. In return for a pledge that the other exporting countries would lower their prices eventually, Saudi Arabia agreed to boost its price to $30 right away and to reduce its production by 1 mb/d sometime in 1981, if it was convinced that the others had adopted moderate pricing policies. For the time being, the other OPEC countries would freeze their prices at their current levels, $32 to $37, and shortly after the meeting concluded, these countries announced plans to cut their production by 10 percent.[128]

Following the September meeting, price unification did not seem far away, but politics again intervened. In September 1980 Iraq invaded Iran, declaring that Khomeini had invalidated the two countries' 1975 agreement by repeated calls for the Iraqi Shiite majority to overthrow the Ba'athist Iraqi movement and by the aid he was providing the Iraqi Kurds. Iraq demanded control of the entire Shatt al Arab waterway, return to Arab control of three islands in the Gulf (which the Shah had seized in 1971), and autonomy for Iran's Kurdish and Arab regional minorities. In acting when it did, Iraq was taking advantage of the disarray in Iran as a result of the revolutionary upheavals and the hostage crisis and was attempting to establish its own predominance in the Gulf.[129]

Once fighting erupted, it was feared that it might spread to other Gulf countries, block the vital Strait of Hormuz (as Iran threatened), or trigger another rapid escalation in oil prices.[130] In fact, the oil installations in Iran and Iraq soon became prime military targets, and oil exports from these two countries came to a halt. The loss of supplies was 3.9 mb/d in October, about 6 percent of the world's production. (In comparison, the loss of supplies from Iran during early 1979 was 5.5 mb/d, about 9 percent of world production.)[131]

While there was an increase in spot prices during this period, there was no increase in official selling prices, for several reasons. At the time the Iran-Iraqi war broke out, world oil production was running between 2 and 3 mb/d above demand, and in response to the war-induced cutbacks, Saudi Arabia boosted its production from 9.5 to 10.4 mb/d and the other OPEC countries rescinded their 10 percent cutbacks. In addition, the large inventories that the consuming countries had accumulated over the previous year provided another cushion and helped stabilize the market. In fact, the consuming countries advised the oil companies to draw on their stocks, rather than bid up prices in the spot market, as they had following the cessation of Iranian exports in the winter of 1978–79.[132]

Nonetheless, the Iran-Iraq war proved a setback to moderation in OPEC pricing and to Saudi Arabia's effort to secure a uniform marker price. After the September OPEC meeting, a compromise marker price of $32 had appeared imminent, but when the OPEC members gathered for their December meeting, there was little prospect of this being realized. Saudi Arabia agreed to raise its price from $30 to $32 (backdated to November 1), but the other OPEC members refused to stay put. They adopted a reference price of $36, to which various countries added premiums as high as $5. As a result, the weighted average OPEC price was about $35—170 percent above its year-end 1978 level.[133]

In December 1980, prices on the spot market began to fall again, and by the spring of 1981 there was a glut, estimated at between 2 and 3 mb/d, on the world market. The impact of higher prices on demand, a mild winter, President Reagan's decontrol of U.S. oil prices, growth in non-OPEC supplies, and recession in the industrialized world (which impacted most severely on the capital goods industry, where energy consumption is normally high) contributed to the glut. Moreover, though the war continued, Iran and Iraq were exporting about 2 mb/d by spring. And despite this addition to supplies, Saudi Arabia kept its production above 10 mb/d throughout this period. Yamani explained Saudi policy as deliberately producing a glut in order to force the other OPEC countries to lower their prices. Moreover, once the market softened, companies became less willing to hold supplies and began reducing their inventories.[134]

In response to the weakness of demand, Mexico, the United Kingdom, and Norway lowered prices about $4 a barrel. Other exporting countries eliminated quality and transport premiums and eased credit terms. Yet aside from Ecuador, no OPEC country made a substantial reduction in its official selling prices. The reasons for this were largely political. With the exporting countries' prestige dependent on their success in boosting prices, their governments were reluctant to risk the consequences of reducing oil prices. Indeed, when Mexico reduced its prices, the political fallout was so great that the director of Pemex, Jorge Diaz Serrano, was forced to resign.[135]

By the summer of 1981 OPEC production was at its lowest level in ten years. Its members were producing just 21.5 mb/d, compared with 31.4 mb/d in 1977, and Nigeria, Libya, and Algeria were most badly affected. Not only did they have the highest-priced crude, they competed directly with the light crudes from the North Sea. Consequently, when the price of North Sea oil was reduced, they were particularly hard hit. By the summer of 1981, Algerian production had fallen to 650,000 b/d, from 900,000 b/d at the end of 1980. Libyan production was down from 1.7 mb/d to 650,000 b/d, and Nigerian production had fallen from 2 mb/d to under 800,000 b/d. Kuwait, which demanded substantial premiums, saw its output drop to half of the 1.5 mb/d it was producing in the summer of 1980.[136]

When OPEC met in May, it attempted to respond to the glut. Saudi Arabia offered to raise its price $2, if the other OPEC countries would reduce their official government selling prices. This represented a considerable hardening in Saudi Arabia's position. Rather than rise to the level of the other OPEC countries, while asking them simply to freeze their prices, Saudi Arabia was asking them to lower their prices—and an OPEC conference had never agreed to lower even a single official government selling price. Consequently, it is hardly surprising that the Saudi proposal was rejected. Unable to agree on prices, the meeting adjourned, leaving all prices unchanged. With the exception of Saudi Arabia, Iran, and Iraq, the other OPEC countries agreed to cut their production 10 percent; however, the base on which this was calculated was significantly higher than their current production. As a result, only a third of the agreed-upon cutbacks—at most—was expected to be realized. Following the meeting, Libya announced a reduction of $1 in its crude price, bringing it down to the $40 level that Nigeria and Algeria charged.[137]

As the problems of oversupply increased, OPEC called a special meeting in August to try once again to reach agreement on a unified price. This time Saudi

Arabia proposed a base price of $34, with various countries allowed to add premiums up to $3. Since some OPEC countries were still selling oil for $40, this would mean a $3 reduction in their prices. Venezuela and Indonesia objected to the Saudi proposal on the grounds that they were able to sell all the crude they produced at $36, and despite their high levels of unused capacity, Libya and Nigeria felt that a market price of $34 was too low. In a last-minute effort to secure a compromise, Venezuela and Indonesia proposed a base price of $35, but Saudi Arabia rejected this. Saudi Arabia announced that it would reduce its production from 10 to 9 mb/d, and a few days after the meeting, Nigeria cut its price by $4—the largest across-the-board reduction an OPEC nation had ever made.[138]

At the end of October 1981, the OPEC countries finally agreed on a uniform price of $34 and announced that it would remain in effect at least until the end of 1982. OPEC also agreed to reduce its maximum surcharge by $1 a barrel, making the new maximum total $38, or $3 less than the previous maximum of $41. In compromising on a price of $34, this was the first time that OPEC officially decided to lower the prices of most of its members. Despite the decision, Standard Oil of California estimated that, as a result of the elimination of discounting and the increase in Saudi prices, the accord would *increase* OPEC's average price by $1 or $2 a barrel. A day after the OPEC meeting, Saudi Arabia announced that it was reducing its production ceiling to 8.5 mb/d.[139]

Despite the October agreement and the Saudi cutback, the glut persisted. Because a weak market prevented countries from charging as much as they were allowed under the October agreement, the U.S. Department of Energy found that OPEC's average price increased only 40¢, rather than the $1–$2 that industry sources had predicted. When OPEC met again in December, the organization cut the prices of the main Gulf crudes, relative to the marker, and reduced the maximum price of its members' best crudes to $37. But with the recession continuing in Western Europe and the United States and companies still reducing their inventories, the glut did not abate. According to IEA, in January and February 1982 oil use in the industrial countries was 5–7 percent below its year-earlier levels, and OPEC production was at its lowest level since 1969; 25 percent of its members' production was idle, and there was still a surplus of roughly 2–3 mb/d.[140]

Iran and Iraq were under strong pressure to increase their sales in order to pay their war costs. With revenues falling below projected levels, Nigeria, Venezuela, and Mexico came under severe budgetary pressure. Indeed, according to *Petroleum Intelligence Weekly,* only four OPEC countries—Saudi Arabia, Qatar, the United Arab Emirates, and Indonesia—were producing enough oil to satisfy their budgetary needs.[141]

In an effort to boost sales, discounting became widespread. In what was seen by other members as a violation of OPEC protocols, Iran cut prices three times in less than three weeks, by a total of $4, bringing its price for Iranian light (comparable in quality to the marker crude) to $30.20. Britain cut prices twice, bringing the cost of its crude from $36.50 in early February to $31 in early March and putting great pressure on Nigeria, Algeria, and Libya. (A year earlier, Britain's price had been $39.25.) By March 1, 1982, the spot market price for the marker crude, Saudi Arabian light, was down to $29—25 percent below its year-earlier level.[142]

The Saudis, who had increased their share of OPEC production from 28 percent in 1978 to 44 percent in 1981, came under great pressure from the other OPEC countries. Qaddafi accused Saudi Arabia of flooding the market with oil, in order to starve others into submission, and called on "the Saudi people and the Arab people in the [Arabian] peninsula to rise in revolution." Iran charged Saudi Arabia with stealing its sales, and hinted that it could easily raid Saudi oil facilities and shut them down.[143]

To deal with the glut, an extraordinary OPEC meeting was called for March 19; but before it was held, on March 5–6, at a meeting of the Organization of Arab Petroleum Exporting Countries (OAPEC) (to which Nigeria and Indonesia, but not Iran, Venezuela, Ecuador, or Gabon had sent representatives), it was agreed that production would be cut by more than 1 mb/d, bringing OPEC production down to 18.5 mb/d. Yet by the time the extraordinary meeting was convened on March 19, OPEC production had fallen to 18.2 mb/d, versus more than 31 mb/d in 1979. Saudi production was down to 7.5 mb/d, but even at this level supply was above demand. As the meeting began, OPEC President Sheik Mana Saeed al-Otaiba declared that "OPEC has never witnessed such a crisis since it was created over 20 years ago."[144]

After two days of meetings, the OPEC ministers announced that the $34 price would be maintained and that, to support this price, the members had committed themselves to production ceilings that would be maintained at least until the organization met again in May. While Saudi Arabia formally dissociated itself from the production program, it agreed to reduce its production by another 500,000 b/d, bringing it down to 7 mb/d. Venezuela, the U.A.E., and Indonesia also agreed to make substantial reductions in their production, while, under the agreement, Libya, Iran, and Algeria were permitted to increase their production. The key to the agreement was the Saudi cutback. While OPEC had committed itself to a 17.5 mb/d ceiling level, Saudi Arabia accounted for 500,000 of the 700,000 b/d reduction in OPEC production. (At this level, OPEC production had dropped by 3 mb/d in three months.) A committee was established to monitor members' compliance with the production agreement. The conference also agreed to reduce the price of OPEC's most expensive oil by another $1.50 and to extend financial aid to Nigeria, which had come under severe strain as a result of the decline in demand for its oil.[145]

In reaching their decision, the OPEC ministers recognized that a price cut of a few dollars a barrel would not have much effect on demand, but might begin a long downward price spiral. Venezuela, which had been badly hurt by the softness of demand for the heavy oil it produces, was reported to be the country most unhappy with the agreement, but acceded to it as a result of pressure from the other members. Above all the agreement demonstrated Saudi Arabia's commitment to maintaining the $34 price. Indeed, Yamani, who has called for a freeze at the $34 price through the end of 1983, appears to be determined to maintain the nominal price, but to allow inflation to erode the real price.[146]

Initially, OPEC's production ceiling program appeared to work. In April and May OPEC production remained below the ceiling level, largely because Saudi Arabia kept its production roughly 500,000 b/d below the 7 mb/d that it had agreed to, and prices began to firm. When they met in Quito in mid-May, the OPEC members decided to continue the program, but by June it was in disarray. Iran, which had never accepted the program, discounted its prices and boosted its production to nearly twice its assigned level. Nigeria and Libya also exceeded their ceiling levels, bringing OPEC production as a whole to 18.2 mb/d— 700,000 b/d more than the ceiling. The only thing keeping the surplus from being even greater was that Saudi Arabia and Iraq (because of war damage) were producing at less than their ceiling levels.[147]

In an effort to firm up the production control program, the OPEC members met in mid-July in Vienna; however, the disagreements among members proved bitter. Iran demanded an increase in its assigned ceiling level and said it should come through a corresponding reduction in Saudi Arabia's quota. The meeting broke up without any agreement. With discounting widespread in the production control program largely ignored, the OPEC countries convened in December 1982. At the meeting, the conflict between Saudi Arabia and Iran over production levels intensified. The OPEC countries did manage to reaffirm their commitment to the official $34 price, but they were again unable to reach agreement on production quotas. As a result, OPEC's ability to maintain the $34 price has become dependent upon the continued willingness of Saudi Arabia to restrict its production far below its capacity and the hope that world oil demand will increase with economic recovery.[148]

In an effort to give stability to the world oil market, in 1979 the OPEC nations began to consider adoption of a plan by their long-term strategy committee to link oil prices to an index that reflects the economic growth in industrial nations, inflation in the goods the exporting countries import, and changes in the value of the dollar. The plan, initially championed by Yamani, was continually deferred during the period in which OPEC was unable to agree on a uniform price for the marker. Once agreement on a uniform price was reached—making it technically feasible to institute such a plan—the plan was put off because, with the market glutted, the exporting countries no longer had the power to impose such a scheme. Nonetheless, once the real OPEC price falls, Yamani hopes to institute the plan.[149]

Were such a plan to be followed, it would give the world oil market greater stability and predictability than it has ever had; but the probability is that an organization that was unable to agree on a uniform price for over two years, and was then befuddled by a world oil glut, will not have either the unity or the power to implement and abide by such a plan. Nor are the consuming countries ready to rationalize the world energy market. Consequently, the world oil market is likely to be jolted again and again by political developments. In any case, the Iranian revolution is another milestone in the history of world oil. While the Shah's return to power in 1953 led to a period of stability in the industry, his downfall, twenty-six years later, created incredible turmoil in world oil markets. That turmoil is not likely to cease until political stability is reestablished in the Middle East.

The Consequences
of the Second Shock

Like the 1973–74 rise in oil prices, the 1979–80 increases have had a major impact on the world economy. Because oil prices went up, economic growth slowed down and inflation increased. Recycling petrodollars and financing the balance-of-payments deficits of the non-OPEC LDCs have again become major problems for the international financial system. The 1979–80 OPEC price increases have also had a dramatic impact on oil company profits and on the operations of the majors in the exporting countries. The consuming countries are now haunted by the possibility that, with economic recovery, demand for oil will outpace available supplies, triggering further price increases. Yet, despite this reality, they remain divided, their response to the problem is still inadequate, and the prospect of renewed political conflict in the highly unstable Middle East threatens to jolt the world oil market once again.

As a result of the 1979–80 oil-price increases, the consuming countries transferred an additional 2–3 percent of their combined gross national product to the oil-exporting countries. As a percentage of GNP, this transfer of wealth is about equal to the cost of the 1973–74 oil-price increases and means that, in 1980, about 4 percent of the consuming countries' total output went to pay for imported oil. Four percent of national income is more than U.S. citizens spend on automobiles and only slightly less than they spend on national defense or social security.[1]

According to the IMF, in 1979 the direct effect of the oil-price increases was to add 1.5 percent to the rate of inflation in the non-Communist consuming countries and to reduce economic growth between 0.67 and 0.75 percent of GNP.[2] Having had to endure the inflationary effects of the 1973–74 oil-price rise during the previous five years, most consuming countries have responded primarily to the inflationary impact of the 1979–80 oil-price rise.[3] This has meant higher unemployment and reduced economic growth.

As a result of the 1979–80 increases, the "OPEC surplus" went up again: from a $1 billion deficit in 1978 to a $63 billion surplus in 1979, and $119 billion in 1980 (see table 9–3). However, by 1981 it had fallen to $67 billion, and in 1982 it was expected to disappear entirely. By the third quarter of 1981, the OPEC countries as a group had become net borrowers from major Western banks for the first time since the end of 1978, and by the fourth quarter they were running a current account deficit.[4]

Despite the magnitude of the surplus, several factors have helped to ease the recycling problem this time. In relation to the overall level of world economic activity, this surplus has been less than the 1974 surplus,[5] and since in 1979–80 the price rise was more spread out than in 1973–74, the resulting surpluses have mounted over a longer time, making it easier to reabsorb them in the world financial system.

In 1979–80 the major consuming countries were also in a better position to accept the rise in import costs than they were in 1973–74 (see table 9–1). When oil-import prices rose in 1973–74, the weaker European economies—Great Britain, France, and Italy—ran a combined balance-of-payments deficit of nearly $20 billion, and the great fear was that one of these countries might default. But in 1979 all three countries ran current-account surpluses. In addition, Great Britain has been greatly strengthened by the development of North Sea oil. In 1979 the U.S. current account also showed a surplus. On the other hand, the rise in oil prices erased the large surpluses that West Germany and Japan had been running, shifting them into substantial deficit positions. Yet, since West Germany and Japan have the strongest capitalist economies, there is little danger that either of them will be unable to finance its balance-of-payments deficit. In fact, in a sharp departure from their policy following the 1973–74 oil-price increases, West Germany and Japan have been encouraging Arab investment in their currencies. Also, West Germany arranged to borrow $5 billion directly from Saudi Arabia, and Japan has been promoting foreign investments in its equity markets.[6]

In addition, Japan again responded to higher oil prices by boosting its exports sharply, prompting a backlash in Western Europe and the United States, so that the danger of protectionism looms again. In fact, on May 1, 1981, Japan was forced to limit its automobile exports to the United States, and Great Britain, France, and Italy have placed restrictions on Japanese car imports as well. Nonetheless, the European Commission responded to the May 1 decision by indicating that it would *make sure* the agreement would not lead to Japan's spilling excess cars in European markets. Japan, in turn, objected to recent inroads by U.S. chemical companies in Japan's traditional market stronghold in Southeast Asia. Japan claims this is due to the unfair advantage these companies gain because the United States continues to maintain price controls on natural gas, the feedstock for many products of U.S. chemical companies.[7]

As in 1974, the so-called "OPEC surplus" is again highly concentrated in just a few OPEC countries—primarily Kuwait, Saudi Arabia, and the United Arab Emirates[8]—but in comparison with 1974, less of it is going to Great Britain and the United States (see table 9–3). Also, the Arab countries are taking more direct control over their money, relying less on the big money-center banks to manage their funds.[9] Kuwait, in particular, has invested in foreign and, especially, foreign-owned oil companies. Its holdings include more than 1.8 million shares of Atlantic Richfield Company, about 1.2 million shares of Phillips Petroleum Company, and roughly 1 million shares of Gulf Oil Corporation, and in October 1981, in the largest Arab investment in the United States, Kuwait purchased

Santa Fe International, a large U.S. oil drilling and production company, for $2.5 billion. Kuwait officials explained that they plan to use their acquisition to expand into foreign oil exploration, production, and distribution.[10]

In part, these trends toward diversification and away from the United States and Great Britain reflect the growing openness of the West German and Japanese economies to Arab funds and the increasing sophistication of Arab investors; yet they are also a consequence of U.S. reaction to the hostage crisis. On November 14, 1979, President Carter froze the $6 billion in Iranian assets held by U.S. banks and the $2 billion in Iranian assets held by the U.S. government. Several hours after the president announced his decision, Citibank seized the Iranian deposits in its possession to cover its huge loan exposure to Iran, and one day later, Chase Manhattan, Banker's Trust, and Manufacturer's Hanover took similar actions. The effect was to greatly weaken the confidence of Arab investors in both dollar-denominated assets and U.S. banks, for if Iranian assets could be seized for essentially political reasons, Arab assets could be seized as well. Moreover, the greatest long-term damage from the episode may be that it will strengthen the oil-exporting countries' preference for oil in the ground over money in the bank—decreasing their willingness to expand oil production in the future.[11]

Ironically, there was no valid financial rationale for freezing Iranian assets. Prior to the freeze, Iran was up to date on its payments, and even after the freeze, Iran's central bank indicated that it did not intend to repudiate its foreign debt.[12] Even had Iran withdrawn its funds from U.S. banks, as it threatened, the effects would not have been major; the U.S. banks could have easily made up the loss of liquidity by borrowing through the international banking market, possibly from the same banks that Iran transferred the money to. And even if Iran had shifted its funds to other currencies, the effect on the dollar would not have been great.[13]

As for the non-OPEC LDCs, their oil bill was $43.5 billion in 1979 and $57.8 billion in 1980, up from $29.2 billion in 1978.[14] This has prompted renewed concern about financing the balance-of-payments deficits in these countries, yet several factors helped to mitigate the problem of non-OPEC LDC oil debts this time around. When oil prices rose in 1973–74, there was no official, institutional mechanism for petrodollar recycling, but by 1979 the $10 billion IMF Witteveen facility had been established to aid countries in financing their oil-related balance-of-payments deficits. This has enabled IMF to play a much larger role in the recycling process. In fact, between January 1980 and mid-May 1981 the IMF committed as much in LDC loans as it had—cumulatively—over the previous seven years. Moreover, this commitment to the LDCs has been possible because, in contrast to 1974–75, the industrial countries have not had to draw on IMF resources, leaving more money available to the LDCs. In fact, between year-end 1977 and April 30, 1981, the share of IMF debt held by the industrial countries fell from 49 percent to 9 percent, while the proportion accounted for by the LDCs increased from 51 percent to 91 percent.[15]

The IMF has also created a $25 billion fund to aid the LDCs in financing energy projects and balance-of-payments deficits, and Saudi Arabia agreed to lend the fund 8 billion in special drawing rights (equal to $9.6 billion) in both 1981 and 1982. Kuwait has committed 3 billion in SDRs to the fund, and the United Arab Emirates has pledged another 3 billion over a three-year period. West Germany, Japan, Great Britain, France, and the Netherlands have together agreed to provide three billion in special drawing rights, but the United States refused to make a contribution to the fund.

Creation of the fund enabled the IMF to lend India $5.8 billion, the largest single outlay it had ever made. Rather than for traditional balance-of-payments financing, the bulk of the loan is to be used to finance oil exploration. The Reagan administration objected to the loan because the terms were too lenient and because it was more for development needs than for meeting specific balance-of-payments deficits. In addition, the oil-exporting countries have transformed their temporary special fund into the OPEC Fund, raising its capital from $2.4 billion to $20 billion. The fund provides aid to the oil-importing LDCs.[16]

Probably the most significant factor in reducing the balance-of-payments financing problems of the non-OPEC LDCs is changes in their internal situation. The reserves held by these countries increased from $30 billion in 1974 to $70 billion in 1979—a substantial cushion against the risk of default. In addition, in 1974 only six of the non-OPEC LDCs were net oil exporters, but by 1979 the number had increased to fourteen.[17]

Despite these advantages vis-à-vis 1973–74, the second oil shock has imposed substantial costs on the non-OPEC LDCs. To reduce oil import costs, many of these countries have had to accept lower growth rates. In fact, in 1980 real per capita income in the non-oil LDCs declined for the first time in twenty years. Moreover, the 1979–80 oil-price increases have reinforced the trend toward even higher indebtedness, and forced many non-OPEC LDCs to devote an even higher percentage of their export earnings to paying back the interest on their external debt. In fact, Morgan Guaranty found that, since 1973, the total external debt of the twelve major non-oil LDCs has risen from 19 percent to 25 percent of their aggregate GDP. Moreover, interest payments on this debt in the early 1980s will account for almost 17 percent of their exports—roughly double the figure during the last half of the 1970s. In addition, the poorest of the non-OPEC LDCs have been hurt by the lack of increase in concessional aid since the 1979–80 oil-price increases.[18]

In 1982, as economic conditions in the industrialized countries worsened— reducing demand for imports—and interest rates escalated—largely because of the restrictive monetary policies pursued by the United States—many non-OPEC LDCs found it increasingly difficult to finance their balance-of-payments deficits and fears of default mounted in international financial circles. The most serious problem arose in Mexico. Mexico, like Iran under the Shah, responded to its new found oil wealth by launching a massive development program. Between 1978 and 1981 its economy grew by 8 percent a year; but inflation accelerated, reaching rates of more than 50 percent a year by 1982; corruption was rampant; and foreign banks, anxious to cash in on the boom and convinced that the country's oil reserves would assure its creditworthiness, flooded the country with loans. By 1982 Mexico had the largest debt of any country—$81 billion, but as a result of the world oil glut and the recession, demand for Mexican oil and nonoil exports slumped. In 1981, Mexico ran a current account deficit of $10.8 billion, its highest ever, and in February 1982 it was forced to devalue the peso. By the summer of 1982 it was clear that Mexico would not be able to meet its mounting debt burden, and investors, fearing that the peso would be devalued again, began withdrawing money from the country. In mid-August European bankers refused to refinance credits that were falling due, and in response the Mexican government closed foreign exchange markets and imposed foreign exchange controls— the first time it had taken such action.[19]

Soon after this the U.S. government, the Bank for International Settlements, the IMF, the leading foreign central banks, and the largest commercial banks put together a multibillion dollar rescue plan for Mexico. The foreign central banks agreed to loan Mexico $1.85 billion, with half of this coming from the United States. Mexico would also receive a $1 billion direct loan from the U.S. government, as a prepayment on purchases of Mexican crude for the strategic petroleum reserve, and another $1 billion U.S.–guaranteed loan from the commercial banks, to finance Mexican imports of U.S. farm products. The plan also provided for Mexico to work out conditions with the IMF, under which the IMF would extend $4.5 billion to Mexico, and the commercial banks agreed that if an IMF/Mexican agreement could be worked out, they would accept a moratorium on principal repayments, totaling $10 billion and due during the remainder of 1982, and would also extend an additional $500 million to $1 billion in new bank loans to Mexico. As part of this package, Mexico agreed to increase its crude oil exports to the United States and to charge no more than $35 for its oil, even if world prices climb higher. This marked the first time that an oil-exporting country had given a guarantee against future price increases. (The United States agreed that it would pay at least $25 for Mexican oil, even if world prices fell below this level.) Also, shortly after the rescue plan was worked out, Mexico, in an effort to prevent the flight of capital, nationalized its privately owned banks— a move that was welcomed by Mexico's foreign leaders, who saw it as putting the credit of the Mexican government behind the country's banking industry.[20]

The Mexican financial crisis focused new concern on the stability of the international financial system. Brazil—the Third World country with the second largest debt ($52.7 billion at the end of 1981), which like Mexico had embarked on an ambitious development program—and the nations of Eastern Europe pose substantial dangers. In addition, Argentina, whose economy has been seriously hurt by the war with Britain over the Falkland Islands, is considered to be particularly vulnerable to the risk of default, as are Chile, Peru, Colombia, Zaire, the Sudan and the Philippines. In an effort to respond to these problems, shortly after the Mexican rescue plan was worked out, the Reagan administration dropped its longstanding objections and agreed that IMF quotas (the amounts countries pay into the fund) should be increased, giving the fund greater resources with which to respond to future balance-of-payments crises. However, while many European nations are seeking quota increases of as much as 100 percent, the United States has indicated that what it envisions is an increase of about 25 percent. Moreover, even if this dispute is resolved, the IMF will not get these additional resources until 1985 at the earliest, making it likely that ad hoc arrangements will be required to respond to any crisis that arises during the next two years.[21]

Since the second shock, the developing countries have renewed their call for a new economic order, but so far have little to show for their efforts. At a fall 1981 meeting of the leaders of twenty-two industrialized and developing nations, held in Cancun, Mexico, for the purpose of planning an agenda for another round of North/South talks, they got only a lecture from President Reagan on the virtues of free enterprise and a vague agreement to hold further preparatory talks.[22]

THE CONSUMING COUNTRIES' RESPONSE TO THE SECOND SHOCK

Despite the 1979–80 oil-price increases, the consuming countries remain divided and their response to the crisis in energy supplies is inadequate. In 1979, as in 1974, many consuming countries sought to assure their oil supplies by concluding direct, government-to-government deals with the exporting countries. In the summer of 1979, France, which already received 30 percent of its oil through direct deals, got Iraq to agree to boost France's entitlement from 500,000 to 600,000 b/d. In return for the extra 100,000 b/d, France agreed to sell Iraq $1.6 billion worth of Mirage F-1s and other arms and to begin negotiations on Iraqi purchases of France's new Mirage Delta 2000 fighter plane. France also promised to deliver a controversial experimental nuclear reactor to Iraq in 1982.[23]

West Germany's state-controlled oil company, Deminex, obtained promises of expanded exploration rights and crude supplies from Libya. Italy's ENI concluded a two and one-half-year deal for 100,000 b/d with Saudi Arabia's Petromin, and in 1979, Sweden, Belgium, and Ireland became direct, government buyers for the first time. The Japanese are seeking to boost the amount of oil produced by Japanese companies or secured by government-to-government agreements to 30 percent by 1990. In the summer of 1979 they secured a 40 percent increase in their imports of Iraqi crude, from 96,000 to 140,000 b/d, and an agreement to purchase 100,000 b/d of Mexican oil.[24]

Of the major consuming countries, only the United States refrained from seeking direct deals on oil, but as former Secretary of Energy James Schlesinger stated, "Other countries are attempting to establish government deals by which they foreclose supplies to the United States. That can be tolerated by us only so long before we get into the competition."[25] By the winter of 1979–80, about one-sixth of the oil in world trade was committed to direct deals. However, with the market having softened, interest in such deals appears to have waned, as it did in 1975–76. Indeed, while between 1978 and 1980 the amount of oil traded in government-to-government deals increased by 3 to 4 mb/d, bringing it to an estimated 6.8–7.8 mb/d, since 1981 the quantities involved in such deals have fallen off almost as much as they had increased previously.[26] On the other hand, if the market tightens again, consuming-country competition for oil could get ugly. In any case, the 1979–80 scramble for oil put additional upward pressure on OPEC prices, and further divided the consuming countries.

In December 1979 the IEA members met to firm up the import quotas they had announced in June. While the United States wanted the countries to reduce their 1980 imports below the levels they had committed themselves to in June, neither the Europeans nor the Japanese agreed to this. They pledged to keep their 1980 imports at 23.1 mb/d, slightly below the 24.2 mb/d that was anticipated for 1979, but meeting this target was based on expectation of a recession. To achieve the 1980 goal, the Europeans agreed to accept country-by-country targets for 1980; however, they would not count North Sea oil as part of their import total.[27]

At this meeting the consuming countries agreed to reduce their 1985 imports from the 26 mb/d they pledged in June to 24.6 mb/d. As part of this agreement, Japan indicated that it would accept a target 6.3 mb/d, the lower end of the range it had committed itself to in June. However, neither the 1980 nor the 1985 targets were ironclad, and there were no sanctions to be applied in the event a country failed to meet its target. Nor were the targets accompanied by a set of actions that countries would take to ensure that they met the target levels. And though the targets were based on the amount of oil that OPEC was expected to export, there was no agreement on how a shortfall would be divided in the event that world oil exports fell short of demand. In addition, the United States indicated that it had done all it could, for the present, and that before it went further, it wanted other countries to take more positive action.[28]

After peaking in 1979, the industrial nations' oil consumption declined 7.5 percent in 1980 and another 6 percent in 1981. While the industrial countries pointed with pride to this accomplishment, it was largely a consequence of a slowdown in economic growth. The industrial countries' economies grew by only about 1 percent in both 1980 and 1981, compared with 3.6 percent in 1979 (see table A8). More significant was the decline in U.S. oil imports, from 8.4 mb/d in 1979 to 6.7 mb/d in 1980 and 5.7 mb/d in 1981—their lowest level since 1972.[29] Yet once economic growth picks up and the immediate impact of oil-price decontrol wears off, U.S. oil imports will undoubtedly increase.

In May 1980 the consuming countries took a significant step by working out a "quick-response plan" to impose legal ceilings on imports in the event the market tightens again.[30] Had such a plan existed in either 1973 or 1979, it probably would have greatly reduced the competitive upward bidding of prices and, as a result, the skyrocketing of prices might well have been contained. Whether this plan will be used and whether it will be effective remain to be seen, but the history of the emergency sharing plan is not an encouraging precedent.

Nor is the experience following the Iran-Iraq war encouraging. While in December 1980 the IEA countries set a loose import-reduction target of 2.2 mb/d for the first quarter of 1981, the plan did not fix import targets for individual countries. In fact, short of an extreme emergency, neither the IEA nor the consuming-country governments have the ability to smooth out allocations and prevent competitive bidding by the oil companies. And with companies reducing their inventories in response to softening world oil prices, the consuming countries' margin of safety is further reduced.[31]

When leaders of the seven leading consuming countries held their annual summit meeting in June 1980 in Venice, they vowed to double their use of coal by 1990[32] and to increase their reliance upon nuclear power and synthetic fuels. They also pledged to increase energy conservation. The leaders maintained that, as a result of these measures, by 1990 they would keep growth in their energy consumption at 60 percent of the growth in their GNP and would reduce the share of oil in their energy consumption from 53 percent to 40 percent. They maintained that this would enable supply and demand for oil to balance in 1990 "at tolerable prices."[33]

A year later, when the heads of state met in Ottawa, they were deeply divided over U.S. interest rates. President Reagan indicated that, to stem inflation, the United States was determined to maintain a restrictive monetary policy, but the leaders from Western Europe were bothered by the fact that a strong dollar tended to raise their oil import costs. Moreover, to prevent a flight of capital to the United States, they were forced to pursue restrictive policies as well, aggravating their serious problems of unemployment and choking off whatever hope of economic recovery they still harbored.[34]

Other differences in interest and approach continue to divide the consuming countries, impeding the prospects for consumer-country cooperation. Their EEC partners have asked Great Britain and the Netherlands to give assurances that, in another supply shortfall, they would increase their production of oil and gas. Yet both countries refused to provide such assurances. West Germany and Switzerland want to rely on higher prices to resolve the crisis, whereas the United States has advocated fixed import quotas and France has advocated market controls. France has proposed placing controls on the spot market, but Germany is unreceptive to this, partly because, historically, its internal market has depended on the spot market for an important part of its oil-product supplies. Moreover, as a Washington official charged, West Germany and Japan act as though "they can buy their way out" of the oil crisis.[35]

Although the Europeans recognize that they need the United States to maintain the security of their oil lines and to mediate the Arab-Israeli conflict, they have pursued an independent approach to the Middle East countries. Steps are being taken to strengthen the Euro-Arab dialogue, and an agreement whereby the Gulf exporting countries guarantee long-term oil supplies to Europe, in exchange for access to Europe's markets, technology, and possible military assistance, has been discussed. To buttress France's special relationship with the Arab states,

French President Giscard traveled to the Middle East in March 1980, pledging support for Palestinian "self-determination" and endorsing the participation of the PLO in Middle East peace talks. Then, in June, the EEC backed full self-determination for the Palestinian people and declared that the PLO should be "associated with" negotiations for a Middle East peace settlement.[36]

There has also been renewed discussion about a consumer/producer dialogue. As early as February 1979, Saudi Arabia called for a meeting of industrialized and exporting countries, and a month later the EEC endorsed the idea of a consumer/producer dialogue. At their meeting in December 1979, the IEA members vowed to pursue all openings for a dialogue with the exporting countries. Also in December, the OECD suggested that consuming governments join moderate OPEC governments in a pact that would guarantee the former the supplies they require in return for an agreement to keep real oil prices rising at a steady but moderate pace. Since it would make price explosions like the one in 1979 less likely, Yamani is reported to favor such an arrangement. However, plans for convening a meeting of oil-exporting and oil-consuming governments have foundered on OPEC's insistence that it not be confined to energy. Moreover, given the lack of unity among the consuming and the exporting countries, it is difficult to see how they could negotiate a meaningful agreement with each other.[37]

Since the 1979 price hikes, OPEC has also come under increasing pressure from the non-OPEC LDCs. While the OPEC countries, as a group, have increased their aid to these countries, they rule out the possibility of preferential pricing. Yet if a full-fledged North/South dialogue gets under way, OPEC may be willing to trade concessions on oil pricing for concessions to the Third World on the part of the industrialized countries.[38]

On the national level, the 1979 rise in oil prices led President Carter to propose a bold new series of U.S. energy measures. On April 5, 1979, he announced that, beginning June 1, he would phase out oil-price controls. To recoup some of the revenues that would accrue to the oil companies as a result, Carter proposed that Congress enact a windfall profits tax, and on June 1, 1979, controls were removed from all newly discovered oil. On January 1, 1980, the price of both upper and lower tier oil began increasing in monthly installments—a process that was to culminate in the removal of all oil-price controls on October 1, 1981. As such, the plan fell slightly short of the president's pledge, made at the Bonn economic summit in 1978, to raise U.S. oil prices to world levels by 1980. At the time of the president's announcement, lower tier oil was selling for $5.85, upper tier oil for about $13, and the world oil price was about $18.[39]

Since the president had the authority to take these actions, no legislation was required for these price increases to occur; however, the windfall profits (or "excise") tax required congressional action. The president proposed that Congress levy a tax of 50 percent on the difference between the current price of upper and lower tier oil and the price it would rise to as a result of his actions. These taxes would be phased out by 1990. In addition, the president proposed the so-called "OPEC tax," a 50 percent tax on the difference between a base price of $16 and the future price of decontrolled oil. This tax, which would be permanent, was intended to prevent oil companies from gaining the full benefits of future OPEC price increases.

Since the companies' profits would be subject to the usual state and federal taxes, the administration estimated that, under its proposal, between 1979 and 1981 the companies would end up with about a third of the increased revenues stemming from decontrol, or an additional $6 billion in after-tax profits. The federal government would get $8.4 billion and state and local governments more than $2 billion. The president proposed to use the federal revenues from the windfall profits tax for development of synthetic fuels, mass transit, and aid to the poor.[40] According to the Congressional Budget Office, Carter's decontrol plan would mean a reduction in oil imports of 620,000 b/d: 405,000 through increased production and 215,000 through increased conservation; but CBO also pointed out that "a significant percentage of this oil . . . represents production that would have become available at a later date as prices increased."[41]

Following further OPEC price increases and the gasoline crisis in the United States, in mid-July the president announced several new measures. He imposed an oil import quota of 8.2 mb/d for 1979—300,000 b/d less than the pledge he had made at the economic summit in Tokyo. While the president pointed to this measure as indicative of the toughness of the U.S. response, in 1979 U.S. oil imports were not expected to exceed this level.[42]

With the June rise in OPEC prices, revenues from the windfall profits tax were expected to increase, reaching $146 billion over the next ten years. Of this enormous sum, the president proposed to spend $88 billion on a crash program to develop synthetic fuels. An Energy Security Corporation, similar to President Ford's proposed Energy Independence Authority, would be created to distribute this money to private industry. As envisioned by President Carter, the Energy Security Corporation would facilitate private development, and undertake that development itself only as a last resort.

The president proposed using $24 billion of the $146 billion to aid low-income groups. Ten billion dollars was to go for mass transit and $6.5 billion to increasing automobile fuel efficiency. The remaining $17.5 billion was to provide tax credits for shale oil, solar energy, and residential and commercial conservation; to encourage utilities to switch to coal; and to promote development of unconventional natural gas.[43] The president also proposed creation of an Energy Mobilization Board to speed development of energy projects, and he decontrolled the price of heavy crude oil.

After a year of debate, at the end of March Congress approved its windfall profits tax, and a few days later the president signed it into law. It was believed to be the largest tax ever levied on an industry. Yet, as Russell B. Long, chairman of the Senate Finance Committee stated, "You're not going to see anyone applying for welfare because he has to pay this tax." Of the $1,000 billion in extra revenue that decontrol was expected to produce, the oil companies would end up with 22 percent after taxes.[44]

The final measure was considerably more generous to the oil industry than what the president initially proposed. By 1990 the final legislation was expected to raise somewhat less than the $280 billion that the original Carter measures would have raised at the new OPEC prices prevailing at the time the bill was passed. More significantly, while the "OPEC tax" that Carter proposed was to be permanent, the measures passed by Congress are to be phased out beginning in January 1988, or after they raise $227.3 billion, whichever is later.[45] Once the tax is phased out, the industry will be left with an enormous windfall.

In addition, any oil produced by a state or local government is exempted from the tax, which will give the oil-producing states huge additional revenues. The final legislation also contained special benefits for small, independent producers. On the oil they discovered before 1979, the majors will be taxed at 70 percent of the difference between $12.89 (the base price) and the price it is sold at, but independents have to pay a tax of only 50 percent on this oil. On "stripper" oil (from wells producing fewer than 11 barrels a day), the majors will be taxed at 60 percent of the difference between $15.30 and the sales price, while the independents pay only 30 percent. On oil discovered after 1978, "heavy" oil, and tertiary oil, both the majors and the independents are taxed at 30 percent of the difference between $16.55 and the sales price.

There are also special benefits for Alaskan oil. While Alaskan oil from the Sadlerochit Reservoir and within 75 miles of the Alaska pipeline will be taxed at 70 percent, on a base price of $13, all other Alaskan oil will be exempt from the tax. The various base prices are to be adjusted periodically for inflation. In addition, while the independents retain their full 22 percent depletion allowance, worth about $13 billion to the companies, the majors get a 30 percent depletion allowance on newly discovered oil. The final legislation contained recommendations on allocating the revenues from the windfall profits tax, but these are not binding; the funds go into general federal revenues.[46]

Upon taking office in January 1981, President Reagan decided to speed up the Carter decontrol program. As of January 28, 1981, he abolished the crude oil entitlements program and all remaining price controls on domestic oil and gasoline—which was estimated to add $2 billion to oil industry coffers. In addition, the oil industry received $11.7 billion worth of special relief as a result of the Reagan-backed tax law enacted in 1981.[47]

The Reagan administration has also been considering removal of all remaining controls on natural gas prices, but decided to delay any such move until after the 1982 elections. Nonetheless, the Federal Energy Regulatory Commission has continued to increase natural gas prices through administrative actions, and gas prices have been rising more rapidly than contemplated under the 1978 Natural Gas Act because producers have learned to take advantage of the complicated classificatory scheme created by the act.[48]

In June 1980, Congress agreed to establishment of a Synthetic Fuels Corporation that will provide legal and financial assistance for development of a synthetic fuels industry. The initial legislation aimed at producing 500,000 b/d of synthetic fuels by 1987 and 2 mb/d by 1992, but under the Reagan administration the target has been reduced to 500,000 b/d by 1990. To induce private companies to produce synthetic fuels, the government-sponsored corporation is authorized to provide loan purchases and price guarantees and up to $20 billion in backup funds.[49]

Also in June 1980, Congress rejected the third part of the energy program that President Carter had proposed the previous July, the Energy Mobilization Board. Conservatives saw it as adding another layer to the bureaucracy and interfering with states' rights, and liberals believed it would be used to back harmful technologies and override environmental safeguards.[50]

In May 1980 the Carter administration had decided to resume filling the strategic petroleum reserve. To ease pressure on the world petroleum market, purchases for the reserve had been suspended in March 1979. Then, in July 1979, when Saudi Arabia raised its oil production, it made it clear that it was not boosting production to enable the United States to fill the SPR. The Saudis later threatened to reduce production if the United States resumed filling the reserve—a threat Yamani enunciated after Carter's May decision but never followed through on. The Saudis oppose the SPR because they believe that, in making the United States less vulnerable to a loss of oil supplies, it will make the United States less responsive to Saudi security and foreign-policy concerns, and once the United States resumed filling the reserve, the Saudis became vulnerable to the charge that they were boosting production to help the United States withstand a future embargo. Despite these Saudi concerns, by the spring of 1980 the world oil market had eased and the administration was coming under increasing pressure from Congress to resume purchases for the reserve. While purchases for the SPR have been continuing, it is still several years short of a reasonably safe level.[51]

Also, in March 1980 President Carter imposed a $4.62 a barrel oil import fee that was aimed at raising gasoline prices 10¢ a gallon, but Congress by early June had voted overwhelmingly to repeal the fee. Carter vetoed the congressional repeal but Congress overrode his veto—the first time since 1952 that a presidential veto had been overridden by a Congress controlled by the same party as the president. Congress's rejection was doubly embarrassing to the president, since he wanted the fee in place, before the economic summit meeting in June, to demonstrate the seriousness of the United States' commitment to reducing its oil consumption. Nonetheless, the administration decided not to submit new proposals to make up for loss of the import fee, deeming it futile to attempt to get Congress to take any action that would raise gasoline prices in an election year.[52] While the import fee was ill conceived, the episode demonstrates how hard it is for the federal government to adopt the tough legislative measures that are needed to deal effectively with the oil crisis. Moreover, with the Reagan administration having proposed abolition of the Department of Energy (with most of its functions to be transferred to the Department of Commerce) and generally pursuing a policy of laissez-faire in this area, it is unlikely that such measures will be adopted in the immediate future. In March 1982, President Reagan vetoed a bill that would have given him authority to allocate oil and control its price in any future supply emergency. The federal government has no plan for handling a future oil cutoff, and as the General Accounting Office recently found, "The U.S. government is almost totally unprepared to deal with disruptions in oil imports."[53]

U.S. energy policy also continues to suffer from overemphasis on encouraging development of domestic oil and gas, a dubious prospect at best. By boosting company profits on U.S. oil, the administration ensured that more money would be spent on boosting U.S. supplies, but from the perspective of boosting total world energy supplies, that is a misallocation of resources. At the same time, the United States has no program for encouraging development of oil and gas resources in the non-OPEC LDCs. In addition, more than a year of congressional time was spent on the windfall profits tax, but, even so, the effect of the decontrol program will be extremely regressive.[54] Nor does the windfall profits tax do anything to recoup the gains the oil companies will derive from higher natural gas prices, despite the fact that these, too, are pulled up by the effect of higher world oil prices.

One area in which the Carter administration failed to propose new initiatives is nuclear power, nor is there any mystery about this. On March 28 a breakdown occurred in the cooling system of the Three Mile Island nuclear reactor near Harrisburg, Pennsylvania, and led to radiation releases, the spilling of radioactive water, and a hydrogen bubble within the containment vessel that threatened a gas explosion. It was as close as any reactor had ever come to a catastrophic meltdown, which would spill large, lethal doses of radioactivity into the countryside. A study later concluded that if a shift foreman had not blocked off a stuck-open valve when he noticed that it was leaking reactor coolant, two hours after the accident began, the reactor fuel would have begun to melt down within 30 to 60 minutes.[55] While officials from the Nuclear Regulatory Commission in Washington rushed in to get the reactor under control, the governor of Pennsylvania, Richard Thornburgh, ordered women and young children to evacuate the area.

Even before Three Mile Island, nuclear power was in trouble. As we have seen, projections for nuclear power have consistently declined. In the United States, thirty-four reactors were ordered in 1973 and seventeen in 1974, but between 1975 and 1978, reactor orders averaged fewer than four a year.[56] Before TMI, in March 1979 the Nuclear Regulatory Commission ordered five reactors to shut down because of questions about their ability to withstand earthquakes. There was also growing concern about the problem of nuclear wastes, the risks of low-level radiation, and the dangers of transporting nuclear materials. In addition, while technically it takes five years to build a nuclear reactor, in the United States the lead time for construction of a nuclear reactor has been extended to ten to fourteen years as a result of regulatory delays.[57]

To remain viable, nuclear power needs government help, but largely because of the opposition aroused by TMI, the government has been unable to extend that help. Indeed, in his April 5 address to the nation, President Carter planned to announce proposals for licensing reform, intended to cut the lead time for building a nuclear plant to seven years, but because of TMI, he struck them from his speech. And as concern for nuclear safety increases, new regulations are instituted that further increase nuclear costs. Since TMI, the NRC has mandated more than 100 improvements that, it says, will cost $30 million per reactor, and the nuclear industry claims that the costs will be even higher.[58]

In the wake of TMI, regulatory uncertainty has become a greater barrier to nuclear expansion. The NRC refused to license new reactors until new regulations, developed in the wake of TMI, were promulgated. TMI has also made the siting of nuclear plants increasingly difficult, because of increased public opposition to nuclear power and because the NRC now requires plans for evacuating all persons within 10 miles of a nuclear plant. (In June 1980, Congress made this a statutory requirement.)[59]

In response to TMI, President Carter declared that it is impossible to "abandon" nuclear power. Yet, while nuclear power accounted for 12.5 percent of U.S. electricity consumption in 1978, by 1980 the figure had fallen to 11 percent.[60] Since TMI, no new reactor orders have been placed in the United States. Prior to TMI, the Energy Department projected U.S. nuclear capacity at 114,000 MW by 1985 and 152,000 MW by 1990; since TMI, these projections have been reduced to 95,000 MW in 1985 and 129,000 MW in 1990.[61]

Still, with more than ninety nuclear plants currently under construction, U.S. dependence on nuclear power is expected to rise from 11 percent of electricity consumption in 1980 to 20 percent in 1985. These partly built plants represent the energy equivalent of about 2 mb/d of oil. Moreover, the nuclear industry is betting that if given a choice between blackouts and brownouts or increased nuclear power (a choice they say is inevitable), the public will choose nuclear.[62] President Reagan, who is seeking to brighten the prospects for nuclear power, announced in October 1981 that he was lifting the ban on reprocessing that President Carter imposed in 1977 and moving ahead with the Clinch River breeder reactor. In addition, he directed Energy Secretary James Edwards to give high priority to recommending a way to speed the licensing process, so that new reactors can be built in six to eight (rather than ten to fourteen) years. And he stated that his administration is committed to moving swiftly to install facilities for the permanent disposal of nuclear waste. Despite the president's statement, no repository is expected to be available until 1997 or 1998 at the earliest; yet the spent fuel pools (that currently store the waste on a "temporary" basis) at 27 of the country's 73 operating reactors are expected to be filled by 1990.[63]

Outside the United States, TMI had its greatest impact on West Germany, where, in response to the accident in Pennsylvania, 35,000 people demonstrated against nuclear power. As a result of public opposition, the West German government agreed to indefinite postponement of the nuclear reprocessing plant and waste disposal facility it was building at Gorlebon. Yet, like nearly all other European governments, the West German government remains committed to nuclear power. Nonetheless, as in the United States, the West German nuclear program has faced a de facto moratorium on new reactor orders in recent years.[64]

In France, in contrast to West Germany, the Giscard government largely ignored nuclear protests and moved ahead with its nuclear program, and in response to the 1979 oil crisis, France decided to accelerate its reliance upon nuclear power. It announced plans to boost nuclear's share from 13 percent of electricity production in 1979 to 50 percent by 1985. France also plans to have the non-Communist world's first commercial breeder reactor, the 1,200-MW Superphenix, in operation by 1983, and is planning two more "breeders" to demonstrate that breeder production costs can be reduced significantly. Following his election in the spring of 1981 President François Mitterand undertook a reevaluation of these plans, but by November 1981 his administration had endorsed the basic framework of the previous conservative government's program. Britain, Canada, Japan, Italy, West Germany, Belgium, the Netherlands, and the Soviet Union are also building breeder reactors or doing research on them.[65]

Following the fall of the Falldin government in October 1978, Sweden has reembarked on a nuclear course. In March 1980 a national referendum was held and 61.4 percent of Swedish voters opted for at least some expansion of nuclear power. The Swedish government therefore plans to increase the number of nuclear reactors from six to twelve.[66]

After the United States, Japan has the next largest nuclear capacity; however, its nuclear program has been plagued by siting and operating problems. After the TMI accident, Japan ordered its eight pressurized water reactors—the kind that malfunctioned at TMI—shut down for safety checks. Nonetheless, in response to the 1979 rise in oil prices, Japan announced plans to double its nuclear capacity by 1985. In fact, in recent years France and Japan have been the only OECD countries to have steadily moved ahead with their nuclear power programs. While nuclear power now accounts for 13 percent of the industrial countries' electricity, this is less than half of what had been forecast ten years ago for this period.[67]

THE IMPACT OF THE SECOND SHOCK ON THE INTERNATIONAL OIL COMPANIES

In 1979–80, as in 1974, the rise in OPEC prices led to remarkably profitable years for the oil companies. According to *Business Week,* in 1979 U.S. oil companies had an average return on common equity of 21.5 percent, compared with the all-industry composite of 16.6 percent. In 1980 the oil companies' return was 23.8 percent, compared with the all-industry composite of 15.3 percent. In contrast, in 1978 the oil companies' average return was only 13.9 percent, compared with the all-industry composite of 15.1 percent. By 1981 the oil companies' return had fallen to 18.6 percent, but it was still above the all-industry composite of 14.0 percent.[68]

Several factors combined to produce these extraordinary profits. When prices went up, companies could sell the oil they had in inventory at a substantial gain. Although changes in accounting methods tended to make inventory profits a lesser factor in the 1979–80 oil profits boom than they had been in 1974, they were still significant. As in 1974, in 1979–80 companies with access to crude at official OPEC prices were able to earn windfall profits by selling it either as crude or as products at the skyrocketing market prices.

Particularly important in this respect was the situation of the Aramco partners, which enjoyed access to lower-priced Saudi crude for much of 1979–81. While the Saudis insisted that the companies pass on their lower prices until the crude entered a refinery, the Saudis acknowledged that they could not control it beyond that point. Consequently, outside the United States, the companies were able to sell the products they made with lower-priced crude for the same amount that other companies charged for their products, pocketing the resulting windfalls. Even in the United States, where up until 1981 price controls put limits on this practice, it could be done to some extent. Moreover, the Aramco partners could bring their higher-priced crude from other sources into the United States, where it would be subject to fixed profit margins, while selling the lower-priced Saudi crude outside the United States.[69]

As OPEC prices rose and crude markets tightened, companies were also able to earn substantial profits by increasing the prices of their non-OPEC production. Indeed, prices went up on North Sea, Canadian, Alaskan, and continental U.S. oil—the latter being made possible by President Carter's program of price decontrol. Moreover, while the popular conception is that higher OPEC prices pulled these other prices up, the reality is that when markets tightened, the price of non-OPEC crude often went up first and reached higher levels than did OPEC prices. In January 1979, North Sea suppliers raised their prices before OPEC did, but without the publicity OPEC receives. At the end of 1979, when OPEC prices clustered around $26, Mexico set $32 for its crude, and in the winter of 1979–80 decontrolled light Texas crudes were selling for $37 a barrel, $3 more than equivalent African or Mideast crudes.[70]

In addition, when markets tightened, the companies were able to raise product prices in the formerly depressed European product markets. Competition from the previously low-priced spot market had been a barrier to this, but with spot prices soaring, this was no longer the case, nor were there controls in most European product markets to limit the prices the companies charged. Similarly, in the United States the companies were able to raise prices substantially on those products that had been decontrolled. For example, between December 1978 and the fall of 1979 retail prices for home heating oil in the United States increased from 55¢ to 80¢ a gallon and wholesale margins widened from 6–8¢ a gallon to

11¢. White House economic officials found that increases in world oil prices could account for only half of the increase in domestic product prices.[71] In addition, profits on the companies' petrochemical operations increased in 1979. Finally, as a result of the increase in oil prices, the value of the companies' oil reserves increased enormously. In fact, in 1979 alone the increase in U.S. oil prices boosted the value of the domestic reserves of the fifteen largest U.S. oil companies from $20 billion to $57 billion, an increase that was nearly three times their reported profits.[72]

Yet many long-term consequences of the 1979–80 oil crisis were not nearly so favorable for the major oil companies. By the fourth quarter of 1980, oil company profits had begun to level out, and by the first quarter of 1981 they had declined below their year-earlier levels. The end of the upward world oil-price spiral, the impact of the windfall profits tax, and the sluggishness of demand for products all played a role in this. Moreover, with Saudi prices higher than those of other OPEC members, who discounted heavily, by 1982 the Aramco partners advantage on Saudi crude, had turned into a disadvantage, costing them several dollars a barrel.

During 1981, the impact of price decontrol only partially offset the decline in U.S. companies' earnings from foreign operations.[73] Longer term, the rise in oil prices and the consequent reduction in oil consumption will only aggravate the surplus of refining capacity in Western Europe and the United States. In fact, once the crude oil market eased, competitive pressures reasserted themselves in the refining industry. As a result, by the first quarter of 1981 only refiners with access to the cheaper Saudi crude were able to make a profit from the sale of petroleum products. Moreover, the desire of OPEC countries to "get into" refining and the reluctance of consuming countries to "export" their refining needs threatens to aggravate the surplus in refining capacity, and small U.S. refiners will be particularly hurt by the elimination of the U.S. entitlements program.

Indeed, between January 1981 and March 1982 more than fifty of the nation's 324 refineries went out of business. Similarly, the industry's other downstream operations—transportation, chemicals, and retailing—have been hurt by the rise in prices and consequent decline in demand. Moreover, with upstream profits leveling off and demand for petroleum products in the industrialized countries expected to continue to decline, the companies are more carefully scrutinizing their downstream operations, withdrawing from unprofitable markets.[74] As a result of developments in 1979, the majors' privileged access to OPEC oil and their control over marketing were seriously eroded. According to estimates by Paul Frankel, the seven largest oil companies, which controlled 70 percent of OPEC's oil in 1975 and 55 percent in 1978, controlled only about 45 percent in early 1980.[75]

Iran, which formerly sold most of its oil through the Consortium, now markets all its oil itself. While the Bazargan government initially considered a new arrangement with the Consortium, opposition from the Iranian oil workers prevented this; consequently, the companies that comprised the Consortium no longer get either a discount on Iranian oil or privileged access to it. While Iran has concluded sales agreements with several companies that comprised the Consortium, they receive much less oil than in the past. For example, after Iran resumed production in the spring of 1979, it concluded sales agreements with BP and Shell, but the agreements provided these companies less than half the oil they received previously. Ironically, prior to his downfall, the Shah had pressed the Consortium to increase its liftings, but the companies had resisted.[76]

Similarly, before its war with Iran, Iraq had cut sales to Western companies in half and sent more of its oil to non-OPEC LDCs. In 1979 Kuwait sold two-thirds of its production to three companies, but in 1980 it reduced this figure to less than one-third, cutting Gulf Oil from 550,000 to 75,000 b/d, British Petroleum from 450,000 to 150,000 b/d, and Royal Dutch/Shell from 360,000 to 175,000 b/d. Kuwait indicated that by 1984 it hopes to sell half its crude as finished products and to transport more than 45 percent of it in its own tankers.[77]

On January 1, 1980, Venezuela also reduced the amount of oil it marketed through the companies, from 65 percent to 50 percent, and at the end of July 1979, BP lost another 276,000 b/d when its operations in Nigeria were nationalized. Nigeria's action was a warning to the British government, which owns half of BP, not to recognize the conservative government that held power in Zimbabwe-Rhodesia or to remove the sanctions that Britain imposed on Rhodesia in 1965.[78] On April 1, 1980, Nigeria reduced the supplies available on contract to other companies operating in the country. Finally, in 1979 Saudi Arabia reduced the amount of oil it sold to the Aramco partners from 7.5 to 6.5 mb/d. The Saudi government then diverted the additional state supplies to non-OPEC LDCs with which it wished to improve relations.[79]

For the first time, as a result of these actions by the exporting countries, the seven major companies found that, together, they had less crude than their refineries required. According to *Petroleum Intelligence Weekly,* in early 1980 these seven companies were forced to obtain 7 percent of their basic needs, or about 1.5 mb/d, on the open market. While Royal Dutch/Shell and Mobil had long been net purchasers of crude, as a result of developments in 1979–80 BP, Exxon, SoCal, and Gulf also found themselves in this situation. With the easing of the world oil market this situation reversed again; nonetheless, while the seven major oil companies' crude supplies exceeded their refining needs by 6.7 mb/d in 1973, by 1978 this was down to 3.65 mb/d and by 1981 to 2.35 mb/d. Moreover, increasingly these companies are shifting the composition of their supplies to crude-oil sources in the industrialized countries.[80]

In 1979 the name of the game became ''hold onto supply.'' Companies were willing to make special deals and pay premiums to lock up supplies. As part of this trend, the majors greatly reduced their third-party sales to the independents, which have had to respond by purchasing more of their oil directly from the exporting countries. However, because of the majors' strength in downstream markets, the independents are likely to increase their market shares only if they secure an independent crude base.[81]

Then, as the market eased in 1980 and 1981, the companies became less concerned about "access to crude" and "security of supply." Consequently, they began to take a tougher line in bargaining about crude prices. Deeming the asking prices "too high," in the summer of 1981 oil companies suspended or phased out an estimated 700,000 b/d in purchases from Mexico, 1 mb/d from Libya, Nigeria, and Algeria, and 500,000 b/d from Kuwait, Indonesia, and the United Arab Emirates.[82] This new aggressiveness on the part of the companies is largely the consequence of a soft market, but it also reflects looser ties between exporting country and company. With the concessions gone and the companies' equity entirely dissolved in many exporting countries, the companies have much less to lose in bargaining over prices. Nonetheless, without assured sources of supply the companies could get caught short, if the market were to tighten again.

In November 1981 Exxon announced that it was ending its operations in Libya—the first time in years that an oil company had voluntarily given up an equity interest in a Middle Eastern/North African production operation. Exxon's move was prompted by the high price of Libyan oil, which meant that it was losing money on every barrel it produced. With oil readily available on the world market and with the Reagan administration threatening to boycott Libyan oil and withdraw U.S. personnel (moves it undertook shortly after the Exxon withdrawal), the benefits of a continued presence in Libya were not worth the political and security risks. Exxon was also concerned about the safety of its U.S. employees, most of whom lived in an area where they were thought to be more vulnerable to attack by Libyans than were the employees of other U.S. companies, who tended to live throughout Tripoli's suburbs. Exxon's diverse worldwide supply sources also made it less dependent upon its Libyan production than were the other U.S. companies that operated in the country. Libya, anxious to improve its image with Western oil companies, agreed to compensate Exxon for the assets it gave up.[83]

Despite their new boldness, the oil companies were not above "maintaining relationships" when they thought this necessary to their long-term interests. Thus when Saudi production fell sharply for short periods in both January and February 1982, the Aramco partners, who had benefited handsomely from Saudi Arabia's lower prices during 1979–81, quickly agreed to buy more oil from the kingdom, though they had little immediate need for it and could find cheaper oil elsewhere. A senior executive with one of the four Aramco partners explained that "when we have a long-term relationship with a supplier, we try to keep a long-term relationship with a supplier, even when it is painful as it is now." Then, in March, fear developed that if oil companies shifted their purchases from Nigeria to North Sea crude, selling for $5.50 less, Nigeria might be forced to cut prices, undermining the March 19 OPEC agreement. Saudi Arabia and Kuwait, therefore, threatened to deny crude supplies to any companies whose purchases of Nigerian oil fell below the levels prevailing before the OPEC meeting. Several companies without extensive interests in Saudi Arabia or Kuwait failed to respond to this pressure, but Mobil agreed to increase its liftings from Nigeria above levels previously planned and other companies that were buying oil from Nigeria agreed to continue doing so for at least a month. Subsequently, demand for Nigerian oil increased, alleviating the crisis.[84]

The events of 1979–80 will also reduce future consumption of oil and lead to greater emphasis on alternative energy sources and conservation—trends that threaten the oil companies' dominance of world energy markets—but the companies have responded in various ways. Following the price rises, SoCal and Texaco began investing heavily in synthetic fuels. In 1981 Gulf made two acquisitions that, together, enabled it to boost its coal producing capacity by 50 percent. Mobil, a leader in the industry's diversification efforts, has been trying to boost its domestic energy reserves, acquiring General Crude Oil Company for $782 million in 1979 and Transocean Oil for $740 million in 1980.[85]

BP, which lost 1.35 mb/d in guaranteed crude supplies in Iran, Kuwait, and Nigeria, launched a $2.6 billion capital spending program aimed at doubling its exploration and production facilities and increasing its refining and trading operations. Not only did it increase its activity in Alaska and the North Sea, it initiated exploration projects in twenty countries. However, because of a lack of "suitable acreage" worldwide, BP's 1980 exploration program was less extensive than the company had hoped initially. Nonetheless, its strong position in both Alaska and the North Sea have enabled the company to compensate for its diminished role in the OPEC countries. On September 1, 1979, following its nationalization in Nigeria, BP suspended all of its crude sales to third parties, and in 1980 made its first major nonenergy acquisition, spending $1 billion to acquire Selection Trust, a minerals company.[86]

Exxon, which lost 600,000 b/d in guaranteed supplies from Iran and Kuwait,[87] responded to the 1979–80 oil crisis by strengthening its position in non-oil sectors. In 1979, for the first time, the world's largest oil company spent more of its research money on nonpetroleum than on petroleum forms of energy. Since the 1979 crisis, Exxon has also gotten involved in three major unconventional hydrocarbon projects. In May 1980 it bought ARCO's 60 percent share of the Colony oil shale project for $400 million. In February 1980 it announced that it would join two Australian firms in producing shale oil in Australia; and a few months before that, Exxon's Canadian affiliate, Imperial Oil Ltd., announced plans for a $6 billion, 160,000 b/d heavy oil project in Cold Lake, Alberta. However, by 1982 all three of these projects had been tabled.[88]

In 1979 Exxon also spent $1.2 billion to acquire Reliance Electric. At the time of the acquisition, Exxon claimed it wanted Reliance in order to develop and market a more efficient electric motor, but two years later Exxon announced that plans to develop the motor had been abandoned. Many industry observers believe that Exxon's real interest in Reliance is to produce and market an electric car.[89]

Other recent oil company acquisitions in nonenergy fields include Sohio's $1.8 billion purchase of Kennecott, the nation's largest copper producer; Indiana Standard's $760 million acquisition of Cyprus Mines, a copper producer; Elf-Acquitaine's $2.7 billion takeover of Texasgulf, a chemicals and natural resources company; Ashland's 1980 purchase of U.S. Filter, an engineering services and pollution control equipment company, and Integon Corporation, an insurance company, for a total of more than $500 million; and Occidental's $831 million takeover of Iowa Beef Processors.[90]

Policies of the consuming countries have also encouraged oil company acquisitions. In 1979 President Carter's decision to decontrol heavy oil triggered a bidding war between Shell and Mobil/Texaco, bidding jointly. Their object was the Belridge Oil Company, which held large reserves of heavy crude in California. Shell eventually won, paying $3.7 billion for Belridge, in what was then the highest-priced corporate takeover in U.S. history. Shell planned to use enhanced recovery techniques, still under development, to extract much more of Belridge's tar-like heavy crude than is possible with conventional methods.[91]

In October 1980 Canadian Prime Minister Elliott Trudeau announced a program to boost domestic ownership of the Canadian oil industry from 28 percent to at least 50 percent by 1990. To achieve this goal, PetroCanada is to acquire several foreign-owned oil companies, and special benefits are provided for private oil companies owned by Canadian nationals. In February 1981, as part of this program, PetroCanada took over Belgian-owned Petrofina Canada. The national oil company's move put it on a par, in terms of book value, with Canada's largest privately owned oil company, Imperial Oil, an Exxon subsidiary.[92]

In May 1981 Dome Petroleum took advantage of the new Canadian policy by buying a 20 percent stake in Conoco for $65 a share and swapping it for Conoco's controlling interest in Hudson's Bay Oil and Gas, a company with large holdings of Canadian acreage. Under Conoco's control, Hudson would not qualify for incentive grants under the Canadian program, but under Dome's control it would be eligible for the maximum incentive, 80¢ for every $1 spent for exploration in high-risk frontier areas.[93] However, Dome's move exposed Conoco as a company vulnerable to takeover. In June, after Conoco's management had spurned several private offers, Seagram began publicly bidding for Conoco, offering $73 a share and triggering the most expensive bidding war for a corporation in history. Conoco's initial response to the Seagram proposal was to seek a merger with Cities Service, but when Seagram upped its bid, the talks between Conoco and Cities Service broke off. Conoco then began talks with Texaco for a cash merger. DuPont soon entered the picture, offering $87.50 a share for 100 percent of Conoco, and then Mobil entered the fray with a bid of $90 a share.

Eventually, DuPont emerged as the winner, paying $7.57 billion, or $98 a share, in the most costly corporate takeover in history. While Mobil raised its offer to $120 a share, the possibility that a merger between the second- and ninth-largest U.S. oil companies would be blocked by the Justice Department made this offer less attractive. (DuPont had already received antitrust clearance.) The merger made DuPont the seventh largest industrial enterprise in the United States. In May, before the bidding started, Conoco was trading for about $50 a share.[94]

The DuPont-Conoco merger was seen as the first of a new wave of takeovers, with Cities Service, Marathon, and Pennzoil as likely targets. Several factors have combined to make these second-tier companies attractive takeover targets. As a result of the 1979–80 rise in world oil prices and the removal of U.S. price controls, the value of these companies' oil reserves has increased enormously, yet, because of the softening of the world oil market and the leveling off of oil company profits, between December 1980 and May 1981, the stock market prices of many of these companies fell by 30–40 percent. The combined effect of these developments reduced the stock prices of many of these companies to only about half their asset value. It has therefore become cheaper to buy oil reserves on Wall Street than to go out and explore for new resources.[95]

At the same time, because of the enormous profits they amassed during 1979–80, many of the major oil companies have huge quantities of cash on hand, and since investing in the Third World is limited by the political risks involved, the companies are attracted to investment opportunities in the United States. In addition, oil companies and chemical companies (such as DuPont), which rely on hydrocarbons for their feedstocks, are anxious to lock up a secure crude supply to meet their own needs, particularly since supplies from the exporting countries have become so insecure.

DuPont claimed that by acquiring Conoco it could reduce the volatility of its earnings, for when oil prices shoot up, chemical industry profits tend to fall, but oil company profits go up. The new emphasis on alternative energy sources also made Conoco attractive, for Conoco owns Consolidated Coal, the largest holder of coal reserves in the United States, and Conoco has been particularly active in developing synthetic fuel technologies. Moreover, the prospect of oil-price increases and the Reagan administration's pro-energy-industry policies and permissive attitude toward mergers helped to spark the bidding for Conoco.[96]

Three months after the Conoco takeover, Mobil offered to pay $85 a share for 67 percent of Marathon Oil Company, then selling for $67. What was particularly attractive about Marathon was that it owned 49 percent of the Yates field, the largest oil field in the continental United States. In an effort to avoid the Mobil takeover, Marathon's management agreed to have the company be acquired by U.S. Steel, which agreed to pay $125 for 51 percent of Marathon's stock and 12.5 percent U.S. Steel notes with a face value of $100 for the remainder (a $6.2 billion package). Mobil quickly countered by raising its offer to $126 a share. However, Mobil again encountered legal obstacles, with a district court ruling that its bid would violate antitrust law, and the FTC threatening to sue if it proceeded with its takeover attempt. As a result, U.S. Steel acquired Marathon, in what was the second largest corporate takeover ever. It was Mobil's fourth loss in a row: Belridge in 1979, Texas Pacific Oil in 1980, and Conoco in 1981. Unlike the Dupont/Conoco merger, the meshing of steel and oil offers no real synergisms that will lead to efficiencies in the combined company, and rather than using Marathon's earnings for the development of oil and gas resources, U.S. Steel will have to use much of the income to pay the high interest costs it incurred in borrowing funds for the takeover.[97]

Nonetheless, the takeover binge continued. In June 1982 Cities Service Company sought to avoid an attempted takeover by Mesa Petroleum Company, by agreeing to a $5.1 billion merger with Gulf Oil. Gulf, which had tried to buy Marathon and which was interested in Cities' domestic reserves, agreed to pay $63 a share for 51 percent of Cities' stock, which had been trading at $37.75. The proposed deal would have created the seventh-largest U.S. industrial corporation, but in August Gulf withdrew its offer, citing the antitrust objections that had been raised by the FTC. However, analysts believed the real reasons for Gulf's withdrawal were that pending tax legislation could have raised the cost of the acquisition by as much as $1 billion, and both falling prices for oil company stocks and the uncertainty about future world oil prices reduced the deal's attractiveness. Spurned by Gulf, Cities Service found a new partner in Occidental Petroleum, which by the end of August agreed to pay $52.50 a share for 45 percent of Cities Service. Like Gulf, Occidental saw the Cities Service acquisition as enabling it to boost its domestic reserves, reorienting the company away from risky foreign production. The merger boosted Occidental from the thirteenth-largest to the eighth-largest U.S. oil company.[98]

Finally, the 1979 oil crisis led to a renewal of public hostility and suspicion toward the major oil companies. In fact, a *New York Times/CBS News* poll, conducted in the fall of 1979, found that more than half the U.S. public believed that the energy shortage had been fabricated, and a fourth of the public said that, if given a choice of ways to deal with the higher earnings of oil companies, they would favor that the government take the companies over and run them. Despite this public sentiment, in September 1981 the Federal Trade Commission announced that it was dropping the antitrust case against the eight largest U.S. oil companies, which it had initiated in 1972.[99]

FUTURE OIL SUPPLIES

Since the second shock, there has been a large increase in oil industry exploration and development expenditures (see table A5); however, most of this effort is in traditional producing areas that are unlikely to yield the large reserves that are needed for the future. These areas are favored because the geological and political risks they pose are small. Since companies are under pressure for immediate returns, they are reluctant to engage in risky, high-cost projects that may begin to yield dividends only after many years. In addition, with the softening of the world oil market, a new complacency has set in in the consuming countries, and because of the effect of higher prices on revenues, many exporting countries are desirous of limiting their long-term production.

Despite these trends—if another major political crisis in the Middle East can be avoided—growth in supplies of energy sources other than oil and weakness in the world economy is likely to keep the world oil market soft until 1985, and possibly until 1990. The key short-term variables are Iranian and Iraqi exports and Saudi production policy. As a result of war damage, both Iran and Iraq will want to maximize their revenues by keeping oil production as high as possible in the immediate future. On the other hand, their capacity to expand production will be limited by the damage the war has done to their production facilities; and as the war continues, the risk of further damage continues.

Iraq's production peaked at 3.5 mb/d in June 1979. Prior to the war with Iran, it appeared that Iraq's capacity would exceed 5 mb/d by the mid-1980s. This expansion was intended in part to increase Iraq's leverage within OPEC by enabling it to hold substantial levels of spare capacity. But given Iraq's moderate-size population and limited dependence upon the West, once it recovers from the war it will probably seek to limit its production to about 4 mb/d.[100]

In Iran the situation is similar. Iran traditionally sought to maximize production, producing about 6 mb/d under the Shah, but in 1979 it averaged only about 3 mb/d, and during 1980 and 1981 it averaged about 1.4 mb/d. Since it seeks to be less dependent upon imports of foreign goods and foreign personnel than under the Shah, the revolutionary Iranian government has indicated that its goal is between 3.5 and 4 mb/d. Even if a new government should come to power, which seeks to alter this plan, its ability to boost production would be limited by the Khomeini government's reduction of Iran's exploration budget and postponement of a gas-injection program that is needed if capacity is to be maintained at 5 mb/d after 1983. Iran has also canceled its agreement to ship natural gas to the Soviet Union, which will reduce the availability of supplies to both Eastern and Western Europe since, upon receiving the Iranian gas, the Soviet Union was to export natural gas to Europe.[101]

In mid-1979 Saudi Arabia embarked upon a plan to raise its capacity to 12 mb/d, but with the world market glutted, in 1982 Yamani indicated that the Saudis were proceeding "much, much more slowly" toward this goal. In early 1982, capacity was estimated at 10.7 mb/d. The Saudis' principal motive in boosting capacity has been to regain their leverage within OPEC, but now that price unity has been reestablished, the Saudis will probably stay below their official ceiling level of 8.5 mb/d and hold the rest of their capacity in reserve. Also, there is pressure from factions within Saudi Arabia for further cutbacks. Those in favor of reducing production further include young, highly trained technocrats, who argue that it is in Saudi Arabia's economic interest to cut back, and traditionalists, opposed to the rapid pace of development in Saudi Arabia.[102] On the other hand, as a result of the high spending levels the Saudi government has committed itself to, it needs production between 6 and 7 mb/d to meet its revenue needs. The Saudis are also committed to supplying 1 mb/d to companies that aid them in their industrialization effort. Moreover, as petrochemical plants and refineries are completed, the Saudis will find that they need larger quantities of oil just to meet their domestic needs, and in addition, the Saudis will probably seek to continue to earn a surplus over their immediate revenue needs. Consequently, in the absence of a major foreign-policy development, the Saudis will probably be reluctant to keep their production much below 7 mb/d for long periods of time.[103]

Kuwait, the fourth of the big Gulf producers, could probably produce 5–6 mb/d if it wanted to. Yet in April 1980 the sheikdom responded to higher prices by reducing its ceiling from 2 mb/d to 1.5 mb/d. A year later, Kuwait announced a further reduction, to 1.25 mb/d, which could be maintained for 150 years from current reserves alone.[104]

In contrast to Kuwait, Libya has been trying to expand both its production and its capacity, but its ability to do so has been greatly limited by the weakness of world oil demand, the age of its oil fields, and the lack of exploration and development in recent years. While the prospects of additional finds in Libya's Sirte basin are thought to be particularly good, Libya's small population and its hostility to the West are likely to lead the government to limit its future production.[105]

Like Libya, Nigeria has substantial prospects for boosting its production, but development has been lagging because of the weakness of world demand and the high-price policies maintained by the government. Nigeria's hopes of becoming an LNG exporter were set back in 1981–82, when both Phillips Petroleum and British Petroleum withdrew from the Bonny LNG consortium, resulting in the liquidation of the 60 percent government-held enterprise. In Ecuador, favorable finds have been made, but disputes within the government and between the government and Texaco hinder development. With 90 percent of its territory still unexplored, Indonesia has the potential to boost its capacity, and oil industry activity in the country has been high since 1979, but production in the near term will be limited by inadequate exploration in the recent past and the depletion of established fields. Given its large population and great internal needs, Indonesia, like Ecuador and Gabon, is expected to become a net oil importer by 1990.

Algeria has sought to boost its reserves by requiring companies that do not undertake exploration to pay more for the oil they take from the country, but this is not likely to prevent its oil production from falling.[106] Algeria's efforts to boost its revenues from the sale of natural gas have also run into trouble. While the concept of paying a price for LNG equivalent to the price of oil on a BTU basis has gained widespread acceptance, the equivalence has generally been between the landed (cif) price of LNG and the price of crude oil. But in March 1980 Algeria demanded price parity between crude oil and its natural gas prior to shipping and liquefaction (fob). This would have increased the landed price of Algerian LNG to U.S. importers from about $5 per mcf to about $8. At the time of the Algerian demand, the United States was paying an average price of less than \$2 for domestic gas and \$4.47 for imports from Mexico and Canada. Consequently, U.S. authorities refused to approve the prices that Algeria was demanding. Algeria made similar demands on the French and, in the spring of 1980, suspended its LNG shipments to both the United States and France, a clear violation of its contractual obligations to concerns in those countries. The U.S. agreements now appear to be dead, and El Paso has written off the \$365 million it invested to import LNG from Algeria.[107]

Shipments to France resumed in August 1980, with Algeria agreeing to sell its gas at a price of \$4.28, close to the old level, but in February 1982 the French socialist government agreed to pay an fob price of \$5.10, the energy equivalent of \$30 a barrel oil, below Algeria's official price of \$37.50 but indexed to a basket of light crude oils. The agreement, which was way out of line with what others were paying in a weak market, was a major victory for the Algerians. France explained its decision as part of its policy of improving relations with developing countries (part of France's payments would come out of its foreign-aid budget) and pointed to the fact that the deal provided for increased Algerian purchases of French goods and machinery. The agreement was expected to strengthen Algeria's hand in negotiating with Italy over the price to be paid for gas supplied through the recently completed trans-Mediterranean pipeline. The pipeline had been completed in October, but no gas had been shipped by the time of the French agreement because Algeria had been holding out for a higher price. Yet with Italy and the United States both resisting its demands, Algeria appears to have retreated from its demand for fob parity pricing. In August 1982 it concluded a deal with Panhandle Eastern Corporation for the importation of LNG into the United States at a price that was less than two-thirds of the fob parity price.[108]

Recently, Indonesia signed several LNG deals with Japan and is now the world's leading LNG producer; nonetheless, in the 1980s the growth in the LNG trade is expected to level off. Sharp increases in price, the impunity with which suppliers (such as Algeria) break contracts, and safety concerns have led consumers to reassess the desirability of LNG as a fuel source, while producers are considering using more natural gas at home or shipping it by pipeline. But in 1980, 58 percent of the natural gas produced in the Middle East was still being flared.[109]

Despite government efforts to counter the trend, Venezuela's conventional production of oil is likely to continue to decline, but the country is pursuing an \$8 billion project to develop the Orinoco heavy oil reserves. Small amounts of oil from the area are currently produced at a cost of about \$14 a barrel. By 1988 the government plans to boost production to 125,000 b/d, and to 1 mb/d by the turn of the century. As for the other OPEC members, Qatar's production has been declining since 1979, and is not expected to increase, but the United Arab Emirates is planning to boost its capacity from roughly 1.5 mb/d to 3 mb/d by 1985.[110]

In the United States, drilling has been at record levels. In mid-1979, just after President Carter announced his decontrol program, 3,300 rigs were operating in the United States, and by mid-1981, 5,100. Yet most of this activity is in traditional producing areas, and at best, this upsurge in drilling is only expected to brake the decline in U.S. petroleum reserves that has been under way since 1971. While U.S. oil production remained level in 1980–81 (see table 10-3), it is likely to resume its downward long-term trend in the next few years. Similarly, between 1980 and 1985 U.S. natural gas production is expected to fall.[111]

In an effort to boost oil production, Reagan's secretary of the interior, James Watt, announced that, beginning in 1982, the United States would lease 200 million offshore acres a year—ten times as much as leased annually in the past. Yet it is extremely doubtful that the oil companies have the capital, drilling rigs, manpower, or geophysical data that would enable them to absorb acreage on this scale. Indeed, several oil company executives have voiced skepticism about the Watt plan. Nor is it likely that with so much acreage being leased so fast, the government can assure that it receives either a fair return on the leased acreage or that adequate environmental safeguards are maintained; nonetheless, Watt appears determined to go ahead with the plan.[112]

Although construction of the southern (Canadian) portions of the Alaskan gas pipeline began in mid-1980, financing for the northern portion of the line remains a problem. As a result, the 1985 target for completion has been pushed back to 1989, when the delivered cost of gas from the pipeline is expected to be $11 per mcf—more than three times the mid-1980 weighted average price of U.S. gas supplies. This has raised further questions about the financial viability of the project. In an effort to move the project along, in 1982 Congress passed several amendments to the 1977 pipeline legislation, including provisions to allow the producing companies (Exxon, Arco, and BP/Sohio) to take up to a combined 30 percent equity in the system and to begin to recover costs from consumers before the line is complete. Yet with energy demand slack, interest rates high, and real world oil prices not expected to increase before 1990, even these changes may not move the pipeline along.[113]

In Canada, important oil and gas discoveries have been made in the Beaufort Sea, the High Arctic, West Pembina, and off the east coast (Newfoundland), but a dispute between the federal government and the provincial government of Alberta over oil pricing and the division of oil revenues has seriously slowed development. In February 1980, after the Progressive-Conservative Canadian government, headed by Joe Clark, proposed an 18¢ gasoline excise tax and doubling the wellhead price of $12.53 over a four-year period, it was voted out of office. In the fall of 1980 the government that replaced it, headed by Prime Minister Elliott Trudeau, proposed that the controlled Canadian price be increased gradually, but not exceed 85 percent of the price of crude in the United States or internationally. Trudeau also called for a gas export tax, and he proposed that oil from the tar sands sell at a base price of $38, which would rise with increases in the world oil price or the consumer price index, whichever was lower. His program of "Canadianization" would give PetroCanada a 25 percent share of all discoveries on Canadian federal land and require that any company that produces oil and gas in the so-called Canada Lands be at least 50 percent Canadian owned.[114]

In response to this program, oil companies cut their 1981 capital expenditures by as much as $2 billion, from a projected $6 billion. To force Trudeau to back down, Alberta's Premier Peter Lougheed held up construction permits for both the Alsands and Cold Lake tar sands projects, and in March he ordered the first of a series of production cutbacks that totaled 180,000 b/d (about 10 percent of Canada's production) by the summer of 1981. To make up for the loss, Canada had to increase its imports of foreign oil, and as a result of the intergovernmental dispute, work on both the Alsands and Cold Lake projects was suspended. Finally, at the end of August, an agreement was reached; it provides for two categories of oil: "old" and "new." "New oil," from new fields, the Arctic, and the oil sands, will sell at the world price. The price of "old oil," which at the time of the agreement was less than half the world price, will rise gradually but will not exceed 75 percent of the world price. The federal government's share of oil revenue will increase to 29 percent from 10 percent, that of Alberta will drop from 45 percent to 34 percent, and that of the industry will fall from 45 percent to 37 percent. (In the fall, Trudeau had proposed a 24/43/33 percent division.) In a major concession to Alberta, Trudeau dropped his proposal for a gas export tax. (In December, the House of Commons approved Trudeau's "Canadianization" proposals, including a provision that PetroCanada receive a 25 percent interest in lands where exploration and discovery had already occurred, but production had not yet begun.)[115]

As a result of Trudeau's policies, well completions in Canada declined by more than 25 percent in 1981, and many investors and independent explorers have shifted their activity to the United States, where the economic (though not the geologic) conditions are more favorable. Moreover, because of Trudeau's low price and interventionist energy policies, large Canadian firms that have the finances to enter the oil industry have shown little interest in "Canadianization." In fact, as we have seen, Seagram's sought to buy Conoco; and Hiram Walker Resources Ltd., the other big Canadian distiller with an interest in oil, spent $600 million on U.S. oil properties in March 1981. And with world oil prices declining, construction and financing costs rising, and Canadian government policies unfavorable, in 1981 Exxon canceled the Cold Lake project and in 1982 the Alsands project was terminated. Development of Newfoundland's offshore resources continues to be delayed by jurisdictional disputes between the provincial and federal governments, and Trudeau's goal of "energy independence" has probably been set back by years.[116]

In comparison with Canada, development in the North Sea has been much more vigorous since the second shock. Production is expected to increase from about 2 mb/d in 1979 to about 4 mb/d in 1985. Moreover, following an upturn in exploration, several important finds were made in the Norwegian sector of the North Sea in 1980 that led Norway to upgrade its recoverable reserves estimate and assured its production at present levels for nearly fifty years. And the prospects for further development in the North Sea are good. In fact, Exxon estimates that only half of the United Kingdom's potentially productive North Sea area has been licensed for exploration so far. Yet as a result of a decline in development work in recent years, production in the British North Sea is expected to level off in the mid-1980s. In addition, the gains from North Sea oil will be somewhat offset by an expected decline in Western Europe's natural gas production.[117]

The biggest enigma in international oil is the Soviet Union. In May 1981 the CIA revised its earlier forecast and said the Soviet Union would be able to meet its own oil needs throughout the 1980s. The CIA estimated that the Soviet Union would produce 10–11 mb/d in 1985, as opposed to the earlier forecast of 8–10 mb/d. The Soviets themselves project a 1985 level of 12.4–12.9 mb/d. Nonetheless, the CIA still thinks that by 1990 Soviet production will drop to 7–9 mb/d.[118]

In contrast to the CIA, the Defense Intelligence Agency believes the Soviet Union will be able to increase both its production and its exports for the foreseeable future. The DIA has also concluded that the Soviets made a major oil find, of mammoth dimensions, in 1980, and while the CIA puts proven Soviet oil reserves at 35 billion barrels, the DIA puts them at 80–85 billion barrels.[119]

In any case, Soviet plans call for its production to increase only 0.7–1.3 percent a year from 1980 to 1985, compared with an average 5.6 percent a year during the 1970s. As a result, Soviet exports to Eastern Europe, which grew by 53 percent between 1975 and 1980, will be significantly reduced between 1980 and 1985, and this will force the East European countries to increase their imports from the OPEC countries. Similarly, Soviet oil exports to the non-Communist world declined from 1.2 mb/d in 1978 to 1.1 mb/d in 1980, and that decline is expected to continue.[120]

Natural gas is the area in which the Soviet Union hopes to substantially increase its exports to the West. The Iranian-Soviet-European deal is now dormant, but plans are under way to have West European banks finance construction of a pipeline to bring natural gas from Siberia to Western Europe. The pipeline would cost at least $10 billion and be the largest East-West transaction in history. Moscow will get the pipeline almost entirely on credit, promising to repay later in gas. With the pipeline, West German dependence upon Soviet gas supplies would increase from 17 percent in the early 1980s to 25 percent in 1990, France's from 13 percent to 32 percent, and Italy's from 23 percent to 35 percent. Austria, Belgium, and Switzerland are also expected to increase gas imports from the Soviet Union, and Spain and Portugal have expressed interest.

The Reagan administration is strongly opposed to the pipeline because it fears that it will give the Soviet Union a stranglehold on Western Europe's energy supplies and because it will give the faltering Soviet economy a much needed boost by providing badly needed foreign exchange. The West Europeans have responded to these criticisms from Washington by pointing out that by 1990 Soviet natural gas will account for only 5–6 percent of the total energy supply in

West Germany, France, and Italy and for only 2 percent in all of Western Europe. To guard against a possible cutoff in Soviet supplies, France has made plans for a strategic supply of Algerian natural gas, West Germany has arranged for emergency supplies from the Netherlands, and Italy has built a new pipeline under the Mediterranean for Algerian gas. In addition, the Europeans argue that by aiding in the development of Siberian gas fields, the plan reduces the likelihood of Soviet dependence on Middle East oil supplies and of a Soviet military foray into the Middle East to secure those supplies. The Soviet gas will also reduce Western Europe's dependence on Middle East oil supplies. Finally, the Europeans question why they should give up the construction jobs and bank loans associated with the project, when Washington continues lucrative grain sales to the Soviet Union.

The Reagan administration opposed the building of the pipeline from the outset, but took no action against it until after the imposition of martial law in Poland. Then in December 1981, the president banned U.S. companies from selling equipment for the pipeline. In June 1982 he announced that this ban was being extended to both subsidiaries of U.S. companies operating abroad and to foreign companies producing under U.S. licenses. Britain, France and Italy all ordered companies within their borders to honor contracts related to the pipeline construction and when the companies did so the United States imposed sanctions—initially prohibiting them from buying any goods or services from the United States, later reducing this to a ban on the purchase of U.S. oil and gas equipment. The Reagan administration's actions outraged the Europeans, who believed it violated both international law and an understanding worked out at the Versailles summit conference, just two weeks before President Reagan announced his decision extending the ban to companies operating abroad. Japan, which would have been hampered by denial of U.S. technology for an oil and gas development project with the Soviet Union off Sakhalin Island, also protested. At most the Reagan administration's actions were expected to delay completion of the pipeline from 1984 to 1986. Yet because of the strains that this policy had placed on U.S.-European relations, in November 1982 the president announced that he was canceling it—removing all sanctions—in return for a new agreement with allies on ways of dealing with the Soviet Union. (The administration is still hoping that the projected pipeline will be reduced from two strands to one.)[121]

Even without the pipeline, Soviet production of natural gas is expected to increase 6–8 percent a year during the 1980s, and with U.S. gas production declining, the Soviet Union will soon be the leading producer. To reduce its need for oil, the Soviet Union, like the rest of Eastern Europe, is increasing its reliance upon nuclear power. In fact, the Soviet bloc plans to increase its nuclear generating capacity from 15–18 million kilowatts in 1979 to 150 million in 1990. The aim is to generate 25 percent of the bloc's electricity with nuclear power in 1990. In the near term, Soviet coal production is expected to remain fairly constant, but by the late 1980s it, too, is expected to increase.[122]

In 1980 China experienced its first year-to-year decline in oil production since

1967, and production is expected to continue to fall in the early 1980s. To keep exports up China plans to rely more on coal to meet its domestic needs. In June 1981 the Chinese were forced to delay an exploration offer in the South China Sea because they were unable to formulate policies on control terms and taxes. Bids were finally opened in 1982, but production from China's offshore areas is not expected to begin until 1987.

Nonetheless, the indications are that China could become a major oil producer. In the spring of 1981 Japanese companies, exploring in Chinese waters, made a major offshore find, which suggests that previous estimates of China's offshore potential may be far too conservative. However, development in the richest offshore area adjacent to China, the East China Sea, is still hampered by disputes over sovereignty among China, Japan, Taiwan, and the two Koreas.[123]

In the non-OPEC LDCs, several countries have emerged as potentially significant oil producers. Mexico is, of course, the most important; its proven oil reserves are estimated at 57 billion barrels—fifth largest in the world—and its potential production may be as high as 7 mb/d, which would put it ahead of all the OPEC countries except Saudi Arabia.[124] Nevertheless, there is strong opposition within Mexico to expanding production, for as a result of the "oil boom," Mexico has experienced unbalanced growth, worsening inequality, and high inflation, with the price of basic commodities rising especially rapidly.

In response to calls for lower production, Mexico's President López Portillo imposed a ceiling of 2.75 mb/d through 1982, with an export ceiling of 1.5 mb/d. Yet, because of the weakness of world oil demand, by the summer of 1981 the export ceiling had not yet been reached, and exports were running around 1.25 mb/d. Its current economic situation may force Mexico to seek higher export levels, but in a soft market it may not be able to find buyers unless it discounts heavily. Indeed Mexico, like many other oil-exporting countries, is likely to seek to export more if prices are low, and less if they are high.[125]

Among the other non-OPEC LDCs that are emerging as significant producers are Cameroun, Ghana, the Ivory Coast, and Angola; the Tierra del Fuego offshore area, in Argentine waters, has promise of becoming an important producing area; and promising finds in Guatemala show geologic similarities to Mexico. Exxon has singled out Brazil and Malaysia as having significant potential and Texaco has noted favorable geological prospects in Zaire. Most U.S.-based international oil companies, however, are trying to allocate at least two-thirds of their investments to domestic ventures; so they are not especially interested in developing resources in the non-OPEC LDCs.[126]

A 1980 study by the World Bank found that natural gas in the developing countries could contribute the energy equivalent of 1.9–2.7 mb/d of oil in 1990, if efforts were begun immediately to exploit their estimated reserves, but the report noted that few developing countries have the capital to build the necessary transportation and distribution infrastructure; and the international oil companies have shown little interest in a resource that is difficult to export. As a result, 40 percent of the associated gas produced in these countries is still flared.[127]

In 1979, to help develop the hydrocarbon potential of the non-OPEC LDCs, the World Bank for the first time agreed to extend credit to these countries for exploration. The Bank also identified sixty LDCs as needing funds for assistance in energy development. Since 1979 the Bank has greatly increased its lending in this area, but while the Bank has identified feasible projects that will require $25 billion in lending in the 1981–85 period, the Bank has only $13 billion available for this purpose. To make up this gap, the Bank proposed creation of an energy affiliate. It was hoped that the energy affiliate would enable the oil-importing LDCs to boost their energy production from its 1980 level of 7.8 mb/d of oil equivalent to 15 mb/d by 1990. The $25 billion that the Bank would invest under this plan is designed to attract another $65 billion in private investment, and it is hoped that, together, this investment would reduce the oil-importing LDCs' oil bill by up to $30 billion a year by 1990.[128]

The plan gained the support of the Arab oil-exporting countries,[129] and most of the industrial countries as well, but the Reagan administration reversed the position taken by the Carter administration and refused participation in the plan, effectively shelving it. The administration opposed the plan on both ideological and budgetary grounds. It wanted funds to come from the private sector, not the Bank, despite the fact that the private sector has repeatedly failed to make the requisite investments in these countries. In addition, in a period of massive budget cutting, the Reagan administration objected to the $250 million in paid-in capital that the United States would have had to contribute to the plan. This, however, is a small fraction of the amount spent annually in almost quixotic efforts to boost U.S. petroleum supplies.[130]

To reduce dependence upon oil, in May 1979 the major consuming countries pledged to use more coal. Yet a recent IEA study has voiced doubts about the West's ability to double its coal production by 1990—the goal set by the industrialized countries. The U.S. coal industry, the West's major source, still has low levels of demand and, consequently, high levels of overcapacity. The U.S. industry still relies heavily on inefficient and antiquated technology, and after another strike in the spring of 1981, there are renewed doubts about its reliability as a supplier. Port inadequacies may also prove a barrier to increasing U.S. coal exports.[131]

In any case, the traditional barriers to greater coal use—difficulties in handling it, environmental problems—are likely to obstruct substantially increased consumption until a viable synthetic fuels industry is developed. But here again, recent signs have not been encouraging. The Reagan administration is giving much less emphasis to synthetic fuels than the Carter administration and has eliminated direct federal subsidies for synfuel programs. Because the outlook for U.S. natural gas supplies has grown more favorable, due largely to exports from Canada and Mexico, interest in coal gasification projects is waning; only one commercial plant is being built in the United States (with another in West Germany); and if natural gas prices are decontrolled, the effect on both the production and the consumption of conventional natural gas will further reduce interest in coal gasification. Similarly, the 1980 decline in U.S. gasoline sales has reduced the interest of U.S. companies in gasohol. The Morgantown coal lique-faction project, which was to involve the participation of the United States (50%), West Germany (25%), and Japan (25%), has been scrapped. Billed in the summer of 1980 as "the most ambitious international energy project ever undertaken," the project was canceled a year later because of escalating costs and the Reagan administration's plan to shift financing for the project to the private sector.

Then in May 1982, Exxon announced that it was withdrawing from the 50,000 b/d Colony shale oil project in Colorado, killing the nation's most ambitious effort to produce synthetic fuels commercially. Escalating costs, due in part to high interest rates, and the world oil glut were cited as reasons for Exxon's decision. Occidental and Tenneco, Gulf and Standard Oil of Indiana, and Mobil and Socal also all announced postponements in plans for shale oil development projects. In fact, by 1982 in the United States only Union Oil was proceeding with a commercial shale oil plant, its 10,000 b/d facility in Western Colorado, and the only other major synthetic fuels project still proceeding was the 20,000 b/d Great Plains Coal gasification project in North Dakota. Thus, there is no possibility of coming anywhere near the original Carter goals of 500,000 barrels a day of oil equivalent by 1987 and 2 mb/d by 1992.[132]

The Reagan administration has also sharply reduced funding for energy con-servation programs and the development of renewable resources, worsening the outlook for both. And while the decline in oil consumption in the consuming countries has prompted numerous self-congratulatory statements, it is too soon to say how much of the decline is structural and how much reflects worldwide recession. Moreover, though recessions save energy, they also deter the kind of capital investments that would boost energy efficiency in the long term.[133]

Yet the greatest danger is that with the easing of the world oil market, compla-cency has become widespread. The energy crisis is viewed as a thing of the past. In early 1982, U.S. sales of big cars were running 20 percent above their year-earlier levels, exploratory activity was falling off, conversions to coal were slowing down, synthetic fuel projects were being canceled, and research on alternative energy sources was being delayed. Rather than having resolved the energy crisis, the consuming countries may well be laying the basis for Oil Shock Three, for the difference between a shortage and a glut is only a few million barrels a day, and the balance can change quickly. As Yamani said, following OPEC's extraordinary meeting in March 1982, "In 1979, when we met in Caracas, I talked about a surplus which would take place. . . . At that time some of my colleagues laughed. Now we are in a huge surplus, and I'm telling you about the possibility of having a serious shortage."[134]

Still, with slow economic growth, favorable Saudi production policies, a return of Iranian and Iraqi exports, and continued growth in Soviet supplies, the consuming countries may well succeed in meeting their energy needs during the next decade. This assumes, however, that there are no major political crises that interfere with oil consumption during this period. That assumption is, of course, open to considerable doubt.

MIDDLE EAST POLITICS

In December 1979 the Soviet Union provoked a storm of outrage in the United States when it toppled the government of Hafizullah Amin in Afghanistan, installed a more compliant leader, Babrak Karmal, and sent 70,000 troops into the country to suppress opposition to the Communist government. This was the first time since 1946, when the Soviets attempted to seize the Iranian province of Azerbaijan, that Moscow had used Soviet troops outside the Warsaw Pact. Islamic foreign ministers condemned the 1979 Soviet military intervention as "a flagrant violation" of international law;[135] critics saw the Soviet move into Afghanistan as part of a Soviet plan to take over the Middle East oil fields. They pointed to the fact that, since November 1977, the Soviets, with the aid of Cubans, had been pouring arms and military manpower into Ethiopia, and in June 1978 a coup brought a pro-Soviet faction into power in South Yemen. Since then, Aden has become a major Soviet naval base and the Soviet Union has helped to double the size of South Yemen's army. In addition, the Soviets have become the main suppliers of military equipment to Libya, Algeria, and Syria.[136]

President Carter demanded that the Soviet Union remove its troops from Afghanistan and, in an effort to get Moscow to comply, postponed Senate consideration of the Strategic Arms Limitation Treaty (SALT II), canceled the sale of 17 million tons of grain to the Soviet Union, and called for a boycott of the Moscow Olympics. In his State of the Union address, January 23, 1980, Carter charged that "the implications of the Soviet invasion of Afghanistan could pose the most serious threat to world peace since the Second World War. . . . The Soviet Union is now attempting to consolidate a strategic position that poses a grave threat to the free movement of Middle East oil." He declared: "Any attempt by any outside force to gain control of the Persian Gulf region will be regarded as an assault on the vital interests of the United States. It will be repelled by use of any means necessary, including military force."[137]

With this declaration the president in effect extended the U.S. security umbrella to the Persian Gulf. Previously, it had been explicitly committed only to Western Europe, the Far East, and Israel. In his address, the president also called for resumption of Selective Service registration to ensure that the United States could "meet future mobilization needs rapidly if they arise." One day later, the United States announced that it was willing to sell military equipment to China, for the first time. As part of his program of reprisals for the Soviet invasion, the president placed restrictions on the sale of oil technology to the Soviet Union, which, in making it more difficult for the Soviet Union to boost its oil production, threatens to worsen the world oil-supply outlook. Finally, as a result of the Soviet invasion of Afghanistan, the Carter administration indicated its interest in maintaining a viable and united Iran and that, following release of the hostages, Washington was prepared to provide Iran with economic and military aid.[138]

Despite the vehemence of the president's reaction—encouraged by his desire to appear as a strong leader when he was being challenged for the Democratic presidential nomination by Senator Kennedy—the Soviet invasion of Afghanistan is hardly the principal threat to the Middle East oil fields that the West confronts. Soviet troops are no closer to Teheran or the Iranian oil fields today than they were before the invasion. Also, the Soviets may have gotten into a quagmire in Afghanistan, where they continue to face opposition from rebel forces in rugged terrain. Moreover, it is important to remember that Afghanistan did not come under Soviet control in December 1979, when the United States began sounding the alarm, but in April 1978, when it provoked little concern, either publicly or in official circles.

Nor is it likely that the president told the Soviet Union anything in his State of the Union address that they did not already know, for the Soviet Union recognizes that a direct attack on the Middle East oil fields would be a fundamental challenge to Western interests and would therefore risk a nuclear confrontation. But this is not what the Soviets were doing in Afghanistan; rather, they sought to preserve a border state that had become part of their sphere of influence, and in taking such drastic action they were probably influenced by a fear of encirclement by hostile forces, following the Iranian revolution, and an assessment that they had little to lose since U.S./Soviet detente was going nowhere. Indeed, even before the Soviet invasion the SALT II Treaty was unlikely to be approved, and Congress showed no signs of granting trade concessions to the Soviet Union. The United States had established diplomatic relations with China and was making an issue of human rights in the Soviet Union. In addition, the United States was proceeding with plans to deploy 572 nuclear missiles in Western Europe.

Rather than direct Soviet aggression, the real threats to the Middle East oil fields stem from internal and regional conflicts. The challenge that the Soviet Union poses is therefore twofold: it may provide protective cover for opposition movements within the region and, in a period of crisis, might openly align itself with one side in a domestic or regional conflict, gaining new power and influence in the region as that side triumphs.

With Iran no longer the "policeman of the Gulf," the danger of regional conflicts breaking out into open warfare has greatly intensified. Many of the Gulf states fear direct Iranian aggression or that Iranian religious leaders might stir up rebellion within their borders, particularly if Iran succeeds in defeating Iraq. Indeed, followers of Ayatollah Khomeini have proclaimed that Bahrain is Iranian territory, and in December 1981 Bahrain uncovered and foiled a plot by an Iranian-backed radical Islamic group to take over the island emirate. Oman is greatly concerned that the Dhofaris, with aid from South Yemen, will resume their struggle. Yet, surprisingly, Iran has offered to support the Sultan of Oman in his efforts to counter the radical forces arrayed against him.[139]

South Yemen is likely to press its claims to North Yemen, and a unified Yemen, closely aligned with the Soviet Union, would pose a threat to the Saudi oil fields and dominate Bab-al-Mandab, the southern entrance to the Suez oil link on the Red Sea. Both Saudi Arabia and Egypt are worried about the threat of Ethiopian-based subversion in the Sudan; Qaddafi has provided money and guns to those trying to topple the shaky Sudan government; and Libya and Egypt are still at odds, which could lead to renewed warfare between them.[140] The most worrisome threat is an attack on Saudi Arabia, which, despite its vast military spending, is not strong enough to repel a major attack.[141]

As a result of the Iranian revolution, many regimes in the other exporting countries have a heightened sense of vulnerability. Indeed, widespread corruption, failure to translate oil revenues into general economic development, and the growth of an educated middle class that is denied political participation—important factors in bringing about the Iranian revolution—are problems in all the oil-exporting countries. Moreover, with their political prestige and budgetary programs now dependent on high oil prices, many of the regimes in these countries could come under severe pressure, if oil prices were to drop precipitously, and ironically, the resulting domestic upheaval might lead to a cutoff in oil supplies, sending world oil prices skyrocketing once again. In the wake of the Iranian revolution, oil-exporting countries also question whether the United States has either the capability or the will to protect them against threats to their security.

Oil-exporting-country governments also fear that the Iranian revolution will lead to an upsurge of Shiite militancy. Iraq, which has a Shiite majority but a ruling group dominated by Sunnis, is vulnerable to this danger, especially since the Shiites have both religious and socioeconomic grievances against the regime.[142] Bahrain is also a country with a Shiite majority ruled by a Sunni regime, and Kuwait, Qatar, and the United Arab Emirates have significant Shiite populations. While the Shiites are a small percentage of the Saudi population, they are concentrated near the oil fields and comprise 35 percent of the Saudi employees of Aramco.[143]

Unlike the Shah, the Saudi ruling family has always maintained close ties with the country's religious elite, but the Saudi government is vulnerable to charges of having desecrated the faith. This became clear in November 1979, when, on the first day of the Islamic fifteenth century, 500 armed men took over the Grand Mosque in Mecca. They claimed that the Saudi leaders had forfeited their role as leaders of Islam. The group included members of five Saudi tribes, as well as foreign students and immigrant workers, and it took the government over two weeks to clear the mosque and put an end to the fighting.[144] Also, when the takeover began, rumors that the United States was involved in seizing Islam's most holy site led militants to occupy the U.S. embassies in Libya and Pakistan.

In December 1979 there were demonstrations in the Saudi oil fields, aimed at getting the government to stop supplying the United States with oil and to support the Islamic revolution in Iran. Leaflets called for a return to Moslem fundamentalism and for ousting all foreigners from Saudi Arabia. Even if these events have little impact on the long-run stability of the Saudi regime, they are likely to strengthen factions in Saudi Arabia that favor slower economic growth, looser ties with the West, and lower oil production.[145]

The Saudi government has also come under attack for corruption, which is believed to be widespread. As James E. Akins, a former U.S. ambassador to Saudi Arabia, recently stated, "Without dramatic internal reforms, the country faces serious problems, as the feelings about corruption are similar to developing feelings in Iran in 1976–77."[146] In contrast with Iran, Saudi Arabia has a smaller population, greater per capita wealth, less inequality, and less urban crowding—factors which make for greater stability. However, resentment about corruption could combine with other factors to produce a coup. Moreover, a power play within the ruling family cannot be ruled out, and even the normal succession patterns could strengthen the factions that are less inclined to raise oil production. Also, foreign workers, who account for a third of the Saudi population, are a continual threat to the regime. The risks to the consuming countries in all this are that turmoil within Saudi Arabia could lead to drastic declines in oil production and that groups less inclined to boost production, and less sympathetic to Western interests, may come to power. (In June 1982 King Khaled died and was succeeded by his half-brother Crown Prince Fahd.)

Yet the oil-exporting country most likely to meet the same fate as Iran is Indonesia, for, as in Iran under the Shah, corruption and violations of human rights in Indonesia are widespread and economic growth is faltering. Also like Iran, but in sharp contrast to Saudi Arabia, Indonesia's vast population greatly dilutes the impact of oil revenues on living standards. The distribution of wealth in Indonesia is extremely unequal, and an impoverished majority coexists with a rich few who regularly engage in conspicuous consumption. (One important difference between Iran and Indonesia is that Indonesia's population consists primarily of Sunnis.)[147]

The other oil-exporting country that is extremely unstable is Iran itself. There are eight major ethnic groups in Iran, each with its own language or dialect and a tradition of resisting the central government. Prior to its approval (in December 1979), the new Iranian constitution prompted widespread opposition from Kurds, Turkomans, and Azerbaijanis, the latter comprising one of every three Iranians. The Kurds, in particular, have a long history of seeking autonomy; they are mainly Sunni Moslems, and since the Iranian revolution there has been continual fighting between them and the central government. In addition, the Soviet Union has given support to the Baluchis in their quest for independence.[148]

Iranians who are ethnically Arab are concentrated in Khuzistan, where the Iranian oil fields are located. Following the revolution, there were repeated clashes in Khuzistan between rightist and leftist oil workers and between Persian and Arab communities.[149] There have also been numerous acts of sabotage in the area, such as the bombing of pipelines. Since Iran's principal pipelines are underground, this has not disrupted oil exports, but it has interfered with refining.[150] However, when Iraq attacked Iran in the fall of 1980, it expected to gain the active support of the Arabs in Khuzistan but failed to do so, indicating that they may be more loyal to the Khomeini government than had been generally believed.

Ethnic conflicts thus threaten the integrity of Iran as a nation, and if they intensify, they are likely to lead to conflict between Iran and either Turkey, Pakistan, or Iraq, each of which has a sizable grouping of at least one of the ethnic groups in Iran. Ethnic conflicts in Iran also pose dangers to the West, portending ethnic turmoil and declining oil production. The Soviet Union may be drawn in in support of a particular group and emerge with new influence in Iran and special access to Iranian oil. Finally, an independent Khuzistan, or a fractionated Iran, would have lower revenue needs than the current Iranian government and, therefore, would probably reduce production well below the 3.5–4 mb/d target of the current government.

Iran is also plagued by serious economic problems. As the Islamic forces have gained control over the government, the urban middle classes have grown increasingly disillusioned. Opposition from the Iranian armed forces is another threat to the Islamic regime. In fact, in January 1980 twenty-five air force officers were arrested on charges of plotting a coup; and a year and a half later, on June 28, 1981, a bomb at the Islamic Republican Party's headquarters in Teheran killed more than seventy government officials, including Ayatollah Mohammed Beheshti, widely considered the second most powerful person in Iran, after the Ayatollah Khomeini. Later that summer, in one week, four senior officials, including the president and the prime minister, were killed in a series of bomb explosions. These bombings demonstrated that opposition groups had penetrated the highest levels of the Iranian government.[151]

Of the various opposition groups, the Mujahedeen is the most effective and best organized. It seeks to combine Islamic traditions with modern socialist political thought and has attracted many young, well-educated supporters. In the summer of 1981 its leader, Massoud Rajavi, escaped to Paris with former President Bani-Sadr, after hiding him from Iranian authorities for several weeks. There are also various right-wing exile groups, which could organize around either Shahpur Bakhtiar, the Shah's last prime minister, or Prince Riza Pahlevi, the Shah's son, who declared himself the new Shah following his father's death in July 1980. The United States has reportedly been financing right-wing paramilitary forces of Iranian exiles.[152]

The mullahs still appear to have the loyalty of the bulk of the Iranian population, but whether they can keep it may depend upon the state of the economy, the course of the war with Iraq, the ability of the highly fragmented opposition groups to offer a real alternative, and, perhaps most importantly, how much longer the eighty-three-year-old Ayatollah Khomeini lives. In any case, the Iranian oil industry has already been hurt by the loss of foreign technicians and many Iranian professional people, and with the country likely to go through another period of turmoil, things could well get worse.[153]

While a change in the Iranian government might ultimately be to the advantage of Western interests, the ensuing conflict could lead to another suspension of Iranian exports. With the market currently slack and Iranian exports averaging only about 1 mb/d since 1980, the consuming countries should be able to withstand another cessation of Iranian exports without much difficulty. However, if Iranian production increases and the world oil market tightens, an abrupt cessation of Iranian oil exports could again send the world oil market reeling.[154]

The Arab-Israeli conflict also remains a threat to the continued flow of Middle East oil. More than three years after the signing of the Egyptian-Israeli treaty, virtually no progress has been made toward resolving the Palestinian issue. The deadline established by the treaty for completing negotiations on Palestinian autonomy—the supposed "link" between the peace treaty and the Camp David framework for resolving the Palestinian issue—has passed. While the Camp David accord provided for the participation of local Palestinians and Jordanians in the autonomy negotiations, so far neither the Jordanians nor any Palestinian group has agreed to participate; and no Arab leader has broken with the Baghdad resolutions of March 1979 and come out in support of Egypt's peace initiative.[155] Meanwhile, Israel has resumed its policy of establishing Israeli settlements in the West Bank, and in an effort to undermine the negotiations on Palestinian autonomy, the PLO has undertaken intensified guerrilla and political activity, which has led to Israeli reprisal raids. In fact, in the spring of 1979 Begin abandoned the policy of limiting Israeli raids to instances of direct retaliation and ordered preemptive strikes.[156]

In the autonomy negotiations, Egypt has sought creation of a Palestinian Governing Council that would have broad executive, legislative, and judicial powers, but not statehood, a standing army, or diplomatic status. Israel has resisted this, making it clear that it is prepared to concede only limited municipal authority to the Palestinians. The position of the Begin government is that there shall be no Palestinian state, that the Israeli military must retain the main security role in the West Bank and Gaza, and that Jewish settlements in this area must be permitted. Under Begin's plan, Israel would also retain control of public lands and water resources in the West Bank and Gaza. While a less intransigent position on the part of the Israeli government would help to move the negotiations along, it is difficult to see how any agreement could win acceptance unless the PLO has a role in drafting it, and Israel is adamantly opposed to this. Nonetheless, in August 1981 Sadat and Begin agreed to resume the autonomy talks, which had been suspended for more than a year, following Israel's formal annexation of Arab East Jerusalem.[157]

Despite the talks, in December 1981 Israel annexed the Golan Heights, a move that the Reagan administration described as a violation of the Camp David agreements. The Israeli action further reduced its options for reaching a future territorial compromise with the Arab states. In the West Bank, the Begin government has been pursuing a policy of de facto annexation, and is attempting to wipe out all PLO influence in the area. In March 1982, elected local Palestinian officials were replaced with Israelis, and Jewish settlements have been expanding from small hilltop clusters into large townships.[158]

When he launched his peace offensive in November 1977, Sadat may not have intended to sign a separate peace agreement with Israel; yet it seems clear that this is what he got. Indeed, the logic of his actions since the October War has led in that direction. In September 1975 Sadat agreed to resolve conflicts with Israel by peaceful means in return for an Israeli withdrawal of only a few kilometers in the Sinai, thereby signaling his willingness to trade an agreement on peace with Israel for return of the Sinai, and this was reaffirmed by his visit to Jerusalem in November 1977. Having gone this far, Sadat could not turn back without an agreement, and in the end he settled for what he could get—not much more than what he probably could have got several years before. Moreover, once the treaty was signed, there was even less pressure on Israel to agree to a comprehensive settlement of the Arab-Israeli conflict.

While Israel has bargained hard and got pretty much what it wanted from Egypt, it is doubtful that its intransigence toward the Palestinians is in its long-term interest. For example, if Israel had been willing to make concessions on the West Bank, Jordan—even Syria—might have joined in the negotiations, and Sadat would not have been so isolated. As it is, the relationship between Israel and Egypt has steadily deteriorated since the signing of the peace agreement and is now mired in mistrust and recriminations.[159]

With Iraq engaged in combat with Iran, Syria and Jordan at loggerheads, and Israel retaining clear military superiority, the chances of an all-out Arab attack on Israel are small, but Lebanon has been a source of continual conflict. In April 1981 Israeli jets shot down two Syrian helicopters that had been introduced into battle in Lebanon. In response, Syria deployed antiaircraft missiles both in Lebanon and within Syria itself, along its border with Lebanon. Begin demanded that the missiles be removed and threatened to attack if they were not, but in the volatile Middle East, the "missile crisis" was soon overshadowed by a more startling event. On June 7, 1981, Israel bombed and destroyed an Iraqi nuclear reactor. Israel claimed its action was to prevent Iraq from building a nuclear bomb, yet Israel is the only Middle East country that has both built nuclear weapons and refused to sign the Nuclear Nonproliferation Treaty.[160]

While Israel's action may have set back Iraq's timetable for acquiring a nuclear weapon, it can only strengthen Arab hostility toward Israel and increase the Arabs' determination to acquire nuclear technology. The Iraqi raid also reduced the likelihood of drawing Arab moderates, such as Saudi Arabia and Jordan, into the peace process, and it increased antagonism toward the United States in the Arab world, especially since U.S.-supplied F-4 Phantoms and F-15s were used in the raid and U.S. sanctions against Israel have been minimal. (The only "sanction" was that delivery of sixteen F-16s was delayed a few weeks.)

Then, in July 1981, Israel said it would no longer refrain from attacking guerrilla targets in civilian areas, and proceeded to bomb a densely populated area of Beirut, in which Palestinian guerrilla headquarters were located. One hundred and twenty-three people were killed in the raid and 550 wounded, but little or no damage was inflicted on the Palestinian guerrillas. Fortunately, with the aid of the Saudis, a cease-fire was arranged shortly after this.[161]

In April 1982 Israel completed its withdrawal from the Sinai. The Begin administration declared that this would be Israel's final territorial concession for peace; no Israeli settlements in the occupied territories would be dismantled in the future. In taking this position, the Israelis conveyed a message to the other Arab states that they could not do what Egypt had done—regain territory by making peace. Then on June 6 Israel invaded Lebanon, declaring that its aim was to free the northern part of Israel from the danger of PLO attacks by creating a security zone reaching 25 miles into southern Lebanon. However, it soon became clear that the Israelis real objectives went well beyond this. They sought to destroy the PLO as a political and military force and to force the removal of all Palestinian and Syrian troops from Lebanon. Showing extraordinary disregard for Arab lives, they pursued the PLO 60 miles north, finally surrounding them in west Beirut. In late August U.S. special envoy Philip C. Habib was able to arrange for the withdrawal of the PLO from west Beirut to various Arab countries—a withdrawal supervised by United States, French and Italian troops. Yet Israeli, Palestinian and Syrian troops still remained in Lebanon. In addition, two weeks after the PLO withdrawal was completed, Christian militiamen were let into two Palestinian camps in west Beirut by Israeli military authorities, who entrusted them with the task of hunting Palestinian guerillas thought to be still in hiding. Once inside the camps, the militiamen proceeded to slaughter roughly six-hundred civilians in one of the most brutal episodes in Middle East history. Following the massacre, United States, Italian, and French troops were sent back into Lebanon.[162]

The Israeli invasion of Lebanon was the first Arab-Israeli war initiated by Israel without major provocation and the first in which its existence was not directly at stake. Indeed, prior to an Israeli attack, the PLO had been observing the cease-fire that had been arranged the previous summer. The invasion and the massacre of Palestinians in the west Beirut camps prompted a crisis within Israel itself, with many Israelis questioning the legitimacy of their government's actions. Nor has Israel achieved its goal of destroying the PLO. While the PLO has been weakened militarily, its political prestige has been enhanced and its leaders have been able to claim that they held off the Israeli army longer than any Arab army in history. The PLO will undoubtedly seek to establish new bases for opposition to Israel, and insofar as its dispersal reduces the centralized control formerly exercised by moderates such as Arafat, the radical factions within the organization are likely to take more militant actions. Moreover, the Palestinians are well aware that when Israel invaded, they received little support from the other Arab states. Indeed, with the world oil market slack and the Arab combatants limited to the Palestinians, there was no serious consideration given to utilizing the oil weapon. (In late August Iran did call for a pan-Islamic oil embargo against the United States for its support of Israel.) Consequently, in the future Arab radicals are likely to direct their hostility at the conservative Arab rulers, as well as at Israel. Indeed, Qaddafi has threatened to send ''revolutionary committees'' beyond Libya's borders to destroy other Arab governments for their failure to intervene militarily on the side of the besieged Palestinians in Beirut and prevent their withdrawal. In addition, the whole episode has worsened U.S. relations with the Arab world, where it is widely believed that the Reagan administration acquiesced in the Israeli invasion. (The Soviets fared no better, with the Arabs resenting their failure to come to the Palestinians aid, and with Soviet-supplied armaments proving inferior to those which the United States had sold to Israel. The Soviet Union's position in the region was also hurt by the defeat of its allies, the PLO and Syria.)[163]

The greatest tragedy of the Israeli invasion of Lebanon is that it has worsened the prospects for an overall settlement of the Arab-Israeli conflict. As a result of the invasion and the subsequent massacre, anti-Israeli sentiment has increased throughout the Middle East, and Israel is likely to be less conciliatory after its costly victory in Lebanon than it was before. As the PLO withdrawal from Lebanon was being completed, President Reagan put forth a new Middle East peace plan, calling for full autonomy for Palestinians in the West Bank and some form of association with Jordan and demanding a freeze on settlements in the West Bank by Israel. The president's plan rejected both a Palestinian state and Israeli annexation of the West Bank. A few days later, Arab leaders meeting at an Arab conference (without Egypt) also announced a Middle East peace plan that declared that all nations in the region, including an independent Palestinian state, had a right to a peaceful existence. In reponse, the Begin government announced immediately that it would not enter negotiations on either plan, that it would continue to pursue a vigorous settlement program in the West Bank, and that it would resume talks only on the basis of the Camp David accords. (The opposition Labor Party endorsed the main elements of the Reagan plan and called for a national debate on it.) Yet Egyptian President Mubarak has indicated that Egypt will not resume talks on Palestinian autonomy until Israeli troops withdraw from Lebanon. Nor is any other Arab country or Palestinian representative likely to join such talks in the aftermath of the Lebanon invasion. Recognizing this, the Begin government appears to be using the Camp David accords as a shield against territorial compromise, with its real aim being the de facto annexation of the West Bank. Indeed, in recent months Begin has been insisting on Israel's claim to eternal sovereignty over the occupied West Bank. The fatal flaw in the Begin government's policy is the underlying assumption that by maintaining and using its military superiority, Israel can bludgeon the Arabs into a settlement. Yet, the only hope of a political compromise now appears to depend upon the emergence of a new Israeli government.[164]

Because the Palestinian issue is unlikely to be resolved in the near future and because of Israel's poor relations with the Arab states, the Arab-Israeli conflict will be a continuing threat to the flow of oil. If another war results, with the United States backing Israel, oil production will probably be cut back, either deliberately (by the Arab exporting countries) or as a result of sabotage. Even in the absence of war, the Arab countries are likely to come under increasing pressure to deploy the oil weapon, and if the current Iranian regime remains in power, they are likely to be joined by Iran. Indeed, following the raid on the Iraqi reactor there were numerous calls in the Arab world for another oil embargo, and as part of the Arab struggle against Israel, Qaddafi has urged guerrillas to sabotage oil fields in the Persian Gulf.[165]

So long as the Palestinian issue remains unresolved, the large number of Palestinians in the oil-exporting countries will pose a threat to the governments of those countries. Palestinians comprise 60–65 percent of the Aramco work force, 20 percent of the population in Kuwait, 22 percent in Qatar, and roughly 30 percent in the UAE.[166] Moreover, if Arab aspirations continue to be frustrated, popular resentment is likely to turn against the moderate and conservative Arab governments that have failed to produce results.

The persistence of the Arab-Israeli conflict weakens U.S. influence in the region and prevents what would otherwise be an alliance between the United States and the conservative Arab oil-exporting countries from solidifying. Even the historic U.S./Saudi alliance is endangered by the failure to resolve the conflict.

From the perspective of Western interests, probably the most encouraging development in the Middle East in recent years has been Iraq's shift from a pro-Soviet regime to a more moderate, nonaligned position. Soviet influence in Iraq reached a high point in 1975, when the fifteen-year treaty of friendship was signed. After that, Soviet aid to Iraq declined and conflict between Iraqi Communist and Ba'athist parties increased. Then, in May 1978, a plot by pro-Soviet Communists to overthrow the Iraqi government was foiled and twenty-one were executed, and in July 1979 the Iraqi government launched a campaign to liquidate Iraqi Communists. Iraq's shift away from the Soviet Union was also encouraged by the Iranian revolution. With the Shah gone, Iraq sought to become the Gulf's regional leader, but it saw its ties to the Soviet Union as a barrier to this. Also, after the fall of the Shah and the weakening of the Iranian military, Iraq no longer needed the Soviet Union to counter Iran militarily. Then, following the Soviet invasion of Afghanistan, Iraq came to fear Soviet expansionism as a threat to the Middle East. Relations have also soured as a result of the Soviet Union's lack of support for Iraq in its war with Iran (the Soviets claim to be neutral), and its willingness to allow Syria to transfer Soviet arms to Iran.[167]

Iraq now wants to keep the Middle East free from domination by either of the two superpowers. In accordance with this policy, the Iraqi government has condemned the Soviet invasion of Afghanistan, and prior to its recent change in government (see below), Iraq vowed to topple the Soviet-aligned regime in South Yemen. To keep the Gulf free of foreign intervention, Iraq has been consulting with both Saudi Arabia and Kuwait. It wants the Saudis to normalize relations with the Soviet Union and to pursue a less one-sided relationship with the superpowers.[168]

On the Arab-Israeli issue, Iraq, which formerly was an ardent rejectionist, has recently encouraged an entente between moderates: the PLO's Arafat and King

Hussein of Jordan. In May 1980, Iraq expelled the two most radical Palestinian organizations, the Popular Front for the Liberation of Palestine and the Democratic Front for the Liberation of Palestine. Still, Iraq maintains that in the current situation, with Israel enjoying military superiority and unquestioned U.S. backing, there is no possibility of a negotiated settlement to the Arab-Israeli conflict. It has therefore launched a campaign to undermine Israel's economic links with Europe and to pressure the United States to choose between its interests in the European alliance and its commitment to Israel. As part of this campaign, Iraq has offered Western Europe guaranteed oil supplies in return for curtailment of trade and all other contact with Israel.[169]

Iraq recognizes that to achieve its foreign-policy objectives it needs Arab League unity. Consequently—aside from its relations with Iran—it has generally pursued a "good neighbor" policy. Historically, Iraq has laid claim to Kuwait, but today the two countries are on good terms, and in recent years Iraq has also sought to improve relations with Saudi Arabia. Nonetheless, Iraq's goal of becoming the regional leader has been greatly set back by its failure to win a decisive victory in the war with Iran.

After Iraq's initial victories, the war appears to have settled down into a long stalemate. The war has tended to unify Iran, strengthening the domestic popularity of the Khomeini regime, but it has badly bled Iraq. The would-be regional leader has been forced to turn to the other Arab states for financial aid, receiving $20 billion by early 1982 from Saudi Arabia, Kuwait, and the United Arab Emirates. Of the Arab states, only Syria and Libya have supported Iran. Despite Khomeini's anti-Israel rhetoric, Iran has received large quantities of arms from Israel. By early 1982 Iraq appeared ready to accept any face-saving compromise that would end the war, but Khomeini seemed determined to continue the fight until the Hussein regime is toppled. If the war continues, it could easily spread to other Arab oil-exporting countries. In the spring of 1982 the United States, fearing the consequences that Hussein's downfall could have on the stability of the Gulf, sought to put pressure on Iran to reach a settlement. In fact, Iran has already bombed Kuwait three times in retaliation for its support of Iraq.[170]

Another development favorable to Western interests occurred in April 1980, when Abdel Fattah Ismail was ousted as head of the government in South Yemen. The new leader, Ali Nasser Mohammed al-Hassani, is also a Marxist, but he is much less pro-Soviet and has been seeking to develop good relations with conservative Arab governments, including Saudi Arabia, and Western countries.[171]

With Iran no longer the regional guardian, the United States has adopted a new strategy for maintaining stability in the Persian Gulf area. The strategy has essentially four parts: assuring its allies that the United States is committed to defending them in the event of attack, searching for new regional guardians, increasing economic and military aid for pro-Western governments in the region, and upgrading U.S. capability for direct military intervention in the area.

Early in 1979, Secretary of State Cyrus Vance, Secretary of Defense Harold Brown, and Secretary of Energy James Schlesinger stated publicly that the United States was prepared to take military action to maintain the flow of oil, and to demonstrate U.S. support for Saudi Arabia, in January 1979 President Carter sent unarmed F-15s on a brief visit to the oil kingdom. Then, in February 1979, when North Yemen was attacked by South Yemen, President Carter ordered the shipment of $400 million worth of military equipment to North Yemen and sent a U.S. weapons training team to the country to show the Yemenis how to use the new equipment.[172] Immediately after the outbreak of the Iran-Iraq war, the Carter administration responded to a Saudi request; it agreed to send four U.S. Air Force radar command aircraft (AWACS) and several hundred support personnel to Saudi Arabia. Washington also warned Iraq against seizing Khuzistan, Iran's oil producing province. While dispatch of the AWACS to Saudi Arabia was supposed to be temporary, the Reagan administration decided to keep the four planes there through 1985 and to sell the Saudis five AWACS of their own, to be delivered in 1985. In addition, on October 1, 1981, President Reagan broadened the U.S. commitment in the Persian Gulf by declaring that the United States would not allow Saudi Arabia to fall into the hands of internal or external forces that threaten to cut off oil supplies for the West.[173]

The Reagan administration also agreed to sell Saudi Arabia 1,100 advanced air-to-air missiles and equipment that would improve the range and fighting power of the sixty-two F-15s that Saudi Arabia purchased in 1978—despite the fact that, at the time of the 1978 sale, the Carter administration pledged to Congress that Saudi Arabia would not receive either the air-to-air missiles or the equipment in question. The cost of the entire package was estimated to be $8.5 billion. The House of Representatives voted overwhelmingly against the sale, but it was narrowly approved in the Senate, enabling it to go forward.[174] France has agreed to sell Saudi Arabia $3.4 billion in arms, and Washington has indicated that it now welcomes French arms sales to the Middle East as complementary to U.S. policy.[175]

Rather than antagonize India, President Carter reversed a ruling of the Nuclear Regulatory Commission and approved nuclear fuel shipments to India, despite India's refusal to accept safeguards to prevent diversion of materials for weapons purposes, and in an effort to bolster a regional ally, the Reagan administration concluded a $3 billion military and economic program with Pakistan. The United States is also seeking to improve its relations with Turkey.[176] The United States has also turned to Egypt to assume (in a limited way) the role of regional guardian formerly played by Iran. As part of this plan, the United States granted Egypt $3.5 billion in arms over a five-year period, plus $800 million in economic aid. The United States also agreed to sell F-15s and F-16s to Egypt, and is helping Egypt upgrade its arms industry and modernize its armed forces.[177]

Yet, as the U.S. government recognizes, there are numerous problems with this approach. The Egyptian armed forces are in near disarray, nor is Egypt, a country widely ostracized in the Arab world, the best ally the United States could have in the region. In addition, while Iran is adjacent to the Gulf and overlooks the strategic Strait of Hormuz, Egypt is several hundred miles away, which greatly limits its ability to police the area. At the same time, none of the pro-Western Gulf countries has either the skills or the population to assume the security role formerly played by Iran.

The greatest problem with relying upon Egypt, however, is the instability of the Egyptian government. That became evident on October 6, 1981, when President Sadat was killed while watching a military parade commemorating the 1973 war against Israel. The assassination, by a group of men in military uniform, is believed to be associated with Egypt's growing Moslem fundamentalist opposition. Sadat was succeeded by Vice President Hosni Mubarak, who immediately ordered a government roundup of religious militants and political opponents. Immediately after the assassination, the United States sent two AWACS to Egypt, and administration officials indicated that they would do whatever was necessary to protect the Egyptian government against external and internal attacks.[178]

Mubarak is a moderate, committed to following the broad outlines of Sadat's policies, but whether he can remain in power and pursue these policies or whether, for reasons of personal proclivity or political necessity, he makes important departures from Sadat's policies remains to be seen. To enhance his legitimacy in the Arab world, he may choose to distance himself from the United States and Israel. And even if he chooses to pursue the same policies as Sadat toward both Israel and the United States, his ability to do so will be limited by the fact that he lacks the political capital that Sadat built up through years of daring moves. In addition, the fact that Sadat was assassinated is likely to deter other moderate Arab leaders from moving toward improved relations with Israel. Yet probably the greatest threat to Mubarak's regime is that the Egyptian economy, despite recent gains, may not be able to keep up with rising expectations. Corruption and disparities between rich and poor are continuing problems, and if the economy falters, Mubarak may be forced to "mend fences" in order to secure financial aid from the rich Arab exporting countries.[179]

Partly because of growing awareness of the limits of relying on regional powers, the United States is upgrading its capability for intervening militarily in the area, creating a rapid deployment force (RDF) of 200,000 U.S. troops and 100,000 reservists that could be sent to the Middle East on short notice. Partly to support this force and partly to maintain a permanent naval force in the Indian Ocean, the United States is also trying to put together a network of bases in the area. Agreement has already been reached permitting the United States to use bases in Oman, Kenya, and Somalia. The United States also plans to use Egyptian port facilities, and it is building up its naval facility at Diego Garcia. In addition, both Israel and Saudi Arabia have indicated that the United States could use their military facilities in an emergency. And in September 1981 the United States announced a policy of "strategic collaboration" with Israel, involving joint cooperation in a broad spectrum of air, sea, and ground operations. (A formal Memorandum of Understanding on Strategic Cooperation, agreed to in November, was suspended less than three weeks later in response to the Israeli annexation of the Golan Heights.)[180]

There are several problems with this new strategy. It is doubtful that the United States has, or will soon have, the military capability to carry it out. A Department of Defense study recently found that U.S. forces could not stop a Soviet thrust into Iran, though the study maintained that they could counter a Soviet invasion of Saudi Arabia or a Soviet threat to oil tankers in the area.[181] And even when the rapid deployment force is fully developed, it will be questionable whether it could be deployed fast enough, even if political factors are ignored.

Still, the main weakness of the U.S. strategy is that it is likely to aggravate the very problems it is designed to counter. The Reagan administration has focused on the Soviet strategic threat to the Middle East, but the main problems that the United States confronts in the area do not stem from the danger of direct Soviet aggression, but from regional and internal conflicts. As Yamani pointedly reminded Washington in April 1981, the Saudis consider Israel a more immediate threat than the Soviet Union.[182]

Moreover, as the experience in Iran should make clear, rather than contribute to stability, indiscriminate arms sales can be destabilizing. Also, they are likely to lead to increased Soviet influence in the area, as the Soviets become the suppliers of the other side in a regional conflict. By building up countries militarily, the United States increases the probability that they will be drawn into conflicts. For example, the arming of Saudi Arabia has made it more, not less, likely that the Saudis will be directly involved in a future Arab-Israeli conflict. Nor would a rapid deployment force be of much use in countering a domestic revolution like the one in Iran. The RDF is intended to deter a conflict in its early stages, but sending U.S. troops to the Middle East is more likely to inflame a crisis situation and lead to the escalation of hostilities. Similarly, the presence of U.S. troops in the area and acquisition of U.S. bases or base rights is likely to provoke radical forces, not contain them. It is precisely for this reason that Saudi Arabia refuses to allow the United States to station forces on its territory, despite its security concerns.

A U.S. presence or military relationship, furthermore, is likely to draw the United States into local conflicts, generally on the side of the right-wing dictatorships that rule most of the countries in the area. Yet this is precisely what the United States does not need, for it is not in the U.S. interest that a reactionary feudal monarchy continue to rule Saudi Arabia. Rather, the U.S. interest is that whoever rules Saudi Arabia should also have an interest in continued oil production. By identifying itself so closely with the existing regimes in the area, the United States makes it almost inevitable that successive or later regimes will be characterized by strong anti-Western feelings that may lead them to cut back on oil production and relations with the West in general, as Iran has done.

By forming military relationships with particular countries, the United States undermines the principle of nonintervention and makes it likely that other countries in the area will seek protection by forming similar alliances with the Soviet Union. Moreover, courting alliances with repressive and unstable countries, such as Turkey and Pakistan, is courting trouble. A U.S.-Pakistan alliance will surely worsen U.S. relations with India; and by having placed so much stress on Sadat, the United States has left itself extremely vulnerable, now that he has been displaced.

In short, the United States would probably do better if it did less. By distancing itself from internal and regional conflicts—by respecting national sovereignty—the United States is likely to find itself better off in the long run. While this policy may have short-term costs—an immediate reduction in Saudi output, for example—the appropriate response is a more effective energy policy on the part of the consuming countries. One element of that policy would be development of oil and gas resources in the non-OPEC LDCs; another would be much greater stress on energy conservation.

U.S. policy, as presently constituted, is insufficiently responsive to the Palestinians' claim for national self-determination, and this is likely to be a major, ongoing source of conflict in the area. To rectify this, the United States should move toward greater contact with and recognition of the PLO. The United States should also be willing to withhold, or cut back on, aid to Israel, if it persists on its intransigent course and particularly if it continues to allow the expansion of settlements in the occupied territory.

U.S. policy has also failed to respond adequately to the recent changes in Iraq's orientation. That a country, formerly closely aligned with the Soviet Union and now the strongest power on the Gulf, should champion nonalignment and moderation and seek to boost its oil production is an enormously positive development from the perspective of U.S. interests. Yet what Iraq wants from the United States is a commitment to nonintervention and greater recognition of Palestinian rights. Indeed, diplomats believe that if the United States were to recognize the PLO, Baghdad would restore diplomatic relations.[183] But by refusing to recognize the PLO and by seeking to establish military bases in the area, the United States may drive Iraq into a bilateral relationship with Western Europe or back into alliance with the Soviet Union.

The weakness of U.S. policy is illustrated by its attempt to rescue the hostages by sending airborne troops into Iran. The United States was probably lucky that the mission was called off when three helicopters broke down, for an "attack" on Iran would undoubtedly have increased anti-U.S. sentiment in the country and might have driven Iran into an alliance with the Soviet Union. As it was, the mission reduced the inclination within Iran to release the hostages and it worsened U.S. relations with other Moslem nations. Indeed, the mission, which was condemned by the Islamic Conference, diverted attention from the Soviet invasion of Afghanistan and encouraged the view that neither superpower can be trusted.[184]

In the end, the hostages were released when the Islamic militants no longer had any interest in keeping them. By the fall of 1980 the Iranian clerics, who used the crisis to increase their control of the Iranian government, had won control of the newly elected parliament and therefore had no further use for the hostages. By this time the sanctions the United States had imposed on Iran were also taking their toll. Consequently, Iran began to express interest in releasing the hostages. Then, with the outbreak of the war with Iraq, obtaining spare parts for the U.S.-made Iranian military equipment became a problem, and the United States indicated that once the hostages were freed, it would allow Teheran to receive $220 million worth of military equipment that had already been purchased but whose delivery had been held up as part of the freeze that President Carter had imposed on Iranian assets in November 1979. Finally, with the election of Ronald Reagan, the Iranians recognized that they would get no better deal from him.[185]

Consequently, in January 1981 Iran agreed to release the hostages in return for release of its frozen assets. But of the $8–10 billion in Iranian assets held by U.S. financial institutions, only about $3 billion went directly back to Iran; another $5 billion went to pay back, in full, Iranian loans to U.S. and European banks. Of the estimated remaining $2 billion, half was to go back to Iran within six months, the other half into a "security fund" at the Algerian central bank to pay off awards by a newly created international tribunal that would resolve U.S. corporations' claims against Iran.[186]

The banks, which right away got all their money back, fared much better under this settlement than the corporations, which must seek recourse through complex international arbitration proceedings. Algeria was an important intermediary in concluding the settlement, yet the episode might have been settled much sooner—and would not have reached the proportions it did—had it not been built up by a president to enhance his reelection prospects (a strategy that ultimately backfired) and a mass media that sought to persuade a susceptible public that the holding of fifty-two Americans for over a year was one of the gravest violations of human rights in the twentieth century.[187] It *was* a violation, but hardly of that magnitude.

The new U.S. emphasis on forceful display has also led to a sharp deterioration in relations with Libya. In May 1981 the Reagan administration expelled Libyan diplomats from the United States; at the same time, the State Department urged U.S. oil companies operating in Libya to cut back their personnel in the country. Administration officials explained that their policy was to refute the claim that U.S. policy in the Middle East/North Africa is simply a function of oil. Yet the administration's "tough line" was made possible by the slackness in the world oil market at the time.[188]

Then, in August, two U.S. Navy F-14 jets shot down two Soviet-built Libyan SU-22s, after being fired on by one of the Libyan aircraft. Libya claimed that the U.S. jets were violating its territorial waters, but the United States maintained that Libya has no right to claim more than a three-mile territorial limit. Administration officials explained that their decision to hold naval exercises in waters claimed by Libya was intended to affirm the right of free passage in international waters and to end any appearance of backing away from a confrontation with Libya. In December 1981 Reagan asked U.S. nationals to leave Libya and invalidated passports for travel to Libya, and in March the president banned imports of Libyan oil and curtailed exports of high technology to Libya.[189]

The Reagan administration's bellicosity toward Libya may well have the effect of driving the country closer to the Soviet Union. By embarrassing Libya, the Reagan administration may be seeking to aid the growing opposition to the Qaddafi regime, an opposition that includes many former members of his government. Yet if internecine struggle were to develop in Libya, it could lead to a loss of oil supplies. As in the case of Iran, in a weak market this might not matter much, but in a tight market it could prove catastrophic. Moreover, a successor government might turn out to be closer to the Soviet Union than Qaddafi or less inclined to keep oil production high. And if the market tightens, the United States may come to regret any impact that its moves have on reducing Libya's future productive capacity.[190]

The final weakness of U.S. strategy is its failure to adequately involve its allies, despite President Carter's admission in January 1980 that, to protect oil supplies in the Persian Gulf, the United States would need the help of its Western allies.[191] Yet the United States did not consult its allies on either the aborted Iranian rescue mission or its response to the Soviet invasion of Afghanistan. The allies, for their part, have been unwilling to reduce trade with the Soviet Union or invoke other sanctions against the Soviet Union for the invasion of Afghanistan, and they initially refused to cut off trade with Iran.[192] In April 1980, they agreed to impose sanctions against Iran on May 17, if the hostages were not released, but after the U.S. rescue attempt, these sanctions were weakened considerably, so that, in the end, only contracts signed since the hostages were taken (on November 4) were invalidated.

The allies have maintained that the Soviet invasion of Afghanistan does not pose the threat that the United States claims, and they have contended that Carter's actions were dictated largely by U.S. electoral considerations. On Iran, they maintained that breaking diplomatic relations would be counterproductive: that blocking commerce would not help free the hostages and that it might trigger an oil embargo. They also feared that actions that would weaken the Iranian state might lead to its disintegration or force it to turn to the Soviet Union. Moreover, they pointed out, while U.S./Iranian trade was blocked by the refusal of longshoremen to load ships bound for Iran, trade with Iran was still important to them, and they objected to the failure of the United States to consult with them before formulating its plans.[193]

As a result of these differences, the consuming countries are as divided as ever—at a time when consuming-country unity is badly needed. The United States has yet to acknowledge the valid claims of either Iranian or Palestinian nationalism, but these claims threaten new disruptions in Middle East oil supplies. Nor have the consuming countries yet reduced their dependence upon those oil supplies to tolerable levels.

Conclusion

The same basic forces produced both the 1973–74 oil crisis and the 1979 crisis. At the heart of each crisis were high levels of consuming-country dependence upon Middle East and North African oil. There was nothing inevitable about this; rather, it was due to the failure of the consuming countries to develop effective energy policies and the major oil companies' emphasis on producing the "easy" oil in these areas. In both cases, moreover, the growth of U.S. demand for imported oil was the underlying factor that put the most pressure on world oil markets.

Both crises were triggered by political events not directly related to oil: the fourth Arab-Israeli war in 1973 and the Iranian revolution in 1979. Each crisis involved only a minor loss of supplies; however, the impact of this loss was greatly aggravated by the competitive bidding among the oil companies that followed and consuming-country policies, particularly in the United States, that misallocated supplies.

These problems, which manifested themselves very clearly during the crisis periods, were rooted in the general patterns of competition within the international oil industry, particularly between the majors and the newcomers, and rivalry among the consuming countries. It was the combination of uncertainty about future supplies and unequal access to crude that led both the oil companies and the consuming countries to seek to protect their own interests, irrespective of the consequences of their actions on the world oil market. All this might have been avoided, had policies been devised to assure consuming countries and oil companies equal access to whatever supplies were available. However, the rivalries among the consuming countries, the refusal of the United States to share its domestic oil supplies (until 1974), and the European and Japanese governments' distrust of the Anglo-American majors all worked against this.

On a broader level, these developments testify to the strength of nationalism and the predominance of nation-states as international actors. The growth of nationalism in the Third World has been nearly continuous. Beginning with Nasser's revolution in 1952 and followed by the overthrow of the monarchy in Iraq in 1958 and the Algerian struggle for independence in the early 1960s, the efforts of national liberation movements to gain control of their countries has had continual impact on the international oil industry. The principal changes in the industry prior to 1973—the fifty/fifty profit-sharing scheme initiated by Venezuela in 1948 and Libya's breakthrough in 1970—were the actions of new regimes' seeking to assert their national rights.

Similarly, Third World nationalism led countries to insist on control over their natural resources—that is, the right to set prices and production rates. Indeed, the Arab oil embargo and production cutbacks, the unilateral price increases, and the agreements on participation are aspects of the successful demand for national sovereignty. As a sign in front of the hotel in Doha, Qatar, where OPEC met in December 1976, proclaimed: "The control of nations over their natural resources is an inalienable right."[1] Therefore it is not surprising that it has not been the policies of the radicals or the pan-Arabists that have won out, but those of the economic nationalists: the Sadats and the Yamanis.

On the other hand, the consuming countries' ability to respond to the challenge posed by the exporting countries has been impaired by the tendency of each consuming country to pursue its own interest, irrespective of the consequences this might have for the consuming countries as a group. While this tendency is inherent in a system of nation-states, where each government is more responsive to its domestic constituency than to the interests of the group, it was greatly encouraged by the uneven resource endowments of the consuming countries and by their different positions vis-à-vis the exporting countries. Whether it was establishment of the Anglo-American majors' predominance at the close of World War II, the refusal of France to cooperate with the other oil-consuming countries following the 1973–74 rise in oil prices, or Japan's heavy bidding in the spot market in 1979, consuming countries have put their national interests ahead of any interest they might have in consuming-country solidarity. Nor have the exporting countries been much better at cooperating with one another or subjecting their national interests to group decisions, but because of the circumstances they found themselves in, they have not had to be.

The attempt to deny the claims of Arab nationalism—to its occupied territory and to a homeland for the Palestinians—led to the Arab-Israeli war in 1973 and to the production cutbacks that resulted in the first skyrocketing of prices in 1973–74. Again in 1979, it was nationalism that led the Iranian people to overthrow the Shah, bringing oil exports to a halt and thereby triggering a second explosion of world oil prices.

These political cataclysms were largely the consequence of the United States' Middle East policy. By ensuring Israel's military superiority from 1970 to 1973, the United States removed the pressures that Israel would otherwise have felt to make the compromises necessary to reach a peace settlement. And even after Sadat expelled the Soviet advisers in 1972, the United States failed to put forward a new peace initiative, which led directly to Sadat's decision to resort to war. Similarly, the United States failed to support the moderate nationalist regime of Mohammed Mossadegh, finally backing the coup that led to his ouster in 1953. The United States then gave unequivocal support to the Shah, training Savak, his hated secret police, and providing him all the armaments that his megalomaniacal desires led him to crave.

The rise in oil prices and the events that surrounded it also indicate that the world has moved to a point where military force is of only limited utility. In response to the Iranian nationalization in 1951, Great Britain threatened military reprisals; then in 1956, in response to the nationalization of the Suez Canal Company, Great Britain and France invaded Egypt. Yet while there were veiled threats, no military reprisals followed the nationalizations of the early 1970s, the use of the Arab oil weapon, or the sharp, unilateral increases in oil prices. Soviet military power, which serves as a counterweight to that of the United States, and the strengthening of international norms, which militate against the use of force, have served to deter military action. Similarly, the Shah's enormous armory did him little good against the opposition of popular forces. Nor is military force likely to resolve the Arab-Israeli conflict, or be a sufficient safeguard against attacks on the Middle East oil fields by a group with popular support that is determined to damage them.

As a result of the rise in oil prices, the oil-exporting countries have increased their economic and political power. Indeed, who would have thought of Saudi Arabia as an international power twelve years ago? Yet, despite their achievements, none of the exporting countries has transformed its increased oil wealth into genuine economic development, and this failure greatly limits the power that they can exercise in world politics. The oil-exporting countries remain dependent upon the developed world for technological aid, oil markets, investment outlets, military equipment, and protection against both external attack and internal subversion. The "rich" oil-exporting countries also stand among the more privileged parts of the capitalist world, and therefore the regimes in these countries are unlikely to pose a radical challenge to that world. Still, if only to help maintain the legitimacy of their position, these countries will continue to provide aid to the non-OPEC LDCs.

It is important to recognize that, rather than part of a transfer of power from the industrial countries to the Third World, the oil-price rises represent a gain for a particular group of strategically situated Third World countries, not for the Third World as a whole. In fact, the non-OPEC LDCs have been hurt by the price rises, some of them severely.

Nor is it likely that other raw material producers will be able to match OPEC's success. There are other commodities whose export, production, and reserves are concentrated in a few countries, as they are in oil (copper, tin, and bauxite are examples). Other commodities also have low price elasticities and few near- or medium-term alternatives (examples include tea, coffee, and copper). Other commodity producers could probably benefit from consuming-country rivalries and, if they control the supply of the commodity in question, they could probably bind the multinational companies in the industry to their interests. But the producers of these other commodities are likely to lack the cohesion to bind one another to group decisions.

OPEC solved this problem with the emergence of several countries that were willing to limit their production because of their interest in conserving their resources and their limited revenue needs. In the case of other commodities, however, those with the capability to produce more are likely to do so. Also, it is doubtful that such commodity-exporting countries will have the foreign-exchange reserves to allow them to sacrifice current revenues long enough to create serious shortages. Nor are they likely to have the overriding political motives for cutting back production that the Arab exporting countries had in 1973.

Duplicating OPEC's success with any renewable resource is particularly unlikely since, while oil and other raw materials can be left in the ground, renewable resources have to be harvested on time or they are lost forever. Also, oil production could be cut back because its highly capital-intensive character meant that relatively few jobs were lost, but most other commodities involve much more labor-intensive production processes. In addition, in comparison with oil, other commodities are easier to stockpile and to substitute for, and tend to be less essential to the world economy and, therefore, easier to do without.

As for its impact on the industrial countries, the oil crisis has not led to the reestablishment of U.S. hegemony, as many in 1974 believed it would. Nor has it led to a stronger and more united Europe. While the economic effects have been significant, they have been far from devastating. Probably the most significant economic impact of the oil crisis on the consuming countries has been the new tradeoff they face between maintaining high economic growth and procuring ample oil supplies at stable prices. The oil crisis has also led the consuming countries to give much greater attention to avoiding shortages of supply, as opposed to the traditional, post–World War II concern with avoiding inadequate demand. As part of this change, attention has shifted from the problem of unemployment to the problem of inflation. Still, what is probably most significant about the oil crisis for the consuming countries is the sense of weakness—the inability to cooperate and take effective action—that it has revealed.

As the power of the exporting countries has increased, that of the international oil companies has declined. Yet to keep this change in perspective, it is necessary to emphasize that the companies were never the all-powerful cabal, conspiring to keep prices up and reaping superprofits in the process, that is popularly imagined. The oil companies' behavior hardly approached the competitive ideal, but since the 1950s it has been characterized by strong elements of competition, particularly between the majors and the newcomers. This competition led to the erosion of world oil prices from 1957 to 1970, but it strengthened the bargaining position of the exporting countries, which were able to exploit the rivalry between the companies. Indeed, had the companies been more unified—had the French been allowed into the Aramco consortium in the late 1940s, had Exxon come to the aid of Occidental in its struggle with Libya in 1970—the ability of the oil companies to resist the rise in exporting-country power would have been greater.

Since the beginnings of the international oil industry, the companies have been dependent upon the power of governments to shape and maintain the political order in which they function. The security that the U.S. government provided enabled the companies to go into the Middle East and develop the area's oil resources after World War II. Today, conversely, the companies are reluctant to invest in the Third World, largely because political institutions can no longer guarantee the security of their investments.

The power that the companies appeared to have in the 1950s stemmed largely from the fact that they had the support of the U.S. government. Yet, as now seems evident, that support was contingent upon the companies' serving U.S. foreign-policy interests. As we have seen, after World War II the U.S. government had an interest in gaining control of as much of the world's oil as possible and countering Soviet advances in the Middle East. The activities of the major oil companies furthered those U.S. foreign-policy interests, and as a result, the companies received strong backing from the U.S. government.

However, in subsequent years, as the foreign-policy interests of the U.S. government and the commercial interests of the companies have diverged, government support for the companies has waned. The U.S. government failed to support its most powerful multinational corporations during the pathbreaking negotiations with Libya in 1970 and again during the crucial Teheran/Tripoli negotiations in 1971. It generally refused to protest when the OPEC countries modified contract terms to the disadvantage of the companies in the early 1970s, and it refused to modify its Middle East policy, despite repeated warnings of the international oil companies.

On the other hand, the companies have frequently been able to resist the entreaties of their home governments. They would not sell the United States part of the Aramco concession following World War II, nor would they boost their liftings in the Iranian Consortium in the late 1960s. Indeed, had the unity between "Big Oil" and "Big Government" been anything like what is popularly imagined, world oil prices would probably be considerably lower today and the world energy situation far more stable.

Still, the international oil companies demonstrated remarkable flexibility in adapting to a changed world order. That companies that after World War II directly served U.S. foreign-policy interests, in Western Europe and in the Middle East, are now widely and to a considerable extent rightly accused of being instruments of the oil-exporting countries is a testament to their ability to maneuver among changing forces. The companies' success in adapting to the changes that the OPEC countries have brought about has been due in large part to the fact that their power is based on control of technology and markets, and not on the physical ownership of assets per se.

Yet the companies' adaptation was not one from which consumers benefited. The companies' failure to take a hard bargaining position in the early 1970s made it easier for the exporting countries to raise prices. Subsequently, it has not been superprofits, or monopolistic behavior, that the companies can be faulted for, but (1) their failure to develop adequate oil and gas resources outside the United States and the Middle East/North Africa and (2) their role in allocating production among the OPEC countries and thereby reducing the likelihood of rivalry among the members of the cartel.

The international oil companies are no longer the dominant powers in international oil. Their ability to shape events is considerably less than that of either the oil-exporting or the oil-consuming countries, and they are increasingly vulnerable to pressure from both these groups of nation-states. Indeed, their bargaining power vis-à-vis governments that can invoke sovereign rights is quite limited. Yet, despite the diminution in their power, the international oil companies are more likely to survive than most of the OPEC governments.

While there is a strong tendency in economic theorizing and popular depiction to regard the rise in oil prices as both a deviation from the workings of a market and a development external to the system of Western capitalism, this study suggests that these claims require qualification. Nothing was more central to the development of the capitalist world since World War II than dependence upon Middle East and North African oil, yet that dependence provided the basis for the increases in oil prices of the 1970s. Consequently, rather than view the rise in oil prices as we view a hurricane or volcano, as external to the system, we should recognize it as a product of advanced capitalism.

In many respects the oil-price revolution is a consequence of the operation of market forces, not their abandonment. It was not that the market did not operate in the period prior to the 1973–74 oil-price rise, but that it gave precisely the wrong signals. Oil prices remained low, encouraging high levels of consumption and discouraging development of alternative energy sources and oil supplies outside the Middle East and North Africa until it was too late. Subsequently, high oil prices have provided a powerful but insufficient incentive for reducing dependence upon Middle East and North African oil. Then, in 1973–74 and again in 1979, the market overreacted to reductions in world oil supplies, accentuating their effects.

The conventional imagery is that competition brings prices down; but as the rise in oil prices demonstrates, in a period of shortages the combination of uncontrolled prices and competitive bidding (both market phenomena) can drive prices up. What makes this particularly damaging to consumer interests is that once oil prices rise, they tend to stay up, exhibiting a strong downside rigidity.

This goes back to the structure of OPEC and the fact that it does not set production quotas for its members. As a result, supply and demand do not interact to determine price; rather, the oil companies adjust supply to the level of demand at the OPEC-administered price. While the temptation for countries to reduce their prices to boost their production is always present, the OPEC countries tend to resist this, for they recognize that by cutting prices this way they jeopardize the high price level that they have established. Similarly, in response to a decline in demand OPEC could lower its official price, but only once (in October 1981) has the organization done this. OPEC's reluctance to cut prices has been due to its recognition that this would be taken as a sign of the weakening

of the cartel. Consequently, most OPEC members are under considerable political pressure not to reduce prices, and they will do so only in the most extreme
situations—as they demonstrated in 1975–76 and again in 1980–81. The OPEC
countries will accept substantial production cutbacks before they reduce official
OPEC prices.

Moreover, while the conventional belief is that producers increase production
in response to higher prices, many of the exporting countries have shown that, in
response to higher prices, they are inclined to reduce their production. But again,
freedom to choose one's production level is a characteristic of a market economy, not a deviation from it.

Since World War II, no other commodity has shown a pattern of price increases comparable to oil. Prices in competitive industries tend to rise and fall in
cyclical patterns. Prices in oligopolistic industries increase in an annual or semi-
annual ratchet-like "stairstep" pattern. And prices for a material in diminishing
supply show a steady secular rise.[2] Only in oil do we find a price evolution
dominated by three dramatic leaps: one at the close of World War II, another in
1973–74, and the third in 1979–80.

This pattern reflects the enormous vulnerability of oil to political developments. Without the political crises, prices probably would have gone up anyway,
as dependence upon Middle East oil increased and demand began to run against
the limits of supply. But they need not have increased as fast or as much, for
without the precipitate cutbacks in supply that the political crises brought on,
markets would not have become as tight as they did. There would not have been
panic buying, which led to the bidding up of prices, and exporting countries
would not have found themselves with more revenue than they could absorb,
which encouraged them to hold back production and led to further price
increases.

While Saudi Arabia has had great difficulty getting OPEC to lower its official
price, it probably could have kept that price from going up as much as it did if
prices in spot markets had not gone up even more and if crisis conditions had not
been created. Had the price rises been gradual, consuming countries would have
had more time to respond to them by reducing their energy consumption and
developing new energy sources, which would have served to counter the price
increases.

The economic consequences of a more gradual increase in prices would have
been far less burdensome. Neither the OPEC surplus nor the depressing impact
on aggregate demand would have been as great. And domestic economies would
have had more time to adjust to high oil prices.

The exporting countries would also have been better off had prices gone up
gradually over a longer period of time rather than precipitously, as they did.
They would have been better able to absorb the revenues that resulted, and they
would have had more revenue when they needed it most and less when they
squandered much of it. Such a steady, gradual increase in prices might have

resulted from an internationally coordinated and planned system. It could hardly result from the anarchic workings of the market.

The problem, then, has not been that market forces were not allowed to operate or that competition was lacking, but that they were given free rein in a world economy whose regulatory structures lag far behind developments in the international marketplace. Yet this lack of regulation is a consequence of a world economy that is global coexisting with a political system that is national. Attempts to coordinate international energy policy and subject it to international control have repeatedly failed because governments have been unwilling to yield real power to international organizations or to subordinate their national interests to the demands of international coordination. This was true of the abortive attempt to organize the world oil market at the close of World War II (through the Anglo-American treaty), the efforts of the United States to organize a coordinated consuming-country energy policy in the early 1970s, the IEA's efforts to develop a consuming-country response to the rise in world oil prices, and the attempt to reach agreement on the pricing of raw materials in the North/South talks. Moreover, the opposition of a single domestic interest group can often block efforts to achieve international coordination. Nor have the exporting countries ceded much real power to OPEC.

Given this lack of international coordination, it is not surprising that stability in the world oil industry coincided with the period in which the United States remained the hegemonically dominant world power and the Anglo-American majors controlled the bulk of the world oil industry. Yet since the decline in both U.S. hegemony and the Anglo-American majors predominance, the oil-exporting countries have been able to exploit U.S.-Soviet rivalries in the Middle East, conflicts among the consuming countries, and growing competition within the international oil industry. The weakness of the dollar has also contributed to the instability of the world oil industry.

What stability there has been in world oil in recent years has been due largely to the efforts of the multinational oil corporations and the multinational banks. Yet these organizations lack both the power and the legitimacy to assume the regulatory role of governments. And, to a considerable extent, they are not the regulators but the ones whose activity needs to be regulated.

While the absence of international coordination places severe limitations on the energy policies that can be pursued and the regulations that can be imposed, international coordination in itself is no guarantee that effective energy policies will result. Indeed, policies at the national level, where governments have control, have also been characterized by a lack of planning and conscious control. Governments failed to plan for adequate long-run energy supplies, and they failed to develop satisfactory backup measures in case of emergency. Of course, it is much easier to do these things on an international basis, where both energy and nonenergy resources can be pooled, than on a national basis.

For the future, it seems that abandoning the world oil market is neither possible nor desirable. Dependence upon Middle East and North African oil may be difficult to endure, but abandonment of supplies from those areas will be intolerable for at least another decade. Still, to make that dependence bearable it should be reduced. That will require more effective consuming-government energy policies and greater efforts to find and develop new oil and gas resources. It is also vitally important that steps be taken to stabilize the Middle East, but that can happen only if the claims for recognition of national rights among the Palestinians, Iranians, and other groups in the region are accommodated. It will not happen if they are opposed, as they have been in the past.

The probability is that, in the absence of some system of regulating the world oil market, the future will be characterized by recurring crises and volatile price movements—the general direction being up. As for efforts to organize the world oil market, several patterns are possible. A consumer/producer agreement on energy prices and supplies might be reached; a hegemonic world power might emerge, capable of organizing the world oil market; or consuming countries might get together and develop effective energy policies. Each of these patterns would provide the world oil market with considerably more stability than it has at present, but none of them is likely. Rather, we will probably see a world oil market characterized by one of the following patterns: East/West rivalry; competition among blocs of consuming countries (possibly the EEC vs. the United States vs. Japan); or an atomized group of consuming countries, competing against one another for scarce supplies. Each of these situations is likely to be highly unstable, but the probability is that we will live with one of them.

APPENDIXES, NOTES, AND INDEX

TABLE A1. U.S. ENERGY CONSUMPTION BY FUEL TYPE, 1938–80 (MILLION METRIC TONS OF COAL EQUIVALENT)

	1938	1950	1955	1960	1965	1970	1973	1975	1978	1979	1980
Indigenous											
Solid fuels	364	508	419	381	458	473.5	467.5	482.6	469.0	531.5	551.6
Liquid fuels	213	428	547	572	642	776.7	749.1	683.2	702.1	691.9	695.5
Natural gas	86	227	341	466	577	780.0	798.8	707.1	704.7	725.9	710.7
Hydro, Nuclear	6	13	15	19	25	33.8	46.1	59.7	69.3	66.6	65.7
Imported											
Solid fuels	(31)	(28)	(51)	(35)	(48)	(66.5)	(45)	(57.9)	(22.2)	(47.7)	(66.9)
Liquid fuels	(43)	24	48	106	164	150.0	338.1	331.2	451.7	415.9	308.4
Natural gas	—	(1)	(1)	6	16	13.1	18.8	19.7	29.1	34.9	34.5
Total	669	1,201	1,370	1,550	1,882	2,227.1	2,418.5	2,283.5	2,428.3	2,470.3	2,369.7
Indigenous (%)											
Solid fuels	54.4	42.3	30.6	24.6	24.3	21.3	19.3	21.1	19.3	21.5	23.3
Liquid fuels	31.8	35.6	39.9	36.9	34.1	34.9	31.0	29.9	28.9	28.0	29.3
Natural gas	12.9	18.9	24.9	30.1	30.7	35.0	33.0	31.0	29.0	29.4	30.0
Hydro, Nuclear	.9	1.1	1.1	1.2	1.3	1.5	1.9	2.6	2.9	2.7	2.8
Imported (%)											
Solid fuels	(4.6)	(2.3)	(3.7)	(2.3)	(2.6)	(3.0)	(.2)	(2.5)	(.9)	(1.9)	(2.8)
Liquid fuels	(6.4)	2.0	3.5	6.8	8.7	6.7	14.0	14.5	18.6	16.8	13.0
Natural gas	—	(.1)	(.1)	0.4	0.9	0.6	0.8	0.9	1.2	1.4	1.5
Ratio of production to consumption	1.084	1.005	1.002	.951	.930	.957	.870	.848	.810	.835	.882

Figures for 1938, 1950, 1955, 1960, and 1965 derived from Darmstadter, *Energy in the World Economy*, table 10, p. 623; figures for 1970, 1973, 1975, 1978, 1979, and 1980 from U.N., *Yearbook of World Energy Statistics 1979 and 1980*, table 6.

TABLE A2. WEST EUROPEAN ENERGY CONSUMPTION BY FUEL TYPE, 1938–80 (MILLION METRIC TONS OF COAL EQUIVALENT)

	1938	1950	1955	1960	1965	1970	1973	1975	1978	1979	1980
Indigenous											
Solid fuels	563	488	533	500	483	356.6	316.4	306.5	288.1	291.9	301.9
Liquid fuels	1	6	14	23	32	29.0	29.3	42.2	127.7	167.0	178.8
Natural gas	—	2	7	16	27	98.9	182.8	214.7	227.1	239.9	232.1
Hydro, Nuclear	8	14	20	29	37	47.1	53.4	61.7	73.9	78.5	79.4
Imported											
Solid fuels	(20)	1	33	30	43	58.7	49.1	33.2	60.6	86.4	83.9
Liquid fuels	47	73	141	252	495	702.6	833.0	730.1	701.0	713.8	637.8
Natural gas	—	—	—	—	1	2.2	9.5	18.3	38.0	41.3	45.1
Total	619	584	748	850	1,117	1,295.0	1,474.0	1,406.5	1,516.4	1,618.8	1,559.3
Indigenous (%)											
Solid fuels	91.0	83.6	71.3	58.8	43.2	27.5	21.5	21.8	19.0	18.0	19.4
Liquid fuels	0.2	1.0	1.9	2.7	2.9	2.2	2.0	3.0	8.4	10.3	11.5
Natural gas	—	0.3	0.9	1.9	2.4	7.6	12.4	15.3	15.0	14.8	14.9
Hydro, Nuclear	1.3	2.4	2.7	3.4	3.3	3.6	3.6	4.4	4.9	4.8	5.1
Imported (%)											
Solid fuels	(3.2)	0.2	4.4	3.5	3.8	4.5	3.3	2.4	4.0	5.3	5.4
Liquid fuels	7.6	12.5	18.9	29.6	44.3	54.3	56.5	51.9	46.2	44.1	40.9
Natural gas	—	—	—	—	0.1	0.2	0.6	1.3	2.5	2.6	2.9
Ratio of production to consumption	.958	.873	.767	.668	.517	.411	.395	.444	.473	.480	.508

Figures for 1938, 1950, 1955, 1960, and 1965 derived from Darmstadter, *Energy in the World Economy*, table 10, p. 623; figures for 1970, 1973, 1975, 1978, 1979, and 1980 from U.N., *Yearbook of World Energy Statistics 1979 and 1980*, table 1.

TABLE A3. JAPANESE ENERGY CONSUMPTION BY FUEL TYPE, 1938–80 (MILLION METRIC TONS OF COAL EQUIVALENT)

	1938	1950	1955	1960	1965	1970	1973	1975	1978	1979	1980
Indigenous											
Solid fuels	49	38	43	52	50	35.8	22.1	17.9	18.0	16.7	17.1
Liquid fuels	1	—	—	1	1	1.1	1.0	0.9	0.8	0.7	0.7
Natural gas	—	—	—	1	3	3.5	3.9	3.7	4.0	3.8	3.4
Hydro, Nuclear	3	5	6	7	9	10.4	10.0	13.7	16.6	19.2	21.7
Imported											
Solid fuels	3	(1)	2	8	17	49.7	54.1	56.9	46.0	53.0	63.4
Liquid fuels	6	3	15	43	109	215.3	280.4	253.2	313.2	313.1	294.4
Natural gas	—	—	—	—	—	1.5	3.5	8.1	20.1	24.8	30.3
Total	62	46	66	111	189	317.4	375.0	354.4	418.7	431.4	431.0
Indigenous (%)											
Solid fuels	79.0	82.6	65.2	46.8	26.5	11.3	5.9	5.1	4.3	3.9	4.0
Liquid fuels	1.6	—	—	0.9	0.5	0.3	0.3	0.3	0.2	0.2	0.2
Natural gas	—	—	—	0.9	1.6	1.1	1.0	1.0	1.0	0.9	0.8
Hydro, Nuclear	4.8	10.9	9.1	6.3	4.8	3.3	2.7	3.9	4.0	4.5	5.0
Imported (%)											
Solid fuels	4.8	(2.2)	3.0	7.2	9.0	15.7	14.4	16.1	11.0	12.3	14.7
Liquid fuels	9.7	6.5	22.7	38.7	57.7	67.8	74.8	71.4	74.8	72.6	68.3
Natural gas	—	—	—	—	—	0.5	0.9	2.3	4.8	5.7	7.0
Ratio of production to consumption	.838	.969	.751	.550	.331	.161	.099	.102	.094	.094	.099

Figures for 1938, 1950, 1955, 1960, and 1965 derived from Darmstadter, *Energy in the World Economy*, table 10, p. 642; figures for 1970, 1973, 1975, 1978, 1979, and 1980 from U.N., *Yearbook of World Energy Statistics 1979 and 1980*, table 6.

TABLE A4. ANNUAL RATES OF GROWTH IN REAL GNP/GDP, ENERGY AND OIL CONSUMPTION, AND OIL IMPORTS, 1950–81 (%)

	1950–55	1955–60	1960–65	1965–70	1970–73	1973–78	1978–79	1979–80	1980–81
U.S.									
Real GNP/GDP	4.3	2.3	4.7	3.2	4.8	2.3	3.2	– 0.2	2.0
Energy consumption	2.7	2.5	4.0	4.4	3.2	0.8	1.2	– 3.5	– 2.4
Oil consumption	5.6	2.7	3.0	4.8	5.6	1.7	–2.3	– 8.5	– 6.4
Oil imports	8.4	7.5	6.2	6.0	22.6	5.5	2.6	–19.7	–12.8
Western Europe									
Real GNP/GDP	4.9	4.4	5.0	4.8	4.4	2.1	3.2	1.4	– 0.3
Energy consumption	5.1	2.6	5.6	5.0	4.4	0.6	4.0	– 3.6	– 3.0
Oil consumption	14.5	12.1	13.9	10.0	6.1	–0.9	2.4	– 7.1	– 7.4
Oil imports	16.1	10.7	12.8	10.9	5.5	–3.0	–0.2	– 9.0	–12.8
Japan									
Real GNP/GDP	9.2	13.9	10.1	11.8	8.8	3.7	5.5	4.2	3.8
Energy consumption	7.7	10.8	11.2	13.2	6.8	0.4	4.3	– 2.8	– 1.7
Oil consumption	39.2	23.6	24.5	17.8	10.6	–0.5	0.9	–10.3	– 5.6
Oil imports	42.1	24.9	21.1	18.9	10.3	–1.5	5.0	–10.8	–10.5

Figures for 1950–55 and 1955–60 are for real GNP. For the U.S. and Western Europe, they are from OECD, *Statistics of National Accounts, 1950–61*, p. 18; for Japan, they are derived from Darmstadter, *Energy in the World Economy*, p. 867. Figures for 1960–65, 1965–70, and 1970–73 are for real GDP and are from U.N., *Yearbook of National Accounts, 1976*, vol. 2, table 4A: 150, 203, 195. Figures for 1973–78, 1978–79, 1979–80, and 1980–81 are for real GNP and are from U.S. Dept. of State, *Economic Growth of OECD Countries, 1968–78*, table 4, p. 9, and *1971–81*, p. 7.

Figures for energy consumption, oil consumption, and oil imports for 1950–55, 1955–60, and 1960–65 are from Darmstadter, *Energy in the World Economy*, table 13, pp. 733–34 and 768. Figures for energy consumption, oil consumption, and oil imports for 1965–70, 1970–73, 1973–78, 1978–79, 1979–80, and 1980–81 are derived from data in BP, *Statistical Review of the World Oil Industry* (various issues).

523

TABLE A5. REAL CAPITAL EXPENDITURES OF THE WORLD OIL INDUSTRY, 1956–80
(MILLION 1972 DOLLARS)

	1956	1960	1970	1973	1978	1979
U.S.						
1) Production	7,127	5,437	4,740	7,039	11,763	15,113
2) Exploration	1,115	910	727	804	1,316	1,597
3) Production + Exploration (1 + 2)	8,242	6,347	5,467	7,843	13,079	16,710
4) Other capital expenditures	2,508	2,096	4,254	3,028	4,548	4,670
5) Total (3 + 4)	10,750	8,443	9,721	10,871	17,627	21,380
Africa, Far East & Latin America						
1) Production	1,656	1,689	1,586	2,110	4,985	5,554
2) Exploration	239	415	383	426	623	799
3) Production + Exploration (1 + 2)	1,895	2,104	1,969	2,536	5,608	6,353
4) Other capital expenditures	1,067	1,586	3,116	2,658	6,468	6,625
5) Total (3 + 4)	2,962	3,690	5,085	5,194	12,076	12,978
Middle East						
1) Production	279	364	306	809	2,033	2,058
2) Exploration	48	58	55	47	100	108
3) Production + Exploration (1 + 2)	327	422	361	856	2,133	2,166
4) Other capital expenditures	199	255	311	506	3,065	3,118
5) Total (3 + 4)	526	677	672	1,362	5,198	5,284
Non-Communist World (excluding U.S.)						
1) Production	2,747	2,729	3,166	5,190	13,365	15,031
2) Exploration	478	670	738	804	1,373	1,674
3) Production + Exploration (1 + 2)	3,225	3,399	3,904	5,994	14,738	16,705
4) Other capital expenditures	3,583	5,058	9,847	13,124	15,892	15,334
5) Total (3 + 4)	6,808	8,457	13,751	19,118	30,630	32,039
Non-Communist World						
1) Production	9,874	8,166	7,906	12,229	25,128	30,144
2) Exploration	1,593	1,580	1,465	1,608	2,689	3,271
3) Production + Exploration (1 + 2)	11,467	9,746	9,371	13,837	27,817	33,415
4) Other capital expenditures	6,091	7,154	14,101	16,152	20,440	20,004
5) Total (3 + 4)	17,558	16,900	23,472	29,989	48,257	53,419
Non-Communist-world oil consumption (million tonnes)	750	932	1,939	2,338	2,480	2,486

Figures on industry capital expenditures are from Chase Manhattan Bank, *Capital Investments of the World Petroleum Industry, 1965*, pp. 22–27, and *1980*, schedule 4, pp. 14–19. These figures were converted to 1972 dollars by implicit price deflators in U.S. Dept. of Commerce, *The National Income and Product Accounts of the United States, 1929–76*, pp. 318–19, *1976–79*, p. 62, and *Survey of Current Business* (June 1982), p. 12. Percentages and rates of increase were also computed by author. Figures on oil consumption derived from BP, *Statistical Review of the World Oil Industry* (various issues). "Tonnes" are metric tons. Figures on production include expenditures on natural gas liquids plants.

| 1980 | % Change | | | | | % of Non-Communist World Total, 1970 |
	1956–70	1970–73	1973–78	1978–79	1979–80	
18,663	−33.5	48.5	67.1	28.5	23.5	60.0
2,171	−34.8	10.6	63.7	21.4	35.9	49.6
20,834	−33.7	43.5	66.8	27.8	24.7	58.3
5,525	69.6	−28.8	50.2	2.7	18.3	30.2
26,359	− 9.6	11.8	62.1	21.3	23.3	41.4
6,611	− 4.2	33.0	136.3	11.4	19.0	20.1
1,128	60.3	11.2	46.2	28.3	41.2	26.1
7,739	3.9	28.8	121.1	13.3	21.8	21.0
6,131	192.0	−14.7	143.3	2.4	−7.5	22.1
13,870	71.7	2.1	132.5	7.5	6.9	21.7
2,791	9.7	164.4	151.3	1.2	35.6	3.9
113	14.6	−14.5	112.8	8.0	4.6	3.8
2,904	10.4	137.1	149.2	1.5	34.1	3.9
3,707	56.3	62.7	505.7	1.7	18.9	2.2
6,611	27.8	102.7	281.6	1.7	25.1	2.9
19,043	15.3	63.9	157.5	12.5	26.7	40.0
2,128	54.4	8.9	70.8	21.9	27.1	50.4
21,171	21.1	53.5	145.9	13.3	26.7	41.7
16,267	174.8	33.3	21.1	−3.5	6.1	69.8
37,438	102.0	39.0	60.2	4.6	16.9	58.6
37,706	−19.9	54.7	105.5	20.0	25.1	
4,299	− 8.0	9.8	67.2	21.6	31.4	
42,005	−18.3	47.7	101.0	20.1	25.7	
21,792	131.5	14.5	26.5	−2.1	8.9	
63,797	33.7	27.8	60.9	10.7	19.4	
2,375	158.5	20.6	6.1	0.2	−4.5	

TABLE A6. CUMULATIVE CURRENT ACCOUNT BALANCE OF THE OPEC NATIONS, 1974–78 (BILLIONS U.S. DOLLARS)

Deficit Countries	1974–78	
Algeria	− 9.2	
Indonesia	− 3.5	
Gabon and Ecuador	− 1.2	
	−13.9	
Surplus Countries		% of Total Surplus
Iraq	13.1	7.3
Libya	7.7	4.3
Qatar	5.3	2.9
Nigeria	.2	.1
Venezuela	.5	.3
United Arab Emirates	22.0	12.2
Kuwait	32.6	18.1
Iran	29.2	16.2
Saudi Arabia	69.9	38.7
	180.5	100.1

Figures for 1974–76 from U.S. Senate, Committee on Housing and Urban Affairs, *International Debt* (Washington, D.C.: Government Printing Office, 1977), p. 220; figures for 1977–78 from U.S. Dept. of Treasury, "Statement by the Honorable C. Fred Bergsten," July 18, 1979, p. 7. Computations by author.

TABLE A7. OECD COUNTRIES' EXPORTS TO OPEC, 1972–81

	Exports to OPEC as % of Total Exports						
	1972–73	1974–75	1976–77	1978	1979	1980	1981
U.S.	5.3	8.8	10.9	11.6	8.3	8.0	9.2
Japan	7.0	13.1	14.5	14.6	13.1	14.3	15.1
France	4.9	7.8	8.6	8.2	7.8	8.9	10.7
W. Germany	3.3	6.4	8.7	8.6	6.1	6.5	8.8
Italy	5.3	9.5	12.3	12.6	10.7	12.7	17.0
U.K.	5.8	9.3	11.8	12.1	8.0	9.2	10.7
Total OECD	4.1	7.2	9.0	9.3	7.3	8.5	9.7

OECD, *Economic Outlook* (Dec. 1979), table 54, (July 1981), table 51, and (July 1982), table 47.

Share of OPEC Market (%)								
1972–73	1974	1975	1976	1977	1978	1979	1980	1981
22.8	23.4	23.0	23.5	21.1	21.1	19.5	17.7	18.3
16.4	19.0	18.0	17.2	17.9	17.9	17.4	18.5	19.4
10.7	9.8	9.8	8.7	8.8	7.9	9.8	9.8	9.2
13.3	14.0	14.4	15.3	16.0	15.5	13.6	12.5	13.1
7.7	7.8	7.9	7.8	8.7	8.9	10.0	9.8	10.9
11.4	9.1	9.9	9.7	10.4	10.9	9.4	10.6	9.4
100.0	100.0	100.0	100.0	100.0	100.0	100.0	100.0	100.0

TABLE A8. RATES OF ECONOMIC GROWTH, 1963–81 (%)

	Annual Average	Change from Preceding Year								
	1963–72	1973	1974	1975	1976	1977	1978	1979	1980	1981
Real GNP										
U.S.	4.0	5.8	-0.6	-1.1	5.4	5.5	4.8	3.2	-0.2	2.0
Japan	9.8	8.9	-1.2	2.8	5.0	5.3	5.1	5.2	4.2	2.9
Canada	5.5	7.6	3.6	1.2	5.5	2.1	3.6	2.9	0.5	3.1
W. Germany	4.5	4.9	0.4	-1.8	5.3	2.8	3.6	4.4	1.8	-0.3
France	5.5	5.4	3.2	0.2	5.2	3.1	3.8	3.3	1.4	0.4
U.K.	3.0	7.2	-1.9	-1.1	2.8	2.2	3.7	1.9	-2.1	-2.2
Italy	4.6	7.0	4.1	-3.6	5.9	1.9	2.7	4.9	3.9	-0.2
All industrial nations	4.7	6.2	0.6	-0.5	4.9	4.0	4.0	3.6	1.3	1.1
Real GDP	1968–72									
Oil-exporting countries	9.0	10.7	8.0	-0.3	12.3	5.9	1.8	2.9	-2.7	-4.6
Non-oil developing countries*	6.0	6.1	5.5	3.9	5.9	5.1	5.5	4.7	4.4	2.5
Africa	4.2	2.5	5.5	3.0	4.7	3.8	3.5	4.2	3.0	2.0
Asia*	4.9	5.3	5.7	3.2	4.9	6.4	6.2	6.1	5.8	5.0
Latin America	5.0	5.0	6.0	4.4	4.6	5.6	6.0	4.8	3.5	5.0
Middle East	6.4	4.9	5.8	7.1	7.3	3.8	7.2	5.2	6.5	5.4

*Excluding China.

IMF, *Annual Report, 1982*, pp. 6 and 12.

Notes

INTRODUCTION

1. In 1974 Abu Dhabi's membership was transferred to the United Arab Emirates, which includes the oil-producing sheikdoms of Dubai and Sharjah, as well as Abu Dhabi.

2. Unless otherwise indicated, throughout this book oil companies will be referred to by their 1982 names, rather than their names at the time of the event under discussion.

3. Joseph A. Yager and Eleanor B. Steinberg, *Energy and U.S. Foreign Policy* (Cambridge, Mass.: Ballinger, 1974), p. 237, and Fuad Rouhani, *A History of OPEC* (New York: Praeger, 1971), p. 190.

4. Paul Leo Eckbo, *The Future of World Oil* (Cambridge, Mass.: Ballinger, 1976), p. 26.

5. Ibid., p. 30.

6. Computed from data in BP, *Statistical Review of the World Oil Industry, 1970*, p. 10.

CHAPTER 1

1. See Karl Polanyi, *The Great Transformation* (Boston: Beacon Press, 1944), and Charles P. Kindleberger, *The World in Depression* (Berkeley and Los Angeles: University of California Press, 1973).

2. Kindleberger, *The World in Depression*, p. 292.

3. On the makeup of the internationalist group in the federal government, see Richard N. Gardner, *Sterling-Dollar Diplomacy* (New York: McGraw-Hill, 1956), pp. 2–4; on corporate support for interventionist policies, see David W. Eakins, "Business Planners and America's Postwar Expansion," in David Horowitz, ed., *Corporations and the Cold War* (New York: Monthly Review Press, 1969). For a statement of internationalist thinking at the time, see Norman S. Buchanan and Friedrich A. Lutz, *Rebuilding the World Economy* (New York: Twentieth Century Fund, 1947).

4. See Raymond F. Mikesell, *United States Economic Policy and International Relations* (New York: McGraw-Hill, 1952), pp. 123 and 192.

5. David Calleo and Benjamin M. Rowland, *America and the World Political Economy* (Bloomington: Indiana University Press, 1973), p. 39. The British Labor Party maintained that in an open world economy Great Britain would be forced to subordinate its domestic economic policy to the demands of the international market, and believed the result would be mass unemployment and social injustice. At the same time, the Conservative Party was sympathetic to the protection of domestic business interests. In contrast to their U.S. counterparts, British business groups supported government controls and development of more effective private agreements to control prices and the flow of trade. Much of British industry also supported the system of "imperial preference." Others wanted to hold the Commonwealth together for political reasons. Most widespread was the fear that free trade would lead to a negative balance-of-payments for Great Britain. See Gardner, *Sterling-Dollar Diplomacy*, pp. 31–38, and Gabriel Kolko, *The Politics of War* (New York: Random House, 1968), esp. chaps. 11 and 12.

6. Robert Gilpin, *U.S. Power and the Multinational Corporation* (New York: Basic Books, 1975), p. 106.

7. See Rayner's statement in U.S. Senate, Special Committee Investigating Petroleum Re-

sources, *American Petroleum Interests in Foreign Countries,* Hearings (Washington, D.C.: Government Printing Office, 1945), pp. 2–3.

8. Gerald D. Nash, *United States Oil Policy, 1890–1964* (Pittsburgh: University of Pittsburgh Press, 1968), p. 158.

9. These three sources of power were highly interconnected. Because the U.S. guaranteed Europe's security, the dollar was accepted as the world's reserve currency. Consequently, countries were ready to accept dollars, thereby facilitating the overseas expansion of U.S. (oil) corporations.

10. Production figures by area and country are from BP, *Statistical Review of the World Oil Industry,* various issues; figures on the control of Venezuelan oil are from Edith T. Penrose, *The Large International Firm in the Developing Countries* (London: Allen & Unwin, 1968), p. 58.

11. See U.S. Senate, *American Petroleum Interests in Foreign Countries,* p. 5. In 1948 the U.S. became a net importer of oil.

12. Cited in Anthony Sampson, *The Seven Sisters* (New York: Bantam Books, 1975), p. 115.

13. In the Western Hemisphere (excluding the U.S. itself), U.S. companies owned 65% of the reserves while British/Dutch interests controlled 24%. In the Eastern Hemisphere as a whole (excluding the Soviet Union), U.S. companies owned 40% of the reserves, British/Dutch interests 53%. Outside the U.S., the world's major oil-producing regions were the Caspian Basin in southern Russia, the Caribbean, the Persian Gulf, and the Netherlands East Indies; but the Persian Gulf was by far the most prodigious. See U.S. Senate, *American Petroleum Interests in Foreign Countries,* pp. 422 and 436.

14. U.S. Senate, Committee on Foreign Relations, Subcommittee on Multinational Corporations, *Multinational Oil Corporations and U.S. Foreign Policy,* Report Together with Individual Views, 93d Cong., 2nd sess. (Washington, D.C.: Government Printing Office, 1975) (hereafter referred to as *MNC Report*), p. 42, and Leonard M. Fanning, *Foreign Oil and the Free World* (New York: McGraw-Hill, 1954), p. 354.

15. Calouste Gulbenkian, an Armenian entrepreneur, had been instrumental in arranging what became the IPC concession and was rewarded with a 5% share for his efforts.

16. SoCal and Texaco were also partners in Bahrain, where their concession was extended in 1940 to the entire sheikdom.

17. *MNC Report,* pp. 36–37.

18. Walter LaFeber, *America, Russia and the Cold War, 1945–1966* (New York: Wiley, 1967), p. 28. The Soviet Union was attempting to secure a concession in the five northern provinces that were not part of the BP concession. The provinces had been exempted from the original D'Arcy concession in 1901 because they were considered to be under Russian influence. In 1946 the Soviet Union gained agreement for a concession in exchange for withdrawal of its troops; however, the Iranian Majlis (parliament) refused to accept the agreement. Benjamin Shwadran, *The Middle East, Oil, and the Great Powers* (New York: Wiley, 1973), pp. 60–62, 71.

19. Mikesell, *United States Economic Policy and International Relations,* p. 220. In 1928–29, net direct investments abroad amounted to nearly 4% of gross private domestic investment; between 1946 and 1949, they were less than 3%. Ibid., p. 231.

20. Ibid., p. 221.

21. See U.S. Senate, *American Petroleum Interests in Foreign Countries,* pp. 91–94.

22. The statement is reproduced in U.S. State Department, *Foreign Relations of the United States* (1944), 5:27–33. The section quoted here is from pp. 27–28.

23. Ibid., pp. 30–31. Though never formally approved by Congress, these objectives were repeatedly reaffirmed by U.S. policy makers. After extensive hearings in 1945–46, a Senate committee, appointed to investigate petroleum resources, endorsed the conservation of U.S. oil resources and federal encouragement for overseas development of foreign petroleum resources by U.S. companies (Nash, *United States Oil Policy,* p. 188). In November 1947 an interdepartmental committee from the State, Interior, Commerce, Army, and Navy departments reiterated the U.S. commitment to obtaining a larger share of Middle East output, while emphasizing the use of Western Hemisphere reserves to meet U.S. needs. Joyce Kolko and Gabriel Kolko, *The Limits of Power* (New York: Harper & Row, 1972), p. 415.

In 1949 the National Petroleum Council, an official group of oil industry executives who advised the federal government, recommended that U.S. petroleum policy be based on the domestic production of petroleum. However, the report said that "the participation of United States nationals in the development of world oil resources is in the interest of . . . our national security. . . . Oil from abroad should be available to the United States to the extent that it may be needed to supplement our domestic supplies." These principles were then endorsed by the Department of Interior. See Shoshana Klebanoff, *Middle East Oil and U.S. Foreign Policy* (New York: Praeger, 1974), pp. 62–63 and 72.

24. Cited in Kolko, *The Politics of War,* p. 297.

25. *MNC Report,* pp. 37–38.

26. Cited in ibid., p. 38.

27. Ibid., p. 39.

28. Joe Stork, *Middle East Oil and the Energy Crisis* (New York: Monthly Review Press, 1975), p. 32.

29. For a brief account of the PRC, see *MNC Report,* pp. 39–41; Nash, *United States Oil Policy,* pp. 172–74; or Klebanoff, *Middle East Oil and United States Foreign Policy,* pp. 19–32. Documents on the history of the PRC are compiled in U.S. Senate, Committee on Foreign Relations, Subcommittee on Multinational Corporations, *A Documentary History of the Petroleum Reserves Corporation, 1943–44* (Washington, D.C.: Government Printing Office, 1974).

30. Rather than take a position on whether the Gulf is the "Persian" or the "Arabian" Gulf, I refer to it as simply "the Gulf." Where this might create ambiguity with the Gulf of Mexico, I have followed convention and used "Persian Gulf." I apologize to any who find this offensive.

31. On the pipeline proposal, see Shwadran, *The Middle East, Oil and the Great Powers,* pp. 329–49.

32. *Department of State Bulletin,* June 15, 1947, pp. 1171–72.

33. Klebanoff, *Middle East Oil and United States Foreign Policy,* p. 47.

34. U.S. Senate, Committee on Foreign Relations, *Executive Sessions of the Senate Foreign Relations Committee,* made public May 1976 (Washington, D.C.: Government Printing Office, 1976), p. 77.

35. See U.S. Senate, Committee on Foreign Relations, *Petroleum Agreement with Great Britain and Northern Ireland* (Washington, D.C.: Government Printing Office, 1947), p. 188.

36. Cited in ibid., pp. 252–53.

37. Ibid., pp. 255–60.

38. Since the treaty had aimed in part at resisting Soviet advances in Iran, interest in the treaty declined in 1947, after the Soviet Union withdrew its bid for a concession.

39. *MNC Report,* p. 45.

40. SoCal and Texaco carefully calculated whether they would earn more from accepting or rejecting the merger, and both concluded that their profits would be greater if they accepted it. However, there is evidence that they miscalculated, failing to take account of the limitations their new partners would place on Aramco's total production and on the marketing of CalTex's Arabian crude. Possibly offsetting this were the gains from control of supply that ultimately accrued to the four Aramco partners. SoCal also considered, but rejected, the alternative of declining the merger and relying on sales to U.S. independent producers. For a discussion of this, see *MNC Report,* pp. 47–49.

41. Robert Stobaugh and Daniel Yergin, eds., *Energy Future* (New York: Random House, 1979), p. 21.

42. To restrict competition in the international industry, in 1928 the IPC partners pledged to refrain from competing with one another. Market-sharing agreements were also worked out in that year. SoCal and Texaco had been able to go into Saudi Arabia because they were not IPC partners.

43. *MNC Report,* p. 52.

44. Ibid., p. 54.

45. This was an old objective of Venezuelan oil policy. In 1943 the government increased tax revenues with the stated intention of obtaining at least half of the companies' future profits. Anxious

to maintain Venezuelan production during World War II, the U.S. State Department urged the companies to take a conciliatory attitude toward the increase. At the same time, the companies were concerned that their concessions would soon run out. Consequently, they agreed to the increase in return for a 40-year extension on their concessions and the opening of new areas for exploration by foreign companies. As a result, in 1944 the Venezuelan government claimed it had met the 50% goal. However, upon coming to power, the new government discovered that the income tax figures had been manipulated to justify the 50% claims. Consequently, the new regime decreed a $27 million levy to bring the figure up to 50%, according to its computations. The 1948 Additional Tax consolidated this victory. See Franklin Tugwell, *The Politics of Oil in Venezuela* (Stanford: Stanford University Press, 1975), pp. 43–45. See also Fanning, *Foreign Oil and the Free World,* pp. 71–88.

46. "Tax-paid cost" refers to both the cost of producing a barrel of oil and the tax payments that must be paid to the host government on each barrel. For example, if the production cost is 20¢ a barrel and the government levies a tax of 80¢ a barrel, the tax-paid cost is $1 a barrel.

47. Peter Francis Cowhey, "The Problems of Plenty: Energy Policy and International Politics" (unpublished Ph.D. thesis, University of California at Berkeley), p. 158.

48. Leonard Mosley, *Power Play* (Baltimore: Penguin, 1974), pp. 182–84.

49. Ibid., p. 184. The figure for Saudi Arabia's profit share is computed from data in Charles Issawi and Mohammed Yeganeh, *The Economics of Middle Eastern Oil* (London: Faber & Faber, 1963), pp. 188–89.

50. The memorandum is reproduced in U.S. Senate, Committee on Foreign Relations, Subcommittee on Multinational Corporations, *Multinational Corporations and U.S. Foreign Policy,* Hearings, 93d Cong., 1st and 2nd sess. (Washington, D.C.: Government Printing Office, 1974) (hereafter *MNC Hearings*), part 7, pp. 122–34; the quoted statement is from p. 128.

51. Kolko and Kolko, *The Limits of Power,* pp. 420–25.

52. Traditionally (and in all other cases), an "income tax" is a payment based on profits while a "royalty" is a payment based on the quantity produced and, therefore, a cost of doing business. According to these definitions, the payments to the oil-exporting countries should have been considered royalties, as they had been prior to 1950, for they were based on the quantity sold, not the total profits earned. The difference this makes for tax purposes is shown by the following hypothetical examples:

	Treated as Royalty	Treated as Income Tax
Price per barrel	$1.80	$1.80
Cost	.20	.20
Royalty	.80	—
Notional profit	$ .80	$1.60
Income tax paid to host government	—	.80
Tax credit	—	.80
Actual profit	.80	.80
Tax owed to home govt. @ 48% corporate tax rate—tax credit	.384	.00*

*In fact, this company carries forward a tax credit of 41.6¢ per barrel.

53. *MNC Report,* p. 85, and Louis Turner, *Oil Companies in the International System* (London: Allen & Unwin, 1978), p. 134.

54. Cited in *MNC Report,* p. 86.

55. Estimates of the profit split between companies and exporting countries vary. See Hanns Maull, "The Price of Crude Oil in the International Energy Market," *Energy Policy,* 5, no. 2 (1977): 150, and Tugwell, *The Politics of Oil in Venezuela,* p. 150, for compilations of some of these estimates.

56. Mosley, *Power Play*, pp. 200–201, and Harvey O'Connor, *The Empire of Oil* (New York: Monthly Review Press, 1955), p. 326.

57. Turner, *Oil Companies in the International System*, p. 80.

58. Mosley, *Power Play*, p. 205.

59. Penrose, *The Large International Firm in the Developing Countries*, p. 69.

60. In 1950, more than a fourth of all refined products supplied to the non-Communist world from outside the Western Hemisphere came from Iran. During the Iranian shutdown, nearly half of these supplies were replaced by increased shipments of refined products from the U.S. Gulf and the Caribbean, and most of the remainder was replaced by increased refinery runs in Western Europe. (See Harold Lubell, *Middle East Oil Crises and Western Europe's Energy Supplies* [Baltimore: Johns Hopkins University Press, 1963], pp. 6–8.) Insofar as problems arose, they were due to a shortage of tanker capacity to carry the oil products from their source in the Western Hemisphere to where they were consumed in the Eastern Hemisphere. Klebanoff, *Middle East Oil and U.S. Foreign Policy*, p. 99.

61. Harvey O'Connor, *World Crisis in Oil* (New York: Monthly Review Press, 1962), p. 291.

62. The officer corps was antagonistic to Mossadegh because it lost many privileges and much power as he increased social welfare spending at the expense of the military budget. The landowners feared his plans for land reform, and other conservative elements were fearful of changes that he might institute. See *MERIP Reports*, no. 18 (June 1973), p. 7. These developments are also recounted in Kolko and Kolko, *The Limits of Power*, pp. 418–19, and in Mosley, *Power Play*, p. 212.

63. In 1954 Gen. George C. Stewart, director of the U.S. Office of Military Assistance, told the House Committee on Foreign Affairs that "when this crisis came on and the thing was about to collapse, we violated our normal criteria and among other things we did, we provided the army immediately on an emergency basis blankets, boots, uniforms, electric generators, and medical supplies that permitted and created an atmosphere in which they could support the Shah. . . . The guns they had in their hands, the trucks that they rode in, the armored cars that they drove through the streets, and the radio communications that permitted their control, were all furnished through the military defense assistance program. . . . had it not been for this program, a government unfriendly to the United States probably would now be in power" (quoted in *MERIP Reports*, no. 40 [Sept. 1975], pp. 6–7). While the oil industry was undoubtedly pleased with the result, there is no evidence that it had a role in putting the coup together. Turner, *Oil Companies in the International System*, p. 73.

64. Despite these problems, a group of State Department officials argued that by getting the majors to relinquish territory in their Middle East concessions and bringing additional companies in, production could be increased and the demands of the oil-exporting countries for more revenue would thereby be met. They believed this approach would satisfy the Shah's need for revenue. See the testimony of Richard Funkhouser, a former State Department official, in *MNC Hearings*, part 7, pp. 135–60. However, this approach was rejected.

65. Ibid., p. 289.

66. Ibid., p. 301.

67. *MNC Report*, p. 67.

68. Acting on the basis of a Federal Trade Commission report, *The International Petroleum Cartel* (filed in 1951), the attorney general called for an investigation of the petroleum industry, and on June 23, 1952, President Truman instructed the Department of Justice to proceed with a grand jury investigation. However, in January 1953 the Departments of State, Defense, and Interior wrote a joint report in which they asked that the grand jury investigation be terminated and replaced by a civil suit. Their report noted that "American oil operations are, for all practical purposes, instruments of our foreign policy" toward the oil-producing countries in the Middle East. What the local inhabitants "think of the oil companies, they think of American enterprise and the American system; we cannot afford to leave unchallenged the assertions that these companies are engaged in a criminal conspiracy for the purpose of predatory exploitation." The report stated that "in both Venezuela and the Middle East a wave of economic nationalism which might endanger American interests is entirely possible.

Once such powerful political and emotional forces are unleashed, it is difficult or impossible to restrain them. The developments in Iran are an example.''

To overcome these problems, the report maintained that the oil industry and the U.S. government had to work together. However, ''if Government and industry are to act together to promote foreign policy and security objectives in petroleum, there must be a basis of mutual confidence between them. Criminal proceedings are not likely to produce such confidence between the two parties in this dispute.'' Hence the report recommended that the grand jury investigation be terminated and that any subsequent legal proceedings take the form of a civil suit. (The report can be found in *MNC Hearings*, part 8, pp. 3–9; the quoted sections are on pp. 5, 7, and 8.)

The Justice Department argued that a civil suit would be far more cumbersome and time consuming and that it was not in the U.S. interest that the oil companies behave monopolistically. On January 11, 1953, President Truman decided to terminate the grand jury investigation and proceed with a civil suit. *MNC Report*, p. 63.

69. See Burton I. Kaufman, ''Oil and Antitrust: The Oil Cartel Case and the Cold War,'' *Business History Review*, 41, no. 1 (1977):55. See also *MNC Report*, pp. 57–74 (esp. pp. 67–70), for a discussion of these developments.

70. In a colloquy with Sen. Frank Church twenty years later, Howard Page explained: ''Now, they—I don't know their reasons for it but they—had a feeling, well, 'Because people were always yacking about it we had better put some independents in there.' '' Sen. Church: ''Put a few independents in?'' Mr. Page: ''Yes.'' Sen. Church: ''Window dressing?'' Mr. Page: ''That's right.'' *MNC Hearings*, part 7, p. 297.

Twelve independent companies applied for a share in the Consortium. Price-Waterhouse certified the financial viability of eleven of them; however, two of these eleven dropped out. The 5% share was then divided among the remaining nine companies in proportion to the total each company had asked for. For independents who had both the capital and the market outlets, it was an extremely lucrative arrangement. For every million dollars invested, each of these companies expected to receive an $850,000 profit annually. O'Connor, *The Empire of Oil*, p. 330.

71. Mosley, *Power Play*, pp. 229–31.

72. *MNC Report*, p. 102.

73. Though the U.S. organized the Baghdad Pact, in the end it decided not to join it for fear of antagonizing the Arab states that were not members. Syria, Egypt, and Saudi Arabia saw the Baghdad Pact not as a means of protecting them from the Soviet Union, but as a means of promoting Iraq as the leader of the Arab world against King Saud (the Iraqi leaders' dynastic enemy) and against the rising power of Nasser in Egypt. The pact was also viewed as a means of strengthening Western entrenchment in the area. See Shwadran, *The Middle East, Oil, and the Great Powers*, p. 534.

74. Cited in LaFeber, *America, Russia and the Cold War*, pp. 157–58.

75. Geoffrey Chandler, ''The Innocence of Oil Companies,'' *Foreign Policy*, no. 27 (1977), p. 53.

76. Roughly two-thirds of Western Europe's petroleum requirements were normally dependent upon the Suez Canal and Middle East pipelines for transportation, and inadequate tanker capacity limited the possibility of shipping the oil around Africa. Klebanoff, *Middle East Oil and U.S. Foreign Policy*, p. 127.

77. Engler states that ''during the critical month of November, 1956, the advisory Middle East Emergency Committee (MEEC) responsible for coordinating oil shipments was suspended. American representatives were temporarily withdrawn from participation in joint United States–European efforts. Plans to meet Europe's oil needs worked out during the preceding summer were not implemented until December.'' Robert Engler, *The Politics of Oil* (Chicago: University of Chicago Press, 1961), p. 261.

78. Seventy-three percent of the decline in oil shipments during the five-month emergency period were compensated by extra shipments from the Western Hemisphere, and roughly three-fourths of this came from the U.S. Gulf. In addition, rationing and mild weather reduced demand in Western Europe. Total shipments of crude and petroleum products fell by only 8% during the five-month

crisis period; however, this decline was 20% below normal in November and 4% below normal in March. Lubell, *Middle East Oil Crises and Western Europe's Energy Supplies,* pp. 13 and 15.

79. See Farouk A. Sankari, "The Character and Impact of Arab Oil Embargoes," in Naiem A. Sherbiny and Mark A. Tessler, eds., *Arab Oil* (New York: Praeger, 1976), pp. 266–67; and Klebanoff, *Middle East Oil and U.S. Foreign Policy,* pp. 130–31.

80. Great Britain maintained bases on Cyprus, but the most important force in the eastern Mediterranean was the U.S. Sixth Fleet.

81. It accounted for only 1.2% of non–North American, non-Communist production in 1950 and only 2.7% in 1957. M. A. Adelman, *The World Petroleum Market* (Baltimore: Johns Hopkins University Press, 1972), p. 80.

82. Ibid., pp. 80–81 and 96. About one-tenth of non-Communist production outside North America is excluded from these figures on the grounds that it was sold in protected markets and was not in competition with other sources of crude. Were this production included, "the difference would be imperceptible." Also, the production figures are based on what a company was entitled to lift rather than what it actually produced (ibid., pp. 78–79 and 81). In 1950 the seven largest firms accounted for 72% of refinery throughput outside North America and the Communist countries. Penrose, *The Large International Firm in the Developing Countries,* p. 78.

83. Adelman, *The World Petroleum Market,* p. 88.

84. The figure for tanker capacity is 29.1%, but this is misleadingly low because it excludes long-term chartered tonnage and control over pipelines, both of which were dominated by the majors. The figures are from Maull, "The Price of Crude Oil in the International Energy Market," p. 148, and Maull's figures are compiled from Neil H. Jacoby, *Multinational Oil* (New York: Macmillan, 1974).

85. Since payments to the exporting countries were essentially fixed on a per barrel basis and did not depend on profits, it was generally in a company's interest to show profits on production and losses on downstream operations.

86. Although it may be argued that limitations on production were necessary to conserve oil and to make sure no company exhausted its partners' reserves, it is doubtful that this was a major consideration in this period because Middle East resources were perceived as almost boundless.

87. *MNC Report,* pp. 77–81, and Christopher T. Rand, *Making Democracy Safe for Oil* (Boston: Little, Brown, 1975), pp. 108–9.

88. Penrose, *The Large International Firm in the Developing Countries,* p. 162, and Rand, *Making Democracy Safe for Oil,* p. 189.

89. This was later modified to a "halfway" price, or the tax-paid cost plus half the difference between the tax-paid cost and the posted price, and still later to the "quarterway" price. See John Blair, *The Control of Oil* (New York: Pantheon, 1976), p. 105.

90. Adelman, *The World Petroleum Market,* pp. 84–85.

91. Blair, *The Control of Oil,* pp. 98–101.

92. Adelman, *The World Petroleum Market,* p. 88.

93. Piercy's statement is from *MNC Hearings,* part 7, p. 334. See also *MNC Report,* p. 95.

94. The eighth major, CFP, failed to enjoy this option, but it was perpetually crude short. On Kuwait as a balancing factor, see Rand, *Making Democracy Safe for Oil,* pp. 174–77.

95. Adelman, *The World Petroleum Market,* p. 100.

96. Mikdashi provides figures that show the cost of Middle East oil going from 18¢ a barrel in 1946 to 12¢ a barrel in 1955. Blair shows the price of Middle East crude oil going from just over $1 in 1946 to $2.22 in 1947, then fluctuating between $1.70 and $2 in the early 1950s. See Zuhayr Mikdashi, *A Financial Analysis of Middle Eastern Oil Concessions: 1901–1965* (New York: Praeger, 1966), pp. 94 and 168, and Blair, *The Control of Oil,* pp. 117–18.

97. Mikdashi, *A Financial Analysis of Middle Eastern Oil Concessions,* p. 168; Blair, *The Control of Oil,* p. 117; and Maull, "The Price of Crude Oil in the International Energy Market," p. 147.

98. How effective the ECA was is unclear. In the latter part of 1950, ECA tried (without success) to get the price lowered further, and it was never able to secure reductions in product prices. Its power

was limited by the probability that, had ECA refused to finance oil purchases, Western Europe and the United States would have objected. By insisting that Middle East oil sell for no more than U.S. oil (parity pricing), the ECA may have inadvertently helped to ensure that it would also sell for no less. See Wayne A. Leeman, *The Price of Middle East Oil* (Ithaca: Cornell University Press, 1962), pp. 143–45 and 148–49.

99. Whether this was a decision by the major companies or the result of competitive behavior is unclear. Penrose takes the first position, stating that "as more Middle East crude became available, and especially as European refineries were completed to process it, the interest of the majors in an f.o.b. price of crude from the Persian Gulf that made it profitable from the narrow point of view of their refining affiliates and subsidiaries to use oil from this source, coincided with the interest of the U.S. Economic Co–Operation Administration in securing a reduction in the cost of oil imports to Europe from the Persian Gulf. Thus, the post-war 'revolution' in crude-oil prices is more easily explained as a deliberate decision of the major Companies (to be sure, taken under government pressure) than as the consequence of competition among sellers of Middle Eastern crude oil forcing prices down as they endeavored to extend their marketing areas." But Adelman, pointing to the fact that all the majors were substantial net sellers of crude, maintains that "the 1948–49 price changes were a substantial but incomplete competitive adaptation to new cost conditions."

Penrose's argument is in *The Large International Firm in the Developing Countries,* pp. 183–91; the quoted section is from p. 187. Adelman's argument is in *The World Petroleum Market,* pp. 131–159; the quoted sentence is from p. 159.

100. Adelman, *The World Petroleum Market,* p. 147.

101. Robert B. Krueger, *The United States and International Oil* (New York: Praeger, 1975), p. 45.

102. Since the high-cost, low-output "stripper" wells were exempt from the prorationing system, the burden of the production cutbacks fell on the larger producers.

103. In retrospect, it might seem that the national security interest would have been best advanced by conserving domestic resources, but the belief was that the U.S. had to maintain a strong domestic industry with the capacity to produce—not just a reserve that could be drawn upon in an emergency (and quickly depleted). The high cost of storing oil was a factor in this debate.

104. Adelman, *The World Petroleum Market,* p. 150.

105. Edward H. Shaffer, *The Oil Import Program of the United States* (New York: Praeger, 1968), p. 18. In the late 1950s the majors appear to have been divided on Middle East imports. Exxon, which had large interests in Venezuela, advocated "Western Hemisphere crude for the Western Hemisphere." In contrast, Gulf, which had access to more oil in Kuwait than it had market outlets for, was a strong and consistent opponent of import restrictions. Exxon's slogan is reported in Adelman, *The World Petroleum Market,* p. 146; for Gulf's position, see Engler, *The Politics of Oil,* p. 233.

106. Between 1954 and 1958 the international majors' share of U.S. imports dropped from 68% to 45%. Shaffer, *The Oil Import Program of the United States,* p. 22.

107. Ibid., p. 18.

108. The quotas were allocated to "traditional" importers of oil and oil products. Since these were mainly the large companies, this provision served to quell the majors' opposition to the import quotas, for these quota rights soon became valuable property. Also, the quota allowed for unrestricted pipeline imports from Canada, but these were limited by informal agreement between the U.S. and Canada. Ibid., p. 215; see also J. E. Hartshorn, *Politics and World Oil Economics* (New York: Praeger, 1967), p. 228. The figures on the rates of growth of U.S. imports are from Peter R. Odell, *Oil and World Power* (Baltimore: Penguin, 1974), p. 34.

109. Over time, the annual costs became greater as the quantities increased and the price of Middle East oil fell. In 1970, President Nixon's Cabinet Task Force on Oil Import Controls estimated that in 1969 the controls cost U.S. consumers roughly $4.8 billion (cited in Richard B. Mancke, "The Genesis of the U.S. Oil Crisis," in Joseph S. Szyliowicz and Bard E. O'Neill, eds., *The*

Energy Crisis and U.S. Foreign Policy [New York: Praeger, 1975], p. 57). Other estimates of the cost of the import quotas to consumers are in Odell, *Oil and World Power*, p. 35; Shaffer, *The Oil Import Program of the United States*, pp. 218–19; and Taki Rifai, *The Pricing of Crude Oil* (New York: Praeger, 1975), p. 315.

110. Peter Odell reports that "the quotas led to some 150 million tons more oil per annum being produced in the U.S.A. than would otherwise have been the case, and so overseas producers have 'lost' an equivalent amount." He also estimated that the higher prices made possible by the quota reduced U.S. oil consumption by an additional 100 million tons a year (*Oil and World Power*, pp. 38–39).

According to BP, *Statistical Review of the World Oil Industry*, in 1965, outside the U.S., non-Communist oil production came to 865.4 million tons. (Of this, the Middle East produced 415.5 million tons, North Africa 91.8 million tons, and Venezuela 182.1 million tons.) Adding 250 million tons (150 + 100) to this figure, one finds the total is reduced by 22.4% (250/(865.4 + 250). Moreover, since the incremental U.S. consumption would probably have been met by increasing the supply in the primary producing areas, the consequent reduction in production in these areas was probably greater than 22.4%. These calculations are rough, but they suggest an order of magnitude.

CHAPTER 2

1. W. G. Jensen, *Energy in Europe, 1945–1980* (London: G. T. Foulis, 1967), p. 11.

2. In 1938 the shares of liquid fuels in total energy consumption were as follows: U.S., 31.8%; Canada, 25.8%; Japan, 11.5%; and Western Europe, 7.7%. Joel Darmstadter with Perry D. Teitelbaum and Jaroslav G. Polach, *Energy in the World Economy* (Baltimore: Johns Hopkins University Press, 1971), table 11, pp. 653–54, and p. 679.

3. In 1938 the developing market economies relied on solid fuels for 48.4% of their energy consumption and on oil for 43.9%. In 1950 oil accounted for 58.1% and coal for 33.6%. After that, coal's share continued to decline, natural gas increased in importance, and oil's position remained relatively constant. The figures for 1970 were coal, 21.2%; oil, 61.3%; and natural gas, 14.3%. Ibid., p. 688, and U.N., *World Energy Supplies, 1971–75*, p. 3.

4. In April 1948, in an effort to halt Yugoslavia's separatist trend, the Soviet Union threatened to cut off its oil supplies. Then, after Yugoslavia was expelled from the COMINFORM, both the U.S.S.R. and Rumania greatly reduced oil exports to the renegade Communist country. However, Yugoslavia was able to secure oil from Western sources. Also, Rumania, the East European country that has pursued the most independent foreign policy in recent years, is the only East European country that is not dependent upon the Soviet Union for its oil supplies. See Arthur Jay Klinghoffer, *The Soviet Union and International Oil Politics* (New York: Columbia University Press, 1977), pp. 195 and 210.

5. Darmstadter, *Energy in the World Economy*, table 11, p. 654, and p. 679.

6. Shoshana Klebanoff, *Middle East Oil and U.S. Foreign Policy* (New York: Praeger, 1974), p. 73.

7. See ibid., p. 75.

8. Wayne A. Leeman, *The Price of Middle East Oil* (Ithaca: Cornell University Press, 1962), p. 148, and *NYT*, May 14, 1951, p. 37.

9. The Marshall Plan legislation had been premised on an anticipated world shortage of petroleum and had advocated that Europe's oil be drawn from outside the U.S. and that petroleum-consuming equipment be discouraged where alternative fuels were available. The figures on the share of Europe's oil that came from the Middle East are from *Business Week*, May 30, 1959, p. 34, and Edward H. Shaffer, *The Oil Import Program of the United States* (New York: Praeger, 1968), p. 13.

10. Edith T. Penrose, *The Large International Firm in the Developing Countries* (London: Allen & Unwin, 1968), p. 82.

11. Peter R. Odell, *Oil and World Power* (Baltimore: Penguin, 1974), p. 126. Oil refining was the only major industry in which Japan relaxed its opposition to foreign capital, and by 1960 foreign

companies accounted for three quarters of the investment in Japanese refining. *Business Week,* Feb. 13, 1960, p. 96.

12. Louis Turner, *Oil Companies in the International System* (London: Allen & Unwin, 1978), p. 60, and Peter Francis Cowhey, "The Problems of Plenty: Energy Policy and International Politics" (unpublished Ph.D. thesis, University of California at Berkeley), pp. 256 and 404.

13. Jensen, *Energy in Europe,* p. 58.

14. Significant automation is now possible with coal boilers, but this was not true in the mid-1950s.

15. M. A. Adelman and Soren Friis, "Changing Monopolies and European Oil Supplies: The Shifting Balance of Economic and Political Power in the World Oil Market," *Energy Policy* 2, no. 4 (Dec. 1974): 283.

16. Taki Rifai, *The Pricing of Crude Oil* (New York: Praeger, 1975), p. 208.

17. See Fred Block, *The Origins of International Economic Disorder* (Berkeley: University of California Press, 1977), pp. 114–19 and 129–37, for an analysis of these developments.

18. Computed from data in U.S. Department of Commerce, *Survey of Current Business* (Aug. 1957), p. 24.

19. Computed from data in U.N., *Yearbook of International Trade, 1972–73,* vol. 1, table A, and 2:331–32.

20. Darmstadter, *Energy in the World Economy,* p. 679; and Odell, *Oil and World Power,* p. 103.

21. Organization for Economic Cooperation and Development, *Oil: The Present Situation and Future Prospects* (Paris: OECD, 1973), pp. 23, 27, and 29.

22. The figures on European coal production are from Darmstadter, *Energy in the World Economy,* p. 623, and U.N., *World Energy Supplies, 1961–70,* pp. 48–49. The estimate of the energy content of Europe's coal reserves is from J. Herbert Hollomon and Michel Grenon, *Energy Research and Development* (Cambridge, Mass.: Ballinger, 1975), p. 129.

23. Darmstadter, *Energy in the World Economy,* p. 642, and U.N., *World Energy Supplies, 1961–70,* p. 71.

24. M. A. Adelman, *The World Petroleum Market* (Baltimore: Johns Hopkins University Press, 1972), p. 272.

25. In 1955 coal output per person-year was only 155 metric tons, 28% below the 1935 level. John Surrey, "Japan's Uncertain Energy Prospects: The Problem of Import Dependence," *Energy Policy* 2, no. 3 (Sept. 1974): 210.

26. Ibid., pp. 210–11.

27. Richard L. Gordon, *The Evolution of Energy Policy in Western Europe* (New York: Praeger, 1970), p. 241.

28. Hollomon and Grenon, *Energy Research and Development,* p. 182.

29. Horst Mendershausen, *Coping with the Oil Crisis: French and German Experiences* (Baltimore: Johns Hopkins University Press, 1976), pp. 26–27.

30. Adelman, *The World Petroleum Market,* pp. 234–35.

31. Cowhey, "The Problems of Plenty," pp. 244–45.

32. Gordon, *The Evolution of Energy Policy in Western Europe,* p. 244. For a discussion of the efforts to formulate a common energy policy, see J. E. Hartshorn, *Politics and World Oil Economics* (New York: Praeger, 1967), pp. 285–96.

33. Romani Prodi and Alberto Clo, "Europe," in Raymond Vernon, ed., *The Oil Crisis: In Perspective,* issued as *Daedalus* 104, no. 4 (1975): 92; and U.S. House of Representatives, Committee on Foreign Affairs, *Foreign Policy Implications of the Energy Crisis* (Washington, D.C.: Government Printing Office, 1972), p. 378.

34. The oil companies tended to oppose the formulation of comprehensive energy policies because they recognized that such policies, whether on a national or an international level, would limit their room to maneuver. Odell, *Oil and World Power,* p. 109, and Hartshorn, *Politics and World Oil Economics,* p. 289.

35. James W. McKie, "The United States," in Vernon, ed., *The Oil Crisis*, p. 75, and Darmstadter, *Energy in the World Economy*, p. 653.

36. Darmstadter, *Energy in the World Economy*, p. 733, and U.N., *World Energy Supplies, 1961–70*, p. 24.

37. For most of the postwar period, natural gas has been available in northern Italy and southern France, but the quantities have been small. Odell, *Oil and World Power*, p. 109.

38. Ibid., pp. 109–12.

39. Bradford Snell, "American Ground Transport," in Jerome H. Skolnick and Elliott Currie, eds., *Crisis in American Institutions* (Boston: Little, Brown, 1976), p. 321.

40. Steven A. Schneider, "Less Is More: Conservation and Renewable Energy," *Working Papers for a New Society* 6, no. 2 (Mar./Apr. 1978): 50.

41. Automobile Manufacturers' Assn., *Automobile Facts and Figures, 1971*, p. 18, and *1974*, p. 22.

42. Lloyd J. Dumas, *The Conservation Response* (Lexington, Mass.: Heath, 1976), pp. 110–11.

43. Snell, "American Ground Transport," in Skolnick and Currie, eds., *Crisis in American Institutions*, p. 323.

44. Transportation Assn. of America, *Transportation Facts and Trends, 1978*, p. 3.

45. Gary A. Tobin, "Suburbanization and the Development of Motor Transportation: Transportation Technology and the Suburbanization Process," in Barry Schwartz, ed., *The Changing Face of the Suburbs* (Chicago: University of Chicago Press, 1976), pp. 106–7.

46. Dumas, *The Conservation Response*, pp. 110–11.

47. When housing is compact, the waste heat from an electric generating plant can be used for heating.

48. M. H. Ross and R. H. Williams, "Energy and Economic Growth," prepared for the Joint Economic Committee, U.S. Congress, *Achieving the Goals of the Employment Act of 1946—Thirtieth Anniversary Review* (Washington, D.C.: Government Printing Office, 1977), 2:8.

49. This account of the development of the natural gas industry in the U.S. is based on an unpublished paper by Christopher T. Rand, "Notes on the Gas Revolution," esp. pp. 7–8.

50. Barry Commoner, *The Poverty of Power* (New York: Knopf, 1976), pp. 195 and 199.

51. Ross and Williams, "Energy and Economic Growth," p. 11.

52. In 1970, 6% of all the electricity produced was used to heat homes, despite the fact that electric heat was only half as efficient as oil or gas heat. U.S. House of Representatives, Committee on Foreign Affairs, *Foreign Policy Implications of the Energy Crisis*, p. 377.

53. Cowhey, "The Problems of Plenty," p. 381. Amory B. Lovins has estimated that electricity is required for only about 4% of our end-use energy needs, but 8% of the delivered energy we use is in the form of electricity. Because most of the energy used to produce this 8% is lost in electrical generation and transmission, electricity accounts for about a quarter of all energy used in the United States. *Soft Energy Paths* (Cambridge, Mass.: Ballinger, 1977), pp. 39 and 80.

54. See note 62 (below) and appendix table A4 on rates of growth in GNP, energy consumption and oil consumption.

55. Yoshi Tsurumi, "Japan," in Raymond Vernon, ed., *The Oil Crisis*, p. 115.

56. Gerald Bloomfield, *The World Automotive Industry* (N. Pomfret, Vt.: David & Charles, 1978), p. 59; and "Motorization in Postwar Japan," *Wheel Extended* (Spring 1972), p. 34.

57. Gerald Leach, "The Impact of the Motor Car on Oil Reserves," *Energy Policy* 1, no. 2 (Sept. 1973):195–97 and 199.

58. Computed from data in Central Intelligence Agency, *Handbook of Economic Statistics, 1976*, p. 147.

59. Mason Willrich, *Energy and World Politics* (New York: Free Press, 1975), p. 36.

60. *Oil and Gas Journal* 75, no. 35 (Aug. 1977) (special 75th anniversary issue):426–28.

61. *Petroleum Press Service* (July 1970), p. 253, and OECD, *Oil: The Present Situation and Future Prospects*, p. 23.

62. In the U.S. the energy/GNP ratio declined gradually from 1947 until 1967 and then increased

until 1970.The reduction is attributed largely to the shift to a service economy, to efficiency improvements in the basic materials processing industries, and to the shift in manufacturing from basic materials to fabrication (see Ross and Williams, "Energy and Economic Growth," pp. 6 and 24). The increase after 1967 is attributed to the greater use of electricity in homes and industry, the increasing use of fuel for nonenergy uses (i.e., petrochemicals), and the leveling off in the conversion efficiency of electric power plants (between 1900 and the early 1960s there had been an eightfold increase in the conversion efficiency of electric power plants). See OECD, *Oil: The Present Situation and Future Prospects,* pp. 14 and 25; *Petroleum Press Service* (July 1971), pp. 257 and 259; and Ross and Williams, "Energy and Economic Growth," p. 12.

63. After shutting down a synthetic fuels program in the 1950s, the U.S. began a small experimental coal gasification program in 1961. West Germany also maintained a coal gasification program in the 1960s, but, like the U.S., it was small and experimental. See John Surrey and William Walker, "Energy R & D—A UK Perspective," *Energy Policy* 3, no. 2 (June 1975):92–93.

64. Heavy crudes and tar sands are highly viscous forms of petroleum; oil shales are rock materials that can be converted into petroleum. The best-known source of heavy crudes is the Orinoco belt in Venezuela, which is estimated to contain 4,200 billion barrels of oil. Large deposits of tar sands have also been found in the Orinoco belt, as well as in Alberta, Canada. Extensive oil shales have been found in the U.S., Brazil, the U.S.S.R., and Zaïre. Though very little exploration has occurred, present sources are known to exceed 3,000 billion barrels. See U.N. Institute for Training and Research and International Institute for Applied Systems Analysis, *The Future Supply of Nature-made Oil and Gas* (New York: Pergamon Press, 1977), pp. 10–12 of the "Summary Report."

65. See Hollomon and Grenon, *Energy Research and Development.*

66. Surrey and Walker, "Energy R & D—A UK Perspective," p. 100.

67. Unlike conventional light-water reactors, which rely on scarce U_{235}, a breeder reactor converts the far more abundant U_{238} to plutonium, which it then uses for fuel. The advantage of the breeder is that while the life span of light-water technology is limited by the supply of U_{235} (estimated by the U.S. Atomic Energy Commission at the time to be sufficient only for reactors built through 1990), the breeder could draw on an almost limitless supply of fuel.

Yet the breeder has other "special" characteristics as well. Unlike the reactors in use today, the density of fuel in a breeder is great enough to trigger an explosion. In addition—unlike the fuel in existing nuclear plants, which would require enrichment plants costing billions before it could be made into bombs—thirteen pounds of plutonium and equipment from a hardware store could become the basis for a home-made atomic bomb. The opportunities that would be opened up to terrorists, if the breeder comes into large-scale use, are staggering.

Moreover, as Sheldon Novick has written, "Plutonium is extremely poisonous; it can burst into flame when divided into fine particles; and when inhaled, it is one of the most potent causes of lung cancer known. And, of course, it can be used to build nuclear weapons. An industry founded on this material—material shipped across the country in thousands of separate packages, handled, fabricated, processed, disposed of—would surely represent a considerable extension of the hazards of the present nuclear industry. These increased hazards are generally conceded." *The Electric War* (San Francisco: Sierra Club, 1976), pp. 282–83.

68. Computed from data in Surrey and Walker, "Energy R & D—A UK Perspective," p. 93. "Nuclear" includes both fission and fusion. "Alternative energy sources" include coal gasification and liquefaction, geothermal, and solar. See also OECD, *Energy R & D* (Paris: OECD, 1975), esp. p. 104. The first attempt to assemble internationally comparable energy R&D statistics was made in 1974. Surrey and Walker, "Energy R & D," p. 91.

69. John Surrey, "Japan's Uncertain Energy Prospects: The Problem of Import Dependence," *Energy Policy* 2, no. 3 (Sept. 1974):213.

70. Computed from data in BP, *Statistical Review of the World Oil Industry, 1971,* p. 16, and *1974,* p. 16. The actual figures are as follows:

Nuclear power as a	% of Total Energy		% of Electricity	
	1970	*1973*	*1970*	*1973*
United States	1.1	1.2	1.3	4.4
Japan	.1	.6	1.3	2.1
Western Europe	.3	1.3	3.8	5.2
Great Britain	.9	2.6	10.4	9.9

The figures on nuclear's share of electricity are from U.N., *World Energy Supplies* (various issues).

71. Figures on proven reserves are published annually in *Oil and Gas Journal* and are widely reprinted. For example, see Joseph A. Yager and Eleanor B. Steinberg, *Energy and U.S. Foreign Policy* (Cambridge, Mass.: Ballinger, 1974), p. 452, and BP, *Statistical Review of the World Oil Industry*.

The concept of "proven reserves" refers to that portion of oil in the ground that has been found and whose production is believed to be economical at commercial prices. However, figures on proven reserves are notoriously unreliable, partly because it is difficult to estimate what portion of the oil in the ground can be recovered at commercial prices. There is no consistent, rigorous definition of proven reserves. Companies have frequently understated them in order to mislead host governments and avoid taxes. And to reduce their neighbors' envy, governments with large reserves and small populations have often sought to keep the estimates of their reserves low, but those with small reserves and large populations have tended to exaggerate their reserves to win the confidence of lenders, attract investors, and support demands for greater production.

Not surprisingly, Saudi Arabia provides the clearest case of a country whose reserves have been underestimated—often estimated at 150 billion barrels but listed by Aramco at the "ultra conservative" level of 90 billion barrels. In July 1973 an Aramco executive, J. J. Johnston, told Saudi Arabia's oil minister, Zaki Yamani, that Aramco estimated its true reserves at 245 billion barrels. In the fall of 1973 James Akins, then serving as ambassador to Saudi Arabia and formerly the energy expert at both the State Department and the White House, estimated Saudi reserves at between 150 billion and 600 billion barrels; he referred to them as quasi unlimited. See *MNC Hearings*, part 7, p. 539, and M. A. Saleem Khan, "Oil Politics in the Persian Gulf Region," *India Quarterly* 30, no. 1 (Jan.–Mar. 1974):28.

72. The assumption of a 10 : 1 ratio may be challenged as too low. Indeed, the Workshop on Alternative Energy Strategies states that "a proven reserves-to-production (R/P) ratio of 10 to 1 is probably the minimum feasible for the world's oil reserves." It reached this conclusion on the basis that, for most oil reserves, it is "impossible to produce more than 10% of the recoverable reserves in any one year without reducing the amount of oil that can eventually be recovered." Reasoning that, at any time, some fields will be under development and unable to produce at this rate, it assumed a maximum R/P ratio of 15 : 1, which is probably appropriate for its purposes. See Workshop on Alternative Energy Strategies, *Energy: Global Prospects, 1985–2000* (New York: McGraw-Hill, 1977), p. 116.

However, if one is trying to estimate potential, one assumes that fields have been developed and are ready to produce. Moreover, in the U.S. the R/P ratio has been below 10 : 1 since 1967 (John Blair, *The Control of Oil* [New York, Pantheon, 1976], p. 5). Even at an R/P ratio of 15 : 1, in 1973 the proven reserves outside the Middle East and North Africa would have been sufficient to meet three quarters of the world's oil demand, reducing dependence upon Middle East and North African oil from more than 40% of total production to about 25%.

Reserves outside the Communist world, the Middle East, and North Africa totaled 144.6 billion barrels and consumption 17.5 billion barrels, making it possible to supply three quarters of the non-Communist world's oil demand without reliance upon Communist, Middle East, or North African reserves at an R/P ratio of 10 : 1. However, as an estimate of dependence upon Middle East and North

African oil, this figure is understated because the Communist world is a net exporter to the West.

Figures on oil consumption/demand are from BP, *Statistical Review of the World Oil Industry;* figures on oil reserves are from Yager and Steinberg, *Energy and U.S. Foreign Policy,* p. 452 (originally from *Oil and Gas Journal,* Dec. 31, 1973, pp. 86–87). The breakdown of reserves by country is as follows.

Proven Oil Reserves by Area, Year-end 1973

	Billion Barrels	Percent of World Total
Asia	35.6	5.7
Indonesia	10.5	1.7
China	20.0	3.2
Australia	2.3	.4
Middle East	350.2	55.8
Abu Dhabi	21.5	3.4
Iran	60.0	9.6
Iraq	31.5	5.0
Kuwait	64.0	10.2
Neutral Zone	17.5	2.8
Saudi Arabia	132.0	21.0
U.S.S.R. and Eastern Europe	83.0	13.2
U.S.S.R.	80.0	12.7
Western Europe	16.0	2.5
Netherlands	.3	<.1
Norway	4.0	.6
United Kingdom	10.0	1.6
Africa*	67.3	10.7
Algeria	7.6	1.2
Libya	25.5	4.1
Nigeria	20.0	3.2
Western Hemisphere	75.8	12.1
Canada	9.4	1.5
United States	34.7	5.5
Ecuador	5.7	.9
Venezuela	14.0	2.2
Total	627.9	100.0

*"North Africa" = Algeria and Libya.

73. Geological estimates of the amount of oil that can ultimately be recovered at economic cost are imprecise and widely disputed. Worldwide, between 1940 and 1960 these estimates tended to increase, from 500 billion to 2,000 billion barrels. Since 1960, studies have tended to converge around 2,000 billion barrels. (See Workshop on Alternative Energy Strategies, *Energy,* p. 115, and M. King Hubbert, "World Oil and Natural Gas Reserves and Resources," in Congressional Research Service, *Project Interdependence: U.S. and World Energy Outlook through 1990* [Washington, D.C.: Government Printing Office, 1977], p. 634.) In 1977 the World Energy Conference released a poll of 29 leading authorities, whose estimates ranged from 1,600 to 3,700 billion

barrels, with a rough consensus around 2,000 billion. (See Peter Nulty, "When We'll Start Running Out of Oil," *Fortune* [Oct. 1977], p. 246.)

However, these more conventional estimates may not take sufficient account of the 1973–74 rise in prices on the supply of the world's ultimately recoverable reserves. A 1976 U.N. conference maintained that in the developing countries alone, there are 1,500 billion to 1,800 billion barrels of oil, already consumed or proven, with "a possibly equal amount of recoverable petroleum" remaining to be discovered. It concluded that the supply of oil and natural gas is adequate for another "hundred years or more." UNITAR and IIASA, *The Future Supply of Nature-made Oil and Gas*, pp. 6 and 28 of the "Summary Report."

74. Adelman and Friis, "Changing Monopolies and European Oil Supplies," p. 278. Since there has been less exploration for natural gas than for oil, the estimates of the ultimately recoverable reserves of natural gas are less reliable; however, these are likely to be greatly increased if gas from geopressurized zones, tight formations, and the hydrates can be made economical. See UNITAR and IIASA, *The Future Supply of Nature-made Oil and Gas*, p. 26 of the "Summary Report."

75. UNITAR and IIASA, *The Future Supply of Nature-made Oil and Gas*, p. 26 of the "Summary Report."

76. Ibid.

77. Bernardo F. Grossling, "A Critical Survey of World Petroleum Opportunities," in Congressional Research Service, *Project Interdependence*, pp. 651–52.

78. Eliot Marshall, "No Rush," *New Republic*, Aug. 20 and 27, 1977, p. 14; UNITAR and IIASA, *The Future Supply of Nature-made Oil and Gas*, pp. 6 and 26; and Steven A. Schneider, "Where Has All the Oil Gone?" *Working Papers for a New Society* 6, no. 1 (Jan./Feb. 1978):39.

79. A December 1968 SoCal memorandum indicates that at least one company thought the problem of a crude surplus was likely to continue for the next five years. The memo discusses the need for the major companies "to maintain politically palatable growth in their liftings from the Middle East." The memo is reproduced in *MNC Hearings*, part 7, pp. 361–63.

80. Ibid., p. 309.

81. *Petroleum Press Service* (Aug. 1971), p. 297. The figures on oil production costs are from Adelman, *The World Petroleum Market*, p. 76. So far, what has distinguished the Middle East from other areas is its much greater density of giant fields—those with more than a billion barrels of recoverable oil (Grossling, "A Critical Survey of World Petroleum Opportunities," p. 653). Moreover, according to Moody, two-thirds of the world's undiscovered potential lies in offshore areas, where costs are higher. Nulty, "When We'll Start Running Out of Oil," *Fortune* (Oct. 1977), p. 247.

82. These are reviewed in Yager and Steinberg, *Energy and U.S. Foreign Policy*, pp. 221–22.

83. In 1973 a Chinese official objected to the proposed Tyumen pipeline on the grounds that it could be used to supply Soviet forces that might invade China. The pipeline would also involve constructing a new road parallel to the Sino-Soviet border. Both the road and the ability to transport oil to border areas were viewed as security threats.

Since gas is less important militarily, the Chinese have had fewer objections to Japanese participation in development of the Yakutsk gas fields. Consequently, in the early 1970s efforts were made to get the U.S. and Japan to participate in development of this area, but efforts to conclude an agreement in the early 1970s foundered on Japanese reluctance and the refusal of the U.S. Congress to authorize Export-Import Bank credits to the Soviet Union. See Ibid., pp. 153–54, and Klinghoffer, *The Soviet Union and International Oil Politics*, pp. 242–65.

84. Prior to the 1970s, the majors were generally unwilling to go into joint ventures with host countries, partly because of the precedent this might establish in their Middle East concessions and partly because it was not necessary for the companies to make such arrangements in order to secure the oil they needed. See Penrose, *The Large International Firm in the Developing Countries*, p. 244.

85. Particularly influential was a study commissioned by the World Bank and done in 1960–61 by the longtime oil-industry consulting firm, Walter J. Levy Inc. The report argued that oil explora-

tion involves great risk and considerable expense in time and skilled labor. Since oil companies have the capital and skilled personnel required, whereas underdeveloped countries lack both, the report recommended that exploration be left to private companies. See Walter J. Levy, *The Search for Oil in Developing Countries: A Problem of Scarce Resources and Its Implications for State and Private Enterprise*, prepared for the International Bank for Reconstruction and Development (1961). See also Michael Tanzer, *The Political Economy of International Oil and the Underdeveloped Countries* (Boston: Beacon, 1969), p. 118, and Jean-Marie Chevalier, *The New Oil Stakes* (London: Allen Lane, 1975), p. 94.

86. The oil depletion allowance permitted the oil companies to deduct 27.5% (later 22%) of their total production revenues, and this deduction was allowed to cover as much as 50% of their taxable income. Unlike normal depreciation, the oil depletion allowance was not based on the initial cost of acquiring the asset, but on current revenues, and as long as companies continued to produce oil, they were able to derive benefits from the allowance. Consequently, companies might recover as much as 10 or 20 times their capital costs in the form of depletion allowances. The government estimated that the use of percentage depletion, rather than cost depletion, cost the Treasury over a billion dollars a year. (See *MNC Hearings*, part 4, p. 13, and Shaffer, *The Oil Import Program of the United States*, p. 222.)

In addition, companies were allowed to treat the sums expended in acquiring an asset (drilling costs, labor, materials, etc.) as expenses, which could be written off immediately, rather than as investments, which had to be depreciated over a period of years. In 1972 alone, this provision was estimated to have saved the oil industry $1.6 billion in taxes. See *MNC Hearings*, part 4, p. 20.

87. Computed from data in Chase Manhattan Bank, *Capital Investments in the World Petroleum Industry, 1965*, p. 22, and *1980*, p. 14.

88. *MNC Hearings*, part 7, p. 336.

89. In comparison, the after-tax return for all manufacturing corporations in the U.S. averaged 9.3% in that year. The 1970 rate of return on U.S. investments in the developing countries averaged 13.5% in mining and smelting and 10.2% in manufacturing. Leonard Mosley, *Power Play* (Baltimore: Penguin, 1974), p. 419; *Economic Report of the President, 1973* (Washington, D.C.: Government Printing Office, 1973), p. 280; and *Middle East Economic Survey* (hereafter *MEES*), May 19, 1972 (supplement), p. 10.

90. The rates of growth in real GDP are from U.N., *Yearbook of National Accounts, 1976*, 2, table 4A:195 and 203. Between 1973 and 1978 the real GNP of the European OECD countries grew at an annual rate of 2.1% and Japan's grew at 3.7% a year. Department of State, Bureau of Intelligence and Research, *Economic Growth of OECD Countries, 1968–78* (Washington, D.C.: Government Printing Office, 1979), table 4, p. 9.

CHAPTER 3

1. On their Middle East operations from 1948 to 1960, Issawi and Yeganeh found that the oil companies' after-tax ratio of net income to total net assets ranged from 51 to 80% a year, the average being 67%. In contrast, on U.S. operations during this period the oil industry return ranged between 7.2 and 14.1% a year, with an average return of 10.8%. The range for Venezuela was 13 to 32%, with the average at 21% (Charles Issawi and Mohammed Yeganeh, *The Economics of Middle Eastern Oil* [London: Faber & Faber, 1963], p. 112). The high Middle East returns reflect the much lower production costs on Middle East oil and the fact that mainly the more profitable production operations were carried on in the Middle East.

Because production cost figures are not available and because most crude oil was not sold on the market, the figures cited are estimates of accounting profits rather than actual profits. Still, even with these qualifications, the magnitude of the estimates indicates the tremendous profitability of Middle East oil. For figures on the profitability of particular Middle East affiliates, see Zuhayr Mikdashi, *A Financial Analysis of Middle Eastern Oil Concessions: 1901–1965* (New York: Praeger, 1966), pp. 195 (IPC) and 221 (the Iranian Consortium), and for the profits of Gulf Oil Co. by area, see pp. 212–14. These figures reveal a similarly high level of profitability on Middle East oil.

2. Horst Mendershausen, *Coping with the Oil Crisis: French and German Experiences* (Baltimore: Johns Hopkins University Press, 1976), p. 28.

3. J. E. Hartshorn, *Politics and World Oil Economics* (New York: Praeger, 1967), p. 263.

4. Several U.S. oil companies had found oil in Libya, not far from deposits the French were exploiting, but they refused to develop it because by their standards it was too costly. Christopher T. Rand, *Making Democracy Safe for Oil* (Boston: Little, Brown, 1975), p. 212.

5. Mendershausen, *Coping with the Oil Crisis,* pp. 20 and 28.

6. Rand, *Making Democracy Safe for Oil,* p. 240, and Leonard Mosley, *Power Play* (Baltimore: Penguin, 1974), p. 324. For example, assume that it cost 10¢ to produce a barrel of oil in Saudi Arabia and 20¢ to produce a barrel in Libya. However, in Saudi Arabia, regardless of the price the oil is sold at, companies had to pay a 50% tax on a posted price of $1.80. The result was that their tax-paid cost came to $1 a barrel (90¢ + 10¢). If they sold the oil for anything less than this, they would lose money on it. However, in Libya taxes were paid on the basis of the actual selling price rather than the posted price. For example, if the oil was sold at $1 a barrel, the companies simply deducted the 20¢ cost and split the 80¢ profit with the Libyan government. In this example, the companies could sell the oil for as little as 20¢ and not incur a loss.

7. Rand, *Making Democracy Safe for Oil,* p. 239, and OPEC, *Annual Statistical Bulletin, 1970,* p. 78.

8. Since offshore drilling began only after World War II in the U.S., the original Middle East concessions had generally not included offshore areas.

9. Mosley, *Power Play,* pp. 271–78; and Edith T. Penrose, *The Large International Firm in the Developing Countries* (London: Allen & Unwin, 1968), p. 74.

10. Edith T. Penrose, "OPEC and the Changing Structure of the International Petroleum Industry," in U.S. Senate, Committee on the Judiciary, Subcommittee on Anti-Trust and Monopoly, *Government Intervention in the Market Mechanism: The Petroleum Industry* (Washington, D.C.: Government Printing Office, 1969), p. 431.

11. Like the U.S. before the 1970s, the Soviet Union has been essentially energy self-sufficient since World War II. During the twentieth century it has been both a net oil importer and a net oil exporter, but it can supply its own needs, if necessary.

12. Arthur Jay Klinghoffer, *The Soviet Union and International Oil Politics* (New York: Columbia University Press, 1977), pp. 39–40.

13. Ibid., pp. 64–66.

14. Ibid., p. 68, and Neil H. Jacoby, *Multinational Oil* (New York: Macmillan, 1974), p. 163. This price discrepancy hardly proves the companies' claims, for it is not surprising that a company would charge lower prices in a market where it is competing to gain entry than in a market where its sales are guaranteed. Indeed, the private Western oil companies continually did this. Also, the high price of Soviet oil to Eastern Europe was somewhat offset by the high price of goods the Soviet Union imported in return.

15. Hartshorn, *Politics and World Oil Economics,* pp. 239 and 280; Peter R. Odell, *Oil and World Power* (Baltimore: Penguin, 1974), p. 52; and Mosley, *Power Play,* pp. 303–5.

16. Taki Rifai, *The Pricing of Crude Oil* (New York: Praeger, 1975), p. 174; Louis Turner, *Oil Companies in the International System* (London: Allen & Unwin, 1978), p. 60; and Klinghoffer, *The Soviet Union and International Oil Politics,* pp. 62–63.

17. Klinghoffer, *The Soviet Union and International Oil Politics,* p. 67.

18. Jacoby, *Multinational Oil,* p. 167, and Hartshorn, *Politics and World Oil Economics,* pp. 236 and 238.

19. While oil played a small role in the initial deterioration of U.S.–Cuban relations, it provided the catalytic event that brought the final break between the two countries. See Turner, *Oil Companies in the International System,* pp. 74–75, and Odell, *Oil and World Power,* p. 61.

20. M. A. Adelman, *The World Petroleum Market* (Baltimore: Johns Hopkins University Press, 1972), p. 161.

21. Fuad Rouhani, *A History of OPEC* (New York: Praeger, 1971), p. 190.

22. Zuhayr Mikdashi, *The Community of Oil Exporting Countries* (Ithaca: Cornell University Press, 1972), p. 49.

23. This is not to say that the long-term impact of the quotas was to reduce prices (see chap. 1).

24. *MNC Report*, p. 88, and Jacoby, *Multinational Oil*, p. 225.

25. Shoshana Klebanoff, *Middle East Oil and U.S. Foreign Policy* (New York: Praeger, 1974), p. 199, and Mosley, *Power Play*, p. 305.

26. Robert B. Krueger, *The United States and International Oil* (New York: Praeger, 1975), p. 59.

27. Penrose, *The Large International Firm in the Developing Countries*, p. 200.

28. To understand the difference this makes, consider the following example. The price of a barrel of oil is $1.80, the cost is 20¢, the tax rate is 50%, and royalties are 22.5¢ (12.5% of $1.80) a barrel. If royalties are included as part of the total taxes owed, the companies simply pay the exporting countries 80¢ (50% of $1.80 − 20¢) a barrel, designating 22.5¢ as a royalty and the other 57.5¢ as taxes owed. But if royalties are expensed, as the exporting countries sought, the companies pay the countries 22.5¢ in royalties and count this as part of their costs, which results in a profit of $1.375 = $1.80 − (22.5¢ + 20¢). On this profit they pay a 50% tax, resulting in an additional payment of 68.75¢ (50% of $1.375) a barrel to the exporting countries. As a result, when royalties are expensed, the companies pay 91.25¢ (22.5¢ + 68.75¢) to the exporting countries, as opposed to 80¢ when they are not.

29. *MNC Report*, p. 90, and Penrose, *The Large International Firm in the Developing Countries*, p. 201.

30. Franklin Tugwell, *The Politics of Oil in Venezuela* (Stanford: Stanford University Press, 1975), p. 66.

31. In Venezuela, the government's per barrel income increased from 84¢ to 96¢ during this period, while the companies' declined from 40¢ to 39¢ a barrel. Computed from data in ibid., p. 150; see also Richard Chadbourn Weisberg, *The Politics of Crude Oil Pricing in the Middle East, 1970–1975* (Berkeley: Institute of International Studies, 1977), p. 20.

32. An Exxon attorney actually wrote the law. *MNC Report*, p. 91.

33. Ruth First, *Libya* (Baltimore: Penguin, 1974), p. 193.

34. Penrose, *The Large International Firm in the Developing Countries*, pp. 203–5, and *MNC Report*, p. 90.

35. Peter Francis Cowhey, "The Problems of Plenty: Energy Policy and International Politics" (unpublished Ph.D. thesis, University of California at Berkeley), p. 345.

36. Joseph A. Yager and Eleanor B. Steinberg, *Energy and U.S. Foreign Policy* (Cambridge, Mass.: Ballinger, 1974), p. 237, and Rouhani, *A History of OPEC*, p. 190.

37. Between 1945 and 1958, Iraq's oil production had grown from 100.1 tb/d to 731.3 tb/d, but Iran's had grown from 357.6 tb/d, to 826.1 tb/d, Saudi Arabia's rose from 58.4 tb/d to 1,058.5 tb/d, and Kuwait's from zero to 1,435.8 tb/d (OPEC, *Annual Statistical Bulletin, 1966*, pp. 27–29 and 31). For a graphic representation, see *MNC Report*, p. 97.

38. Edith Penrose and E. F. Penrose, *Iraq: International Relations and National Development* (Boulder, Colo.: Westview Press, 1978), p. 147; Rand, *Making Democracy Safe for Oil*, p. 190; and *MNC Hearings*, part 7, p. 310.

39. Joe Stork, *Middle East Oil and the Energy Crisis* (New York: Monthly Review Press, 1975), p. 81, and Rand, *Making Democracy Safe for Oil*, p. 210.

40. Penrose and Penrose, *Iraq*, p. 259.

41. In 1920, as part of the San Remo agreement between Britain and France, Iraq had been promised a 20% share in any public company the IPC partners might form. But since IPC remained a privately owned subsidiary of its parent companies, Iraq never received its 20%.

42. Stork, *Middle East Oil and the Energy Crisis*, pp. 105–6.

43. *MNC Report*, pp. 101–2.

44. Throughout these negotiations the IPC partners were somewhat divided. Exxon and BP, which had large supplies of oil elsewhere, were reluctant to make a deal with Iraq for fear of the precedent it would establish. Shell and CFP, both of which were crude short, were anxious to

maintain and expand access to Iraqi oil. In their joint efforts to reduce France's dependence upon the Anglo-American majors, CFP and the French government were particularly concerned about access to Iraqi oil. See Penrose and Penrose, *Iraq,* p. 383.

45. Ibid., pp. 387–90.

46. Klinghoffer, *The Soviet Union and International Oil Politics,* pp. 50, 68–69, 70, and 72; Lincoln Landis, *Politics and Oil: Moscow in the Middle East* (New York: Dunellen, 1973), p. 68; and Yager and Steinberg, *Energy and U.S. Foreign Policy,* p. 196.

47. *MNC Report,* p. 102; Penrose, *The Large International Firm in the Developing Countries,* pp. 73 and 218; and Penrose and Penrose, *Iraq,* p. 426.

48. As a percentage, the Iraqi increase was 56.0%, Iran's 184.9%, Kuwait's 59.8%, and Saudi Arabia's 118.5%. However, Iraq started from a much lower base than the others. BP, *Statistical Review of the World Oil Industry,* various issues.

49. *Basic Petroleum Data Book,* sec. 14, table 1 (originally from *Oil and Gas Journal*).

50. Tugwell, *The Politics of Oil in Venezuela,* pp. 48 and 83.

51. The differences in the share of the take received by Venezuelan and Eastern Hemisphere governments were not as great as the difference in these official tax rates would imply because Venezuela taxed the companies on the basis of realized (market) rather than posted prices. Consequently, because of the fall in market prices, in 1958 the split in the Eastern Hemisphere was actually 56/44, in favor of the countries. In the Eastern Hemisphere, exporting countries received 76¢ a barrel whereas Venezuela received $1.04 a barrel. Between 1958 and 1960 the fall in market prices reduced Venezuela's per barrel income by 20¢ while reducing the Eastern Hemisphere exporting countries' income by only 5¢ a barrel. Ibid., p. 150.

52. This remained a limited operation, accounting for only 2.2% of Venezuelan production in 1973. Ibid., p. 53.

53. Yager and Steinberg, *Energy and U.S. Foreign Policy,* p. 82.

54. Tugwell, *The Politics of Oil in Venezuela,* pp. 87–89.

55. Ibid., pp. 100–108.

56. For the period 1950–63, Mikdashi estimated that per barrel production costs averaged $1.65 in the U.S., 41¢ in Venezuela, and 14¢ in the Middle East (*A Financial Analysis of Middle Eastern Oil Concessions,* p. 168). Issawi and Yeganeh estimate Middle East production costs in this period at under 20¢ a barrel, Venezuelan at about 80¢ a barrel, and U.S. at $1.75 a barrel (*The Economics of Middle Eastern Oil,* p. 91). Adelman estimated the total per barrel development-operating costs in the 1960s at about 10¢ in the Persian Gulf, about 15¢ in Libya and Nigeria, 46¢ in Venezuela, and $1.22 in the U.S. *The World Petroleum Market,* p. 76.

57. Adelman, *The World Petroleum Market,* pp. 69 and 146.

58. Tugwell, *The Politics of Oil in Venezuela,* pp. 73–75.

59. Computed from tables in U.N., *World Energy Supplies,* "World Movement of Crude Petroleum," various issues.

60. Tugwell, *The Politics of Oil in Venezuela,* p. 79.

61. *Basic Petroleum Data Book,* sec. 14, table 1 (originally from *Oil and Gas Journal*).

62. Krueger, *The United States and International Oil,* p. 59, and *Petroleum Press Service* (Oct. 1963), p. 385.

63. With the fall in market prices, the Middle East governments were receiving more than 60% of the actual profits by the 1960s (see Maull, "The Price of Crude Oil in the International Energy Market," *Energy Policy* 5, no. 2 [June 1977]: p. 150). Consequently, the Indonesian agreement was not really a breakthrough. Also, as part of the agreement the companies were granted new exploration areas, the first time since before World War II. *Petroleum Press Service* (Apr. 1965), p. 146.

64. Between 1953 and 1963, Middle East production grew at an annual average rate of 11%, going from 118 million tons to 334 million tons. During this period, Indonesian production grew at an average annual rate of 8%, going from 10 million tons to 23 million tons. BP, *Statistical Review of the World Oil Industry, 1963,* p. 18.

65. Krueger, *The United States and International Oil,* p. 60.

66. OECD, *Oil: The Present Situation and Future Prospects* (Paris: OECD, 1973), p. 91; Sevinc

Carlson, *Indonesia's Oil* (Boulder, Colo.: Westview Press, 1977), p. 18; and *NYT*, Jan. 4, 1967, p. 68.

67. *Petroleum Press Service* (Feb. 1966), pp. 55–56.

68. BP, *Statistical Review of the World Oil Industry, 1970*, p. 6.

69. Yager and Steinberg, *Energy and U.S. Foreign Policy*, p. 117.

70. Many of Nigeria's oil fields were in Biafra—the province that sought to secede from Nigeria and the locus of much of the fighting. In fact, the war began over a dispute whether the Shell-BP joint venture should pay its royalties to the federal government or the eastern province. In a move that was widely interpreted as motivated by oil, France intervened on behalf of the Biafran secessionists. In sharp contrast to the French actions, the Netherlands imposed an arms embargo on Nigeria during the latter part of the war, despite the fact that this antagonized the ascendant Nigerian federal authorities and might have endangered Shell's extensive interests in Nigeria. See Turner, *Oil Companies in the International System*, pp. 76 and 110.

71. Odell, *Oil and World Power*, pp. 89–90, and Yager and Steinberg, *Energy and U.S. Foreign Policy*, p. 109.

72. As indicated, the National Iranian Oil Co. was established in 1951, Venezuela's CVP in 1960, and the Iraq National Oil Co. in 1964. In 1960 the Kuwait National Petroleum Co. was established, in 1962 Saudi Arabia established the General Petroleum and Mineral Organization (Petromin), and in 1968 a Libyan national company was organized. Sam H. Schurr and Paul T. Homan, *Middle Eastern Oil and the Western World* (New York: American Elsevier, 1971), p. 127.

73. By 1970 only 1.5 million barrels per day—less than 5% of world exports—were produced, or about to be produced, by companies operating in a contract or joint-venture arrangement. Cowhey, "The Problems of Plenty," p. 373; and BP, *Statistical Review of the World Oil Industry, 1970*, p. 10.

74. Thomas R. Stauffer, "Price Formation in the Eastern Hemisphere: Concessionary versus Non-Concessionary Oil," in Zuhayr Mikdashi, Sherril Cleland, and Ian Seymour, eds., *Continuity and Change in the World Oil Industry* (Beirut: Middle East Research and Publishing Center, 1970), p. 182.

75. Ibid., pp. 197–98.

76. Mikdashi, *The Community of Oil Exporting Countries*, p. 48.

77. In the mid-1960s the view that, unless something was done, the impact of these new arrangements would further reduce the price level was widely shared by academic observers of the industry, officials of the oil-exporting countries, and oil company executives. For a summary of these views, see Schurr and Homan, *Middle Eastern Oil and the Western World*, pp. 143–51.

78. Penrose, *The Large International Firm in the Developing Countries*, p. 209.

79. Yamani had attempted to conclude a participation deal with Aramco since 1963. Mosley, *Power Play*, p. 395.

80. Yamani's speech is reprinted in Mikdashi, Cleland, and Seymour, eds., *Continuity and Change in the World Oil Industry*, pp. 211–33. The quoted sections are from pp. 214–16.

81. Ibid., pp. 208 and 222.

82. See Schurr and Homan, *Middle Eastern Oil and the Western World*, pp. 152–53.

83. Compared with the majors, the oil-exporting countries were less likely to be able to maintain the price level; they lacked the companies' experience. And though they had joined together in OPEC, they could not match the linkages among the majors, with their joint production and marketing ventures. Finally, because they were not established in downstream markets, they lacked the informational advantages that came with vertical integration. See Adelman, *The World Petroleum Market*, p. 224.

84. Quoted in Schurr and Homan, *Middle Eastern Oil and the Western World*, p. 155.

CHAPTER 4

1. Despite this price decline and the increase in government per barrel take, the companies' return on investment does not appear to have declined in this period because investment per barrel declined

as well. Robert Stobaugh and Daniel Yergin, eds., *Energy Future* (New York: Random House, 1979), p. 271.

2. *MNC Hearings,* part 11, p. 7.

3. Seijiro Matsumura, " 'Participation Policy' of the Producing Countries in the International Oil Industry," *Developing Countries* 10, no. 1 (Mar. 1972):32.

4. Quoted in Klaus Knorr, "The Limits of Economic and Military Power," in Raymond Vernon, ed., *The Oil Crisis : In Perspective,* issued as *Daedalus* 104, no. 4 (1975):229.

5. OECD, *Oil: The Present Situation and Future Prospects* (Paris: OECD, 1973), p. 14.

6. John Blair, *The Control of Oil* (New York: Pantheon, 1976), p. 20; Adelman and Friis, "Changing Monopolies and European Oil Supplies," *Energy Policy* 2, no. 4 (Dec. 1974):275 and 277. See also M. A. Adelman, " 'World Oil' and the Theory of Industrial Organization," in U.S. Senate, Committee on Interior and Insular Affairs, *Oil and Gas Imports Issues* (Washington, D.C.: Government Printing Office, 1973), part 3, p. 1002, and Richard Chadbourn Weisberg, *The Politics of Crude Oil Pricing in the Middle East, 1970–75* (Berkeley: Institute of International Studies, 1977), p. 16.

7. It would probably be several years before substantial new oil and gas reserves were found. Development of reserves takes several years, depending upon where they are found and the geological properties of the reservoirs. Nuclear reactors take 5 to 10 years to build, and according to Akins, it would be 8 to 15 years before shale oil, Canadian tar sands, or heavy Venezuelan oil could make a significant contribution to world energy supplies ("The Oil Crisis," in U.S. Senate, Committee on Interior and Insular Affairs, *Oil and Gas Imports Issues,* part 3, p. 1046). Some conservation measures could be implemented quickly but others would depend on basic changes in land use, turnover of motor vehicle stock (a 10-year cycle), and replacement of energy-inefficient buildings and machinery.

8. In 1973 Akins estimated the cost of alternative sources at $5 a barrel in 1970 dollars or $7.50 in 1980 dollars, which, based on subsequent experience, appears to have been too low (James E. Akins, "International Cooperative Efforts in Energy Supply," *Annals of the American Academy of Political and Social Science* 410 [Nov. 1973]:80). In 1973 an OPEC economic commission estimated the comparative price of alternative energy sources at $17 a barrel (cited in Marwan Iskandar, *The Arab Oil Question* [Beirut: Middle East Economics Consultants, 1974], p. 120). Other estimates during the year were that shale oil would cost $7.50 a barrel; see *MEES,* Sept. 21, 1973 (supplement), p. 3.

9. Akins, "International Cooperative Efforts in Energy Supply," pp. 78–79.

10. The oil companies' net profits came to 6.3% of the total. Other costs were production, 2.7%; refining, 3.3%; tanker freight, 6.3%; and storage, handling, distribution, and dealer's margin, 26%. Taki Rifai, *The Pricing of Crude Oil* (New York: Praeger, 1975), p. 35.

11. Most studies have estimated the short-term elasticity of demand for oil between -0.1 and -0.5. The short-term elasticity of demand for gasoline is even less, with estimates ranging from -0.06 to -0.16. See Weisberg, *The Politics of Crude Oil Pricing in the Middle East,* p. 133, and Blair, *The Control of Oil,* p. 324.

12. In the less developed countries the relationship between economic growth and energy demand was even stronger—a 10% increase in GNP was associated with a 13 to 16% increase in energy demand. Joseph A. Yager and Eleanor B. Steinberg, *Energy and U.S. Foreign Policy* (Cambridge, Mass.: Ballinger, 1974), p. 163.

13. There are other commodities, in which a small number of countries account for as large a share of world exports as the OPEC countries account for in oil, but these commodities frequently have close substitutes. For example, in 1970 the four largest copper exporters accounted for 61% of world copper exports while the four largest oil exporters accounted for 52% of world oil exports. However, efforts to boost the price of copper have repeatedly been beset by the fact that aluminum is a close substitute. On the prospects of "cartelizing" other commodities, see the debate "One, Two, Many OPEC's . . . ?" *Foreign Policy,* vol. 14 (Spring 1974). Included in this debate are Zuhayr Mikdashi, "Collusion Could Work"; Stephen Krasner, "Oil Is the Exception"; and C. Fred Bergsten, "The Threat Is Real." See also Philip Connelly and Robert Perlman, *The Politics of*

Scarcity (New York: Oxford University Press, 1975); Zuhayr Mikdashi, *The International Politics of Natural Resources* (Ithaca: Cornell University Press, 1976); and Ian Smart, "Uniqueness and Generality," in Vernon, ed., *The Oil Crisis,* pp. 259–81.

14. *MNC Hearings,* part 7, p. 570, and Neil H. Jacoby, *Multinational Oil* (New York: Macmillan, 1974), p. 89.

15. Computed from IPAA data on spare capacity and export figures in OPEC, *Annual Statistical Bulletin, 1970,* p. 80.

16. Cabinet Task Force on Oil Import Control, *The Oil Import Question* (Washington, D.C.: Government Printing Office, 1970), p. 184. The committee also considered importing and storing crude oil for use in an emergency, but rejected this option because of cost and physical problems. It also rejected greater reliance upon imported oil, as a way of conserving domestic resources, because, in the absence of direct government involvement in oil production, it would weaken the domestic industry, which would make it impossible for the U.S. to increase production in times of emergency.

17. Richard B. Mancke, "The Genesis of the U.S. Oil Crisis," in Joseph S. Szyliowicz and Bard E. O'Neill, eds., *The Energy Crisis and U.S. Foreign Policy* (New York: Praeger, 1975), p. 60.

18. As a result of the high cost, or nonavailability, of low-sulfur steam coal, oil's share of utility fuels increased from 6% in the mid-1960s to 16% in 1972. Darmstadter and Landsberg, "The Economic Background," in Vernon, ed., *The Oil Crisis,* p. 28.

19. Quoted in U.S. House of Representatives, Committee on Foreign Affairs, *Foreign Policy Implications of the Energy Crisis* (Washington, D.C.: Government Printing Office, 1972), p. 380.

20. Sam H. Schurr and Paul T. Homan, *Middle Eastern Oil and the Western World* (New York: American Elsevier, 1971), pp. 77 and 79; *Petroleum Intelligence Weekly,* Dec. 14, 1970, p. 4, and Dec. 4, 1972, pp. 5 and 6.

21. BP, *Statistical Review of the World Oil Industry,* various issues.

22. William Quandt, "U.S. Energy Policy and the Arab-Israeli Conflict," in Naiem A. Sherbiny and Mark A. Tessler, eds., *Arab Oil* (New York: Praeger, 1976), p. 280, and BP, *Statistical Review of the World Oil Industry,* various issues.

23. The situation had changed considerably since the mid-1950s. Now, with U.S. oil prices about $1.50 above world prices, the international companies benefited more from the protection the import quotas provided for their U.S. production than they would have from an increase in Middle East oil imports, and substitution of foreign for domestic oil would have entailed a costly rerouting of their well-established oil supply and refining patterns. Moreover, the industry preferred the import program to a tariff system since the import tickets issued to "traditional importers" were worth about $1.50 per barrel, while under a tariff system this windfall would go to the federal government.

24. Franklin Tugwell, *The Politics of Oil in Venezuela* (Stanford: Stanford University Press, 1975), pp. 134–38, and BP, *Statistical Review of the World Oil Industry, 1971,* p. 6, and *1974,* p. 6.

25. See Darmstadter and Landsberg, "The Economic Background," in Vernon, ed., *The Oil Crisis,* pp. 17 and 22–25, and *MNC Hearings,* part 5, p. 213, and part 7, pp. 334, 342, and 371.

26. The main reason for this was that coal's contribution to the world's total energy supply was projected to be far greater than it was. See Darmstadter and Landsberg, "The Economic Background," in Vernon, ed., *The Oil Crisis,* p. 24, and *MNC Hearings,* part 7, pp. 371–372.

27. Yuan-li Wu, *Japan's Search for Oil* (Stanford: Hoover Institution Press, 1977), pp. 62–72.

28. Joe Stork, *Middle East Oil and the Energy Crisis* (New York: Monthly Review Press, 1975), p. 114.

29. Don Peretz, "Energy: Israelis, Arabs, and Iranians," in Szyliowicz and O'Neill, eds., *The Energy Crisis and U.S. Foreign Policy,* p. 92.

30. Stork, *Middle East Oil and the Energy Crisis,* p. 115.

31. Benjamin Shwadran, *The Middle East, Oil and the Great Powers* (New York: Wiley, 1973), p. 514.

32. The argument has been made that the dependence of the Arab countries on food imports was a source of vulnerability, for in the early 1970s Saudi Arabia imported roughly 80% of its wheat and wheat flour while Kuwait was almost entirely dependent upon imported feed. However, their food needs were quite modest, relative to world production, and could be satisfied by many sources. Don

Peretz, "Energy: Israelis, Arabs, and Iranians," in Szyliowicz and O'Neill, eds., *The Energy Crisis and U.S. Foreign Policy*, pp. 105–6.

33. James E. Akins, "The Oil Crisis," in U.S. Senate, Committee on Interior and Insular Affairs, *Oil and Gas Imports Issues*, part 3, p. 1041.

34. Fred Halliday, *Arabia without Sultans* (New York: Vintage, 1975), pp. 74–75.

35. In 1969 a Rand Corp. report stated that, as a result of U.S. assistance, the Shah was able to control Iran "without achieving popularity or winning popular support outside the army." *MERIP Reports*, no. 36 (Apr. 1975), pp. 18–19.

36. In 1972 the U.S. established a "communications facility" on Diego Garcia in the Indian Ocean; however, this remained a very modest "base" and was a considerable distance from the Persian Gulf. Moreover, the National Security Council criticized the navy's efforts to expand this facility, fearing this would lead to an arms race with the Soviet Union in the Indian Ocean.

37. Since Democratic Yemen is nearly 1,000 miles from the lower Gulf (with a desert in between), it posed much less of a direct threat than a radical Oman.

38. In the summer of 1969 a plot by Saudi air force officers was discovered and several hundred officers were arrested. The military remained a possible source of revolt, but to minimize the likelihood it was kept dispersed and divided. Another source of instability stemmed from disputes within the royal family. In Kuwait, the main potential sources of opposition were the "guest workers," who outnumbered the native Kuwaitis, and the nationalist minority in parliament.

39. *MNC Hearings*, part 5, p. 1.

40. Ibid., p. 2, and Ruth First, *Libya* (Baltimore: Penguin, 1974), p. 243.

41. *PIW*, June 1, 1970, p. 5, and Stork, *Middle East Oil and the Energy Crisis*, p. 158.

42. Quoted in *MEES*, Sept. 14, 1973 (supplement), p. 8.

43. In May 1969 a leftist military junta took power from a conservative government in Sudan.

44. *The Gulf: Implications of British Withdrawal* (Washington, D.C.: Center for Strategic and International Studies, Georgetown University, 1969), Special Report series, no. 8, p. 90.

45. U.S. House of Representatives, Committee on Foreign Affaris, Subcommittee on the Near East and South Asia, *New Perspectives on the Persian Gulf*, Hearings (Washington, D.C.: Government Printing Office, 1973), p. 8.

46. Between 1968 and 1972 U.S. military aid and arms sales to Iran came to $1.7 billion, nearly three times the level of Johnson's 1968 commitment; moreover, sales to both Iran and Saudi Arabia increased dramatically after 1970. See table 5–3.

47. Dadant, "American and Soviet Defense Systems vis-à-vis the Middle East," in Willard A. Beling, ed., *The Middle East: Quest for an American Policy* (Albany: State University of New York Press, 1973), p. 184, and William B. Quandt, *Decade of Decisions* (Berkeley: University of California Press, 1977), p. 65.

48. Only Jordan accepted the plan. For an account of the plan and the negotiations that accompanied it, see Quandt, *Decade of Decisions*, pp. 89–93.

49. Richard Nixon, *RN: The Memoirs of Richard Nixon* (New York: Grosset & Dunlap, 1978), p. 483.

50. Computed from figures in Quandt, *Decade of Decisions*, p. 163.

51. Cited in Marvin Kalb and Bernard Kalb, *Kissinger* (New York: Dell, 1975), p. 125.

CHAPTER 5

1. The statement is reproduced in Dankwart A. Rustow and John F. Mugno, *OPEC: Success and Prospects* (New York: New York University Press, 1976), pp. 166–72.

2. According to this doctrine, countries had the legal right to unilaterally alter contractual agreements with foreign concessionaires if there had been substantial changes in the conditions that prevailed at the time those agreements were reached. The companies never accepted the validity of this doctrine.

3. Quoted in Edith Penrose, "The Development of Crisis," in Raymond Vernon, ed., *The Oil Crisis: In Perspective*, issued as *Daedalus* 104, no. 4 (1975):40.

4. In 1960–61, oil accounted for 16.8% of Iran's GDP and 77% of its exports; by 1965–66 the

figures were 18 and 81% respectively. Joseph A. Yager and Eleanor B. Steinberg, *Energy and U.S. Foreign Policy* (Cambridge, Mass.: Ballinger, 1974), pp. 58–59.

5. *MNC Report*, pp. 102–9.

6. As a result of the Arab oil embargo during the Arab-Israeli war, Iranian production increased by 22% in 1967. Ibid., p. 109.

7. Yager and Steinberg, *Energy and U.S. Foreign Policy*, pp. 58–60.

8. With a ratio of 1 SAVAK agent for every 450 Iranians, Iran was one of the most repressive, dictatorial regimes in the world. Despite its oil wealth, it is also a nation of incredible poverty. As Frances FitzGerald reported: "In Teheran two-thirds of all families have an income of less than $200 per person per year. Dollar comparisons may be misleading, but the living conditions are almost as bad as the sum indicates. In the rural areas, where 58 percent of the population still live, over a third of all families earn less than $400 a year, while another 40 percent earn less than $800, and the inflation rate this year is 18 to 20 percent. The poor have not gotten poorer in twenty years, but the inequalities have become much greater. . . . About 70 percent of Iranians are illiterate." See FitzGerald, "Giving the Shah Everything He Wants," *Harper's* (Nov. 1974), pp. 58 and 72.

9. Ibid., pp. 58 and 67; *MNC Report*, p. 103; and Christopher T. Rand, *Making Democracy Safe for Oil* (Boston: Little, Brown, 1975), p. 156.

10. *MNC Hearings*, part 7, pp. 274–75.

11. Ibid., part 7, p. 275.

12. Ibid.; *MNC Report*, p. 111; and Rand, *Making Democracy Safe for Oil*, p. 156.

13. *MNC Hearings*, part 7, p. 275.

14. *MNC Report*, pp. 116–17.

15. *NYT*, Apr. 16, 1969, p. 7, and Rand, *Making Democracy Safe for Oil*, p. 157.

16. Rand, *Making Democracy Safe for Oil*, pp. 157–58. After all this, Palestinian guerrillas sabotaged Tapline, leading to a temporary decline in Saudi Arabia's oil production and an increase in Iran's. As a result, in 1969 the Consortium's output increased by 13.8%. From 1960 through 1970 the Consortium's growth averaged 13%, compared with 10.5% for industry exports from all Middle East areas and 10.1% for industry exports from Middle East areas in which Consortium members had interests. Computed from data in *MNC Report*, p. 103.

17. *Petroleum Press Service* (June 1969), p. 224.

18. Rand, *Making Democracy Safe for Oil*, pp. 157–58, and *NYT*, May 16, 1969, p. 67, and May 21, 1969, p. 14.

19. John Blair, *The Control of Oil* (New York: Pantheon, 1976), p. 212.

20. Richard Chadbourn Weisberg, *The Politics of Crude Oil Pricing in the Middle East, 1970–1975* (Berkeley: Institute of International Studies, 1977), p. 43.

21. *MNC Hearings*, part 5, p. 146.

22. Only about 2 million people live in Libya. Weisberg, *The Politics of Crude Oil Pricing in the Middle East*, p. 136.

23. Akins, "The Oil Crisis," in U.S. Senate, Committee on Interior and Insular Affairs, *Oil and Gas Imports Issues*, part 3, p. 1028.

24. *MNC Hearings*, part 5, p. 77.

25. Ibid., part 6, p. 2.

26. Ibid.; *MNC Report*, p. 122; and *Petroleum Intelligence Weekly*, Mar. 9, 1970, p. 1.

27. *MNC Hearings*, part 5, p. 3.

28. For example, say Libya secures a 40¢ freight differential, boosting its per barrel revenue from $1.40 to $1.80. Then the Gulf exporting countries would demand that their per barrel revenue also be increased to $1.80. If this is granted, Libya will demand that, like the Gulf countries, it too should receive $1.80 for its crude oil, plus the 40¢ differential already agreed to. That pushes its per barrel revenue to $2.20 and brings the Gulf countries back with demands for $2.20 per barrel; and so on. As this process continues, Libya will insist it simply seeks to "level up" to basic terms equivalent to those the Gulf countries receive, while the Gulf countries will claim they are only asking for an increase comparable to Libya's.

29. *MNC Hearings*, part 5, p. 7.

30. Weisberg, *The Politics of Crude Oil Pricing in the Middle East*, p. 40.

31. *MNC Report*, p. 122, and *PIW*, Apr. 13, 1970, p. 1.

32. U.S. Senate, Committee on Foreign Relations, Subcommittee on Multinational Corporations, *Chronology of the Libyan Oil Negotiations, 1970–71* (Washington, D.C.: Government Printing Office, 1974), pp. 4–5, and *MNC Report*, p. 122.

33. Rand, *Making Democracy Safe for Oil*, p. 279.

34. *MNC Report*, p. 122; *MERIP Reports*, no. 27 (Apr. 1974), p. 18; and Taki Rifai, *The Pricing of Crude Oil* (New York: Praeger, 1975), p. 254.

35. *MNC Hearings*, part 5, p. 214.

36. See Rand, *Making Democracy Safe for Oil*, p. 285, and *MEES*, Apr. 20, 1973, p. 8.

37. *MNC Hearings*, part 6, p. 3, and *PIW*, July 27, 1970, p. 2.

38. *MNC Report*, p. 123.

39. Ibid., p. 122; *MNC Hearings*, part 5, p. 16; and U.S. Senate, Committee on Foreign Relations, *Chronology of the Libyan Oil Negotiations*, p. 10.

40. Rand maintains that this was the case (*Making Democracy Safe for Oil*, pp. 271–73), but Akins questions it, as did Occidental's engineers at the time. *MNC Hearings*, part 5, p. 11.

41. *MNC Report*, pp. 122–23, and Anthony Sampson, *The Seven Sisters* (New York: Bantam, 1975), p. 253.

42. Michael Tanzer, *The Energy Crisis* (New York: Monthly Review Press, 1974), p. 121.

43. *MNC Report*, p. 124.

44. *PIW*, Sept. 21, 1970, pp. 3–4.

45. Ibid., Sept. 28, 1970, p. 2.

46. Ibid., pp. 1–2.

47. *MNC Hearings*, part 5, p. 16.

48. Ibid., p. 6.

49. *MNC Report*, p. 125.

50. *MNC Hearings*, part 8, p. 771.

51. Louis Turner, *Oil Companies in the International System* (London: Allen & Unwin, 1978), p. 155.

52. Rand, *Making Democracy Safe for Oil*, p. 283; Sampson, *The Seven Sisters*, pp. 255–56; and *MNC Hearings*, part 8, p. 771.

53. *MNC Hearings*, part 8, pp. 768–69. Despite their differences, the U.S. government (and the U.S. companies) sought to maintain the U.S. companies' position in Libya. As Akins testified: "There was certainly interest in maintaining the companies in Libya and this was essentially, there was no difference in that as far as I know among anybody that I talked to in government or in industry; that is, we wanted to maintain a company presence in all of the oil-producing countries, there was a difference in opinion on how this could be done." Idem, part 5, p. 13.

54. Penrose, "The Development of Crisis," in Vernon, ed., *The Oil Crisis*, p. 42.

55. Rifai, *The Pricing of Crude Oil*, p. 257.

56. *Petroleum Press Service* (Feb. 1971), p. 42; M. A. Adelman, *The World Petroleum Market* (Baltimore: Johns Hopkins University Press, 1972), p. 191; and *PIW*, Oct. 12, 1970, pp. 2–3. Since market prices began to fall in the mid-1950s, the exporting countries had been receiving more than 50% of the total per barrel profits. However, their per barrel payments were still derived by taking 50% of the essentially fixed posted price. Libya had increased the posted price and raised the tax rate. Also, while Occidental agreed to a 58% tax, part of this was in payment for commitments it had made on a Libyan agricultural project. *PIW*, Sept. 28, 1970, p. 2.

57. *MNC Hearings*, part 6, p. 6.

58. Joe Stork, *Middle East Oil and the Energy Crisis* (New York: Monthly Review Press, 1975) p. 163, and *PIW*, Nov. 9, 1970, p. 5.

59. Since the 1950s the exporting countries had most-favored-nation clauses in their agreements with the companies, which gave the host governments the right to call on their concessionaires to

discuss revisions of agreements if other countries received better terms. However, this merely required the companies to discuss changes, not make them. Zuhayr Mikdashi, *The Community of Oil Exporting Countries* (Ithaca: Cornell University Press, 1972), pp. 24–26.

60. *PIW*, Dec. 14, 1970, pp. 1–2, and Dec. 21, 1970, p. 3.

61. Rand, *Making Democracy Safe for Oil*, p. 284; *PIW*, Nov. 9, 1970, p. 5, and Nov. 16, 1970, p. 3; and Penrose, "The Development of Crisis," in Vernon, ed., *The Oil Crisis*, p. 42.

62. M. A. Adelman, "Is the Oil Shortage Real?" *Foreign Policy*, no. 9 (1972–73), pp. 79–80. See also Adelman, *The World Petroleum Market*, p. 254.

63. Akins, "The Oil Crisis," in U.S. Senate, Committee on Interior and Insular Affairs, *Oil and Gas Imports Issues*, part 3, p. 1028.

64. *MNC Hearings*, part 6, pp. 6 and 233.

65. Weisberg, *The Politics of Crude Oil Pricing in the Middle East*, p. 53, and Rand, *Making Democracy Safe for Oil*, p. 293.

66. *Petroleum Press Service* (Feb. 1971), p. 42.

67. *MNC Hearings*, part 5, p. 146, and *PIW*, Jan. 18, 1971, p. 2.

68. *MNC Report*, p. 126.

69. *PIW*, Feb. 8, 1971, p. 2.

70. *MNC Report*, pp. 127–28.

71. Turner, *Oil Companies in the International System*, p. 167.

72. *MNC Hearings*, part 5, pp. 81 and 249. The agreement is reproduced in part 6, pp. 224–30.

73. Ibid., part 5, p. 81, and Rand, *Making Democracy Safe for Oil*, p. 288.

74. *MNC Hearings*, part 5, pp. 82 and 93–94, and part 6, p. 8.

75. *MNC Report*, p. 130.

76. *MNC Hearings*, part 5, p. 147.

77. Ibid., p. 72, and part 6, pp. 10–11.

78. Ibid., part 5, p. 147.

79. Ibid., pp. 84 and 156, and "Don't Blame the Oil Companies: Blame the State Department," *Forbes*, Apr. 15, 1976, p. 74.

80. *MNC Hearings*, part 6, pp. 11–12. Libya and Algeria believed that the demands of the Gulf states were "much too low." Also, while the other OPEC countries had accepted the "Message to OPEC" as a basis for negotiations, Libya and Algeria had denounced it as a tactic to gain time and avoid negotiations on their demands. *MEES*, Feb. 5, 1971, p. 15, and *PIW*, Jan. 25, 1971, pp. 1–2.

81. *MNC Hearings*, part 5, pp. 148–49 and 171, and part 6, pp. 12 and 63–66.

82. Ibid., part 5, pp. 152 and 169.

83. *MNC Report*, p. 131.

84. *MNC Hearings*, part 5, p. 265.

85. Saudi Arabia and Iraq exported from the eastern Mediterranean as well as from the Gulf.

86. *MNC Report*, p. 133, and *MNC Hearings*, part 6, pp. 20–21.

87. *MNC Hearings*, part 6, p. 23.

88. Marwan Iskandar, *The Arab Oil Question* (Beirut: Middle East Economics Consultants, 1974), p. 9; Akins, "The Oil Crisis," U.S. Senate, Committee on Interior and Insular Affairs, *Oil and Gas Imports Issues*, part 3, p. 1030. For the OPEC resolutions, see *MNC Hearings*, part 6, pp. 123–24.

89. Quoted in Sampson, *The Seven Sisters*, p. 273.

90. Adelman, *The World Petroleum Market*, p. 255, and "Don't Blame the Oil Companies," *Forbes*, Apr. 15, 1976, p. 70.

91. *MNC Hearings*, part 6, p. 122.

92. Sampson, *The Seven Sisters*, p. 273, and *PIW*, Feb. 1, 1971, p. 4.

93. *PIW*, Mar. 8, 1971, p. 5, and *MNC Hearings*, part 5, p. 238.

94. A copy of the agreement is in *MNC Hearings*, part 6, pp. 169–72. Figures on the financial impact and the various offers are from *PIW*, Feb. 22, 1971, p. 6; Weisberg, *The Politics of Crude Oil Pricing in the Middle East*, pp. 60–61; and *MNC Report*, p. 133.

95. *PIW*, Feb. 22, 1971, p. 1, and *MNC Report*, pp. 133–34.

96. This provision was limited to a maximum payment to the Gulf countries of 21.5¢ a barrel. *MNC Hearings*, part 5, p. 140.

97. *PIW*, Feb. 8, 1971, p. 2.

98. *MNC Hearings*, part 5, pp. 157 and 271.

99. *PIW*, Mar. 2, 1971, p. 4.

100. *MEES*, Mar. 12, 1971 (supplement), p. 3.

101. *Petroleum Press Service* (Apr. 1971), p. 123, and *PIW*, Apr. 5, 1971, p. 48.

102. Figures on tanker rates are in OPEC, *Annual Statistical Bulletin, 1972*, p. 84. *PIW*, Feb. 1, 1971, p. 1, and Mar. 22, 1971, pp. 3–4.

103. *Oil and Gas Journal*, Mar. 8, 1971, p. 36; Mar. 15, 1971, p. 34; and Mar. 22, 1971, p. 48.

104. Ruth First, *Libya* (Baltimore: Penguin, 1974), p. 203, and *MEES*, Mar. 19, 1971 (supplement), p. 3.

105. *MNC Hearings*, part 6, pp. 39, 211, and 212, and *PIW*, Apr. 5, 1971 (supplement), p. 4.

106. *MNC Hearings*, part 6, p. 40.

107. *MEES*, Apr. 2, 1971, pp. 3–4, and *PIW*, Apr. 5, 1971 (supplement), p. 4.

108. *Petroleum Press Service* (May 1971), pp. 162–63; *PIW*, May 3, 1971, p. 2; and *MNC Hearings*, part 6, p. 42.

109. *Oil and Gas Journal*, Apr. 12, 1971, p. 23, and *PIW*, May 10, 1971, pp. 1–2.

110. "Recent Negotiations: Background Paper Prepared by the Department of State," in U.S. House of Representatives, Committee on Foreign Affairs, *Oil Negotiations, OPEC, and the Stability of Supply* (Washington, D.C.: Government Printing Office, 1973), p. 238, and Rifai, *The Pricing of Crude Oil*, pp. 279–80.

111. Edith Penrose and E. F. Penrose, *Iraq: International Relations and National Development* (Boulder, Colo.: Westview Press, 1978), p. 404.

112. *PIW*, July 5, 1971, p. 1.

113. See *MNC Hearings*, part 6, pp. 36–37.

114. Adelman, *The World Petroleum Market*, p. 251, and *PIW*, May 24, 1971, p. 3.

115. In 1957 the Eastern Hemisphere exporting countries' per barrel revenues were 78¢, and in 1969 they were 84¢. In 1957 Venezuela's per barrel revenue was 95¢, and in 1969 it was 96¢. Franklin Tugwell, *The Politics of Oil in Venezuela* (Stanford: Stanford University Press, 1975), p. 150.

116. Between 1970 and 1971 the increase in per barrel government take was about 40¢ in the Middle East, more than 90¢ in Libya and Algeria, 30.6¢ in Indonesia, 79¢ in Nigeria, and 47¢ in Venezuela (*PIW*, May 24, 1971, p. 5, and *Petroleum Press Service* [July 1971], p. 243). In evaluating these figures, it is important to recognize that countries started from different base levels and had different advantages in terms of location and crude quality.

117. Rifai, *The Pricing of Crude Oil*, p. 301, and *PIW*, May 24, 1971, p. 1, and Apr. 19, 1971, p. 5.

118. *PIW*, Mar. 27, 1972, pp. 5–6.

119. *Petroleum Press Service* (Apr. 1971), p. 124.

120. *PIW*, Apr. 5, 1971, p. 1, and June 28, 1971, p. 5. It is unlikely that this was due to the growth in demand, since the non-Communist world's oil consumption, which had increased at an annual 8.3% between 1965 and 1970, increased by only 4.9% in 1971. BP, *Statistical Review of the World Oil Industry, 1970*, p. 8, and *1971*, p. 8.

121. See Iskandar, *The Arab Oil Question*, p. 4, and *MNC Hearings*, part 5, p. 24. In the 1960s, both Kuwait and Venezuela had endorsed reserve conservation in principle, but had done little to implement it. Also, in Venezuela, it has been argued, this policy was a cover for the fact that Venezuelan oil was overpriced and not desired. Peter Francis Cowhey, "The Problems of Plenty: Energy Policy and International Politics" (unpublished Ph.D. thesis, University of California at Berkeley), p. 446.

122. *MNC Hearings*, part 7, pp. 332 and 340.

123. U.S. House of Representatives, Committee on Foreign Affairs, *New Perspectives on the Persian Gulf,* Hearings (Washington, D.C.: Government Printing Office, 1973), p. 11, and Fred Halliday, *Arabia without Sultans* (New York: Vintage, 1975), pp. 25 and 29.

124. Robert O. Freedman, *Soviet Policy toward the Middle East since 1970* (New York: Praeger, 1975), p. 105, and *MERIP Reports,* no. 30 (Aug. 1974), p. 23, and no. 36 (Apr. 1975), p. 20.

125. On the Dhofari rebellion and the Iranian intervention, see R. P. Owen, "The Rebellion in Dhofar—A Threat to Western Interests in the Gulf," *The World Today* (June 1973); Yager and Steinberg, *Energy and U.S. Foreign Policy,* p. 62; Freedman, *Soviet Policy toward the Middle East,* p. 105; Halliday, *Arabia without Sultans,* pp. 24 and 360–66; John Duke Anthony, *Arab States of the Lower Gulf: People, Politics, Petroleum* (Washington, D.C.: Middle East Institute, 1975), pp. 43, 226–28, and 232; and Alvin J. Cottrell, "The Foreign Policy of the Shah," *Strategic Review* 3, no. 4 (1975):37–38.

CHAPTER 6

1. The "participation demand" was proposed by Saudi Arabia's Sheikh Zaki Yamani in 1963 and formally endorsed by OPEC in 1968. In Dec. 1970 OPEC established a ministerial committee "to study implementation of the principle of participation." *Petroleum Intelligence Weekly,* Dec. 20, 1970, p. 2.

2. In a clear break with the Bretton Woods system, in August 1971 President Nixon ended the link between gold and the dollar (\$35 = 1 ounce), allowing the value of the dollar to float on the world market. For an analysis of these developments, see Fred Block, *The Origins of International Economic Disorder* (Berkeley: University of California Press, 1977), pp. 203–25.

3. *MNC Report,* p. 134, and *Petroleum Press Service* (Nov. 1971), p. 402.

4. *PIW,* Sept. 13, 1971, pp. 3 and 4, and *MNC Hearings,* part 6, pp. 169 and 213.

5. *PIW,* Sept. 27, 1971, p. 2; Edith T. Penrose, "The Development of Crisis," in Raymond Vernon, ed., *The Oil Crisis: In Perspective,* issued as *Daedalus* 104, no. 4 (1975): 44; and Akins, "The Oil Crisis," in U.S. Senate, Committee on Interior and Insular Affairs, *Oil and Gas Imports Issues* (Washington, D.C.: Government Printing Office, 1973), p. 1033.

6. *PIW,* Sept. 20, 1971, p. 1. Only Libya, Venezuela, and Nigeria required payment in local currencies. Saudi Arabia was paid in dollars and the other Gulf countries in sterling. Ibid. and Sept. 25, 1971, p. 1.

7. Penrose, "The Development of Crisis," in Vernon, ed., *The Oil Crisis,* p. 44, and *PIW,* Jan. 24, 1972, pp. 3 and 4.

8. *MNC Report,* p. 135; *PIW,* Jan. 24, 1972, p. 3, Feb. 21, 1972, p. 5, and May 5, 1972, p. 1; and Richard Chadbourn Weisberg, *The Politics of Crude Oil Pricing in the Middle East, 1970–1975* (Berkeley: Institute of International Studies, 1977), p. 77.

9. Analysts and those directly involved in the changing relationship between governments and companies have maintained that there are basic differences between nationalization and participation. For example, Lenczowski maintains that participation differs from nationalization in that (1) it was not punitive, (2) it was negotiated and provided for compensation, (3) it ensured continuous services of the former concessionaire through a "service contract," and (4) it enabled companies to "buy back" substantial quantities of oil. George Lenczowski, *Middle East Oil in a Revolutionary Age* (Washington, D.C.: American Enterprise Institute, 1976), p. 11.

While these are useful distinctions, they can be very misleading if they are taken to be a description of the differences between governments that "nationalized" the oil companies in their countries and those that sought "participation" in them, for in the end, the terms on which a company was nationalized were negotiated and compensation was provided. Moreover, in several instances of nationalization the former concessionaire retained a "service contract" role and/or special buy-back rights. While nationalization generally occurred in a more hostile political context, both nationalization and participation were punitive in that they adversely affected the concessionaire; and while most oil company executives viewed participation as gradual nationalization, there were 51% "nationalizations" and 100% "participations."

10. If the producing countries owned the refineries, it would probably increase the likelihood of their cutting prices, since the capital-intensive nature of refining makes it costly to run refineries below capacity.

11. See Zaki Yamani, "Prospects for Cooperation between Oil Producers, Marketers and Consumers: The Issue of Participation and After," in U.S. House of Representatives, Committee on Foreign Affairs, Subcommittee on Foreign Economic Policy, *Foreign Policy Implications of the Energy Crisis* (Washington, D.C.: Government Printing Office, 1972), pp. 368 and 371, and *PIW*, Sept. 25, 1974, p. 4.

12. Mira Wilkins, "The Oil Companies in Perspective," in Vernon, ed., *The Oil Crisis*, p. 174. The case of Mexico's national oil company is also instructive; it took Pemex more than 30 years to make major finds on Mexican territory. Louis Turner, *Oil Companies in the International System* (London: Allen & Unwin, 1978), p. 92.

13. Quoted in *MEES*, Jan. 5, 1973, p. 3.

14. U.S. House of Representatives, Committee on Foreign Affairs, *Foreign Policy Implications of the Energy Crisis*, p. 370.

15. *PIW*, Sept. 20, 1971, p. 1, and *MEES*, Sept. 24, 1971, p. 4.

16. *MNC Hearings*, part 6, p. 4.

17. Christopher T. Rand, *Making Democracy Safe for Oil* (Boston: Little, Brown, 1975), p. 216, and Jean-Marie Chevalier, *The New Oil Stakes* (London: Allen Lane, 1975), p. 81.

18. Taki Rifai, *The Pricing of Crude Oil* (New York: Praeger, 1975), p. 290.

19. Chevalier, *The New Oil Stakes*, pp. 79 and 83–85, and Rifai, *The Pricing of Crude Oil*, pp. 288–90.

20. *NYT*, May 2, 1971, p. E5; *Petroleum Press Service* (July 1971), p. 273; and Joe Stork, *Middle East Oil and the Energy Crisis* (New York: Monthly Review Press, 1975), p. 187.

21. Robert O. Freedman, "The Soviet Union and the Politics of Middle Eastern Oil," in Naiem A. Sherbiny and Mark A. Tessler, eds., *Arab Oil* (New York: Praeger, 1976), p. 310, and *Petroleum Press Service* (June 1971), p. 204.

22. *Petroleum Press Service* (July 1971), pp. 263, 304, 323, and (Aug. 1971) 313; Chevalier, *The New Oil Stakes*, pp. 80–81; and Rifai, *The Pricing of Crude Oil*, pp. 289–92. Algerian officials later stated that it had taken them six years to prepare for these takeovers. *PIW*, June 12, 1972, p. 3.

23. Stork, *Middle East Oil and the Energy Crisis*, p. 187, and *PIW*, July 17, 1972, p. 1.

24. *Petroleum Press Service* (Mar. 1971), p. 87 and (Feb. 1972) pp. 53–55; and Stork, *Middle East Oil and the Energy Crisis*, p. 187.

25. Quoted in Penrose, "The Development of Crisis," in Vernon, ed., *The Oil Crisis*, pp. 44–45.

26. In practice, the companies treated these bonds as a loss, implying that they would do little to keep their facilities in a condition to justify return of the deposit. Franklin Tugwell, *The Politics of Oil in Venezuela* (Stanford: Stanford University Press, 1975), pp. 118–21.

27. *MEES*, Sept. 24, 1971, pp. 1–2, and *PIW*, Sept. 27, 1971, pp. 1–2, and Oct. 4, 1971, p. 6. Nigeria also rejected OPEC bargaining and sought an initial 35% share. *PIW*, Mar. 20, 1972, p. 2, and *MEES*, Sept. 24, 1971, p. 2.

28. David Long, "United States Policy toward the Persian Gulf," *Current History* (Feb. 1975), p. 71; Joseph A. Yager and Eleanor B. Steinberg, *Energy and U.S. Foreign Policy* (Cambridge, Mass.: Ballinger, 1974), pp. 62–63; and David Holden, "The Persian Gulf: After the British Raj," *Foreign Affairs* 49, no. 4 (July 1971):733.

29. *MNC Hearings*, part 6, p. 48.

30. *Petroleum Press Service* (Jan. 1972), p. 5, and *PIW*, Dec. 12, 1971, p. 2, and Dec. 20, 1971, p. 1.

31. *MNC Hearings*, part 5, p. 21, and part 6, pp. 47 and 52–53, and *PIW*, Oct. 16, 1972, p. 2.

32. *MNC Hearings*, part 6, p. 53.

33. *PIW*, July 31, 1972, p. 3, Aug. 7, 1972, p. 5, Sept. 11, 1972, p. 3, and Oct. 2, 1972, p. 2; *MEES*, July 28, 1972, p. 3; and Edith Penrose and E. F. Penrose, *Iraq: International Relations and National Development* (Boulder, Colo.: Westview Press, 1978), p. 433.

34. A 20% share would be roughly equal to the amount of oil the majors sold to third parties. *MEES,* Sept. 15, 1972, p. 2.

35. Michael Field, "Oil: OPEC and Participation," in U.S. House of Representatives, Committee on Foreign Affairs, Subcommittee on Foreign Economic Policy, *Oil Negotiations, OPEC and the Stability of Supply* (Washington, D.C.: Government Printing Office, 1973), p. 268.

36. Akins, "The Oil Crisis," in U.S. Senate, Committee on Interior and Insular Affairs, *Oil and Gas Imports Issues,* p. 1033.

37. *MNC Hearings,* part 6, p. 50. An example may help to clarify this: posted price = $2.60, production cost = 10¢, taxes + royalty = $1.50, tax-paid cost = $1.60, market price = $1.90, halfway price = $2.10 = ($2.60 + $1.60)/2.

38. *PIW,* Jan. 31, 1972, p. 3, and Mar. 20, 1972, p. 2.

39. *MNC Hearings,* part 5, p. 229, and part 6, p. 50.

40. Quoted in ibid., part 6, p. 50.

41. Ibid., part 5, p. 229, and *MEES,* Mar. 17, 1972, pp. 1 and 2.

42. *MNC Hearings,* part 5, p. 229, and *PIW,* Mar. 20, 1972, p. 1, and Mar. 27, 1972, p. 3.

43. *MEES,* June 2, 1972 (supplement), p. 8, and Stork, *Middle East Oil and the Energy Crisis,* p. 192.

44. Quoted in Penrose and Penrose, *Iraq,* p. 410.

45. Basrah Petroleum Co. was an affiliate of IPC, organized in 1938, with rights to southern Iraq. Penrose and Penrose, *Iraq,* pp. 406–11, and *MEES,* June 16, 1972 (supplement), pp. 1–7.

46. Freedman, "The Soviet Union and the Politics of Middle Eastern Oil," in Sherbiny and Tessler, eds., *Arab Oil,* pp. 310–12; Robert O. Freedman, *Soviet Policy toward the Middle East* (New York: Praeger, 1975), pp. 71–73; and Arthur Jay Klinghoffer, *The Soviet Union and the Politics of International Oil* (New York: Columbia University Press, 1977), p. 137.

47. Penrose and Penrose, *Iraq,* p. 412, and *MEES,* June 9, 1972 (supplement), p. 1.

48. In evaluating this it is important to recognize that, prior to nationalization, IPC's exports were also far below capacity. *MEES,* July 7, 1972, p. 1, and Jan. 5, 1973, p. 3, and *PIW,* June 19, 1972, p. 3, and Oct. 2, 1972, p. 2.

49. *PIW,* Oct. 2, 1972, p. 3.

50. Stork, *Middle East Oil and the Energy Crisis,* p. 193.

51. Penrose and Penrose, *Iraq,* p. 434; *MEES,* June 16, 1972, p. 6; and Turner, *Oil Companies in the International System,* p. 168.

52. Yamani, "Prospects for Cooperation between Oil Producers, Marketers, and Consumers," in U.S. House of Representatives, Committee on Foreign Affairs, *Foreign Policy Implications of the Energy Crisis,* p. 370.

53. *MNC Report,* p. 103, and *MNC Hearings,* part 5, p. 229.

54. Turner, *Oil Companies in the International System,* p. 170, and *MEES,* July 7, 1972, p. 7.

55. *MNC Report,* p. 137.

56. Ibid., p. 140; *MNC Hearings,* part 7, pp. 455–56 and 528–29; and Marshall I. Goldman, "The Soviet Union," in Vernon, ed., *The Oil Crisis,* p. 140.

57. *MNC Hearings,* part 5, p. 229, and *PIW,* June 26, 1972, p. 2.

58. The compensation that each country would have to pay for a 25% share was estimated as follows: Saudi Arabia, $500 million; Abu Dhabi, $162 million; Kuwait, $150 million; Qatar, $71 million; Iraq (Basrah affiliate), $68 million. In contrast, the net book value of the Aramco 25% share was estimated at $200 million. *PIW,* Oct. 30, 1972, p. 5.

59. *MEES,* Jan. 5, 1973, p. 4; *MNC Hearings,* part 5, p. 230; and *PIW,* Oct. 9, 1972, pp. 1–2, and Oct. 30, 1972, p. 6.

60. *PIW,* Sept. 24, 1973, p. 1.

61. Quoted in *PIW,* Nov. 20, 1972, p. 2.

62. The Kirkuk fields (nationalized by Iraq) were no longer directly involved in the participation negotiations, but the IPC's holdings in southern Iraq, the Basrah Petroleum Co., were supposed to be part of the Oct. 5 settlement.

63. *MEES*, Oct. 27, 1972 (supplement), pp. 1–2.

64. Cited in ibid., Nov. 17, 1972, p. 7.

65. In contrast to Saudi Arabia, Libya was not interested in making downstream investments in the consuming countries. Aside from its greater militance, Libya also wanted a higher share sooner, because its reserves were not expected to last as long as those of the Gulf states. *MEES*, Nov. 3, 1972 (supplement), pp. 2–3, and Nov. 10, 1972, p. 1; and *PIW*, Nov. 13, 1972, p. 5.

66. Turner, *Oil Companies in the International System*, p. 169; *MNC Hearings*, part 6, p. 53; and *PIW*, Oct. 9, 1972, pp. 5–6, Oct. 16, 1972, p. 3, Oct. 23, 1972, p. 2, and Mar. 5, 1973, p. 6.

67. *PIW*, Oct. 16, 1972, p. 1, and *MNC Hearings*, part 6, p. 53.

68. On Nov. 30, 1972, the five U.S. majors took a firm stand against Libya's participation demands. They formed a "shadow team" to represent them in the subsequent stages of the Libyan/Bunker Hunt negotiations. Though it played no direct role in negotiations, it was active behind the scenes. *MEES*, Dec. 22, 1972, pp. 1–2.

69. *MEES*, Dec. 15, 1972, p. 1; *MNC Hearings*, part 5, p. 230; and *PIW*, Dec. 12, 1972, p. 8, and Dec. 25, 1972, pp. 1–2.

70. *MNC Hearings*, part 5, p. 230, and *PIW*, Jan. 8, 1973, pp. 1–2.

71. *MNC Report*, p. 137.

72. *PIW*, Jan. 15, 1973, p. 3, and *MNC Hearings*, part 5, p. 55.

73. *PIW*, Feb. 12, 1973, pp. 5–6.

74. Ibid., July 30, 1973, pp. 3 and 8.

75. *MNC Hearings*, part 5, pp. 230–31; *PIW*, Mar. 5, 1973, pp. 1–3, Apr. 16, 1973, p. 3, and July 23, 1973, p. 6; and Adelman and Friis, "Changing Monopolies and European Oil Supplies," *Energy Policy* 2, no. 4 (Dec. 1974):276.

76. Penrose and Penrose, *Iraq*, p. 440.

77. *MEES*, Mar. 23, 1973, pp. 5–6, Mar. 30, 1973, pp. 4–5, and Apr. 6, 1973, p. 1; Yager and Steinberg, *Energy and U.S. Foreign Policy*, pp. 38–39; Long, "United States Policy toward the Persian Gulf," *Current History* (Feb. 1975), p. 72; and Freedman, *Soviet Policy toward the Middle East*, p. 106.

78. *PIW*, Jan. 8, 1973, p. 1.

79. *PIW*, Feb. 19, 1973, p. 4, May 7, 1973, p. 1, and May 21, 1973, p. 3; and *MNC Hearings*, part 5, p. 231.

80. In February, 1973 an Italian court ruled against BP's claim that it still owned the nationalized crude. The ruling was based on technical grounds and did not address the legal merits of BP's contention. BP appealed, and Western firms continued to fear legal action in the event they purchased "hot" oil. *MNC Hearings*, part 6, p. 56, and *PIW*, Apr. 30, 1973, p. 3.

81. *PIW*, May 14, 1973, p. 5.

82. Ibid., July 16, 1973, p. 1.

CHAPTER 7

1. Quoted in Walter J. Levy, "An Atlantic-Japanese Energy Policy," *Survey* 19, no. 3 (1973):68.

2. Akins, "The Oil Crisis," in U.S. Senate, Committee on Interior and Insular Affairs, *Oil and Gas Imports Issues* (Washington, D.C.: Government Printing Office, 1973), part 3, pp. 1043–44, and *Petroleum Intelligence Weekly*, June 11, 1973, p. 5, and June 18, 1973, p. 7.

3. Akins, "The Oil Crisis," in U.S. Senate, Committee on Interior and Insular Affairs, *Oil and Gas Imports Issues*, part 3, p. 1033.

4. *MEES*, May 18, 1973, p. 5, and June 1, 1973, p. 2, and *The Economist*, July 7, 1973 ("Survey"), p. 19.

5. Louis Turner, "The European Community: Factors of Disintegration," *International Affairs* 5, no. 3 (July 1974):407.

6. Levy, "An Atlantic-Japanese Energy Policy," *Survey* 19, no. 3 (1973):64.

7. *PIW*, Oct. 9, 1972, pp. 3–4, and William Quandt, "U.S. Energy Policy and the Arab-Israeli

Conflict,'' in Naiem A. Sherbiny and Mark A. Tessler, eds., *Arab Oil* (New York: Praeger, 1976), p. 282.

8. *PIW*, Apr. 2, 1973, p. 8.

9. Akins, "The Oil Crisis," in U.S. Senate, Committee on Interior and Insular Affairs, *Oil and Gas Imports Issues*, part 3, p. 1044.

10. V. H. Oppenheim, "Why Oil Prices Go Up—The Past: We Pushed Them,'' *Foreign Policy*, no. 25 (1976–77), p. 38, and Joe Stork, *Middle East Oil and the Energy Crisis* (New York: Monthly Review Press, 1975), p. 221.

11. Geoffrey Chandler, "Energy: The Changed and Changing Scene," *Petroleum Review* 27, no. 319 (July 1973):269.

12. Oppenheim, "Why Oil Prices Go Up," *Foreign Policy*, no. 25 (1976–77), pp. 36–37.

13. Surrey, "Japan's Uncertain Energy Prospects," *Energy Policy* 2, no. 3 (Sept. 1974):213.

14. N. J. D. Lucas, *Energy and the European Communities* (London: Europa Publications, 1977), pp. 46–47.

15. Stingelin, "Europe and the Oil Crisis," *Current History* 68, no. 403 (Mar. 1975):100.

16. Turner, "The European Community," *International Affairs* 50, no. 3 (July 1974):406; J. E. Hartshorn, "Oil Diplomacy: The New Approach," *The World Today* 29, no. 7 (July 1973):287; and *PIW*, Mar. 13, 1972, p. 4.

17. *NYT*, June 5, 1971, pp. 1 and 57, and July 7, 1971, p. 24.

18. Only about 10% of this oil is recoverable with present technology, but even that is a huge amount. However, the capital costs of developing it were estimated at $5,000 to $6,000 a barrel. In contrast, capital costs for Middle East oil were from $400 to $500 a barrel. Joseph A. Yager and Eleanor B. Steinberg, *Energy and U.S. Foreign Policy* (Cambridge, Mass.: Ballinger, 1974), p. 80, and *PIW*, Oct. 16, 1972, p. 1.

19. Franklin Tugwell, *The Politics of Oil in Venezuela* (Stanford: Stanford University Press, 1975), pp. 138–40.

20. Richard Nixon, *RN: The Memoirs of Richard Nixon* (New York: Grosset & Dunlap, 1978), p. 983, and *PIW*, Mar. 26, 1973, p. 3.

21. *MNC Hearings*, part 7, p. 344, and Mancke, "The Genesis of the U.S. Oil Crisis," in Joseph S. Szyliowicz and Bard E. O'Neill, eds., *The Energy Crisis and U.S. Foreign Policy* (New York: Praeger, 1975), p. 61.

22. *PIW*, Nov. 6, 1972, p. 1, and Dec. 18, 1972, p. 1; BP, *Statistical Review of the World Oil Industry, 1973*, p. 6; and Robert Engler, *The Brotherhood of Oil* (Chicago: University of Chicago Press, 1977), p. 96.

23. *PIW*, Jan. 8, 1973, p. 3, and Jan 22, 1973, pp. 1–2.

24. Ibid., Apr. 2, 1973, p. 2, Marwan Iskandar, *The Arab Oil Question* (Beirut: Middle East Economics Consultants, 1974), p. 31.

25. Akins, "International Cooperative Efforts in Energy Supply," *Annals of the American Academy of Political and Social Science* 410 (Nov. 1973):83, and *PIW*, Apr. 16, 1973, p. 4.

26. In April 1973, Texaco and Exxon publicly called for elimination of restrictions on imports. Engler, *The Brotherhood of Oil*, p. 97.

27. *Business Week*, Apr. 21, 1973, pp. 51 and 53, and *PIW*, May 14, 1973, p. 4.

28. *Petroleum Economist* (June 1974), p. 240.

29. See table 7–2. (p. 198).

30. See Otto Eckstein, Suzanne Lorant, and Gobind Nankani, "Oil and the World Business Cycle," in U.S. Senate, Committee on Interior and Insular Affairs, *Implications of Recent Organization of Petroleum Exporting Countries (OPEC) Oil Price Increases* (Washington, D.C.: Government Printing Office, 1974), p. 667, and U.S. Department of Commerce, *International Economic Indicators* (June 1978), p. 37.

31. U.N., *Yearbook of National Accounts, 1976*, vol. 2, table 4A.

32. Computed from data in BP, *Statistical Review of the World Oil Industry*, various issues.

33. *MNC Hearings*, part 4, p. 57.

34. Penrose, "The Development of Crisis," in Raymond Vernon, ed., *The Oil Crisis: In Perspective,* issued as *Daedalus* 104, no. 4 (1975):48. With oil prices rising, the Soviet Union sought to maximize its hard currency earnings by selling oil to the West. Consequently, in mid-1973 the Soviet Union openly encouraged the East European countries to attempt to purchase oil in the Middle East and North Africa. Yager and Steinberg, *Energy and U.S. Foreign Policy,* p. 202.

35. MITI criticized Japan Line for paying such high prices for this oil and took steps to control the bidding of Japanese companies. Penrose, "The Development of Crisis," in Vernon, ed., *The Oil Crisis,* p. 56; *Petroleum Press Service* (Nov. 1973), p. 404; and *The Economist,* July 7, 1973 ("Survey"), p. 12.

36. Japanese firms took 27.4%, U.S. firms 24.7%, European 18.2%, and state-owned companies in the developing countries 29.7%. *MEES,* May 25, 1973, pp. 3–4; *PIW,* Aug. 6, 1973 (supplement), p. 1; and *PE* (Feb. 1974), p. 45.

37. *PE* (Feb. 1974), p. 45.

38. *PIW,* June 25, 1973, p. 1, and July 30, 1973, p. 1, and Penrose, "The Development of Crisis," in Vernon, ed., *The Oil Crisis,* pp. 48–49.

39. *PIW,* Aug. 20, 1973, p. 7.

40. *PIW,* Sept. 3, 1973, p. 4.

41. *MEES,* June 6, 1973, p. 5, and *PIW,* June 18, 1973, p. 3.

42. See *MNC Hearings,* part 6, p. 308; *MEES,* June 15, 1973, p. 4, and Aug. 10, 1973, p. 2; and *PIW,* June 25, 1973, p. 2, and Aug. 13, 1973, pp. 1–2.

43. See *MNC Hearings,* part 5, p. 26, part 6, pp. 57–58, and *PIW,* Aug. 20, 1973, p. 3.

44. See *MNC Hearings,* part 5, pp. 93–94, and part 6, p. 54.

45. *PIW,* Aug. 20, 1973, pp. 1 and 6.

46. Ibid., pp. 2, 3, and 6, Aug. 27, 1973, p. 1, Sept. 10, 1973, p. 6, and Sept. 19, 1973, p. 7.

47. Ibid., Aug. 20, 1973, p. 4., and Aug. 27, 1973, p. 8.

48. See *MNC Hearings,* part 7, p. 504, and *PIW,* Aug. 20, 1973, p. 6, and Aug. 27, 1973, p. 2.

49. *PIW,* Sept. 10, 1973, pp. 1 and 5, Sept. 24, 1973, pp. 3 and 4; *MNC Report,* p. 143; and *MEES,* Sept. 7, 1973, p. 2, Sept. 28, 1973, p. 8, and Oct. 12, 1973, p. 8. At this point, the majors also stopped supplying Bunker Hunt with oil under the terms of the Libyan Sharing Agreement. Richard Chadbourn Weisberg, *The Politics of Crude Oil Pricing in the Middle East, 1970–1975* (Berkeley: Institute of International Studies, 1977), p. 83.

50. Quoted in *MNC Report,* p. 138.

51. New England Petroleum Co. needed Libya's low-sulfur crude for its New England markets. Moreover, it was not particularly concerned about the price it had to pay for this oil since most of the utilities it sold it to (after refining) had fuel-adjustment clauses that enabled them automatically to pass increased costs on to the public (see *MNC Hearings,* part 5, pp. 39–49). As a NEPCO spokesman later told a Senate subcommittee, "We did not feel that we could prudently sit and wait for the major oil companies to negotiate something with the Libyan government because, at that point in time, you would have substantial blackouts and brownouts in the northeastern part of the United States." Idem, p. 40.

52. *MNC Report,* p. 139; *PIW,* Jan. 14, 1974, p. 3; and *PE* (Feb. 1974), p. 52.

53. *Oil and Gas Journal,* Oct. 8, 1973, p. 48.

54. *MNC Hearings,* part 7, p. 438; *PIW,* July 2, 1973, pp. 1–2, and Feb. 4, 1974, p. 2.

55. *MNC Report,* p. 139, and *MNC Hearings,* part 7, pp. 438–49.

56. *MNC Hearings,* part 7, pp. 438–39, and *PIW,* Oct. 13, 1973, p. 2, and Feb. 4, 1974, p. 9.

57. The "spot market" is an open market where petroleum products not under long-term contract are sold on a short-term basis. Price fluctuations on the spot market are generally more volatile than the prices of petroleum products sold under long-term contract or through the vertically integrated structure of the oil companies. However, trends established on the spot market are typically a harbinger of things to come in the channels where the bulk of the world's petroleum products are sold.

58. Oppenheim, "Why Oil Prices Go Up," *Foreign Policy,* no. 25 (1976–77), pp. 33–34;

Penrose, "The Development of Crisis," in Vernon, ed., *The Oil Crisis*, p. 49; and *PIW*, Sept. 17, 1973, p. 2.

59. Penrose, "The Development of Crisis," in Vernon, ed., *The Oil Crisis*, p. 47. Despite these increases, in countries where currencies had appreciated against the dollar the real landed cost of crude oil was generally less in Aug. 1973 than it had been in 1957. However, as the following table from *Petroleum Intelligence Weekly*, Sept. 24, 1973, p. 7 shows, this was not true for countries with depreciating currencies.

Index of Real Landed Crude Prices (Iranian Light), 1957, '71, '73
(Apr. 1970 = 100)

	1957	2/15/71	1/1/73	8/1/73
Hamburg, Germany	174.2	136.2	129.3	128.6
Rotterdam, Netherlands	166.5	133.0	131.5	143.1
Gothenburg, Sweden	157.8	133.1	134.9	154.0
London, U.K.	115.3	136.4	149.2	192.9
Lavera, France	86.0	136.6	135.2	145.5
Genoa, Italy	134.6	134.6	136.6	187.1
Yokohama, Japan	183.7	133.4	147.9	174.5
New York, U.S.	125.7	136.6	145.3	201.5

60. Weisberg, *The Politics of Crude Oil Pricing in the Middle East*, p. 73.

61. *MEES*, Sept. 21, 1973, p. 2.

62. Penrose, "The Development of Crisis," in Vernon, ed., *The Oil Crisis*, p. 49.

63. *MEES*, May 19, 1972 (supplement), p. 8; *PIW*, June 11, 1973, p. 1; and Jean-Marie Chevalier, *The New Oil Stakes* (London: Allen Lane, 1975), p. 54.

64. *PIW*, July 2, 1973, p. 1, and July 9, 1973, p. 1, and *MEES*, June 29, 1973 (supplement), p. 1. According to Iran's oil minister, Amouzegar, between 1947 and spring of 1973 the price of Persian Gulf oil increased by 20% while the index of the oil-exporting countries' manufactured imports had increased by more than 50%. Jahangir Amouzegar, "The Oil Story: Facts, Fiction, and Fair Play," *Foreign Affairs* 51, no. 4 (July 1973):682.

65. Edith Penrose and E. F. Penrose, *Iraq: International Relations and National Development* (Boulder, Colo.: Westview Press, 1978), pp. 502–3; *PIW*, July 2, 1973, p. 1, and July 9, 1973, p. 1; and *MEES*, Mar. 23, 1973, p. 2, and June 29, 1973 (supplement), p. 1.

66. The OPEC calculations were as follows:

	Cost	Posted Price	Realized Price	Company Take	Country Take	Country/Company Profit Ratio
Mar.-June 1971	$0.10	$2.18	$1.70	$0.33	$1.27	80/20
Sept. 1973	0.10	3.00	3.00	1.04	1.86	64/36

From *MEES*, Sept. 21, 1973, p. 2; see also, Sept. 7, 1973, p. 1.

67. Penrose, "The Development of Crisis," in Vernon, ed., *The Oil Crisis*, pp. 48 and 57; and *MEES*, Sept. 7, 1973 (supplement), p. 1.

68. *MEES*, Sept. 21, 1973, p. 3.

69. Naiem A. Sherbiny, "Arab Oil Producers' Policies in the Context of International Conflicts," in Sherbiny and Tessler, eds., *Arab Oil*, p. 41.

70. *MEES*, Oct. 15, 1973, p. 1.

71. Computed from U.S. Bureau of Mines, *International Petroleum Annual* (Mar. 1973), table 6, and (Mar. 1975), table 1.

72. Neither Alaskan nor North Sea oil was expected to make a significant contribution to world oil production before 1976. *MEES,* June 15, 1973 (supplement), p. 2.

73. Christopher T. Rand, *Making Democracy Safe for Oil* (Boston: Little, Brown, 1975), p. 326, and *PIW,* May 14, 1973, pp. 1, 6, and 8.

74. BP, *Statistical Review of the World Oil Industry, 1971,* p. 6.

75. John Blair, *The Control of Oil* (New York: Pantheon, 1976), p. 282.

76. *PIW,* May 15, 1972, p. 3, and Michael Field, "Oil: OPEC and Participation," in U.S. House of Representatives, Committee on Foreign Affairs, *Oil Negotiations, OPEC and the Stability of Supply* (Washington, D.C.: Government Printing Office, 1973), p. 270, and *Petroleum Press Service* (Jan. 1972), p. 6.

77. *MEES,* Nov. 3, 1972, p. 4.

78. *MNC Hearings,* part 7, p. 339. In 1968 SoCal had estimated that Libyan production would increase to 4.4 mb/d by 1973. See ibid., p. 332.

79. Actually, the pattern was much more erratic, decreasing by 26% in 1971, then increasing by 42.5% in 1972 and by 1.8% in 1973. BP, *Statistical Review of the World Oil Industry, 1971–74.*

80. Yager and Steinberg, *Energy and U.S. Foreign Policy,* pp. 28–29, and *PIW,* May 14, 1973, p. 8.

81. After the 1973 presidential election, Rafael Caldera, the outgoing president, urged his successor to nationalize the petroleum industry posthaste, and the newly elected Acción Democrática president declared his intention to nationalize the companies within two years, which he did. Tugwell, *The Politics of Oil in Venezuela,* p. 143.

82. See ibid., pp. 122–25 and 143.

83. BP, *Statistical Review of the World Oil Industry, 1973,* and *1974.*

84. Quoted in Blair, *The Control of Oil,* p. 285.

85. Rand, *Making Democracy Safe for Oil,* p. 233.

86. *MNC Hearings,* part 7, p. 344.

87. Ibid., p. 519.

88. Rand, *Making Democracy Safe for Oil,* p. 126.

89. See *MNC Hearings,* part 7, pp. 403, 406–10, and 442–43.

90. Ibid., p. 528.

91. *PIW,* Oct. 9, 1972, p. 4, and George Lenczowski, *Middle East Oil in a Revolutionary Age* (Washington, D.C.: American Enterprise Institute, 1976), p. 5.

92. The Arab "oil weapon" is as old as the Arab-Israeli conflict. During the 1948 Arab-Israeli war, the Arab oil-exporting countries embargoed oil to states that supported Israel and closed the IPC pipeline between Iraq and Haifa. However, these actions were completely ineffective, mainly because of the industrialized world's minimal dependence upon Arab oil at the time (Sankari, "The Character and Impact of Arab Oil Embargoes," in Sherbiny and Tessler, eds., *Arab Oil,* p. 266, and Stork, *Middle East Oil and the Energy Crisis,* p. 211). As we have seen, the effect was slight; but the flow of Arab oil to the consuming countries also was interrupted in 1956 and 1967.

93. See *MEES,* May 15, 1973 (supplement).

94. Penrose and Penrose, *Iraq,* pp. 505–6, and *MEES,* Aug. 11, 1972, p. 8.

95. *PIW,* Oct. 9, 1972, p. 3, and May 14, 1973, p. 3; and *MEES,* Aug. 31, 1973, p. 1.

96. Nixon, *RN,* p. 1012.

97. *MNC Hearings,* part 7, p. 526.

98. John C. Campbell, "Oil Power in the Middle East," *Foreign Affairs* 56, no. 1 (Oct. 1977):96.

99. George Lenczowski, *Soviet Advances in the Middle East* (Washington, D.C.: American Enterprise Institute, 1972), p. 163; John C. Campbell and Helen Caruso, *The West and the Middle East* (New York: Council on Foreign Relations, 1972), p. 38; and William B. Quandt, *Decade of Decisions* (Berkeley: University of California Press, 1977), pp. 136–37.

100. Robert O. Freedman, *Soviet Policy toward the Middle East since 1970* (New York: Praeger, 1975), pp. 54–55.

101. Qaddafi believes (probably correctly) that he is more loyal to Nasser's "mission" than any

other Arab leader of his time (see Ruth First, *Libya* [Baltimore: Penguin, 1974], p. 21), and his hostility toward Sadat was due in large part to the fact that he viewed Sadat as unfaithful to Nasser's goals.

102. *MERIP Reports*, no. 27 (Apr. 1974), p. 21, and Freedman, *Soviet Policy toward the Middle East*, pp. 115—16.

103. Freedman, *Soviet Policy toward the Middle East*, p. 74.

104. Quandt, *Decade of Decisions*, p. 151; and Lenczowski, "Egypt and the Soviet Exodus," *Current History* (Jan. 1973), pp. 13—16.

105. After Egypt came Israel (18.2%), South Vietnam (17.4%), Jordan (17.4%), and Syria (11.5%). Peretz, "Energy: Israelis, Arabs, and Iranians," in Szyliowicz and O'Neill, eds., *The Energy Crisis and U.S. Foreign Policy*, p. 98.

106. Freedman, *Soviet Policy toward the Middle East*, p. 77, and Quandt, *Decade of Decisions*, p. 151.

107. Freedman, *Soviet Policy toward the Middle East*, pp. 75 and 77, and *MERIP Reports*, no. 39 (July 1975), p. 20.

108. *MERIP Reports*, no. 27 (Apr. 1974), p. 21, and Freedman, *Soviet Policy toward the Middle East*, p. 116.

109. Marvin Kalb and Bernard Kalb, *Kissinger* (New York: Dell, 1975), p. 510.

110. Ibid., and Stork, *Middle East Oil and the Energy Crisis*, p. 218. Johnston's cable is in *MNC Hearings*, part 7, p. 505.

111. Rand, *Making Democracy Safe for Oil*, p. 319; Stork, *Middle East Oil and the Energy Crisis*, p. 218; and Ian Smart, "Oil, the Super-Powers and the Middle East," *International Affairs* 53, no. 1 (Jan. 1977):22.

112. *PIW*, Apr. 23, 1972, p. 6, and Lenczowski, *Middle East Oil in a Revolutionary Age*, p. 6.

113. M. A. Saleem Khan, "Oil Politics in the Persian Gulf Region," *India Quarterly* 30, no. 1 (Jan.–Mar. 1974):33.

114. *MEES*, May 18, 1973, p. 5.

115. Quoted in Khan, "Oil Politics in the Persian Gulf Region," *India Quarterly* 30, no. 1:33—34.

116. *MNC Hearings*, part 7, p. 506.

117. Ibid., p. 509.

118. Ibid., p. 504.

119. Ibid., p. 509.

120. Similarly, the CIA failed to anticipate the October War and concluded that, in the absence of war, the Arab states would not employ oil as a political weapon. Senate Select Committee on Intelligence, *U.S. Intelligence Analysis and the Oil Issue, 1973–74* (Washington, D.C.: Government Printing Office, 1977), p. 6.

121. *MNC Hearings*, part 6, p. 308, and part 7, pp. 429 and 528.

122. McKie, "The United States," in Vernon, ed., *The Oil Crisis*, p. 81.

123. *MNC Hearings*, part 7, p. 511.

124. Szyliowicz, "The Embargo and U.S. Foreign Policy," in Szyliowicz and O'Neill, eds., *The Energy Crisis and U.S. Foreign Policy*, p. 159, and McKie, "The United States," in Vernon, ed., *The Oil Crisis*, p. 81.

125. *MNC Hearings*, part 7, p. 512, and Stobaugh, "The Oil Companies in the Crisis," in Vernon, ed., *The Oil Crisis*, p. 183.

126. Stork, *Middle East Oil and the Energy Crisis*, p. 219, and *PIW*, July 16, 1973, pp. 5—6.

127. Stork, *Middle East Oil and the Energy Crisis*, p. 219; U.S. Senate, Committee on Foreign Relations, Subcommittee on Multinational Corporations, *U.S. Oil Companies and the Arab Oil Embargo: The International Allocation of Constricted Supplies* (Washington, D.C.: Government Printing Office, 1975) (hereafter *MNC Embargo Report*), p. 13; *MEES*, July 13, 1973, p. 10, and July 27, 1973, p. 6; and Smart, "Oil, the Super-Powers and the Middle East," *International Affairs* 53, no. 1 (Jan. 1977):22.

128. Freedman, *Soviet Policy toward the Middle East*, p. 116, and Peretz, "Energy: Israelis, Arabs, and Iranians," in Szyliowicz and O'Neill, eds., *The Energy Crisis and U.S. Foreign Policy*, p. 98.

129. Anthony Sampson, *The Seven Sisters*, (New York: Bantam, 1975), p. 295, and Lenczowski, *Middle East Oil in a Revolutionary Age*, p. 6. Faisal's statement is reproduced in part in *PIW*, Sept. 10, 1973, p. 10.

130. *MEES*, Aug. 31, 1973, p. 4.

131. Ibid., Sept. 7, 1973, p. iii.

132. *Wall Street Journal*, Sept. 6, 1973, p. 2, and *PIW*, Sept. 10, 1973, p. 1.

133. *MEES*, Aug. 31, 1973, pp. 1–2, and Sept. 7, 1973, p. 1.

CHAPTER 8

1. Marvin Kalb and Bernard Kalb, *Kissinger* (New York: Dell, 1975), pp. 513 and 523.

2. William B. Quandt, *Decade of Decisions* (Berkeley: University of California Press, 1977), pp. 162 and 168.

3. Kalb and Kalb, *Kissinger*, pp. 519–21.

4. Joseph Szyliowicz, "The Embargo and U.S. Foreign Policy," in Joseph S. Szyliowicz and Bard E. O'Neill, eds., *The Energy Crisis and U.S. Foreign Policy* (New York: Praeger, 1975), p. 184.

5. Kalb and Kalb, *Kissinger*, pp. 533–40, and Quandt, *Decade of Decisions*, pp. 176, 178–79, and 181–84.

6. Joe Stork, *Middle East Oil and the Energy Crisis* (New York: Monthly Review Press, 1975), p. 222; *Oil and Gas Journal*, Oct. 22, 1973, p. 15; and *MEES*, Oct. 12, 1973, p. 4.

7. *MNC Embargo Report*, p. 15; Edith Penrose ane E. F. Penrose, *Iraq: International Relations and National Development* (Boulder, Colo.: Westview Press, 1978), p. 507; *PIW*, Oct. 15, 1973, p. 2; and Richard Chadbourn Weisberg, *The Politics of Crude Oil Pricing in the Middle East, 1970–1975* (Berkeley: Institute of International Studies, 1977), p. 103.

8. *MNC Report*, p. 149; *MNC Hearings*, part 5, pp. 216–17; and U.S. House of Representatives, Committee on Foreign Affairs, *The U.S. Oil Shortage and the Arab-Israeli Conflict* (Washington, D.C.: Government Printing Office, 1973), p. 12.

9. *MEES*, Oct. 12, 1973, p. 11.

10. *MNC Report*, p. 149.

11. The memo is reproduced in *MNC Hearings*, part 7, pp. 546–47.

12. *MNC Report*, pp. 149–50; *MNC Hearings*, part 5, pp. 216–17; and *MEES*, Oct. 19, 1973, p. 8.

13. *Petroleum Intelligence Weekly*, Oct. 22, 1973, p. 3, and Nov. 5, 1973, p. 5. In addition, individual countries were free to set their own sulfur premiums, which many of them did, following Abu Dhabi's lead.

14. The idea of linking posted and realized prices was reported to be Yamani's. *MEES*, Oct. 19, 1973, p. 6.

15. *PIW*, Oct. 22, 1973, p. 2, and Nov. 26, 1973, p. 2.

16. *PIW*, Oct. 22, 1973, p. 2.

17. If the sulfur premium is included, the increase in government take averaged about $1.30, or 75%, according to industry calculations. *PIW*, Nov. 26, 1973, p. 9.

18. *PIW*, Oct. 22, 1973, p. 10.

19. *MEES*, Oct. 19, 1973, p. 7, and *PIW*, Nov. 26, 1973, p. 9.

20. *PIW*, Oct. 22, 1973, pp. 4 and 9.

21. In January 1974 columnist Jack Anderson claimed to have seen documents that showed that, early in 1973, the Aramco partners had encouraged Saudi Arabia to raise prices. According to Anderson, the companies did this because an increase in the world price would tend to push prices in the U.S. up and enable the companies to develop more productive capacity in the U.S. An extensive investigation by the Senate Subcommittee on Multinational Corporations found that SoCal had

assumed that a rise in the price of imported oil would lead to an increase in domestic oil prices and that this would make it economical for them to recover more oil from their U.S. fields by undertaking costly secondary and tertiary recovery processes. However, the subcommittee was unable to establish a link between the companies' desire for increased U.S. prices and their acquiescence in the October price increases. Nor did the subcommittee find hard evidence of the companies' directly encouraging the exporting countries to raise prices.

Anderson, who claimed that his story was based on the overall documentary record, provided the subcommittee staff with some, but not all, of the documents he relied upon. In addition, the subcommittee investigation included a search of SoCal's files, the source of the documents Anderson claimed to have relied upon.

In his original story, Anderson also stated it was likely that the oil-exporting countries would have raised prices even if they had not been encouraged to do so by the companies, and that in the fall the companies had sent a delegation to urge Yamani to hold down the price demands. But the only reason for this, according to Anderson, was that the companies were concerned about political repercussions in the consuming countries.

Anderson's articles are reprinted in *MNC Hearings*, part 7, pp. 470–74; see also pp. 1–11, 401–5, 424, 446, and 467.

22. Penrose, "The Development of Crisis," in Raymond Vernon, ed., *The Oil Crisis: In Perspective*, issued as *Daedalus* 104, no. 4 (1975):50, and *PIW*, Nov. 5, 1973, p. 5, and Nov. 12, 1973, p. 4.

23. Quoted in U.S. House of Representatives, Committee on Foreign Affairs, *The U.S. Oil Shortage and the Arab-Israeli Conflict*, p. 15.

24. Kuwait's militant position was due in part to the presence of 150,000 Palestinians in the country.

25. *MNC Embargo Report*, p. 14.

26. Kalb and Kalb, *Kissinger*, pp. 541–42.

27. Though created in 1969 as an organization of the conservative oil-exporting countries (Kuwait, Libya, and Saudi Arabia), OAPEC's character changed following the 1969 revolution in Libya. In 1970 the organization's membership was increased to include Algeria, Abu Dhabi, Dubai, Bahrain, and Qatar; then, in Oct. 1971, Abu Dhabi announced that it would support the admission of Iraq, and in December Saudi Arabia proposed a change in the membership rules that paved the way for the admission of Syria and Egypt. In Mar. 1972, Syria, Egypt, and Iraq were accepted as OAPEC members.

28. See *MNC Hearings*, part 7, p. 517.

29. *MNC Report*, p. 144.

30. *MNC Embargo Report*, p. 15.

31. Marwan Iskandar, *The Arab Oil Question* (Beirut: Middle East Economic Consultants, 1974), p. 95, and *MNC Embargo Report*, p. 15.

32. Edward R. F. Sheehan, *The Arabs, Israelis, and Kissinger* (New York: Reader's Digest Press, 1976), p. 69; Kalb and Kalb, *Kissinger*, p. 545; and *MEES*, Oct. 19, 1973, pp. 2–3. Nixon had not read the memo from the Aramco executives when he made this decision, but it is doubtful that he would have acted differently if he had. Lenczowski, "The Oil-producing Countries," in Vernon, ed., *The Oil Crisis*, p. 68.

33. The Dutch, who had offered to replace Austria as a relay center for emigrating Soviet Jews, had permitted volunteers to be recruited on their territory for service in Israel, and the Dutch airline, KLM, had been used for chartered flights to Israel in connection with the Israeli war effort (Lenczowski, "The Oil-producing Countries," in Vernon, ed., *The Oil Crisis*, p. 65). It was feared that the embargo would prevent transshipment of supplies to Western Europe through Rotterdam; however, the Arabs soon made it clear that the embargo on the Netherlands would be limited to supplies for the internal Dutch market. *PIW*, Nov. 5, 1973, p. 1.

34. U.S. House of Representatives, Committee on Foreign Affairs, *The U.S. Oil Shortage and the Arab-Israeli Conflict*, p. 13.

35. Quoted in Stork, *Middle East Oil and the Energy Crisis*, p. 238.

36. On October 12, 1973, Kissinger stated that "After hostilities broke out, the United States set itself two principal objectives. One, to end the hostilities as quickly as possible. Secondly, to end the hostilities in such a manner that they [*sic*] would contribute to the maximum extent possible to the promotion of a more permanent, more lasting solution in the Middle East" (quoted in Quandt, *Decade of Decisions*, p. 181). Similarly, Nixon later stated: "We would make Israel strong enough that they would not fear to negotiate, but not so strong that they felt they had no need to negotiate." Richard Nixon, *RN: The Memoirs of Richard Nixon* (New York: Grosset & Dunlap, 1978), p. 1018.

37. Nixon, *RN*, pp. 936 and 938–39; Kalb and Kalb, *Kissinger*, pp. 541–64; and Quandt, *Decade of Decisions*, pp. 194–200.

38. *MNC Hearings*, part 7, p. 530.

39. The 25% reduction from September levels was equivalent to a 32% reduction from Aramco's projected November production (*MNC Embargo Report*, p. 16). While the official figure was 25%, at its peak the cutback came to 24%, as shown in table 8–1.

40. *MNC Report*, p. 145.

41. Lenczowski, "The Oil-producing Countries," in Vernon, ed., *The Oil Crisis*, p. 65.

42. Christopher T. Rand, *Making Democracy Safe for Oil* (Boston: Little, Brown, 1975), p. 318. Iraqi production declined in October as a result of wartime damage to the Banias terminal; however, by mid-November this was fully repaired. Iskandar, *The Arab Oil Question*, p. 102.

43. On October 22 Iraq nationalized 60%—the Dutch share—of Royal Dutch/Shell's interest in Basrah Petroleum Co.

44. Quoted in Rand, *Making Democracy Safe for Oil*, p. 318.

45. *MERIP Reports*, no. 23 (Dec. 1973), p. 14; *MEES*, Nov. 19, 1973, pp. 5–6; Wilkins, "The Oil Companies in Perspective," in Vernon, ed., *The Oil Crisis*, pp. 162–63; Edith Penrose and E. F. Penrose, *Iraq: International Relations and National Development* (Boulder, Colo.: Westview Press, 1978), pp. 509–11; and Stork, *Middle East Oil and the Energy Crisis*, p. 225.

46. Lenczowski, "The Oil-producing Countries," in Vernon, ed., *The Oil Crisis*, p. 64.

47. Stobaugh, "The Oil Companies in the Crisis," in ibid., p. 180.

48. *PE* (Jan. 1974), p. 17; Sam H. Schurr and Paul T. Homan, *Middle Eastern Oil and the Western World* (New York: American Elsevier, 1971), pp. 77 and 79; and Iskandar, *The Arab Oil Question*, p. 106. Figures on oil production are from table 8–1 and BP, *Statistical Review of the World Oil Industry, 1967*, p. 7. Figures on U.S. spare productive capacity are from the Independent Petroleum Assn. of America.

49. Schurr and Homan, *Middle Eastern Oil and the Western World*, p. 79; *PIW*, Nov. 15, 1973, p. 5; and *Petroleum Press Service* (Nov. 1973), pp. 413–14.

50. *MNC Hearings*, part 7, p. 344.

51. Rand, *Making Democracy Safe for Oil*, p. 310. Though it lacked the capacity to substantially increase oil production, the Soviet Union increased its exports to the U.S. during the embargo, and there are indications that its deliveries to the Netherlands increased during this period as well, despite the fact that the Soviet Union officially supported the Arab oil embargo—even urging its extension to Western Europe and Japan and its continuation in Mar. 1974. See Arthur Jay Klinghoffer, *The Soviet Union and International Oil Politics* (New York: Columbia University Press, 1977), pp. 165 and 173–75, and Goldman, "The Soviet Union," in Vernon, ed., *The Oil Crisis*, p. 137.

52. Stobaugh, "The Oil Companies in the Crisis," in Vernon, ed., *The Oil Crisis*, p. 180, and *MNC Hearings*, part 7, p. 344. Since the need to transport and refine oil creates a lag between the time a barrel of oil is produced and the time it is consumed, it would be about a month before consumers felt the effect of this shortfall.

53. *OECD Observer* (Dec. 1973), p. 20.

54. Louis Turner, *Oil Companies in the International System* (London: Allen & Unwin, 1978), p. 171, and *MEES*, Oct. 19, 1973, p. 4. Figures for the U.S. are computed from data in BP, *Statistical Review of the World Oil Industry, 1974*, p. 8, and *Oil and Gas Journal*, Nov. 5, 1973, pp. 118–19.

55. Public support for Israel increased in the U.S. from 47% in October 1973 to 50% in Decem-

ber 1973, reversing a slow but steady downward trend from 1967, when support stood at 56%. Support for the Arabs, which was only 6% in October 1973, increased to 7% in December 1973. In June 1967 it had been only 4%.

In February 1974, 61% of the public disagreed with the statement "We need Arab oil for our gasoline shortage so we had better find ways to get along with the Arabs, even if that means supporting Israel less." Only 23% agreed. In December 1973, when asked "Who or what do you think is responsible for the energy crisis?" the most frequent responses were oil companies (25%), the federal government (23%), the Nixon administration (19%), and U.S. consumers (16%); only 7% of the respondents blamed the Arab nations and less than 1% blamed Israel. See David Garnham, "The Oil Crisis and U.S Attitudes toward Israel," in Naiem A. Sherbiny and Mark A. Tessler, eds., *Arab Oil* (New York: Praeger, 1976), pp. 298, 300, 301, and 303.

56. Kalb and Kalb, *Kissinger,* p. 582.

57. There is a partial transcript of the meeting in Sheehan, *The Arabs, Israelis, and Kissinger,* pp. 70–73; the quoted section is from p. 72.

58. *PIW,* Nov. 19, 1973, p. 8.

59. Klaus Knorr, "The Limits of Economic and Military Power," in Vernon, ed., *The Oil Crisis,* p. 236, and Khan, "Oil Politics in the Persian Gulf Region," *India Quarterly,* vol. 30, no. 1 (Jan.–Mar. 1974), pp. 95–96.

60. Knorr, "The Limits of Economic and Military Power," in Vernon, ed., *The Oil Crisis,* pp. 236–37.

61. Halliday suggests five explanations for the invasion "threat": it might have been (1) "part of a U.S.-Saudi understanding to give the Saudis a nationalist reputation"; (2) "standard contingency preparations"; (3) designed "to deter radical Arab states"; (4) rooted in "a division of opinion within the U.S. government between the diplomatic sector (Kissinger plus the State Department) and the military sector"; (5) "a way of letting it be known that if the embargo was maintained for a long time with damaging international effect, military pressure would be exerted." Fred Halliday, *Arabia without Sultans* (New York: Vintage, 1975), p. 22.

62. Lenczowski, "The Oil-producing Countries," in Vernon, ed., *The Oil Crisis,* p. 62, and Prodi and Clo, "Europe," in ibid., p. 106.

63. *MEES,* Oct. 19, 1973, p. 3.

64. Quoted in Khan, "Oil Politics in the Persian Gulf Region," *India Quarterly* 30, no. 1 (Jan.–Mar. 1974):35.

65. Tsurumi, "Japan," in Vernon, ed., *The Oil Crisis,* pp. 123–24.

66. *MNC Embargo Report,* p. 16.

67. Lenczowski, "The Oil-producing Countries," in Vernon, ed., *The Oil Crisis,* p. 67.

68. *MNC Embargo Report,* p. 16. Yamani is quoted in *MEES,* Dec. 12, 1973, p. 2.

69. *MNC Embargo Report,* p. 16; George Lenczowski, *Middle East Oil in a Revolutionary Age* (Washington, D.C.: American Enterprise Institute, 1976), p. 20; Lenczowski, "The Oil-producing Countries," in Vernon, ed., *The Oil Crisis,* p. 67; and *MNC Report,* p. 144.

70. *PIW,* Dec. 17, 1973, pp. 6 and (supplement) 2.

71. *PIW,* Mar. 26, 1973, p. 2.

72. *MEES,* Apr. 20, 1973, p. 8.

73. Despite this, the exporting countries were unable to agree on how the market price would be determined. Several possibilities were considered: (1) tying crude prices to the rise in the price of petroleum products, (2) basing it on state sales of participation oil to third parties, and (3) linking it to the cost of alternative energy sources. *PIW,* Nov. 12, 1973, p. 5, and Taki Rifai, *The Pricing of Crude Oil* (New York: Praeger, 1975), p. 349.

74. *MEES,* Oct. 19, 1973, p. 6.

75. *MEES,* Sept. 21, 1973, p. 2.

76. *PIW,* Oct. 29, 1973, pp. 7–8.

77. *PIW,* Nov. 26, 1973, pp. 2 and 9.

78. *PIW,* Oct. 29, 1973, p. 8.

79. Anthony Sampson, *The Seven Sisters* (New York: Bantam, 1975), p. 306.

80. *MEES*, Dec. 21, 1973, p. 2.

81. *MEES*, Dec. 28, 1973, p. 17.

82. *PIW*, Dec. 17, 1973, pp. 1–2.

83. *PIW*, Dec. 29, 1973, p. 4, and Tsurumi, "Japan," in Vernon, ed., *The Oil Crisis*, p. 125.

84. The U.S. defended its opposition to inclusion of its domestic supplies in any sharing agreement by pointing out that, in the current situation, it would have to share its domestic supplies while being denied Arab oil (*PIW*, Oct. 22, 1973, p. 5). Yet during the embargo the U.S. fared better than Western Europe, despite the fact that the U.S. was the embargoed country.

85. *MNC Hearings*, part 7, p. 342.

86. Lenczowski, *Middle East Oil in a Revolutionary Age*, p. 26.

87. Iskandar, *The Arab Oil Question*, p. 120; Lenczowski, "The Oil-producing Countries," in Vernon, ed., *The Oil Crisis*, p. 69; and Lenczowski, *Middle East Oil in a Revolutionary Age*, p. 27.

88. *PIW*, Dec. 31, 1973, p. 3; *MEES*, Jan. 11, 1974 (supplement), p. 3; and *MNC Hearings*, part 5, p. 296. The Shah is quoted in *PIW*, Dec. 31, 1973, p. 8.

89. *PIW*, Dec. 31, 1973, p. 8, Jan. 7, 1974, pp. 5 and 7, and Jan. 14, 1974, p. 4; and *MEES*, Jan. 14, 1974, p. 5.

90. Lenczowski, "The Oil-producing Countries," in Vernon, ed., *The Oil Crisis*, p. 66.

91. Kalb and Kalb, *Kissinger*, pp. 596–97, and *MEES*, Dec. 28, 1973, pp. 8 and 10.

92. Lenczowski, "The Oil-producing Countries," in Vernon, ed., *The Oil Crisis*, p. 69.

93. Maull, "The Price of Crude Oil in the International Energy Market," *Energy Policy* 5, no. 2 (June 1977):146, and Oppenheim, "Why Oil Prices Go Up," *Foreign Policy*, no. 25 (1976–77), p. 40.

94. In practice, the U.S. and the Netherlands did not suffer more than the (other) nations of Western Europe, but the flexibility of the embargo/cutback strategy seems to have remained an important Saudi consideration. Lenczowski, "The Oil-producing Countries," in Vernon, ed., *The Oil Crisis*, p. 70.

95. Ibid.

96. *MNC Hearings*, part 7, p. 514.

97. See ibid., p. 427.

98. Ibid., p. 514.

99. Ibid., part 6, p. 59, and part 7, p. 533.

100. *MNC Report*, p. 163, and *PIW*, Feb. 4, 1974, pp. 3–4, and Feb. 11, 1974, p. 2.

101. *MNC Hearings*, part 6, p. 59; *MNC Report*, p. 163; and *PIW*, Mar. 25, 1974, p. 3.

102. *PE* (Mar. 1974), p. 95.

103. *PE* (May 1974), p. 173, and *MNC Report*, p. 163.

104. *PE* (July 1974), p. 256, and *PIW*, Feb. 11, 1974, p. 3.

105. *MNC Report*, p. 163, and Frank Church, "The Impotence of Oil Companies," *Foreign Policy*, no. 27 (1977), p. 43.

106. In January, *PIW* estimated that the increases from changes in the participation agreement boosted Saudi Arabia's average per barrel take from the $7 established in December to $8.57. In Nigeria and Libya, the increases from changes in concession agreements were estimated at an additional $4 a barrel. *PIW*, Jan. 21, 1974, p. 2.

107. Nixon, *RN*, p. 987.

108. Knorr, "The Limits of Economic and Military Power," in Vernon, ed., *The Oil Crisis*, p. 236.

109. William Griffith, "The Fourth Middle East War, the Energy Crisis, and U.S. Policy," *Orbis* 17, no. 4 (1974):1168; *Oil and Gas Journal*, Jan. 14, 1974, p. 18; and *MEES*, Jan. 11, 1974, p. 9.

110. Quandt, *Decade of Decisions*, p. 226; *MEES*, Jan. 25, 1974, p. 1; and Nixon, *RN*, p. 987.

111. Lenczowski, *Middle East Oil in a Revolutionary Age*, p. 24, and Quandt, *Decade of Decisions*, p. 231.

112. Quandt, *Decade of Decisions*, p. 235, and Quandt, "U.S. Energy Policy and the Arab-Israeli Conflict," in Sherbiny and Tessler, eds. *Arab Oil*, p. 289.

113. Szyliowicz, "The Embargo and U.S. Foreign Policy," in Szyliowicz and O'Neill, eds., *The Energy Crisis and U.S. Foreign Policy*, p. 206, and Quandt, *Decade of Decisions*, p. 236.

114. Lenczowski, *Middle East Oil in a Revolutionary Age*, p. 24.

115. Lenczowski, "The Oil-producing Countries," in Vernon, ed., *The Oil Crisis*, p. 67.

116. Quandt, "U.S. Energy Policy and the Arab-Israeli Conflict," in Sherbiny and Tessler, eds., *Arab Oil*, p. 288, and Quandt, *Decade of Decisions*, pp. 220–21 and 231.

117. Smart, "Oil, the Super-Powers, and the Middle East," *International Affairs* 53, no. 1 (Jan. 1977):26.

118. These were fairly minor. In the U.S. they involved only a shift to daylight saving time and lower speed limits. In Japan, the government called for a voluntary 10% reduction in oil and electric power use and the closing of gasoline stations on holidays. In Western Europe, countries introduced new automobile speed limits, banned driving on Sundays and holidays, rationed gasoline, and placed restrictions on heating and lighting. Tsurumi, "Japan," in Vernon, ed., *The Oil Crisis*, p. 121, and Prodi and Clo, "Europe," in ibid., p. 100.

119. *MNC Report*, p. 147. These efforts were not coordinated, but undertaken by each company individually, and companies' criteria varied. For example, Mobil allocated supplies on the basis of a country's past use (historical base) while Exxon allocated on the basis of current/projected demand (*MNC Embargo Report*, p. 4). Since being the international allocator was a "no win" role, the companies would have preferred to have the consuming countries establish the allocation criteria, but the consuming countries declined; they were not anxious to make unpopular decisions, they lacked the information and logistical skills to handle the crisis, and their only emergency allocation scheme applied to Europe but not Japan or the U.S., which made it highly inappropriate to a situation in which the U.S. was the principal target. Hence, rather than invoke this plan, possibly provoking the Arabs in the process, OECD decided to rely on the companies to allocate the shortfall. *PIW*, Jan. 7, 1974, p. 2, and Turner, *Oil Companies in the International System*, pp. 176–77.

120. Stobaugh, "The Oil Companies in the Crisis," in Vernon, ed., *The Oil Crisis*, p. 187, and *MNC Embargo Report*, pp. 1 and 5.

121. *MNC Embargo Report*, p. 10.

122. If indirect imports (i.e. imports originating in Arab countries but passing through non-Arab countries for refining, etc.) are included, the figure rises to about 28% of U.S. oil imports or 10% of U.S. oil consumption (*MEES*, Oct. 19, 1973, p. 4). The Arabs embargoed direct and indirect imports, and the companies are believed to have observed this.

123. Computed from data in *Basic Petroleum Data Book*, sec. 9, table 9.

124. Prodi and Clo, "Europe," in Vernon, ed., *The Oil Crisis*, p. 101.

125. *MNC Embargo Report*, p. 6.

126. U.S. independents increased their deliveries to Japan by 35.8% over their year-earlier levels while reducing deliveries to Western Europe by 12.6% and to the U.S. by 13.6% under year-earlier levels. However, these figures overstate the difference in treatment, because during 1973 Japanese energy demand was growing by 17% while demand in the U.S. and Western Europe was growing at only 5%. *MNC Embargo Report*, pp. 8–9, and Stobaugh, "Oil Companies in the Crisis," in Vernon, ed., *The Oil Crisis*, p. 180.

127. Weisberg, *The Politics of Crude Oil Pricing in the Middle East*, p. 109, and Stobaugh, "Oil Companies in the Crisis," in Vernon, ed., *The Oil Crisis*, p. 189.

128. Horst Mendershausen, *Coping with the Oil Crisis: French and German Experiences* (Baltimore: Johns Hopkins University Press, 1976), p. 41, and Stobaugh, "Oil Companies in the Crisis," in Vernon, ed., *The Oil Crisis*, p. 190.

129. Wilkins, "The Oil Companies in Perspective," in Vernon, ed., *The Oil Crisis*, p. 173; Stobaugh, "The Oil Companies in the Crisis," in ibid., p. 188; Weisberg, *The Politics of Crude Oil Pricing in the Middle East*, pp. 107 and 109; and *MNC Report*, p. 145.

130. *MNC Report*, p. 148, and Stobaugh, "The Oil Companies in the Crisis," in Vernon, ed., *The Oil Crisis*, p. 199.

131. Prodi and Clo, "Europe," in Vernon, ed., *The Oil Crisis*, p. 100.

132. Ibid., pp. 101 and 103.

133. *Oil and Gas Journal*, Dec. 10, 1973, p. 52. In Western Europe, countries also sought to spare the industrial sector by shifting the bulk of the shortfall onto gasoline. Prodi and Clo, "Europe," in Vernon, ed., *The Oil Crisis*, p. 100.

134. *Oil and Gas Journal*, Jan. 14, 1974, pp. 23 and 25.

135. Federal Trade Commission, "An Evaluation of Mandatory Petroleum Allocation Program," in U.S. Senate, Committee on Interior and Insular Affairs, *Oversight—Mandatory Petroleum Allocation Programs* (Washington, D.C.: Government Printing Office, 1974), appendix pp. A40 and A41, and ibid., part 1, p. 112.

136. Ibid., part 1, pp. 13 and 97–98; Federal Trade Commission, "An Evaluation of Mandatory Petroleum Allocation Program," in ibid., appendix p. A146; Mancke, "The Genesis of the U.S. Oil Crisis," in Szyliowicz and O'Neill, eds., *The Energy Crisis and U.S. Foreign Policy*, p. 66; and Stork, *Middle East Oil and the Energy Crisis*, p. 233.

137. U.S. Senate, Committee on Interior and Insular Affairs, *Oversight—Mandatory Petroleum Allocation Programs*, part 1, p. 65.

138. McKie, "The United States," in Vernon, ed., *The Oil Crisis*, p. 87.

139. U.S. Senate, Committee on Interior and Insular Affairs, *Oversight—Mandatory Petroleum Allocation Programs*, part 1, pp. 58 and 126, and FTC, "An Evaluation of Mandatory Petroleum Allocation Program," in ibid., appendix pp. A33 and A53.

140. FTC, "An Evaluation of Mandatory Petroleum Allocation Program," in ibid., appendix pp. A170–72, and *Oil and Gas Journal*, Jan. 14, 1974, p. 25.

141. U.S. Senate, Committee on Interior and Insular Affairs, *Oversight—Mandatory Petroleum Allocation Program*, part 1, pp. 44 and 64; and FTC, "An Evaluation of Mandatory Petroleum Allocation Program," in ibid., appendix pp. A42 and A45.

142. The FEA compromised, bringing 250 oil executives into the government to help run the allocation program. *PIW*, Dec. 3, 1973, p. 9.

CHAPTER 9

1. In 1977 the Central Intelligence Agency, the Organization for Economic Cooperation and Development, and the Workshop on Alternative Energy Systems issued reports that predicted that demand for oil would outpace growth in supplies, leading to serious shortfalls between 1980 and 1990. These reports emphasized that the most critical factor was not availability of resources but the willingness of Saudi Arabia to expand production. Oil company forecasts generally conformed with these predictions (CIA, *The International Energy Situation: Outlook to 1985* [Washington, D.C.: Government Printing Office, 1977]; OECD, *World Energy Outlook* [Paris: OECD, 1977]; WAES, *Energy: Global Prospects 1985–2000* [New York: McGraw-Hill, 1977]; *BW*, May 30, 1977, pp. 25–6; and *PE* [May 1977], p. 172).

One of the earliest and most persistent critics of these studies was oil economist M. A. Adelman, who said: "The crunch that [U.S. Energy Secretary] Schlesinger talks about so eloquently is like the horizon—it recedes as you approach it" (cited in J. E. Hartshorn, *Objectives of the Petroleum Exporting Countries* [Nicosia, Cyprus: Middle East Petroleum and Economics Publications, 1978], p. 53). Then, a year after the forecasts of doom were heralded, with the world oil market characterized by glut, the Petroleum Industry Research Foundation, National Economic Research Associates, and Stanford Research Institute International came out with reports that disputed the predictions of shortages by 1990. Nonetheless, the International Energy Agency continued to project a shortfall by 1985, and most energy experts maintained that a shortfall would materialize by 1990. Alberto Quiros Corradi, "Energy and the Exercise of Power," *Foreign Affairs* 57, no. 5 (1979): 1153; *PE* (Aug. 1978), p. 328; Edith T. Penrose, "OPEC's Importance in the World Oil Industry," *Interna-*

tional Affairs 55, no. 1 (Jan. 1979): 24. Both sets of studies are reviewed and compared in U.S. Senate, Committee on Energy and Natural Resources, *Energy: An Uncertain Future* (Washington, D.C.: Government Printing Office, 1978).

2. *PE* (Mar. 1975), p. 85.

3. Edward R. Fried and Charles L. Schultze, eds., *Higher Oil Prices and the World Economy* (Washington, D.C.: The Brookings Institution, 1975), p. 2.

4. Cited in Geoffrey Barraclough, "Wealth and Power: The Politics of Food and Oil," *New York Review of Books,* Aug. 7, 1975, p. 26.

5. *BW,* Feb. 10, 1975, p. 15.

6. Paul A. Volcker, "Inflation, Recession, Oil and International Financial Markets," *Journal of International Affairs* 9, no. 1 (1975):26.

7. Robert J. Lieber, *Oil and the Middle East War: Europe in the Energy Crisis* (Cambridge, Mass.: Center for International Affairs, 1976), p. 30; *PIW,* Mar. 18, 1974, p. 4; and *PE* (Feb. 1974), p. 51 and (Mar. 1974), p. 87.

8. Taki Rifai, *The Pricing of Crude Oil* (NewYork: Praeger, 1975), pp. 373–74; Richard Chadbourn Weisberg, *The Politics of Crude Oil Pricing in the Middle East, 1970–1975* (Berkeley: Institute of International Studies, 1977), p. 126; and *PE* (Feb. 1974), p. 51.

9. *Wall Street Journal,* Dec. 13, 1973, p. 2.

10. Cited in Dankwart A. Rustow and John F. Mugno, *OPEC: Success and Prospects* (New York: New York University Press, 1976), p. 51.

11. While by 1980, Britain's oil production exceeded its oil consumption, Britain cannot be insensitive to a loss of Middle East supplies. Because its refineries require heavy crude, it will continue to import substantial quantities of Middle East oil, even as it becomes a substantial net exporter. In addition, if Britain's trading partners suffer, it will suffer too.

12. John A. Cicco Jr., "The Atlantic Alliance and the Arab Challenge: The European Perspective," *World Affairs* 137, no. 4 (1975):317.

13. Barraclough, "Wealth and Power," *N.Y. Review of Books,* Aug. 7, 1975, p. 27.

14. Lieber, *Oil and the Middle East War,* p. 21.

15. Ibid., p. 22.

16. *NYT,* Feb. 15, 1974, p. 43.

17. Lieber, *Oil and the Middle East War,* p. 49.

18. *NYT,* Feb. 14, 1974, p. 1, and Henry R. Nau, "Continuity and Change in U.S. Foreign Energy Policy," *Policy Studies Journal* 7, no. 1 (1978):124.

19. Lieber, *Oil and the Middle East War,* p. 30.

20. Ibid., p. 38.

21. Oystein Noreng, "Friends or Fellow Travelers? The Relationship of Non-OPEC Exporters with OPEC," *Journal of Energy and Development* 4, no. 2 (1979):325.

22. Lieber, *Oil and the Middle East War,* p. 23.

23. Cicco, "The Atlantic Alliance and the Arab Challenge," *World Affaris* 137, no. 4 (1975):317 and 319, and Barraclough, "Wealth and Power," *N.Y. Review of Books,* Aug. 7, 1975, p. 27.

24. N. J. D. Lucas, *Energy and the European Communities* (London: Europa Publications, 1977), pp. 62–64.

25. Kenneth I. Juster, "Foreign Policy-Making during the Oil Crisis," *Japan Interpreter,* vol. 9, no. 3 (1977), pp. 294 and 307–9.

26. This was because most of the oil purchased in government-to-government deals was invoiced at 93% of the posted price or the equivalent cost of participation oil, rather than at the average price of participation and equity oil. Rifai, *The Pricing of Crude Oil,* p. 374.

27. *BW,* Dec. 14, 1974, p. 44.

28. Joe Stork, *Middle East Oil and the Energy Crisis* (New York: Monthly Review Press, 1975), p. 244; Szyliowicz, "The Embargo and U.S. Foreign Policy," in Joseph S. Szyliowicz and Bard E. O'Neill, eds., *The Energy Crisis and U.S. Foreign Policy* (New York: Praeger, 1975), p. 207;

Weisberg, *The Politics of Crude Oil Pricing in the Middle East,* p. 127; *PE* (May 1974), p. 174, and (July 1974), p. 251; Lieber, *Oil and the Middle East War,* p. 34; and Louis Turner, *Oil Companies in the International System* (London: Allen & Unwin, 1978), p. 180.

29. *PE* (Aug. 1974), p. 295; Stingelin, "Europe and the Oil Crisis," *Current History* 68, no. 403 (Mar. 1975):133; and Turner, *Oil Companies in the International System,* p. 180.

30. Tom Cutler, "Recycling Petrodollars to the Third World: A Critique of the IMF Oil Facility," *World Affairs* 139, no. 3 (1976–77):204.

31. See ibid. for details on the regulation and operation of the oil facility. *PE* (Nov. 1974), p. 402, and (Mar. 1976), p. 87.

32. Sidney S. Alexander, "Background Paper," in Twentieth Century Fund Task Force on the International Oil Crisis, *Paying for Energy* (New York: McGraw-Hill, 1975), p. 115.

33. Ibid., p. 125, and Peter Francis Cowhey, "The Problems of Plenty: Energy Policy and International Politics" (unpublished Ph.D. thesis, University of California at Berkeley), p. 562.

34. U.S. Senate, Committee on Foreign Relations, Subcommittee on Foreign Economic Policy, *International Debt, the Banks, and U.S. Foreign Policy* (Washington, D.C.: Government Printing Office, 1977) (hereafter *MNC Debt Report*), pp. 26–27.

35. *BW,* Sept. 14, 1974, p. 144.

36. *PE* (Apr. 1974), p. 132.

37. Paul Jabber, "Conflict and Cooperation in OPEC: Prospects for the Next Decade," *International Organization* 32, no. 2 (1978):383.

38. *PE* (July 1974), p. 251, and Rifai, *The Pricing of Crude Oil,* pp. 359–60.

39. This can be seen from the following calculations. The equity price was $7.108 and the participation price was $10.835. Then, at 25% participation, the cost of 100 barrels would be $803.975 = (75 × 7.108) + (25 × 10.835), yielding an average per barrel price of $8.04. But at 60% participation, the cost of 100 barrels would be $934.42 = (40 × 7.108) + (60 × 10.835), yielding an average per barrel price of $9.34. The figures on the cost of equity and participation oil are from Rustow and Mugno, *OPEC: Success and Prospects,* p. 132.

40. Oppenheim, "Why Oil Prices Go Up," *Foreign Policy,* no. 25, (1976–77), p. 42, and *PE* (Sept. 1974), p. 333.

41. Hartshorn, *Objectives of the Petroleum Exporting Countries,* p. 65.

42. During this period the intelligence agencies anticipated a fall in prices and indicated that Saudi Arabia could and would reverse the price increases. See U.S. Senate, Select Committee on Intelligence, *U.S. Intelligence Analysis and the Oil Issue, 1973–74* (Washington, D.C.: Government Printing Office, 1977).

43. *BW,* Sept. 28, 1974, p. 116.

44. *BW,* Nov. 23, 1974, p. 81. See, for example, Miles Ignotus (pseud.), "Seizing Arab Oil: The Case for U.S. Intervention: Why, How, Where," *Harper's* (Mar. 1975), pp. 45–62; *The Economist* (May 1975), "Survey," pp. 35ff.; and Edward Friedland, Paul Seabury, and Aaron Wildavsky, *The Great Detente Disaster* (New York: Basic Books, 1975).

45. Klaus Knorr, "The Limits of Economic and Military Power," in Raymond Vernon, ed., *The Oil Crisis: In Perspective,* issued as *Daedalus* 104, no. 4 (1975):237.

46. *BW,* Jan. 13, 1975, p. 69.

47. M. A. Adelman, "The World Oil Cartel: Scarcity, Economics and Politics," *Quarterly Review of Economics and Business* 16, no. 2 (1976): p. 17.

48. *BW,* Oct. 5, 1974, p. 24.

49. *BW,* Nov. 23, 1974, p. 80.

50. *BW,* Jan. 13, 1975, p. 67.

51. Ralph H. Magnus, "Middle East Oil," *Current History* 68, no. 402 (Feb. 1975):88; *PE* (Dec. 1974), p. 454; and *BW,* Nov. 23, 1974, p. 80.

52. OPEC's success inspired other Third World countries to attempt to form cartels in other commodities, but their efforts have had little success. Brazil, Colombia, the Ivory Coast, and Angola tried unsuccessfully to boost the price of coffee, but frosts in Brazil eventually pushed the price up

anyway. Phosphate producers quintupled the price of phosphate, only to see it fall when demand fell, and a copper exporters' group had to abandon a plan to proration exports when it became apparent that members would not comply with the plan. *BW,* May 9, 1977, p. 78.

53. *PE* (Apr. 1975), p. 133.

54. The Lomé Convention between the EEC and 46 developing countries, mostly from Africa and the Caribbean, was held in Feb. 1975. The countries agreed to pursue greater economic cooperation and establish a $450 million fund to stabilize the earnings on 12 commodity exports of the participating LDCs. Rustow and Mugno, *OPEC: Success and Prospects,* p. 76, and *PE* (Dec. 1975), p. 443.

55. Wilfrid L. Kohl, "The International Energy Agency: The Political Context," in J. C. Hurewitz, ed., *Oil, the Arab-Israeli Dispute and the Industrial World* (Boulder, Colo.: Westview Press, 1976), pp. 252–53.

56. Quoted in Barraclough, "Wealth and Power," *New York Review of Books,* Aug. 7, 1975, p. 27.

57. Hartshorn, *The Objectives of the Petroleum Exporting Countries,* pp. 68–69, and *NYT,* June 3, 1977, pp. A1 and A4.

58. In March 1976 the IMF oil facility was replaced by a trust fund whose lending was limited to the LDCs. Cutler, "Recycling Petrodollars to the Third World," *World Affairs* 139, no. 3 (1976–77):189, and Nazli Choucri with Vincent Ferraro, *International Politics of Energy Interdependence: The Case of Petroleum* (Lexington, Mass.: Heath, 1976), pp. 67–72.

59. *MNC Debt Report,* pp. 36 and 43.

60. Ibid., p. 46.

61. Computed from figures in table 9–1.

62. See table 9–5, p. 291.

63. *MNC Debt Report,* p. 36.

64. The rise in oil prices must be responsible for more than three quarters of this sum, for in addition to the direct increased cost of oil imports, the rise in oil prices boosted the cost of LDC imports and contributed to both the recession in the developed countries and the restrictions they imposed on imports from the LDCs.

65. Of course, the non-OPEC LDCs varied in how they responded to the oil/balance-of-payments crisis. In Africa, countries generally tried to maintain the momentum of existing development programs, borrowing heavily to meet their balance-of-payments deficits. In Latin America, governments tended to rely on changes in the exchange rate, import controls, or export promotion to reduce their deficits. And the Asian non-OPEC LDCs generally undertook stringent contractionary policies in 1974–75, leading to more rapid reduction in their balance-of-payments deficits. Morgan Guaranty Trust Co., *World Financial Markets* (May 1979), p. 7.

66. *BW,* Feb. 14, 1977, p. 13.

67. Walter J. Levy, "The Years that the Locust Hath Eaten: Oil Policy and OPEC Development Prospects," *Foreign Affairs* 57, no. 2 (1978–79):292.

68. Of an estimated private bank debt to non-OPEC countries of $123.4 billion, Brazil accounted for $31.9 billion, Mexico for $23.4 billion, Argentina for $6.9 billion, Peru for $3.4 billion, Egypt for $1.6 billion, Korea for $7 billion, the Philippines for $4 billion, Taiwan for $4 billion, Thailand for $2.7 billion, Morocco for $2.2 billion, and Colombia for $2.1 billion. Citibank, *Monthly Economic Letter* (Mar. 1980), pp. 10–11.

69. *MNC Debt Report,* p. 56.

70. Between 1973 and 1978 higher-income non-OPEC LDCs financed 10.6% of their imports with inflows of private long-term capital; but the lower-income LDCs were able to finance only 2.3% of their imports in this way. IMF, *Annual Report, 1979,* p. 27.

71. Ibid., p. 25.

72. Morgan Guaranty Trust Co., *World Financial Markets* (May 1979), p. 8.

73. Peru was eventually forced to turn to the IMF, and the conditions the Fund imposed led to a

general strike and then, when Peru failed to meet the IMF's terms, to suspension of a $106 million standby credit. *BW*, June 19, 1978, p. 45.

74. *BW*, Mar. 21, 1977, pp. 117–18, and July 2, 1979, p. 79; IMF, *Annual Report, 1979*, p. 24; and *MNC Debt Report*, p. 57.

75. *BW*, Mar. 28, 1977, pp. 24 and 88.

76. *BW*, Oct. 3, 1977, p. 80, Oct. 10, 1977, p. 40, and Feb. 27, 1978, p. 86.

77. The reluctance of the industrial countries to grant them power in the IMF led the Arab oil-exporting countries to start their own Arab Monetary Fund in 1976. The fund began with a capitalization of $900 million. Membership and loans were limited to Arab nations. *NYT*, May 25, 1977, p. D1.

78. *NYT*, Nov. 17, 1977, p. D1, and Jan. 20, 1978, p. D1.

79. Morgan Guaranty Trust Co., *World Financial Markets* (May 1979), p. 2.

80. Barraclough, "Wealth and Power," *New York Review of Books*, Aug. 7, 1975, p. 26, and Hollis B. Chenery, "Restructuring the World Economy," *Foreign Affairs* 53, no. 2 (Jan. 1975):257.

81. Many are summarized in Rustow and Mugno, *OPEC: Success and Prospects*, p. 50, and Choucri and Ferraro, *International Politics of Energy Interdependence*, p. 58.

82. U.S. Department of the Treasury, "Statement by the Honorable C. Fred Bergsten," July 18, 1979, p. 7. To be consistent with the figures in table 9–3, these estimates would have to be revised, but this would not alter the basic point that even while some OPEC countries had significant deficits, others still had large surpluses.

83. IMF, *Annual Report, 1977*, p. 14.

84. At the end of 1978 the OPEC countries accounted for less than 10% of all liabilities to foreigners reported by U.S. banks and for less than 1% of all deposits in U.S. banks; however, the OPEC funds constituted a significant portion of the deposits of the largest U.S. banks. A survey by the Federal Reserve System found that, at the end of 1975, funds from the oil-exporting countries accounted for 5% of the deposits of the largest U.S. banks. U.S. Department of the Treasury, "Statement by the Honorable C. Fred Bergsten," July 18, 1979, p. 4, and *NYT*, Mar. 12, 1976, p. 45.

85. *MNC Debt Report*, p. 38.

86. *NYT*, June 17, 1976, p. 55, and Apr. 16, 1977, p. 31, and *BW*, Mar. 14, 1977, p. 81.

87. *MNC Debt Report*, p. 38, and *NYT*, June 8, 1976, p. 1.

88. *NYT*, Jan. 4, 1977, p. 37.

89. *NYT*, Jan. 13, 1977, p. 49, Jan. 18, 1977, p. 50, and Apr. 16, 1977, p. 31.

90. *BW*, Mar. 14, 1977, p. 42, Nov. 14, 1977, p. 56, Dec. 12, 1977, p. 68, and Mar. 27, 1978, p. 56, and *NYT*, Apr. 17, 1977, p. 1.

91. Hartshorn, *The Objectives of the Petroleum Exporting Countries*, p. 87.

92. Turner, *Oil Companies in the International System*, p. 218; *BW*, Mar. 14, 1977, p. 99; and Rustow and Mugno, *OPEC: Success and Prospects*, p. 46.

93. U.S. Department of the Treasury, "Statement by the Honorable C. Fred Bergsten," July 18, 1979, table 5. For more information on this, see ibid., tables 2, 3, and 5.

94. Computed from ibid., table 2.

95. It is for this reason that several OPEC countries have repeatedly expressed concern about the confidentiality of their investments in the U.S. Since countries have indicated that, in the absence of confidentiality, they would be less inclined to invest in the U.S., the U.S. government has sought to keep information about the investments of particular countries secret. Ibid., p. 18.

96. *BW*, Jan. 24, 1977, p. 42.

97. The OPEC countries have also hired many prominent Americans to give them legal, financial, and political advice. Frederick G. Dutton, assistant secretary of state under President Kennedy, has been retained as an adviser to Saudi Arabia and earns well over $200,000 a year for his services. The law firm of former Senate Foreign Relations Committee Chairman J. William Fulbright has been registered as a foreign agent for the United Arab Emirates, and the law firm of Nixon's secretary of

state, William P. Rogers, handled legal work for Iran's Pahlevi Foundation. Other prominent Americans who have advised the OPEC countries include John Connally, Nixon's former treasury secretary and a recent presidential candidate; Gerald L. Parsky, assistant secretary of the treasury for monetary affairs under Ford and Nixon; William C. Armstrong, assistant secretary of state for economic affairs under Nixon, Richard M. Helms, former CIA director and ex-ambassador to Iran; and Kermit Roosevelt, who engineered the 1954 coup in Iran. *BW*, Jan. 23, 1978, pp. 85–86.

98. *BW*, July 10, 1978, p. 38.

99. Ibid.

100. Cowhey, "The Problems of Plenty," pp. 555A, 556, and 558, and Williamson, "The International Financial System," in Fried and Schultze, eds., *Higher Oil Prices and the World Economy*, pp. 208–9.

101. Data Resources Inc. found that as a result of the oil price hikes, the 1974 U.S. inflation rate, as measured by the consumer price index, was 11.08% rather than 8.1%. *BW*, Oct. 13, 1975, p. 34.

102. George L. Perry, "The United States," in Fried and Schultze, eds., *Higher Oil Prices and the World Economy*, p. 103.

103. Neil H. Jacoby, "Oil and the Future: Economic Consequences of the Energy Revolution," *Journal of Energy and Development* 1, no. 1 (1975):45, and *BW*, July 24, 1978, p. 71.

104. Fried and Schultze, eds., *Higher Oil Prices and the World Economy*, pp. 25–26.

105. *BW*, Oct. 3, 1977, p. 69.

106. *BW*, July 7, 1975, p. 45, Aug. 9, 1976, p. 80, and Aug. 30, 1976, p. 54.

107. *BW*, Aug. 8, 1977, p. 36, and Aug. 15, 1977, p. 102.

108. The British Labor government had only a slim parliamentary majority and the governments in France and Italy faced strong opposition from Socialists and Communists.

109. At Rambouillet, France abandoned its insistence on a return to fixed exchange rates and the U.S. agreed to take steps to stabilize the value of the dollar. An international committee was established to take responsibility for stabilizing exchange rates. *BW*, Dec. 1, 1975, p. 21.

110. *BW*, Aug. 9, 1976, p. 80.

111. Ironically, a year later, when the recession had passed, France and Italy were intervening in exchange markets to keep their currencies overvalued. Since oil was priced in dollars, an overvalued currency reduced one's oil-import bill. *BW*, Mar. 29, 1976, pp. 83, 84, and 86, and Oct. 3, 1977, p. 130.

112. *NYT*, Aug. 1, 1979, p. 29.

113. *BW*, June 19, 1978, p. 50.

114. *BW*, May 1, 1978, p. 31.

115. *BW*, Nov. 14, 1977, p. 194.

116. *BW*, July 31, 1978, pp. 30–31.

117. Along with this plan, the Federal Reserve Board raised the discount rate from 8.5% to 9.5% and imposed a 2% reserve requirement on large negotiable certificates of deposit. The U.S. raised $15 billion by borrowing Swiss francs, Japanese yen, and West German marks; $10 billion by selling government securities denominated in marks, yen, and Swiss francs; and $5 billion by drawing on U.S. IMF accounts (for details of the plan, see *BW*, Nov. 13, 1978, p. 28). Between September 1977 and the end of October 1978, the U.S. dollar had depreciated by 19% while the yen and the mark appreciated by 40 and 13% respectively. IMF, *Annual Report, 1979*, p. 17.

118. Ibid., pp. 15 and 17, and *1982*, p. 6.

119. *BW*, Oct. 3, 1977, p. 37.

120. Britain participates in certain parts of the new arrangement, but has not agreed to keep its currency in any fixed relationship with the other European currencies. Italy became a member on special terms that give it a wider margin in determining its exchange rate relative to the rest of the European Community.

121. *BW*, Oct. 2, 1978, p. 99, and Mar. 12, 1979, p. 67.

122. For a discussion of these agreements, see *BW*, May 9, 1977, pp. 64–79.

123. Arnold E. Safer, *International Oil Policy* (Lexington, Mass.: Heath, 1979), p. 45.

124. Fried and Schultze (*Higher Oil Prices and the World Economy*, p. 21) present the following estimates:

Changes in Real GNP, 1973–74 (Percent)

	Pre-Embargo Outlook	Actual	Total	Change from Pre-Embargo Outlook Attributable to	
				Oil	Other Factors
United States	2.6	−2.1	−4.7	−2.5	−2.2
Western Europe	4.8	2.3	−2.5	−2.7	+0.2
Japan	5.2	−1.8	−7.0	−4.2	−2.8

125. *BW*, July 7, 1975, pp. 45–46, and Jan. 30, 1978, p. 46.

126. International Economic Policy Assn., *America's Oil and Energy Goals: The International Economic Implications* (Washington, D.C.: IEPA, 1977), pp. 3–4.

127. Because oil is a major input into fertilizer, the connections between food shortages and high oil prices were often direct.

128. IMF, *Annual Report, 1979*, p. 10.

129. Iran and Venezuela were the main forces behind creation of the fund; Ecuador and Indonesia refused to participate in it. It was originally intended to be a $1 billion fund. *PE* (Mar. 1976), p. 87.

130. Moran, "Why Oil Prices Go Up," *Foreign Policy*, no. 25 (1976–77), p. 74.

131. *PE* (June 1975), p. 222. The OECD Development Assistance Committee calculated that in 1974 ten OPEC donors gave 1.8% of their GNP in "official development assistance," as opposed to only 0.33% for 17 OECD member countries (Rustow and Mugno, *OPEC: Success and Prospects*, p. 67). Moreover, in 1974 Kuwait's aid represented 4.5% of its GNP and Saudi aid nearly 3% of its GNP (*PE* [Mar. 1976], p. 88). OPEC aid peaked in 1975 at 2.7% of members' GNP and fell to 0.9% in 1979. However, OPEC officials maintain that these official statistics fail to take account of the unilateral aid that many OPEC members provide. They claim that in the late 1970s Qatar and the United Arab Emirates provided as much as 10% of their GNP in aid and Saudi Arabia 6%. In contrast, in 1978 aid and bank loans from the industrialized countries averaged only 1.3% of GNP. *BW*, Feb. 4, 1980, p. 42.

132. In March 1976 the *Petroleum Economist* reported that since the 1973 oil-price rise, two-thirds of OPEC's direct concessionary aid went to various Arab states, most of it to Egypt and Syria (both net exporters of oil). Non-Arab Islamic states received another 25% of OPEC's aid, and non-Islamic states received about 10%. *PE* (Mar. 1976), p. 88.

133. Computed from data in CIA, *Handbook of Economic Statistics, 1980*, p. 66.

134. The EMS has created a new monetary unit, the ECU, and EMS members hope it will soon rival the dollar as a means of international payment.

135. *PIW*, Oct. 21, 1974, p. 9.

136. Church, "The Impotence of Oil Companies," *Foreign Policy*, no. 27 (1977), p. 48.

137. Other retaliatory actions would include freezing OPEC-country assets, withdrawing trained personnel, and imposing excise taxes on trade with OPEC countries; but each involves risks. Freezing OPEC-country assets is likely to jeopardize the international financial system and lead to a cutoff of oil supplies; withdrawing technical personnel would also lead to a loss of supplies; an excise tax would reduce the exports of the consuming country (or countries that impose it) to the OPEC countries, aggravating the recycling problem.

138. See *BW*, Aug. 28, 1978, p. 100.

139. *Washington Post*, Sept. 21, 1976, p. C23.

140. Oppenheim, "Why Oil Prices Go Up," *Foreign Policy*, no. 25 (1976–77), p. 44.

141. *BW*, Jan. 13, 1975, p. 67.

142. Oppenheim, "Why Oil Prices Go Up," *Foreign Policy,* no. 25 (1976–77), p. 45, and *Washington Post,* Sept. 21, 1976, p. C23.

143. Production from these fields covered about 65% of Israel's internal demand of about 140,000 b/d. The extra cost to Israel of buying oil on the world market was estimated at $300–350 million a year. *PE* (Oct. 1975), p. 375.

144. George W. Ball, "The Coming Crisis in Israeli-American Relations," *Foreign Affairs* 58, no. 2 (1979–80):241, and William B. Quandt, *Decade of Decisions* (Berkeley: University of California Press, 1977), pp. 273–74.

145. *BW,* Nov. 27, 1978, p. 48.

146. At the same time, Libya was using its oil wealth to supply armaments to radical groups all over the world. Libya gave Soviet-made arms to the Irish Republican Army in Northern Ireland, to Moslem guerrillas in the Philippines and Thailand, and to rebels in Chad and Ethiopia. It also helped finance the more radical Palestinian groups. *NYT,* July 16, 1976, p. A1.

147. *Wall Street Journal,* June 2, 1977, p. 1; *NYT,* Jan. 30, 1977, p. 16; and *BW,* Jan. 10, 1977, p. 62.

148. *BW,* Jan. 10, 1977, p. 63, and June 19, 1978, p. 43, and *PIW,* Apr. 9, 1979, pp. 7–8. In the summer of 1974 Iran also agreed to provide Egypt with $750 million in development loans and $100 million in suppliers' credit. *PE* (July 1974), p. 266.

149. *NYT,* Nov. 11, 1976, p. 10.

150. *NYT,* Dec. 26, 1976, p. 1.

151. *PE* (Feb. 1976), p. 52.

152. *NYT,* Apr. 6, 1975, p. 3.

153. Louis Turner and James Bedore, "Saudi Arabia: The Power of the Purse Strings," *International Affairs* 54, no. 3 (1978):412–13; Paul Jabber, "Petrodollars, Arms Trade, and the Pattern of Major Conflicts," in J. C. Hurewitz, ed., *Oil, the Arab-Israeli Dispute and the Industrial World,* pp. 151–52; Rustow and Mugno, *OPEC: Success and Prospects,* p. 33; *NYT,* Apr, 6, 1975, p. 3; and *PE* (Aug. 1975), p. 301.

CHAPTER 10

1. *PE* (Oct. 1979), p. 428, and U.S. Department of the Treasury, "Statement by the Honorable C. Fred Bergsten," July 18, 1979, p. 7.

2. While in recent years Saudi Arabia's proven reserves have been officially listed at about 170 billion barrels, according to knowledgeable industry sources a more realistic figure is more than 200 billion barrels, and possibly close to 300 billion. *BW,* June 18, 1979, p. 113, and *PE* (Dec. 1981), p. 541.

3. Comptroller General of the U.S., *More Attention Should Be Paid to Making the U.S. Less Vulnerable to Foreign Oil Price and Supply Decisions* (Washington, D.C.: General Accounting Office, 1978), p..15; and Zuhayr Mikdashi, "The OPEC Process," in Raymond Vernon, ed., *The Oil Crisis: In Perspective,* issued as *Daedalus* 104, no. 4 (1975):207.

4. Cited in Dankwart A. Rustow and John F. Mugno, *OPEC: Success and Prospects* (New York: New York University Press, 1976), p. 102.

5. *PE* (Dec. 1978), p. 500.

6. J. E. Hartshorn, *Objectives of the Petroleum Exporting Countries* (Nicosia, Cyprus: Middle East Petroleum and Economics Publications, 1978), pp. 82, 87–88, and 100.

7. Ibid., p. 87; and Theodore H. Moran, *Oil Prices and the Future of OPEC* (Washington, D.C.: Resources for the Future, 1978), p. 19.

8. Hartshorn, *Objectives of the Petroleum Exporting Contries,* pp. 68 and 171.

9. Moran has estimated that in 1980 the Saudis would experience difficulties below an annual revenue level of $35–46 billion (1977 prices) (Moran, *Oil Prices and the Future of OPEC,* p. 26). In 1977 Saudi oil revenues totaled $42.4 billion and in 1978 $35.8 billion (*PE* [June 1979], p. 224). Consequently, had prices not gone up in 1979, Saudi Arabia may well have experienced financial problems in the early 1980s.

10. *MNC Saudi Oil Report*, p. 552, and *NYT*, June 24, 1979, p. 2E.

11. *PE* (Aug. 1978), p. 356, and *BW*, Nov. 6, 1978, p. 105, and Mar. 12, 1979, p. 58.

12. *BW*, Jan. 13, 1975, p. 68.

13. *NYT*, Dec. 18, 1976, p. 29.

14. Quoted in *NYT*, Dec. 19, 1976, p. 8.

15. The one exception occurred after the December 1976 OPEC meeting, when Saudi Arabia refused to raise prices by 10%, as the other countries did. Saudi Arabia then lifted the ceiling and boosted production in an effort to bring prices down. After the dispute was resolved, the 8.5 mb/d ceiling was reimposed, but by the time Saudi Arabia had done so, production had fallen below the ceiling level.

16. "Facility capacity" refers to the total installed capacity while "maximum sustainable capacity" is the maximum production rate that can be sustained for several months, usually six or more.

17. *MNC Saudi Oil Report*, p. 16.

18. Ibid., p. 6. The cost of expanding capacity from 10 to 16 mb/d was estimated at more than $25 billion. *NYT*, Mar. 5, 1979, p. D3.

19. *NYT*, Dec. 25, 1977, p. 1. If a field is continually worked at reduced pressure, its ultimate recovery may be reduced. U.S. government officials blamed the technical problems in the Saudi fields on poor management and overproduction by Aramco. However, Aramco management tended to dismiss the problems as routine. In any case, Yamani told a GAO investigative team that three of Saudi Arabia's largest fields, accounting for more than 90% of its total production, had been damaged by overproduction. He ordered production cutbacks in those fields, pending reservoir pressure tests by a British consulting firm. See *NYT*, Feb. 8, 1978, pp. D1 and D10.

20. *MNC Saudi Oil Report*, p. 19.

21. Hartshorn, *Objectives of the Petroleum Exporting Countries*, p. 173.

22. *PE* (Mar. 1975), p. 124.

23. Hartshorn, *Objectives of the Petroleum Exporting Countries*, p. 171.

24. Ibid., pp. 169 and 1974, and CIA, *The World Oil Market in the Years Ahead* (Washington, D.C.: Government Printing Office, 1979), pp. 6 and 48.

25. CIA, *The World Oil Market in the Years Ahead*, p. 48.

26. Hartshorn, *Objectives of the Petroleum Exporting Countries*, p. 177.

27. Ibid., pp. 168 and 174.

28. "United Arab Emirates" is something of a misnomer. The seven emirates are not united on oil policy nor do they have comparable oil reserves. The bulk of the oil is found and produced in Abu Dhabi, and Abu Dhabi has complete control over its oil resources.

29. CIA, *The World Oil Market in the Years Ahead*, p. iv, and Moran, *Oil Prices and the Future of OPEC*, p. 51.

30. Hartshorn, *Objectives of the Petroleum Exporting Countries*, pp. 201–2.

31. Moran, "Why Oil Prices Go Up," *Foreign Policy*, no. 25 (1976–77), p. 70.

32. Hartshorn, *Objectives of the Petroleum Exporting Countries*, p. 190.

33. *PE* (June 1975), p. 211, and (May 1977), p. 169.

34. Claudia Wright, "Iraq—New Power in the Middle East," *Foreign Affairs* 58, no. 2 (1979–80):261.

35. Moran, *Oil Prices and the Future of OPEC*, p. 41, and CIA, *The World Oil Market in the Years Ahead*, p. 47.

36. Hartshorn, *Objectives of the Petroleum Exporting Countries*, p. 124, and Edith Penrose and E. F. Penrose, *Iraq: International Relations and National Development* (Boulder, Colo.: Westview Press, 1978), pp. 517 and 520.

37. BP, *Statistical Review of the World Oil Industry, 1978*.

38. Penrose and Penrose, *Iraq*, p. 515.

39. *BW*, Nov. 24, 1975, p. 42, and *NYT*, Dec. 7, 1978, p. D11.

40. Joseph Kraft, "Letter from OPEC," *The New Yorker*, Jan. 20, 1975, p. 65.

41. *BW*, Dec. 17, 1979, p. 42.

42. BP, *Statistical Review of the World Oil Industry,* various issues.

43. For an estimate of the various countries' 1980 revenue needs, see Moran, *Oil Prices and the Future of OPEC,* p. 52.

44. It has been suggested that to break OPEC, all consumers need do is target their sales on the "rich" OPEC countries. If this were done, it is argued, the other OPEC countries would be forced to cut prices in order to sell their crude. But the "rich" OPEC countries would foil this plan simply by limiting their production.

45. The OPEC countries produce more than 130 varieties of crude. Comptroller General of the U.S., *More Attention Should Be Paid to Making the U.S. Less Vulnerable to Foreign Oil Price and Supply Decisions,* p. 12, and Penrose, "OPEC's Importance in the World Oil Industry," *International Affairs* 55, no. 1 (Jan. 1979):22.

46. After the December 1977 decision to freeze prices, Yamani indicated that in the future Saudi Arabia would assume the role of "swing supplier." He stated: "When there is a glut in the market Saudi Arabia is obliged to preserve the unity of OPEC and to reduce its oil production. There is no need to study any production programme. Saudi Arabia will take the responsibility of fixing prices" (quoted in Hartshorn, *Objectives of the Petroleum Exporting Countries,* p. 81). Yet Saudi Arabia's reluctance to absorb the full world surplus, during the glut of 1981–82, casts doubt on the extent to which it is ready to assume this role.

47. In 1975 both Venezuela and Saudi Arabia offered to lend Ecuador money after Ecuador's production fell because the companies deemed its price too high. Rustow and Mugno, *OPEC: Success and Prospects,* p. 105, and Jabber, "Conflict and Cooperation in OPEC," *International Organization* 32, no. 2 (1978):383.

48. In June 1978 several OPEC members agreed to a nonbinding six-month plan, aimed at sopping up a 2–3 mb/d oil surplus. According to Qatar's petroleum minister, the effort eliminated the surplus. *Petroleum Intelligence Weekly,* Dec. 25, 1978, p. 9.

49. For example, if market prices rise from $12.70 to $13.50, the companies will pocket the extra 80¢, until OPEC raises its official price.

	Before Rise in Market Price	Before OPEC Price Rise	After Rise in Market Price and OPEC Price Rise
Market price, of which	$12.70	$13.50	$13.50
OPEC country take	12.48	12.48	13.28
Company Profit	.22	1.02	.22

50. *PIW,* July 2, 1979, p. 2.

51. *PIW,* Apr. 2, 1979, p. 3.

52. Moran, "Why Oil Prices Go Up," *Foreign Policy,* no. 25 (1976–77), pp. 63–64.

53. Walter J. Levy, "The Years that the Locust Hath Eaten: Oil Policy and OPEC Development Prospects," *Foreign Affairs* 57, no. 2 (1977–78):299, and Eliahu Kanovsky, "Saudi Arabia's Moderation in Oil Pricing—Political or Economic?" *Occasional Papers* (Tel Aviv Univ., Apr. 1977), p. 15.

54. Since 1974 the exporting countries (except Iran and recently Kuwait) have not shown much interest in acquiring downstream facilities in the consuming countries; the excess capacity in these countries and the huge capital costs involved discouraged them. OPEC's product exports still equal only about 7% of its production, and the OPEC countries account for only 6% of world refining capacity and 3.2% of the world's petrochemical industry. Also, only 2.9% of OPEC's oil exports are shipped in OPEC tankers (Ali M. Jaidah, "Downstream Operations and the Development of OPEC Member Countries," *Journal of Energy and Development* 4, no. 2 [1979]: 309, and *PE* [Nov. 1978], p. 477). The main exception is Venezuela, where refined products account for 50% of exports. Hartshorn, *Objectives of the Petroleum Exporting Countries,* p. 33.

55. While there is a need for specialized refining facilities that can produce a higher proportion of light products, the consuming countries are more likely to adapt their own refineries or build such facilities, rather than turn to the OPEC countries for them.

56. This development strategy has other consequences as well. As a result of the energy intensity of their development programs and the low prices they charge for petroleum products, demand for oil in the OPEC countries is rising rapidly. Also, insofar as the exporting countries move into downstream activities, their ability to cut back on oil production declines since they need the oil to keep their expensive refineries operating; and the market in products is far more competitive than the market in crude, increasing the likelihood of OPEC price cutting. Moreover, to make their refineries competitive, OPEC countries would be tempted to transfer crude to them at lower prices than they charge the international oil companies.

An exporting country with an energy-intensive development program also has a special interest in conserving its oil resources. Because its economy requires large inputs of hydrocarbons, it does not want to become an oil importer in a period of even higher oil prices. This concern is likely to lead such a country to favor higher prices in the near term, which would conserve resources, rather than a precipitous jump in the future, when it would have to import oil.

57. *NYT,* Dec. 5, 1978, p. A1, Jan. 22, 1979, p. D1, and Oct. 8, 1979, p. 3E.

58. According to the London-based Economist Intelligence Unit, only Iran, Iraq, Oman, Bahrain, and Dubai (of the Gulf countries) have the potential to build nonoil-based economies. And as Walter Levy stated, "The odds at this time are that when the oil revenues begin to peter out, a number of the OPEC countries will find themselves not too much better off than before" (Levy, "The Years the Locust Hath Eaten," *Foreign Affairs* 57, no. 2 [1977–78]:301). Moreover, much of the money invested in the OPEC countries since 1974 could have been used far more profitably in other parts of the world.

59. *BW,* Dec. 24, 1979, p. 88.

60. S. A. Van Vactor, "Energy Conservation in the OECD: Progress and Results," *Journal of Energy and Development* 3, no. 2 (1978):244. In the U.S. since 1973, half of all home owners have added insulation, raising the energy efficiency of private houses by 5 to 10%. *BW,* July 30, 1979, p. 60.

61. *PE* (Nov. 1974), p. 404.

62. Yager and Steinberg, "Trends in the International Oil Market," in Edward R. Fried and Charles L. Schultze, eds., *Higher Oil Prices and the World Economy* (Washington, D.C.: The Brookings Institution, 1975), p. 242, and Van Vactor, "Energy Conservation in the OECD," *Journal of Energy and Development,* p. 247.

63. Morgan Guaranty Trust Co., *World Financial Markets* (May 1979), p. 3.

64. CIA, *The World Oil Market in the Years Ahead,* p. 12.

65. OPEC, *Annual Statistical Bulletin, 1978,* p. 63.

66. Morgan Guaranty Trust Co., *World Financial Markets* (May 1979), p. 2.

67. The ratio of primary energy consumption to GNP improved only slightly, as the following figures show:

Primary Energy Consumption/GNP, 1973 and 1978

	U.S.	Japan	Western Europe	All Industrial Countries
1973	.97	.44	.52	.69
1978	.90	.38	.48	.64

Computed from figures in BP, *Statistical Review of the World Oil Industry, 1978,* p. 32, and CIA, *Handbook of Economic Statistics, 1979,* p. 22. Energy consumption is measured in million tonnes of oil equivalent, GNP in billions of U.S. dollars.

68. *PE* (Dec. 1979), p. 527.

69. According to OECD, in mid-1974 the composite selling price of an average barrel of petroleum products was $24. Of this, 40% went to the producing countries, 36% to the consuming countries in the form of various taxes, and 24% to the companies to cover their costs and profits. Prior to Oct. 1973, the breakdown was 17%, 54%, and 29% respectively. Cited in Joe Stork, *Middle East Oil and the Energy Crisis* (New York: Monthly Review Press, 1975), p. 276.

70. CIA, *The World Oil Market in the Years Ahead*, p. 1.

71. Robert Stobaugh and Daniel Yergin, "Energy: An Emergency Telescoped," *Foreign Affairs* 58, no. 3 (1979):584, and *BW*, July 30, 1979, p. 57.

72. *BW*, Sept. 4, 1978, p. 70.

73. Joseph A. Yager and Eleanor B. Steinberg, *Energy and U.S. Foreign Policy* (Cambridge, Mass.: Ballinger, 1974), p. 241, and *NYT*, May 3, 1977, p. 63.

74. CIA, *The World Oil Market in the Years Ahead*, p. 1.

75. By 1973–74, Western Europe and Japan had well-developed mass transit systems and small, energy-efficient vehicles, and since petroleum-product prices had always been higher in Western Europe and Japan than in the U.S., these areas also had more efficient patterns of industrial and residential energy consumption. In fact, U.S. citizens, on average, have larger homes than Europeans and a higher proportion of detached, single-family dwellings. In the U.S., homes, stores, and offices are heated to higher temperatures than in Europe, and homes in the U.S. are generally less well insulated than in Europe (Kenneth Paul Erickson, "Public Policy and Energy Consumption in Industrialized Societies," *Policy Studies Journal* 7, no. 1 [1978]:117). West Germany's industrial sector uses 38% less energy per unit of output, and Sweden uses 40% less energy to produce each dollar of GNP. *BW*, Apr. 25, 1977, p. 71.

76. Quoted in Robert B. Krueger, *The United States and International Oil* (New York: Praeger, 1975), p. 87.

77. *MNC Report*, p. 151.

78. Quoted in George A. Lincoln, "Background to the U.S. Energy Revolution," in Joseph S. Szyliowicz and Bard E. O'Neill, eds., *The Energy Crisis and U.S. Foreign Policy* (New York: Praeger, 1975), p. 42. The Ford administration eventually established an "invulnerability target" of 3–5 mb/d in oil imports. *PE* (Mar. 1977), p. 91.

79. *MNC Report*, p. 151; *PE* (Nov. 1974), p. 405; and BP, *Statistical Review of the World Oil Industry, 1974*.

80. *PE* (Apr. 1974), pp. 124–25.

81. Taki Rifai, *The Pricing of Crude Oil* (New York: Praeger, 1975), p. 374, and *BW*, Jan. 27, 1975, p. 47.

82. *BW*, Dec. 1, 1975, p. 19, and *NYT*, Nov. 13, 1975, p. 35.

83. *BW*, Jan. 12, 1976, p. 24, and Nov. 15, 1976, p. 79.

84. *NYT*, Oct. 18, 1976, p. 48.

85. *NYT*, Nov. 18, 1976, p. 71.

86. *BW*, Sept. 27, 1976, p. 69, and Feb. 14, 1977, p. 101; and *PE* (Mar. 1976), p. 85.

87. *BW*, July 7, 1975, pp. 18–19, and Sept. 27, 1976, p. 70, and *NYT*, Jan. 30, 1977, p. 26.

88. This was later changed to 93¢, but at that point a 1¢ per year escalator was added (*PE* [Dec. 1976], p. 476). Though it was charged with regulating gas prices, the FPC had long advocated deregulation of natural gas prices.

89. *PE* (Sept. 1976), p. 354.

90. *NYT*, Oct. 30, 1977, p. 1.

91. *NYT*, Feb. 23, 1977, p. 3E.

92. *NYT*, Feb. 26, 1977, p. 27.

93. *NYT*, Apr. 21, 1977, p. 48.

94. For details of the president's National Energy Plan, see "Energy Program Fact Sheet," reprinted in *NYT*, Apr. 21, 1977, pp. 48–49. Also consult *The National Energy Plan* (Washington, D.C.: Government Printing Office, 1977). For a summary of how the various proposals fared in the House and Senate, see *NYT*, Nov. 6, 1977, p. 2E.

95. *NYT,* Apr. 22, 1977, p. 1.

96. For example, the GAO charged that, because supplies of coal, natural gas, and nuclear power would fall short of administration estimates, imports would increase, not decrease, between 1977 and 1985 (*NYT,* July 26, 1977, p. 3). The Carter administration responded to such criticism by indicating it was prepared to accept tougher measures if Congress would enact them.

97. An analysis by World Energy Models Ltd. found that the crude oil equalization tax would have an insignificant impact on the prices paid by final consumers. The study found that, as a result of the tax, U.S. refiners and distributors would have to pay an additional $16.6 billion for oil, but would be able to pass only $5.5 billion on to consumers. *PE* (Aug. 1978), p. 331.

98. Consumers questioned whether this would actually happen. Their fears were encouraged when one day after presenting the plan, the president said he could not guarantee that all the money collected through the taxes proposed in the plan would be returned to the American public through rebates and refunds (*NYT,* Apr. 23, 1977, p. 1). Similarly, James Schlesinger, the president's chief energy adviser, said that while the administration proposed to recycle all energy taxes to the public "in the early years," it might not do so later on. *NYT,* Apr. 25, 1977, p. 1.

99. See, e.g., Barry Commoner's critique of the plan in Barry Commoner, *The Politics of Energy* (New York: Knopf, 1979), or preferably Barry Commoner, "The Natural Energy Plan: A Critique" (St. Louis: Center for the Biology of Natural Systems, 1977), which circulated shortly after the Carter plan was announced.

100. *NYT,* June 30, 1977, p. 46. In one of the less partisan studies, the Congressional Budget Office found that total price deregulation would increase natural gas production in 1985 by 5% over the levels that would be obtained under the original Carter proposals. The additional cost from deregulation would be $10 billion a year between 1977 and 1985. *NYT,* Sept. 8, 1977, p. D1.

101. To obtain equivalent energy from heating oil would have cost about $2.50. *NYT,* Oct. 5, 1977, p. 51.

102. *PE* (Nov. 1978), p. 450.

103. *Los Angeles Times,* Oct. 16, 1978, part 1, p. 10.

104. Public understanding of the problem had never been very great. In fact, in June 1977 a Gallup poll found that only slightly more than half of the U.S. public knew that the U.S. needed to import petroleum, and a third of those responding believed the U.S. was self-sufficient in oil (*NYT,* Feb. 6, 1978, p. A18). Only 9% of all adults were aware of the approximate magnitude of U.S. oil imports. International Economic Policy Assn., *America's Oil and Energy Goals: The International Economic Implications* (Washington, D.C.: IEPA, 1977), p. 1.

105. Increased gas production was estimated as saving 1.4 mb/d, tax breaks for energy conversation 0.4 mb/d, and the weak provisions on industrial conversion to coal, utility rate changes, and other conservation measures 1.1 mb/d. *Wall Street Journal,* Oct. 27, 1978, p. 1.

106. Yergin and Stobaugh, "Energy: An Emergency Telescoped," *Foreign Affairs* 58, no. 3 (1979):579.

107. *Los Angeles Times,* Oct. 8, 1978, part 6, p. 3.

108. *PE* (Mar. 1975), p. 96.

109. Cowhey, "The Problems of Plenty: Energy Policy and International Politics" (unpublished Ph.D. thesis, University of California at Berkeley), p. 75.

110. Mason Willrich and Melvin A. Conant, "The International Energy Agency: An Interpretation and Assessment," *American Journal of International Law* 71, no. 2 (Apr. 1977):215.

111. Robert O. Keohane, "The International Energy Agency: State Influence and Transgovernmental Politics," *International Organization* 32, no. 4 (1978):943.

112. Prior to 1980, the stockpiling requirement was only 60 days. It can also be met by a capacity to switch to other fuels or increase oil production; alternatively, extra stockpiling can substitute for demand reduction. In addition, countries that reduce oil imports below 1973 levels get credit for this in their emergency reduction quotas.

113. Walton, "Atlantic-Relations: Policy Coordination and Conflict," *International Affairs* 52, no. 2 (Apr. 1976):191. Since the Treaty of Rome forbids quantitative restrictions on trade among

EEC members, France could expect to derive benefits from the sharing agreement without making a commitment to it. N. J. D. Lucas, *Energy and the European Communities* (London: Europa Publications, 1977), p. 62.

114. The IEA designates 10% of total stocks "working stocks" and not part of the stipulated 90-day level. But "working stocks" are actually much higher than this, probably equal to 30–45 days' supply. The U.S. plans to exceed the 90-day level, but its stockpiling program is way behind schedule. Japan has considered building stockpiles to the 180-day level in the 1980s, but none of the other major IEA members plans to build stocks beyond the 90-day level. *PE* (July 1978), pp. 291–93.

115. Willrich and Conant, "The International Energy Agency," *American Journal of International Law* 71, no. 2 (Apr. 1977), p. 210, and *PE* (July 1978), p. 294.

116. Robert J. Lieber, *Oil and the Middle East War: Europe in the Energy Crisis* (Cambridge, Mass.: Center for International Affairs, 1976), p. 26, and *PE* (Nov. 1978), p. 459.

117. Lucas, *Energy and the European Communities*, p. 77.

118. At that point EEC adopted a scheme compatible with IEA's program, but designed to include fuels other than oil. Turner, "European and Japanese Energy Policies," *Current History* (Mar. 1978), p. 107.

119. Werner J. Feld, "West European Foreign Policies: The Impact of the Oil Crisis," *Orbis* 22, no. 1 (1978):67.

120. Lieber, *Oil and the Middle East War*, pp. 26, 28, and 51.

121. *BW*, Mar. 17, 1975, pp. 36–37; *NYT*, Nov. 9, 1976, p. 18; and *PE* (Oct. 1975), p. 377.

122. *Los Angeles Times*, Dec. 18, 1977, part 1, p. 32.

123. In the U.S. it takes 10–12 years to build a nuclear power plant; coal-fired plants can be built in 6 years. *NYT*, Sept. 21, 1977, p. 50.

124. *PE* (Dec. 1977), p. 480, and (Mar. 1978), p. 108.

125. The fuel used in conventional reactors, uranium 235, cannot be used for the manufacture of nuclear weapons because it is not concentrated enough. Plutonium is found in the spent fuel from these reactors, but, to separate it out, a reprocessing plant is required. Plutonium is the fuel used in breeder reactors, and is obtained after spent fuel is sent through a reprocessing plant.

126. An "enrichment" plant can also produce weapons-grade fuel.

127. With the Europeans building their own enrichment capacity and with enrichment services available in the Soviet Union, this was less a concern than it would have been several years before, when the U.S. accounted for nearly all of the non-Communist world's enriched uranium.

128. At the same time, U.S. reactor manufacturers complained that the Carter policy was jeopardizing the U.S. position in world markets.

129. *NYT*, Nov. 4, 1979, pp. 1 and 8, and Mar. 1, 1980, p. 27.

130. *NYT*, Oct. 28, 1979, p. 4E.

131. *NYT*, Apr. 7, 1980, p. A4.

132. Pakistan secured financing for its enriched uranium from Libya's Qaddafi, who has long sought a "Moslem bomb" (*NYT*, Apr. 29, 1979, p. 5E). India has warned that it might be forced to amass nuclear weapons if Pakistan went ahead with efforts to assemble an atomic bomb. U.S. officials believe that an India/Pakistan nuclear arms race may now be inevitable. *NYT*, Aug. 16, 1979, p. A6, and Aug. 24, 1979, p. A4.

133. Iraq has used its position as a major oil exporter to gain access to nuclear technology. In 1975 France agreed to provide Iraq with 12–13 kilograms of 93% enriched uranium—weapons-grade material—by the end of 1980 or early 1981. In 1978 a group of Italian companies agreed to sell Iraq four nuclear laboratories, one of which could be used to work with weapons-grade enriched uranium. Iraq is a major oil supplier to both France and Italy, and State Department officials have said that Italy's desire to gain access to Iraqi oil was probably a central factor in its nuclear export policy. *BW*, Apr. 14, 1980, p. 55, and *NYT*, Mar. 18, 1980, p. A1.

134. *PE* (July 1977), p. 265.

135. President Ford vetoed two strip-mine bills, but President Carter signed a strip-mine bill into law in August 1977.

136. Ulf Lantzke, "Expanding World Use of Coal," *Foreign Affairs* 58, no. 2 (1979–80):351; Stobaugh and Yergin, "Energy: An Emergency Telescoped," *Foreign Affairs* 58, no. 3 (1979):581; and *Wall Street Journal*, June 9, 1977, p. 1.

137. Federal Energy Administration, *Project Independence: A Summary* (Washington, D.C.: Government Printing Office, 1974), p. 8.

138. *BW*, Aug. 11, 1975, p. 19.

139. *BW*, Apr. 25, 1975, p. 87, and Apr. 24, 1978, p. 84.

140. *BW*, July 30, 1979, p. 53.

141. *PE* (Oct. 1976), p. 392, and *BW*, July 26, 1976, p. 46.

142. *BW*, Sept. 12, 1977, p. 52, Sept. 19, 1977, p. 39, and Apr. 23, 1979, p. 128.

143. *BW*, July 23, 1979, p. 146, and July 30, 1979, pp. 53–54; *NYT*, July 15, 1979, sec. 3, p. 1; and *PE* (Dec. 1979), p. 509.

144. In 1972 shale oil was considered profitable at $6.60 a barrel—three times the price of imported oil (*PE* [July 1975], p. 245). During 1973–74 it was estimated to cost between $7 and $9 (Corradi, "Energy and the Exercise of Power," *Foreign Affairs* 57, no. 5 [1979]:1149). But by 1975, when the price of OPEC oil had climbed to $12, projections for shale oil jumped to about $21 (*BW*, July 30, 1979, pp. 53–54). By 1978 estimates had increased to $25–30, about twice the price of OPEC oil at the time (*BW*, Apr. 24, 1978, p. 84). Estimates of the cost of coal gasification are also up, to about $30 per barrel of crude oil equivalent. These estimates increased because of inflation and because, as experimental work proceeded, companies found that these technologies were more expensive than initially envisioned. *BW*, July 30, 1979, pp. 53–54.

145. *PE* (Aug. 1979), p. 326.

146. *BW*, Sept. 19, 1977, pp. 39–40, Dec. 4, 1978, p. 106, and Apr. 23, 1979, p. 72.

147. *NYT*, July 4, 1976, p. 18.

148. *BW*, June 27, 1977, p. 24.

149. *BW*, Oct. 20, 1975, p. 45.

150. South Africa is the only country with a commercial coal-liquefaction program. However, its commercial viability is based on cheap coal (largely a product of cheap labor) and lax environmental standards. See *BW*, July 9, 1979, p. 70, and July 16, 1979, p. 58; and *PE* (Feb. 1979), p. 67.

151. West Germany, which has significant coal reserves, has spent more than $350 million since 1974 on 10 coal gasification and liquefaction pilot plants (*BW*, Apr. 21, 1980, p. 76). The Soviet Union and China both have commercial oil shale programs. *PE* (Dec. 1979), p. 529.

152. OECD, *Energy R & D: Problems and Perspectives* (Paris: OECD, 1975), p. 46.

153. *BW*, Mar. 6, 1978, p. 42.

154. Brian Brinkworth, "UK Solar Policy—The Way Forward?" *Energy Policy* 4, no. 2 (June 1976):180.

155. OECD, *Energy R & D*, p. 46.

156. *BW*, Jan. 29, 1979, p. 36. While in recent years the cost of solar cells has fallen from $50 per watt to less than $10, to produce electricity at competitive prices they will have to fall to 50¢ a watt. *BW*, Sept. 3, 1979, p. 192.

157. *BW*, June 18, 1979, p. 67.

158. Israel is the country with the largest per capita use of solar energy, getting 2% of its total energy from the sun (*BW*, Feb. 5, 1979, p. 44). Brazil has long blended ethyl alcohol (ethanol), made from biomass materials, with gasoline to produce gasohol, and in 1974 this program was stepped up. Brazilian vehicles can run on 20% ethanol, and the Brazilian government plans to have ethanol meet 20% of Brazil's motor fuel demand by the mid-1980s (originally, this was to be achieved by 1980). (*PE* [Aug. 1979], p. 329, and [Oct. 1979], p. 418). While several companies began selling gasohol in the U.S. in 1979 (90% gasoline, 10% grain alcohol), differences in gasoline prices, the cost of

agricultural labor, and suitable farm land all make direct comparisons between the U.S. and the Brazilian situations hazardous.

CHAPTER 11

1. See *PE* (Aug. 1978), p. 338, (June 1982), p. 233, and (July 1982), p. 266, and Arnold Safer, *International Oil Policy* (Lexington, Mass.: Heath, 1979), p. 106.

2. World Energy Congress, *World Energy Resources, 1985–2020* (New York: IPC Technology Press, 1978), p. 9.

3. Halbouty, "Acceleration in Global Exploration—Requirement for Survival," *American Association of Petroleum Geologists' Bulletin* 62, no. 5 (May 1978):751.

4. CIA, *The World Oil Market in the Years Ahead* (Washington, D.C.: Government Printing Office, 1979), p. 14.

5. Ibid., p. 15.

6. *PE* (Sept. 1979), p. 314.

7. *PE* (Feb. 1979), p. 47.

8. *Petroleum Intelligence Weekly,* Sept. 10, 1979, p. 6.

9. CIA, *The World Oil Market in the Years Ahead,* pp. 76–77.

10. Halbouty, "Acceleration in Global Exploration," *American Association of Petroleum Geologists' Bulletin,* p. 746.

11. *PE* (Dec. 1979), p. 501.

12. Of these 33 supergiants, 11 are in Saudi Arabia. CIA, *The World Oil Market in the Years Ahead,* p. 78.

13. Ibid., p. 74.

14. Richard Nehring, who did a study of the discovery of giant and supergiant fields for the CIA, maintains that 90–100% of the giant fields in a "province" are discovered with the drilling of no more than 25–200 new-field exploratory wells. Congressional Budget Office, *A Strategy for Oil Proliferation: Expediting Petroleum Exploration and Production in Non-OPEC Developing Countries* (Washington, D.C.: Government Printing Office, 1979), p. 8.

15. *Los Angeles Times,* Sept. 28, 1978, p. 16. Since the extent of a field's reserves can be determined only after further drilling, it is often many years before its size is established. Discoveries of giant and supergiant fields are indicated by the following table:

	Giant Fields		Supergiant Fields		Giants and Supergiants
	Number	Recoverable Oil (Billion Barrels)	Number	Recoverable Oil (Billion Barrels)	Recoverable Oil (Billion Barrels)
1848–1900	9	10	0	0	10
1901–1910	6	7	0	0	7
1911–1920	12	12	1	32	44
1921–1930	21	21	3	37	58
1931–1940	24	22	3	99	121
1941–1950	19	21	3	104	125
1951–1960	45	57	11	124	181
1961–1970	69	80	12	117	197
1971–1979	40	35	2	15	50

CIA, *The World Oil Market in the Years Ahead,* p. 76.

16. CIA, *The World Oil Market in the Years Ahead,* pp. 14, 15, and 78.

17. Safer, *International Oil Policy,* p. xiii.

18. The economic assumptions behind reserve estimates are rarely made clear, and information on a field's technical possibilities is not readily available.

19. *PE* (Oct. 1975), p. 370.

20. "Primary" recovery normally amounts to less than 25% of the oil in place. This can be increased through "secondary" and "tertiary" recovery, but so far most secondary and tertiary work has been limited to the U.S. *PE* (Oct. 1977), p. 382.

21. *PE* (Oct. 1975), p. 370.

22. *PE* (Apr. 1978), p. 142.

23. *BW,* Dec. 5, 1977, p. 19.

24. *NYT,* Jan. 26, 1978, p. A21.

25. *BW,* July 10, 1978, p. 64.

26. He breaks it down as follows:

| | (Billion Barrels) | |
	Low Estimate	High Estimate
Latin America	215	790
Africa and Madagascar	160	625
South and Southeast Asia	90	300
Total Non-Communist Non-OPEC LDCs	465	1,715
China	27	172
Total	492	1,887

BW, July 10, 1978, p. 64.

Other geologists have objected to Grossling's thesis on the grounds that geophysical surveys have eliminated large areas because they do not have sufficient sediment thickness (1,000 meters) to generate temperatures adequate for the conversion of organic material into petroleum or to produce sufficient pressure to assure migration to areas of accumulation. U.S. House of Representatives, Committee on Interstate and Foreign Commerce, Subcommittee on Energy and Power, *Are We Running Out? A Perspective on Resource Scarcity* (Washington, D.C.: Government Printing Office, 1978), p. 12.

27. *PE* (Oct. 1978), p. 406.

28. Quoted in *San Francisco Bay Guardian* (May 1979), p. 3.

29. Computed from figures in BP, *Statistical Review of the World Oil Industry, 1981*.

30. *PIW,* Sept. 10, 1979, p. 6.

31. Ibid. (supplement), p. 1; World Energy Congress, *World Energy Resources,* pp. 10–11; and *PE* (Feb. 1975), p. 67.

32. M. A. Adelman, "Oil Import Auctions," reprinted in U.S. Congress, Joint Economic Committee, *Multinational Oil Companies and OPEC: Implications for U.S. Policy* (Washington, D.C.: Government Printing Office, 1977), p. 325.

33. *Wall Street Journal,* Nov. 13, 1978, p. 24.

34. R. Vedavalli, *Petroleum and Gas in Non-OPEC Developing Countries: 1976–1985,* World Bank Staff Working Paper no. 289 (Apr. 1978), p. 2.

35. *PE* (Nov. 1979), p. 486.

36. CIA, *The World Oil Market in the Years Ahead,* p. 28.

37. Ibid.

38. In 1978 only about 10% of globally marketed natural gas moved in international trade, and

LNG accounted for about 16% of this. (In contrast, exports accounted for 54% of all oil production in 1978 [BP, *Statistical Review of the World Oil Industry, 1978*].) The leading natural gas exporter in 1978 was the Netherlands (45 billion cubic meters or 28.6%), followed by the Soviet Union (31.9 billion cubic meters or 20.3%) and Canada (26.3 billion cubic meters or 16.7%) (*PE* [Sept. 1979], p. 315). Between 1974 and 1978 the world LNG trade increased by 26.8%; however, the projections for 1985 have been declining. Worldwide in 1978, LNG imports provided the energy equivalent of 830,000 barrels of oil a day. *PE* (Nov. 1978), pp. 466–67.

39. *PE* (July 1976), p. 250.

40. It costs twice as much to transport gas by pipeline as to transport crude oil; LNG transport costs are 5 times the cost of transporting crude oil. In addition, the cost of manufacturing LNG is equivalent to about $5 per barrel of crude oil. *PIW*, Sept. 10, 1979 (supplement), p. 2.

41. *PIW*, Sept. 10, 1979, p. 5.

42. *PE* (Feb. 1979), p. 47. In 1973 two-thirds of the gas produced in the Middle East, as opposed to 13% worldwide, was flared (*PE* [July 1976], p. 250). In 1978 28.4% of the world's associated gas output was flared; in the Middle East the figure was 60%, in Africa 65.6%, and in the Far East 38.7%. High though the figures are, they have been declining. *PE* (Aug. 1979), p. 313.

43. In Western Europe, only Norway has large undeveloped natural gas resources. CIA, *The World Oil Market in the Years Ahead*, p. 22.

44. In September 1978 the U.S. agreed to a price for Indonesian LNG that was linked to the price of Indonesian oil and a U.S. wholesale price index; however, similar deals with Algeria have not been approved. Part of the difficulty in setting a price for natural gas stems from the fact that consumers vary in what they use it for (i.e. heating, boiler fuel). It is therefore difficult to set its price on the basis of some alternative fuel, such as home heating oil.

45. Surveying U.S. oil companies, the GAO was told by several nonmajor oil companies that "the U.S. government had failed to provide them with meaningful support against actions by OPEC governments to expropriate their physical assets and concessionary rights. The companies claimed that they have received inadequate compensation for physical assets and no compensation for oil in the ground which they were entitled to by concessionary rights. They complained that the U.S. government had failed to uphold the legal principle of sanctity of contracts. Instances were cited in which OPEC governments had repeatedly abrogated previously agreed-to contracts. As a result, the companies said foreign investment by the oil companies is being curtailed which, in turn, would eventually have a negative effect on future production levels and the world petroleum supply." Comptroller General of the U.S., *More Attention Should Be Paid to Making the U.S. Less Vulnerable to Foreign Oil Price and Supply Decisions* (Washington, D.C.: General Accounting Office, 1978), p. 32.

46. While independent producers account for the bulk of exploration drilling, these companies are dependent upon the majors for much of their financing. The majors also tend to do the drilling in the least accessible areas, such as the Arctic or the North Sea. Other companies lack the expertise for this. *PE* (Aug. 1976), p. 314.

47. In frontier areas, 9 of 10 exploratory wells are usually dry. Safer, *International Oil Policy*, p. 99.

48. *BW*, July 10, 1978, p. 64.

49. The actual figures, in millions of U.S. dollars, are:

	1973	1978
1. Cash flow	20,023	30,587
2. Capital expenditures	14,637	29,893
3. Ratio 1/2	1.37	1.02
4. Available Cash Flow	15,901	23,634
5. Ratio 4/2	1.09	.79

(Computed from data in Chase Manhattan Bank, *Financial Analysis of a Group of Petroleum Companies*, 1978, pp. 22–23.) After-tax cash flow equals total revenues minus operating costs and other expenses and all taxes. Writeoffs and dividends are not deducted from cash flow, but available cash flow equals cash flow minus dividends.

50. Surveying more than 800 of the U.S.'s largest nonfinancial corporations in 37 industries, *Business Week* found that the "natural resources (fuel)" group, which consists almost entirely of oil companies, had a lower debt ratio and a higher percentage of five-year cash flow in relation to its economic growth needs than the all-industry composite. The figures since the survey was first taken in 1977 are as indicated in the following table.

	1977	1978	1979	1980
Short-Term Debt as a % of				
Total Investment Capital				
Natural resources (fuel) cos.	3.4	3.2	3.2	3.5
All industry	5.1	5.5	5.9	6.8
Long-Term Debt as a % of				
Total Invested Capital				
Natural resources (fuel) cos.	25.2	27.1	26.7	24.4
All industry	32.0	32.3	31.7	31.3
Five-Year Cash Flow as a %				
Five-Year Growth Needs				
Natural resources (fuel) cos.	77.4	75.7	74.6	76.1
All industry	73.9	73.6	74.2	73.8

BW, Oct. 17, 1977, pp. 87 and 100, Oct. 16, 1978, pp. 135 and 150, Oct. 15, 1979. pp. 94 and 115, and Oct. 13, 1980, pp. 84 and 103.

The five-year cash flow as a percent of five-year growth needs is defined as the "five-year sum of (1) net income available for common stockholders, plus (2) depreciation and amortization, plus (3) income from discounted operations and extraordinary items of net taxes divided by five-year sum of (1) capital expenditures, plus (2) difference between fiscal year-end 1978 and 1973 inventories (except utilities), plus (3) common dividends." *BW*, Oct. 15, 1979, p. 115.

51. *BW*, June 13, 1977, p. 83.
52. *Forbes*, Aug. 15, 1977, p. 38.
53. *NYT*, Aug. 22, 1979, p. D1.
54. The Bank estimated that from 1976 to 1985 the developing countries would need $7 billion (in 1977 prices) per year for petroleum exploration and development. Congressional Budget Office, *A Strategy for Oil Proliferation*, pp. vii and 18, and *PE* (Nov. 1979), p. 487.
55. *NYT*, Aug. 22, 1979, p. D1.
56. Quoted in *NYT*, Aug. 22, 1979, pp. D1 and D5.
57. *NYT*, Aug. 22, 1979, p. D5.
58. At the Conference on International Economic Cooperation in 1976 the U.S. proposed an International Energy Institute and International Resources Bank to facilitate technology transfers, generate financing, and provide limited-risk insurance to encourage private development of new oil resources. The bank would begin operations with capital funds of $1 billion. However, this proposal was never approved because of the opposition of Third World countries that feared it was intended mainly to give the U.S. greater access to their raw materials and to create profitable conditions for multinational corporations. Roy A. Warner, "Oil and U.S. Security Policies," *Orbis* 21, no. 3 (1977):665–66, and *NYT*, June 19, 1976, pp. 27 and 29.
59. CIA, *The World Oil Market in the Years Ahead*, p. 19. In 1975 the U.S. Geological Survey revised its estimate of the U.S.' undiscovered oil reserves from 200–400 billion barrels to 50–127 billion barrels (*NYT*, Nov. 19, 1978, p. 20). The lower estimate is consistent with estimates by the Project Independence Task Force (134 billion barrels) and the National Academy of Science (113

billion barrels). The Geological Survey estimated gas reserves between 322 and 655 trillion cubic feet, down from its earlier estimate of 990 to 2,200 trillion cubic feet. *PE* (June 1975), p. 228; *BW*, Mar. 10, 1976, p. 76; and *NYT*, Feb. 22, 1977, p. 14.

60. *BW*, July 30, 1979, p. 48.

61. *NYT*, June 17, 1979, p. 14.

62. *NYT*, Aug. 31, 1979, p. 12.

63. Figures are computed from Exxon annual reports. See chapter 12, note 48 for the actual breakdown.

64. *BW*, July 30, 1979, p. 50, and U.S. Congress, Joint Economic Committee, *Achieving the Goals of the Employment Act of 1946—Thirtieth Anniversary Review* (Washington, D.C.: Government Printing Office, 1975), vol. 2: Energy, Paper No. 1, "Oil Profits, Prices and Capital Requirements," p. 10.

65. Safer, *International Oil Policy*, p. 18.

66. *BW*, June 14, 1976, p. 32. In July 1979 *Business Week* reported that while the average OPEC price was $20 a barrel, tertiary oil was estimated to cost a minimum of $25. *BW*, July 30, 1979, p. 53.

67. *BW*, July 30, 1979, p. 53.

68. U.S. House of Representatives, Committee on Interstate and Foreign Commerce, Subcommittee on Energy and Power, *Are We Running Out?* p. 15. The U.S. Geological Survey estimates total offshore oil prospects, including Alaska, at 10–49 billion barrels, compared with onshore prospects of 37–81 billion barrels. Of the remaining gas prospects, about 20% are thought to be offshore. Offshore production accounts for about 16% of U.S. oil production and about 21% of U.S. natural gas production. *NYT*, Feb. 5, 1978, p. 4E.

69. *BW*, July 30, 1979, p. 50.

70. Richard J. Barnet, "The World's Resources," *The New Yorker*, Mar. 17, 1980, p. 53; *BW*, Feb. 26, 1979, p. 85; and *NYT*, Jan. 29, 1979, p. D1.

71. *PE* (Aug. 1978), p. 343, and (Apr. 1979), p. 166, and *NYT*, Feb. 15, 1979, p. E1, Mar. 1, 1979, pp. D1 and D4, and Oct. 23, 1979, p. D7.

72. Part of the reason was that the industry expected the West Coast to absorb more Alaskan oil than it actually did. *Wall Street Journal*, Feb. 16, 1979, p. 1.

73. *BW*, Mar. 26, 1979, p. 36.

74. *NYT*, July 25, 1979, p. D1, Sept. 4, 1979, p. D1, and Aug. 29, 1982, p. E19.

75. *BW*, Feb. 26, 1979, p. 74.

76. *BW*, Feb. 10, 1975, p. 46, and May 19, 1975, p. 118.

77. In 1977, with the price at $10.75, Alberta took $4.12 in royalties; federal and provincial taxes accounted for $3.23, operating costs for $1.10, and company profits for $2.30. *PE* (Aug. 1977), p. 318.

78. *BW*, May 30, 1977, p. 26.

79. *BW*, June 21, 1976, p. 52, and Dec. 6, 1976, p. 38, and *PE* (Apr. 1978), p. 150, and (Aug. 1978), p. 320.

80. *PE* (Apr. 1979), p. 165.

81. *BW*, Feb. 4, 1980, p. 114. However, only 26 billion barrels are on the surface; the rest are as deep as 2,000 feet. *NYT*, Jan. 15, 1979, sec. 3, p. 1.

82. *PE* (Sept. 1978), p. 390, and *BW*, Feb. 4, 1980, p. 114.

83. *PE* (Feb. 1975), p. 55, and (Mar. 1975), p. 108; *BW*, Feb. 4, 1980, p. 116; and *NYT*, Feb. 15, 1982, p. D2. Since it takes the energy equivalent of half a barrel of oil to produce a barrel of "syncrude," oil-price increases also drive up the cost of syncrude production. *NYT*, Nov. 27, 1979, p. D16.

84. *BW*, Dec. 25, 1978, p. 42, and *PE* (Jan. 1979), pp. 32–33, (Sept. 1979), p. 381, and (June 1982), p. 251.

85. *BW*, Apr. 10, 1978, p. 106.

86. *BW,* Apr. 21, 1975, pp. 116 and 118, and Nov. 10, 1975, pp. 51–52.

87. *BW,* Apr. 10, 1978, p. 108.

88. *BW,* Apr. 10, 1978, p. 107, and *NYT,* June 8, 1979, p. E4, and Oct. 31, 1979, p. E5.

89. *NYT,* Apr. 1, 1977, p. D13, and July 25, 1978, p. E15.

90. *PE* (Apr. 1979), p. 147, and (Feb. 1982), p. 43.

91. *PE* (July 1979), p. 266, and (Aug. 1979), p. 321, and Mallakh, "OPEC: Issues of Supply and Demand," *Current History* (Mar. 1978), p. 126.

92. U.S. Congress, Joint Economic Committee, *Multinational Oil Companies and OPEC: Implications for U.S. Policy* (Washington, D.C.: Government Printing Office, 1977), p. 320; *PE,* (May 1979), p. 189; and *Oil and Gas Journal,* Dec. 31, 1979, p. 70.

93. *PE* (Jan. 1979), pp. 19–21; *BW,* Aug. 16, 1982, p. 37; and *NYT,* Nov. 23, 1982, p. D6.

94. See CIA, *The International Energy Situation: Outlook to 1985* (Washington, D.C.: Government Printing Office, 1977).

95. *Oil and Gas Journal,* Dec. 28, 1981, pp. 86–87, and John D. Moody and Robert E. Geiger, "Petroleum Resources: How Much Oil and Where," *Technology Review* (Mar./Apr. 1975), p. 41.

96. *PE* (May 1977), p. 191.

97. BP, *Statistical Review of the World Oil Industry,* various issues.

98. *NYT,* June 30, 1979, p. 28, and Nov. 20, 1979, p. D1. In Rumania, the other East European oil producer, production fell below internal requirements in 1978, the first time that had happened in the post–World War II period. *PE* (Sept. 1979), p. 361.

99. *PE* (Dec. 1977), p. 492, and CIA, *The World Oil Market in the Years Ahead,* p. 38.

100. *PE* (May 1977), p. 191, and *NYT,* Jan. 24, 1978, p. 49, and Nov. 20, 1979, p. D11.

101. The Soviet Union experienced delays in getting sophisticated equipment. The U.S. government debated whether the contribution this equipment would make to increased Soviet oil production would outweigh its impact in improving Soviet military capability. Prior to 1980, the most controversial deal was a $144 million agreement between Moscow and Dresser Industries of Dallas for technology and plans to produce high-quality drill bits. After bitter debate, the Carter administration gave final approval in December 1978 and promised that, in the future, the Soviet Union would have less trouble getting U.S. oil equipment. However, following the Soviet invasion of Afghanistan in December 1979, restrictions were placed on shipments of oil equipment to the Soviet Union.

102. Arthur Jay Klinghoffer, *The Soviet Union and International Oil Politics* (New York: Columbia University Press, 1977), pp. 270–71.

103. *PE* (Mar. 1975), p. 97, and (July 1978), p. 304, and *BW,* Apr. 19, 1976, p. 50.

104. *Los Angeles Times,* Oct. 9, 1978, part 1, pp. 1 and 15.

105. *NYT,* Nov. 20, 1979, pp. D1 and D11.

106. *BW,* Apr. 19, 1976, p. 51, and Dec. 3, 1979, p. 57, and *NYT,* Nov. 21, 1977, p. 55.

107. The East Europeans were also required to invest heavily in the Soviet oil industry, in effect raising the prices they paid even further. The Soviet Union also charged the full world price for quantities supplied in excess of a country's quota. Klinghoffer, *The Soviet Union and International Oil Politics,* p. 93, and *NYT,* Feb. 3, 1980, sec. 12, p. 41.

108. *PE* (Aug. 1977), p. 320.

109. *PE* (May 1978), p. 217.

110. *BW,* Oct. 30, 1978, p. 156.

111. This could be offset somewhat through development of China's huge hydro potential, only about 3% of which has been developed to date (*BW,* Sept. 17, 1979, p. 37). Only about 15% of China's oil production is currently available for export. *Oil and Gas Journal,* Dec. 31, 1979, p. 31.

112. Congressional Budget Office, *A Strategy for Oil Proliferation,* p. 19.

113. *PE* (May 1976), p. 122.

114. China has long regarded oil concessions by Taiwan to U.S. companies as payoffs, in exchange for which Taiwan receives military and financial support. *NYT,* Sept. 18, 1977, p. 21.

115. *PE* (Jan. 1978), pp. 9–10, and (May 1979), pp. 185–86.

116. The split also cost Vietnam at least 20% of its oil supply and left it almost totally dependent upon the Soviet Union for oil. *PE* (July 1978), p. 305, and (Feb. 1979), p. 64, and *NYT,* June 15, 1978, p. D11.

117. *NYT,* Apr. 24, 1979, p. 27.

118. *PE* (Sept. 1975), p. 338, and (May 1978), p. 212.

119. *PE* (Feb. 1979), pp. 62 and 63, and *NYT,* Mar. 24, 1979, p. 27.

120. *PE* (June 1976), pp. 212–13, and *Oil and Gas Journal* (various issues).

121. *NYT,* Feb. 18, 1977, p. D1.

122. Cited in *PE* (Mar. 1979), pp. 105–6.

123. *BW,* Jan. 15, 1979, p. 67, and *NYT,* Feb. 18, 1979, p. D5.

124. George W. Grayson, "Mexico's Opportunity: The Oil Boom," *Foreign Policy,* no. 29 (1977–78), p. 72; *NYT,* Dec. 31, 1977, p. 23; and *PE* (May 1978), p. 198.

125. *NYT,* Nov. 29, 1978, p. D1; *Oil and Gas Journal,* Dec. 28, 1981, pp. 86–87; and *PE* (Sept. 1979), p. 314.

126. BP, *Statistical Review of the World Oil Industry, 1980,* and *PE* (Mar. 1979), p. 111, and (Aug. 1981), p. 344.

127. Because of its proximity to the U.S., Mexico is able to set higher prices than any OPEC country and still keep the landed price of its crude in the U.S. Gulf below that of any OPEC crude. Until 1979, Mexico set its prices to assure that its crude would sell in a period of oversupply. *PE* (Mar. 1979), p. 111.

128. Because of Mexico's sales of oil to Israel, most Arab members of OPEC are not anxious to have Mexico as a member.

129. *NYT,* Feb. 13, 1979, p. 1.

130. *NYT,* Jan. 6, 1979, p. 25, and Feb. 3, 1979, p. 27.

131. In early 1979 85% of Mexico's oil exports still went to the U.S., but Pemex had agreed that, beginning in 1980, 100,000 b/d would be sold to both France and Canada. Mexico has also concluded oil export deals with Spain, Israel, Japan, and Cuba; however, it is likely that much of this oil will end up in the U.S. as a result of swap deals. *NYT,* Feb. 3, 1979, p. 27, and *BW,* July 3, 1978, p. 44.

132. *NYT,* Aug. 5, 1977, pp. D1 and D11.

133. *BW,* May 29, 1978, p. 50, and *NYT,* Feb. 11, 1979, p. 52.

134. Since, for internal distribution, Mexico continued building its gas pipeline during the period of the dispute, the controversy over the price of natural gas has not delayed delivery very much, if at all; and the fact that the gas would flow through a major pipeline suggested that larger quantities might ultimately be involved. *NYT,* Sept. 22, 1979, p. 1, and *PE* (Nov. 1979), pp. 479–80.

135. *PE* (Dec. 1975), p. 461.

136. *NYT,* Sept. 21, 1979, p. D12, and *PE* (Nov. 1978), p. 481, (Nov. 1980), p. 490, and (Apr. 1982), p. 149.

137. While more than 30% of the oil in U.S. fields is typically recovered, Argentine oil fields were recovering only 10% of their reservoir volume. *NYT,* July 29, 1976, p. 53.

138. *NYT,* Oct. 3, 1977, p. 49, and *Elements* (Feb. 1976), p. 8.

139. *PE* (Oct. 1979), pp. 409–10. The number of wildcats drilled in Argentina was: 1973, 139; 1974, 117; 1975, 78; 1976, 83; 1977, 143; and 1978, 81. *Oil and Gas Journal* (various issues).

140. Grossling, "A Critical Survey of World Petroleum Opportunities," Congressional Research Service, *Project Interdependence: U.S. and World Energy Outlook through 1990* (Washington, D.C.: Government Printing Office, 1977), p. 651.

141. *PE* (June 1978), pp. 243–44. Gulf, the main company operating in Angola, was uneasy about the aid the U.S. government provided to UNITA and the FNLA. At one point the State Department asked Gulf to halt payments to the MPLA, a suggestion that Gulf resisted on the grounds that halting payments would jeopardize the safety of its personnel and installations. Louis Turner, *Oil Companies in the International System* (London: Allen & Unwin, 1978), p. 78.

142. BP, *Statistical Review of the World Oil Industry,* various issues; *BW,* Oct. 4, 1976, p. 42; and *NYT,* Feb. 3, 1980, p. 47.

143. *NYT*, Feb. 3, 1980, p. 47, and *PE* (Oct. 1975), p. 375.

144. CIA, *The World Oil Market in the Years Ahead*, p. 15.

145. *PE* (Oct. 1975), p. 371.

146. J. E. Hartshorn, *Objectives of the Petroleum Exporting Countries* (Nicosia, Cyprus: Middle East Petroleum and Economics Publications, 1978), p. 115; *Oil and Gas Journal*, Dec. 28, 1981, pp. 86–87; *NYT*, Oct. 24, 1979, p. D2; and *BW*, June 18, 1979, p. 113.

147. The figures in the *Oil and Gas Journal* are estimated.

148. *PE* (Sept. 1977), p. 347.

149. *MNC Saudi Oil Report*, p. 31, and *Oil and Gas Journal* (various issues).

150. *PE* (Sept. 1977), p. 347, and (Aug. 1978), p. 333. In comparison with LNG, the export of LPG and natural gas liquids requires less specialized transport systems and is considerably less costly.

151. *PE* (Nov. 1979), p. 465.

152. *PE* (Nov. 1976), p. 424, (Aug. 1976), p. 481, and (Jan. 1981), p. 30; and Hartshorn, *Objectives of the Petroleum Exporting Countries*, p. 149.

153. CIA, *International Energy Statistical Review*, Sept. 29, 1981, p. 3.

154. CIA, *The World Oil Market in the Years Ahead*, p. 50.

155. *PE* (July 1976), p. 262, and (June 1978), p. 243, and BP, *Statistical Review of the World Oil Industry*, various issues.

156. *PE* (Jan. 1978), p. 27, (Mar. 1978), p. 107, (June 1978), p. 244, and (Nov. 1978), p. 475.

157. To prevent this, Indonesia recently began encouraging development of other energy sources. *PE* (Sept. 1976), p. 358 (Sept. 1977), p. 368, and (Oct. 1978), p. 438; Hartshorn, *Objectives of the Petroleum Exporting Countries*, p. 185; and BP, *Statistical Review of the World Oil Industry, 1978*.

158. *PE* (May 1976), p. 188, and (Apr. 1977), p. 143, and Safer, *International Oil Policy*, pp. 140–41.

159. *Oil and Gas Journal*, Dec. 31, 1979, p. 69.

160. *NYT*, Sept. 9, 1979, p. 20E.

161. BP, *Statistical Review of the World Oil Industry, 1978*, and *PE* (Sept. 1977), p. 349.

162. *PE* (Sept. 1977), p. 350, and CIA, *The World Oil Market in the Years Ahead*, p. 49.

163. *PE* (Sept. 1977), p. 350, and (May 1980), p. 194.

164. The Soviet Union is also producing heavy oil at Yarega, in the Komi Autonomous Republic. CIA, *The World Oil Market in the Years Ahead*, pp. 49 and 80; *NYT*, Mar. 23, 1979, p. E3; and *BW*, Aug. 20, 1979, p. 38.

165. *PE* (Oct. 1978), pp. 416–18.

166. Ibid., and Hartshorn, *Objectives of the Petroleum Exporting Countries*, p. 213.

167. *PE* (Sept. 1977), p. 345, (Nov. 1977), p. 456, and (Jan. 1978), p. 22.

168. CIA, *The World Oil Market in the Years Ahead*, p. 50.

169. The deals were finally rejected in Dec. 1978, partly because the gas would not have been economical unless its price was "rolled in." An earlier agreement between El Paso and Sonatrach has been approved, and imports began in 1978. *BW*, Apr. 23, 1979, p. 78.

170. Hartshorn, *Objectives of the Petroleum Exporting Countries*, p. 107.

171. Ibid., p. 203, and *PE* (July 1979), p. 295.

172. *PE* (Mar. 1974), p. 117.

173. Yager and Steinberg, "Trends in the International Oil Market," in Edward R. Fried and Charles L. Schultze, eds., *Higher Oil Prices and the World Economy* (Washington, D.C.: The Brookings Institution, 1975), p. 237, and George Lenczowski, *Middle East Oil in a Revolutionary Age* (Washington, D.C.: American Enterprise Institute, 1976), p. 33.

174. Taki Rifai, *The Pricing of Crude Oil* (New York: Praeger, 1975), p. 365; Hartshorn, *Objectives of the Petroleum Exporting Countries*, p. 76; and *PE* (Aug. 1974), p. 293.

175. Rifai, *The Pricing of Crude Oil*, pp. 361–62, and Yager and Steinberg, "Trends in the International Oil Market," in Fried and Schultze, eds., *Higher Oil Prices and the World Economy*, pp. 235 and 265–66.

176. *PE* (Dec. 1974), p. 455.

177. Dankwart A. Rustow and John F. Mugno, *OPEC: Success and Prospects* (New York: New York University Press, 1976), p. 27, and *PE* (Jan. 1975), p. 14.

178. The OPEC countries differed on their interpretation of this. Iran and most other OPEC countries held that the average government take should be the same on each barrel, regardless of how much equity and how much participation oil the companies lifted. However, Saudi Arabia maintained that the average government take assumes that 60% will be participation oil and 40% equity oil and that therefore, if the companies take proportionally more equity oil (i.e. all the participation oil is not sold), then the average government take will decrease. Rifai, *The Pricing of Crude Oil*, pp. 366–67.

179. Ibid., p. 367; Penrose, "The Development of Crisis," in Raymond Vernon, ed., *The Oil Crisis: In Perspective*, issued as *Daedalus* 104, no. 4 (1975):52; and *BW*, Dec. 21, 1974, p. 28.

180. How much of this increase came during 1974 depends upon how one treats the retroactive price increases that OPEC imposed. If one accepts the average tax-paid cost of $8.20 that appeared to be established on Jan. 1, 1974, as the starting point, then the increase is from $8.20 to $10.12. But if one takes the retroactive price of $9.54 that was eventually established for Jan. 1, 1974, as the starting point, then the 1974 increase appears far more modest.

181. *PE* (Apr. 1975), p. 133.

182. *PE* (Aug. 1975), p. 290, and (Sept. 1975), p. 360.

183. Yager and Steinberg, "Trends in the International Oil Market," in Fried and Schultze, eds., *Higher Oil Prices and the World Economy*, p. 238, and Mikdashi, "The OPEC Process," in Vernon, ed., *The Oil Crisis*, p. 210.

184. *PE* (Apr. 1976), p. 160.

185. *PE* (Sept. 1976), p. 338.

186. *BW*, Nov. 17, 1975, p. 58.

187. *PE* (Apr. 1976), p. 130, and *NYT*, Nov. 17, 1977, p. 71.

188. Quoted in Edith Penrose and E. F. Penrose, *Iraq: International Relations and National Development* (Boulder, Colo.: Westview Press, 1978), p. 519.

189. *PE* (Oct. 1975), p. 373, and *NYT*, Sept. 20, 1975, p. 37.

190. *PIW*, Apr. 30, 1979 (supplement), p. 3.

191. *BW*, Sept. 22, 1975, p. 23, and Oct. 13, 1975, p. 35.

192. Penrose and Penrose, *Iraq*, p. 519, and *NYT*, Oct. 15, 1975, p. 4.

193. Penrose and Penrose, *Iraq*, p. 519, and *PE* (Nov. 1975), p. 417.

194. *PE* (July 1976), p. 246. The Petroleum Industry Research Corp. found that, from third quarter 1975 to third quarter 1976, the price of OPEC's imports increased no more than 2.7% on a weighted average basis. *PE* (Dec. 1976), p. 464.

195. The moderation in Iran's position may have been linked to its desire to secure additional arms sales from the U.S. The Ford administration denied that it had ever linked arms sales and oil prices, but whether this was true or not, the Shah may have believed that a link was implicit. *NYT*, Nov. 11, 1976, p. 8.

196. Frank R. Wyant, *The United States, OPEC and Multinational Oil*, (Lexington, Mass.: Heath, 1977), pp. 110–11, and *NYT*, Dec. 15, 1976, p. D1, and Dec. 18, 1976, pp. A1 and D7. Inflation in the West cut both ways this time, depending upon whose estimates were used. According to OPEC experts, the cost of the exporting countries' imports had risen by 26.9% since the last oil price increase, but a study by the U.S. Treasury maintained that OPEC import costs had risen no more than 1 or 2% during this period (*NYT*, Dec. 15, 1976, p. D1). As Yamani pointed out, the differences were mainly due to the fact that the high estimates included exporting-country port dues in their cost comparisons while the low estimates excluded them on the grounds that they were due to exporting-country inefficiency and not to the rising cost of Western goods per se (*NYT*, Dec. 18, 1976, p. 32). Also, while the OPEC countries often attributed the rising cost of their development projects to inflation, the rise had more to do with the difficulty of arriving at the original cost estimates and the consequent underestimation in these initial figures. *PE* (Dec. 1976), p. 465.

197. *NYT*, Dec. 18, 1976, pp. 1 and 32.

198. Hartshorn, *Objectives of the Petroleum Exporting Countries,* p. 78.

199. *PE* (Jan. 1977), p. 3.

200. In Nov. Yamani told *Business Week:* "We need a strong economy in the West to achieve our industrial and development targets inside Saudi Arabia. And we do not want a recession in the West that will definitely weaken the present political systems, especially in certain areas in Europe, and would increase the rate of unemployment and bring about a different type of system." *BW,* Nov. 29, 1976, p. 66.

201. Between the second half of 1976 and the first half of 1977, production declined by 25.9% in Kuwait, 18.4% in Qatar, 16.2% in Iraq, 11.5% in Iran, 5.6% in Venezuela, 3.1% in Gabon, 2.9% in Ecuador, and 2.8% in Algeria. During this period Saudi Arabia's production increased by 1.5% and the UAE's by 1.4%. Production also increased in Indonesia (9.7%), Nigeria (4.7%), and Libya (3.7%). *PE* (Aug. 1977), p. 329.

202. Comptroller General of the U.S., *More Attention Should Be Paid to Making the U.S. Less Vulnerable to Foreign Oil Price and Supply Decisions,* pp. 20–21, and *PE* (Feb. 1977), p. 71.

203. See *MNC Saudi Oil Report,* p. 13; *PE* (Feb. 1977), p. 42, and (July 1977), p. 329.

204. *PE* (Mar. 1977), p. 118, and (Aug. 1977), p. 329.

205. The fire was the worst in Aramco's 40-year history. At its peak, it engulfed a square-mile area that contained pipelines, pumping stations, storage tanks, and processing equipment through which the bulk of Saudi production flowed en route to tanker terminals on the Persian Gulf Coast. *NYT,* May 14, 1977, p. 1.

206. *PE* (Aug. 1977), p. 329, and Theodore H. Moran, *Oil Prices and the Future of OPEC* (Washington, D.C.: Resources for the Future, 1978), p. 79.

207. *PE* (Mar. 1977), p. 102.

208. Hartshorn, *Objectives of the Petroleum Exporting Countries,* p. 78.

209. *PE* (Mar. 1977), p. 102.

210. *NYT,* Dec. 21, 1976, p. 60.

211. *NYT,* Dec. 19, 1976, p. 1.

212. Libya did not accept the compromise until the end of June, and Iraq waited until the first week of July to accede. *NYT,* July 6, 1977, p. D1.

213. This decline in demand for light crudes created major problems in Nigeria, where the government was committed to heavy expenditures under its Third National Development Plan. To deal with this problem, the government began borrowing heavily and discounted its oil. *PE* (Mar. 1978), p. 105.

214. *Christian Science Monitor,* Nov. 18, 1977, p. 62, and *NYT,* Jan. 13, 1977, p. 43, Nov. 15, 1977, p. 57, and Nov. 18, 1977, p. 62.

215. *NYT,* Dec. 22, 1977, p. 1, and *PE* (Jan. 1978), p. 2.

216. Calculated from data in *PE* (Aug. 1978), p. 356.

217. One could accept payment in dollars and still set the price in some other currency or combination of currencies. For example, if pricing were in terms of SDRs and a barrel of oil cost 12 SDRs (when $1 = 1 SDR), it would cost $15 when 1 SDR = $1.25.

218. *Petroleum Intelligence Weekly* (July 17, 1978, p. 7) gives the following figures for the delivered cost of crude oil to the major consuming countries in April 1978:

	Apr. Index (1974 = 100)	Delivered Cost (Dollars per Barrel)
U.S.	116.7	14.41
Japan	97.2	13.81
West Germany	96.2	14.22
Netherlands	103.8	13.90
France	130.1	14.01
Italy	159.1	13.20
U.K.	164.8	13.43

219. According to *Business Week,* in June 1978 more than 80% of Saudi Arabia's foreign reserves and assets, estimated at some $65 billion, were denominated in dollars. *BW,* June 26, 1978, p. 38.

220. The sale was part of a "package" deal that originally included 15 F-15s and 75 F-16s for Israel and 50 F-5E fighter-bombers for Egypt, but the Saudi part was the most controversial. Opponents of the sale argued that in the event of another Arab-Israeli war, the planes would be used against Israel. They maintained that merely having the planes would make the Saudis a party to any new Middle East war, making its airfields—and perhaps its oil fields—targets. Israel's supporters also feared that the Saudi sale was but the beginning of an overall buildup in Arab strength, and they were concerned that, for the first time, Arabs were gaining access to the most sophisticated U.S. jets, a development that threatened Israel's traditional technological edge.

Supporters of the sale maintained that the F-15s were for defensive purposes—to be used mainly against Iraq and Southern Yemen—and that the Saudis had given assurances that they would not be used against Israel. For example, the Saudis had pledged that the planes would not be based at Tabuk, the airbase closest to Jerusalem. They held that by selling the advanced fighters to the Saudis, the U.S. would cement ties with Saudi Arabia and strengthen Saudi security.

In May, to win passage of the deal, President Carter promised to sell Israel an additional 20 F-15s at a later date. Also, Israel reluctantly admitted that it would rather see the Saudi sale go through than be denied its part of the package. Another factor influencing Congress and the Israelis was that if the sale were denied, Saudi Arabia could buy French fighter aircraft of nearly equal capability. *BW,* May 15, 1978, p. 26, and *NYT,* May 16, 1978, pp. 1 and 12, and May 31, 1978, p. A6.

221. From the beginning of 1977 until the middle of 1978, the dollar declined 9.7% against a basket of 12 major currencies. *PE* (Nov. 1978), p. 477.

222. *NYT,* June 20, 1978, pp. A1 and D13.

CHAPTER 12

1. More than three quarters of the industry's assets were in pipelines, tankers, refining, and petrochemical and marketing facilities that were outside the exporting countries and could not be nationalized by them. Jacoby, "Oil and the Future," *Journal of Energy and Development* 1, no. 1 (1975):52.

2. *PE* (Sept. 1978), p. 359.

3. In many exporting countries the companies still hold an equity interest and are therefore not properly referred to as "former concessionaires." However, to avoid the awkwardness of a more accurate term, this expression has been used throughout this section.

4. Church, "The Impotence of Oil Companies," *Foreign Policy,* no. 27 (1977), p. 46.

5. *PE* (Apr. 1976), p. 140. In April 1975 the Aramco partners agreed to increase Mobil's share of the jointly owned subsidiary from 10% to 15% over a five-year period. The three other partners would each sell Mobil a 1⅔% share, reducing their respective shares in Aramco to 28⅓%. The companies were entitled to the Saudi crude roughly in proportion to their equity in Aramco.

6. *PE* (Jan. 1975), p. 14, (Apr. 1976), p. 140, and (Nov. 1981), p. 465; and *NYT,* Feb. 10, 1982, p. D7.

7. Comptroller General of the U.S., *More Attention Should Be Paid to Making the U.S. Less Vulnerable to Foreign Oil Price and Supply Decisions* (Washington, D.C.: General Accounting Office, 1978), p. 30.

8. J. E. Hartshorn, *Objectives of the Petroleum Exporting Countries* (Nicosia, Cyprus: Middle East Petroleum and Economics Publications, 1978), pp. 175–76, and *PE* (Dec. 1975), p. 450.

9. Hartshorn, *Objectives of the Petroleum Exporting Countries,* pp. 201–2.

10. *PE* (Oct. 1976), p. 388, and (Apr. 1977), p. 155.

11. *PE* (July 1976), p. 264. According to Abu Dhabi's oil minister, Mana Saeed al-Otaiba, in 1975 the companies urged Abu Dhabi to take 100% participation as soon as possible. *PE* (June 1975), p. 215.

12. Hartshorn, *Objectives of the Petroleum Exporting Countries,* pp. 162–63.

13. Ibid., p. 102.

14. Despite the change of name, Oil Service Co. of Iran will be referred to as "the Consortium" since it remained essentially the same organization.

15. *Petroleum Intelligence Weekly,* Mar. 26, 1979, p. 3.

16. Hartshorn, *Objectives of the Petroleum Exporting Countries,* p. 107, and *BW,* Feb. 9, 1976, p. 39.

17. Hartshorn, *Objectives of the Petroleum Exporting Countries,* pp. 121 and 123.

18. Ibid., p. 198.

19. *PE* (Oct. 1974), p. 383.

20. Hartshorn, *Objectives of the Petroleum Exporting Countries,* p. 149, and *PE* (Nov. 1976), p. 425, and (Nov. 1977), p. 430.

21. *PE* (Dec. 1975), pp. 450 and 452, and Hartshorn, *Objectives of the Petroleum Exporting Countries,* p. 202.

22. *PE* (Jan. 1976), p. 12, and (Sept. 1979), p. 377.

23. Figures on direct sales for the following OPEC countries in 1976 are

	Volume (mb/d)	Percentage of Total Production
Abu Dhabi	.435	27
Iran	.800	14
Kuwait	.950	44
Iraq	2.000	95
Algeria	.800	80
Qatar	.114	23

Comptroller General of the U.S., *More Attention Should Be Paid to Making the U.S. Less Vulnerable to Foreign Oil Price and Supply Decisions,* pp. 16 and 17. Between 1973 and 1978 third-party crude oil sales by the seven largest international oil companies declined from 6.7 mb/d to 3.7 mb/d. *PE* (July 1982), p. 270.

24. Chandler, "The Innocence of Oil Companies," *Foreign Policy,* no. 27 (1977), p. 67.

25. Vertical divestiture bills would prevent an oil company from operating in each of the various sectors of the industry: refining, marketing, transportation, and production. Proponents argued that a company with only marketing and/or refining operations would bargain harder for lower crude prices than one with production interests to protect. Opponents denied this and stressed the efficiency of vertical integration. Horizontal divestiture bills prohibit oil companies from involvement in coal, uranium, or other nonhydrocarbon energy resources. Proponents of horizontal divestiture argued that the oil companies would slow development of alternative sources since they have interests in oil and gas to protect; opponents argued that the companies' capital and expertise were needed for development of alternative sources.

26. Anthony Sampson, *The Seven Sisters* (New York: Bantam, 1975), p. 337.

27. In October 1975, when a vertical divestiture proposal was offered as a surprise amendment to another bill, it got 45 votes in the Senate, but since then, following heavy industry lobbying, the proposal has made little legislative progress. The Ford administration opposed both horizontal and vertical divestiture. Jimmy Carter came out for horizontal divestiture during the 1976 presidential campaign, but after his election he did little to promote the idea.

28. U.S. Senate, Committee on Interior and Insular Affairs, *A Study of the Relationships between the Government and the Petroleum Industry in Selected Foreign Countries: The Federal Republic of Germany* (Washington, D.C.: Government Printing Office, 1975), p. 5.

29. *PE* (Jan. 1976), p. 6 (Apr. 1976), p. 123, and (Nov. 1978), p. 462. While Japan sought to "lock up" as much oil as possible through special arrangements with OPEC countries and non-OPEC governments and by increasing its nationals' control of foreign oil, oil in these categories accounted for only about 15% of Japan's oil imports by 1977. Moreover, this represented an increase of only about 2% since 1973. *PE* (Dec. 1977), p. 474.

30. Noreng, "Friends or Fellow Travelers?" *Journal of Energy and Development* 4, no. 2 (1979):332–33. The number of government-owned oil companies has increased from 7 in 1950 to 17 in 1960, 33 in 1970, and 51 in 1978; and in 1978 there were 12 partially government-owned or

-controlled companies. Halbouty, "Acceleration in Global Exploration," *American Association of Petroleum Geologists' Bulletin* 62, no. 5 (May 1978):739.

31. A bill to create such a company was introduced by Sen. Adlai Stevenson in 1973, but it received little support.

32. For independent producers, the allowance was gradually scaled back to 15% on the first 1,000 barrels a day, or the first 6 million cubic feet of natural gas. *PE* (May 1975), p. 174.

33. Ibid., and *BW*, Apr. 14, 1975, p. 21.

34. *BW*, July 19, 1976, p. 23.

35. *NYT*, May 15, 1979, p. D2.

36. *BW*, Jan. 28, 1980, p. 120; Hartshorn, *Objectives of the Petroleum Exporting Countries*, p. 27; *NYT*, May 15, 1979, p. D2; and Arnold E. Safer, *International Oil Policy* (Lexington, Mass.: Heath, 1979), p. 79.

37. *BW*, June 23, 1975, p. 56, and Mar. 6, 1978, p. 29; and *PE* (June 1979), p. 233.

38. *PE* (June 1979), p. 233.

39. Great Britain, which wants as much North Sea Oil as possible refined at home, blocked the plan. Great Britain has also opposed other EEC efforts to reduce European refining capacity. *PE* (Nov. 1976), p. 371, (Aug. 1977), pp. 294–96, (Sept. 1977), p. 338, (Feb. 1978), p. 43, (July 1978), p. 295, and (Mar. 1978), p. 118.

40. *PE* (Sept. 1978), p. 375.

41. *BW*, Sept. 12, 1977, p. 72. In addition to higher average costs these small refineries also tend to extract less in products from a barrel of crude than their larger competitors. *NYT*, Nov. 15, 1977, p. 61.

42. For example, if the average price of all the crude oil consumed in the U.S., both imported and domestic, was $10.50 a barrel, then a refiner that bought imported oil at $14 received an entitlements credit of $3.50, effectively reducing the price of the imported oil.

43. The main exception involved residual oil, which U.S. refineries are not geared to producing and, therefore, import in large quantities. *PE* (Dec. 1976), p. 486.

44. *PE* (Mar. 1975), p. 91 (May 1975), p. 181, and (Mar. 1976), p. 93; *MNC Report*, pp. 158–59 and 162; and *NYT*, Mar. 11, 1979, p. 11.

45. *PE* (May 1975), p. 183.

46. See Daniel M. Holland and Stewart C. Myers, "Trends in Corporate Profitability and Capital Costs," Sloan School of Management, Massachusetts Institute of Technology, WP #999–78. Since, to the author's knowledge, calculations for the oil industry have not been made, this conclusion is tentative. It is based on the following reasoning. Given that the real rate of return in U.S. industry has declined and given that the nominal rate of return in the U.S. oil industry has followed a course broadly similar to the nominal rate of return in all U.S. industry, then the real rate of return in the U.S. oil industry must also have declined.

47. *MNC Report*, p. 162.

48. Exxon's rate of return on average capital employed was as follows (all figures are from Exxon annual reports; the 1975–78 and 1979–81 averages were computed by the author):

	1975	1976	1977	1978	1979	1980	1981	Average 1975–78	Average 1979–81
U.S.									
Exploration and production	26.1	21.2	20.2	20.5	22.6	29.2	24.8	22.0	25.5
Refining and marketing	9.6	11.6	10.0	10.7	4.0	7.9	3.5	10.5	5.1
Chemical	21.8	26.4	18.0	14.6	16.1	8.7	7.5	20.2	10.8
Foreign									
Exploration and production	46.7	30.3	25.9	25.7	30.5	36.7	37.0	32.2	34.7
Refining and marketing	5.7	4.2	9.1	10.5	24.1	22.6	11.6	7.4	19.4
Chemical	9.6	9.5	7.1	9.8	20.4	20.5	8.9	9.0	16.6
Total	12.4	12.0	12.0	12.5	16.6	18.4	14.4	12.2	16.5

49. George L. Perry, "The United States," in Edward R. Fried and Charles L. Schultze, *Higher Oil Prices and the World Economy* (Washington, D.C.: The Brookings Institution, 1975), p. 79, and *Monthly Energy Review* (Dec. 1979), p. 77.

50. Hartshorn, *Objectives of the Petroleum Exporting Countries*, p. 26; *PE* (Mar. 1975), p. 122, and (Jan. 1976), p. 37; Franklin Tugwell, *The Politics of Oil in Venezuela* (Stanford: Stanford University Press, 1975), p. 150; *BW*, July 14, 1975, p. 140; and *MNC Hearings*, part 7, pp. 226–27.

51. Odell, "The International Oil Companies in the New World Oil Market," *Year Book of World Affairs, 1978*, p. 77.

52. *NYT*, Sept. 30, 1979, p. 46.

53. See *NYT*, Oct. 11, 1977, p. 55.

54. *NYT*, Oct. 11, 1977, p. 55.

55. *NYT*, Feb. 15, 1980, p. A1, and *Wall Street Journal*, Apr. 19, 1982, p. 21.

56. *PE* (Jan. 1976), p. 3.

57. *BW*, Sept. 24, 1979, p. 104.

58. *BW*, Oct. 4, 1976, p. 33, and Aug. 20, 1979, p. 36.

59. *BW*, Apr. 24, 1978, p. 79, and Barnet, "The World's Resources," *The New Yorker*, Mar. 17, 1980, p. 71.

60. Robert Engler, *The Brotherhood of Oil* (Chicago: University of Chicago Press, 1977), pp. 46–47; *PE* (June, 1978), p. 250; and *Wall Street Journal*, May 25, 1977, p. 21.

61. *BW*, Jan. 13, 1975, p. 110.

62. *PE* (Nov. 1978), p. 456. For a more complete listing of U.S. oil companies nonenergy acquisitions, see *BW*, Apr. 24, 1978, p. 77.

63. *BW*, July 24, 1978, p. 88.

64. *BW*, June 13, 1977, p. 80, and July 16, 1979, p. 81.

65. *NYT*, Sept. 25, 1979, p. D15.

66. *BW*, June 13, 1977, p. 82.

67. *BW*, Aug. 11, 1975, p. 54, and May 8, 1978, pp. 79–80.

68. *BW*, Nov. 23, 1974, p. 36.

69. *BW*, Nov. 14, 1977, p. 177.

70. In this period the share of the eight largest oil companies also declined, from 52.4 to 49.3%. National Petroleum News, *Fact Book* (Mid-May 1974), p. 109, and (Mid-June 1979), p. 118.

CHAPTER 13

1. The PLO objected to U.N. Resolution 242 because it referred to the Palestinians only as refugees and made no mention of Palestinian national rights. While the majority of the groups that make up the PLO probably would have been willing to recognize Israel if they had gotten something in return, they would not throw this trump card away in the absence of concessions from Israel. In addition, since the more radical Palestinian groups opposed recognizing Israel under any circumstances, changing the charter would have led to a major crisis within the organization. To avoid this, the charter was left alone, especially since there were few incentives for doing otherwise.

2. *BW*, June 19, 1978, p. 43.

3. *NYT*, Jan. 24, 1977, p. 3.

4. *BW*, Feb. 7, 1977, p. 42.

5. *NYT*, July 21, 1977, p. A4.

6. *NYT*, Nov. 7, 1977, p. 3.

7. *NYT*, Dec. 6, 1977, pp. 1 and 7.

8. Amos Perlmutter, "A Race against Time: The Egyptian-Israeli Negotiations over the Future of Palestine," *Foreign Affairs* 57 (1979):1000, and *NYT*, Dec. 5, 1977, p. 3.

9. *NYT*, Dec. 17, 1977, p. 10.

10. *NYT*, Mar. 13, 1978, p. A10.

11. *NYT*, Mar. 18, 1978, p. 1.

12. *BW*, Oct. 8, 1979, p. 47.

13. *Los Angeles Times*, Nov. 3, 1978, p. 15.

14. Ibid., Nov. 6, 1978, p. 1.

15. *BW,* Mar. 22, 1976, p. 58, and *NYT,* Nov. 26, 1978, p. 2E.

16. George Lenczowski, "The Arc of Crisis: Its Central Sector," *Foreign Affairs* 57, no. 4 (1979):806, and *Berkeley Gazette,* Oct. 24, 1978, p. 1.

17. *NYT,* Nov. 11, 1978, p. 5, and *BW,* Nov. 27, 1978, p. 48.

18. *NYT,* Feb. 14, 1979, p. 2E.

19. Lenczowski, "The Arc of Crisis," *Foreign Affairs* vol. 57, no. 4 (1979):806, and *NYT,* Nov. 23, 1978, p. 2.

20. Between 1956 and 1976 the educated middle class increased from 6% to 13% of Iran's employed population. James A. Bill, "Iran and the Crisis of '78," *Foreign Affairs* 57, no. 2 (1978–79):333.

21. *NYT,* Apr. 2, 1978, p. E5, and Feb. 12, 1979, p. A12.

22. *NYT,* May 6, 1979, p. E25.

23. *NYT,* Dec. 31, 1978, p. 1, and *PE* (Dec. 1978), p. 503.

24. *PE* (Feb. 1979), p. 54.

25. *BW,* Dec. 18, 1978, p. 36.

26. *NYT,* Dec. 31, 1978, p. 1.

27. See, e.g., Penrose, "OPEC's Importance in the World Oil Industry," *International Affairs* 55, no. 1 (Jan. 1979): 25, and *PE* (Dec. 1978), p. 509.

28. *Petroleum Intelligence Weekly,* Dec. 25, 1978, p. 9. Morgan Guaranty estimated that since 1974 OPEC's real per barrel income had declined at least 20%. *World Financial Markets* (May 1979), pp. 2 and 3.

29. *PE* (Dec. 1978), p. 499.

30. *PE* (Sept. 1979), p. 391. There is considerable controversy about Saudi Arabia's sustainable capacity in this period. *Petroleum Intelligence Weekly* listed it as 11.84 mb/d, the U.S. Energy Department at 10.7 mb/d, and the CIA at 10.4 mb/d (*PIW,* Jan. 29, 1979, p. 9; *BW,* Mar. 19, 1979, p. 28; and *International Energy Statistical Review,* Nov. 29, 1978, p. 3, and Jan. 10, 1979, p. 3). According to a report by the Senate Subcommittee on International Economic Policy, it was only 10.1 mb/d (*MNC Saudi Oil Report,* p. 15). In any case, it is possible to produce at levels somewhat above capacity for short periods, and this may have been what Saudi Arabia was doing.

31. *PE* (Jan. 1979), p. 3, and *NYT,* Dec. 15, 1978, p. D5.

32. *PE* (Jan. 1979), p. 2.

33. *NYT,* Dec. 27, 1978, p. 1, and Dec. 28, 1978, p. 1.

34. The Soviet Union played little, if any, role in the Shah's downfall; nor did it attack the Shah as it might have, if it wished his downfall (*NYT,* Jan. 2, 1979, p. 3). In fact, in the years preceding his downfall, the Soviet Union had maintained good relations with the Shah, and appeared to prefer the Shah to an anti-Communist Islamic government on its southern flank.

35. *NYT,* Apr. 25, 1979, p. 23.

36. *BW,* Feb. 19, 1979, p. 36.

37. *BW,* Jan. 15, 1979, p. 34, Feb. 5, 1979, p. 43, and Oct. 8, 1979, p. 46.

38. The text of the treaty is reprinted in *NYT,* Mar. 27, 1979, pp. A14 and A15.

39. Even before the treaty, Egypt and Israel were the two largest recipients of U.S. aid. Since the 1973 Arab-Israeli war, the U.S. had poured more than $10 billion into Israel; since 1975, the U.S. had given Egypt $3.4 billion in aid, making Egypt the largest recipient of U.S. civilian aid. According to calculations by the Agency for International Development, U.S. per capita assistance to Egypt exceeded what the Marshall Plan provided to all of Europe, even when adjusted for inflation. *NYT,* Feb. 16, 1979, p. 2, Mar. 20, 1979, p. 1, and Mar. 26, 1979, p. 5.

40. *NYT,* Mar. 15, 1979, p. A14.

41. *NYT,* Mar. 27, 1979, p. A1.

42. Quoted in *MEES,* Mar. 26, 1979, p. 2.

43. *NYT,* Mar. 18, 1979, p. 17.

44. *BW,* June 18, 1979, p. 112.

45. *NYT*, Mar. 27, 1979, p. A12.

46. Of the Arab states, only Oman, the Sudan, and Egypt did not attend the meeting.

47. *NYT*, Mar. 27, 1979, p. A13.

48. Ibid., p. A10.

49. *MEES*, Apr. 2, 1979, p. 8.

50. *NYT*, Mar. 28, 1979, p. A13, and Apr. 9, 1979, p. A3.

51. Arab economic aid to Egypt had been running at about $1 billion a year. *NYT*, Apr. 12, 1979, p. A14.

52. *NYT*, Apr. 1, 1979, pp. 1 and 4.

53. *BW*, May 28, 1979, p. 64, and *NYT*, Apr. 1, 1979, p. A1, and Aug. 27, 1979, p. A3.

54. *NYT*, Aug. 26, 1979, p. A3, and *BW*, Sept. 24, 1979, p. 86.

55. Iran also stopped exporting natural gas, which caused serious economic problems in the Soviet border republics of Armenia and Azerbaijan. *NYT*, Jan. 24, 1979, p. A1.

56. *PE* (Sept. 1979), p. 391, and BP, *Statistical Review of the World Oil Industry, 1978*.

57. *PE* (Apr. 1979), p. 138.

58. *NYT*, June 27, 1979, p. A30; *PE* (Feb. 1979), p. 82, and (Sept. 1979), p. 391; and BP, *Statistical Review of the World Oil Industry, 1978*.

59. During the first quarter of 1979, stocks were drawn down by 3.3 mb/d rather than the normal 2 mb/d. *PIW*, May 28, 1979, p. 6.

60. *NYT*, Feb. 18, 1979, p. F16.

61. *PE* (Apr. 1979), p. 138.

62. *PIW*, Mar. 19, 1979, p. 2.

63. *NYT*, Mar. 22, 1979, p. D11.

64. *BW*, Apr. 9, 1979, p. 98, and *NYT*, Mar. 26, 1979, p. D1.

65. *NYT*, Mar. 28, 1979, p. D11; *PE* (May 1979), p. 182; and *BW*, Apr. 9, 1979, p. 96.

66. There were long- and short-term factors behind the growth in differentials. In February 1978 Saudi Arabia decided to limit the light crude it lifted for export from 80% to 65% of its exports. The Saudi policy was intended to bring its light/heavy export ratio into closer line with its light/heavy ratio of reserves (*PE* [Apr. 1978], p. 173). In addition, much of the Iranian oil that was lost was light crude, not easily replaced (*NYT*, Feb. 11, 1979, p. E3).

Only an estimated 40% of U.S. refining capacity could use heavy sour crudes on a sustained basis. Refiners had not invested in desulfurization facilities, claiming that a price differential of $1.50–$2 was needed to justify the investment and that, until recently, differentials had not been that great (*PE* [Feb. 1979], p. 66). Coal and nuclear power had replaced demand for heavy products, but demand for light products (gasoline, aviation fuel, etc.) continued to grow rapidly, increasing the value of light crudes, from which more of these products can be derived. As a result, differentials that had generally been within $2 a barrel widened to $4 early in 1979. *PIW*, July 2, 1979, p. 2.

67. *PE* (Sept. 1979), p. 391.

68. *BW*, July 16, 1979, p. 33, and *PE* (June 1979), pp. 225 and 239.

69. Imports of crude products had generally not been covered by the entitlements program, but under the new program, importers of home heating oil, who paid up to $5 a barrel more than the average U.S. price for their supplies, could claim reimbursement from a fund financed by those who sold cheaper domestic supplies. This evened out the prices in the U.S., as those with domestic supplies raised prices to finance their contributions to the fund while purchasers of imported supplies reduced their price to consumers by the amount they were subsidized. *NYT*, June 2, 1979, p. 31.

70. *NYT*, June 2, 1979, p. 31, and June 5, 1979, p. D4.

71. *NYT*, May 10, 1979, p. D1, June 1, 1979, p. D1, June 2, 1979, p. 31, and June 20, 1979, p. D14.

72. *NYT*, June 27, 1979, p. A1, and June 28, 1979, pp. A1 and D15.

73. *PIW*, July 2, 1979, p. 1.

74. *PE* (Aug. 1979), p. 310.

75. Ibid. According to OPEC officials, as a result of inflation in the cost of OECD exports and the

depreciating value of the dollar, a marker price of $19.50 would be required to match the price that prevailed in the fall of 1974. *PIW*, May 20, 1979, p. 1.

76. *PE* (Oct. 1979), p. 308.

77. *PIW*, July 2, 1979, p. 6, and *NYT*, May 23, 1979, p. D4.

78. *BW*, Dec. 3, 1979, p. 37, and *NYT*, June 16, 1980, p. D7.

79. *PIW*, June 4, 1979, p. 5, and GAO, *Analysis of the Energy and Economic Effects of the Iranian Oil Shortfall* (Washington, D.C.: Government Printing Office, 1979), pp. 3–4.

80. *NYT*, June 23, 1979, p. 29, and June 29, 1979, pp. A1 and D15.

81. *NYT*, June 27, 1979, p. D12.

82. *NYT*, June 30, 1979, pp. 1 and 29.

83. Ibid., and *PIW*, July 9, 1979, p. 4.

84. *BW*, July 16, 1979, p. 33.

85. The U.S. strategic petroleum reserve was of little help in the crisis. It was supposed to have reached 250 million barrels by the end of 1978, and 1 billion barrels ultimately, but in early 1979 it contained only about 70 million barrels, less than 10 days' imports. *BW*, Jan. 22, 1979, p. 78, and Mar. 12, 1979, p. 61, and *PE* (Feb. 1979), p. 48.

86. Calculated from figures in *PE* (June 1979), p. 227, BP, *Statistical Review of the World Oil Industry, 1978,* and *Monthly Energy Review* (Dec. 1979), p. 32. Figures on imports include crude and product imports but not imports for the strategic petroleum reserve.

87. Louis Turner and Audrey Parry, "The Next Steps in Energy Cooperation," *The World Today* 34, no. 3 (Mar. 1978):1, and U.S. Dept. of Energy, *An Analysis of the World Oil Market, 1974–1979* (Washington, D.C.: Government Printing Office, 1979), p. 29.

88. *PE* (Mar. 1979), p. 90, and (Apr. 1979), p. 139. In the first half of 1978 the U.S. imported 7.932 mb/d; in the second half, 8.467 mb/d. In the first half of 1979, U.S. imports fell to 8.245 mb/d. *Monthly Energy Review* (Dec. 1979), p. 32.

89. Turner and Parry, "The Next Steps in Energy Cooperation," *The World Today* 34, no. 3 (Mar. 1978):2, 25, 26, and 30; *BW*, Dec. 3, 1979, p. 37; *NYT*, May 29, 1979, p. A1; and *PIW*, Apr. 9, 1979, p. 5, and June 4, 1979, p. 4.

90. *NYT*, May 29, 1978, p. D8, and Sept. 5, 1979, p. E5.

91. *PE* (Sept. 1979), p. 391.

92. *NYT*, July 8, 1979, p. 30.

93. Stobaugh and Yergin, "Energy: An Emergency Telescoped," *Foreign Affairs* 83, no. 3 (1979):571.

94. *NYT*, May 25, 1979, p. A13.

95. Ibid., p. A1.

96. Part of President Carter's concern with building home heating oil supplies was due to his interest in winning the upcoming New Hampshire Democratic primary in February 1980. He was likely to be challenged by Sen. Kennedy, who would have a good chance of defeating him, especially if the residents of New Hampshire were experiencing shortages of heating oil.

97. Yergin and Stobaugh, "Energy: An Emergency Telescoped," *Foreign Affairs* 83, no. 3 (1979):571, and *NYT*, June 15, 1979, p. E3, and July 8, 1979, p. 30.

98. New York City got only 1 gallon per registered vehicle from the state set-aside in June 1979 and Nassau County got only 1.08 gallons per vehicle, but upstate Hamilton County got 10.14 gallons per vehicle and Essex County got 5.52 gallons. *NYT*, June 24, 1979, p. 22, and July 29, 1979, p. 30.

99. *BW*, Dec. 24, 1979, pp. 84–85, and *NYT*, July 29, 1979, p. 30.

100. Shell's problem was prompted by the allocation system. Because of price controls, it had to keep its price lower than that of other refiners. As a result, consumers rushed to buy Shell, prompting the eventual allocation restrictions. *BW*, Dec. 18, 1978, p. 31.

101. *NYT*, May 6, 1979, p. 18, and May 25, 1979, p. A13.

102. An increase in allocations helped ease the California crisis, as did more effective use of the 5% of available supplies put under state control. *NYT*, May 11, 1979, p. 16, May 25, 1979, p. A1, June 15, 1979, p. E4, and June 24, 1979, p. 22.

103. Stobaugh and Yergin, "Energy: An Emergency Telescoped," *Foreign Affairs* 83, no. 3 (1979):571.

104. Japan also required gasoline stations to close on Sunday, shortened work weeks, and mandated workers to take their one-week vacations. Curbs were placed on the use of air conditioning and neon signs. *NYT,* July 8, 1979, p. 33.

105. Twice in July, dissident ethnic Arabs, who worked in the Iranian oil fields, sabotaged pipelines carrying crude to the giant refinery in Abadan, causing brief disruptions of supply. *PE* (Aug. 1979), pp. 311 and 346, and *BW,* July 30, 1979, p. 46.

106. In the summer of 1979, Algeria, Nigeria, and Kuwait were reported to be considering production cutbacks. *BW,* July 30, 1979, p. 46, and Sept. 24, 1979, pp. 62–63.

107. *BW,* July 16, 1979, p. 33, and July 30, 1979, p. 46, and *PE* (July 1979), p. 306.

108. Supporters of Israel feared that a deal had been struck, with the U.S. agreeing to force concessions from the Israelis on the Palestinian issue in return for increased Saudi oil; but this is unlikely. If Carter failed to deliver, the consequences of such a deal would be disastrous. *NYT,* July 9, 1979, pp. D1 and D5, and July 12, 1979, p. 3, and *BW,* July 16, 1979, p. 32.

109. *PE* (Sept. 1979), p. 394; *BW,* Sept. 24, 1979, p. 63; and *PIW,* Aug. 27, 1979, p. 1.

110. *BW,* Oct. 22, 1979, p. 71; *NYT,* July 25, 1979, p. E3; *PIW,* July 2, 1979, p. 3; and *PE* (Dec. 1979), p. 498.

111. *NYT,* Oct. 9, 1979, pp. D1 and D5, and Oct. 16, 1979, pp. A1 and D12.

112. If ever there was a case of diplomatic incompetence, it was the decision to allow the Shah into the U.S. The U.S. had every reason to suspect that, if the hated Shah was allowed into the U.S., the Iranians would retaliate. The Iranian people knew that the U.S. had placed the Shah on the throne in 1953; that the U.S. had trained Savak, the Shah's intelligence agency; and that the U.S. had supplied the Shah with massive armaments throughout the 1970s. Moreover, the U.S. continued to back the Shah in 1978, as opposition to his regime mounted, and in that year U.S. arms were used against the Shah's opposition. The U.S. then supported the Bakhtiar government, which the Shah had installed in a last-ditch effort to prevent the forces loyal to Ayatollah Khomeini from coming to power.

Despite this history, the Ayatollah indicated, upon coming to power, that he favored maintenance of good relations with the U.S., provided it withdrew its support for the Shah and stayed out of Iran's internal affairs. In fact, during the summer of 1979 U.S./Iranian relations improved, with the U.S. agreeing to send spare parts for weapons delivered during the Shah's rule, and negotiations resumed for the sale of additional arms. However, when the Carter administration allowed the Shah into the U.S., all the old fears of the "imperialist monster" were rekindled; nor is what happened surprising. The U.S. embassy had been seized briefly in Feb. 1979, and in earlier discussions of admitting the Shah into the U.S., President Carter had asked, "When the Iranians take our people in Teheran hostage, what will you advise me then?" *NYT,* Nov. 19, 1979, p. A1.

113. Minutes after Carter announced his decision, Iran said it would stop all its oil exports to the U.S. *NYT,* Nov. 13, 1979, pp. A1 and A10.

114. *PE* (Dec. 1979), p. 538, and *NYT,* Nov. 7, 1979, p. D5, and Nov. 13, 1979, p. A8.

115. Stobaugh and Yergin, "Energy: An Emergency Telescoped," *Foreign Affairs* 83, no. 3 (1979):575, and *NYT,* Dec. 14, 1979, pp. A1 and D5, and Dec. 17, 1979, p. A1.

116. *NYT,* Dec. 23, 1979, p. F4, and Jan. 6, 1980, sec. 12, p. 13.

117. *NYT,* Dec. 21, 1979, pp. A1 and D3, and Dec. 23, 1979, p. F4.

118. *BW,* Jan. 14, 1980, p. 27, and *NYT,* Jan. 7, 1980, p. D1, and Feb. 26, 1980, p. D15.

119. *BW,* Jan. 14, 1980, p. 27, and *NYT,* Dec. 18, 1979, p. D2, Dec. 19, 1979, p. D14, and Dec. 21, 1979, pp. A1 and D3.

120. *BW,* Apr. 7, 1980, p. 34. According to *Petroleum Intelligence Weekly,* 75% of the 1.2 mb/d in OPEC production cutbacks in Jan. were unplanned, i.e., due to reduced liftings by oil companies rather than to explicit decisions by exporting countries. Cited in *NYT,* Mar. 11, 1980, p. D15.

121. *NYT,* Jan. 28, 1980, p. A1, and Jan. 30, 1980, p. D1; and *BW,* Feb. 11, 1980, p. 36.

122. *BW,* June 2, 1980, p. 27.

123. Of course, the distinction between "voluntary" and "involuntary" cuts is often not clear.

124. *NYT*, Mar. 6, 1980, p. D3, Mar. 8, 1980, p. 27, Mar. 10, 1980, p. D1, and Mar. 18, 1980, p. E5.

125. Despite its hard-line position, Iran was quietly reducing its prices as much as $3 a barrel because it lacked customers at the high price it was charging. *NYT*, June 10, 1980, pp. D1 and D11.

126. *NYT*, June 9, 1980, pp. A1 and D10.

127. *NYT*, June 11, 1980, pp. A1 and D4, and June 12, 1980, p. D4.

128. *NYT*, Sept. 15, 1980, pp. D1 and D6, Sept. 16, 1980, pp. A1 and D19, Sept. 17, 1980, p. D16, Sept. 19, 1980, pp. A1, D3, and D11, and Sept. 24, 1980, p. D11.

129. *NYT*, Sept. 25, 1980, p. A16, and Oct. 4, 1980, p. 4.

130. *NYT*, Sept. 25, 1980, p. A1.

131. Computed from data in *PE* (Sept. 1979), p. 391, and (Aug. 1981), p. 368.

132. *NYT*, Sept. 24, 1980, p. D11; *PE* (Nov. 1980), pp. 462 and 506; and *BW*, Dec. 22, 1980, p. 16.

133. *PE* (Jan. 1981), p. 7, and *NYT*, Oct. 16, 1980, p. D1, and Dec. 17, 1980, pp. A1 and D15.

134. *PE* (Jan. 1981), p. 40, (May 1981), pp. 186 and 223 (June 1981), p. 276, and *BW*, Feb. 25, 1981, p. 105. With interest rates high, it costs between $6 and $9 a year to hold a barrel of oil in storage. When prices are rising, companies can recoup these costs through the appreciation in the value of their stocks, but when prices are stagnant or declining, the incentive to unload stocks becomes particularly strong. Indeed, by July 1981 companies were reported to be reducing their stockpiles at rates of 500,000 to 1 mb/d. *NYT*, June 28, 1981, p. F2, and July 15, 1981, p. D3.

135. *PE* (July 1981), p. 319; *BW*, Mar. 9, 1981, p. 28; and *NYT*, May 11, 1981, p. D1.

136. *BW*, June 29, 1981, p. 49, and Aug. 31, 1981, pp. 46 and 47, and *PE* (Aug. 1981), p. 368.

137. *NYT*, May 26, 1981, p. A1, and May 27, 1981, p. A1; *BW*, June 8, 1981, p. 57; and *PE* (July 1981), p. 319.

138. *NYT*, Aug. 19, 1981, pp. D1 and D4, Aug. 20, 1981, p. D13, Aug. 22, 1981, pp. 1 and 39, and Aug. 27, 1981, pp. A1 and D11.

139. *NYT*, Oct. 30, 1981, pp. A1 and D13, and Oct. 31, 1981, p. 33.

140. *NYT*, Nov. 10, 1981, p. D1, Dec. 12, 1981, p. 40, Mar. 8, 1982, p. D10, Mar. 14, 1982, p. D11, and Mar. 16, 1982, p. D6; *PE* (Jan. 1982), p. 3; and *BW*, Mar. 22, 1982, p. 69.

141. Cited in *NYT*, Feb. 22, 1982, p. D8.

142. *NYT*, Feb. 9, 1982, p. A1, Feb. 23, 1982, pp. A1 and D14, and Mar. 3, 1982, pp. A1 and D14, and *BW*, Mar. 22, 1982, pp. 66 and 69.

143. *PE* (Jan. 1982), p. 5; *NYT*, Feb. 16, 1982, p. D12, Mar. 4, 1982, p. D11, Mar. 7, 1982, p. 17, and Mar. 16, 1982, p. D6; and *Wall Street Journal*, Mar. 8, 1982, p. 1.

144. *NYT*, Mar. 4, 1982, p. D1, Mar. 7, 1982, pp. 1 and 17, and Mar. 19, 1982, pp. D1 and D11.

145. *PIW*, Mar. 29, 1982, p. 6 and (supplement), p. 1, and *PE* (Apr. 1982), p. 122.

146. *NYT*, Mar. 20, 1982, p. 1, and Mar. 21, 1982, pp. 1 and 4, and *PIW*, Mar. 29, 1982, p. 6.

147. *NYT*, May 19, 1982, p. D1, May 20, 1982, p. D19, May 22, 1982, pp. 41–2, July 8, 1982, p. D18, and July 10, 1982, p. 35; *BW*, June 7, 1982, p. 26; and *PE* (Aug. 1982), p. 315.

148. *NYT*, July 12, 1982, p. D1, and *PE* (Aug. 1982), p. 315.

149. *PIW*, Mar. 29, 1982, p. 6.

CHAPTER 14

1. *NYT*, Dec. 20, 1979, p. D1, and Dec. 21, 1979, p. 34, and Hollis B. Chenery, "Restructuring the World Economy: Round II," *Foreign Affairs* 59, no. 5 (1981):1113.

2. IMF, *Annual Report, 1979*, p. 2.

3. Shonfield, "The World Economy, 1979," *Foreign Affairs* 58, no. 3 (1979):619, and *BW*, May 5, 1980, p. 70.

4. *NYT*, Feb. 15, 1982, p. D5, and Mar. 16, 1982, p. D6; Morgan Guaranty Trust Co., *World Financial Markets* (Mar. 1982), p. 4; and *BW*, Mar. 22, 1982, pp. 67 and 69.

5. Healey, "Oil, Money and Recession," *Foreign Affairs* 58, no. 2 (1979–80):222.

6. *NYT*, Dec. 29, 1981, pp. A1 and D5, and *BW*, June 30, 1980, p. 10, and Apr. 13, 1981, p. 127.

7. *BW*, Mar. 16, 1981, pp. 57–58, Apr. 27, 1981, pp. 64–65, May 18, 1981, pp. 58 and 63, and July 27, 1981, p. 22.

8. *BW*, Oct. 6, 1980, p. 73. According to the OECD, the "low absorbers"—Saudi Arabia, Kuwait, the United Arab Emirates, Oman, Qatar, and Libya—ran a combined current account surplus of $42 billion in 1979 and $95 billion in 1980, while the other OPEC countries had a combined surplus of $24 billion and $25 billion in those years. *OECD Economic Outlook* 29 (July 1981):121.

9. *BW*, June 30, 1980, pp. 39 and 40, and Oct. 6, 1980, pp. 70–84, and *NYT*, Jan. 19, 1982, p. D1, and Feb. 15, 1982, p. D5.

10. *PE* (June 1981), p. 257; *NYT*, June 4, 1981, p. D4, and Oct. 6, 1981, p. A1; and *BW*, Jan. 11, 1982, p. 36. In May 1982 Kuwait acquired roughly 25 percent of Hoechst, the West German chemical giant. Kuwait had previously acquired significant minority shares in Daimler-Benz, the auto maker; Korf-Stahl, a steel company; Metallgesellschaft, a metals concern; and Volkswagen do Brasil. Also in May 1982, Saudi Arabia purchased a 17.87 percent interest in IBH Holding, a West German construction machinery company. *NYT*, May 18, 1982, pp. D1 and D4.

11. *BW*, Dec. 3, 1979, p. 110, and June 30, 1980, p. 39.

12. Credit Suisse claims it had "absolutely reliable information" that Iran intended to repay all its foreign obligations and that moves to declare default were therefore unnecessary. *NYT*, Nov. 23, 1979, p. D1, and Dec. 3, 1979, p. D4.

13. *BW*, Nov. 26, 1979, p. 31.

14. *BW*, Feb. 4, 1980, p. 42, and *PE* (Jan. 1981), p. 2.

15. *World Financial Markets* (May 1981), p. 8, and *BW*, July 27, 1981, p. 70.

16. *NYT*, May 8, 1981, p. D1, and Nov. 10, 1981, p. A1, and *PE* (Oct. 1980), p. 430, and (Dec. 1981), p. 542.

17. *BW*, Nov. 18, 1979, p. 179, and *NYT*, Feb. 3, 1980, sec. 12, p. 61.

18. *World Financial Markets* (May 1981), pp. 5 and 11; *BW*, July 27, 1981, p. 15; and Chenery, "Restructuring the World Economy," *Foreign Affairs* 59 (1981): 1118.

19. *NYT*, Feb. 21, 1982, p. E3, May 13, 1982, p. D6, Aug. 20, 1982, p. D15, Aug. 23, 1982, p. A4, and Sept. 7, 1982, p. A1.

20. *NYT*, Aug. 21, 1982, pp. 1 and 32, Aug. 31, 1982, pp. D1 and D5, and Sept. 2, 1982, pp. D1 and D6.

21. *NYT*, Aug. 26, 1982, p. A27, Sept. 2, 1982, pp. D1 and D2, and Sept. 7, 1982, p. D5, and *BW*, Sept. 13, 1982, p.30.

22. *NYT*, Oct. 24, 1981, p. 6, and Oct. 25, 1981, p. 12.

23. *BW*, Dec. 24, 1979, p. 83. The reactor that France was initially to send was blown up by saboteurs. *NYT*, July 12, 1979, p. D14, and *PE* (Sept. 1979), p. 351.

24. *BW*, July 30, 1979, p. 38; *Petroleum Intelligence Weekly*, Oct. 15, 1979, p. 3; and *PE* (Sept. 1979), p. 370.

25. *BW*, Dec. 24, 1979, p. 83.

26. Ibid.; *NYT*, Dec. 30, 1979, p. E2, and May 5, 1980, p. D1; and *PE* (July 1981), p. 319.

27. *BW*, Dec. 24, 1979, p. 86, and *NYT*, Sept. 27, 1979, p. D4.

28. *NYT*, Sept. 27, 1979, p. D1, and Dec. 11, 1979, pp. D1 and D12, and *BW*, Dec. 3, 1979, p. 37, and Dec. 24, 1979, p. 86.

29. *Economic Report of the President, 1982* (Washington, D.C.: Government Printing Office, 1982), p. 355; *NYT*, Feb. 14, 1982, sec. 12, p. 18; BP, *Statistical Review of the World Oil Industry*, various issues; *PE* (Jan. 1982), p. 2; and *Wall Street Journal*, Jan. 27, 1982, p. 1.

30. *NYT*, May 23, 1980, p. E5.

31. *PE* (Dec. 1980), p. 544, and (Jan. 1981), p. 7.

32. The consuming countries' commitment to coal was encouraged by the "World Coal Study,"

done by a group of scientists, headed by Professor Carroll L. Wilson of M.I.T., and released in May 1980. The study concluded that by 1990 coal production could be doubled and provide two-thirds of the energy needed to fuel the world's economic growth over the next two decades. Moreover, the study maintained that this could be done without significant harm to the environment. However, the U.S. coal industry maintains that without relaxation of environmental standards, there will not be large increases in coal production. *NYT*, June 18, 1980, p. D2, and June 24, 1980, pp. D1 and D5.

33. *NYT*, June 24, 1980, p. A7.

34. *NYT*, July 22, 1981, p. D18.

35. *PE* (July 1979), p. 292; *NYT*, June 11, 1979, p. D5; and *BW*, July 2, 1979, p. 19, and Dec. 3, 1979, p. 36,

36. *BW*, Aug. 20, 1979, p. 10, and *NYT*, Mar. 13, 1980, p. 5.

37. *NYT*, June 29, 1979, p. D4, Dec. 11, 1979, p. D12, and Dec. 30, 1979, p. E2; *BW*, Jan. 24, 1980, p. 24; and *PIW*, Mar. 5, 1979, p. 6, Apr. 2, 1979, p. 4, and July 2, 1979, p. 4.

38. *BW*, Feb. 4, 1980, p. 42.

39. *NYT*, Apr. 3, 1979, p. D13, and May 9, 1979, p. D1.

40. *BW*, May 14, 1979, p. 34, and *NYT*, Apr. 27, 1979, p. A1.

41. *NYT*, Apr. 22, 1979, p. E4.

42. *BW*, Aug. 13, 1979, p. 99.

43. *PE* (Aug. 1979), p. 332, and *NYT*, July 17, 1979, p. A12.

44. *NYT*, Jan. 23, 1980, p. D1, and Mar. 28, 1980, p. D3.

45. *NYT*, Feb. 25, 1980, p. D2. The phaseout, at 3% a month, will last 33 months, ensuring that more than the $227.3 billion initially agreed to will ultimately be raised by the windfall profits tax. This sum does not include the additional federal revenues from the corporate income tax. *NYT*, Feb. 25, 1980, p. D2.

46. *NYT*, Jan. 23, 1980, p. D1, and Feb. 25, 1980, pp. D1 and D2.

47. *NYT*, Jan. 29, 1981, pp. A1 and D6, and *BW*, Aug. 17, 1981, p. 30.

48. *NYT*, Dec. 16, 1981, p. D1, and Mar. 2, 1982, p. D1, and *BW*, Mar. 15, 1982, p. 36.

49. *NYT*, Sept. 11, 1980, p. D1, and *PE* (Feb. 1982), p. 56. To promote development of a synthetic fuels industry, the West German government is providing subsidies to German industry. The West German program is aimed at having as many as 14 demonstration plants on line by 1992. *BW*, Apr. 21, 1980, p. 74.

50. *NYT*, June 28, 1980, p. 1.

51. *NYT*, Mar. 6, 1980, p. D1, May 22, 1980, pp. D1 and D5; *BW*, Mar. 24, 1980, p. 58; and *PE* (Feb. 1982), p. 44.

52. *NYT*, Mar. 15, 1980, p. A1, June 5, 1980, p. 1, June 6, 1980, p. 1, June 7, 1980, p. 1, and June 10, 1980, pp. A1 and D12.

53. *NYT*, Dec. 17, 1981, p. A1, and Mar. 25, 1982, p. D1, and *BW*, Nov. 23, 1981, p. 136.

54. *BW*, Apr. 30, 1979, p. 15.

55. *NYT*, Jan. 25, 1980, p. A13.

56. *NYT*, Apr. 2, 1979, p. A15.

57. *NYT*, Mar. 14, 1979, p. A1, and Apr. 8, 1979, sec. 4, p. 1.

58. Stobaugh and Yergin, "Energy: An Emergency Telescoped," *Foreign Affairs* 58, no. 3 (1979):581–82, and *NYT*, Mar. 16, 1980, sec. 3, p. 9.

59. *BW*, Nov. 19, 1979, p. 43, and *NYT*, Dec. 2, 1979, p. E22, Mar. 16, 1980, sec. 3, p. 1, and June 17, 1980, p. E17.

60. *Monthly Energy Review* (July 1981), p. 72.

61. *NYT*, Apr. 11, 1979, p. A1, Mar. 16, 1980, sec. 3, p. 1, Aug. 16, 1981, p. A33, and *BW*, Feb. 18, 1980, p. 64.

62. *Monthly Energy Review* (July 1981), pp. 72 and 74; *NYT*, May 29, 1979, p. 23, July 5, 1979, p. A14; and Barnet, "The World's Resources," *The New Yorker*, Mar. 17, 1980, p. 77.

63. *NYT*, Oct. 9, 1981, p. A1, and Aug. 24, 1982, p. A12.

64. Reactor manufacturers in West Germany, France, and the U.S. were hurt by the cancellation

of Iranian nuclear deals following the fall of the Shah. Iran was the only OPEC country with a large nuclear power program. J. E. Hartshorn, *Objectives of the Petroleum Exporting Countries* (Nicosia, Cyprus: Middle East Petroleum and Economics Publications, 1978), p. 38; *NYT*, Jan. 30, 1979, p. 13E, Apr. 1, 1979, p. 32, May 17, 1979, p. A7, June 8, 1979, p. 1, June 10, 1979, p. 16, and Mar. 14, 1982, p. 17; CIA, *The World Oil Market in the Years Ahead* (Washington, D.C.: Government Printing Office, 1979), p. 53; and *BW*, Feb. 23, 1981, p. 52.

65. *NYT*, Apr. 6, 1979, p. 11, Feb. 27, 1980, p. D1, Nov. 9, 1980, p. 14, and March 14, 1982, p. 17, and *PE* (July 1981), p. 308.

66. *PE* (May 1979), p. 210, and *NYT*, Apr. 24, 1980, p. A1.

67. CIA, *The World Oil Market in the Years Ahead*, pp. 56–57; *PE* (June 1979), p. 255, (July 1982), p. 284; and *NYT*, Dec. 27, 1979, p. D4.

68. *BW*, Mar. 19, 1979, pp. 89, 90, and 104, Mar. 17, 1980, pp. 3 and 116, Mar. 16, 1981, pp. 87 and 100, and Mar. 15, 1982, pp. 91 and 104.

69. *NYT*, Mar. 11, 1979, sec. 3, p. 11, and July 30, 1979, p. D3; *PIW*, Apr. 2, 1979, p. 4; and *BW*, Oct. 8, 1979, p. 31.

70. *PIW*, Apr. 30, 1979 (supplement), p. 2; Stobaugh and Yergin, "Energy: An Emergency Telescoped," *Foreign Affairs* 58, no. 3 (1979):575; and *BW*, Feb. 25, 1980, p. 51.

71. *PE* (Oct. 1979), pp. 430 and 442, and *NYT*, Aug. 23, 1979, p. D6, and Nov. 8, 1979, p. D5. The oil companies tried to explain their huge 1979 profit increases by claiming they stemmed primarily from increases in foreign profits, but the distinction between domestic and foreign profits is hardly clearcut. If companies choose to sell their low-priced Saudi oil in Western Europe and their higher-price Iranian oil in the U.S., have they really earned more in Western Europe than in the U.S.? Similarly, if a company makes a large profit on the "sale" of crude oil to its refinery in the Caribbean and then that refinery "loses" money by selling the products made from that crude in the U.S., has the company really earned money overseas and lost it in the U.S.? In any case, in 1980 profits from U.S. operations rose by 42% while profits from foreign operations rose by 25%. *PE* (Mar. 1981), p. 103.

72. *PE* (Sept. 1979), p. 379, and *BW*, Aug. 18, 1980, p. 87.

73. *PE* (Mar. 1981), p. 103, (June 1981), p. 268, (Mar. 1982), p. 98 and (May 1982), p. 173.

74. *PE* (Sept. 1980), p. 383 (Apr. 1981), pp. 153, 163, and 170, (July 1981), p. 285, (July 1982), p. 272, and *NYT*, Mar. 18, 1982, p. D1.

75. *Fortune*, Jan. 28, 1980, p. 55. The majors position in downstream markets has also eroded. While the seven major oil companies accounted for 51% of all noncommunist oil product sales in 1973, by 1978 this had fallen to 44% and by 1981 to 41%. *PE* (July 1982), p. 272.

76. *PIW*, Mar. 5, 1979, p. 2, Mar. 26, 1979, p. 3; *BW*, Mar. 19, 1979, p. 29; and *PE* (Feb. 1979), p. 56 (Apr. 1979), p. 153, and (May 1979), p. 218.

77. *NYT*, Jan. 21, 1980, pp. D1 and D2, and Apr. 17, 1980, pp. D1 and D28.

78. The "official" reason for the nationalization was that BP planned to sell Nigerian oil in South Africa, in contravention of Nigeria's export embargo, but both BP and the U.K. Foreign Office denied this. Nigeria was able to nationalize BP largely because Shell, BP's partner in the joint venture, had been supplying almost all of the expatriate staff, and the tight market made it easy for Nigeria to sell its additional participation crude. Nigeria warned Washington that if it lifted economic sanctions against the government of Bishop Muzorewa, it should expect "an appropriate response." *NYT*, Aug. 1, 1979, p. D3, Aug. 2, 1979, p. A2, and Oct. 27, 1979, p. 19, and *PE* (Sept. 1979), p. 377.

79. *NYT*, May 29, 1979, p. D8, and Mar. 3, 1980, p. E4.

80. *NYT*, Apr. 17, 1980, p. D23; *BW*, Dec. 24, 1979, p. 82; and *PE* (May 1979), p. 218, and (July 1982), pp. 271–2.

81. *PE* (July 1980), pp. 329–31.

82. *NYT*, July 13, 1981, pp. D1 and D4.

83. *NYT*, Nov. 13, 1981, pp. A1 and D15, Dec. 23, 1981, p. D2, and Jan. 6, 1982, pp. D1 and D11. In June 1982 Mobil announced that it too was withdrawing from Libya, but a month later the

company withdrew its "notice of surrender". Both Exxon and Mobil were reported to have been pressured by Saudi Arabia to withdraw from Libya. Then on Dec. 30, 1982, Mobil terminated its activities in Libya. *NYT,* Apr. 14, 1982, p. D10, June 10, 1982, p. D1, July 21, 1982, p. D4, and Jan. 5, 1983, p. D6.

84. *NYT,* Feb. 22, 1982, p. D8, Mar. 27, 1982, p. 29, Mar. 29, 1982, p. D9, and Apr. 1, 1982, p. D1; *PE* (Apr. 1982), p. 154, (July 1982), p. 297; and *Wall Street Journal,* Apr. 5, 1982, p. 2.

85. *BW,* Oct. 13, 1980, p. 118, Dec. 22, 1980, pp. 55 and 61, Mar. 23, 1981, p. 48, and *NYT,* July 15, 1981, sec. 3, p. 20.

86. *PE* (July 1981), p. 283; *BW,* Apr. 23, 1979, p. 46, Aug. 25, 1980, p. 66 and May 24, 1982, p. 100; and *PIW,* Aug. 27, 1979, p. 1.

87. Prior to Kuwait's cutbacks, Exxon bought 350,000 b/d of Kuwait's oil from BP. *PE* (May 1979), p. 218.

88. *NYT,* May 19, 1979, p. D2, and *BW,* June 2, 1980, pp. 27–28, and June 7, 1982, p. 89.

89. *BW,* July 16, 1979, pp. 82 and 84, and *NYT,* Aug. 5, 1981, p. D5.

90. *NYT,* Mar. 13, 1981, p. A1, and Mar. 28, 1982, p. F1; *PE* (Aug. 1981), p. 331; and *BW,* June 15, 1981, p. 37.

91. *BW,* Dec. 3, 1979, p. 92.

92. *NYT,* June 4, 1981, p. D1, and *PE* (Mar. 1981), p. 119.

93. *NYT,* June 2, 1981, p. D13, and Aug. 6, 1981, pp. A1 and D6.

94. *BW,* July 13, 1981, p. 21, and *NYT,* July 7, 1981, pp. A1 and D4, July 24, 1981, p. D1, and Aug. 6, 1981, pp. A1 and D6.

95. *PE* (Aug. 1981), p. 331, and *NYT,* Aug. 7, 1981, p. D1.

96. *NYT,* Mar. 17, 1981, p. D1; *BW,* July 20, 1981, p. 53; and *PE* (Aug. 1981), p. 331. Since 1979, energy company acquisitions of oil companies include Tenneco's $1.6 billion purchase of Houston Oil and Minerals Corp., Getty's Jan. 1980 $631 million purchase of Reserve Oil and Gas Co., Occidental's merger with Crestmont Oil and Gas Co., and Dome's takeover of Siebens Oil and Gas, Mesa Petroleum, and Kaiser Petroleum. *BW,* June 23, 1980, pp. 99 and 102, July 7, 1980, p. 86, Dec. 22, 1980, p. 60, and Dec. 29, 1980, p. 89.

97. *NYT,* Dec. 1, 1981, p. A1, Dec. 11, 1981, p. D6, Jan. 7, 1982, p. D4, and Jan. 8, 1982, p. D3.

98. *NYT,* June 18, 1982, p. A1, June 19, 1982, p. D1, Aug. 7, 1982, pp. 1 and 35, Aug. 14, 1982, p. 36, Aug. 16, 1982, p. D3, and Aug. 26, 1982, p. 1.

99. *NYT,* Nov. 6, 1979, p. D6.

100. CIA, *International Energy Statistical Review* (Sept, 29, 1981), p. 3, and *PE* (Feb. 1980), p. 75.

101. *PE* (Jan. 1982), p. 6; CIA, *The World Oil Market in the Years Ahead,* pp. iv and 47; and *PIW,* Aug. 6, 1979, p. 1.

102. *NYT,* June 25, 1979, p. D4, Apr. 15, 1980, p. D7, Dec. 11, 1980, p. D1, and Jan. 13, 1982, p. D13.

103. *BW,* Mar. 9, 1981, p. 28, and July 27, 1981, p. 41; *PE* (Dec. 1981), p. 544; and *NYT,* Jan. 13, 1982, pp. D1 and D13. Saudi Arabia is planning to build the world's largest oil stockpile as a hedge against disruptions that might affect its oil production. When completed (in the 1990s), the 1.5-billion-barrel stockpile will enable Saudi Arabia to pump more than 4 mb/d, even if all its productive capacity were destroyed. *NYT,* Oct. 14, 1981, p. D2.

104. *PE* (July 1981), p. 311.

105. *PE* (Sept. 1979), p. 365, and (Jan. 1981), p. 30, and *NYT,* Oct. 15, 1979, pp. D1 and D5.

106. *BW,* Aug. 10, 1981, p. 53; *PE* (Sept. 1980), p. 370 (Feb. 1981), p. 53 (July 1981), p. 283 (Nov. 1981), p. 463, and (Mar. 1982), p. 107; and *NYT,* Jan. 12, 1981, pp. D1 and D6.

107. *PE* (Sept. 1980), p. 375, and (Dec. 1980), p. 513; *BW,* Sept. 22, 1980, p. 123, Apr. 13, 1981, p. 164, and Apr. 27, 1981, p. 39; and *NYT,* Dec. 27, 1980, p. 30.

108. *NYT,* Feb. 4, 1982, pp. A1 and D5, May 10, 1982, p. D1, and Aug. 16, 1982, p. D3, and *PE* (Mar. 1982), p. 105.

109. *PE* (Dec. 1980), pp. 513 and 515, and (Aug. 1981), pp. 335, 337, and 339.

110. *NYT,* Nov. 2, 1980, p. A6, Mar. 4, 1981, p. D3, June 26, 1981, p. A26, and May 24, 1982, p. D11; *PE* (May 1980), p. 194 (Jan. 1982), p. 6, and (Mar. 1982), p. 86; CIA, *The World Oil Market in the Years Ahead,* p. 6; *Wall Street Journal,* Jan. 27, 1982, p. 24 and table 11–4.

111. *NYT Magazine,* Aug. 30, 1981, p. 22; CIA, *The World Oil Market in the Years Ahead,* pp. 2 and 3; and *PE* (June 1980), p. 291, and (Aug. 1981), p. 335.

112. *BW,* June 1, 1981, p. 32, and June 8, 1981, p. 124, and *NYT,* July 21, 1982, p. A18.

113. *BW,* Apr. 13, 1981, p. 165, and June 8, 1981, p. 66; *PE* (July 1981), pp. 305 and 307, and (Jan. 1982), p. 25; and *NYT,* June 13, 1981, p. 29.

114. *PE* (Dec. 1980), pp. 510 and 512, and *BW,* Nov. 17, 1980, pp. 164 and 166.

115. *BW,* Dec. 8, 1980, p. 24, and Mar. 16, 1981, pp. 43–44; *NYT,* Nov. 21, 1980, p. D4, Sept. 3, 1981, p. D11, and Dec. 9, 1981, p. D1; and *PE* (Oct. 1981), p. 435.

116. *BW,* July 13, 1981, p. 21, Aug. 17, 1981, pp. 41 and 42, May 17, 1982, p. 30, and June 28, 1982, p. 80; *PE* (Feb. 1982), p. 74; and *NYT,* Mar. 26, 1982, p. D3.

117. *BW,* July 30, 1979, p. 45, and *PE* (Aug. 1979), p. 316 (Jan. 1981), p. 19, (Apr. 1981), p. 156, and (June 1982), p. 232.

118. *NYT,* May 19, 1981, pp. A1 and D11, and July 13, 1981, p. A15.

119. *NYT,* Sept. 3, 1981, pp. A1 and D14.

120. *BW,* July 7, 1980, p. 20, and Apr. 27, 1981, p. 67; Exxon, *World Energy Outlook* (Dec. 1980), p. 22; *PE* (Aug. 1981), p. 355, and (Jan. 1982), p. 28; and *NYT,* Dec. 6, 1981, p. 17.

121. *NYT,* Nov. 21, 1981, p. A1, Feb. 14, 1982, p. E5, June 19, 1982, p. 1, June 21, 1982, p. D1, Aug. 27, 1982, pp. A1 and D14, and Sept. 2, 1982, p. A1; *BW,* July 5, 1982, p. 21; and *PE* (Jan. 1982), p. 13.

122. *BW,* Apr. 27, 1981, p. 67; *NYT,* July 26, 1981, p. 8, and Sept. 3, 1981, p. D13; and *Wall Street Journal,* Dec. 18, 1979, p. 32.

123. *PE* (Feb. 1981), p. 58, and (May 1981), p. 218, and *NYT,* June 11, 1981, p. D16, June 30, 1981, p. D18, Jan. 19, 1982, p. D13, and Mar. 26, 1982, p. D4.

124. *PE* (Sept. 1980), p. 369, and (Nov. 1980), p. 498, and *Oil and Gas Journal,* Dec. 28, 1981, pp. 86 and 87.

125. *NYT,* Aug. 17, 1980, p. 6, Apr. 6, 1981, pp. D1 and D6, July 6, 1981, p. D4, and Sept. 2, 1981, p. D9; *PE* (Aug. 1981), p. 343; and *BW,* May 25, 1981, p. 58.

126. *PE* (Jan. 1981), p. 6 (Mar. 1981), pp. 98 and 121; *BW,* Aug. 10, 1981, pp. 53 and 63; *NYT,* May 8, 1981, p. D1; and Exxon, *World Energy Outlook* (Dec. 1980), p. 22.

127. *PE* (Oct. 1980), p. 429.

128. *PE* (Feb. 1980), p. 63; *NYT,* Aug. 30, 1980, p. 20, and Oct. 2, 1980, p. D3; and Walter J. Levy, "Oil: An Agenda for the 1980's," *Foreign Affairs* 59, no. 5 (1981):1092.

129. In a strategy document, OPEC has suggested that a new international organization be established jointly by OPEC and the industrialized countries to provide financial aid and technical expertise for the development of the LDCs' energy resources. In the meantime, the OPEC Fund for International Development has been lending on the order of $500 million a year for these purposes. Walter J. Levy, "Oil: An Agenda for the 1980's," *Foreign Affairs* 59, no. 5 (1981):1091, and *PE* (Mar. 1981), p. 98.

130. *NYT,* Feb. 20, 1981, pp. D1 and D8, and Aug. 13, 1981, p. D15.

131. *NYT,* Nov. 12, 1980, p. D1, Nov. 19, 1980, p. D6, Dec. 9, 1980, p. D1, and Mar. 23, 1981, p. D1.

132. *BW,* Mar. 30, 1981, p. 77, and Apr. 13, 1981, p. 164; *PE* (Aug. 1981), p. 350, and (Mar. 1982), p. 101; and *NYT,* Aug. 1, 1980, p. A1, May 12, 1981, p. D1, June 25, 1981, p. D1, May 3, 1982, pp. A1 and D4, and May 5, 1982, pp. D1 and D2.

133. *PE* (Aug. 1981), p. 328, and (Sept. 1981), p. 384, and *NYT,* Oct. 9, 1981, p. A31.

134. *NYT,* Mar. 8, 1982, p. D10, and Mar. 21, 1982, p. F4; *Wall Street Journal,* Mar. 8, 1982, p. 20; and *PIW,* Mar. 29, 1982 (supplement), p. 3.

135. *BW,* Jan. 21, 1980, p. 78, and *NYT,* Jan. 30, 1980, p. A1.

136. *NYT,* June 4, 1979, p. A3; *BW,* Feb. 11, 1980, p. 50; and William B. Quandt, "The Middle East Crises," *Foreign Affairs* 58, no. 3:556.

137. *NYT,* Jan. 24, 1980, pp. A1 and A12.

138. *NYT,* Jan. 25, 1980, p. A1, Feb. 6, 1980, p. A11, and Mar. 19, 1980, p. A1.

139. *BW,* Aug. 13, 1979, p. 53, Nov. 12, 1979, p. 55, and Feb. 11, 1980, p. 50, and *NYT,* Nov. 25, 1979, p. E1, Jan. 24, 1982, p. 7, and July 25, 1982, p. 3.

140. *BW,* June 18, 1979, p. 75. Border clashes between Egypt and Libya broke out in the summer of 1977.

141. *NYT,* June 14, 1979, p. A5.

142. In contrast to Iran, Iraq's Shiite clergy appears to lack both a single leader and a cohesive organizational network, nor does it have the same tradition of oppositional activity. *NYT,* June 26, 1980, p. A9.

143. *NYT,* Nov. 1, 1979, p. A23, and Dec. 2, 1979, p. 17, and John K. Cooley, "Iran, the Palestinians, and the Gulf," *Foreign Affairs* 57, no. 5 (1979):1019.

144. *NYT,* Feb. 25, 1980, pp. A1 and A10.

145. *NYT,* Dec. 4, 1979, p. 16, and Dec. 20, 1979, p. A18.

146. *NYT,* Apr. 16, 1980, p. A8.

147. *NYT,* June 3, 1979, p. 3.

148. *NYT,* Apr. 11, 1979, p. A8, and May 31, 1980, p. 5, and *BW,* Jan. 21, 1980, p. 51.

149. *BW,* Oct. 15, 1979, p. 44, and *NYT,* Apr. 9, 1980, p. A14. In September 1979 intense clerical pressure led to the forced resignation of Hassan Nazih as chairman of the National Iranian Oil Co. Nazih was closely aligned with Prime Minister Bazargan, and since his ouster the oil industry has been under the influence of the mainly clerical pro-Khomeini Komitehs. *BW,* Oct. 15, 1979, pp. 42 and 44.

150. *NYT,* Dec. 6, 1979, p. A20, and Mar. 10, 1980, p. 12.

151. *NYT,* Aug. 31, 1981, p. A1, and Sept. 6, 1981, p. 1.

152. *NYT,* Mar. 8, 1982, p. A10.

153. *NYT,* Sept. 6, 1981, pp. 1 and 26.

154. *PE* (June 1981), p. 232, and (July 1981), p. 311.

155. The only Arab League members to retain diplomatic relations with Egypt are the Sudan, Somalia, and Oman, but differences among the Arab countries and their preoccupation with other issues—southern Lebanon, the guerrilla war in the western Sahara, renewed hostility between Syria and Iraq—have greatly weakened their campaign against Egypt. Moreover, Morocco and Yemen have sought Egypt's protection against their neighboring rivals, Algeria and South Yemen. *NYT,* Nov. 19, 1979, pp. A1 and A3.

156. *NYT,* Sept. 3, 1979, p. A4.

157. *NYT,* Aug. 27, 1981, pp. A1 and A13.

158. *NYT,* Dec. 15, 1981, p. A1, Mar. 27, 1982, p. 4, and Mar. 28, 1982, p. E3.

159. *NYT,* Aug. 18, 1980, p. A1.

160. *NYT,* Feb. 18, 1981, p. A6, May 23, 1981, pp. 4–5, June 9, 1981, p. A8, June 21, 1981, p. E23, and Jan. 25, 1982, p. A1.

161. *NYT,* July 18, 1981, p. A1, and July 25, 1981, p. 4, and *BW,* Aug. 17, 1981, p. 47.

162. *NYT,* Apr. 26, 1982, p. A1, Apr. 27, 1982, p. A10, May 4, 1982, p. A3, June 17, 1982, p. A20, Sept. 26, 1982, p. 1, and Sept. 27, 1982, p. 1.

163. *NYT,* June 16, 1982, p. A31, June 20, 1982, pp. E1 and E2, Aug. 11, 1982, p. A14, Aug. 20, p. A13, Aug. 25, 1982, p. A7, and Sept. 3, 1982, p. A9.

164. *NYT,* Apr. 27, 1982, p. A10, Aug. 21, 1982, p. 4, Aug. 27, 1982, p. A7, Sept. 2, 1982, pp. A1 and A11, Sept. 3, 1982, pp. A1 and A9, Sept. 5, 1982, p. E1, and Sept. 10, 1982, p. A1.

165. *NYT,* Dec. 23, 1979, p. 5, and *PE* (July 1981), p. 320. The West may also face an African "oil weapon," if it fails to resolve the issue of Namibia. Nigerian President Shehu Shagari has said

that Nigeria is prepared to use "all means at our disposal, including oil if necessary," to put pressure on the U.S. to oppose South Africa's apartheid system more forcefully, *NYT*, Oct. 4, 1980, p. 4.

166. *BW*, Mar. 12, 1979, p. 52, and Cooley, "Iran, the Palestinians, and the Gulf," *Foreign Affairs* 57, no. 5 (1979):1020 and 1026.

167. *NYT*, June 11, 1978, p. 3, July 2, 1978, p. E4, Apr. 13, 1980, p. E3, and May 24, 1982, pp. A1 and A7.

168. *NYT*, Jan. 18, 1980, p. A3, and Apr. 13, 1980, p. E3.

169. *BW*, May 26, 1980, p. 79, and *NYT*, June 22, 1980, p. E3.

170. *Wall Street Journal*, Feb. 24, 1982, p. 1; *BW*, Mar. 22, 1982, p. 54; and *NYT*, Feb. 11, 1982, p. A13, Mar. 28, 1982, p. 11, Apr. 1, 1982, p. A7, and May 23, 1982, p. 7.

171. *NYT*, June 15, 1980, p. 4.

172. Cooley, "Iran, the Palestinians, and the Gulf," *Foreign Affairs* 57, no. 5 (1979):1032, and *NYT*, Apr. 9, 1979, p. 19.

173. *NYT*, Sept. 29, 1980, p. A14, Sept. 30, 1980, p. A10, Apr. 16, 1981, p. A11, and Oct. 2, 1981, p. A1.

174. *NYT*, Mar. 7, 1981, pp. 1 and 7, Aug. 15, 1981, p. 5, Aug. 22, 1981, p. 1, and Oct. 29, 1981, p. A1.

175. *BW*, Mar. 24, 1980, p. 69, and Oct. 27, 1980, p. 53.

176. *NYT*, June 16, 1981, p. A1.

177. *NYT*, Aug. 10, 1979, p. A3, and Feb. 26, 1980, p. A1.

178. *NYT*, Oct. 7, 1981, pp. A1 and A9, Oct. 18, 1981, pp. A1 and E1, and *BW*, Oct. 19, 1981, p. 40. The U.S. also agreed to accelerate arms shipments to the Sudan to deter a possible invasion of that country by Libya. *NYT*, Oct. 13, 1981, p. A1.

179. *BW*, Nov. 16, 1981, p. 74.

180. *NYT*, Sept. 26, 1980, p. A24, Feb. 18, 1981, p. A6, Sept. 21, 1981, p. A5, and Dec. 19, 1981, p. A1.

181. *NYT*, Feb. 2, 1980, p. 1.

182. *NYT*, Apr. 24, 1981, p. A1.

183. *NYT*, Feb. 3, 1980, p. 12.

184. It is also difficult to see how the mission could have succeeded, especially since the Iranians could have responded by rounding up any or all of the 220 non-hostage U.S. citizens in Iran (*NYT*, Apr. 30, 1980, p. A18). On Jan. 8, 1980, Carter himself said that "a strike force or military action that might be oriented toward the release of the hostages would almost certainly end in failure and almost certainly end in the death of the hostages" (*NYT*, Apr. 26, 1980, p. 6, and Apr. 28, 1980, p. A10). Of all the Islamic countries, only Syria and Libya supported the seizing of U.S. hostages. *BW*, Dec. 3, 1979, p. 37.

185. *NYT*, Oct. 4, 1980, p. 4, Oct. 30, 1980, p. A1, and *NYT Magazine*, May 16, 1981, pp. 98 and 100.

186. *BW*, Feb. 2, 1981, p. 14, and *NYT*, Jan. 20, 1981, p. A5.

187. *NYT Magazine*, May 16, 1981, pp. 116–17.

188. *BW*, May 25, 1981, p. 113.

189. *NYT*, Aug. 20, 1981, p. A1, Aug. 21, 1981, p. A1, Dec. 11, 1981, p. A1, and Mar. 11, 1982, p. A1.

190. *NYT*, May 27, 1981, p. A1, and June 25, 1981, p. A19.

191. At present, if a conflict in the Persian Gulf were to emerge, the allies would be militarily capable of providing the U.S. only minimal support. *NYT*, Feb. 17, 1980, p. 11.

192. Initially, Japan rushed to buy oil earmarked for the U.S., but on Dec. 14 the Japanese government imposed a ceiling, limiting oil imports from Iran to their pre-hostage-crisis level. Then, in April, with the world oil market soft, Japan refused to pay the high oil prices demanded by Iran. Whether political factors played a role in this decision is unclear; in any case, Japanese banks undercut Carter's freeze on Iranian assets by providing credits and banking services to Iranian

importers. *NYT,* Jan. 5, 1980, p. 27, and Apr. 24, 1980, p. D5, and *BW,* Dec. 24, 1979, p. 40, and June 2, 1980, p. 25.

193. *NYT,* Jan. 18, 1980, p. A1, Jan. 30, 1980, p. A15, Feb. 17, 1980, p. E2, and May 19, 1980, p. A1, and *BW,* Dec. 24, 1979, p. 40, and June 2, 1980, pp. 25 and 26.

CONCLUSION

1. Cited in *NYT,* Dec. 15, 1976, p. D12.
2. John Blair, *The Control of Oil* (New York: Pantheon, 1976), p. 276.

Index

613

and differentials, 320–21
and embargo, 156, 234, 237
and inflation, 392–404
investments of, 276, 277–81
and Iranian revolution, 429–31, 447–50
and Libyan breakthrough, 146, 148
and Mexico, 381
and most favored company clause, 85
and non-OPEC LDCs, 268–71, 290,
   609n.129
and oil companies, 83–86, 139, 154–55,
   223–24
and oil glut, 451–56
and oil price, 206, 225, 264–65, 318–20,
   390–404, 429–31, 438–39, 440–41,
   447–56
on participation, 99–100, 169, 176–77
production ceiling program of, 454–56
prorationing attempts by, 4, 87, 117, 234,
   321, 394–96
on split negotiations, 149–50
and split pricing episode, 398–401
role of members in, 303, 311, 313, 314,
   315, 316, 317
stability and success of, 317–18, 320,
   511–12
and surplus, 254, 276–81, 457–58
and Teheran/Tripoli agreements, 158, 164,
   204–7
and U.S. balance-of-payments, 292
See also OAPEC
OPEC countries
characteristics of, 302–5
cumulative current account of, 526
development efforts of, 322–24
direct sales of, 411
and dollar devaluation, 167–68
Egyptian-Israeli peace treaty and, 423–27,
   433–36
exploration and development in, 358, 385–90
foreign exchange reserves, ratio of reserves
   to imports, and oil as percentage of exports, 119
and IMF oil facility, 277
imports of, 273, 276–77
natural gas reserves of, 352–53, 359–60
OECD exports to, 288, 523
and oil companies, 405–11, 417–18
oil policy of, 302–24
oil production in, 97, 480, 482
and petrodollar recycling, 272
settlement of long-standing disputes in,
   298–99
surplus of, 276–79, 290

See also Gulf-exporting countries; Oil-ex-
   porting countries; specific countries
OPEC Fund, 460
Organization of Arab Petroleum Exporting
   Countries. See OAPEC
Organization of Petroleum Exporting Coun-
   tries. See OPEC
Orinico reserves, 388, 389, 482
al-Otaiba, Mana Saeed, 400

Page, Howard, 33–34, 68, 534n.70
Pahlevi, Muhammed Reza. See Iran, Shah of
Pahlevi, Prince Reza, 494
Pakistan, 121, 380
Palestinian autonomy, 495–99. See also PLO
Palestinians, 123, 132–33, 312–13
Panarctic, 371
Panhandle Eastern Corporation, 482
Participation agreements, 407–11
of Gulf countries, 175–87
and nationalization, 100, 556n.9
oil companies and exporting countries, in-
   terest in, 168–70
revised, 199, 239–42
and rise in market prices, 197–203
and threat of falling prices, 97–100
Pemex, 380, 381
Penrose, Edith, 199, 204
People's Democratic Republic of Yemen, 122,
   123–24, 129–30
Perez, Carlos Andres, 323
Pertamina, 317, 387–88, 396–97
Peru, 275
Petrobras, 200
PetroCanada, 370, 389, 477, 484
Petrochemicals industry, 62–64, 323–24,
   414–17, 419, 420, 473
Petrodollar recycling, 8, 254–55, 263,
   271–81, 458, 459. See also Balance-of-
   payments
Petroleum products
price of, 204, 325, 472–73
supply of, 247–48, 249
Petroleum Reserves Corporation, 22–24, 26,
   110
Petroven, 388, 389
Phillips, 171
Piercy, George, 44, 142, 158, 209, 236–37
PLO, 222, 295, 297, 434–35
and Egyptian-Israeli peace treaty, 422, 423,
   425
and Israeli invasion of Lebanon, 497–98
rejection of U.N. Resolution 242 by, 599n.1
revised, 199, 239–42

The Johns Hopkins University Press

THE OIL PRICE REVOLUTION

This book was composed in Times Roman text and Eurostyle display type by The Composing Room of Michigan, Inc., from a design by Lisa S. Mirski. It was printed on S. D. Warren's 50-lb. Sebago Cream Offset paper and bound in Holliston Roxite A by Universal Lithographers, Inc.